D1559358

Saint Sergius of Radonezh, His Trinity Monastery, and the Formation of the Russian Identity

NORTHERN ILLINOIS UNIVERSITY PRESS / DEKALB

SAINT SERGIUS OF RADONEZH, HIS TRINITY MONASTERY, AND THE FORMATION OF THE RUSSIAN IDENTITY

David B. Miller

Published by the Northern Illinois University Press, DeKalb, Illinois 60115

using postconsumer-recycled, acid-free paper.

Design by Julia Fauci

Title page illustration: "The Trinity-Sergius Monastery." Photograph by William Craft Brumfield, professor of Slavic Studies at Tulane University and honorary fellow of the Russian Academy of the Arts. A selection of his work is available online at http://www.cultinfo.ru/brumfield.

Library of Congress Cataloging-in-Publication Data

Miller, David B.

Saint Sergius of Radonezh, his Trinity Monastery, and the formation of the Russian identity / David B. Miller.

p. cm.

Includes bibliographical references (p.) and index.

ISBN 978-0-87580-432-3 (clothbound : alk. paper)

1. Sergii, Radonezhskii, Saint, ca. 1314–1391 or 2. 2. Troitse-Sergieva lavra—History. 3. Orthodox Eastern monasteries—Russia (Federation)—Sergiev Posad—History. 4. Sergiev Posad (Russia)—Church history. I. Title.

BX597.S45M55 2010

271'.8147—dc22

2010015389

TO JOAN JACOBUS MILLER

Contents

Acknowledgments

I take great pleasure in thanking the people and institutions that assisted me in writing this book. First and foremost, I thank Gregory and Marilyn Shesko, who gave me photocopies and transcriptions of the Trinity-Sergius Monastery's copybooks, land documents of the State's *Kollegiia ekonomiki*, and a photocopy of Trinity's *sinodik*. Without their generosity, I could not have written this book. Although it is too late to thank him, I wish to recognize the assistance given me by the late Richard Hellie. Richard gave the penultimate version of the book a careful reading and his comments and criticisms were invaluable. From the time we were doctoral candidates as members of the cohort of 1963–64 of the US-USSR cultural exchange and throughout my career, Richard has been a source of enthusiastic advice and encouragement. I owe him a great deal. I also am grateful to Barbara Rosenwein, who read and commented on my initial investigation of Trinity's property; to my publisher's three anonymous readers; to editors Amy Farranto, Susan Bean, and Tracy Schoenle; and the production manager, Julia Fauci at Northern Illinois University Press. Their patience and wisdom made this a better book. William Brumfield very kindly contributed three photographs, one of the Trinity-Sergius Monastery (which graces the book cover) and two of its churches, for the book. I am most grateful. I also thank Aleksei Sirenov and Maria Korogodina, who procured for me a copy of an illumination from the Illuminated Codex, and Marianna Tax Choldin, who provided me a copy of the cover of the program marking the celebration of the 600th anniversary of Sergius's death, and Ann Kleimola who supplied the source describing the event. Finally, I thank Jeff Liem for his expertise in preparing and printing illustrations, and Cory Johnson, XNR productions, for producing two excellent maps and a genealogical chart for the book.

Needless to say, I owe a great deal to many institutions. Institutions are made up of people, and I would be remiss if, where possible, I did not express my thanks to those special individuals by name; to Norman Ingham and Valentina Pichugina, who hosted workshops at the University of Chicago, and to Gail Lenhoff, whose conferences and workshops at The University of California at Los Angeles afforded me opportunities to test my ideas; to the organizers Tat'iana Manushina, Svetlana Nikolaeva, and Archimandrite

Makarii (Veretennikov), who invited me to participate in biennial conferences at the Trinity-Sergius Monastery sponsored by the Moscow Theological Academy and Seminary, and the Sergiev Posad Museum-Reserve. I owe special thanks to Archimandrite Makarii of the Theological Academy. For many years he has shared his research with me, arranged my participation in one of the annual *Makar'evskie chteniia*, and kindly assisted in the translation and publication of my work in Russia. Finally, I thank Tat'iana Isachenko, archivist of the Manuscript division of the Russian State Library in Moscow. She arranged for me to use the Trinity Monastery archive at that institution and to work in the Russian Archive of Ancient Acts. I deeply appreciate her hospitality and advice on numerous summer trips to Moscow. I also thank the International Research and Exchanges Board for summer grants that in part assisted me in making these trips.

In this country I have had the privilege of working in two great Slavic collections. With assistance from the Summer Program of the Russian and East European Institute, I have used the University of Illinois Library for many years. The staff of its Slavic Reading Room, particularly Helen Sullivan, have been indispensible in finding materials for me there or elsewhere. I am grateful also for being able to use the rich collection at the University of Chicago Library, and for the assistance of its Slavic librarians, June Farris and Sandra Levy.

Note: Throughout, I use the names Sergius, Moscow, and tsar (instead of Sergii, Moskva, and tsar') common to the English-speaking world. I transliterate all other Russian names and words according to the Library of Congress system, except for the omission of hard signs and diacritical marks.

Saint Sergius of Radonezh, His Trinity Monastery, and the Formation of the Russian Identity

Видъ Троицко-Сергіевой лавры XVII вѣка.

1. Church of the Holy Trinity (1422)
2. Chapel of St. Nikon (1548)
3. Refectory (1469)
4. Kitchen (1469)
5. Church of the Holy Spirit (1476)
6. Gate Church of St. Sergius (1512)
7. Tsar's Residence (*chertog*, 1550s)
8. Cellarer's Residence (1550s)
9. Cathedral of the Dormition (1559-1585)

Gravure, "View of the Trinity-Sergius Lavra, XVII Century" (before 1686). Author's print.

Introduction

About the year 1339, a youth named Varfolomei, having carried out his last obligation to his parents by burying them, set out to fulfill his destiny. He renounced his inheritance and, with his older brother Stefan, left the little town of Radonezh to dedicate his life to God. They had not gone far when, above a shallow, forested valley watered by a streamlet called the Konchura on the southerly slope of Makovets Hill, 15 kilometers northeast of Radonezh and 80 kilometers northeast of the ruling city of Moscow, Varfolomei received a sign from God that this was the place. He and Stefan stopped, built a hut and a tiny chapel dedicated to the Trinity, and began to live as hermits. Stefan could not endure this harsh existence, and departed; Varfolomei carried on alone, honing his zeal on solitude and adversity. Word of his piety and fortitude spread and he collected around him other pious souls. Circa 1342 Varfolomei took holy orders as the monk Sergius. Still seeking the humble way, until 1353 Sergius resisted entreaties of his fellow monks that he become abbot of the hermitage he had founded. It is uncertain whether Sergius established a rule of common life and governance for Trinity's brotherhood then or much later. But when he did, he did so in the face of considerable opposition. Sergius died 25 September 1392. By then reverence for him and his Trinity Monastery had spread beyond Muscovy, even to the Patriarchal court in Constantinople.

Trinity's development after its founder's death is one of the great success stories of late medieval and early modern Russia. The monastery's monks proclaimed Sergius a miracle worker early in the fifteenth century. By mid-century Muscovites came to consider Sergius the intercessor who secured divine support for the Russian land to free itself from Mongol rule; both Russian and Greek Orthodoxy recognized him as a saint, and by example and deed he was the catalyst to a wave of monastic foundations in rural areas of Rus'. Princes, including the grand princes of Moscow, gave Trinity immunities from taxes and other obligations, and joined thousands of other landowners in giving Trinity land and money so that its monks, by prayer, would summon Sergius's intercessory powers to save their souls and those of their kin. In the sixteenth century they made the monastery a destination for pilgrimages and feasts. Trinity grew rich. As Moscow expanded to dominate Rus', Trinity's spiritual reach expanded with it.

Historians who seek to comprehend Trinity's remarkable history first must take the measure of Sergius and his achievement. This is not as easy as it might seem, primarily because of the nature of the sources by which we know him. Vasilii Kliuchevskii and Evgenii Golubinskii began the serious study of these sources a century ago, and their conclusions remain of value to this day.[1] And while their work and those of others who followed provide us with knowledge of the source base, they also reveal its inadequacies, not to mention the difficulties in interpreting it. For example, the basic sources were hagiographical biographies of Sergius. Hagiography is a genre that operates according to different rules of narrative and chronology from those employed by historians: it uses topoi to describe decisive events in Sergius's life that cannot be taken seriously as causal descriptions of his motives; it describes events unverifiable in other sources; it prefers an idealized pattern of saintly behavior to chronological order in its narrative; and usually it is bereft of dates for events about which other sources are silent, vague, or in conflict. Thus, from the hagiographical material Golubinskii concluded that Sergius was born in 1314, whereas Kliuchevskii said 1321/22. Golubinskii thought Sergius founded the hermitage in 1337 and almost immediately became a monk; Kliuchevskii cautiously placed the foundation "no earlier than 1341" and Sergius's tonsure in 1345/46. They agreed only that Sergius became Trinity's abbot in 1353 and established a cenobitic rule about 1355. Nor have Golubinskii's and Kliushevskii's successors reached consensus on these and other benchmarks in Sergius's life. Most glaring are their conclusions about when Sergius established a cenobitic rule at Trinity: for Pierre Gonneau, I. I. Bureichenko, and N. S. Borisov it was around 1355, while B. M. Kloss, K. A. Aver'ianov, and V. A. Kuchkin placed it much later, Gonneau between 1365 and 1373, the others in 1375 or 1377.[2] No less disputatious are attempts, notably of G. M. Prokhorov, Kuchkin, Aver'ianov, and Jean Meyendorff, to use the "life" (subsequently used without quotation marks) and other sources to establish Sergius's role in the protracted struggle to succeed Aleksei at his death in 1378 as metropolitan of Russia.[3]

Contributing to the difficulty in making sense of Sergius's career is the fact that no true and complete edition of the original life of the saint, which his disciple Epifanii the Wise completed in 1418, survives. Recently Kloss assembled, examined, and categorized the known versions of Sergius's life, only to conclude that the single surviving text attributable solely to Epifanii is an incomplete version of the so-called Extended Edition of 1518. V. M. Kirillin's study of stylistic elements in the various editions supports Kloss's opinion that only this incomplete text reflects Epifanii's efforts.[4] Also, despite its undeniable merits, Kloss's scheme for defining subsequent editions, written by the famous hagiographer Pakhomii the Serb, is open to criticism.[5] And while most everyone agrees that the Extended Edition contains Epifanii's final chapters, they know that these are "corrupted" by altered episodes and new information provided by Pakhomii the Serb, who in the interim rewrote Epifanii's original numerous times.[6] It is not surprising, then, that scholars have had free rein to let their vision of Sergius's era dictate what in the Extended Edition came from Epifanii and what was altered or added by Pakhomii or others. Resolving these issues in essence means deciding which episodes were events in the life of the historical Sergius and which were elements of his cult. As things stand, one can only accept as a matter of faith that Epifanii, who knew Sergius, wrote the episode recounting the central miracle on which Sergius's reputation as an intercessor rested, that in which the Mother of God appeared to him and promised that his house would be under her protection. By the same logic we cannot be certain whether Epifanii or a later writer created the episode in which Sergius interceded to assure the army of Prince Dmitrii Donskoi of Moscow victory in 1380 over Emir Mamai and his invading Tatars on Kulikovo Field.

Ecclesiastical, princely, and private records, available in published critical editions, supplement hagiographical information about Sergius, and chronicle accounts are essential. Although specialists disagree about the origin and dating of crucial hypothetical compilations of metropolitans Kipriian and Photios, and the compilation of 1448, our knowledge of chronicles that contain them rests on solid scholarship.[7] I conclude with the happy observation that we now have fair appraisals of the historical Sergius by contemporary historians to supplement Golubinskii's original assessment. There is no consensus, but their work rests on a skilled parsing of sources and a sensitive awareness of the historical context in which Sergius and his devotees lived.[8]

However influential Sergius was in life, in death his impact on the emergence of Russia was greater. The cult, to which his reputation as intercessor for the Russian land was central, made the Trinity-Sergius Monastery a unifying center of the sort that Edward Shils wrote, "gives meaning to the major events of existence and which explains why things happen and why some things are better than other things."[9] It is difficult to understand how religious fervor transforms the behavior of a human being. Yet we recognize intuitively that creative individuals—religious prophets in one age, philosophers in another, demagogic politicians always—may burst on the scene to define values that a community has yet to articulate. Emile Durkheim, in formulating a sociological explanation of religious belief, put it well when he wrote that "if society happens to fall in love with a man and if it thinks it has found in him the principal aspirations that move it, as well as the means of satisfying them, this man will be raised above the others and, as it were, deified."[10] Durkheim, of course, knew that societies have created false gods. For that matter, societies can call into doubt a person's status, not only when he or she is alive, as the historian Aviad Kleinberg has noted writing about saints, but after he or she is dead. But Kleinberg, with Durkheim, is surely correct to argue that sainthood is a social creation. That is, it is an accumulative formulation that takes on meaning after the death of a "performer"; that sainthood emerges out of an ongoing negotiation between the candidate's promoters on one hand and succeeding generations with their baggage of aspirations and expectations on the other. A contemporary hagiographer might know the candidate intimately and the candidate's life is the more factual for it. Moreover, writing for a community that knew the candidate in all of his or her ambiguity, compromises, or collaborations, the hagiographer had to walk a fine line between what that community expected to find in the narrative and the exalted ideals of the hagiographic canon. Over time there is a blurring of memory, and factuality lapses or is bent to correspond with idealized models of sainthood and cultural expectations of later generations.[11]

If the cultural milieu that spawns a cult is largely self-generating and not an invention of cultural elites as Shils argued, then it behooves us to reconstruct the historical Sergius with particular care for context. This I attempt in Chapter 1. As a corollary it will be necessary to explore how Sergius's deeds caused contemporaries to view him as a charismatic figure. It will be apparent, I hope, that this was an extraordinary process. In Muscovite Rus' in the fourteenth century there were numerous Sergiuses, pious hermits who founded rural cenobitic monasteries. Tradition may ascribe the movement to Sergius's example and make Trinity its fountainhead, but its roots were more complicated: for example, it is unclear whether Sergius inspired Evfimii of Suzdal' and others who founded houses at about the same time he founded Trinity; also, the *Rogozhskii letopisets* records the establishment of a cenobitic rule at two other houses simultaneously with or earlier than Sergius's at Trinity, and says that an Archimandrite Ivan in his monastery of St. Peter (*Vysokopetrovskii*) in Moscow was the first to establish a cenobitic rule.[12] This is part of the context within which we shall examine the moral world Sergius sought to construct, who were the helpmates and disciples that came to Trinity to help make his vision reality, and what influence they had on the wave of monastic foundings that followed.

In Chapter 2 I discuss the inauguration of Sergius's cult. It emerged through negotiations between his disciples and the generation that followed his death, from which his deeds came to be accepted as divinely inspired and his reputation as a miracle worker became a social artifact revered throughout the Muscovite principality and beyond. Chapter 3 concerns the question of princely patronage in the emergence and development of the cult throughout Russia and eastern Orthodoxy from the mid-fifteenth century to 1605. Here I devote attention to how Muscovite bookmen, often in a dialogue with Trinity's brothers, appropriated the cult and transformed it in creating myths of Muscovite Russian identity.

Subsequent chapters concern the Trinity-Sergius Monastery as the first and arguably the most vital sacred center of the emerging Muscovite Russian state. It is indisputable that the site housing the relics of the miracle worker for centuries to come became invested with the charisma of the living saint. Clifford Geertz, in a gloss on Shil's imagery of the unifying power on peripheries of charismatic central places, called them "animating centers of society."[13] The reader should be forewarned that my study focuses on Trinity's interaction with the wider world. It was, I argue, constant and transforming, both for the spiritual and economic regimen of Trinity's monks and for the world they inhabited. The sources for my study may be found primarily in the immense fund of state, ecclesiastical, and private charters regarding Trinity's property in government archives and in Trinity's cartularies (*kopeinye knigi*), and in its donation book (*vkladnaia kniga*), lists of those to be prayed for (*sinodiks*), and feast book (*kormovaia kniga*). Sergei Shumakov cataloged, described, and published in part or in full land documents relating to Trinity in the archive of the State College of the Economy, now in Fund 281 of the Russian State Archive of Ancient Acts (RGADA).[14] The publication in the 1920s of charters from northern districts (*uezds*) continued Shumakov's pre-revolutionary catalogs.[15] Subsequently S. B. Veselovskii undertook a comprehensive inventory of charters of Russia's major monasteries, resulting in the appearance of a three-volume collection of land documents, judicial rulings, and immunity charters published in 1952–1964.[16] Volume one in its entirety and volume three in part contain documents pertaining to Trinity's property from its founding to 1505/6. Another three-volume collection of documents on the agricultural economy published in 1951–1961 contains further materials relating to Trinity for this period.[17] Three more volumes, bringing the series to 1584, have been ready for press for some time, but all we have is a list of the charters, probably for the first of these volumes (2007), and a volume containing records relating to Trinity's property from 1506/7 to 1526/27 (1975).[18] For the period from 1526/27–1605, apart from published collections of documents relating to other topics, a catalog of immunity charters for the period 1506/7–1610, a study and description of Trinity's charters for 1584–1641,[19] and Shumakov's archival descriptions, investigators must look to manuscript collections in Fund 281 of RGADA and in Fund 303 of the Manuscript Division of the Russian State Library (RORGB), which contains the copybooks of the Trinity-Sergius Monastery, to write the history of Trinity's property. The history of Trinity's property also resides in the stone of its buildings and the artifacts that decorated them or were in its treasury.

From these materials I have constructed a database with over 4,000 entries, annotated by date, the names of donors, the nature of the grants, their locations (if landed property), and the nature of the services or remembrances requested from Trinity. To make the materials speak to questions I raise, I divide the records into 11 chronological periods determined by three criteria. The first is that the periods make historical sense. Thus, Period 1, 1392–1422, extends from Sergius's death to his local recognition as a saint in 1422. Period 2, 1423–45, spans the initial period of the local cult and the Muscovite dynastic struggle, a struggle that left its mark on Trinity's formative years. Period 3, 1445–61, encompasses the climax of that struggle and recognition of Sergius's cult throughout the metropolitanate. Periods 4, 1461–78, and 5, 1478–1501, were years of prosperity for Trinity and for the Muscovite state. In the first of these Grand Prince Ivan III's mastery of appanage princes changed the climate for gift-giving and patronage. In the second Ivan's determination to create a landed service class and successful expansion challenged Trinity's property rights; simultaneously, it opened the way for the cult's expansion. Periods 6 through 9—1501–22, 1522–September 1533, October 1533–46, and 1547–64—were years of expansion and prosperity for Trinity and the Muscovite state. The first two fall within the reign of Vasilii III; their divide is the year of Vasilii's divorce and the concomitant rearrangement of clan power relationships. The "good" years of the reign of Ivan IV "the Terrible" are the background of the second pair, a time that witnessed Ivan's emergence as ruler in his own right, with the title of tsar. Period 10, 1564–18 March 1584, contains records for the years of Ivan's *oprichnina* and its aftermath, years that proved decisive for Trinity as well as for Russia. Trends apparent in its records continued in the final period, 19 March 1584–13 April 1605, which covers the reigns of Fedor and Boris Godunov, and ends with the "time of troubles" (*smuta*). A second priority for this periodization is that it provides a rational arrangement for aggregative purposes of charters with estimated dates. Finally, variations in the length of the periods are not so great as to make comparisons unrealistic.[20]

Chapter 4 has as its focus the "culture of remembrance" that grew up at the monastery. Sergius's reputed intercessory powers attracted celebrants to Trinity and generated thousands of gifts from every social class and from every part of Muscovy, later the Russian tsardom, in return for its prayers for the souls of donors, their families, and their ancestors. Historians of such phenomena in that part of Europe under the Roman Church have noted the complex combination of spiritual and social considerations that caused families to maintain long-term memorial arrangements with a particular house.[21] We shall look to these studies in framing answers to questions about the significance of the culture of gifts for prayers at Trinity, how it originated, and how it became institutionalized. Information in the database allows us to frame answers to numerous questions, one of which is how the land politics, piety, and personality of Moscow's rulers and their consorts shaped the memorial culture. It also helps us to comprehend how Sergius's cult and Trinity's reputation as a sacred center prospered, even after they became institutionalized in ways that from the late fifteenth century seem self-serving. Trinity's memorial culture engendered feasts and pilgrimages to the great house or to its outposts. Such acts were a means by which participants achieved a temporary "crossing of the barrier" to the sacred from the profane to renew a clan's bonds of kinship. Public acts of piety legitimized the distinction or authority of one's family in this world by linking it to the charisma of a sacred center.[22]

Donation charters provide the earliest evidence for other rites that linked families to the Trinity-Sergius Monastery and to each other. One took the form of requests for tonsure for oneself or one's kin; another ensured that one or more of a person's family might enter into Trinity's service. The requests took several forms, indicating that they were made for a variety of reasons. In one a donor might request immediate initiation as a monk; in another he might ask to be tonsured as the hour of his death approached. In Chapter 5 I use this material to discuss the size of Trinity's brotherhood, profiles of its social and geographical composition, and the monastery's organization, lifestyle (*byt*), and governance. In theory, taking the habit was a form of "social death" by which the novice cut his or her ties to the secular world.[23] I shall argue that Trinity's monks remained very much in touch with the wider world. The same evidence, upon examination, has a gendered quality, which I discuss in Chapter 6. Trinity received numerous gifts and requests from women, and women were executors of testaments and charters by which their spouses made grants. Women also appear in the database as memorial subjects in prayers requested by both men and women, and as nuns at Trinity's subsidiary convents. These phenomena bear out historian Peter Brown's observation that, in the worship of saints, women found "respite and protection which they lacked the freedom to find elsewhere."[24] In Trinity's charters familial relationships between men and women, and between women and the Trinity-Sergius Monastery, appear in all their complexity. Their study reveals the importance of women in maintaining and, in the case of Moscow's grand princesses and tsarinas, adding a gendered quality to Sergius's cult. In Chapter 7 I discuss requests for burial at Trinity, when and why they were initiated, and who made them. Literature about death practices in western Christendom, inspired by Philippe Ariès, informs my inquiries into what those requesting burial at Trinity expected to happen, what they hoped to gain by it, and why Trinity encouraged it.[25] As I shall demonstrate, interment at Trinity reflected as well Russian customs of rank and place.

My Conclusion holds an argument that Sergius's cult and the Trinity-Sergius Monastery were vital elements of an emerging Russian identity. By acts of devotion described in previous chapters, Trinity's benefactors—free peasants, provincial smallholders, townspeople, great magnates, princes, and Moscow's grand princes and tsars—coalesced morally, economically, and socially into a horizontal community of venerators, one that cut across traditional lines of authority, class, and custom and reached people in every part of what by 1600 had become the Russian tsardom. This process had various dimensions. In the first place the monastery became a "memory site" energized by Sergius's cult with a moral dimension implanted in the minds of Russia's inhabitants and in expressions of national identity employed by bookmen. Sergius's cult and Muscovite national consciousness developed together, so much so that in determining what it meant to be Russian, people thought of them as inseparable. Secondly, contact with Trinity contributed to the social bonding of elites by drawing them into the sphere of Trinity's economic life and memorial culture. In doing so it forged ties between local families and between families from diverse parts of the realm and with persons above and below them in the social order. In these spheres I shall stress "the power of rites"—whether accompanying donations, feasts, pilgrimages, tonsures, or burials—to bring to life Sergius's power to intercede for celebrants and link them together as a community centered on Trinity's affiliated churches and houses, and on the great house itself.[26] Thirdly, these processes transformed the Trinity-Sergius Monastery into an economic engine, second only to the state, in unifying Russia. Finally, I shall present evidence from my database of the development of literacy of a basic sort among those who did business with Trinity, a literacy in part explained by Trinity's insistence that property transactions be recorded in written charters. By insisting on documentation the Trinity-Sergius Monastery propelled those who dealt with it into a larger and more sophisticated culture based on the written word that around 1600 was beginning to be called Russian.

When the Russian tsardom, its economy, and its society collapsed under the weight of Ivan IV's wars of expansion and *oprichnina* terror, and when Moscow's line of grand princes and tsars came to an end in 1605, the Trinity-Sergius Monastery survived. It remained the greatest institution in Russia that was statewide and possessed a charisma commanding the respect of a demoralized people. During the *smuta* its stature reached new heights when it survived a Polish siege and assisted society to drive the Poles from central Russia and establish a new political order. In doing so, its monks presented the house as the sacred center that defined the Russian land. As it turned out, most were willing to accept that definition as their own. These events take us beyond the scope of my investigation. It is hoped, however, that my analysis of Sergius's cult and the memorial culture that grew up around Trinity and its properties will enable us to understand how they created a community that proved dynamic, resilient, and important in the construction of the Russian identity.

Chapter One

The Historical Sergius

About 1418, some 26 years after the death of his hero in 1392, the Trinity monk Epifanii the Wise began his great work, saying, "I am astounded that so many years have passed without a life of Sergius being written."[1] Epifanii might well have been astonished. Sergius had died a famous man, respected throughout Rus'. And between then and Epifanii's writing, his fame, if anything, had grown. Nowhere was this truer than at the Trinity Monastery, whose monks had come to think of Sergius as a miracle worker. To appreciate what this meant it is necessary to establish the facts of Sergius's life; in other words, to reveal the historical Sergius, stripped of accretions of legend.

When Sergius died, and even when Epifanii wrote, a monk at Trinity would have had to be either foolhardy or possessed of supernatural vision to be optimistic about the future. True, Grand Prince Dmitrii Donskoi, before his death in 1389, had made Moscow the permanent capital of the Grand Principality of Vladimir and had ruled it more firmly than any prince before him. Northern Rus', despite the onset of plague in the 1350s, enjoyed an economic resurgence, when compared to the disastrous depression that had followed the Mongol conquest of 1237–38 and had run well into the fourteenth century. In the 1360s Dmitrii used some of his wealth to wall Moscow's kremlin with stone. More spectacularly, and to what must have been everyone's relief, he defeated an invading army of the Mongol Emir Mamai in 1380. In one stroke Dmitrii relieved northern Rus' of the burden of Mongol overlordship and tribute it had born for almost a century and a half. Yet Epifanii and his contemporaries could hardly have viewed Dmitrii's victory as other than as a false portent of better times. In 1382 the Mongol Khan Tokhtamysh drove Dmitrii from Moscow, breached the stone walls of his kremlin, looted and burned the city, and ravaged its countryside. Dmitrii retained the grand princely title but the price was prohibitive. Tokhtamysh restored the Mongol tribute, held hostage Dmitrii's oldest son Vasilii for three years to assure that it was paid, and weakened Dmitrii's power over other princes. It must be remembered too that plague remained endemic in Rus' in the first half of the fifteenth century. As if that were not enough, in 1408 a Mongol raid ravaged Moscow and burned the Trinity Monastery to the ground.[2]

Yet the world would have seemed darker and prospects even bleaker to Muscovites in 1322, the year a boy named Varfolomei, the future Sergius, was born.[3] Northeastern Rus' was firmly under Mongol rule, with all that it implied; a heavy tribute and Mongol-Tatar intervention in local affairs to set prince against prince. Its inhabitants knew that a Mongol raiding party might appear at any time to loot, burn, and kill. The more prosperous the town or the more ambitious or recalcitrant its prince, the more it might expect a Mongol raid.[4] Only four stone buildings had been built or restored in northeast Rus' since the Mongol invasion. For Varfolomei's parents, landowners of the principality of Rostov, the situation must have seemed hopeless. In 1316 their Prince Vasilii Konstantinovich returned from the Horde with a Mongol troop that proceeded "to inflict great harm on Rostov." In the year of Varfolomei's birth Khan Uzbek sent a Mongol detachment with his envoy Akhmyl, this time in assistance of Prince Ivan Danilovich Kalita of Moscow (1322–41), to plunder northeastern Rus'.[5]

Epifanii wrote that during Varfolomei/Sergius's childhood his father Kirill, a wealthy boiar, underwent a series of reversals that left the family impoverished. These he ascribed to trips to the Horde in the entourage of Rostov's prince—occasions on which the khans expected expensive gifts, frequent Mongol raids, and visits by Mongol envoys (again, more gifts)—and to burdensome Mongol levies and to famine. Epifanii then wrote the following:

> But the worst of these misfortunes occurred at the time of the great Tatar invasion led by Fedorchuk [and] Turalyk after which the savagery continued for one year because Ivan Danilovich became grand prince and sovereignty over Rostov also went to Moscow. Alas! How bad it was then in the town of Rostov, and especially for Rostov's princes since they were stripped of their power, the principality, property, honor and glory, and everything thenceforth went to Moscow. Then the grand prince commanded and sent from Moscow to Rostov a governor from among his magnates named Vasilii called Kocheva, and with him one Mina. When they came to the town of Rostov they inflicted great hardship on the town, yea and on its inhabitants, and heaped many persecutions [on them]. Not a few of Rostov's inhabitants against their will

> had to forfeit their property to Muscovites, and in return they received blows and were left with reproaches and empty hands. . . . And as a result of these persecutions the servant of God Kirill left this Rostov land. Gathering his family and his kinsmen, he went away from Rostov to settle in Radonezh.[6]

The invasion, undertaken to punish Tver' and strip its ruler Aleksandr Mikhailovich of the grand princely title and deliver it to Ivan Kalita, occurred at the end of 1327 and early in 1328. N. S. Borisov connected Rostov's misfortune and Kirill's resettlement to the invasion, but B. M. Kloss and others argued that it occurred no earlier than 1334. In evidence of this was a passage in Epifanii's life, preceding the news of the move in Rostov, noting his mother's concern that Varfolomei, though not yet 12, agonized over Rostov's sinfulness. V.A. Kuchkin suggested another dating. Ivan Kalita's marriage of his daughter Mariia to the younger of Rostov's brother princes, Konstantin Vasil'evich, in 1228, Kuchkin argued, was one step of several by which Ivan took over the principality. The final step, Kuchkin wrote, occurred in 1331. Konstantin's older brother Fedor died, allowing Ivan Kalita to take control of Rostov and appoint a governor who in 1332 punished Fedor's boiars, including Kirill. In that year chronicles recorded the famine Epifanii said was concurrent with the event. Bureichenko and Gonneau dated the resettlement to 1337, and Aver'ianov argued that it occurred in 1341 under Grand Prince Semen (1341–53), after Ivan Kalita's death. Bureichenko's chronology rests on the conviction that Moscow was on good terms with Rostov, the proof being the marriage between Mariia and Konstantin in 1328. Bureichenko related Kalita's punishment of Rostov and the resettlement to his engineering the Horde's summons to Prince Aleksandr Mikhailovich of Tver' and his allies, and Aleksandr's death at the Horde in 1339. Bureichenko also assumed that, because Varfolomei's family retained its social standing and well-being in Radonezh and because Varfolomei/Sergius and his older brother Stefan later were intimates of Moscow's princes, their resettlement could not have been the result of punishments to Rostov's elite. Aver'ianov instead argued that Moscow's ill treatment and resettlement of Rostov's elite followed from Semen's need for cash to pay off bribes and promises of tribute to the Mongols made in order to secure the grand princely title.[7]

The two scenarios hold different implications regarding Sergius's initiatory relationship with the Muscovite princely house and whether the move happened when he was an impressionable 10 or a mature 20 or 21. In my view Kuchkin was correct in dating the event to 1332. It is consistent with the tight chronology in Epifanii's narrative of events, a chronology not undermined by the reference to Varfolomei's age. When he wrote Sergius's life, Epifanii was no enemy of Moscow's ruling house and would not lightly have cast it as villain in telling the story of his hero. Nor was he so unskilled in the hagiographer's craft, nor so ignorant of the facts of his hero's early life, that he would have inadvertently implied that Sergius's family endured Moscow's wrath when it did not. Even the illumination in the Illuminated Codex, written circa 1570 to glorify Moscow's rulers, portrayed the subjugation of Rostov as a brutal act (see fig. 1). Nor is there evidence that the events at the Horde in 1339 were tied to Ivan Kalita's hostility to Rostov. Finally, it is erroneous to base conclusions about Sergius's childhood on the conviction that his subsequent fame was in part the result of an intimate alliance with Moscow's princely house. Quite the contrary; it was Sergius's moral courage in facing harsh conditions and uncertain political realities that caused people, including Moscow's grand princes, to revere him.

So it was that Varfolomei, then ten years old, saw his world fall to pieces, his parents ruined and adrift, ultimately transported to the Muscovite town of Radonezh. All this was at the hands of Kalita's agents in Rostov. Varfolomei could not but have been scarred by the change in his family's fortunes, nor could he have passed through it without animus toward those who had inflicted these blows on his family. At least the family maintained its social status as landowners. And, if we can believe Epifanii—for there is no other source for it—its fortunes improved rapidly. Kinsmen accompanied the family to Radonezh, providing the material and spiritual benefits of clan solidarity in the family's new life. Among those kinsmen, Epifanii mentions a Protasii who, with Kirill's uncle Anisim, settled there and subsequently became "thousand man" (*tysiatskii*) at the Muscovite court. This could only be Protasii Fedorovich Vel'iaminov, Ivan Kalita's senior boiar. Kirill and his family landed on their feet, so to speak, and quickly. Epifanii said Ivan Kalita gave Radonezh to his youngest son Andrei as an appanage. In reality Kalita's testament of 1339 bequeathed it to his widow Ul'iana and her children, Andrei being the youngest and still a minor. Lacking a prince, a governor ruled Radonezh, and evidently he did so benignly, granting its landowners tax privileges that brought prosperity.[8] Before leaving this episode I might suggest that for those of Epifanii's generation a defining component of Sergius's sanctity was his ability to live a life personifying love and mercy despite the traumas of his youth.[9]

The first mention of our hero in a source other than Epifanii's life—that is, the moment in which Sergius became an historical person—came 40 years later. The source is a chronicle, the only copy of which was found at the Trinity-Sergius Monastery in the eighteenth century and, because of its provenance, was called the Trinity chronicle. Although it perished during

Napoleon's occupation of Moscow, its text has been reconstructed from common entries in the Rogozhskii and the Simeonovskii chronicles, and from transcriptions of the original made by historian Nikolai Karamzin. There is a consensus that the Trinity chronicle was based on a compilation of 1408 and that the Rogozhskii and Simeonovskii chronicles reflect a reworking of it done in Tver' no earlier than 1412. Ia. S. Lur'e and earlier historians thought the scriptorium of Metropolitan Kipriian (1378–1406) prepared the compilation; Kloss has argued that it was done at Trinity by none other than Epifanii the Wise.[10] Epifanii's life and the chronicle contain undeniable textual similarities and the chronicler is unusually well informed about Sergius and his house from the mid-1370s, when Epifanii might have taken residence there. We know too that when Edigei's Mongols raided Muscovy in 1408 Epifanii took refuge in Tver' and might have become acquainted with its chronicle writing. If Kloss's reasoning is correct, though, the contemporary historian risks confirming the historicity of one account by reference to another written by the same person. That said, there remain puzzling differences in the accounts' content that cast doubt on Kloss's theory. One is that the chronicle says nothing of Sergius's earlier life although his formidable presence was known to people in Moscow and elsewhere before 1374. Most likely, entries in the Trinity chronicle about Sergius and his brothers reflect the fact that its author had at his disposal a chronicle written at the monastery.[11]

But regarding the reference in the Trinity chronicle, under 1374 it reported that Prince Vladimir Andreevich, the son of the first prince of Radonezh and Dmitrii Donskoi's cousin, founded the town of Serpukhov and asked Sergius to establish a monastery there. He did so and appointed his disciple Afanasii as abbot. It was called the Vysotskii Monastery and its church was dedicated to the Miraculous Conception. Then, under 25 November 1374, it said that in Pereiaslavl' a son was born to Grand Prince Dmitrii Ivanovich of Moscow. His name was Iurii and Sergius baptized him.[12] So by then Varfolomeii had become Sergius the monk and abbot of his Trinity Monastery, revered by his lord, Prince Vladimir, and respected by Dmitrii of Moscow, the grand prince of Vladimir. He had become a holy man, so well known in the capital that the greatest lay figures in the land sought his benefactions. It is this remarkable turn of events that lends credence to Epifanii's description of Sergius's earlier life.

Forty days after his birth in 1322 Kirill and Mariia had their baby son baptized with the name Varfolomei. If, as seems likely, this occurred on the date on which the apostle Varfolomei was celebrated, or 11 June, Varfolomei was born on 3 May.[13] Epifanii tells us that while in Rostov Kirill had his three sons—

Stefan, Varfolomei, and Petr—schooled in reading and writing and implies that Varfolomei completed his mastery of the written word in Radonezh. In a society in which literacy was a rarity among the elite, this in itself was remarkable.[14] Varfolomei as a child reportedly agonized over the omnipresence of evil, acted piously, and desired to dedicate himself to God's service by becoming a monk. But it did not come about at once or easily. His brothers married, the elder producing two sons. Varfolomei remained celibate, lived at home, and cared for his parents. When their time neared, they underwent tonsure; when they died, Varfolomei buried them and mourned the obligatory 40 days. Both the tonsures and the burials probably occurred in nearby Khot'kovo at what was likely the family's seignorial monastery of the Intercession of the Mother of God.[15] Only then did Varfolomei make his break.

Varfolomei turned over the family's property to his brother Petr and sought out his elder brother Stefan who, Epifanii tells us, upon the death of his wife, had become a monk at the monastery of the Intercession in Khot'kovo. Together they set out into the wilderness to found a hermitage, build a chapel, and live as solitaries. The "wilderness" was nearby and very likely on a site that was a family domain, perhaps coming to Varfolomei from Stefan when the latter became a monk.[16] Young Varfolomei had taken the first step into a life in which he emerged as the historical Sergius. If we pare away Epifanii's eloquent yet clichéd description of Varfolomei's piety and monkish existence, a simple truth remains. In his adolescent dreams the youth fashioned for himself an idealized adult persona, the core of which was the conviction that he had to break with the world in which he had grown up if he were to save his soul. I know of no psychological theory of adolescence that explains it. Yet I cannot but think that the grim events of his childhood had an important bearing on his fateful decision to turn his back on the world.

It was Stefan who suggested the brothers dedicate their chapel to the Trinity. Metropolitan Theognostos sent them a priest to consecrate it at the beginning of the reign of Grand Prince Semen Ivanovich. Stefan, however, unable to withstand the rigors and solitude of their existence, soon left to enter a house in Moscow. Thereupon Varfolomei summoned an abbot, one Mitrofan, probably from the monastery at Khot'kovo, to tonsure him. This occurred on 7 October, the feast day of the martyrs Sergius and Bacchus. Epifanii does not tell us what year it was, but in his encomium to Sergius, probably written in 1411 or 1412, he said Sergius died in 1392 at the age of 70 after having lived 50 of those years as a monk. From this and our knowledge that Semen became grand prince in 1340 and held the title until plague took both him and Theognostos in 1353, we can conclude that Varfolomei became the monk Sergius in 1342.[17]

Sergius then began a mythic existence in the "empty place" devoid of human contact. He lived alone and shared meager provisions with animals, all the while tormented by evil spirits and the devil. To survive Sergius displayed traits that were to bring him fame: a physical strength to overcome hardship and a mental toughness grounded on stubborn faith to ward off psychological trials. The description of Sergius's torments may well have come from stories related by his first disciples, for we have no evidence that Epifanii knew Sergius before 1380, if then. However, parallels between Epifianii's narrative of these ordeals and those in the life of the hermit and founder of the "Great Lavra" in Palestine, St. Sabas the Sanctified (d. 532), indicate that his model for Sergius's struggles came from traditional hagiography.[18] Regardless, Sergius's ordeal became an icon that disciples sought to emulate and that lay admirers found awe-inspiring. Word about this wondrous man got around: settlers appeared, villages grew up nearby, even a small town. Pious solitaries, appropriately 12 in number, gathered around Sergius, built their own cells, and sought to live as he did.

Epifanii's story, however, contains inconvenient inconsistencies, one of which continued to dog his narrative. Epifanii called Mitrofan Trinity's abbot. Yet he admitted that, despite Sergius's entreaties that he stay, Mitrofan blessed Sergius and departed, leaving the young monk to his solitude. Later, having successfully endured his trials and having attracted fellow solitaries, Sergius was ready for the next step in the divine plan, to become abbot of his house. His fellow hermits had urged him to do this and Sergius had resisted, fearing that the "love of rank" (*sanoliubia*) would corrupt his soul. Or so Epifanii explained with words taken from the life of St. Sabas. To make Sergius accept the abbacy, Epifanii had Mitrofan reappear so that he might die and open up the vacancy. In his words, "A year went by and the aforementioned abbot who had tonsured the blessed Sergius took sick and, after lingering on for a while, died."[19] The other inconsistency is that the land, to begin with, was hardly empty. It was part of a princely appanage spanning the main road from Moscow to Pereiaslavl', thence to Uglich on the northern Volga, and was filling up with settlers *before* Sergius founded his hermitage. The Zubachev family, for instance, at the outset of the fourteenth century had assembled a large estate that abutted Trinity. Not far away were several monasteries, one of which was the house in Khot'kovo. Epifanii made the miracle worker the cause of this flowering.[20] It may have been partially so, but who of Epifanii's contemporaries would doubt that such a marvelous phenomenon could have anything other than a wondrous cause?

There is also a problem of chronology. Simply put, twice Epifanii referred to the length of time Sergius lived alone. At one point he said Sergius lived two years, more or less, as a solitary. Further on he mentioned that Mitrofan's final illness began a year after he tonsured Sergius.[21] These references understate the length of time between Sergius's tonsure and his decision to become abbot, and probably the duration of his hermetic existence. We know this because Epifanii provides information allowing us to date Sergius's installation as abbot precisely. When Sergius at last consented and they sent for a bishop to install him, Epifanii wrote, Metropolitan Aleksei was in Constantinople. So Sergius went with his request to Bishop Afanasii of Volyniia, whom Aleksei had left in charge during his absence and who was then in nearby Pereiaslavl'. Afanasii already knew of Sergius's piety. In one day Afanasii made Sergius subdeacon, then deacon; on the next he raised Sergius to the rank of priest-abbot.[22] Aleksei, in fact, was not yet metropolitan, although he was Grand Prince Semen's choice for the job and Theognostos had designated Aleksei as his successor and made him bishop of Vladimir. But metropolitans of Rus' were under the jurisdiction of the patriarch of Constantinople and had to go to them for installation. Aleksei went to Constantinople twice to make his case. The first time he arrived in the summer of 1353 and remained until the fall of 1354. He also wintered there in 1355–56. Mitrofan probably died from the same epidemic that took Semen and Theognostos in the first half of 1353. If so, Afanasii installed Sergius as abbot during Aleksei's first absence, probably during the summer of 1354.[23] Thus Sergius became abbot 12 years after he was tonsured. Albeit grudgingly, he had taken the first of a series of steps by which he was to reintegrate himself into the society he had forsaken to become a monk.

Epifanii was only slightly premature in dating Sergius's fame, the monastery's growth, and the area's prosperity to the reign of Grand Prince Ivan Ivanovich (1353–56).[24] In his own words Trinity was a small house of no more than 12 monks and Sergius; that is, until an Archimandrite Simon came from Smolensk "with his property" (*eshche zhe i imenie prinese*) to join the brotherhood. This probably occurred between 1356 and 1359 when Grand Prince Algirdas of Lithuania on three occasions invaded the Smolensk principality. Only that, one may assume with Kuchkin, could have induced Simon to abandon his abbacy of the SS. Boris and Gleb Monastery in Smolensk, and a significant place in the church hierarchy, for a life in Muscovy.[25] Once there, he chose to live at Trinity. The choice makes sense only if he had foreknowledge that its abbot was a remarkable holy man. Others also thought so. "Many persons from different towns and lands came to live with him," wrote Epifanii. They built more cells and became monks, "and still who would have thought, that where once there was only forest, thicket and wilderness inhabited by rabbits, foxes, wolves and an occasional bear, and where demons lurked, now stands a church and a great monastery has come into existence, many monks have gathered and the doxology sounds in churches and monastic cells, and [that] ceaseless prayers to God are heard?" Sergius, Epifanii wrote, welcomed rich and poor, young and old into the brotherhood.[26]

Epifanii's colorful stories, showing that Sergius continued to live the simple life he had known as a solitary and by example and scolding taught his fellow monks to emulate him, although drawn from models in the hagiography of monk-saints, ring true. Sergius continued to dress in rags and to work the fields like a peasant. He refused to beg for alms or allow his monks to do so, even in time of need. This probably referred to the famine of 1371.[27] Sergius treated great and humble alike, winning the love and respect of peasant and princely pilgrims who came to see him. Indeed, it is tempting to identify his unnamed princely visitor as Vladimir Andreevich, who between 1372 and 1374 became lord of Radonezh and who, in 1374, acquainted with Sergius's regimen at Trinity, sought Sergius's aid in founding the Vysotskii Monastery at Serpukhov.[28]

We are now at the moment Sergius became the historical figure mentioned in other sources. Some historians believe that in 1374 or soon after Grand Prince Dmitrii Ivanovich made Sergius one of his confessors. The evidence is Metropolitan-designate Kipriian's letter of 23 June 1378, entreating Sergius and his nephew Fedor, by then abbot of the Simonov Monastery near Moscow, as "keepers of the soul" of the grand prince to persuade Dmitrii to accept Kipriian as Aleksei's successor.[29] In 1374 Patriarch Philotheos had chosen Kipriian, a Bulgarian monk who had come from Mt. Athos to Constantinople, as his envoy to Aleksei.[30] He met Aleksei in Tver' and accompanied the metropolitan to Pereiaslavl' for the assembly of princes convened by Dmitrii to decide the momentous issue of whether to resist the Mongols. Kuchkin thought Sergius, as Dmitrii's confessor, was there too, having baptized his son Iurii in Pereiaslavl' earlier that year. If not there, Kipriian probably met Sergius at the Trinity Monastery while accompanying Aleksei on his return to Moscow. We know that by 1380 Dmitrii made Fedor his confessor; it probably happened in 1377 or 1378. We know too that by 1378 Dmitrii chose Archimandrite Mikhail of the Moscow Monastery of Our Savior to be his confessor and his nominee as Aleksei's successor. That Sergius was a third seems likely. The Trinity chronicle for 1374 has another entry confirming the abbot's historicity. During lent, it related, Sergius became ill, but that "with the Lord's help" he was better by St. Simeon's Day, 27 April.[31]

* Epifanii viewed the subsequent section of Sergius's life, in which he established a rule of communal living at Trinity, as a defining moment in his career, as indeed it was. By it Sergius concluded a journey of reintegration into society, becoming a central figure in the development of Russian monasticism. Sergius could hardly have done this without considerable inner turmoil and probably would not have carried it through without assistance. To understand how it came about it is important to realize that it was preceded and in some manner precipitated by the return to Trinity of Sergius's brother Stefan and his son Ivan. Only from Epifanii's information about Stefan do we learn that, having left Sergius at his hermitage, Stefan went to Moscow and lived in the monastery of the Epiphany along with the future metropolitan Aleksei, a member of the Biakont boiar family. Epifanii said that Stefan and Aleksei stood together and sang in the choir during services, implying that they were otherwise close to one another. Grand Prince Semen, he remembered, learned about Stefan and his exemplary life and saw that he was made a presbyter, then a priest, and later abbot of the prominent Epiphany Monastery. He said also that Semen made Stefan his confessor, as did Boiar Vasilii Vasil'evich Vel'iaminov, successor to the title of "thousand man" formerly held by his forebear Protasii and his brother Fedor. Vasilii and Fedor's clan was patron to the Epiphany Monastery and had ties to Stefan and Sergius's family.[32] Yet Semen's testament mentioned another as his confessor and, to repeat, only Epifanii said anything about Stefan.[33]

There is also a problem in dating Stefan's return to Trinity and with Epifanii's explanation of why it happened. Epifanii placed it immediately after his account of Sergius's installation as abbot in 1353 and said that Stefan returned in order that Sergius tonsure his son. He also said that Ivan, who accompanied his father Stefan to Trinity, was 10 or 12 years old. Ivan must have been born no later than 1342, when his father was widowed and became a monk.[34] If so, then Ivan's tonsure took place no later than 1354. Stefan's sudden return must have been connected to political events in Moscow in the aftermath of Grand Prince Semen's death in 1353. His brother Ivan Ivanovich (1353–59) succeeded him and immediately replaced Stefan's patron Vasilii Vel'iaminov as thousand man with Aleksei Khvost. The Rogozhskii chronicle dated it to 1356, but it most likely occurred not long after Ivan assumed power.[35] Stefan, out of favor in Moscow, one may surmise, returned to the monastery he had helped to found and Sergius tonsured Stefan's son as the monk Fedor. Epifanii described the return as a joyous occasion. There was nothing to suggest that Stefan might have been disappointed by the prospect that he and Fedor were fated to remain at Trinity. Yet, given his prominence in founding and naming Trinity, and his meteoric rise to prominence in Moscow, it would hardly be surprising if he was bitter when contemplating that he would spend the rest of his life at Trinity as an ordinary monk under a vow of obedience to his younger brother.

At this point the manuscript containing an unadulterated text of Epifanii's life breaks off. For subsequent events leading to the implementation of a cenobitic rule one must rely on later editions of Sergius's life, the oldest being Pakhomii's first rewriting of Epifanii in the late 1430s. They differ in telling Sergius's story, so one must consider all of them to piece together what happened. The points of issue are many, but the key to understanding them is again in the dating. When did Sergius establish a cenobitic rule? Golubinskii, Bureichenko, Meyendorff, and Borisov concluded that it occurred between 1354 and 1356. But Kloss, Kuchkin, and Aver'ianov believed it happened only in the 1370s, well after Sergius became abbot and well after Stefan's return, and I can add supporting arguments for their conclusion. But first the story of what happened.

Pakhomii's First Edition and the Extended Edition (1518) of Sergius's life said that Greek envoys brought Sergius a letter and gifts from Patriarch Philotheos of Constantinople. The gifts consisted of a case (*futliar'*) containing a small cross to be hung on Sergius's chest, and two articles of monastic dress. The cross survives, and in 1918 an investigation revealed that it was a reliquary; the inscription on it said that it contained part of the True Cross and remains of various martyrs among whom were the "new Lithuanian martyrs." Sergius took the letter to Metropolitan Aleksei and read it in his presence. Philotheos's letter said Sergius's monastic existence was praised everywhere and well known to Aleksei, yet was deficient in that Sergius had not instituted a rule of common living in his house. Sergius thereupon turned to Aleksei for direction and the metropolitan urged that Sergius implement its charge immediately. This Sergius did. Trinity's monks no longer were to have their own property and Sergius appointed monastic officers to manage what they held in common.[36] Pakhomii's first rewriting of Epifanii and the Extended Edition of the life agree about what happened next:

> Not long after the trouble began. [The devil], detesting virtue, who could not endure the brilliant radiance of the saint, resolved to triumph over and extinguish that light, and implanted the idea [among the brothers] that [they] did not want Sergius to be abbot. [It came about] one day, it was a Saturday, while at evening prayer. The abbot Sergius, robed in priestly garments, was at the altar. His brother Stefan stood on the left in the choir [and] asked the Canonmaster (*kanonarkh*), "Who gave you that book?" The Canonmaster answered, "The abbot gave it to me." To which [Stefan] replied, "Just who is the abbot here; did I not previously occupy that position?" [Stefan] also

> said other improper things. The saint at the altar heard all of this and said nothing. But when he came out of the church the saint did not go to his cell, but immediately left the monastery without anyone seeing him and set out alone along the road leading to Kinela.[37]

After a night on the road Sergius found refuge at the Makhrishchskii Monastery of the Trinity in the principality of Pereiaslavl', 30 kilometers from Trinity. He inquired of its abbot, Stefan, where he might find an empty place at which to found another house. The site Sergius selected was nearby on the Kirzhach River. Of course, Trinity's brothers discovered that Sergius had disappeared. Eventually they located him with the help of Makhrishchskii's abbot. They pleaded with Sergius to return, but he refused. The new monastery flourished; two or three, then more, monks left Trinity to join Sergius. They built a church. Princes and boiars donated silver to the new house. This caused Trinity's monks to complain to the metropolitan that they were without a pastor and to ask that he order Sergius to return. Aleksei thereupon sent archimandrites Gerasim and Pavel to Sergius to see that it was done. Only after Aleksei promised to consecrate the church of the Annunciation at Kirzhach and appoint Sergius's disciple Roman as its abbot did Sergius obey, returning to Trinity to the rejoicing of its brothers.[38]

Along with protestations about the love that Sergius had for Stefan, Pakhomii thereafter wrote that Fedor decided to leave Trinity to establish his own monastery, that he obtained Sergius's blessing to do so, and that he left, taking with him some brothers (and, presumably, Stefan). In his First Edition Pakhomii said Metropolitan Aleksei helped Fedor find a site at a place called Simonovo located under the walls of the capital on the Moscow River. Fedor became its first abbot and initially dedicated its church to the Birth of the Mother of God. Pakhomii's Second Edition, in contradiction to other versions, revealed that Sergius initially resisted Fedor's request, saying that it might lead him to seek "worldly glory." It also said that Grand Prince Dmitrii Ivanovich and Aleksei overruled Sergius to obtain Fedor's release. But it too said that Sergius helped Fedor to select the site for his house. In the Extended Edition this episode appears several chapters removed from the description of Sergius's return to Trinity and (like late editions of Pakhomii's life) insisted that Sergius, rather than Aleksei, helped Fedor to secure a site and found the monastery. These were elements of the Sergius cult. They served to obscure the obvious; that Sergius's triumphal return had been the cause of the ignominious departure from Trinity of Fedor, Stefan, and other malcontents.[39]

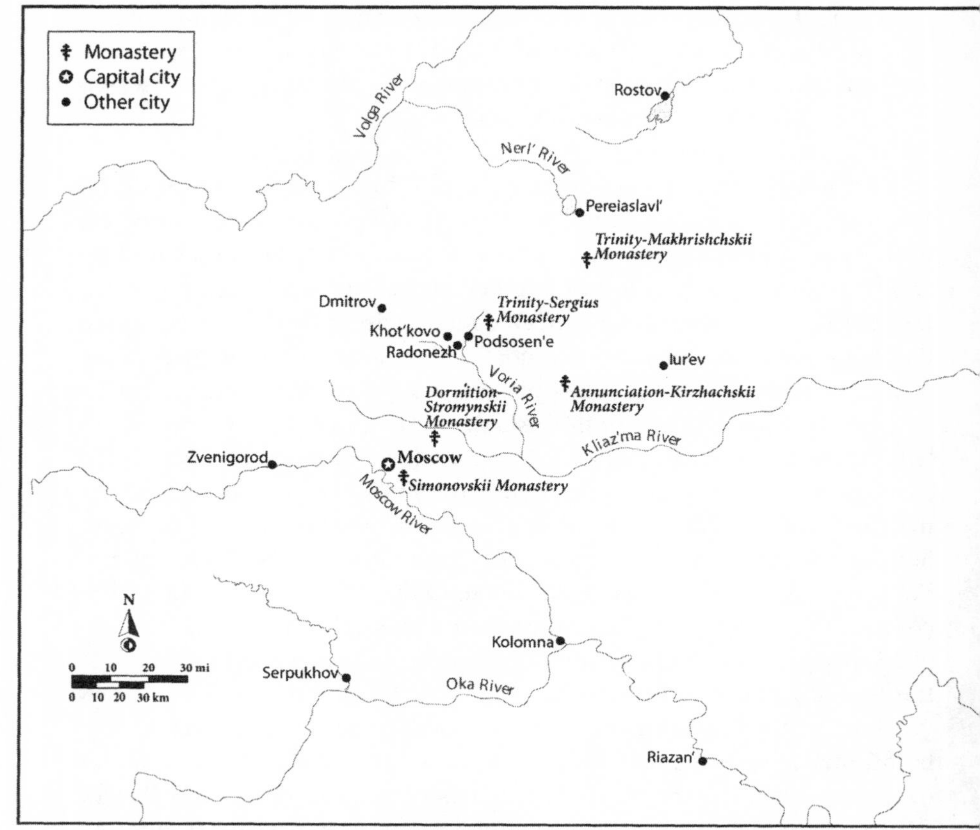

MAP 1—The Trinity-Sergius Monastery and Its Environs in the Sixteenth Century

The departure point for putting a date to these events is our knowledge that it happened during the patriarchate of Philotheos Kokkinos. Philotheos was twice patriarch, the first time from November 1353 to 22 November 1354, the second from 8 September 1364 to September 1376. As mentioned previously, historians Golubinskii, Bureichenko, Meyendorff, and Borisov connected the coming of Greek envoys with Philotheos's letter to the return of Aleksei from one of his two trips to Constantinople. For Golubinskii, Meyendorff, and Bureichenko it was in 1354, after his first trip; for Borisov it was in 1355, after his second.[40] Bureichenko's argument for the date is notable for its clever hypothesis about how a letter from Patriarch Philotheos might have been addressed to Sergius even though neither Philotheos nor Aleksei could have known that Sergius had become abbot of Trinity during

Aleksei's absence. Aleksei, he reasoned, not Philotheos, was the prime mover in instituting a cenobitic rule at Trinity. Arriving in Moscow in 1354 and learning that Sergius had become abbot of Trinity, Bureichenko said, Aleksei conspired with the patriarchal envoy Georgios Perdikos, who had accompanied him, to prepare the letter in Philotheos's name and present it with gifts to Sergius. The hypothesis makes understandable the succeeding episode in which a bitter Stefan, jealous of his younger brother, led a faction of monks in opposition to the new rule. Given the penury and instability of the patriarchate, that Aleksei and Georgios would forge the patriarch's name to a letter was not as unlikely as it might seem. Moreover, there is no copy of the letter in the patriarchal archive; it comes down to us *only* in Sergius's life. Also, the inscription on the cross/reliquary allegedly sent from Constantinople is not in Greek but in the Rus' language and the relics in the cross were in part those of three Orthodox saints martyred in Lithuania in 1347. T. V. Nikolaeva, an authority on applied arts, tentatively dated its creation to the early fifteenth century.[41] These assessments lend credence to Bureichenko's supposition that someone also crafted the letter in Rus' and that it happened in the 1350s. Bureichenko dated Sergius's implementation of the rule to 1356, but his attempt to link it to political rivalries at the Muscovite court is at best speculative. Bureichenko theorized that Grand Prince Ivan Ivanovich replaced Vasilii Vel'iaminov as thousand man in 1353 with Khvost while Stefan's ally Metropolitan-designate Aleksei was in Constantinople, precipitating Stefan's return to Trinity and the squabble that broke out when Sergius implemented a cenobitic rule. Sergius subsequently returned to Trinity with Aleksei's help and the cenobitic rule was preserved.

Compelling as Bureichenko's arguments are, it is more likely that the transformation of Trinity into a cenobitic house occurred during Philotheos's second tenure as patriarch. It is unlikely that the patriarchal letter was a forgery. Aver'ianov finds an echo of it in a letter from an anonymous patriarch to an unnamed abbot about monastic life in manuscripts of a fifteenth-century Russian *Kormchaia kniga*, a collection of church canons, sermons, and legislation.[42] Like Aleksei, Philotheos was a reformer of monastic practices.[43] Only in the 1360s did Aleksei begin to establish cenobitic rules in monasteries of his see.[44] And only then did Sergius begin to attract attention to his austere lifestyle and moral strength. Patriarchal embassies frequently made their way to Moscow at that time and could have brought word of Sergius to Constantinople. Another reason to connect the implementation of a rule of common life at Trinity to Philotheos's second term is that Sergius's life called Gerasim and Pavel, Aleksei's emissaries to Sergius at Kirzhach, archimandrites. According to the Trinity chronicle for 1363, Gerasim was an abbot when Aleksei sent Pavel and him as envoys to Nizhnii Novgorod in support of Dmitrii Donskoi's demands. Gerasim became an archimandrite in 1365.[45] Additionally, the reference to Abbot Stefan of the Makhrishchskii Monastery must refer to a period after 1370, the most likely date for the founding of his house. The Makhrishchskii Monastery where Sergius took refuge and the house Sergius soon established on the Kirzhach River were in Pereiaslavl', a domain of Grand Prince Dmitrii. By going there, Kuchkin pointed out, Sergius placed himself under Dmitrii's protection. The life of Sergius confirms this in noting that Metropolitan Aleksei immediately blessed the undertaking and that boiars from the court underwrote its foundation with gifts. It was with their patronage that Sergius returned to Trinity on his own terms to restore a cenobitic rule.[46]

Finally, the nature of the relics in the cross/reliquary that came with Philotheos's letter suggests that it came to Moscow in the mid or late 1370s. Grand Prince Algirdas of Lithuania burned three Orthodox believers in Vilnius in 1347. It is hardly possible that the patriarch of Constantinople canonized them as martyrs or that Aleksei in Moscow might have possessed some of their remains and placed them in the reliquary less than a decade later. In the mid-fourteenth century Moscow and Lithuania battled to control Rus'. This rivalry had ecclesiastical repercussions: in Lithuania, Catholic and Orthodox churches struggled for supremacy at the Lithuanian court and Patriarch Philotheos was an ardent defender of the latter's cause there against Catholic influence. But the Orthodox metropolitanate of Kiev and all Rus' extended over both Muscovy and Lithuania, and its head Aleksei used the church's power on behalf of the interests of the grand princes of Moscow. Lithuania's rulers demanded a separate metropolitanate. In 1355 Byzantine Emperor John V replaced Philotheos with Callistos, who pursued an ecclesiastical policy designed to win Algirdas for Orthodoxy, appointing one Roman Orthodox metropolitan of Lithuania, thereby removing its bishops from Aleksei's jurisdiction. This was hardly a propitious time for Constantinople to canonize Orthodox faithful whom Algirdas had martyred. Aleksei, by the same token, never ceased to rally Orthodox opinion in Moscow, Byzantium, and Lithuania to protect his jurisdiction over the entire see. He may well have promoted the canonization of the Lithuanian martyrs. But their veneration had to wait until 1374, when Philotheos once again was patriarch in Constantinople and the attempt to divide the Rus' metropolitanate was repudiated.[47] Knowing this is one more reason to suppose the initiative to institute a cenobitic rule at Trinity came after this date and that Philotheos crafted the letter and the gift in Constantinople.

But exactly when? Aver'ianov thought Philotheos's envoys Kipriian and Georgios Perdikos brought his letter and the cross/reliquary to Sergius in March 1374 as part of their mission to rally Russian and Lithuanian princes to make peace, keep the Russian see united, and challenge Mongol rule. Accepting, as I do not, that Sergius already carried out a successful mission to Nizhnii Novgorod in the 1360s, Aver'ianov argued that the letter and gift were but a small episode in an effort to groom Sergius to succeed Aleksei, then 69, as metropolitan. Kuchkin, on the other hand, proposed that patriarchal envoys Georgios Perdikos and John Dokianos arrived in Moscow with Philotheos's letter and gifts to Sergius in January 1377 (the Rogozhskii chronicle says in the winter of 1376–77), or at least three months after the aforementioned patriarch was again removed from office.[48] Both dates are plausible, but I think Aver'ianov's the more likely, even if I think his evaluation of its significance mistaken.

Sergius instituted the reform sometime in 1374. From his life we may be certain that a faction of brothers opposed the rule and that Stefan either instigated or came to lead those who caused Sergius to abandon Trinity. And well Stefan might have. For 20 years he had remained at Trinity in obedience to his younger brother, who was its abbot, a post Stefan had coveted. During that same period, Stefan, who once had moved in the highest political and ecclesiastical circles in Moscow, saw his brother replace him in the affection of Aleksei, now the metropolitan, and become a court favorite who baptized the grand prince's second son and perhaps was the ruler's confessor. Pakhomii's first two editions of Sergius's life reveal that Grand Prince Dmitrii and Aleksei resolved the quarrel at Trinity by arranging for Fedor and dissident monks to depart and found the Simonov Monastery.

* The institution of a cenobitic rule in 1374 was a crucial moment in the monastery's history,; indeed, in the history of Russian monasticism. By creating an environment for cooperative administration and the pooling of resources, it allowed Trinity and other monasteries to flourish. Philotheos urged it; Aleksei may have instigated it; but Sergius made it work and by his lifestyle defined the ideal by which monks were to live. Sergius and his disciples founded numerous houses and inspired the foundation of still more.

The times were propitious for establishing monasteries. The marginal quality of Muscovy's boggy and forested lands and a harsh climate contributed to low population densities and the availability of vacant land in Muscovy, even at its center. Reoccurring epidemics of plague in the fourteenth and into the fifteenth century, after over a century of Mongol raids and tribute, caused more demographic attrition and land abandonments in an economy that was just beginning to recover. Land was plentiful and cheap.[49] After trips to Constantinople, Metropolitan Aleksei promoted monastic reforms in a manner designed to take advantage of economic and demographic trends. One element was the introduction of the Jerusalem *typikon*, a rule designed to standardize liturgical practices, rules of behavior, and institutional life. Constantinople adopted it a century earlier and it spread gradually throughout the Orthodox world. There are references to it in Rus' in the late thirteenth century; the earliest edition of it in Moscow is in manuscripts of the second half of the fourteenth century. Its implementation continued into the fifteenth. In versions known in Muscovite Rus' the section containing rules of communal life for monasteries drew on the rule of the Studios house in Constantinople. While not stringent in its specifics, it nevertheless set down principles for common liturgical observance, communal dining in the monastic refectory, and communal organization of monastic property. The monastery might own property but austerity was to guide the daily life of the individual monk. Equally important, monks in most things were to submit to their chosen abbot, and to lay and clerical lords.[50] Houses with a cenobitic rule were ideally organized to pool resources to acquire lands, to institute an efficient division of labor to exploit their property, and to develop economic networks with subsidiary houses and urban yards.[51]

Archimandrite Ivan was said to have established the first cenobitic rule in Moscow at his Vysokopetrovskii Monastery. It was mentioned under 1379 in connection with an account of Ivan's presence in a delegation traveling to Constantinople. L. A. Beliaev thinks it was founded in the 1350s or 1360s, if not earlier.[52] Metropolitan Aleksei founded the cenobite Chudovskii Monastery in the Moscow kremlin in 1365. Claims that he established the Vladychin Monastery in Serpukhov and the Alekseevskii convent in Moscow for his sisters, each with a cenobitic rule, are in late sources and possibly legendary. Pakhomii's First Edition of Sergius's life and subsequent editions mention that Aleksei founded a monastery with a church dedicated to the image of "Christ not drawn by human hands" on the Iauza River just east of Moscow, possibly in 1366 in order to fulfill a vow made after what he considered a divine intervention that had saved him from a storm when returning from Constantinople. Aleksei provided the funds, but Sergius set the project in motion and sent Andronik, a fellow native of Rostov whom he had tonsured ten years earlier and who just then had vowed to found his own house, to be its first abbot. The Extended Edition of Sergius's life said the house had a cenobitic rule. The pattern, in which Metropolitan Aleksei implemented and encouraged the creation of new houses with a cenobitic rule rather than imposing the rule on recalcitrant monks in established houses who lived from their own incomes (as was the case at Trinity), characterized the explosion of monastic foundings that followed. His successor, Metropolitan Kipriian, also promoted the movement.[53]

Sergius was at the forefront of these foundings and appeared larger than life in their stories. In 1374, at the behest of Prince Vladimir Andreevich of Serpukhov, Sergius supplied his disciple Afanasii as abbot for the cenobitic Vysotskii Monastery. Kloss mentioned other houses that adopted cenobitic rules in Pereiaslavl', Vladimir, and Nizhnii Novgorod before or soon after Aleksei's death in 1378. Sergius's hagiographers linked him to many of them.[54] Sergius founded the cenobitic monastery of the Annunciation at Kirzhach circa 1374 and made his disciple Roman its abbot.[55] That year or the next Sergius's nephew Fedor left Trinity. Whatever the circumstances, we know Sergius assisted him in founding the monastery of the Birth of the Mother of God at Simonovo, near Moscow. Fedor moved his house to a nearby site in 1379. It too had a cenobitic rule.[56] In Pakhomii's Third Edition, dated by Kloss to 1437–40, we have the earliest claim that Sergius, late in life, founded another monastery for Grand Prince Dmitrii at a place called Golutvin, near Kolomna at the juncture of the Moscow and Oka rivers. He dedicated it to the Epiphany, and as its abbot Sergius installed the Trinity priest-monk Grigorii. Kloss thought the passage drew on Epifanii's original biography. Indeed, it seems to be an inflated version of the account in the Extended Edition, which, with emendations, contained Epifanii's original text. The most likely date is 1385, when Sergius passed through Kolomna to and from Riazan' on a diplomatic mission for Dmitrii.[57] Both Kuchkin and Kloss doubted later stories, credited by Golubinskii, that Sergius created the monastery of Saints Boris and Gleb near Rostov and the Georg'ev hermitage in Gorokhovets, there being no mention of them in editions of Sergius's life or in early sources. Aver'ianov revisited the sources about Sergius's founding of the Georg'ev hermitage. He found them creditable and dated the founding to 1365, during Sergius's purported mission to Nizhnii Novgorod.[58] I am not convinced.

Sergius also established the cenobite house of the Dormition at Stronym on the Dubenka River. It was mentioned in the Trinity chronicle under the year 6887, or 1378/79:

> That same year the venerable elder, Abbot Sergius, built a church in the name of the holy Mother of God in honor of her esteemed dormition and decorated it with icons and books, and established a monastery and put up cells on the Dubenka river at Stronym, and recruited monks and sent out a single presbyter named Leontii from the big monastery, the great laura [sic], whom he appointed and installed to be abbot in that monastery. That same fall on the

> first day of December, the name day of the holy prophet Naum, the church was consecrated. Sergius built this monastery on the order of Grand Prince Dmitrii Ivanovich.[59]

Kuchkin theorized that Dmitrii sponsored the monastery's founding to fulfill a pledge made while visiting Sergius before his victory over Khan Begich in 1478 on the Vozha River; Kloss dated the founding to 1381, or after Dmitrii's famous victory at Kulikovo in 1380. This was "correct" in that it validated Pakhomii's claim in his life of Sergius, one expanded in later editions, in chronicles and tales, that it followed Sergius's blessing and intercession for Dmitrii, ensuring his victory over Emir Mamai. Borisov would have it both ways, positing the existence of two monasteries of the Dormition founded by Sergius for Dmitrii at different sites on the Dubenka River, one before, the other after the victory of 1380. This was a conclusion reached earlier by Evgenii Golubinskii. I see no reason, however, not to accept the date of 1378/79 in the Trinity chronicle. In my next chapter I shall argue that the story that Dmitrii communicated with Sergius before one or another battle emerged later as an element in the development of Sergius's cult.[60]

Sergius early on inspired others to emulate his deeds. Although most of our knowledge of their acts come from hagiography, it is possible to confirm some from independent testimony. For others one needs rely on the apparent historicity of the life, even if it originated well after the event it described. Despite the difficulties involved in dating exactly what transpired in the lives of monastic founders, some of the foundings probably occurred before Trinity began to celebrate Sergius's sanctity in 1422. In other words, Sergius's example, rather than his cult, inspired these acts. Thus, in 1398 or 1399 Prince Iurii Dmitrievich of Zvenigorod, whom Sergius had baptized, invited the monk Savva to found a seigniorial monastery for him at a place called Storzhi near Zvenigorod. Although Savva's veneration cannot be attested earlier than 1505, his life, recounted by Markel of that house about 1552, referred to events that could only have been known to Savva's contemporaries or that can be confirmed in earlier sources: that Savva (d. 1406) had been elected abbot of Trinity by its monks in 1392 when Sergius's nominee Nikon refused to serve; that previously Savva had been abbot of the Dormition Monastery at Stronym founded by Sergius, and before that the confessor of Trinity's monks.[61] Another legend had it that one Mefodii, a disciple of Sergius, perhaps as early as 1361 founded the cenobite monastery of St. Nicholas at the junction of the Iakhroma and Pesnosha rivers in the Dmitrov principality. Like Sergius, he died in 1392. Again, a later source lent credence to the story: an immunity charter to the monastery issued in April

1547. It said that Prince Petr Dmitrievich, whom Sergius baptized in 1385, had given the monastery a village.[62] Like Savva's house it was in a domain of Prince Iurii Dmitrievich. Finally, another life, that of St. Dmitrii Prilutsk, says the saint visited Sergius, possibly in the late 1370s, before setting off to found the Monastery of Our Savior on the Vologda River before Dmitrii Donskoi's death in 1389. Dmitrii also was said to have died in the same year as Sergius, on 11 February 1392.[63]

* Metropolitan Aleksei, age 85, died on 12 February 1378.[64] For 24 years he had presided over the Russian see in a manner that served Moscow well. For the first 12 years he was regent of the realm during Dmitrii's minority. In 1359 he intervened at the Horde to reverse its decision to bestow the grand princely title on Dmitrii Konstantinovich of Suzdal'. In 1367 he presided over the replacement of Moscow's wooden walls with those of stone. His diplomacy strengthened Moscow against Tver' and Lithuania. All this in addition to his energetic administration of the metropolitanate of Kiev and all Rus'. Moscow's princes understood how important it was to have a metropolitan of their liking and insisted on nominating candidates for that office. But their choice had to be acceptable to bishops and to leaders of the monastic establishment, such as Sergius and Fedor of Simonov. Most importantly, the patriarch of Constantinople, whose tenure depended on serving the political interests of whoever was emperor, with his synod, had jurisdiction over the Russian see and had to approve that choice and install the candidate in office. In 1378 this was extraordinarily difficult. Byzantium was weak, under attack by Turkish armies, its economy controlled by Genoese and Venetian commercial interests, and it secular and spiritual establishments divided as to how to deal with these staggering problems. During the struggle for the Russian see that ensued even before Aleksei's death, contending parties in Constantinople raised four men to the patriarchal throne: Philotheos (second term, 1364–76), Makarios (1377–79), Neilos (1380–88), and Anthony (1389–90, 1391–97). Between February 1388 and January 1389, there was no patriarch.[65]

That the Russian metropolitanate was torn by conflicting international forces complicated the problem further. The metropolitan, like the patriarch, had to heed the Mongol khan at a time the Horde itself was in turmoil. Princes and Orthodox leaders in Lithuania demanded a metropolitan who would help them to stem Catholic influence from Poland and who would rule evenhandedly between their interests and those of Moscow. If a metropolitan residing in Moscow ignored their interests, they said, the see had to be split, with Lithuania having its own metropolitan. Patriarch Philotheos had promoted Lithuanian-Muscovite amity in order to preserve the unity of the Russian see and to persuade its princes to unite against the Mongols. In 1371 he encouraged Prince Vladimir Andreevich to marry a daughter of the Lithuanian prince Algirdas to bring peace between Moscow and Lithuania. In the spring of 1374, he sent Kipriian to Russia in furtherance of this policy. With Aleksei, Kipriian consecrated an erstwhile ally in Dionisii, a monk of the Monastery of the Caves in Kiev, as bishop of Suzdal'.[66] But within a year Lithuania and Moscow were at odds and Algirdas threatened Philotheos that he would turn to the Catholics if he did not have an independent metropolitan. In a desperate attempt to salvage the Russian see, Philotheos on 2 December 1375 consecrated Kipriian metropolitan of Kiev, which was within the Lithuanian state, with the implied promise that on Aleksei's death Kipriian would rule the whole see. On 9 June 1376 Kipriian arrived in Kiev to assume office.[67]

The anti-Kipriian act of 1380, issued by Patriarch Neilos and his synod and surviving only in part, said Aleksei wrote to Constantinople that Kipriian's appointment caused grief in Rus'. Even so, the act was noticeably vague regarding Aleksei's position.[68] But Grand Prince Dmitrii did not hesitate. No later than 16 April 1376, he arranged that his keeper of the seal, Dmitrii, be tonsured as the monk Mikhail (but called Mitiai), and made archimandrite of the Monastery of Our Savior in Moscow and metropolitan-designate to succeed Aleksei. The Muscovite court supported the nomination of one of their own, but Aleksei, despite pressure from Moscow boiars, refused to endorse Dmitrii's choice, saying that Mikhail had only just been tonsured and that only the patriarch of Constantinople and his synod could consecrate him. The source for this is the Tale of Mitiai. It is the most detailed account of the crisis over the metropolitanate, but no less tendentious than other sources. Its earliest text is in the metropolitan's compilation of 1408 as rendered in the Trinity chronicle. For this and other reasons G. M. Prokhorov, its foremost investigator, thought Kipriian produced it, perhaps in 1382, when for a moment he occupied the metropolitan's throne with Dmitrii's approval.[69] Pakhomii's first and later editions of Sergiuis's life had a different description of the state of affairs in 1378. Aleksei, they said, summoned Sergius and told him that, with the approval of the grand prince and his boiars, Aleksei wanted Sergius to be the next metropolitan. Sergius, ever humble, refused, saying he was unworthy.[70] Aside from its statement about the views of the grand prince and his boiars, which is contrary to everything we know about the affair, the text rings true. Aleksei at the time might well have put forward Sergius's candidacy, knowing that both Kipriian and Constantinople were favorable to him. But the dying Aleksei was powerless to influence events.

When he died, according to the Tale of Mitiai, Dmitrii buried him with honor behind the alter of the Dormition cathedral and Mitiai moved into the metropolitan's residence, took over its treasury, and proceeded to treat bishops and abbots as if he were metropolitan. It left Sergius at the center of the firestorm.[71]

On news of Aleksei's death, Kipriian set out from Kiev and on 3 June 1378 wrote to Sergius of Trinity and Fedor of Simonov addressing them as pious men who, "despise all worldly pursuits and concern [themselves] only with the will of God" and wrote that he was coming,

> to Moscow to my son the Grand Prince bringing peace and a blessing as once Joseph was sent by his father to his brother (Gen. 45). Whatever some say about me, I am a bishop, not a military man. I bring a blessing, as the Lord who sent his disciples to preach, teaching them saying, "He that receiveth you, receiveth me" (Mat. 10:40; John 13:20). So be ready to see me, wherever it pleases you. I am looking forward to seeing you and being consoled with spiritual comfort.[72]

Either ignorant of Dmitrii's state of mind or, if forewarned, determined to press the issue, Kipriian turned to Sergius and Fedor to prepare the way. He knew Sergius and probably Fedor as like-minded clerics, and Patriarch Philotheos may have advised Kipriian that they would be his allies. Also, patriarchal envoys Perdikos and Dokianos had come to Moscow in 1377, probably to explain the patriarch's appointment of Kipriian as metropolitan of Kiev and as Aleksei's successor.[73] But neither they nor Sergius and Fedor—if they tried—swayed Dmitrii, who was well aware of Sergius's family history: its Rostov roots and its ties to the Vel'iaminov family that, having lost its hegemony at court in March 1375, had plotted against his line in Tver', then at the Horde. Dmitrii had also seen his court embroiled in the troublesome monks's dispute with his relatives and monks at Trinity over its rules and had had to intervene with Metropolitan Aleksei to resolve the matter by establishing Fedor at Simonov. Sergius was now master of his house and respected for a stubborn piety and independence; now in the matter of the metropolitanate, Dmitrii might suspect that his candidate Mikhail would never have Sergius's endorsement, especially if Aleksei had balked at the appointment and had asked Sergius to succeed him, and that this self-appointed guardian of righteousness, if not muzzled, might publicly embrace the cause of one he knew and respected, namely Kipriian. Sergius could not but be aware of this and that an intervention would be futile.

Eventually Kipriian realized this, as is evident from the impassioned letter he wrote to Sergius and Fedor on 23 June 1378. It was now common knowledge, Kipriian said, that although the patriarch had made him metropolitan of "the entire Russian land," Grand Prince Dmitrii had sent troops to block his entry into Moscow. Having apprehended him, the prince's men put him in prison, stole his baggage and horses, and treated him and his entourage brutally before releasing them. Kipriian then rebuked Sergius and Fedor, lamenting, "was there nobody left in Moscow concerned about the soul of the grand prince and his entire domain? Did everyone stand aside without coming to his aid? It may be that lay people would do nothing out of fear for themselves, their families, or their property."

> But you who have renounced the world and all the things within it and who live for God alone, why did you remain silent, seeing such evil? If you are concerned about the soul of the grand prince and about his patrimony, why did you remain silent? Should not you have torn apart your garments and spoken before the princes without fear? Had they heeded you, it would have been well; had they killed you, you would be saints. Do you not know that the sin of the people falls on the princes, and the sin of princes on the people? Do you not know Scripture tells us that the curse of worldly parents falls upon children's children? Then how much more so the curse of spiritual fathers uproots the very bases [of life] and leads to perdition (Eccles. 3:9?)? Why do you content yourself with silence, when you see the sanctuary blasphemed, for Scripture tells us: "The abomination that maketh desolate pollutes the sanctuary" (Dan. 11:30, 12:11; Mat. 24:15)? Is this how the prince and the boiars should venerate the metropolitanate and the graves of the holy metropolitans? Is there nobody who reads the holy canons? Does nobody know what is written there?

Kipriian protested that since he arrived in Kiev he not once had spoken ill of the grand prince. Rather, he had offered acclamations of "many years" to him in celebrating the liturgy, and had cursed his critics. The grand prince blamed Kipriian for going first to Lithuania, he admitted. But Aleksei had neglected that part of his see so that he had to go there to promote Orthodoxy. Now Dmitrii wishes to divide the Russian see. Kipriian then pronounced excommunication on all who had treated him badly and said that he was going to Constantinople to seek vindication. "As to yourselves, venerable elders and abbots," he concluded, "answer me quickly, write me at once, what is your judgment, ere I withdraw my blessing for that place [Moscow]."[74]

Sergius evidently took Kipriian's second letter to heart. In yet a third letter, which he wrote from Kiev on 13 October 1378 while en route to

Constantinople, Kipriian addressed Sergius and Fedor cordially. Whatever it was they had promised to do, we don't know, but Kipriian clearly was satisfied. Perhaps Sergius had appealed to Dmitrii to remain open to Kipriian's claim to be metropolitan of all Rus', or at least to keep the see from being divided. Pakhomii's life of Sergius leaves no doubt that, whatever it was, it angered Mitiai/Mikhail so much that Trinity's brotherhood feared he would remove Sergius as abbot and destroy the monastery.[75] Sergius had become a partisan, if not the leader, of those in the church opposed to Mikhail's candidacy. It is at this point in 1379, the historian N. S. Borisov theorized, that Sergius announced that he experienced a vision of the Mother of God accompanied by the apostles Peter and John with promises of her protection for the monastery. This famous incident is in all full editions of Sergius's life, but historians still differ about when it happened. Aver'ianov dated the vision to 1382 when Sergius returned to the ruins of his monastery after Khan Tokhtamysh destroyed it. Kloss thought it occurred in 1385 when Sergius returned from his successful mission to Riazan' for Dmitrii. Kloss also opined that Pakhomii, writing in the 1430s, may have been the first to describe the miracle. This is also my conclusion. In the following chapter I argue that Nikon, Sergius's designated successor as abbot, probably invented the story, that Pakhomii then recorded it and added a new miracle in which Sergius interceded with her to bring Dmitrii victory in 1380 over Mamai.[76]

Unable to obtain consecration by the patriarch, Mikhail persuaded Dmitrii to call a council of bishops of the Russian see to install him as metropolitan with jurisdiction only in Muscovite Rus'. The council met between the fall of 1378 and the summer of 1379. According to the Tale of Mitiai, the bishops, excepting Dionisii, whom Aleksei and Kipriian had consecrated as bishop of Suzdal' in 1374, were afraid to oppose Mikhail. Prokhorov gives us a vivid sketch of this remarkable man. Dionisii had visited Byzantium and was highly literate. His bishopric included Nizhnii Novgorod. There, in the tradition of former patriarch Philotheos and of Kipriian (and Sergius?), he encouraged its Prince Boris Konstantinovich to resist the Mongols, a policy that brought tragedy when Emir Mamai sacked the city in 1378. Like Sergius, Dionisii promoted cenobite reforms of monastic life. Now he denounced Mikhail's use of the council as uncanonical. Dmitrii was about to punish him for this when Sergius intervened again to swear surety that Dionisii would remain in Moscow and no longer oppose Dmitrii's plans for the metropolitanate.[77] Dmitrii's plans received further endorsement in the form of a letter from Patriarch Makarios. Writing under pressure from Emperor Andronikos IV (1376–79), whose position depended on support of the Genoese and close ties to Mamai's Mongols, Makarios announced that he withdrew support for Kipriian's claim.

Mikhail might now administer the Russian see and come to Constantinople to be consecrated as metropolitan of all Rus'.[78]

What followed might seem farcical were it not fact. Receiving a charter (*iarlyk*) from the Horde recognizing him as metropolitan, Mikhail set out for Constantinople in July 1379 to be consecrated. But while Mikhail was at sea, Turkish and Venetian machinations in July 1379 provoked a civil war to bring about the return of Emperor John V. If it had been successful, it would have brought to power a new patriarch and a shift in ecclesiastical orientation. Next, Mikhail died just as his ship approached Constantinople. The Tale of Mitiai said that his delegation settled on Pimen, one of their own, and forged his name on a blank charter as the grand prince's nominee in order to preserve Dmitrii's ability to designate the metropolitan-to-be. In the city Kipriian sat in the patriarchal synod with the title of Metropolitan of Kiev and all Rus'. And as if that were not enough, Dionisii broke the surety that Sergius had arranged with Dmitrii, fled Moscow, and made his way to Constantinople to plead his case, one option of which was to put himself forward as another nominee to be metropolitan. Supposedly with lavish bribes, Pimen won a compromise from the new patriarch Neilos; he would be metropolitan in Moscow while Kipriian would have authority in Kiev and Lithuania. On the latter's death, Pimen was to have jurisdiction over a reunited see.[79]

Now things changed in Moscow. Dmitrii decided to resist Mamai, a perilous policy that required peace, if not cooperation, with Algirdas's sons in Lithuania. Dmitrii's gamble succeeded and he won a glorious victory on Kulikovo Field in 1380. This was a policy that Philotheos and Kipriian had promoted. So it is not surprising that Dmitrii put aside his concern about Kipriian's independence and recognized him as metropolitan. Kipriian entered Moscow on 23 May 1381.[80] But Dmitrii and Sergius remained estranged. Dmitrii had turned to Sergius, whose monastery had become a veritable factory turning out leaders of new cenobitic houses, to assist him in establishing a house at Dubenka in 1379, but there is no record that Dmitrii was there when it was consecrated. Nor did he call Sergius to his service for six years after 1379 (another reason to doubt that he asked Sergius's blessing before setting out in 1380 against Mamai). It was Fedor, not Sergius, whom Dmitrii sent to Kiev in 1380–81 to bring Kipriian to Moscow; it was Fedor he called in August 1382 to baptize his son Andrei; and it was Fedor and Archbishop Dionisii, not Sergius, whom he sent to Constantinople in June 1383 after he again found Kipriian unacceptable as metropolitan.[81] The first and third of these chronicle entries refer to Fedor, but not Sergius, as Dmitrii's confessor. In 1382 Tokhtamysh devastated Muscovy, took Moscow, and stormed its kremlin. Dmitrii retired northeast to his town of Kostroma; Kipriian found refuge in Tver', the capital of Dmitrii's principal rival for control of northeast Rus', Prince Mikhail Aleksandrovich. The Trinity chronicle, so praising of Sergius, was silent about his whereabouts, but a later chronicle reported that he too took refuge in Tver'. Learning that Kipriian was in Tver' and fearing that he supported Mikhail's bid to the Horde to replace him as grand prince, Dmitrii sent two boiars to order Kipriian to return, and, when he did, Dmitrii removed him from office.[82] Kipriian went to Kiev and Dmitrii released Pimen from jail and recognized him as metropolitan on 1 October 1382. The only other news of Sergius in this critical period is the entry in the Trinity chronicle that he and Kipriian baptized a son of Prince Vladimir Andreevich of Serpukhov in the spring of 1381.[83]

In retrospect there probably were deeper reasons for Dmitrii's wariness of Sergius than the abbot's hostility to Mikhail's elevation. Sergius may well have come around to Kipriian's vision of a Russian see, not only united but independent of princes of Moscow and Lithuania. If so, it should not surprise. As a boy Sergius had endured vicissitudes brought about by the policies of Moscow's princes. The experience, albeit unconsciously, shaped his conception of the monastic ideal, whose purity and independence of worldly power would be worth fighting to preserve. In this spirit Sergius heeded Aleksei and Philotheos's appeal to restructure his house with a cenobitic rule that provided it with an internal order autonomous of secular power. Dmitrii perhaps suspected that Sergius with Kipriian supported Prince Mikhail of Tver' when he went to the Horde seeking the grand princely title after Tokhtamysh sacked Moscow. In Sergius's case the suspicion was unfounded. Sergius never plotted against the Muscovite (or any other) prince and it would have been entirely out of character for him to have done so in 1382 or 1383.

* Kipriian did not return to Moscow as metropolitan until after Dmitrii Donskoi's death in 1389. Sergius, though, was once more at the Muscovite court on 29 July 1385 to baptize Dmitrii's newborn son Petr.[84] One can only speculate about Dmitrii's motive in asking Sergius to take part in this family ceremony. Had Dmitrii come to realize, as did others, that in the matter of the metropolitanate Sergius displayed not only his characteristic humility but an uncompromising moral strength? If so, it is understandable why that same year Dmitrii asked Sergius to go to Riazan' to persuade its prince Oleg Ivanovich to make peace with Moscow, presumably on the same terms as their pact of 1381, by which Oleg had recognized Dmitrii as his "elder brother." In the spring of 1385 Oleg had used Tokhtamysh's victory over Dmitrii to seize Moscow's border town of Kolomna and repulse the Muscovite counteroffensive

commanded by Prince Vladimir Andreevich. This was a critical moment in Moscow's political history. Temporarily enfeebled and beset with other problems, Dmitrii could not maintain the predominance he had won over the other princely centers of northern Rus'. He needed time to recover and for that he needed to persuade Oleg to restore their previous relationship. Perhaps it was Vladimir Andreevich who advised Dmitrii that Sergius was the ideal, perhaps the only, person who could bring it about. Sergius's mission to Riazan' took place between 15 November and 24 December, 1385. Knowing that Riazan' could not remain for long safely independent of outside interference, particularly by the Mongols, Oleg chose peace. But to the compiler of the Trinity chronicle it was Sergius's reputation for disinterestedness and the moral way that induced Oleg to respect him as a mediator and to reconcile himself with Dmitrii:

> That autumn during Advent the venerable elder Abbot Sergius went by himself to Riazan' to Grand Prince Oleg regarding peace. Previously many others had gone to him but none of them were able to pacify him. The venerable elder though with gentle words, a quiet voice and affectionate speeches by grace given to him spoke for a long time with him in a way beneficial to his soul and about peace and love. By this Prince Oleg saw his truculence become tenderness and submitted, became humble and most affected in his soul and so shamed before the holy man [that he] concluded an eternal peace with Grand Prince [Dmitrii].[85]

Sergius's prestige was never higher, making it still more difficult for Dmitrii to believe that the monk could be a loyal adherent, allowed to be privy to his private thoughts as confessor. This had to have been on his mind when in the winter of 1388–89, knowing he was dying, Dmitrii ordered his affairs so that his son Vasilii (1389–1425), would be securely in control of his hereditary principality of Moscow and the grand principality of Vladimir. Doing so put him in conflict with his powerful and heretofore loyal cousin and Sergius's lord Prince Vladimir Andreevich. As historian A. E. Presniakov presciently noted, the texts of treaties between Dmitrii and Vladimir were "profoundly ambiguous," so much so that it is impossible to know the substance of their quarrel. What seems to have happened is that Vasilii took over Dmitrov and Galich, appanages Vladimir had administered since the 1370s. Vladimir must have objected and Dmitrii's response, described in the Trinity chronicle, said that they resolved their differences on 25 March 1389; but the pact between them with that date makes no mention that Vladimir retained these appanages. Dmitrii had coerced Vladimir into recognizing the new order, but he could not compel his cousin to reconcile himself to it. Dmitrii died on 19 May 1389. In a sense Sergius gave this tenuous arrangement his moral blessing when he came to Moscow on 20 May 1389 for the service by which Dmitrii was buried alongside his ancestors in the kremlin church of the Archangel Michael.[86] Before the year was out, however, Vladimir renewed his opposition to the settlement, moving to the border of Novgorod and Tver', thereby implicitly threatening to ally himself with these independent states against Vasilii I. It is hard to believe that he meant to go that far. The pact of March 1389, after all, had reaffirmed Vladimir's right to a third of Moscow itself in addition to his hereditary domains. Indeed, he and Vasilii settled sometime before 6 January 1390. Vasilii compensated Vladimir for his loss of Dmitrov and Galich with appanage properties of Volok and Rzhev. Their reconciliation, which created a new political balance at the Muscovite court, held until Vladimir died in 1410.[87]

To the new grand prince, who had returned to Moscow in 1387, having endured three years at the Horde as Tokhtamysh's hostage and several more in Kiev after his release, Sergius must have seemed truly venerable. To Sergius the young Vasilii was a ruler with whom there were no grudges, only a soul to fill with piety and good works. Indeed, the atmosphere in Moscow was so quickly transformed in a manner that boded well for Sergius, that contemporaries might have thought his pious benevolence had been its cause. In the spring of 1390 Kipriian returned to Moscow as Metropolitan of Kiev and all Rus'. Again there was a metropolitan in Moscow who respected Sergius and supported the monastic movement he personified. Sergius probably also looked favorably on the rapprochement between Moscow and Lithuania that Kipriian had nurtured as early as 1387 when Vasilii was in Kiev, one which on 9 January 1391 brought to Moscow as Vasilii's consort Sofiia Vitovtna, the daughter of Grand Prince Vytautas of Lithuania.[88] The union, like Sergius's success in reconciling Oleg with Dmitrii, promised harmony in the Rus' land and, implicitly, resistance to Mongol depredations.

The next reference to the historical Sergius was the report of his death in 1392. But shortly before that, according to hagiographical accounts of the two abbots who succeeded him as abbot, Sergius, in anticipation of his death, designated the Trinity monk Nikon to take his place.[89] Then, as reported in the Trinity chronicle,

> That autumn in the month of September on the 25th day, the feast day of the venerable saint Ephrosinia [of Alexandria] the venerable Abbot Sergius, that holy elder, so estimable, unimpeachable and benevolent, gentle humble,

> plainspoken, whose life surpasseth anything one can say or write, died. Formerly no one like him existed in our land who was pleasing to God and [whom] tsars and princes deemed honorable, [who] drew praise from a patriarch, in whose life unbeliever tsars and princes marveled so that they sent him gifts; [who] was universally beloved for his saintly life, who was the shepherd not only of his flock but [was] the teacher and mentor of our entire Russian land; [who was] a guide to the blind, [who helped] the lame to walk, [who was] to the sick a healer, to the hungry and thirsty a provider, [who] clothed the naked, [who] gave solace to the miserable, [and] to all Christians was the beacon without whose prayers we sinners would not receive God's mercy, to the glory of God forever, amen.[90]

Nikolai Karamzin, who saw the Trinity chronicle before it perished in 1812, said that an encomium (*pokhvalnoe slovo*) filling 20 folio pages followed this passage. It could have been none other than that Epifanii the Wise wrote and probably read in 1411 over Sergius's relics at the consecration of the wooden Trinity Church built in the aftermath of the destruction of the monastery by Edigei's Mongols in 1408.[91] Epifanii, as well he should have, admired Sergius as an ideal monk in the tradition of the Eastern Church: had he not deliberately withdrawn to live in a silent world disciplined by inward prayer and physical labor? To cause Epifanii and others to enter his world to learn to live as he did, or to emulate his way of life elsewhere, Sergius must have embodied this ideal to an unusual degree. In order that their hopes and aspirations be met, Trinity's brothers inevitably requested that Sergius be their abbot.. Sergius may not have been aware of it, but in doing so he took the first steps back into the world he had abandoned as a young man.

Hagiographical convention guided those who wrote about Sergius when they said that he repeatedly asserted his reluctance to depart from the solitary way. But cannot one argue that it was because Sergius so faithfully *lived* such conventions that he became more famous than other solitaries? Sergius could envisage, when it was urged on him, that only by accepting a rule by which solitaries could live a communal life could he preserve his calling in this world. Sergius made such a choice despite the resistance of his brother and other monks at Trinity, and he made it work for his house, then for others. Marveling at his achievement, princes and their boiars began to demand that Sergius bless their world with his spirituality; he was to baptize their children or found their monasteries. These deeds involved him in the political struggle over the appointment of a new metropolitan in 1378. Sergius did not retreat from this challenge; but neither did he allow it to cause him to give up his monastic calling. Indeed, by remaining rooted in it, he spoke about the affairs of men as they concerned the faith in a manner that was disinterested and founded on a moral plateau. Knowing that he descended from a family whose roots were outside the clan loyalties of the Muscovite court, one might predict that Sergius's loyalties in the matter of the metropolitanate would not be those of Grand Prince Dmitrii. Even so, by refusing to endorse Mitiai/Mikhail's appointment in defiance of the will of the grand prince, Sergius acquired an aura of unassailable moral courage. Was it not for this that Dmitrii asked the monk to go to Oleg of Riazan' to establish the peace he so desperately needed in 1385?

The anonymous writer who so eloquently eulogized Sergius in the Trinity chronicle under 1392, and Epifanii in his encomium (if not the same person) were the first to praise Sergius as a moral beacon to the world. No doubt by then others at the Trinity Monastery had come to see him in that light. Yet there is no evidence that anyone at the Muscovite court or elsewhere in 1392 thought of him as a saint. However much the admiring world wished to reward him, it seems certain that Sergius went to his grave true to his vow of poverty; he might have accepted simple charity for his house, but there is no record that Trinity acquired landed property in his lifetime.[92]

Chapter Two

Sergius the Saint

How does respect and love for a person become a cult? How is it that a community, such as that which during Sergei's life thought him exceedingly pious and his deeds occasionally wondrous, after his death attributed to him supernatural qualities and considered some of his deeds miraculous? Or that this community so venerated him that it organized its existence around ceremonies that celebrated him as a saint? Sergius's death in 1392 occasioned no immediate claims of healings, visions, or miraculous events. Nor is there evidence that Trinity's brotherhood raised claims for such while Savva, a Trinity monk whom Sergius once had installed as abbot of the Dubenka monastery, was abbot. That was from 1392 to 1398, a span when the Trinity monk Nikon, Sergius's first choice to be abbot, demurred to pursue vows of silence and solitude. Epifanii tells us that even then he began to collect and record testimony about Sergius with the intention of writing his biography, but does not mention miracles as the reason behind it. Nor did Nikon take measures to recognize Sergius as a saint for some time after he became abbot in 1399.[1] Indeed, Trinity's fortunes and Sergius's reputation might seem to have reached a low point when Emir Edigei destroyed the monastery in his raid on Moscow in 1408, a raid causing Epifanii, and probably his fellow monks, to flee to Tver'.[2] As it turned out, in the aftermath of this tragedy the cult of Sergius was born. In this chapter I discuss the emergence of Sergius's cult, from its origin to his recognition about 1448 as a saint throughout the Orthodox world.

Modern sociology rejects that sainthood is an individual quality and its proponents passive observers. Sainthood involves interaction between "performer," or testimony about him or her, and the immediate community. The process is one in which the terms of sainthood are negotiated. Regarding sainthood in the Catholic West, Aviad Kleinberg wrote that debates about sainthood rarely are conclusive while a candidate is living; therefore, supernatural acts characterizing sainthood should be thought of as attributive qualities of hagiography upon which a community could agree.[3] Those who came to revere Sergius as a saint and then publicly proclaimed his sanctity—monastic brothers and disciples, sympathetic clerics and, perhaps, local princes—were persons who had known him. Epifanii, already a monk, came to Trinity by 1380, at least 12 years before Sergius's death. Nikon's tonsure by Sergius, Kloss proposed, was on 30 June 1381.[4] In making a case that Sergius was a saint, Epifanii and Nikon not only had to convince "the converted" but to establish their claim in a larger, less-committed, community that had little or no direct knowledge of Sergius. Nikon's statement of faith in the aftermath of Edigei's raid was to build a wooden church of the Trinity at the site of Sergius's grave; Epifanii's was to compose an encomium to Sergius.

It is likely that Epifanii recited his encomium to Sergius on the occasion of the consecration of the wooden church. Kloss cites a manuscript in which one Varlaam, probably a monk from Novgorod, described the church's consecration and said it occurred on 25 September 1412, the twentieth anniversary of Sergius's death. What better time to glorify his memory and to make it a statement of faith in the house that he had founded? Veneration of Sergius may have been spontaneous and self-generating, maintained in the memories of those who had known him. For its transmogrification into a cult we must look to the genius of Epifanii, Nikon, and Andrei Rublev. Epifanii's encomium is highly personal, yet rests on familiarity with eastern hagiography and respect for the genre. E. M. Vereshchagin has shown that Epifanii relied heavily on a Slavonic translation of the life of his name-saint, Epiphanius of Cyprus, written by the latter's disciple. In the encomium Epifanii says he visited Constantinople, Jerusalem, and Mt. Athos, a journey that could only have enriched his hagiographical resources. Kloss, based on a Russian source, suggested Epifanii made the trip in 1411 in the company of the Muscovite princess Anna who was sent to Constantinople as a prospective bride for the Byzantine emperor.[5] Whether or not this is so, the encomium remains a gem in the canon of Old Russian literature, at once prolix and eloquent.

Epifanii at the outset protests his unworthiness to compose an encomium to such a holy man; but he does so in an excessive, even showy manner that suggests he thought himself equal to the task. He praises Sergius extravagantly in what is an attenuated and stylistically complex version of Sergius's death notice in the Trinity chronicle.[6] Epifanii marvels at how Sergius for 50 years personified the traits of the ideal monk dedicated to poverty, humility, and prayer. He was one "adorned in the manner of a monk, but even more [he looked] like an angel."[7] Epifanii describes how princes and boiars, clerics and all the people marveled at Sergius's lifestyle and mourned his passing. But nowhere does he call Sergius a miracle worker, describe miracles he performed, or mention visions or omens to which he was privy. Only once, to convince his audience that God gloried in how Sergius lived such a divinely dedicated life, Epifanii says that Sergius by prayer cured many who were sick and made well the infirmities of many more.[8] As if Trinity's monks, many of whom had known Sergius, needed convincing as they stood there in 1412 in the little wooden church they had raised to house the bones of their teacher and founder. They above all must have had faith that by prayer this purest of mortal souls could reach God and move Him to accomplish wonders. Elements of a service to Sergius survive—three hymns (*stikhira*), two anthems (*tropar'*), and a song (*kondak*)—that antedate the service Pakhomii wrote between 1440 and 1460, but it is impossible to determine their authorship or whether they were written in 1412 or to celebrate the translation of Sergius's relics in 1422.[9]

It is likely that Andrei Rublev painted his famous icon of the Trinity (see fig. 2) for this church (and not for the dedication of the stone church of the Trinity erected in 1422–28). V. N. Lazarev and more recently G. V. Popov wrote that Rublev painted the icon while at the height of his powers or soon after he finished his fresco cycle in the Church of the Dormition in Vladimir in 1408. The best proof of this, wrote Lazarev, was the likeness of the three angels in the icon to the figures of apostles Peter and Paul in one of the Vladimir frescos. Moreover, Varlaam's description of the consecration contained a sketch of Rublev's icon done with great verisimilitude.[10] If we accept their dating, it is not difficult to imagine how it must have appeared to Trinity's monks, who then numbered at the least two dozen, and other witnesses who crowded into the humble church to celebrate its consecration.[11] In the darkness of this small, stuffy room they must have wondered at the icon, illuminated with candles and occupying a space to the right of the holy doors in the hastily improvised iconostasis. There were the three angels around a table, representing the triune God to whom in the form of three youths Abraham and Sara gave hospitality by the oaks of Mamre (Gen. 18:1–22). Each wore robes freshly painted in glowing, yet soft, tones. The central angel, the incarnate Christ, wore a chiton in various shades of brown and a blue himation. Above him arises the tree of life. He looks to the angel on his right, who, most believe, represents the Father and is clothed in subdued tones of brown laced with gold and a chiton of light blue. The angel on Christ's left, the Holy Spirit, wears a green himation, a symbol of renewal, over a light-blue chiton. He and the Father gaze serenely at the chalice on the table containing the head of the sacrificial calf symbolizing the Eucharist with its New Testament hope of salvation. Rublev, a monk whose work was steeped in currents of hesychast spirituality, bathed the three figures in the "uncreated light of God" by which he appeared to the apostles on Mt. Tabor at the time of Christ's transfiguration (Mt. 17:1–8, Mk. 9:2–8). It was a light hesychast solitaries found accessible by means of disciplined prayer, a practice that probably was not lost on Sergius's disciples. Few if any Slavonic translations of the hesychast corpus that might account for Rublev's spiritual aesthetics were available in Rus' by 1400. But we know next to nothing about Rublev's life. Art historian O. S. Popova observed that such icons, produced in Rus', were composed in simple lines with a laconic disregard for classic forms, qualities unlike those of their Byzantine models. Another art historian, E. S. Smirnova, observed that the inclination of the bodies and heads of the three figures formed the arc of a circle uniting them in an "ideally perfect form." Even if only few of those present had knowledge of recent models for the icon in eastern iconography, here where their master lay buried, they gazed on a new symbol of hope, made wondrous by the quiet power exuded by its figures.[12] Rublev offered the image and its promise in open denial of the misery and fear that washed over the land in the wake of Edigei's Mongol raiders.

Trinity's first patron, Vladimir Andreevich of Serpukhov, having died in May 1410, could not be there and it is unknown whether his son Andrei, who became prince of Radonezh, was present. Although it is attested in a later edition of Sergius's life, Prince Iurii Dmitrievich of Zvenigorod and Galich occupied a place of honor among those present when Nikon consecrated the wooden church in 1412, just as he did when Nikon consecrated its stone successor in 1422. To start with, Sergius had baptized this second son of Grand Prince Dmitrii Donskoi. Thenceforth Iurii's patronage to Sergius's monastery appeared in various forms: beginning in 1398 or 1399 he underwrote the foundation of a house dedicated to the birth of the Mother of God "at the outskirts" (*na storozhakh*) of Zvenigorod as his court monastery and Savva, Sergius's disciple and head of Trinity to 1398, was its first abbot. Like those of his teacher, Savva's remains were interred in Trinity's main church at his death. About 1399 Iurii also built the Church of the Dormition "in the kremlin" (*na gorodke*) for his appanage capital of Zvenigorod and commissioned Rublev to paint icons for its iconostasis. Iurii's brother Petr, the appanage prince of Dmitrov whom Sergius also baptized, might well have been there too, although no one mentioned it. In Trinity's precarious early days Petr had sold it a yard (*dvor*) in Dmitrov and in 1423 subsidized Nikon's construction plans by granting it rights to beaver and fish in the Voria River.[13]

This was the first, tentative claim for Sergius's sanctity. Within a few years Epifanii in his life and Nikon in ritual were to make the new and gloriously decorated stone church of the Trinity that held Sergius's relics the holiest center in northeast Rus'. Epifanii began to write a life of Sergius in 1418. He probably finished it in 1419, but certainly before he died, sometime before 1422. It went quickly because he had, in his words, collected information beginning within 2 years of Sergius's death, and had for 20 years set down episodes from Sergius's life.[14] For information about Sergius's early life and first years as a monk Epifanii sought out older monks,

> [those] most knowledgeable, who truly knew about his life, for according to Scripture: Ask thy father, and he shall make known to thee, so also [ask] thy elders, and they shall tell thee. Everything that I heard and found out, elders told me, all that these elders heard, all that I saw with my own eyes, all that I heard from Sergius's own mouth, and all that I learned from one who had long served him and was his intimate (v'zliavshago vodu na rutsi ego), and much more that I heard from his brother the elder Stefan who was the birth father of Fedor, archbishop of Rostov; other things I found out from other aged elders, from reliable witnesses to his birth, upbringing, and schooling, his maturation and youth to the very time he was tonsured; and other elders bore witness and provided true evidence about his tonsure, the beginning of his life in the wilderness, and his appointment as abbot; and others testified or recounted concerning other episodes.[15]

But neither in his introduction nor in the telling of Sergius's life, *up to the point where the incomplete text that we can be certain contains his and only his words breaks off*, did Epifanii describe a miracle that Sergius performed. And, although he came close to doing so, he did not call Sergius a miracle worker.

Of course, Sergius's birth and childhood were occasions of wondrous events, some of them portents of his later life that would become clear only when he became a monk. One time, when his pregnant mother listened in church to the singing of the liturgy, the babe in her womb thrice cried out so loudly that not only the women standing nearby, but the men, heard him. It was a portent of Sergius's future dedication to the Trinity, but of a sort harkening back to Scripture (Luke 1:41–42). From the moment of his birth, Varfolomei/Sergius, true to his future calling, declined his mother's breast on monastic fast days and whenever she ate meat. George Fedotov terms this a topos common to Orthodox hagiography.[16] Epifanii explained the youth's sudden ability to read with yet another miracle tale. Varfolomei/Sergius met a mysterious elder to whom he lamented his inability to learn. The elder offered him a morsel of eucharistic bread. Sergius ate it and, thenceforth, could read Scripture. Having passed on to the boy the gift of learning, the elder predicted that he would use it to serve the Trinity, then became invisible. Sergius's book learning was God-given, not something he had initiated. As a hermit Sergius's praying and fasting, and rejection of worldly goods and company—so pleasing to God, but not miracles—allowed him mastery in relation with wild animals and duels with demons. These were clichéd struggles common to solitaries whose lives inspired Epifanii and other hagiographers of monastic figures. As abbot, Sergius inspired his flock to live as his did: to scorn other than simple apparel, to revel in physical labor, and to have faith that God would provide for them if they prayed zealously. And God heard the prayers and answered them. It was the same when Epifanii said that tonsure transformed Sergius "in the image of an angel" (*v angel'skii obraz*) or, once, called him a "miraculous zealot" (*chudnyi strastotr"pets'*).[17] Lives of monk-saints of the fourteenth and fifteenth centuries in the Eastern Church abounded in such characterizations. Epifanii's narrative and rhetorical ploys perfectly fitted the hero he had known and whose memory he revered. They brought Sergius to life so vividly for contemporaries at Trinity and those who came there soon after Sergius's death that it did not take much for them to take the next step and view him as a miracle worker. But we cannot be certain that Epifanii went on to ascribe to Sergius the miracles that later manuscripts of his life attributed to the saint.

Nikon's revelation that it was necessary to disinter Sergius and translate his remains to the site of a stone church of the Trinity, the construction of which had just begun, and to celebrate Sergius as a miracle worker on 5 July 1422, could hardly have been unexpected. Nor could Trinity's monks have been surprised when Nikon told them of miraculous visions that had preserved the brotherhood and revealed the necessity of reinterring Sergius, or that further miracles would accompany the translation of Sergius's remains. Pakhomii, in rewriting Epifanii's life of Sergius in the late 1430s, in variants of the 1440s and in the life of Nikon he wrote in the mid-1440s, was the sole source for the discovery and translation of Sergius's remains and in praise of Nikon for his revelation of Sergius's sanctity; he was the first to proclaim Nikon a saint in Sergius's image. Aver'ianov dated these texts slightly differently than Kloss and convincingly argued that they were initiated at Trinity to promote recognition of Sergius's sainthood throughout the metropolitanate.[18] Pakhomii skillfully pared away the historical trivia by which Epifanii authenticated Sergius's holiness. Gone were the hardships of his youth. Epifanii's account about how Muscovite officials punished Rostov and deported his family also was left out.[19] To later generations such "facts" would have been incomprehensible; by the 1430s, when Pakhomii first wrote, the man authenticated the acts, not the other way around. To what was left, Pakhomii added elegant but conventional rhetorical flourishes and descriptions of miracles that Sergius initiated in life and which, after his death, his remains brought about. He treated Nikon's life in the same manner, with the result that we must parse Pakhomii's writings carefully to ascertain which miracles Nikon claimed for Sergius in 1422, and which 15 years later Pakhomii anticipated his readers would expect.

In his initial recasting of Epifanii's life in the late 1430s, Pakhomii related eight miracles for which Sergius was responsible during his life and said that after his death "many healings occurred at his grave even to the present day."[20] But he described none of the latter and said nothing about reburying his remains in the wooden church in 1412, or their transfer to the site of the new stone church on which construction began in 1422 and the special service to Sergius that accompanied it. A close variant, which Kloss called Pakhomii's Second Edition and dates to 1440 or soon after, also said nothing of the transfer of the relics, although it elaborated on some of Sergius's miracles.[21]

Pakhomii wrote a third version dated by Kloss to 1442; it was the first to mark the translation of Sergius's relics and the inauguration of his worship as a miracle worker at Trinity. Rulers of many lands, it said, made pilgrimages to Sergius's grave. In doing so, they followed the precedent of the "aforementioned" Prince Vladimir [Andreevich], thus revealing that Vladimir had supported Trinity during Sergius's lifetime and after. It then said that in 1422, precisely 30 years after Sergius's death, one of the brothers had a vision in which Sergius told him to inform Abbot Nikon that water had inundated his coffin and that he should be reburied. The news brought "happiness to the great ruling prince, the holy council, the monks, and to ordinary people of many lands." The prince of Radonezh then was Andrei Vladimirovich. He probably participated in what was to follow, but it was the "worthy Prince Georgii" (Iurii, of Zvenigorod and Galich), Dmitrii Donskoi's second son whom Sergius had baptized, who so revered Sergius, according to Pakhomii, that he came to Trinity's assistance in disinterring Sergius's body and having it translated. The occasion revealed to all Sergius's sanctity. His body survived whole and exuded a sweet aroma; even the clothes in which he had been buried were unspoiled. Trinity's monks put his body in a new coffin and reburied it with a ceremony that celebrated Sergius as a miracle worker. Then Nikon, again with Prince Iurii's assistance, erected a new Church of the Holy Trinity, this time of stone. It was decorated until it resembled "heaven on earth," and the coffin was placed in it. This was the earliest text that said Sergius's translation occurred on 5 July 1422. The Third Edition of Sergius's life also mentioned Nikon's death. It described his deeds as being like those of his teacher, and said that in dying Nikon swore Trinity's brothers to maintain Sergius's way and that they in turn buried him near Sergius's grave. Following this, we find 11 miracles that were said to have occurred at Sergius's gravesite. Finally, Pakhomii introduced a new and momentous element into the narrative: the Mother of God was said to have graced the wondrous decoration of the new church. Thenceforth the brotherhood invoked her along with the Trinity in addressing Nikon on his deathbed as Sergei's disciple.[22]

In his life of Nikon, Pakhomii built the narrative leading to the celebration of Sergius's sanctity from a vision. In it Sergius, with Metropolitan-Saints Petr and Aleksei, appeared to warn Nikon of Emir Edigei's impending invasion of 1408. Forewarned, Nikon and Trinity's monks fled to safety, presumably hauling Sergius's coffin with them. They returned to rebuild the monastery, including a wooden Trinity church. All this occurred, it said, thanks to an inpouring of gifts for which its monks sang prayers to cleanse their benefactors' souls and those of their kin. Soon the brothers brought in masons and carpenters to build the stone Trinity church and the monks Daniil Chernyi, Andrei Rublev, and others to decorate it so that it was consecrated shortly before Nikon's death.[23]

The graceful stone church that arose around Sergius's grave from 1422 (fig. 3), its frescos and icons (which were repainted numerous times thereafter), and lives describing the event but written 15 or more years after it, testify to the celebration of Sergius as a saint at Trinity. So does documentary material that thenceforth designated the house as the Trinity-Sergius Monastery. But none of these sources tell us precisely what was in the minds of Nikon and Trinity's brothers in 1422 when they proclaimed him a saint. Restorations carried out in 1918–1919, 1946, and again in 1990 and 2000, provide some idea of which icons Andrei and Daniil painted, and which date to the end of the fifteenth century and after. Most specialists believe Nikon had Rublev's icon of the Old Testament Trinity installed in a place of honor in the "local," the lowest row of icons, immediately to the right of the Royal Doors to the sanctuary. To the left from the Doors in the same row, then, as now, was an icon of Mother and Child Hodegetria, "indicator of the Way." The icon of Sergius with scenes from his life presently at the left end of the local row, however, dates to the 1490s and was the work of the painter Dionisii or his school. Another icon depicts Savva Storozhevskii with Sergius and Nikon. It was done at the end of the sixteenth century. Both represent later emendations of Sergius's cult.[24] From the beginning Rublev's Old Testament Trinity was the signature icon of the monastery. The presence of an icon "Mother and Child," common in fourteenth-century churches, may have been part an initial attempt to associate the Mother of God with the well-being of the monastery. I shall return to this theme. These icons were elements in the earliest, if not the first, high iconostasis, in which rows icons of apostles, church fathers, and saints stretched almost to the ceiling of the sanctuary, surrounding a central icon over the Holy Doors of Christ in Glory, with his promise of salvation. Other than the icons I have mentioned, it is impossible to read this glorious creation as a calculated enhancement of Sergius's cult. The restored frescos, dating from the seventeenth century, are thought to replicate the originals. Nevertheless, even more than as is the case with the icons in the iconostasis, it is impossible to uncover Rublev's and Daniil Chernyi's work of the 1420s. The only possible exception is a major fresco in the central apse of the Mother of God, enthroned with Child and surrounded by angels. Like the icon on the same theme, it was typical of fourteenth-century churches but does not indicate a special veneration of her at Trinity.[25]

Finally, there is the remarkable pall bearing Sergius's visage (fig. 4) that survives in Trinity's treasury. Apparently it was sewn to cover his coffin in the new church. No one knows who commissioned it. The best guess is that it was Prince Iurii Dmitrievich. From its angular face its deeply sunken eyes transfix the viewer with a burning gaze of an ascetic monk of the sort described by Epifanii, and which Trinity's monks in 1422 thought embodied the sanctity of the living Sergius. It remains the closest visual representation we have of the historical Sergius.[26]

Written testimony was more forthright. Of the eight miracles in Pakhomii's first life, the initial three might well have been taken from Epifanii.[27] If so, they would have been known to Trinity's brothers in 1422. Together with other "facts" about their hero, they offered compelling evidence of Sergius's sanctity. The first recounted the discovery of a spring where none had previously been detected; Sergius found the source after praying for guidance. He had a witness, unnamed, and Pakhomii said that the water cured many people. In essence the vignette resembles that described by Epifanii, in which Sergius's prayers were connected to the arrival of provisions for his brothers. The difference was that Pakhomii's story about the source concluded with the observation that its waters had healing qualities. In that the version of Epifanii's life in the Extended Edition did *not* mention the spring as having healed people, one may conclude that this conviction must have come into currency at Trinity about 1422, by which time Epifanii was dead, and became common currency only after Pakhomii mentioned it in his biography. Pakhomii's second "miraculous" episode was that in which Sergius revived a sick boy, whose father thought him dead when he brought him to Trinity. But in the narrative Sergius insisted the boy had not died, had only been unconscious, and that the warmth of his cell had revived him. Sergius also forbade the father to claim that he had brought him back from the dead. In the third episode Sergius blessed a deranged and violent boiar with a cross. The crazed one, terrified by a pillar of fire he saw emanating from the cross, jumped into some water that had collected in the monastery, was instantly cured, and departed sane. In these episodes one cannot detect a happening, or manner of describing what had happened, that Epifanii could not have written.

On the other hand it is likely that Pakhomii recast significantly or was the author of the remaining miracles. It is instructive to look at four of them together. In the first a voice roused Sergius while at prayer in his cell one night. He emerged and saw a "great light" from which many birds approached. The voice told him that it was a portent that many monks would flock to him. He related the experience to the monk Simon who was with him, but Simon said that he saw only part of the vision, or in Pakhomii's Second and Third Editions, "some of the light."[28] In the next miracle the monk Isaakii told Sergius that he saw a fourth person with Sergius, his brother Stefan, and nephew Fedor as they conducted the service. Asked to describe this person, Isaakii said he could not because the person's face "shone like the sun so that he could not gaze on it" (*svetiatshchesia, iako sol'ntse iako ne mogushchem zreti na ti*). Sergius said he had not noticed this fourth worshiper, but he made inquiries nevertheless. Ascertaining that the stranger hadn't come to Trinity with Prince Vladimir Andreevich, Sergius concluded that he was the angel of the Lord who served always with them and whom God chose to reveal to the monk.[29] Another, more famous, miracle was the apparition of the Mother of God to promise Sergius that she would take the Trinity Monastery under her protection and that neither in his lifetime nor after would it be in need. The situation, Pakhomii tells us, arose from the fact that Trinity had attracted more monks than it had the means to support. Sergius, as usual, sought a solution in prayer. He was praying in his cell to the Mother of God for help and reciting the *akathistos* to her on the fortieth day after Christ's birth, February 3, at five in the evening, when a voice told him to expect her. Sergius left his cell and saw "suddenly a light shining with the great glare of a brilliant sun" (*abie svet vosia velik zelo solntsa iasneishii*). Before him came the Mother of God, accompanied by the apostles John the Prophet and Peter "glowing brilliantly in indescribable glory" (*v neizrechennei svetlosti zareiu blistaiushchesia*). Sergius fell to his knees while his cellmate Mikhei, in fear, fell to the ground. Our Lady then stretched out her hand to Sergius, saying "Do not fear my chosen one! For I have come to visit thee. Do not lament on thy brothers' account nor for [thy] monastery, nor should thou become impoverished, because henceforth the holy monastery shall not want for anything, not only in thy lifetime, but even after thou hast passed away it will not lack for anything." She disappeared and Sergius raised up his disciple, who asked his teacher to confirm what he had seen "and the indescribable light" (*i svet' neizrechennyi*). Sergius did so and asked Mikhei to inform Isaakii and Simon about the vision, after which they rejoiced at the Mother of God's promise to protect their monastery.[30] Pakhomii wrote that the fourth of the miracles occurred soon after the apparition of the Mother of God to Sergius. During the liturgy, he said, the ecclesiarch Simon saw a "divine fire" cross the altar in the sanctuary and circle the refectory three times. Then, as Sergius prepared to take communion, the fire disappeared into the chalice. Afterward Sergius noticed Simon's fright and asked him what had so terrified him. Simon explained to him that he "had seen a miraculous vision—the divine fire that is the grace of the Holy Spirit conferred upon thee" (*videv chiudnoe videnie—bozhestvenyi ogn', pache zhe blagodat' Sviatogo Dukha deistviushchia s toboiu*). Hearing this, Sergius asked Simon to keep silent about what he had seen until after the saint's death.[31]

Grouped in this manner, it is obvious that these episodes have one thing in common: miraculous happenings occur against a background of dazzling light or, as in the last of these miracles, they are distinguished by what Pakhomii called a divine fire. Jostein Børtnes pointed out that Pakhomii often employed "light mysticism" in hagiographical writings. By contrast, Epifanii did not use it at all in that part of his life of Sergius that comes down to us in an early edition, nor in describing miracles in his life of St. Stefan of Perm'. In other words, either Pakhomii added elements of light mysticism in rewriting Epifanii's description of these four miracles or, more likely, he was the first to record the miracles. It is tempting to think that Pakhomii came by his use of light imagery from hesychast hagiography. Greek texts or Slavic translations would have been available to him in the Balkans (texts not yet available in Rus').[32]

Light imagery is so central to Pakhomii's account of the Mother of God's apparition to Sergius, and to Mikhei's terrified reaction to the vision, that it is difficult to envisage this episode without it. Nor should one forget that Sergius, when he founded his monastery, dedicated it to the Trinity, not to the Mother of God. Yet Kloss and Aver'ianov argued for the historicity of the miracle—or Epifanii's testimony for it. Kloss pointed out that Sergius chose the names of the two apostles in the vision in baptizing Prince Vladimir Andreevich's son (Ioann) in 1381 and to Prince Dmitrii Ivanovich's son (Petr) in 1385, events within Epifanii's memory. The deaths of the witnesses to Sergius's vision, Mikhei in 1386 and Isaakii in 1397–98, attested in Trinity's burial records and in the second instance also in the Trinity chronicle, mark the endpoint for Kloss's dating.[33] The argument is ingenious, that is until one realizes that it is more plausible to think that the choice of baptismal names followed traditional Christian naming practice. Vladimir's son was born in the spring of the year probably close to 8 May, the feast date of John the Prophet, and Petr was born on 29 June, the feast Day of Peter and Paul. Also, the chronological sequence supplied by Kloss works only if one posits that Sergius had the vision before giving the babes baptismal names of the personages accompanying the Mother of God. Lacking other evidence that Epifanii wrote about the vision, and strong reason to believe he did not, one may question whether he thought it appropriate or possible to pass off such a story to brothers whose memory stretched as far back as his. In using his or her imagination to reconstruct how such episodes came about, the historian is complicit with the hagiographer. Each seeks to make a case for what he or she thinks could have happened. Admitting this, would it not be more logical to posit that it was Pakhomii, writing later to a receptive audience in which there was no one left who might question his claims, who invented the story of the vision, and the other miracles that occurred in a flash of divine light? In claiming this it should be realized that there is no iconographic evidence of a special celebration of the Mother of God at Trinity that can be dated to Sergius's lifetime or any time before the translation of his relics in 1422.

There is an icon, "The Mother of God Hodegetria," in the Sergiev Posad Museum at the Trinity-Sergius Monastery that, according to its catalog, dates to the second half of the fourteenth century. The monastery's inventory of 1641 called it "[the object] of prayer of Sergius the miracleworker," from which T. V. Nikolaeva concluded that it probably stood in Sergius's cell.[34] The Hodegetria is a frontal view of the Mother of God with the Christ child perched on her left arm. It is well attested in Orthodox iconography. Nothing in its imagery refers to the episode I recounted, although it could be inferred that Sergius was praying to such an icon when she appeared to him. Or that Sergius venerated the Mother of God. But so did all Christians. It was not evidence that Sergius established a worship of the Mother of God as the monastery's protector. The passage in the inventory of 1641, and the assumption that this icon stood in his cell, could as easily reflect a conviction that arose at a later date that the Mother of God had appeared to Sergius.

If specialists who question the antiquity of the icon and date its creation to sometime after 1450 are correct, then the importance imputed to the icon reflected a later consensus that the legend was fact.[35] The earliest references to the existence of an icon entitled "The Apparition of the Mother of God to Sergius" are in chronicle entries for 1442 and 1446.[36] The earliest reported that Abbot Zinovii compelled Dmitrii Shemiaka to make peace with his uncle Vasilii Dmitrievich. Each swore to uphold the armistice on an icon entitled "The Apparition of the Virgin to St. Sergius." The second described a later and critical incident in their struggle for Moscow. Seeking sanctuary from Dmitrii at the monastery, Vasilii, it said, took the icon from Sergius's grave to church doors of the Trinity Church and held it before him, hoping that its definition of holy space would save him from Dmitrii's pursuing force. No such icon dating from the mid-fifteenth century survives. The earliest image we have is one carved on a wooden chancel (*naprestol'nyi*) cross that probably dates to the 1450s and its rendition of the miracle is hardly "canonical." Only the apostle John accompanied the Mother of God; Nikon, not Mikhei, was the witness; and Sergius and Nikon are standing in her presence (fig. 5). The artisan carved on another chancel cross later in the fifteenth century a "correct" version with two apostles and Mikhei.[37]

I think that in 1422 Nikon inaugurated a ceremony linking the Mother of God to the monastery's well-being.[38] Pakhomii's reference to Nikon's search for means to sustain the growing monastery was especially apt then. Exactly how many monks there were at Trinity in 1422 is not known, but I can identify at least 35.[39] In Sergius's time and for some time after, Trinity did not acquire landed property. Nikon decided this had to change when he undertook the restoration of Trinity after Edigei's campaign. The first record of his success is an immunity charter issued to Trinity by its lord, Prince Andrei Vladimirovich of Uglich and Radonezh, and dated March 1411 for the village of Udinskoe in Uglich. Nikon had witnessed the testament of Uglich and Trinity's lord, Vladimir Andreevich, in 1401; when Vladimir died in 1410 their new lord, his son Andrei, on coming to power very likely gave the village to Trinity.[40] Nikon aggressively moved to acquire property, though only in 1422 in conjunction with plans to build a stone church to house Sergius's remains. It is then that Prince Iurii Dmitrievich's boiar Semen Fedorovich Morozov gave Trinity half of a salt mine and a saltworks in Sol'-Galich.[41] Soon after that Nikon acquired three nearby villages, Klement'evo, Afanas'evo, and Kniazhe. These probably came from the estate of Prince Andrei and were to commemorate his death and those of his brothers Prince Semen of Borovsk and Prince Iaroslav of Maloiaroslavets in the plague of 1426. The earliest accounts said Nikon tonsured Semen as the monk Sava (spelled "Savva" elsewhere) and mentioned the burial of Andrei and, less likely, Semen in the Trinity Church.[42] Of one thing we can be certain. Without their generosity Nikon might never have been able to build, decorate, and consecrate the Trinity Church before he died. Nikon's honor to Semen and Andrei also created a bond between Trinity and Andrei's surviving brother and heir, Vasilii, Andrei's niece Mariia—who in 1433 would marry Grand Prince Vasilii II of Moscow—and with magnates related by service or marriage to this line. From the 1420s on Trinity collected a great deal of property.[43] So it was fortuitous, one might even say logical, that in 1422 Nikon proposed, and Trinity's brotherhood would quickly confirm, that the Mother of God had made known to Sergius that she would take his house under protection and ensure that it did not need.

Although Nikon proclaimed Sergius's sanctity in 1422, it was Pakhomii who in his Third Edition of Sergius's life provided the earliest description of the ritual celebrating the translation of his remains. It drew on the observation, present even in Pakhomii's First Edition at the conclusion of his description of her appearance to Sergius, that St. Athanasius (d. 1003) of Mt. Athos had experienced a similar vision. Indeed, the life of Athanasius recorded that at a moment of desperate need, the Mother of God appeared to Athanasius and told him that she would assure that his monastery would not want. The life of Athanasius was available to Pakhomii in a collection (*sbornik*) at the Trinity-Sergius Monastery with the inscription, "in the year 6339 (1431) this book was copied at the holy mountain of Athos, . . . in the laura of the great Athanasius. . . . It was copied (by hand) by the most sinful and humble monk Afanasii the Russian (*rusin*). Subsequently on the order of lord Zinovii, abbot of the Sergius monastery (1436–45) it was copied by the sinful monk Iona, abbot [of the] Ugreshskii [monastery]."[44] Afanasii or, less likely, Iona also must have translated it from the Greek. It is doubtful that the life of Athanasius was available to Nikon in 1422. Therefore, it must have been Pakhomii, who knew that the Orthodox celebrated Athanasius's feast on 5 July, for the first time, in his Third Edition, dated the translation of Sergius's relics and his celebration as a saint in Athanasius's image *to this very date*.

A large icon in the State Historical Museum in Moscow is further evidence that from this time Trinity's monks thought Sergius had placed their house under the Mother of God's protection. On the right in large scale the Mother of God sits enthroned. She holds the infant Jesus on her left knee while extending her right hand to a standing figure who is represented in smaller scale. He wears a monk's cowl and beard, has a halo, and extends his right hand toward them. In a circle above him is an angel, possibly one of the archangels. The provenance of the icon is well established as far back as 1641 in the inventory of that date of the Trinity-Sergius Monastery as one of the icons in the "local" row of the iconostasis of its subsidiary house (since 1615), the Makhrishchskii-Trinity Monastery. Stefan founded the house in the name of the Trinity about the time Sergius founded his house of the same name 35 kilometers to the southwest. The icon was not part of the original "local" row of the Makhrishchskii iconostasis, it being larger than the others, and there is reason to believe that the devout monk in the icon is Sergius and that the icon was painted at the Trinity-Sergius Monastery. The inventory of 1641 identified the monk in the icon as Sergius, for one thing. Also, there exists an icon modeled on this one, but without the angel, which was painted at the Trinity-Sergius Monastery in the sixteenth century and which identified the adoring monk as Sergius. The primitive quality and laconic spirituality displayed in the image of the Mother with Child Enthroned from the Makhrishchskii-Trinity Monastery are typical of a large number of icons influenced by late Byzantine mysticism that were painted in Rus' in the fourteenth and early fifteenth centuries. Dating it to the 1420s would not be out of line. Because the icon was of a type that in Rus' was placed at the foot of a person's tomb (a *nadgrobnaia ikona*), is another reason to suppose that it was painted in 1422 to be placed aside Sergius's coffin in the Trinity church. Whoever painted the sixteenth-century copy of the icon at Trinity thought so, judging by the fact that on it Sergius holds a parchment in his left hand on which is visible the phrase, "Therefore brothers, do not grieve for [me . . .]."[45] E. S. Smirnova accepted this line of reasoning, but added that this iconographic type resembled donor (*ktitorskii*) portraits. Sergius, the donor, stands before the throne, liturgically the altar where the house of God resides. Extending his right hand he offers himself and, symbolically, his house to God; from the extended hand of the Mother of God he receives the intercessory promise of grace and wisdom.[46]

The generosity of Trinity's lord Prince Vladimir, his son Andrei, and of Prince Iurii Dmitrievich were not inventions and must have been well known; Pakhomii's description of their generosity, however, was a not-too-subtle plea to the elite of northeast Rus' to emulate their magnanimity as well as a petition that the church recognize Sergius's sanctity. Indeed, the inclusion of a feast honoring Sergius on the date of his death, September 25, in a liturgical calendar dated 1422–25, indicates that many within the metropolitanate had begun to venerate him.[47] Pakhomii revised his life of Sergius to further Trinity's campaign of the 1440s to have him canonized throughout Rus'. It contained new episodes from Sergius's life and miracles wrought posthumously at his grave. Some of them underscored the virtue the landed elite might accrue from supporting Trinity; others, the unworthiness of those who did not. In the latter vein Pakhomii recounted a tale of a sinful emissary of Prince Vladimir Andreevich who had withheld supplies that his lord had meant for Trinity, then lied about it. Under Sergius's moral gaze he was unable to maintain his deception, confessed his sins, and dedicated the rest of his life to venerating Sergius.[48] Then there was Zakharii Borozdin, a member of a great family in Tver' who came to Trinity thinking that if he prayed and ate bread served in its refectory, his sick stomach might be made healthy. In several days Zakharii's stomach felt so much better that he vowed to give thanks at Sergius's grave and to reward his monastery. But he forgot to do so and again took sick. During a sleepless night his soul cried out to Sergius, who appeared to him and told him to return to Trinity. He had himself taken to Sergius's grave, and again he returned home a well man. Subsequently he returned to Trinity to give thanks and reward its brothers, and remained healthy.[49]

Pakhomii told a similar story of a military servitor wounded in battle with the Tatars. A Christian army sent by an unnamed ruler and led by unnamed princes, he wrote, defeated Ulu Mehmet's horde. Some of its officers, however, out of greed for spoils, refused to accept Ulu Mehmet's surrender. The battle resumed and the Christian army was routed. Then, Pakhomii turned his readers' attention to a warrior named Ioann syn Mikhailov "from the court of a great ruler who loved him." Wounded and expecting capture and death, God inspired Ioann to ask Sergius to save him. No sooner did he do so than his horse delivered him safely "on invisible wings" from the pagans. Ioann came upon his commander, told him of his miraculous escape, and announced that he was setting out to the "holy hermitage" to fulfill his vow to do reverence at Sergius's tomb. But, en route, he reflected that it would impoverish him to feast and give alms to Trinity's many brothers. Thought engendered catastrophe; his horse collapsed, he fell to the ground, and pursuing Tatars seized and disarmed him. Now the familiar reversal of fate: the warrior reproached himself for forsaking his vow and pleaded with Sergius to give his unworthy self a second chance. Again he was saved; he went to the "holy hermitage," feasted its brothers "in double measure," gave them alms, and did reverence at Sergius's casket. Pakhomii's telling of the event, namely the battle of Belev between Vasilii and Khan Ulu Mehmet in 1438, triggering the miracle was purposely opaque. Khan Ulu Mehmet in 1434 had awarded the grand princely title to Vasilii II instead of to his cousin Vasilii Iur'evich Kosoi. In 1437 Ulu Mehmet broke from the Horde to establish a rival horde near Belev on the Oka River abutting Moscow and Lithuania, and offered to live in peace with Moscow and to forsake demands for tribute. But either Vasilii II decided to rid himself of Tatar rule by force and sent out the army mentioned in the tale, or the decision was made by the army's commanders, whom we know were Vasilii II's past and future nemeses Dmitrii Iur'evich Krasnii and Dmitrii Iur'evich Shemiaka. Pakhomii, writing within recent memory of the event while the dynastic conflict raged, omitted their names, knowing that they were ostensibly Vasilii's allies, but might have initiated the conflict to alienate Ulu Mehmet from Vasilii. The Dmitriis, at first victorious, were then routed although they outnumbered the enemy. While not daring to reveal their names, Pakhomii blackened their memory by attributing the continuation of hostilities to their greed. Nor did he mention Vasilii's name and defeat in the same sentence, even though to contemporaries his ignominious part in the defeat was clear enough. Simultaneously, Pakhomii validated the fiction of Sergius as intercessor in a manner appropriate to a contest everyone knew was not a test of Christian survival, yet taught everyone, including Vasilii, that Sergius's intercessory promise was contingent on generosity to Trinity. Other miracle stories described how prayers to the saint cured people, usually from merchant and landowning families, of lameness, blindness, sleeplessness, inability to eat, paralysis, injury, insanity, and indefinable physical ills, and of moral defects of bribery, extortion, and doubting Sergius's sanctity.[51]

It was also but a small step from Nikon's inauguration of worship of the Mother of God as protector of the Trinity-Sergius Monastery to Pakhomii's invention of a miracle in which the Mother of God appeared to Sergius and promised to watch over his house. Over the next decade Pakhomii wrote the same episode into new editions and by the 1450s, if not already by 1446, her apparition attained iconographic representation. Subsequently, images of "The Apparition of the Mother of God to Sergius" became ubiquitous. Trinity's inventory of 1641 recorded 1,163 items in its possession—icons, textiles, carved objects—with images that mostly were faithful renditions of Pakhomii's description of the miracle. The same may be said of the many copies of the life of Sergius.[52] Her patronage also turned up in the address, "for the mercy of the life-giving Trinity and the most pure Mother and the [Her] adherent [*molebnika*] Sergius" of a donation charter issued between 1467 and 1474 and copied into Trinity's earliest copybook.[53] And by the 1450s Andrei Rublev's icon of the Old Testament Trinity became the Monastery's logo and palladium. Compelling proof of this was its presence, usually at the top center but always in a prominent location, on many images of the apparition of the Mother to God to Sergius. Its presence represented the house that she had taken under her protection.[54s]

1. Miniature, "The Subjugation of Rostov by the Moscow Voevoda," Illuminated Codex, BAN, 31.7.30–2, folio 382. Courtesy of the Library of the Russian Academy of Sciences, St. Petersburg.

2. *(above)* Andrei Rublev. Icon, "Old Testament Trinity." ca. 1411. 1.42 x 1.14 m. Moscow. Tretiakovskaia Gallery. V. N. Lazarev, *Andrei Rublev i ego shkola* (Moscow, 1966), 48.

3. *(right)* Church of the Holy Trinity, 1422–ca. 1428, and the Chapel of St. Nikon, 1548. Trinity-Sergius Monastery. Photograph by William Brumfield.

4. *(left)* Pall (*Pokrov*). Sergius of Radonezh. 196 x 84 cm. 1420s. Sergiev Posad Museum-Reserve, no. 412. T. V. Nikolaeva, *Sobranie drevnerusskogo iskusstva v Zagorskom muzee* (Leningrad, 1968), 149, no. 53.

5. *(below)* Detail, chancel cross. The Apparition of the Mother of God to Sergius. Wood. Work of Trinity monk Amvrosii? Sergiev Posad Museum-Reserve, no. 1847. Photograph by the author.

The eighth and final miracle in Pakhomii's initial biography was that in 1380 Sergius urged Grand Prince Dmitrii of Moscow to defend Rus' from the Mongols and then interceded to bring him victory on Kulikovo Field on the Don River, and a safe return. To this day Sergius is remembered throughout Russia as intercessor for the Russian land against its enemies. The numerous and often different retellings of this story have provoked debate over what was the earliest narrative and who wrote it.[55] A modern person, one would think, would not need to be persuaded that the story of Sergius's intercession in 1380 was a part of the cult rather than an actual event in Sergius's life. But this is not so. In either case, one must ask when and how the story originated. In addition to difficulties posed by textual "tangles," the issues themselves are charged with elements of religious and patriotic conviction. Rehashing them is a sensitive and painstaking process.[56] I hope to persuade the reader that Pakhomii at the end of the 1430s, rather than Epifanii, Sergius's first biographer, brought to life the image of Sergius as intercessor for Rus'. I shall also argue that Pakhomii did so in part to satisfy new popular aspirations that had arisen in northeast Rus'. In 1422 Sergius's worship was a local cult; by the 1430s this was still true, although, thanks largely to Pakhomii, his reputation as a miracle worker resonated at the Muscovite court and attracted devotees from other parts of Rus'. The time was ripe, the audience receptive. As in similar instances recorded throughout history, a venerator appeared, in this case Pakhomii, who could explicate the nature of Sergius's sanctity and in the process introduce ingredients that had not been noticed before.

Two early texts, appearing about the same time, stated that Sergius had a role in the victory on the Don. One was Pakhomii's life of Sergius. It was written at the end of 1430s and reworked several times in the early 1440s. The other was the so-called Chronicle Tale of Dmitrii's battle on the Don ("*o poboishchi izhe na Donu i o tom, chto Kniaz' Velikii bilsia s Ordoiu*"). It comes to us in almost identical versions in the Sofiia First and the Novgorod Fourth chronicles. Ia. S. Lur'e argued that at the core of these chronicles was a hypothetical compilation that he termed the first all-Rus' compilation since the Trinity chronicle. He dated it to 1448; later he hedged on the date, but M. A. Salmina showed it could have been compiled no earlier than 1437.[57]

Pakhomii wrote that Grand Prince Dmitrii came to Trinity with news that Mongol Emir Mamai had set out to attack Rus' to kill Christians and asked Sergius to pray to God for their salvation. Sergius urged Dmitrii to resist Mamai and said God would grant him victory and the army a safe return. Thereupon Dmitrii vowed that if he were victorious he would build a church dedicated to the Mother of God's dormition, and there found a cenobitic monastery. Warned of Mamai's approach, Dmitrii departed. He was victorious, fulfilling Sergius's prophecy, and returned to fulfill his vow. Sergius picked out a site on the Dubenka River where the monastery was to stand and when it was completed he appointed a disciple as its abbot.[58] In the Second Edition of his life of Sergius Pakhomii reinforced the ideological power in the message with more florid rhetoric, but no new "facts." He doted upon fears engendered by Emir Mamai's "Godless Tatars'" onslaught on the "Rus' land" (not "lands"), which he called Dmitrii's patrimony (*otchina*). Sergius then addressed Dmitrii with "our lord and Russian tsar, thou art the pastor of the whole Christian flock," and predicted his victory with the help of God and the Mother of God.[59] In his Third Edition Pakhomii said Dmitrii held the sceptre of the "land of Moscow," called him "Orthodox tsar" in urging him to resist Mamai, and added new information, namely that a messenger sent by Sergius intercepted Dmitrii as he prepared to do battle. In the message he told the "Great Tsar" not to fear Mamai's host because Christ's strength was greater and would assure him victory. And, indeed, following an extended description of the battle, "they perceived the fulfillment of a wonderful miracle: where formerly weapons glistened, now they saw everything covered with the blood of their enemies, and all Orthodoxy rejoiced [as it] beheld this sign of victory. And so the prophesy was fulfilled, 'should one drive out a thousand, then two can drive out tenfold more.'" Pakhomii also wrote that Sergius and Trinity's monks prayed for the dead and, describing the establishment of a monastery on the Dubenka, said that Sergius appointed Trinity's confessor Savva as its abbot.[60] The Chronicle Tale is a lengthy contrived narrative in which Sergius is heard offstage. When the grand prince came to the Don River, two days before the feast of the Nativity of the Mother of God (8 September), he received a message from Sergius in which the saint blessed him and urged him to fight the Tatars. If he engaged them, Sergius promised, he might expect the support of God and the Mother of God.[61] Dmitrii went to battle and, thanks to the appearance of a heavenly host, won. Although the Chronicle Tale, like Pakhomii's Third Edition, mentioned a message from Sergius, it said nothing of Sergius the intercessor, of a visit by Dmitrii to Trinity before or after the battle, or of any vow to build a monastery.

Although it allocated to Sergius a minor role in the victory on the Don, the Chronicle Tale was a critical text in the transformation of Sergius's cult from a local affair at Trinity into an all-Russian celebration. If we juxtapose it to accounts in various editions of Pakhomii's life of Sergius, it is evident that the Serbian hagiographer wrote the first version of Sergius's intercession. In the Second Edition Pakhomii added the Mother of God as an intercessor for Rus', an allusion that made particular sense when we remember that Pakhomii had given dramatic form to the belief at Trinity that Sergius's faith could summon her protection. In the Third Edition he added information about a letter to Dmitrii from Sergius. What the author of the Chronicle Tale did was to appropriate the elements added by Pakhomii to these editions in order to introduce Sergius as prophet of Dmitrii's victory to a "national" audience. Some historians, including Kuchkin, thought the Chronicle Tale with its episode of Sergius's messenger to Dmitri on the eve of the battle was present in a hypothetical compilation, dated variously to 1419 or 1423, for Metropolitan Photios.[62] If so, then it was Pakhomii's Third Edition that drew on the Chronicle Tale for this episode and not the other way around. But, as I indicated previously, Lur'e's arguments against the existence of such a compilation are persuasive. More to the point, M. A. Salmina has demonstrated that the Chronicle Tale, the first literary description of the battle, could not have been written earlier than 1437. Therefore, Pakhomii's "full" narration of Sergius's intercession was primary to that in the Chronicle Tale.[63] Another reason to think the Chronicle Tale appeared in the 1440s is that its author's excoriation of Prince Oleg of Riazan' for cooperating with the Mongols echoed an accusation Metropolitan Iona hurled at Vasilii II's rival Prince Dmitrii Shemiaka in 1448.[64] Iona charged Dmitrii with conspiring in 1439 or, more likely, 1445 with the Mongols to unseat Vasilii. In this respect the reference to Oleg would provide a context for condemning Shemiaka's "treason" against Rus'.

There are others who argue that the description of Sergius's intercession in the Extended Edition of Epifanii's live of 1518 was the earliest. That view is mistaken; yet it needs to be confronted directly if one is to appreciate the transformation that Pakhomii brought in Sergius's cult. This requires resolving the complex interrelationship among the texts about the Kulikovo battle. First of all, a passage in the Extended Edition relating to Sergius as intercessor clearly derived from a tale of the battle on the Don known as "The Tale of the Battle with Mamai" (*Skazanie o Mamaevom poboishche*): in it Sergius told Dmitrii, who visited Trinity before the battle, "Go against the godless, and God will help thee, thou shalt be victorious and return safely to thy patrimony with great acclaim" (*Poidi protivu bezbozhnykh, i bogu pomagaiushchu ti, pobedishi i zdrav v svoe otech'stvo s velikymi pokhvalami v"zvratishisia*). The writer of the Extended Edition repeated the sentence, only "correcting" the epithet "pagȧn Polovtsy" for the Mongols in the former—an anachronism that suggests the author of "The Tale" had at his disposal a copy of the twelfth-century "Tale of the Host of Igor'"—to "the Godless." Second, Kloss demonstrated that "The Tale of the Battle with Mamai" was written no earlier than 1500, by Mitrofan, Bishop of Kolomna (1507–18), who probably had been a Trinity monk and subsequently died and was buried there in 1521. Mitrofan's Tale introduced fictitious monks from Trinity as warriors at Kulikovo and named as participants in the battle persons unattested in earlier accounts, but whose names may be found in memorials arranged by their descendents at Trinity at the end of the fifteenth century. In other words, Sergius's venerators, Trinity's monks and patrons, were the heroes of Kulikovo. To argue conversely, that the phrasing jumped from Epifanii's pen to The Tale, while being ignored in the interim by Pakhomii and the author of the Chronicle Tale, makes no sense.[65]

There is one other textual curiosity in the Extended Edition's account of the Kulikovo battle. Unlike either the Chronicle Tale or "The Tale of the Battle with Mamai," it described the vision of the victory and the prophecy fulfilled in almost the same language with which Pakhomii introduced it in his Third Edition of Sergius's life.[66] Logic would have it that the passage migrated from Pakhomii's Third Edition to the Extended Edition. To argue otherwise, that Epifanii wrote it and Pakhomii appropriated it, one would have to posit that Pakhomii chose not to use it in writing about the Kulikovo in his initial and second recastings of Epifanii's original life of Sergius, then inserted it into his Third Edition. Still, several aspects of the text in the Extended Edition can be used to argue its primacy: for one, while flattering of Dmitrii, it did not inflate his title to that of tsar, and it said that he "holds the sceptre of the Russian lands" (not "land"). Also, if it were secondary to Pakhomii and the Chronicle Tale, one would think it would have recognized Sergius's ability to call on the Mother of God as intercessor, but that is not the case. Sergius was intercessor but God alone heard his prayers and aided Dmitrii. These oddities, however, are not enough to overturn my conclusion that the image of Sergius as intercessor in 1380 in the Extended Edition was secondary to Pakhomii's, and to other accounts of the battle on the Don.

Another reason to believe Dimitrii did not visit Trinity in search of support (and that Sergius did not act as intercessor for him) is that Sergius's house was neither in Dmitrii's patrimony nor favored by Dmitrii in 1380. The dispute over who should succeed Aleksei as metropolitan estranged Dmtrii from Sergius. One can think of any number of other holy men to whom Dmitrii might have turned for moral support and prayers in 1380. More importantly, Sergius was nowhere mentioned in the account of the battle of 1380 in the Trinity chronicle.[67] This work derived from the metropolitan's compilation of 1408 and is the closest source we have to the event. Its failure to mention that Sergius might have urged Dmitrii to resist the Mongols, or interceded on Dmitrii's behalf, is all the more glaring in that the Trinity chronicle has many references to Trinity Monastery of that period that must have come from a chronicle written there, if not from Epifanii himself! We should also remember the Trinity chronicle dated Dmitrii's underwriting and Sergius's founding of the Dormition monastery at Stronym on the Dubenka River to 1379. Kloss's redating of this to 1381 is speculative; and if one accepts his view that Epifanii wrote the chronicle, the redating makes less sense because it says nothing about Sergius's role in the victory as a motive for its founding. Furthermore, the Trinity chronicle said Sergius installed his disciple Leontii as abbot of the new monastery. Pakhomii, in his Third Edition, as Kloss knew, erroneously (but perhaps purposefully to flatter its lord and son of Trinity's longtime patron Iurii Dmitrievich) said it was Savva, the future abbot of the Storozhevskii Monastery near Zvenigorod. The Extended Edition of Epifanii's life repeated Pakhomii's version.[68]

It is conceivable that Sergius urged Dmitrii to resist the Mongols in 1380 and it is possible that he predicted that Dmitrii would defeat them. But it defies the imagination to think that anyone writing soon after the battle, or for decades thereafter, would be so bold as to claim that God or the Mother of God had a special interest in protecting Moscow or the Russian land from the Mongols. Only two years after Dmitrii's victory, Khan Tokhtamysh cut a swath through northeastern Rus', sacked Moscow, and stormed its kremlin. In its aftermath Tokhtamysh forced Dmitrii to resume paying tribute to the Mongols and for several years held his son and heir Vasilii hostage at the Horde to ensure that Dmitrii did it. In 1399 another Mongol force led by Mamai's rival Khan Timur-Kutlugh and by Emir Edigei thoroughly trounced an army of Lithuanian and Rus' princes led by Grand Prince Vitautas of Lithuania. Edigei returned in 1408 to devastate northeastern Rus' and besiege Moscow. He withdrew only after Moscow paid him a ransom. In 1411 a Mongol army again appeared in northeast Rus'. And long after Epifanii was in his grave a Mongol force reached the walls of Moscow in 1439. But by then the Mongols no longer enjoyed an overwhelming military superiority and had split into rival hordes; northeast Rus', despite plague and other calamities, was increasingly prosperous and united under Moscow's control.[69] By then a Rus' patriot might be bold enough to believe that God was with his people. Or a hagiographer, Pakhomii for instance, seeking to promote Sergius's cult as a Russian saint, might advance the claim that he possessed the ability to intercede for Rus'. And only then might he think it appropriate to utilize the conviction of Trinity's brothers that Sergius could call on the Mother of God to protect them, to make her the vehicle of the salvation of Rus'. In the fourteenth century Moscow had been an embattled outpost of the Mongol empire; toward the middle of the fifteenth century it was the most powerful state in north Rus'. Was it not, then, logical that Muscovites could accept that the victory in 1380 set in motion the dramatic transformation in their status and to attribute it to the charismatic Sergius they knew from Trinity's celebrations and Pakhomii's lives? The person in whom they saw the cause of their well-being resembled those sketched by Max Weber in his essay on the origins of charisma. They were not men of affairs, accustomed to leadership in normal times; rather they were persons who in difficult times exhibited "special gifts of the body and spirit," gifts "believed to be supernatural, not accessible to everybody."[70]

There are two different ways to explain such appearances. Garry Wills recently stated the one I call spontaneous combustion, saying (with reference to Jesus), "the original story that reaches us does not begin with literal facts that are later 'embellished' as the seminarists put it. The first reports spreading from such figures are all a blaze of holiness and miracle. . . . It is their impact on the faith of others that makes these men noticeable in the first place. Miracles, as it were, *work themselves*, around such men." The other approach credits the hagiographer, in this case Pakhomii, with crafting a miracle story to fit the expectations of his contemporaries. In Eric Hobsbawm's terminology, Pakhomii was inventing tradition.[71] Pakhomii was a professional wordsmith who hired out his skills to credulous Muscovites. Yet, even in a more optimistic time it remains difficult to see how his assertion that Sergius summoned divine power to protect Rus' from its enemies could have become a broadly accepted organizing fiction had not Moscow's ruling elite found it useful. To put it another way, the emergence of Sergius's cult at Trinity and general admiration for him may have been largely self-generating; but the diffusion of his cult could not have happened had not the political and ecclesiastical authorities in Moscow come to see Trinity as a sacred place capable of bestowing transcendental authority on their power. Pakhomii understood this. Whereas in his initial life he wrote simply that Sergius urged Dmitrii to resist Mamai on behalf of Christianity in Rus', in the second he transformed Rus' Christianity into Dmitrii's patrimony and Dmitrii from a grand prince into "lord and Russian tsar" and "pastor of the Christian flock." In the third Rus' became "the land of Moscow," and Dmitrii's dignities were subsumed in the term "Orthodox tsar."

But Pakhomii's patronizing of the Muscovite grand prince went beyond flattery. At the end of the Third Edition of his life of Sergius was a final miracle with the cryptic title "What we wrote already, should not to be covered by silence" (*Nizhe se molchianiam da pokryetsia, iako zhe predpisakhom*).[72] In it Pakhomii brought Sergius to life in a vision to assist Vasilii II to ward off heresy. The heresy was Roman Catholicism, specifically the union of the Orthodox and Catholic Churches that the Papacy proposed at the Council of Ferrara-Florence in 1438–39, and which the Byzantine emperor and patriarch accepted in the hope that it would summon Catholic military power to relieve an Ottoman siege of Constantinople. The title wasn't the only curious thing about it. Compared to the miracle tales that preceded it, it is full of corruptions and oddities of usage and vocabulary, so different from Pakhomii's style that they suggest either another author or an aberrant copyist. The tale drew on information gleaned from the polemical account of the council and its aftermath by Simeon of Suzdal'. Simeon, a cleric in the entourage of Bishop Avraamii of Suzdal', went to Italy in the delegation of Isidore, a Greek who for his unionist views the patriarch of Constantinople had appointed Metropolitan of Kiev and all Rus'. While in Venice after the council, Simeon broke with Isidore and, with one Foma, the Prince of Tver's envoy in the Rus' delegation, made a difficult journey that brought him to Novgorod. The Lithuanian prince Lugven then lured him to Smolensk, shackled him, and turned him over to Isidore, who brought him to Moscow in 1441. He was confined at the Trinity-Sergius Monastery, perhaps at first at Isidore's request but, after Vasilii deposed Isidore and repudiated the union, because his Orthodoxy seemed suspect. At Trinity Simeon had time to rethink the significance of the council and write a "proper" account of it; and, possibly, to acquaint Pakhomii with his story. Pakhomii, utilizing the skeleton of Simeon's account, about 1442 wrote one of the first of the anti-Latin stories that emerged in Moscow after Vasilii rejected the union.[73] Pakhomii truncated Simeon's description of the Florence council but preserved his unfavorable reading of Isidore's pro-unionist activities and Simeon's break with him in Venice. This was prelude to the story of Simeon's arduous journey across Catholic Europe to Novgorod, and thence in chains to Moscow and the Trinity Monastery. At some point after crossing the Danube River, when things seemed hopeless, Pakhomii wrote, Simeon encountered a monk who identified himself as Sergius. Sergius assured Simeon that, because he had supported Bishop Mark of Ephesus in opposition to union at Florence, he need not fear. He foretold the adventures that would befall him on his return and that at last he would be brought to his Trinity Monastery. Pakhomii concluded, correctly, that Vasilii II would eventually perceive Isidore's perfidy, depose and confine him, then permit his escape, and he praised Vasilii for upholding Orthodoxy. The words were an appeal in the guise of praise. When Pakhomii wrote, it was by no means certain who the custodians of secular and ecclesiastical power in Moscow might be. The Russian see was vacant and Moscow's political elite was convulsed by a struggle for power between Vasilii Vasil'evich of the senior line of

Dmitrii Donskoi and the junior line led by his uncle Iurii Dmitrievich. The quarrel reverberated throughout Eastern Europe, with each party finding support at the Horde and in Lithuania.[74] Given that Constantinople lived under continuous siege by the Turks, no metropolitan could be appointed and no person or institution in Moscow was in a position to make the choice.

* The Trinity-Sergius Monastery was at the vortex of the Muscovite dynastic conflict between the senior line of Grand Prince Vasilii I and his son Vasilii II, and the line of Vasilii I's younger brother Iurii Dmitrievich and his son Dmitrii Shemiaka. Both factions wooed Trinity with property and privileges; but the shifting fortunes of this often-violent struggle tested the monastery's image as a holy center above the fray of worldly affairs. Invariably, it tested the loyalty of Trinity's brotherhood. Trinity's early history would lead one to believe that its allegiance would be with the line of Iurii Dmitrievich, whom Sergius had baptized and who had been a generous patron of Trinity in Abbot Nikon's time. Abbot Nikon also went out of his way to cultivate other princely patrons, the earliest and most important of whom was Prince Vladimir Andreevich of Radonezh. In 1401 Nikon journeyed to Kashin to baptize the son of its Prince Vasilii Mikhailovich; this Vasilii was the son of one prince of Tver' and brother of another, both hostile to Moscow. In 1410 Nikon interceded in Tver' politics again, blessing its Grand Prince Ivan Mikhailovich's reconciliation with his nephew Ivan Borisovich.[75] By contrast, until Nikon's death Trinity's relationship to the senior line in Moscow had been distant. Neither Dmitrii Donskoi nor his son Vasilii I, at least until 1415, issued an immunity charter to Trinity, let alone gave it land. Subsequently, Vasilii courted Trinity with fishing rights and immunities.[76] His son Vasilii II created even closer ties to Trinity. On 25 September 1433, after beating back Iurii's claim to be grand prince at the Horde, Vasilii must have gone to Trinity to give thanks on Sergius's feast day. It was the first time one of his line visited Trinity. The next day Vasilii issued Trinity a charter of immunities for Priseki, the administrative center of its newly acquired properties in Bezhetskii Verkh on the Novgorod frontier. Other favors followed. The following year on February 8, Vasilii, not yet 18, married Princess Mariia Iaroslavna. Mariia was the niece of Princes Andrei of Radonezh and Semen, who were buried next to Sergius, and of Prince Vasilii of Borovsk and Serpukhov, the reigning lord of Radonezh.[77]

Vasilii II and his rivals frequently visited Trinity to resolve their quarrels. They found partisans of both parties among Trinity's monks; Trinity's abbot Zinovii (1432–45) perforce had to maintain a delicate balance between rivals who sought Trinity's support. Envoys of the warring princes met at

Trinity in an unsuccessful effort to arrange a truce in April 1433, soon after Vasilii's marriage.[78] In 1434, having gained the upper hand, Prince Iurii met his nephew and ally Ivan Andreevich of Mozhaisk at Trinity to sign a treaty of alliance. They thereupon rode to Moscow, where Iurii ruled one month before dying.[79] Judging by their grants of immunities to Trinity and the nearby Kirzhach Monastery of 27 October 1438, Grand Prince Vasilii II and his mother Sofiia Vitovtna very possibly made a pilgrimage through Pereiaslavl' to Trinity. A. V. Gorskii thought Vasilii returned to Trinity again when he issued it another immunity charter in September 1439. And he must have been there on 22 January 1440 when Zinovii baptized the son of Vasilii and Mariia, the future Ivan III.[80] Iurii's son Dmitrii Shemiaka also courted Trinity with privileges and property.[81] Subsequently, Vasilii II came to Trinity to compel Abbot Zinovii to intervene on his behalf to halt Prince Dmitrii Iur'evich Shemiaka's march on Moscow. The date was either 1441 or 1442. Zinovii mediated an armistice and Vasilii and Dmitrii on Sergius's tomb swore an oath to uphold it.[82] For the descendents of Dmitrii Donskoi, Sergius had become a "family" saint, the benevolent guardian of the clan, nurturing its unity and interceding for its members. The site of Sergius's relics had become a place enjoying a moral ascendancy greater that that of any secular court in northeast Rus'. Its status bestowed a special dimension on the power of those who sought its sanction; in Emile Durkheim's words, it lent to "a profane object the sanctifying virtues of a sacred one."[83]

What the Trinity-Sergius Monastery gained in patronage and prestige owing to the competition between Vasilii and Dmitrii Shemiaka, it paid for in its vulnerability to their meddling. After Zinovii died in 1445, the rivals intervened to persuade or compel Trinity to appoint a sympathetic abbot. In 1445 Gennadii Samatov became abbot with the approval, if not by the instigation, of Grand Prince Vasilii II.[84] During his tenure the dynastic struggle came to a conclusion in a manner that transformed Trinity's status. From a private religious center of Moscow's ruling family, it became a public shrine whose saint was intercessor for Rus' and patron of the Muscovite-Russian state. In February 1446 Grand Prince Vasilii II made a pilgrimage to Trinity in the hope that he would be "reborn" as monarch and he and his line "relegitimitized." Certainly he was in need of any charisma that might accrue from his presence there. In the aftermath of plague, a destructive Tatar raid and siege in 1439, and the chaos of the dynastic struggle, in July 1445 Vasilii allowed Khan Ulu Mehmet to defeat his army and take him captive. Muscovites then witnessed the sorry flight of Vasilii's family and boiars, fearing Shemiaka's arrival to seize the grand princely title. And it suffered a terrible fire. On 17 November, the hapless Vasilii returned with an escort of Tatar troops, the meaning of which soon became apparent. He had bought his freedom with a promise that Moscow would pay a ransom, reported variously as 25,000 or 200,000 rubles. Supporters of Dmitrii Shemiaka circulated the rumor that Vasilii had undertaken a more onerous, secret obligation to allow the khan to rule as "tsar" in Moscow and other towns, leaving Vasilii to rule in Tver'.[85]

Vasilii's pilgrimage to Trinity was a public ritual of atonement: "The Grand Prince, expressing his desire to do reverence to the life-giving Trinity and to the relics of the miracle worker Sergius" on 12 February 1446, "proceeded with his illustrious children, Princes Ivan and Iurii, and a very small entourage [to the Trinity Monastery], expecting only to fête the brothers who lived at that great laura." With a public act of contrition for the misfortunes that he had brought upon his people, Vasilii could manifest publicly the blessing—and forgiveness—bestowed upon him through Sergius's intercessory power.[86] But not immediately. In Vasilii's absence Dmitrii Shemiaka seized the grand princely throne, imprisoned Vasilii's mother Sofiia, his wife Mariia, and his boiars, seized his treasury, and sent a troop commanded by Prince Ivan of Mozhaisk to capture Vasillii and his sons. The boys evaded capture and a sacristan (*ponomar'*) at Trinity named Nikifor helped Vasilii flee into the monastery, where he took refuge in the Church of the Holy Trinity. However, Abbot Gennadii must have denied him sanctuary. The earliest account of what happened, the Ermolin chronicle, which was also the source for Shemiaka's charge that Vasilii intended to turn over Moscow to a Tatar khan, was explicit about this. Numerous monks, including relatives of prominent Moscow merchant families, were adherents of Dmitrii Shemiaka. One was Dionisii who, before his tonsure, was the "great [Moscow] merchant Dmitrii Ermolin." The citation is from a miracle tale Pakhomii appended to his life of Sergius in 1447–49 that portrayed Dionisii as a malefactor at Trinity. He was one of several Ermolins tonsured at Trinity both before and after 1446. The Surmins, another Moscow merchant family, also had ties to Trinity and perhaps were part of the anti-Vasilii cabal.[87] Prince Ivan and his men entered the monastery and surrounded the church.[88] Accounts reflecting his later triumph said Ivan of Mozhaisk's man rode his horse up the steps to the doors of the Church of the Holy Trinity to flush out Vasilii. Vasilii took the icon "The Apparition to Sergius of the Mother of God with the two Apostles" from above Sergius's tomb, appeared in the doorway of the church, held it over his head, and swore in Sergius's name that he meant no one harm and that they had no cause to harm him. Ivan objected that Vasilii intended to subject Moscow to ransom and Tatar rule. Vasilii retreated into the church, replaced the icon, and, crying, threw himself on Sergius's tomb. Ivan and his men rushed in, seized Vasilii, and brought him to Moscow. Three days later Dmitrii Shemiaka ordered Vasilii's eyes be put out—as Vasilii had ordered the blinding of Dmitrii's brother Vasilii Kosoi in 1436—and that he be exiled. By the end of May 1446, Dmitrii replaced Trinity's abbot Gennadii Samatov with Dosifei, who came from the Storozhevskii Monastery of the Birth of the Mother of God in Dmitrii's appanage of Zvenigorod.[89]

Shemiaka's triumph was short-lived. Exiled to Vologda, Vasilii visited the Kirillov Monastery; where its abbot Trifon and an elder Simon Kartmazov, possibly an immigrant from the Trinity-Sergius Monastery, in 1446 released him from his oath of obedience to Dmitrii, said to have been given under duress.[90] By February 1447 Dmitrii's adherents had deserted him and Vasilii was in Moscow as grand prince. He compelled Dmitrii to release his mother Sofiia Vitovtovna, and she and Vasilii were reunited at the Trinity Monastery.[91] It was now Vasilii's turn to transform Trinity's leadership. Dosifei was out as abbot and another outsider, Martinian, was in. Martinian was a disciple of Kirill Belozerskii and was the founder of the Ferapontov Monastery. Vasilii met him during his exile in Vologda. Martinian supported Vasilii and became his confessor. So great was his influence that as abbot of Trinity he once summoned Vasilii and rebuked him for disregarding his advice.[92] Martinian brought recalcitrant monks at Trinity into line behind Vasilii, one being Dmitrii/Dionisii Ermolin.[93] In December 1447 Martinian put his signature on the letter of a church council threatening Dmitrii Shemiaka that if he did not end his rebellion, he would be excommunicated. One of its counts of treason against Shemiaka was that he accused Vasilii II falsely of plotting with the Mongol khan to conceal his own dealings with the Mongols in 1445. Martinian also witnessed a treaty, dated to the period 31 March–6 April 1448, by which Prince Ivan of Mozhaisk capitulated to Vasilii.[94] Although I have no evidence for it, Martinian also must have been present at the church council of December 1448, which on Vasilii's initiative elected Bishop Iona of Riazan' and Murom metropolitan of Kiev and all Rus'. It may not have intended it so, but with the fall of Constantinople to the Turks in 1453, the council's election of Iona became the precedent on which subsequent councils chose autocephalous metropolitans of Russia.[95] Subsequently Martinian was host at Trinity to a meeting in 1449 between Vasilii and Grand Prince Boris Aleksandrovich of Tver'. Vasilii was there again to celebrate the birth of a son that July, whom he named Boris. Out of these visits came an alliance—sealed by the marriage of Boris's daughter Mariia and Vasilii's twelve-year-old son Ivan in 1452—that isolated the fugitive Dmitrii Shemiaka.[96]

Trips to Trinity became regular occurrences. Vasilii stopped there at the beginning of 1451 at the outset of his final campaign against Shemiaka and again to celebrate the Epiphany in 1452.[97] To make Martinian's tenure palatable, Moscow's ruling family awarded Trinity grants of property and were lavish in the number and terms of its immunities. Vasilii gave Trinity two vacant properties in Vladimir and, with his mother Sofiia Vitovtovna, a village in Suzdal'.[98] Sofiia, in her own right, in 1449, probably on a visit, gave Trinity a chalice (*potir'*) and, in execution of her testament after her death on 5 July 1453, Vasilii issued a charter giving Trinity two villages in Pereiaslavl'. The charter has no date but he probably issued it in the short interregnum between 3 March 1454, when he released Martinian as abbot and allowed him to return to the Ferapontov Monastery, and 22 September 1454, when Vassian Rylo became abbot.[99] During Martinian's tenure Vasilii issued 16 immunity charters to Trinity, Sofiia Vitovtovna issued four, and Vasilii's wife Mariia Iaroslavna issued three.[100] In all they issued 23 immunity charters, or almost as many (25) as Vasilii, his mother, and his father had issued in all of Trinity's previous history. At some point Vasilii also granted Trinity a yard within the Moscow kremlin where in 1460 the monastery built a stone Church of the Epiphany.[101] Such generosity should not surprise. The treaty between Vasilii and Ivan of Mozhaisk of March–April 1448 and a circular letter issued at the end of 1448 by Metropolitan Iona to hierarchs within his eparchy, concerning Shemiaka's treason and excommunication, invoked the same divine witnesses in a virtually identical formula. I quote from the treaty: "The lord God, the most pure Mother of God, and the great saints and miracle workers, Nicholas, Petr the Metropolitan (of Rus', d. 1326), Leontii, bishop of Rostov (eleventh century), and the venerable elders Sergius and Kirill."[102] Sergius had become a star in a galaxy of saints who were, excepting Nicholas, from the see of Kiev and all Rus', to be worshiped as miracle workers throughout Russian and Greek Orthodoxy. It is thought that a church council placing Sergius and Kirill in that company must have met in 1447 after Vasilii II returned to power, although no record of such a council survives. Sergius's feast day was 25 September.

* Epifanii in his life, Andrei Rublev with his icon of the Trinity, and Nikon by proclaiming him a miracle worker with access to the benevolence of the Mother of God established Sergius as the object of a local cult. On this basis Nikon and his successors solicited the veneration and patronage of local landowners and princes. From these beginnings Pakhomii the Serb took the cult to a new level by enriching it with descriptions of miracles apparent during Sergius's life and posthumous ones at the site of his grave. Above all,

he dramatized the conviction that the Mother of God was Trinity's protector with a vision in which she appeared to Sergius and either Nikon or Mikhei. His words caught the imagination of icon painters, craftsmen, and scribes not only at Trinity but in Moscow and elsewhere. Pakhomii made this relationship the basis for claims, made more specific in succeeding editions of his life, that Sergius was the instrument by which divine grace gained victory for Dmitrii Donskoi at Kulikovo in 1380. The legend attained the status of a state cult in the Chronicle Tale of the battle sometime between the late 1430s and 1448. The tale in Pakhomii's Third Edition in which Sergius's miracles supported Vasilii as protector of the faith after the Council of Ferrara-Florence, also promoted Sergius as a "national" saint. Finally, during the Muscovite dynastic struggle rival claimants utilized Trinity's prestige and connections to advance their cause. Both parties approached Trinity asking that Sergius intercede for them. In so doing they made his veneration a family cult. In 1446 Trinity itself was the arena where Vasilii II was humiliated in the final crisis of the dynastic war, then the destination of his triumphal pilgrimage after winning out. In the aftermath of those events the prince and the hierarchy proclaimed Sergius's sainthood.

Chapter Three

Sergius, a Russian Icon

On 21 September in 1504, in the penultimate year of his reign, "Grand Prince Ivan Vasilevich and his son Grand Prince Vasilii Ivanovich and [his other] children departed Moscow and were that fall at the life-giving Trinity Sergius monastery."[1] Their pilgrimage was timed to celebrate St. Sergius's feast day, 25 September. By then Sergius's cult had become an "all-Rus'" celebration and his monastery something like a national shrine. It attracted pilgrims from all parts of Rus' and inspired deeds far beyond its walls. Such fame had serious consequences for Trinity. Powerful constituencies sought to share in Trinity's charisma. In turn they expected to share in defining and redefining Sergius's significance. Trinity lost its monopoly to shape the cult. Although its financial, artistic, and intellectual resources, and ultimately its inviolability as preserver of Sergius's relics, allowed it considerable influence, its brothers perforce had to develop antennae sensitive to how their inventions played at the court of Moscow's rulers or in the chancellery of the metropolitanate, later the patriarchate. In some instances Trinity formed "joint ventures" with these patrons in interpreting Sergius's cult.

* Pakhomii the Serb continued to work at Trinity. He described and appended to his Third Edition of the life new miracles attributed to Sergius that happened in 1448–49, during Martinian's tenure. He also produced a "prologue" edition of Sergius's life to be read on feast days. Then there are variants of Sergius's life, the earliest manuscripts of which date from around 1450, which Kloss called Pakhomii's Fourth Edition and others which he called Pakhomii's Fifth and dated to 1459.[2] The later editions in all their variants contained the episode in which Sergius's intercession was instrumental in Dmitrii Donskoi's victory over the Tatars in 1380.[3] A standard hagiographical narrative had come into being. Clifford Geertz described such narratives as a master fiction. It had four acts. In act one Dmitrii came

to Trinity for Sergius's blessing; Sergius, who possessed a "gift of prophesy," foretold that with God's help, for which he would offer prayers, Dmitrii would win and with his army return safely; Dmitrii thereupon vowed that he would found a monastery dedicated to the Mother of God to celebrate the victory. In the second act Dmitrii, en route to meet the Tatars, received Sergius's message urging him to press on. The battle was the third act, one punctuated by a miraclulous vision of gleaming, bloody armor that prophesied victory for Dmitrii's army. In the last act Dmitrii returned victorious to Trinity to fulfill his vow to build a monastery dedicated to the Mother of God. Editions of Sergius's life containing this story survive in over 100 manuscripts copied in many places from the mid-fifteenth through the seventeenth century. The story was present in the Extended Edition of 1518 and thereafter in over 40 manuscripts. One was an illuminated version containing 651 (or 652) miniatures that the tsar's masters produced about 1590 in Moscow. By then the narrative was an authenticating strategy.[4] Its salient quality, aside from repetition, was that it enlisted fiction to demonstrate the "truth" that Sergius was the agent and the Kulikovo battle the proof of a divine solicitude for Orthodox Russia. Another way of putting it is that society's optimistic expectations for the future of the Muscovite Russian state could only be justified by a powerful master fiction in which Sergius was the vessel through which God protected his chosen people.

Sergius's cult now grew rapidly in popularity in areas beyond Moscow's domains, earliest of all in the grand principality of Tver'. Epifanii had had longstanding ties there, as had Abbot Nikon and his successors. In his turn Pakhomii described a posthumous miracle in which a visit to Sergius's remains cured the Tver' citizen Zakharii Borozdin; in another miracle composed in 1448–49, Pakhomii said pilgrims flocked to Trinity to celebrate the feast of the Epiphany "from many towns and countries, not only from [towns] of Muscovy, but from far away areas, that is from [towns in] Lithuania, Riazan', and Tver'."[5] As tangible evidence of this Grand Prince Boris Aleksandrovich of Tver' (d. 1461) and his brothers gave Trinity a village with surrounding hamlets near Kashin on the north bank of the Volga. Boris also issued six charters assuring Trinity tax immunities on its commerce with Novgorod on the Volga and Sheksna Rivers and judicial immunities for the yard it founded in the appanage town of Kashin.[6] Novgorod's titular head of state, Archbishop Evfimii II, granted a charter of immunities to Abbot Martinian that exempted Trinity's trade in Vologda and on the Northern Dvina to its port of Kholmogory from duties and the jurisdiction of Novgorod's courts. His successor, the pro-Moscow Archbishop Iona, immediately on arriving in Novgorod in 1459 introduced Sergius's cult. While en route to his eparchy, the story went, Iona stopped at the Trinity-Sergius Monastery. There Iona made a vow, and in fulfillment of it he constructed and decorated a gate church to the Novogord kremlin where he resided, and dedicated it to Sergius. It was finished in 1463. Its fresco cycle depicting Sergius's life and miracles is poorly preserved, but enough remains to see that of its 16 scenes one was of the appearance to him of the Mother of God.[7]

Late in life Pakhomii moved to the Russian north to write in 1452 a life of St. Kirill. In it he added one more legend to Sergius's cult. On a visit to the Simonov Monastery, he wrote, the saint met Kirill and inspired him to follow a divine path that led to the establishment of the famous monastery of the Dormition near Beloozero. Kirill died in 1427. There is no other source for this.[8] Nor can we know whether Pakhomii was the sole agent by which Sergius's cult became part of the lore of northern monastic foundings. Pierre Gonneau's tabulation of images of Sergius showed that by 1505, he was venerated in Vologda and at the Kirill-Belozerskii and Ferapontov monasteries, as well as in Moscow, Novgorod, and Tver'.[9] Drawing on this heritage, lives written in the sixteenth century of four founders of trans-Volgan houses said their heroes were Sergius's contemporaries or disciples. One was an Avraamii, said to have died in 1375, who founded a house at Chukhlomsk; another was a Sil'vestr, said to have died in 1379, who founded the monastery of the Ascension on the Obnora River; a third was Sergii, who founded the Transfiguration Monastery on the Nur'ma river before his death in 1412; a fourth was a Pavel, said to have lived 15 years at the Trinity Monastery, who founded a house on the Obnora River with the authorization of Metropolitan Photios in 1414. He dedicated it to the Trinity and gave it a cenobitic rule. His hagiographer said he was 112 when he died in 1429.[10] No one knows when these houses were actually founded. But for the hagiographers who wrote about them, Sergius's inspiration was a logical part of the process.

To this list one can add Murom in the Grand Principality of Riazan', where a Trinity Monastery came into existence in the 1450s. It was founded in honor of Sergius, probably to celebrate his recent elevation to sainthood. Murom's reigning prince Ivan Fedorovich was the grandson of Grand Prince Oleg, whose grudging self-definition as the "younger brother"—or vassalage—to Dmitrii Donskoi Sergius had arranged in 1385, and whose son Fedor had wed Donskoi's daughter Sofiia in 1387 to seal the relationship. Sofiia probably had known Sergius, so it is not difficult to envisage how in her son's time the legend arose that 70 years earlier Sergius had founded the monastery during his peacemaking mission. Monks of the Solotchinskii Monastery near Riazan'—which Grand Prince Oleg founded in the 1390s, where he was tonsured and lived, and where he died and was buried in 1402—embraced Sergius's cult too. Oleg had dedicated its main church to the Intercession of the Mother of God, making it the family monastery of his dynasty. His son and grandson and their descendents were its patrons and at some point, but no earlier than the 1450s, the monastery built a church over the main gate and dedicated it to Sergius.[11]

Sergius's cult found its richest expression in Moscow. Stories of miracles that sustained the cult, however, did not travel between Trinity and Moscow in a vacuum; they intersected with material and political issues in which Trinity's brothers and Moscow's court had divergent or conflicting interests. We find examples of Muscovite generosity to Trinity alongside measures to assert its dominance there and to limit its economic privileges. And in ways that resemble the situation in Capetian France of the eleventh century described by Patrick Geary, Muscovite bookmen introduced the energizing force of Sergius's cult into Muscovite elite culture to mobilize the past to "give meaning to a transformed present."[12] By 1500 the cult became so "real" at the Muscovite court that its ruling family began to act it out in politics and in their personal lives.

Vasilii II's patronage of Trinity and good faith in seeking charisma there did not stop him from imposing on it an abbot who favored his political interests. His control of Trinity ostensibly was complete when on 10 July 1456 Vasilii arrested his wife's brother, Prince Vasilii Iaroslavich, abolished his appanage of Radonezh, and sent him in confinement to Uglich, where he remained until he died. Perhaps the Muscovite prince thought Vasilii too powerful, having inherited titles of Borovsk, Serpukhov, and Radonezh; perhaps too, with Shemiaka dead, Vasilii II no longer needed his brother-in-law as an ally and considered him a rival to the future succession of his son. Vasilii II thereupon canceled immunities previously granted Trinity's properties in Radonezh, Sol'-Galich, and Bezhetskii Verkh. Gonneau suggested that Vassian Rylo might have remonstrated with Moscow on behalf of Vasilii Iaroslavich, causing Vasilii to put Trinity in its place. Alternatively, M. S. Cherkasova cited the not unbiased testimony of Iosif Volotskii in letters written about 1510 to the effect that Vasilii took Trinity under his protection from Vasilii Iaroslavich because the latter did not treat it well. Whatever the case, from that moment Moscow's ruler became Trinity's lord. At Vasilii's death in 1462 Moscow was all-powerful in northern Rus'. Vassian Rylo understood this and made peace with Vasilii. A year later the privileges Vasilii had revoked were restored.[13] Subsequently, Vassian went to Kiev in 1459 to urge its prince to recognize Iona, Vasilii's choice to be metropolitan of Moscow and all Rus', and not the Uniate metropolitan Grigorii, whom

Kazimierz, ruler of Poland and Lithuania, had accepted. For this Iona publicly made known his esteem for Vassian.[14]

The earliest story about Sergius's life that bookmen outside Trinity's walls came up with was an entry for 1365 in what Lur'e called the all-Russian compilation of 1448. It concerned Prince Boris Konstantinovich's claim to rule Nizhnii Novgorod against the wishes of Moscow in the 1360s. To force Boris to relinquish Nizhnii Novgorod, Dmitrii Donskoi sent Abbot Sergius to summon Boris to judgment. When Boris refused to come to Moscow, Sergius closed Nizhnii Novgorod's churches. Dmitrii then sent an army to place Boris's brother Dmitrii in Nizhnii and to relegate Boris to Gorodets.[15] Many historians have doubted the historicity of the entry. Neither Pakhomii's many editions, nor the later Extended Edition of Sergius's life, mentioned his involvement in the affair. Most importantly, the earliest source regarding this episode, the Trinity chronicle, had an account that rings more true. First, it accurately dated the episode to 1363, not 1365. At that time Metropolitan Aleksei was regent for the 14-year-old Dmitrii. Prior to this a Muscovite army had defeated Boris's brother Dmitrii of Suzdal' to thwart his attempt to seize the title Grand Prince of Vladimir from Moscow. Afterward Moscow annexed Suzdal' and intended that Dmitrii rule in Nizhnii Novgorod in place of his brother Boris, who instead was to receive the lesser principality of Gorodets. Also, Metropolitan Aleksei took the latter two towns under his spiritual jurisdiction from the bishop of Suzdal'. The entry in the Trinity chronicle said Aleksei sent an archimandrite Pavel and an abbot Gerasim as emissaries to Nizhnii Novgorod to carry out his coup. Pavel was abbot of the Monastery of the Birth of the Mother of God in Vladimir; Gerasim, Aleksei's disciple, was abbot of the Spaso-Andronikov Monastery in Moscow. Subsequently Aleksei made Gerasim archimandrite of the Chudovskii Monastery in the Moscow kremlin. Aleksei had founded that house and as metropolitan resided there. Sergius, who did not live in the Muscovite principality and was still a relative nonentity, wasn't mentioned. When Boris refused to submit, Pavel and Gerasim closed Nizhnii Novgorod's churches, an act that only the metropolitan could authorize, and sent Boris's boiars to Moscow. Giving credence to this version is the fact that Aleksei made Pavel and Gerasim his agents in another delicate matter in the 1370s, sending them to the Kirzhach Monastery to ask Sergius to return to Trinity.[16] From the 1440s, however, it seemed more "truthful" to ascribe Moscow's policies to Dmitrii, the hero of Kulikovo, and to Sergius. That is how the story came down in the Moscow grand princely compilation of the 1470s, the Nikon chronicle of Metropolitan Daniil (1524) and in the Voskresenskaia Chronicle of the 1540s.[17]

The establishment of the cult of Sergius in Moscow as intercessor for the lands of Rus'—subsequently, the Russian land—we should remind ourselves, initially appeared in the same all-Russian compilation in the Chronicle Tale of the battle of Kulikovo. It then became a familiar theme in Muscovite narratives about Kulikovo and later struggles. The Moscow grand princely compilation of the 1470s, following the Chronicle Tale, had an emissary bring Dmitrii a message from Sergius with a blessing, an admonition to push on against Mamai and a promise that God and the Trinity would assist him.[18] In the grandiloquent "Tale of the Battle with Mamai," composed in 1500 or after by the former Trinity monk Mitrofan, Sergius, Trinity, and Trinity's lord Prince Vladimir Andreevich occupied center stage with Dmitrii Donskoi. On the eve of the battle, Grand Prince Dmitrii, his "brother" Prince Vladimir Andreevich, and other princes of Rus' made a pilgrimage to Trinity to do reverence to Sergius. He blessed them and, it being Sunday, the feast of the martyr-saints Florus and Lauras (18 August), asked Dmitrii to celebrate the liturgy with him and dine at Trinity. Dmitrii hesitated, fearing that to delay his departure would be dangerous. To that Sergius replied that if he hurried away, he would be doubly late. Dmtrii stayed to feast with Trinity's monks. Sergius blessed him and his army with holy water that had washed the relics of Florus and Lauras, saying God would help him and predicting that Dmitrii would wear a "crown of victory" and obtain many other crowns. As he left, Dmitrii asked that Sergius dispatch two monks to fight with them. Sergius complied, sending Aleksandr Peresvet and Andrei Osliaba to fight for the faith. Sergius dressed them in monks' robes emblazoned with a cross and in gold helmets. Returning to Moscow en route to meet Mamai, Dmitrii related Sergius's prediction of victory to Metropolitan Kipriian. Like the Chronicle Tale, the narrative said Sergius sent Dmitrii a message, here described as books, in which were written Sergius's greeting and admonition to engage the enemy. It added that he also sent a portion of the host (*khlebets*") set aside from communal loaf for a special rite, said to be from the Mother of God. Accepting these, Dmitrii prayed to the Trinity and the Mother of God for help and asked for Sergius's prayers. In the battle itself Vladimir Andreevich was a hero and Sergius's warrior-monk Peresvet figured prominently, charging off crying, "Abbot Sergius, help me with prayer!" to challenge a Tatar warrior. As victory neared, Vladimir Andreevich proclaimed that Russian arms were victorious owing to the mercy of God, the Mother of God, the (Russian) prince-saints and martyrs Boris and Gleb, and the prayers of "the Russian saint (Metropolitan) Petr, and our abettor and inspiration Abbot Sergius." Dmitrii concurred and singled out the deeds of Aleksandr Peresvet, "who was blessed by Abbot Sergius" and emerged victorious in his duel.[19]

The "Tale of the Battle with Mamai," composed at a time far-removed from the event it described, was full of errors: it placed Dmitrii's visit to Trinity on a Sunday whereas the feast of Florus and Lauras in 1380 was on a Saturday, it said Kipriian was metropolitan although he was not so recognized in Moscow in 1380, and in one instance it called the enemy Pechenegs instead of Tatars. The two warrior monks were inventions. Aleksandr Peresvet was a historical person, listed in the Trinity chronicle as one of lay warriors slain in the battle on the Vozha River in 1378. Osliaba was also the name of a real person, probably a boiar of the metropolitan's court in the late fourteenth century, but never a monk.[20] By 1500 these errors, like the greater story in which they appeared, were the truth that explained how things had come to be what they were. Muscovites liked this version more than the others. Between its origin and the end of the sixteenth century it appeared in four main variants, one of which went into Metropolitan Daniil's Nikon chronicle of 1524; during the sixteenth and seventeenth centuries it appeared in over 60 other manuscripts.[21]

Thenceforth Muscovite icon painters and chroniclers constantly introduced the image of Sergius as intercessor along with other all-Russian saints to explain Muscovite victories. According to the Moscow grand princely compilation, Metropolitan Gerontii ordered prayers at the graves of Russian saints in Moscow, at Sergius's grave at the Trinity Monastery, and throughout the realm to secure victory on the eve of Grand Prince Ivan III's forthcoming campaign against Novgorod.[22] The famous letter in which the bishop of Rostov and former abbot of Trinity Vassian Rylo urged Ivan III to stand firm in 1480 against the Tatars invoked Russian saints Sergius, Kirill Belozerskii, and Varlaam Khutynskii of Novgorod as intercessors to assure victory. Numerous chronicles, beginning with the offshoot of the grand princely compilation known as the Vologda-Perm' chronicle, contained the letter.[23] Another sort of evidence that Sergius's cult flourished in Moscow is an icon cloth (*pelena*) preserved in the Kremlin Museum in Moscow on which the central image is that of the appearance of the Mother of God to Sergius (fig. 6). It is attributed to the shop of the grand prince and princess and dated to the period 1450–1500, possibly to the 1480s. The image was canonical; that is, disciples John and Peter accompanied her, Sergius knelt before her, and Sergius's disciple Mikhei looked on in wonder from his cell. The bottom border contained images of five Russian saints: Evfimii of Suzdal', Kirill, Savva Visherskii, Varlaam, and, perhaps, Antonii Pecherskii.[24] Written and graphic evidence agree; in Moscow the cult of Sergius was primary, that of the other Russian saints secondary.

* Vasilii II's son Grand Prince Ivan III (1462–1505) began a transformation of the Muscovite state that institutionalized legal and bureaucratic structures that heretofore had been rudimentary forms of clientage and household management. His policies to rationalize fiscal and judicial control of the realm inevitably impacted on the economic interests of monasteries, Trinity included.[25] Those policies took several forms. One was to limit the number and generosity of fiscal and judicial immunities granted to autonomous institutions, and to renegotiate old ones. Another was to continue Vasilii II's oversight of Trinity's leadership and that of other important positions within the church. But this was only part of the story. The ruling family had forged palpable personal ties to Trinity, which political developments could only hope to redefine. Also, Muscovite bookmen had begun to write Sergius's cult into rationalizations of Muscovite power. As a result government policies at times seemed in harmony with the cult, at others in opposition to it. Yet they were integral parts of the same story.

Between 1462 and 1501, or four years before Ivan III's death, my database shows a sharp rise in the number of cases—56 compared to 12 up to 1461—brought to grand princely courts in which peasants or the ruler's officials were embroiled with Trinity, or which resulted in directives to his officials to enforce judicial decisions involving Trinity's properties. Pierre Gonneau, employing somewhat different categories and chronological divisions than mine, noted 13 litigations concerning Trinity before 1462; 29 in the first part of Ivan' reign, 1462–82; and 90 in the latter part, 1482–1505.[26] Such cases concerned land ownership, the burden of obligations that Trinity might expect from its tenants, and Trinity's tax immunities. By its command of documentary evidence, Trinity more often than not prevailed. For example, a clause in one directive substantiated Trinity's rights to taxes, described as *dan'* and *obrok*, in Vladimir from forests given to bee-keeping on properties in Gorokhovets and Iaropolch; another clause validated its income from streams and lakes in the valley of the Kliazma River.[27] Or, in a dispute over ownership of several villages that occurred around 1474–75 with a representative (*sotnik*) of state peasants in the Mishutinskii district (*stan*) of Pereiaslavl', Ivan's judge ruled for Trinity because it could produce an agreement showing its cellarer Login in 1462 had purchased the properties. The agreement named witnesses and Ivan III had registered it.[28] Between 1478 and 1501, 17 charters recorded proceedings in which Trinity's outpost of Verkhnii Berezovets in Kostroma prevailed in disputes with tax-paying peasants over land titles and borders.[29] The number of immunity charters issued by the grand prince to Trinity increased, but in the majority of cases they did not offer new immunities to existing properties or grant privileges to new ones; rather, they defined more precisely or, rarely, reduced the immunities that Trinity enjoyed.[30] Ivan's transfer of the "great market," controlled by the monastery and situated outside its walls, to the town of Radonezh in 1492 was exceptional in its harshness. Coming, as it did, on 25 September, the one hundredth anniversary of Sergius's death, it can only be interpreted as a calculated insult. No one knows the pretext; yet in the context of the squeeze Ivan's government exerted on monastic properties and privileges to support his service-class cavalry, its timing was hardly coincidental.[31]

Overall, Trinity retained generous privileges on a widely dispersed portfolio of properties and acquired more properties, albeit at a diminished rate. Appendix Table 2 shows 113 transactions—donations, purchases, exchanges, or judicial awards—by which Trinity acquired property, a significant decrease from the 171 recorded between 1423 and 1461. One might argue that in part it was the result of a rise in land values in a period of growing prosperity and the decreasing incidence of plague. But then one might expect that those making memorial donations, a phenomenon to be discussed in the following chapter, might instead have made money donations, but this didn't happen until later. The only other explanation is that the state limited Trinity's ability to acquire property. This may not have been the whole story, but it was the most important.

An immunity charter attesting to Ivan's presence at Trinity on 30 October 1472 is the earliest record of his patronage after becoming grand prince. After a fire damaged the Church of the Epiphany in Trinity's court in the Moscow kremlin on 4 April 1473, it was quickly rebuilt. Probably Ivan supported that effort, but we have no record of it. Gonneau thought that Ivan could not abide Trinity and ascribed his alleged antipathy to his having witnessed as a boy his father's capture there in 1446. This seems unlikely. Vasilii II made happy pilgrimages there after having won back his the throne, trips on which Ivan probably accompanied him.[32] On 4 April 1479 Ivan brought Vasilii, his infant son by his second wife the Greek princess Sophia Palaeologa, to Trinity to be baptized, just as his father had baptized him there. Paisii, an austere monk from a northern monastery whom Ivan imposed on Trinity as abbot in 1478, and former abbot and archbishop of Rostov Vassian Rylo, presided. The next year Ivan brought his second son by Sophia, Iurii, to Trinity to be baptized by Paisii. Ivan must have thought it important to make public these rites and the processions from Moscow to Trinity that accompanied them. Chronicles do not record where he baptized his son Ivan "the Younger," born in 1458 during his father's reign, or where his grandson Dmitrii Ivanovich, born in 1483, was baptized. Perhaps this was because the chronicles were written after Sofiia's son Vasilii won out over them in the succession.[33] With these acts Ivan reaffirmed his family's ties to Trinity and lent Paisii's administration the cachet that went with it. In 1481 Trinity's monks drove Paisii from office. Ivan, evidently, did not forgive them for this and ceased to visit Trinity.

In 1503, probably in the late summer–early fall, Ivan III convened a church council. The council's response (*sobornyi otvet*) said he intended to gain control of church lands. It and other sources about the council are in some respects contradictory in their testimony; not a few of them were polemical in intent. The earliest may have appeared in 1517, but the others were of later provenance. But because the sources emanated from diverse parties, and addressed common themes regarding Ivan's intentions and the clerical factions involved, it is likely that such a council took place.[34] Given his consistent record of using church lands to pay for his service cavalry, I think Ivan's intentions were radical. Trinity's land fund would have been a primary target. Nothing came of it. The hierarchy was a necessary ally and Ivan's servicemen, by reason of grants to monasteries for memorial prayers, had a stake in the existing order. Also, at the end of July 1503, Ivan showed signs of failing health (*nachat iznemogati*).[35] Grand Princess Sophia and her boiar allies, who in 1502 had persuaded Ivan III to recognize her as-yet-unmarried son Vasilii as grand prince and heir to the throne, would hardly have endangered his chances by following through with whatever Ivan had in mind.

Sophia's triumph occurred almost three years after disgruntled boiars brought about Ivan Patrikeev's disgrace in 1499. The Patrikeev family had been dominant at court since the 1450s. In 1480 Ivan Patrikeev solidified its position with the marriage in 1480 of Ivan III's son, Ivan the Younger, to their mutual first cousin once removed, Princess Elena of Moldavia. In 1497 Ivan Patrikeev prevented a coup by Grand Princess Sophia, her eldest son Vasilii, and their allies, after which Ivan III crowned Ivan the Younger's son Dmitrii co-ruler and heir apparent in 1498. This was too much for his rivals, and Patrikeev was gone.[36] Sophia, sensing that the coup would work to her son's advantage, had ready and presented Trinity a magnificent icon cloth (*pelena*, fig. 7) in 1499.[37] The iconography of the icon cloth brought Sergius's intercessory powers into play on behalf of Sophia's eldest son's claim to be Ivan III's successor. It was to establish the saint as protector of the ruling family as well as of the Russian land. I shall discuss its significance in Chapter 6. Sophia died 4 April 1503. The next year, on 21 September, Vasilii celebrated his victory by setting out for Trinity for Sergius's feast day. It was with a description of that pilgrimage that I began this chapter. At the conclusion of the feast of St. Sergius, a procession—Vasilii, his family, the court, and a military guard—left the Trinity-Sergius Monastery to parade its awesome might through Pereiaslavl', Rostov, and Iaroslavl'.[38] This was a public act in which his siblings and the court recognized Vasilii's preeminence. Ivan III was in tow to affirm the legitimacy of the succession. In an age in which communication was mostly visual and personal, the royal progress had the power of rites to give meaning to the world, "by linking the past to the present and the present to the future"; that is, to legitimize the transformation of power from Ivan III to Vasilii Ivanovich III (1505–33). For provincials who rarely, if ever, had seen such a sight, the spectacle, to paraphrase Clifford Geertz, stamped the land with ritual signs of dominance.[39] Probably with an icon of St. Sergius at its front, the procession made known to all who witnessed its passing that with such an intercessor Vasilii's rule was secured by divine favor. Vasilii then returned to Moscow on 9 November having demonstrated that his kremlin was a sacred center of power.[40]

In the sixteenth century the master fiction of Sergius as intercessor became ubiquitous in Moscow. Its rulers, who by the 1550s said they ruled all Russia, had their differences with Trinity, but it did not stop them from basking in its charisma; their bookmen and artisans wrote, wove, and worked this theme into a variety of creations. Vasilii III was more hospitable to Trinity than his father had ever been. He gave 60 rubles to Trinity in 1505 to pray for his father's soul; on 29 November 1516 he donated 50 rubles to memorialize the deceased son of a boiar; in 1519 he donated 30 rubles in memory of his late brother Semen. Subsequently, he gave Trinity a silver ladle (*kovsh*).[41] On the other hand, the government's policies regarding monastic lands, including Trinity's, changed little from those of Ivan III. During Vasilii's reign of 32 years, Trinity acquired 107 properties, not much less than the 124 acquired in the 42 years of his father's reign. The 67 that were donations was slightly higher than the 60 recorded under Ivan III. Vasilii's government, like his father's, reviewed immunity charters and issued about half as many as had Ivan's. As S. M. Kashtanov noted, after 1511 in substance they were inconsistent, extending some privileges while reining in others. Trinity received over twice the number of immunity charters enjoyed by any other monastery (and almost a quarter of the charters issued to all beneficiaries), but lagged far behind the Iosifo-Volokolamskii Monastery in exemptions from various taxes. Although Vasilii's government established uniform fiscal and land policies and extended them across the realm, it allowed Trinity and other great houses considerable autonomy and even abetted their piling up of wealth.[42]

On 13 December 1512 Grand Prince Vasilii III was at Trinity to consecrate a new brick entrance gate atop which was a church dedicated to St. Sergius and a side chapel dedicated to his name-saint Basil of Parius. Abbot

Pamba and Bishop Mitrofan of Kolomna, who probably had been tonsured at Trinity, presided.[43] Vasilii returned to Trinity seven times:[44] On the eve of his campaign against Zygmunt of Poland in 1518 Vasilii went to Trinity to pray for victory and to fête its monks. He next was at Trinity for the feast of Pentecost in 1524. Vasili and Grand Princess Elena Glinskaia, his second wife, visited Trinity on 4 September 1530 to baptize their infant son and heir, the future Ivan IV. Abbot Ioasaf Skripitsyn baptized him and probably participated in selecting the holy elders Daniil of Pereiaslavl', the 100-year-old Kassian Bosoi of the Iosifo-Volokolamskii Monastery, and Iov Kurtsev of Trinity to be Ivan's godfathers. Ivan was the third of his line to be baptized at Trinity; it had become a family tradition. On 17 September 1531 Vasilii with Elena and baby Ivan embarked on a major pilgrimage: they were at Trinity for an entire week for the feast of St. Sergius. Subsequently, "for his imperial diversion" (*na svoiu tsar'skuiu potekhu*), probably to hunt, they went to Volok and Mozhaisk, returning to Moscow on 19 November. In addition to doing reverence to Sergius for their son on his first birthday, Vasilii used the procession to exhibit his young heir. One year later Vasilii repeated the pilgrimage to Trinity and went on to his palace at Aleksandrovskaia Sloboda, returning to the kremlin on 3 October. Abbot Ioasaf with Daniil of Pereiaslavl' baptized Ivan's and Elena's second son Iurii at Trinity's yard in the kremlin 27 days later. And when Vasilii was dying in 1533, Abbot Ioasaf came to bless him. Vasilii asked Sergius's protection for his heir. They then went to Trinity, where Vasilii was tonsured and prayed for before returning to Moscow to die.

Muscovite bookmen continued to embellish Sergius's reputation as intercessor for the dynasty, often in events in which Sergius figures as an historical actor. The tale entitled "Citations drawn from sacred writings," a polemical retelling of the conquest of Novgorod that appeared in the first decade of the sixteenth century, portrayed Ivan III's campaign as a crusade to save the city from Latin heresy. Prayers invoked Sergius, among a galaxy of Russian saints, to summon a heavenly host to assure Moscow's victory.[45] Compilers of the Sofiia Second chronicle in the 1520s appended to the story of the battle of Belev (1438) with Ulu Mehmet's Horde a text of the double-edged miracle tale of the warrior saved from pagans that Pakhomii had written into several editions of Sergius's life. In the 1540s the compilers of the L'vov chronicle repeated these entries.[46] The Sofiia Second and other chronicles also recorded an episode best described as an "acting out" of the cult. In 1518 Vasilii with his brother went to the "Trinity Monastery of the venerable Sergius the miracle worker" to pray and feast its brothers, presumably, to solicit the saint's support in the impending war with Zygmunt of Poland.[47] Images of Sergius as intercessor also formed a thread running through Metropolitan Daniil's Nikon chronicle, a work unprecedented in its integration of information from many sources to create a history of Russia within the context of Christian world history. Under 1392, the year of Sergius's death, Daniil inserted a fresh version of his life. Its sources were the Extended Edition and an early edition of Pakhomii. It mentioned Sergius's blessing of Dmitrii Donskoi's resistance to Mamai and prediction that, with the help of God and the Mother of God, he would win and return safely. It did not mention a message from Sergius to him on the eve of the battle but had Dmitrii returning to fulfill his vow to found a monastery dedicated to the Mother of God. This version also used news from "The Tale of the Battle with Mamai" that Sergius sent monks Peresvet and Osliabia into the battle.[48]

* Sergius's cult in greater measure shaped the personal lives of Vasilii's son Grand Prince, and from 1547 Tsar, Ivan IV "the Terrible" (1533–84), his grandson Tsar Fedor (1584–98), and Fedor's successor Tsar Boris Godunov (1598–1605). These rulers and their advisors, bookmen, and artists employed Sergius's cult as if it were an activating force to shape affairs of state. Ivan IV and Metropolitan Makarii (1542–63) produced as well historical narratives, ceremonies, and monuments that enlisted Sergius's cult to explain the events of their age. Ivan IV's personal relationship to Trinity and Sergius's cult, however, like so many of his actions, abounded in contradictory acts of extreme generosity and reverence on one hand and a puritanical zeal to renovate the monastery on the other. Even his government's policies regarding Trinity's properties were anything but consistent.

Between 1533 and 1605 Trinity received 149 immunity charters. Some were exceedingly generous; most only confirmed existing charters on the basis of periodic government surveys of monastic privileges; and some narrowed Trinity's immunities. Upon coming to power, the regency that ruled during Ivan's minority instituted the first general survey of monastic properties. It compelled Trinity to copy its land documents and revoked or modified privileges granted in some of them before ratifying the rest. This process led to the production of the oldest of Trinity's surviving copybooks in February 1534, to the affixing of ratifying postscripts on existing charters and to the issuance of new immunity charters dated 9 February 1534. In all it confirmed 92 immunity charters issued since Ivan III's campaign to define immunities.[49] From the fall of the regency in 1538 to 1548, a period of so-called boiar domination, Trinity and other monasteries acquired many new properties, often with liberal immunities. Ivan himself in 1548 gave Trinity a yard in Kholmogory near the mouth of the Northern Dvina river, conferring on it tax immunities and relief from tariffs on the river route to Vologda.[50]

And how is one to make sense of the contradictions between Ivan's generosity to Trinity and the anti-monastic policies of the "government of compromise" that had his favor from 1548 to 1553? Ivan's government set a course directed at restricting the ability of monasteries to acquire taxable properties, one that included another review of immunity charters.[51] On 17 May 1551 it reconfirmed 97 charters, but in many instances curtailed previous privileges. Trinity notated these in its copybook, in the process providing a bogus signature to a charter dating from the reign of Vasilii II giving Trinity fishing rights in Pereiaslavl'.[52] Conversely, several times in 1551 Ivan's government examined and confirmed a charter issued in September 1550 that allowed Trinity to collect customs duties at its properties in Radonezh, Pereiaslavl', and Dmitrov. In this and its obligation to provide its peasants for government corvée, local government officials (the *iamskii dvor, prikazshchiki*) were not to be involved. Subsequently, Ivan granted Trinity new charters with liberal immunities: a charter of 12 October 1571 gave Trinity financial immunities for three years in areas devastated by the Crimean khan's raid on Moscow; on 20 June 1577 he issued another that barred his officials from recruiting corvées on Trinity's rural properties; and on 28 April 1578 he issued a charter promising more privileges for its rural properties that were in ruin. Kashtanov doubted whether the state was committed to the more liberal promises in these charters, noting that those of 1577 and 1578 specified that previous charters with restrictive provisions—those confirmed in 1551—were to be observed.[53] No one can be certain how they were interpreted. Yet I suspect Ivan's courts treated Trinity generously in that the tsar continually rewarded Trinity with privileges to support commercial endeavors in new territories. Thus, in 1554 he extended Trinity's exemption from commercial duties on the Northern Dvina route from Vologda to the monastery and on to Moscow. The same act halved the periodicity of tax collections and provided judicial independence for Trinity's factory at Ust' Kur'ia on the Dvina. In February 1553 Trinity received a charter giving it the right to branding fees (*piatna*) on Nogai horses traded in newly conquered Kazan'.[54]

On another front, in January and February 1551 Ivan's government convened the church council known as the Council of the Hundred Chapters (*Stoglav*). The great monasteries, Trinity in particular, were the primary targets of its reform efforts. Ivan opened the council with an address in which he railed at monks in the great houses who spent too much time piling up wealth and lived a raucous life of ceaseless feasting. Their acceptance of gifts and properties, he said, was at the root of the problem, singling out Trinity for "entertaining an unending number of guests both day and night." Ivan's displeasure at such behavior, perhaps exaggerated because it profaned a sacred site, seems real. Although the council had to accept restrictions on the acquisition of property of secular owners, Ivan and his reformers obviously were dissatisfied with the outcome.[55] That spring Ivan summoned non-possessor monk Artemii from the northern hermitages and housed him at the Chudovskii Monastery in the kremlin. Probably in May Ivan deposed Serapion Kurtsev as abbot of Trinity and compelled the brotherhood to accept Artemii as his replacement. Ivan propitiated the brotherhood by appointing Serapion archbishop of Novogorod in July 1551 and awarding Trinity immunities from judicial oversight for its large village of Remenka in Bezhetskii Verkh in October. Trinity's elders were not appeased and forced Artemii to flee six months later. In 1553–54 Trinity elders Iona Shchelepin and Ignatii Kurtsev, and cellarer Andreian Angelov, gave testimony in Moscow to convict Artemii of heresy.[56] There was no more talk of reform.

Paradoxically, throughout the "reform" period Ivan favored Trinity with unparalleled acts of generosity. In the 1540s his government subsidized the construction of stone walls at Trinity, ordering that peasants recruited to do the building be freed from customs duties (*podati*) and compulsory labor obligations (*povinnosti*). Ivan personally granted Trinity 3,000 rubles for the construction. In addition, next to Trinity's south and east walls workers built wooden dormitories for its monks, and on the west side of the monastery they built a stone cellarer's residence, a hospital, and a wooden residence for the tsar (Frontispiece). Judging from an entry in Trinity's donation book stating that he ordered court favorite Aleksei Adashev to provide Trinity another 7,000 rubles, Ivan underwrote these constructions. Subsequently, at Abbot Serapion Kurtsev's request, Ivan ordered townspeople of Pereiaslavl', Dmitrov, and Radonezh to strengthen Trinity's walls. For this they were freed from construction levies elsewhere. Then there is the stone church of St. Nikon, adjoining the south side of the Holy Trinity church that replaced a wooden church of the same name. The consensus has been that it was built in 1548 as recorded in Trinity's chronicle (written no earlier than 1637), following Nikon's recognition as a saint at a church council in 1547.[57] (fig. 3) Ivan subsidized more construction, but it is impossible in most cases to ascertain whether the sums expended were private or public monies. Perhaps it is a distinction without meaning.

Moscow's grand princes had made pilgrimages to Trinity since the reign of Vasilii II for devotional reasons or to solicit Sergius's charisma to justify their rule. Some clearly were public processions. Vasilii III introduced a new custom in 1531 when he made a pilgrimage to Trinity—and thence to other places—accompanied by his wife and children to celebrate Sergius's feast day. During the regency his widow Elena made a regular practice of such displays of familial piety. Ivan gave new meaning to the custom of royal pilgrimages. Trinity was his primary destination. He might go to Trinity two or three times a year, then journey on to other monasteries to pray. Often he was on the road for months, traveling north to the Kirillov monastery, west to Novgorod and Pskov, and south to Moscow's border between Kolomna and Tula. But always to Trinity. Between 1536 and 1567 Ivan visited Trinity at least 45 times, usually on feast days: for the feast of the Appearance of the Holy Spirit to the Apostles or Pentecost Sunday, which in sixteenth-century Russia was called Trinity Day; on July 5, the anniversary of the discovery and translation of Sergius's relics in 1422; and on 25 September.[58] After 1567 chronicle entries are too irregular to track the frequency of his pilgrimages, but we know he made them. Except for the distance traveled, the pilgrimage he began on 21 May 1545 was not atypical. Taking brother Iurii and cousin Vladimir Andreevich, Ivan went to Trinity to celebrate Easter. The service extended through the night and into the morning. When it was over they feasted Trinity's abbot and brothers in the refectory and gave them gifts after which they went to Pereiaslavl' to pray. Brother and cousin returned to Moscow; Ivan went on to Rostov and Iaroslavl', north to the Kirillov and Ferapontov monasteries and the Monastery of Our Savior at Priluki near Vologda, and on to the Kornil'ev Vvedenskii, Pavel Obnorskii, and Boris and Gleb houses in Ust'e, where he fed their brothers and gave them alms. Ivan returned to Moscow 7 July. On 15 September Ivan again set out for Trinity with his brother. He must have remained there ten days because the chronicle said that, after praying night and morning and feasting and rewarding its brothers, presumably on the 25th, he went to his retreat at Aleksandrovskaia Sloboda. He returned to Moscow on 5 October.[59]

Initially Ivan, like his forefathers, made Trinity the agent for family baptisms, a custom that called forth images of Sergius as the dynasty's protector. On 18 August 1550 Abbot Serapion Kurtsev and two brothers baptized Ivan's daughter Anna in Moscow at the Church of Saints Joachim and Anna; in December 1552, Ivan, his wife Anastasiia, his brother Iurii, and "many boiars" went to Trinity to witness the baptism of Ivan's son and heir Dmitrii. Dmitrii died six months later and, perhaps brooding over that unfortunate event, Ivan baptized his son Ivan, born 28 March 1554, in the Kremlin Chudovskii Monastery.[60] Later he was to regret his decision. Trinity was also a favorite destination at which to celebrate other occasions. After his coronation as tsar, between 25 and 28 December 1547, Ivan went to Trinity to pray at Sergius's grave and to take part in a service at which the brothers ordered prayers for his health and well-being and a strengthening of his *tsarstvo.* Most likely in their procession to Trinity of 21–28 June 1548, or coincident with the feast of the Pentecost as Kloss suggested, Ivan and Anastasiia presented Trinity with an elaborate icon cover (*oklad*) for Rublev's icon of the Trinity. Only parts of it survive, but information in Trinity's inventory of 1641 and T. V. Nikolaeva's investigation allow us to assess its magnificence. The engraved metal cover concealed all but the central image of the icon. Its canopy supported three gold crowns set with emeralds, rubies, and sapphires. From it hung a panagia on gold with a chain of diamonds and three coinlike pendants (*tsaty*) with enamels. Engraved plating to hold the icon covered all but the central image. Appended to it were 22 circular medallions on which various saints were inscribed in niello. The medallions contained a complex ideological message that Kloss decoded in part. Figures on the nine medallions on each side were of baptismal name-saints of members of the imperial family. Ivan IV's baptismal name-saint, the apostle Titus, is on the lower left; that of the martyr Justina (d. 324), the baptismal name of Anastasiia, is on the lower right. Other medallions contained images of saints associated with the dynasty's self-definition of divinely inspired imperial rule: the martyr saints of old Rus' Boris and Gleb, who were among the earliest "ancestors" claimed by Ivan, were on the top right and paired on the top left by the Roman Emperor Constantine and his mother Helen. Elsewhere one finds Petr and Aleksei, metropolitan-saints who had supported Moscow's princes, and the paired images of Varlaam Khutynskii and Sergius. Cellarer Andrean Angelov's tale of the conquest of Kazan' in 1552 recorded that Ivan prayed at Trinity before the icon that he had decorated before setting out on the campaign. Kloss thought Rublev's icon of the Trinity had become the dynasty's palladium. Perhaps so: Ivan, having been baptized at Sergius's tomb under that icon in 1530, might well have thought it symbolized Sergius's promise of protection for his person and his cause. Returning from his conquest, Ivan stopped at Trinity on 27 or 28 December 1552 before entering Moscow. He dined with its brothers and gave thanks at Sergius's grave for interceding with the Mother of God for the Russian land.[61] Between 1548 and 1563 Ivan IV and his wife Anastasiia commissioned and donated to Trinity five other icons with lavish covers. The images on several of the covers suggest they celebrated the conquest of Kazan' or victories in Livonia; the images on others honored family members. For example, Kloss suggested that Anastasiia and Iul'iana Paletskaia, the wife of Ivan's brother Iurii, commissioned and donated to Trinity an icon of St. Nicholas in 1559 with images of SS. John and Basil in honor of their sons Ivan and Vasilii.[62]

Subsequent pilgrimages brought more gifts. On 11 October 1556, probably upon receiving news of the conquest of the Khanate of Astrakhan, Ivan ordered the gilding of the cupola of the Church of the Holy Trinity. That year he also ordered that rest stations be established on the pilgrimage route from Moscow to Trinity in the villages of Kopilovo, Taininskoe, Bratovshchino, Sofrino, and Vozdvizhenskoe.[63] In September 1558 Ivan again was at Trinity to celebrate the feast of St. Sergius. Before he departed he received Prince Petr Shuiskii and his party, who brought news of a victory in Livonia. Elated, Ivan decided to build another Church of the Trinity next to the old one on the site of the ancillary Church of St. Nikon. He consulted Trinity's abbot Ioasaf Chernyi and elders and solicited Metropolitan Makarii's approval for his plan. They must have suggested alternative purposes for his beneficence, because the following year Ivan and his family were present to witness the laying of the foundation of the Basilica of the Dormition at the center of Trinity's sacred space. It was his wife Anastasiia's last pilgrimage to Trinity. She died the following summer. The basilica was completed in 1585, the year after Ivan's death. With chapels dedicated to his and Anastasiia's name-saints, it stands as a memorial to their marriage.[64] It remains the largest church at the monastery, and its liturgical center. In January 1561 Metropolitan Makarii and a council of bishops elevated Abbot Eleuferii of Trinity to the rank of archimandrite. The enabling charter said the tsar recommended it, although the Illuminated Codex, commissioned by Ivan, said Ivan ordered it on the metropolitan's recommendation. Both said Eleuferii and his successors ranked above other archimandrites, the charter saying, "of the Russian metropolitanate," the chronicle reading, "of the Russian state." For Kremlin ideologues they were synonymous.[65]

Three years later, following the feast of St. Sergius, 25 September, at "the Trinity-Sergius monastery the refectory and monastic treasury in the [cellarer's?] residence [*v polatakh*] burned and many bells melted. The entire kitchen, the guest house and that for servants, and the cells burned from the main gate [*ot Krasnykh vorot*] of the upper row along the mill pond behind the refectory to the cellarer's [residence], and the cells near the cellarer's treasury burned. [The fire] consumed all the monastery's stores so thoroughly that not a day's ration remained for its brothers." Having only left Trinity and having heard of it, and, "having great faith in the life-giving Trinity and in St. Sergius," Ivan gave the monastery 1,000 rubles, saw to other needs, and ordered the monastery be rebuilt to its former standard.[66]

These were public acts of beneficence, most of them calculated but no less sincerely proffered. Because Ivan's processions went to Trinity before going elsewhere, Sergius's cult became a regular and familiar component of Muscovite imperial symbolism. There were other private acts, mostly memorial donations on behalf of kin and for members of his court. The phenomenon of donations for prayers for the dead, usually at the grave of a miracle worker, was of huge proportions at Trinity and elsewhere. It was how most people came to Sergius and I discuss it in the following chapter. Ivan made 47 donations, 29 explicitly for memorial prayers. They came to 13,251.40 rubles, 36 gold coins, over 9 villages, 57 hamlets and wastes, 1 salt works, 2 factories, over 3 urban courts, 2 subsidiary monasteries, and a generous award of personal property.[67]

The campaign of terror between 1565 and 1572 known as the *oprichnina* benefited Trinity, albeit fortuitously. *Oprichnina* agents did seize some lands and houses but these acts were incidental to attacks on secular landowners. Trinity's "good fortune" was to acquire estates from families ruined by the terror, by purchase, made cheap owing to the economic distress, or by donation for memorial prayers for those who had perished. If one interprets the charters of immunity issued by Ivan in 1571, 1577, and 1578 as liberal in intent, then the government helped Trinity to consolidate its acquisitions. Ivan also issued Trinity generous immunity charters in Kazan' (15 March and September 1576) and in Astrakhan (8 July 1578), and freed Trinity's fisherman in the far north from taxes on their catch (1581).[68] In 1580, reacting to the growing economic crisis, Ivan's government reversed course. It forbade monasteries to expand their holdings and ordered another land survey, which was completed after his death in 1584.[69]

In his last years Ivan gave compulsively. And, although he visited the Kirillov Monastery less frequently than Trinity, his gifts to Kirillov from 1570 to 1584 were greater.[70] Gifts usually were calibrated public statements by which a person, family, or group established its place in the social hierarchy. Throughout his reign Ivan had calculated what might be expected of a tsar in giving to Trinity. Like his pilgrimages, gift-giving was a ritualized activity that showed the ruler as a sacred source of power and demarcated the heartland of his realm as sacred space. But now, I suspect giving was as much a means to salve a conscience as it was a display of the ruler's wealth and magnanimity. A grant to a religious institution such as Trinity transcended social definitions of honor in that it was an appeal for grace; that is, "a free gift from God unmerited by men." As such it was above the obligatory or predictable.[71] I will make more of this in the following chapter in discussing the memorial culture that bound secular society to Trinity. But, remembering Ivan's troubled reverence for a monk's life displayed at the *Stoglav* and during the *oprichnina*, this splurge of giving calls up the image of a tormented soul restlessly seeking spiritual solace. Knowing how he agonized over the souls of those whom he did away with in the *oprichnina*, efforts to assuage feelings of guilt and sinfulness must have entered into it. Historians, viewing Ivan as a paranoid, sadistic butcher, have undervalued the depth of Ivan's religiosity, despite the fact that he organized his life as a succession of ritual acts, many of them devoted to Sergius's intercessory powers.[72]

Ivan's conflicted piety was never more evident than in the aftermath of the death of his son and heir, Tsarevich Ivan. The circumstances were tragic. On 19 November 1581 the tsarevich attempted to restrain the tsar Ivan during one of his rages. Ivan struck the tsarevich with his staff and killed him. Ivan brooded constantly over what he had done. A year later, recalling, one might think, that 27 years earlier he had departed from ancestral custom and had Tsarevich Ivan baptized in the kremlin rather than at Trinity, unable to find peace of mind and in constant physical pain from the degenerative condition of his spine, the tsar made a final visit to Trinity. It was recorded in Trinity's *sinodik* of 1575 and in its donation book:

> On the 6th of January, 1583, the tsar and sovereign was at the monastery of the life-giving Trinity and the great miracle workers Sergius and Nikon on the feast of the Epiphany and took part in morning prayer and evensong in the main church [of the Holy Trinity] and summoned unto himself the cellarer and elder Evstafii [Golovkin], the elder Varsunofii Iakimov, and near him also stood his confessor the archimandrite (1569–73) Feodosii—only three of them. And the sovereign began to sob and lament, and sought solace about it secretly from the elders Evstafii and Varsunofii Iakimov, but did summon the archimandrite (1577–84) Iona, asking that [they] undertake to perform a special memorial [service] weekly from Saturday to Saturday for his son the lord and tsarevich Ivan in the Church of St. Nikon and to sing a panikhida daily at the center of the main church and [to sing] memorial prayers at evensong for ever and ever so long as the holy monastery stands even to the end of time. And [the tsar] from [his] treasury gave money to the treasurer for [services] in the Church of St. Nikon and for the main church for ever and ever, or as long as the holy monastery stands. And so that his words and requests be observed the sovereign ordered that the archimandrite, cellarer, treasurer, council of elders, priests, deacons, or whoever will be archimandrite, cellarer, treasurer, priest, or elder not alter the tsar's behest, disobey his command, or terminate his request, lest he answer to God on the day of judgment on Christ's second coming at the end of time. And the tsar and sovereign continued to lament and weep and seek solace, bowing his head against the ground six times with tears and lamentations.[73]

Compared to these, the devotions that Ivan's successors Tsars Fedor and Boris Godunov manifested toward Trinity were mundane, but hardly less grand. They occurred against a background of acts by Fedor's government, which his brother-in-law Boris Godunov controlled, and by Boris in his own right, even more stringent than those of Ivan IV, to prohibit monasteries from making further inroads on the fund of taxable land in Russia. The government supervised a thorough survey and registration of secular and clerical properties in 1592–94. The results for Trinity may be seen in copybooks numbered 520–526 prepared by cellarer Evstafii Golovkin now in the fund of Trinity's acts in the Russian State Library.[74] And, as I shall demonstrate in Chapter 5, Boris sought to regulate Trinity's governance to an unprecedented degree.

At the same time in public and private acts Fedor and Boris honored Sergius's cult and the Trinity Monastery. At Fedor's coronation in May 1584 the metropolitan had an archdeacon pray for Fedor's protection, addressing those prayers to the Holy Trinity, the Mother of God, and the Russian saints Aleksei and Sergius. Archimandrite Iona of Trinity assisted in the ceremony and presented Fedor with a cross made from the "life-giving wood [of the True Cross]" after proclaiming him tsar.[75] Soon after, between 10 and 17 June, Fedor and his wife Irina went to Trinity to pray for an heir. Irina reportedly went on foot. They were there again twice in 1585: in July they presented Trinity with a silver casket to hold Sergius's remains and prayed again for a child. On 15 August Fedor returned with Metropolitan Dionisii to consecrate the completed Basilica of the Dormition and it chapels dedicated to his and Irina's birth saints, Theodore Stratilatus and the martyr Irene (fig. 10), and to establish yet another feast dedicated to Sergius. The casket and the church had been commissioned by his father, the former in 1556, the latter in 1558 or 1559.[76] In 1591 Fedor celebrated the feast of the Trinity on Pentecost Sunday at Trinity. Probably it was then that Fedor and Irina donated a cover for an icon of St. Sergius with scenes from his life painted by cellarer Evstafii Golovkin (fig. 12). Its inscription says it was to mark the birth of an heir and to stand over Sergius's casket.[77] In 1592 Fedor and Irina undertook a grand pilgrimage that began at Trinity, extended west to the Monastery of St. Nicholas in Mozhaisk and to the Pafnut'ev Monastery in Borovsk, returning via the Savva-Storozhevskii Monastery in Zvenigorod.[78] Fedor's record of giving—in addition to the casket, 12 gifts on 9 occasions—suggests he was at Trinity many more times. Most of his donations were for memorial prayers for his father, his sister, and two daughters. They amounted to 4,333.33 rubles. In 1587 Fedor gave Trinity a pall depicting the apparition to Sergius of the Mother of God and another with Nikon's image.

With Irina he donated an icon cloth that bore Sergius's image in 1592. Fedor also gave Trinity properties in Zvenigorod, Murom, and Nizhnii Novgorod. Irina made the last of these memorial gifts, a sum of 3,000 rubles, in 1598 to commemorate Fedor.[79]

Boris Godunov's first gift to Trinity was 50 rubles in 1572, when he was a boiar. As Fedor's regent, Boris made seven increasingly munificent donations. Five were for memorial prayers for relatives, the largest being 500 rubles for feasts in memory of his ancestors and for prayers for his own health and that of his immediate family in 1585. A special gift recorded under 1594 was a bell weighing 22,536 pounds. But was this the bell registered in Trinity's donation book for 16 January 1594 as a gift worth 200 rubles (which Boris's kinsman Boiar Grigorii Vasil'evich Godunov gave Trinity, along with 100 rubles cash) in order for Boris be tonsured as the monk Khristofor?[80]

Boris must have visited Trinity on pilgrimages led by Ivan and Fedor and probably went there annually after becoming tsar in 1598. In 1599 his son Fedor wrote his "baptismal father and confessor, the elder Varsunofii Iakimov" of Trinity asking forgiveness that Boris was too ill to go to Trinity that year to celebrate Sergius's feast day. But when he recovered, Fedor continued, Boris would come to pray at Trinity and its subsidiary convent of "[the Dormition of] the most Pure Mother of God" (at Podsosenie).[81] I have evidence of three other visits. The first occurred in 1600 and I shall return to it in a moment; the second was in 1602 after he received the prince of Denmark as a suitor for his daughter. The third was in March 1605 to give thanks upon news that his army had been victorious at Putivl' over an invading force supporting the Pretender, a young man claiming to be Ivan IV's son, Dmitrii.[82] Boris's gifts to Trinity arrived regularly: an icon cloth, the central panel of which depicted Sergius, several villages in the regions of Pereiaslavl' and Moscow in 1602, a jeweled hat inscribed with the Trinity below which Sergius is one of its saintly worshipers in 1602/3, two memorial gifts of 100 rubles in 1603 (or one gift recorded twice), yet another icon cover for what was surely Rublev's icon of the Trinity, and another bell. The icon cover, probably intentionally, outdid in splendor that which Ivan had given Trinity for the same icon. In the middle of its central crown an angel held a cameo in which a six-faceted emerald contained an image of the Trinity. From the crown hung a panagia with cameos on the rear of which were SS. Boris and Gleb. Other angels dangled cameos with figures depicting Godunov's patron saints.[83] We are fortunate that Englishman William Parry, a clerk in a Persian embassy travelling through Moscow to the West, left us a wide-eyed description of the procession of 1600 in which Boris and his wife delivered the icon cover and the bell to Trinity.[84]

At noon the crowd saw a guard of 500 cavalrymen in a column riding three abreast, followed by monks chanting prayers and carrying icons and candles, and by Moscow's merchant elite. The patriarch, archbishops, bishops, and other clergy came next. Tsar Boris then appeared, his son on his left, his crown (*shapka*) on his right, followed by his wife and her female escorts, their horses led by men on foot, and surrounded by richly attired riders. Horses loaded with precious goods accompanied them and three teams of ten white horses in tandem pulling three very large carts followed. Next came the court and the icon, with its new cover guarded by 500 men. Lastly, in a huge frame pulled by what Parry estimated to be 3,500 men, came the bell, weighing 20 tons. Parry called the procession a pilgrimage. How long it took it to reach Trinity and to return he did not say, but we can imagine the throngs of people who viewed its passing and who were recruited to provision it. For those who took part or witnessed it, it was a living icon of royal power on which signs of Sergius's cult were the proof of the dynasty's divine favor. S. V. Nikolaeva calculated that, apart from Irina's memorial donation, Fedor and Boris gave Trinity 7,461 rubles in addition to the treasures I have mentioned.[85]

* Beginning in the 1550s, bookmen employed by the tsar and the metropolitan, not without assistance from Trinity's monks, explained what was behind such devotion to Sergius and his monastery. They did so by integrating Sergius's cult into five great works that codified notions developing in Moscow of what we can call a history of Russia. They were continuations of Metropolitan Daniil's Nikon chronicle, the court-inspired history of the first decades of the reign of Ivan IV known as the *Letopisets nachala tsarstva*; the Book of Degrees of the Imperial Genealogy compiled for Metropolitan Makarii before his death in 1563; the History of Kazan', an anonymous work probably composed in the mid-1560s but certainly before 1600; and the gigantic Illuminated Codex that Makarii's successor as metropolitan Afanasii prepared for Ivan between 1568 and 1576.[86]

The continuations contained the life of Sergius, with stories of his intercessions found in the Nikon chronicle. The compiler of the Book of Degrees employed an alternative source, the Tale of the Life and Death of Grand Prince Dmitrii Ivanovich, Tsar of Russia, to describe the victory at Kulikovo; but he appended to it under 1492 a necrology to Sergius saying that he had interceded to bring Dmitrii victory. Throughout the Book of Degrees were episodes chosen from various editions of Sergius's life. A version of Sergius's life similar to that in the Nikon chronicle, supplemented by entries about Sergius from the Book of Degrees and other sources, appeared in the Illuminated Codex. The life in the first and third of these works said Sergius blessed Dmitrii's resistance to the Mongols in 1380 and interceded to bring victory.[87]

All these works repeated descriptions in the Nikon chronicle of Sergius's intercessions assuring the conquest of Novgorod and Ivan III's stand against the Mongols in 1480. To these, compilers cleverly added entries from earlier works describing how Muscovites prayed to Sergius to intervene on their behalf for new intercessions and invented miracles in which Sergius secured Russia's destiny in their own time. The author of the Book of Degrees coupled claims from earlier chronicles that Vasilii went to Trinity to pray in 1518 before going to war with a story that made the conflict a defense of the faith against Latin invaders. A Polish-Lithuanian army of the "oath breaking apostate," Konstantin Ostrozhskii besieged Muscovy's border town of Opochka. Although defenseless, the townspeople decided to resist, saying, "it is better to die here than be converted to the Latin faith." A local woman had a vision in which Sergius told her that stones sufficient to fortify the town lay buried under the church altar. And so it was; with the stones they built walls that made the town invulnerable.[88]

This was but the first of the narratives in these midcentury histories in which Sergius's intercessory power was an explanatory force in the making of a Russian history. The Book of Degrees and, after it, the Illuminated Codex, for example, contained a tale commissioned by Metropolitan Makarii describing the raid on Moscow by the Crimean Horde in 1521. Recalling earlier sieges, particularly that of Edigei in 1408, it repeated passages in which Muscovites prayed for salvation to icons, including the Vladimir icon of the Virgin, and to Russian saints, among whom Sergius and Varlaam Khutynskii received special reverence. Miraculous happenings caused terror among the invaders and saved Moscow.[89] The writer of the *Letopisets* provided another example in describing how Moscow defeated the Lithuanians at Sevezh in 1536 "thanks to God's help, the intercession of the most pure Mother of God and the prayers of the miracle worker Sergius." The compiler of the Book of Degrees added that in honor of the victory Grand Princess Elena, mother and regent of Ivan IV, built a church at Sevezh dedicated to the Trinity, with chapels dedicated to the Dormition of the Mother of God, her Intercession, and Sergius.[90]

Works portraying the birth and accession to the throne of Ivan IV in August 1530 and December 1533, respectively, and Moscow's conquest of Kazan' in 1552 as events of universal importance accorded Sergius a central role in each. The Book of Degrees had the seminal story about Ivan's birth and it was repeated in the Illuminated Codex.[91] The material for the story came mainly from an extended narrative of Vasilii's death in the Sofiia Second chronicle and an anonymous encomium to Vasilii III done sometime after 1533. Its author, however, appropriated Sergius's charisma and the monastery's sacred space to enhance the dynasty's claim to rule a Russian *tsarstvie* from St. Volodimer of Kiev, the baptizer of Rus' (d. 1015), to Ivan IV of Moscow.[92] Ivan's baptism took place at Trinity under the icon of the Trinity in the Church of the Holy Trinity. There Grand Prince Vasilii placed his newborn son on Sergius's casket and prayed to the saint:

> Oh venerable most saintly miracle worker Sergius: Thou father of fathers [who] boldly stood before the Holy Trinity and with thy prayer gave me this child, now preserve him from harm, from every calumny and danger seen and unseen. Watch over him with thy holy prayers and preserve him, venerable one, until he dies. And then, should God preserve us, our mouths [shall] raise praise and thanks to God and for thy prayers. For I always seek refuge through thee before God and place all my hopes in entreaties though thee to God. Intercede for us to the Holy of One Essence Trinity, yea, grant us that which we desire!

Abbot Ioasaf lifted Ivan from Sergius's casket, handed him to his father and said, "Take, o God-loving tsar, the long-awaited child that God has given thee, raise him in knowledge of God's law and your imperial decorum, so that thy son will [grow up] according to thy aspirations, as it is written: 'Sons shall replace their fathers and shall establish their princes in every land, and their names shall be remembered from generation to generation.'" Thereupon the tsar received his newly baptized son "bestowed upon him by God . . . for the strengthening of his great empire." Part two commenced with an enumeration of Vasilii's qualities of kingship drawn from a Byzantine encomium, yet to be identified, although its maxims were a selective rendering of the portrait of an ideal emperor composed in Constantinople by the Deacon Agapetus in the sixth century.[93] The following narrative encapsulated the description in the Second Sofiia chronicle of Vasilii's last days: after having made a pilgrimage to the Trinity Monastery for the feast of St. Sergius and his return to Moscow, Vasilii became ill. On 3 December he ordered his confessor to give him the last rites, for which Trinity came to Moscow in the person of Abbot Ioasaf. Vasilii asked Ioasaf to pray "for the well being of the land, for my son Ivan and for my transgressions" and reminded him that,

> by your prayer and supplication God and the great miracle worker, Sergius gave me [my] son Ivan, and I baptized him at [the monastery] of the miracle worker, and I gave him to the miracle worker and placed him on the tomb of

> the miracle worker, and I place my son in your hands, father. So pray to God and the most pure Mother of God and the great miracle workers for [my] son Ivan and for my wife.[94]

Vasilii received the last rites and made his testament in which he requested to be tonsured before death. The text said Metropolitan Daniil silenced objections to this. Indeed, although unusual elsewhere in the Orthodox world, tonsure before death was an established custom for Russian landowners and princes. Vasilii blessed his son before the court with regalia said to have come down from his ancestor Prince Volodimer Monomakh [of Kiev, d. 1125], a myth drawn from the Tale of the Princes of Vladimir. Metropolitan Daniil exclaimed, "We bless thee, venerable father Sergius, and honor thy holy memory; now make [him] a monk, with the substance of an angel." Vasilii asked that an elder from the Kirillov Monastery tonsure him. None was present so Ioasaf of Trinity, whom Vasilii had requested to remain with him to the end, conducted the ceremony of tonsure and Daniil performed the act.[95] Thirteen years later Ivan and Metropolitan Makarii convened an assembly of boiars on 17 December 1546 to announce that he would marry and be crowned tsar. The Illuminated Codex said Ivan uttered Sergius's name along with those of metropolitan-saints Petr, Aleksei, and Iona to justify his decision, an invocation that went unnoticed by the writer of the *Letopisets*, the basic source for the episode.[96]

The conquest of the Khanate of Kazan' in 1551–52 was the other great event. The author of the *Letopisets* described it as the climatic event of Ivan's reign in an extended narrative which made clear that the conquest substantiated Moscow's imperial destiny. His account became the model for those in continuations of the Nikon chronicle and the Illuminated Codex, as well as in the "fragment" (*otryvok*) appended to the Second Sophiia chronicle; it also influenced accounts of the conquest in the Book of Degrees and the History of Kazan'. However, two texts produced at the Trinity Monastery soon after the campaign by authors who said they had witnessed what had happened were primary sources for Sergius's presence in all these narratives. The first, an anonymous work, described how Ivan founded a fort at Sviiazhsk on the Volga near Kazan'. There, it said, he built churches to the Birth of the Mother of God and to St. Sergius. Trinity cellarer Andreian Angelov, a descendent of Greek courtiers who had accompanied Sophia Palaeologa to Moscow to marry Ivan III, wrote the second tale. It took the story through Ivan's victory and return to Moscow. Abbot Gurii, he wrote, sent him to Ivan's camp before Kazan' in 1552 bearing the monastery's most holy images of the Trinity and of the Apparition of the Mother of God with two apostles to Sergius and Nikon, along with communion bread and holy water. That the former was an image of the Rublev Trinity follows from information in the first tale that Ivan, before embarking on his campaign, retired to the Trinity-Sergius Monastery to pray at Sergius's grave and to the Trinity icon that he had decorated, a reference to the icon cover fashioned for the icon in 1547. It may be that the two images Gurii sent to Ivan IV were those in the wooden portable diptych (*skladen'*) that Vasilii Karacharov, a benefactor who had been tonsured at Trinity, gave that house in 1540 (fig. 8).[97] The first tale is particularly important in that it said Ivan's prayers at Trinity before the campaign emulated those of Dmitrii Donskoi in 1380 before resisting Mamai. In each case Sergius's intercession with the Mother of God was Russia's salvation. The second tale said that before the conquest Ivan's warriors dreamt that on a stroll through Tatar Kazan' they met a monk who revealed himself as Sergius and who assured them of their imminent triumph.[98]

The tales inspired numerous passages in the *Letopisets*: on 24 May 1551, it said, having seized Sviiazhsk and made it his outpost, Ivan ordered the construction of churches dedicated to the birth of the Mother of God and to Sergius. It added that the icon of Sergius in the latter church, like Sergius's grave at Trinity, was immediately the source of miracles.[99] Using material in the Trinity tales, the author of the *Letopisets* noted Sergius's presence in every stage of the conquest and its aftermath: his text of a letter from Metropolitan Makarii to Ivan invoked Sergius's name along with that of other saints as intercessors. When Ivan arrived for the final attack on 13 August 1552, it said boiars greeted him with crosses at the gates of Sviiazhsk and led him to the new churches, where the tsar prayed to Sergius's icon "for assistance and the salvation of Christians from pagans." In camp, before assaulting Kazan' on 23 August, Ivan ordered the erection of three tent-churches. One he dedicated to Sergius and attended daily; after a successful skirmish Ivan returned there to thank God for the victory. On the eve of the final attack Ivan heard bells, entered the church, and stood before icons of Christ, the Mother of God, and Sergius. Before Sergius's icon he placed a candle, prayed, and sought the aid of Christ and the Mother of God. After the conquest Ivan returned to the same church to utter a prayer of thanks and, on his triumphal return to Moscow, he stopped at the Trinity-Sergius Monastery, prostrated himself before Sergius's tomb, and, weeping profusely, gave thanks to God, the Mother of God, and the great saints. Afterward he thanked Abbot Ioasaf and brothers for their sacrifices and prayers. They in turn cried and did obeisance over his salvation of Christians.[100] The same episodes reappeared in narratives of the conquest in the continuation of the Sofiia Second chronicle, in continuations of the Nikon chronicle, and in the Illuminated Codex. These works added that in

1553 Ivan made a grand pilgrimage to Trinity on which he gave thanks for the victory and for the birth of an heir. The Book of Degrees contained a different narrative. By comparison, it minimized the import of Sergius's intercession; but it, too, following the *Letopisets*, reported that the tsar stood before the icon of Sergius, lit a candle, and prayed to it, and that he stopped first at Trinity on his pilgrimage in 1553.[101]

The History of Kazan', a history-*cum*-military tale, differed in style and plotting from the other works, but drew from the *Letopisets* considerable information and numerous entries involving Sergius's cult: the construction of the Church of St. Sergius in Sviiazhsk in June 1551 and the miracles associated with it; Makarii's letter to Ivan citing Sergius among saints supporting his cause; Ivan's prayer of supplication to icon of Sergius on the eve of the final assault; and his celebration of the victory at Trinity on his return.[102] The History of Kazan' also incorporated parts of the two Trinity tales: it used Andrian's information that Trinity's abbot sent two monks to Ivan's camp before Kazan' bearing icons of the Trinity; from the anonymous tale it took the report that Ivan received an icon of the Apparition of the Mother of God to Sergius, communion bread, and holy water. An alternative version of the History said Andreian and several priests brought an old cross containing relics and an image of the Apparition to Sergius of the Mother of God, in addition to the Host and holy water.[103] Both versions said Ivan received them with joy; in the first he intoned a prayer to Sergius adapted from the first Trinity tale that concluded, "And thou venerable father Sergius, so pleasing to Christ, speed now to our assistance and aid us with prayers just as once [thou did assist] our ancestor on the Don [win out] over the pagan Mamai." The History of Kazan' repeated the analogy in describing Ivan's visit to Trinity to celebrate his victory and the birth of an heir, saying that throughout "great Russia" God "had revealed to him a great victory and conquest like that granted to his ancestor Dmitrii Ivanovich over the godless Mamai on the Don."[104] The History also incorporated from Andrian's tale the report that Ivan's warriors had seen Sergius in a dream sweeping the streets of Kazan' before the conquest and that he had told them that he was expecting guests there. Once inside Kazan', vanquished Tatars allegedly confirmed the reality of the dream and added that Sergius had blessed the city with a cross.[105]

Describing events subsequent to the conquest of Kazan', the compiler of the Illuminated Codex appropriately invoked Sergius's cult in describing the storming of Polotsk in the Livonian War in 1563 and in Tsar Fedor's coronation in 1584. Finally, one extension of the Nikon chronicle contained the Tale of the Honorable Tsar and Grand Prince of all Russia Fedor Ivanovich, an account of an attack on Moscow by the Crimean Horde in

1591. It said Boris Godunov built a fort where he stationed his army and in it built a church dedicated to Sergius, hoping to save Moscow from "pagan barbarians" as ancient Israel had been saved. Tsar Fedor prayed to God and an icon of the Mother of God, asking her intercession in the tradition of his forefather Dmitri Ivanovich, who had defeated Mamai on the Don. Patriarch Iov led a procession that paraded the icon around Moscow and then into the Church of St. Sergius to solicit his intercession against the "pagan barbarians."[106]

* Sergius's cult had become a totem cherished by Moscow's rulers, and their bookmen. Court and monastery continually enriched it in ways that served their needs. Indeed, the cult became so real that Moscow's rulers acted out its stories by staging family baptisms at Trinity, mounting pilgrimages, and providing munificent gifts. Both Trinity and court narratives of the Kazan' campaign confirm Kloss's conclusion that Ivan IV made Rublev's Trinity icon, already the monastery's symbol, a palladium of his dynasty. Muscovite bookmen wove Sergius's intercessory legends into historical works in which Moscow's dynasty ruled a Russian *tsarstvie* with ancient roots.

Chapter Four

TRINITY'S PATRONS

Sometime between 1398 and 1427 a landowner named Ivan Svatko, who lived in Pereiaslavl' near the Trinity Monastery, had a scribe write a charter addressed to "my lord, the Abbot Nikon." Ivan said he owed Nikon ten rubles. But in lieu of cash he was giving the monastery three uncultivated settlements (*pustoshi*) and a forest that he owned and paid taxes on (*potiaglo*). The charter ended with this request: "And [when] death comes for me, he should pray for my soul."[1] Although it was not strictly a donation charter, in that it described a payment of a debt, the document was one of the earliest grants, if not the first, of property to Trinity by a lay person accompanied by a request that Trinity's brothers pray for the issuer's soul. Ivan's bequest was one of the earliest of 3,507 grants to Trinity of land, fiscal and judicial immunities, cash, moveable property, and combinations of these, down to 1605 in my database (Appendix Table 1). Of these grants, 3,135 were of property described in donation (*dannye*) charters, testaments (*dukhovnye gramoty*), or Trinity's donation book and register of feasts (*kormovaia kniga*). Of these, 1,698 contained requests for memorial prayers. In many others such requests were implied. The documents reveal that Trinity's benefactors manifested a faith that Sergius's intercessory powers might save their souls and those of their kin and ancestors. But in their detailed instructions about possessions and familial relationships they also evinced a lively interest in social and business arrangements in this world. The number of memorial grants to Trinity far surpassed totals for other houses in Muscovite Russia. The data in Appendix Table 2 shows that donors came from every geographical area as well as from every social class of Muscovite Russia, testimony to the universality of Sergius's cult and the "national" scope of Trinity's wealth. Thousands of Russians came to consider the relationship they forged with the Trinity-Sergius Monastery an ingredient of their social identity. Well before 1605 they had become a community of venerators. Over time the relationship between Trinity and those who sought prayers there became formalized and complex. In this it reflected hierarchical divisions in the community and the sophistication of elite persons in defining their identity.

After Sergius's death in 1392 and for 20 years thereafter there is little evidence that people sought prayers at Trinity in return for grants, or that the monastery encouraged the practice. The turning point seems to be Edigei's destructive raid, after which Abbot Nikon began to recruit patrons to restore the monastery. But only after 1422, when Nikon discovered and translated Sergius's remains and proclaimed him a miracle worker, does the documentary evidence of a "grants for memorial prayers" culture become plentiful. It is impossible to date its origin exactly. Most of the early documents recording land acquisitions mentioned Nikon as abbot but few were dated. It is logical, though, to ascribe those addressed to the Trinity Monastery to period 1, 1392–1422, and those addressed to the Trinity-Sergius Monastery as coming in 1422, the year Nikon proclaimed Sergius a saint, or after. Even this classification is arbitrary. Scribal practices were primitive and some acts that did not mention Sergius as part of the name of the monastery may have recorded grants that should be dated in 1422 or after. With this in mind it is likely that benefactors gave Trinity six properties and three personal items before 1422, and that in 1422, in honor of Sergius's sainthood the monastery received ten more grants. Eight of them were of land (including Ivan Svatko's) and one was a large *Apraksos* (a New Testament organized for weekly and daily liturgical readings) with a bejeweled silver cover (*oklad*), commissioned by Boiar Fedor Koshka in 1392 and given to Trinity by his son Fedor Goltiai.[2] But it is possible that these might have come to Trinity in Nikon's last years, 1423–27. Most of the 14 grants of property recorded in period 1 were from local people. Vasilii Borisovich Kopnin was a boiar serving the prince of Radonezh and Afanasii Elizarovich Kniazhnin was a Radonezh landowner. One grant of land was in nearby Dmitrov, and seven others were in a district of Pereiaslavl' adjacent to Trinity. Boiar Semen Fedorovich Morozov's grant of a salt mine and one half of a salt works in Sol'-Galich and three grants by landowners in the principality of Uglich were the only donations in more remote lands. But Galich was a possession of Trinity's patron Prince Iurii Dmitrievich of Zvenigorod and Trinity's lord and benefactor Prince Andrei Vladimirovich of Radonezh ruled Uglich. During period 1 Trinity purchased a court in Dmitrov, then ruled by Petr Dmitrievich, whom Sergius had baptized; three properties in Pereiaslavl'; five in Uglich; and one in Moscow. It also received an immunity charter from Prince Andrei for the village of Udinskoe, later Priluki, in Uglich. Andrei probably gave Trinity the property as well. Grand Prince

Vasilii I gave Trinity three immunity charters for properties in Pereiaslavl', one of which Trinity had acquired from his boiar Fedor Ivanovich Koshkin and another for an undocumented acquisition that might have come from another boiar, Ivan Dmitrievich Vsevolozhskii. Requests for prayers for the dead accompanied seven of the 19 donations in period 1. Like that of Ivan Svatko, they were simple and followed no formula. Fedor Andreevich Korovai requested "commemorations (*na pominok*) of the souls of my ancestors and my wife." Elizar Ivanovich Filiksov asked that "he (Nikon) write me in the commemoration list" (*A im napisati menia v pominanie*). The nun (and widow) Evpraksiia, in granting Trinity a village in Pereiaslavl', asked that Trinity commemorate "my lord Prince Dmitrii Ivanovich [Riapolovskii?], myself, (his) princely line and mine."[3]

Nikon's successors were no less aggressive in soliciting donations. Appendix Table 2 shows that in period 2 (1423–45) Trinity acquired 99 properties and in period 3 (1445–61) 72. As in period 1, Trinity acquired most of its properties in areas near the monastery: in Radonezh 11, in Pereiaslavl' 39, in Dmitrov 19, and in Moscow 22. On the upper Volga it added to its holdings in Uglich and acquired for the first time 14 properties in Kostroma. Northwest of the Volga it acquired 10 properties in Bezhetskii Verkh and Novyi Torg, and 1 in Tver'. Trinity also added 20 properties to the east in Vladimir, Suzdal', Starodub, and Murom; and in 1458/59 Vasilii I's daughter Anastasiia, the wife of Prince Aleksandr (Olel'ko) Vladimirovich of Kiev, gave Trinity a substantial grant of entire districts (*volosti*) in Maloiaroslavets, a land well to the southeast of Trinity along the Oka River.[4] In period 2 34, and in period 3 25 land grants came with requests for commemorations, and many of the grants without such requests in both periods were obviously formulated by benefactors as they neared the end of their life. These landowners believed prayer at the site of Sergius's tomb an efficacious means to save them and their kin and gave Trinity land to make it possible. A donation of money and personal items accompanied one of the grants (in period 2), and in each period there were two donations of personal property.[5] The simplest was a golden chest cross that an unknown prince of Suzdal' gave Trinity about 1427; more ornate and expensive was the intricate frame of gold and wood fashioned by Trinity monk Amvrosii Kuchetskii for a triptych icon. In addition to commemorative prayers, benefactors in eight or nine instances in period 2 and four in period 3 requested that annual commemorative feasts be held near Sergius's remains. Prince Andrei's brother Semen probably requested tonsure at Trinity before he died in the plague of 1425.[6]

Further on I shall say more about the motives of Trinity's benefactors because they were often complex, as were their requests for commemoration.

But one pattern emerged early on: landowners who donated property to Trinity began to create networks of cooperation radiating out from the monastery or one of its outposts. Aleksei Bobosha Voronin, who, like his father and other relatives, was a benefactor, became the Trinity monk Avraamii and eventually Trinity's cellarer. In that office he did business with landowners in Pereiaslavl' who had been his neighbors, and with his own family. Another well-documented example is the network in Bezhetskii Verkh involving the Golovkin and Irzhevskii families. They did business with one another as early as the 1420s, intermarried, and, within several generations, became involved with Trinity, giving it property, witnessing its transactions with others, and becoming its monks.[7]

Land was cheap. As Lawrence Langer observed, after a century of hardship under Mongol rule, divided by political rivalries and depopulated by plague, much of northeast Rus' was empty and untilled, or otherwise underutilized.[8] Additionally, there was not a political center strong enough to restrain or regulate Trinity's activities; indeed, to encourage economic growth princes encouraged monasteries to bring their capital and entrepreneurial skills to open new lands and restore old ones. Trinity bought 26 parcels in period 2, 15 more in period 3, and made exchanges of property for 11 others. Appendix Table 1 shows that most of its acquisitions by period, 61 and 44, were from grants, a measure of the growing power of Sergius's cult. By 1461 Trinity held a dense cluster of properties around the monastery in the lands of Radonezh, Moscow, Pereiaslavl', and Dmitrov. They amounted to 55 percent of the parcels under its control. Trinity also owned land in an unbroken arc along the upper Volga and had significant holdings in the northwest anchored by subsidiary churches in Bezhetskii Verkh on the Mologa River, and to the northeast of the Volga in Galich. In the east it had acquired significant properties in Vladimir and Suzdal', single holdings in Starodub and Murom; and it owned one very large property in Maloiaroslavets in the southwest. With the exception of a single grant in Kashin across the Volga from its outpost in Priluki (from Grand Prince Boris of Tver', who betrothed his daughter to Vasilii II's son Ivan at Trinity in 1449), Trinity's property was entirely within the Grand Principality of Moscow.

Trinity's acquired 55, 58, and 65 parcels, respectively, in periods 4 (1462–78), 5 (1478–1501), and 6 (1502–22). These included 37, 23, and 37 donations of land, or less each period than in periods 2 and 3. One reason was that land had become more valuable. Secondly, by 1478 Moscow ruled all of central Rus', but Tver' and its ruler, Ivan III, was anxious to restrain the hemorrhage of taxable property to the "dead hand" of the church.[9] In period

5, however, Trinity recorded a land grant supplemented by cash, three donations consisting only of cash, and 11 donations of personal property. In period 6 the number of grants of money skyrocketed to 60 (11 of which were accompanied by property).

Although Trinity received fewer donations of land in periods 4 through 6, their geographical scope grew apace with the growth of the Muscovite state. By 1522 Trinity had acquired five parcels in lands formerly part of the Grand Principality of Tver' and nine north of the Volga in Beloozero. To the west it acquired properties in the former appanage principalities of Borovsk and Volok, and one in Ruza. In the south it picked up fewer parcels, four more properties in Maloiaroslavets and one in Kolomna. Acquisitions in outlying areas in these periods increased relatively compared to those in the central region around Trinity (35% of the total). It is also worth noting that Tver's rulers, before capitulating to Moscow in 1485, gave Trinity immunities from taxation on its commerce and that, perhaps to consolidate his position in these areas, Ivan III issued Trinity commercial immunities in Nizhnii Novgorod and on the route from the Northern Dvina to Moscow in Vologda.[10] These were a departure from Ivan's otherwise stingy policies regarding immunities. Finally, in period 6 one finds the first records—seven in all—in which persons from Tver', Riazan', Novgorod, and Kolomna made donations of money to Trinity. Three were from bishops or an archbishop, the later being Serapion of Novgorod, a former abbot of Trinity who returned to live there in 1508/9 when Ivan removed him from office. Three others were from one person, Anastasiia, the widow of former boiar Ivan Zakhar'evich Ovinov.[11] Although state policies and rising land prices dampened the giving of memorial gifts of land, the significant increase in cash donations and the geographical expansion of donors show that Sergius's cult continued to spread.

By the 1490s Trinity's brotherhood had assumed a large number of memorial obligations. They came with gifts that varied widely in their nature and value. The memorial requests themselves increasingly became complex. These factors caused Trinity to regularize the way memorial requests were observed and to render more uniform the services it provided. Historians of rituals of death and commemoration in Catholic Europe have considered such issues for some time. Only recently have historians begun to study the commemorative culture of Muscovite Rus'. Notable are Ludwig Steindorff and A. I. Alekseev, based primarily on documents of the Iosifo-Volokolamsk Monastery (founded by Iosif Sanin in 1479) and the Kirillo-Belozerskii Monastery (1397).[12] Trinity's culture of commemoration was oldest and had its own idiosyncrasies.

MAP 2—The Trinity-Sergius Monastery. Its Centers of Economic Privileges and Properties in the Sixteenth Century

From the first charter that provided Trinity a grant in return for prayers, down to the last, donors sought to assure themselves a life after death. Such quests had a long history. They influenced human conduct and engendered death rituals long before the Christian era. What was new in Rus' from the fifteenth century was how persons went about it. The culture of commemoration that took form at Trinity and other houses and spread throughout Rus' had three ingredients. The first was an exchange of property that obligated monks to pray in perpetuity for the soul of a person who was facing death or had just died, or for the souls of his or her ancestors. In this memorial donations resembled exchanges common to many cultures in which the bestowal of a gift created a mutual obligation for the recipient toward the giver. In archaic "segmented" societies, such as that of the early Germans, it was often a public act that joined clans or created bonds between chief and retinue; it existed in the Roman world as well, as a means of holding society together.[13] Eastern Slavs also engaged in ritualized exchanges from the moment they entered recorded history.[14] Giving a gift to a religious corporation lent greater strength to a bond created by an exchange because it conferred grace on the giver; that is, a "free gift of God unmerited by men."[15]

The second ingredient was that donations, ostensibly from a single benefactor seeking salvation, involved his or her surviving kin. Bonds of kinship involving the living and the dead probably had roots in pre-Christian customs, but as familial inheritance customs became intertwined in a web of complex property rights, they took on additional constraints. The living were expected to respect the grant and, as I shall discuss later, participate in services of remembrance to assure that their dead ancestors benefited from perpetual prayer. By the same token services of remembrance kept the dead alive in the minds of the living.[16] In a charter issued soon after 1422 giving Trinity a land grant, Prince Fedor Andreevich of Starodub asked for "prayers [for the souls] of his grandfather, his father, himself and his entire line. If his children or nephews contest it, he continued, they will face judgment before God."[17] Hartmut Rüss, in his history of Rus' nobles, said familial memorial customs were the chief form of aristocratic piety. But, he concluded, their material manifestation and concern with external behavior lacked the profundity of internal religiosity; rather, elites saw salvation in terms of fate rather than acts. The resiliency of memorial customs and frequently with which benefactors sought tonsure for themselves or their kin tell a different story. High churchmen, secular elites, and untutored provincials were intimately involved in this culture. This being the case, it behooves us to ponder carefully Peter Brown's strictures against models of religious experience that distinguish between elite, or high, and popular, or vulgar, expressions of piety.[18]

The final ingredient of this memorial culture was the selection of a holy site that might best mediate between the natural and the supernatural world on behalf of one's soul. In Muscovite Rus', as in the Catholic West from the tenth century on, foundations that housed holy relics were thought to be the best of all. At his or her tomb, a saint was thought to be immanent and accessible to Christians. Writing about cult centers in Catholic France, Thomas Head explained it, saying that, "relics were the manifestation of the saints in the physical world . . . [that made possible] a joining of heaven and earth."[19] Among monasteries in Rus', Trinity was privileged. Not only did it house the remains of one who by the mid-fifteenth century was regarded as the greatest local intercessor and miracle worker in Rus'; it contained monks knowledgeable in memorial rites and eager to conduct the bereaved and mourners through the final moments. Finally, Trinity possessed the means to properly celebrate them and exuded a sense of permanence that donors expected. The charter in which Princess Anastasiia and her sons made a grant in 1458/59 stipulated that Trinity could not alienate the grant, implying that its reciprocal obligation for prayers also was perpetual.[20]

From the moment they accepted Christianity Eastern Slavs performed death rituals that included a regular sequence of prayer for the souls of the dead. But the exchange of property for perpetual prayer at monasteries as an element in their devotions began no earlier than the second half of the fourteenth century in northeast Rus'. S. V. Sazonov, in his study of chronicle writing, marked the divide at 1300. In chronicles written before then he found over 20 entries in which the living invoked dead ancestors to mediate on their behalf with God. In chronicles dating from after 1300 there were no more such entries; instead, he wrote, the living became concerned about the fate of the dead. Sazonov cited prayers at the death of Prince Volodymer Vasil'kovich in the Galich-Volyn chronicle for 1288 as a transitional entry that combined appeals to the dead to ensure a good life of a surviving descendent with entreaties for the dying prince's salvation. In Byzantium and in pre-Mongol Rus' elites had established patrimonial (*ktitorskii*) monasteries as family sanctuaries where they might be tonsured to find peace in life or prepare for the next world as they neared the end of their days; but in neither place did they infuse death rituals with exchanges of property for perpetual prayers.[21]

Dating the transition is one thing; explaining what an individual who approached the end of his or her life, or mourners for one deceased, expected prayers to accomplish is another. At all times and in all places death is a mystery. No wonder that a preoccupation with death and the hereafter is at the core of Christian belief. In the liturgy the faithful reconstruct symbolically Christ's death and resurrection, believing that by following his way they might find salvation when their time is up.[22] In its death rituals the Orthodox never formulated a doctrine, such as the Catholic concept of purgatory, defining a limited period after death during which the soul found its way to a permanent destination. Yet they did believe that after death there existed a transition period in which the soul had yet to find rest, a time during which final judgment is rendered on the deceased. Death rituals, attested from at least the 1350s, provided for daily memorial masses for the deceased for 40 days, the *sorokoust'*.[23] Such customs began in the Catholic world sometime in the tenth century.

Beginning in the late fourteenth century, however, in Rus' the living, as they approached death, began to seek out an intercessor for their souls and did so with urgency. A *sorokoust'* was not enough. Consequently, the Rus' began to parse the writings of Church fathers about how to be saved. One senses that they did so out of a palpable fear and possibly an awareness of the imminence of the fate that awaited them. In the fourteenth century a memorial culture was well underway in Novgorod. Initially, it took the form of founding patrimonial monasteries. In the fifteen century a memorial-for-grant (*vklad*) culture became the norm as it did in northeast Rus', where at Trinity and other houses the recitation of memorial prayers for the dead became a regular responsibility. Even so, the earliest requests for commemoration were expressed so laconically that it is difficult to read anything in to them.[24]

The most obvious communality between the situation in the Catholic world in the tenth century and Rus' in the fourteenth is that the cult of saints with its sacred sites emerged as a distinguishing mode of religiosity. Then there is the connection between the emergence of memorial cultures and conditions in which people lived and died. Medieval people were familiar in normal times with a high incidence of infant mortality, and for the mature the prospect of death at an early age. Calamities such as war, famine, and plague were frequent visitors. Even in good times, death was omnipresent. Northeast Rus' had endured one and one-half centuries of Mongol depredations. In 1400 the end was nowhere in sight. Even in the 1440s prospects for liberation remained unsettled. Nor could people envisage that plague, which ravaged Rus' from the 1350s through 1440s, might pass. Living in such times, people might well judge the road to salvation equally perilous, and fear for their souls.[25] In Rus' it is easy to imagine that such fear generated a collective mind set in which the usual 40 days of mourning seemed inadequate. There, at least until the 1460s, as it had been in the West in the tenth century, nobles judged relationships with bishops or princes relatively unimportant. So they forged relationships with monasteries wherein they or their kin might be prayed for forever.

In each area the availability of land, often vacant or underutilized, and the emergence of a class of landowners, for the most part unrestrained by higher authority in their control of hereditary properties, facilitated the growth of such a culture. Also, in the Orthodox world as well as in the Catholic West, family traditions shaped personal authority, social relationships, and the property ownership among the living. Through rituals that reconstructed memory, family traditions extended beyond the grave to one's ancestors and shaped the way people worshipped. Peter Brown, observing this, concluded that historians must view the Christian church through "kinship colored glasses." There is also a psychological element in death rituals. In the protective security of the family, and by participating in prescribed, public rituals of prayer, the mourner could find the strength to call forth appropriate responses that sublimated the anger or fear brought on by the shock of death.[26] Yet sixteenth-century Russians who wrote testaments and donation charters evinced what Eamon Duffy has described as a "pragmatic sense of the value of life." Their charters abounded in fond detail listing personal possessions, instructing survivors how to arrange the property they left behind, and how to order family relationships.[27] Finally, in Catholic Europe from the ninth century, so later in Muscovite Rus', there came into being new sorts of religious foundations. Usually they were monasteries. What was important, however, was that they were self-governing, in possession of relics thought to be miraculous, and administered by leaders who promoted their foundations as cult centers in order to solicit property in exchange for prayer. Such was the Trinity-Sergius Monastery under Nikon and the abbots who succeeded him. It was there when despair weighed on local landowners overtaken by personal or familial crises associated with the approach of death. These were the micro-events that generated donations.[28]

To facilitate the bond created by gifts in return for memorial prayers, monasteries in Muscovite Rus', including Trinity, recorded terms and conditions of the exchange in a manner that would ensure that appropriate prayers were said at the proper time. As donations and requests for prayers rolled in, the written notation of those to be prayed for took the form of a list of names or memorial book called a *sinodik*. It had as its model a document of the same name, sometimes called the "ecumenical" *synodicon*, issued in Constantinople in 843 at the end of the iconoclast controversy. The ecumenical *synodicon* commemorated the emperors and hierarchs who had opposed the iconoclasts, and listed iconoclast heretics to be anathematized. It was read as part of the Orthodox service on the first Sunday in Lent. The Iosifo-Volokolamsk Monastery had a *sinodik* listing donors to be prayed for almost from the moment of its founding in 1479.[29] However, the earliest surviving *sinodiks* in Muscovite Rus' date from the early sixteenth century and the earliest surviving Trinity *sinodik* dates from 1575. It was of the type, as I shall explain, known as "daily" (*povsednevnyi*) *sinodik* in which those making major benefactions were commemorated.[30] Comparing various redactions, S. V. Konev concludes that Trinity had a *sinodik* at the end of the fifteenth century.[31] But Elizar Filiksov's request in a donation charter, noted above and written between 1410 and 1427, that, "he [Abbot Nikon] write me in the commemoration list," suggests that Trinity's *sinodik* existed much earlier.[32]

Historians have made little use of *sinodiks*, largely because they are difficult to decode. Those commemorated were recorded only by their given names. Making it even more difficult, if not impossible, to connect the given name to a historical person is that the name might be the one he or she assumed when baptized or tonsured. The problem vexed those charged with performing commemorations long before historians encountered it. Their remedy, as seen in Trinity's *sinodik* of 1575, was to enter the family name in interstices between lines. But not always. The task of identifying entries is further complicated by the fact a *sinodik* contains blocks of names added to earlier versions (that don't survive independently), making it difficult to break down the lists chronologically. Finally, the entries are difficult to read. Scribes made entries hurriedly and squeezed some of them in the interstices in a tiny script.

Although Elizar Filiksov's charter is evidence for the early existence of a Trinity *sinodik*, well into the sixteenth century donors requested memorial prayers in a variety of ways without mentioning a list. Mariia, the wife of landowner Aleksandr Redrikov in the Kinel' district of Pereiaslavl', gave Trinity an uncultivated parcel "for the soul of my husband" (*po dushe muzha svoego*); a Rodion Potapov from Verkhnii Berezovets in Kostroma made his grant "for my ancestors, for [my] father and mother, and for myself" (*po svoikh roditelekh, po otse i po materi i po sobe*) "so that they commemorate my ancestors" (*a oni pominaiut moi roditeli*). Both charters were written either in 1427/28 or 1432.[33] In another a Grigorii Muromtsev in 1446/47 gave Trinity a village in the Moscow land "to commemorate my father, my mother and my clan" (*na pominok svoemu ottsu i svoei matere i svoemu rodu*).[34]

The earliest Trinity charter to use the word *sinodik* was one in which Gorianin Mordvinov in 1523/24 donated a hamlet (*derevnia*) in Rostov "for my kin, that is, for my father and mother, and for my soul." To this he added, "I, Gorianin, wish to be tonsured, and for this grant, when God sends for my, [that is,] Gorianin's soul, bury me at the house of the life-giving Trinity and inscribe me in the *sinodik*" (*A pokhochiusia iaz Gorianin postrichi, ino to mne i vklad, a b(o)go po dushu poshlet po moiu Gorianovu, ino im menia polozhiti v domu zhiv(o)nachalnyia Tro(i)tsi da v senanik napis(a)ti*).[35] The same year, on 8 September, Afanasii Karachev donated his hereditary village of Stanishino together with its hamlets and untilled areas in Staritsa to Trinity. In return he specified that it grant "a commemoration to my kin, and so the abbot and brothers would inscribe my kin in the daily *sinodik*" (*na pominok svoim roditelem, i igumen by z brat(')eiu pozhalovali, napisali moikh roditelei v sinanik v vsednevnai*).[36] These entries mirror a significant change in the manner Trinity provided commemorations, the nature of which we know best from the fifth chapter of the Book of Rules (*obikhod*) of the Iosifo-Volokolamsk Monastery. It was composed about 1575, but Ludwig Steindorff's analysis of the letter Iosif Sanin, its founder, wrote to a disgruntled donor between 1508 and 1513 shows that its rules were then in effect. The chapter specified the books in which ceremonies to be followed were set forth, their purposes, the prices for various kinds of commemoration, and when they were to take place. For donations of 50 rubles or more, it said, Iosif's monastery would record the name of a person to be commemorated into the daily *sinodik*. It was read publicly in front of the iconostasis at specific moments for commemorations of the dead in the liturgical cycle, supposedly in perpetuity. In this it resembled the diptychs. The person's name also went into a more voluminous book called the "eternal" (*vechnyi*) *sinodik*, along with names of those whose donations amounted to less than 50 rubles. Monks read their names independently of the liturgy but ostensibly also forever.[37] Distinguishing between the two books, Trinity and other houses could accommodate everyone's wish to achieve immortality by having their name set down and commemorated forever; but it reserved liturgical honors for the "big" people. Until the advent of inflation that characterized the economic crisis beginning in the 1570s, 50 rubles was a considerable sum. M. S. Cherkasova calculated it could buy between 75 and 100 *desiatina* (2.7 acres) of land. By the 1630s Trinity divided commemorations into at least three different *sinodiks*, the placement made according to the size of the benefaction.[38] The practical side of this was that monasteries, by limiting those to be mentioned during the service, kept them to reasonable time limits.

Gorianin Mordvinov's request for entry in a *sinodik* was not specific, although from his explicit and detailed request for tonsure and burial one might think that he expected to be entered into the daily *sinodik*. The donation book valued his gift at 20 rubles, however, indicating that he wasn't. But a short time later, in a testament dated 23 December 1525, his son Daniil made another donation to Trinity that specified that his father, among other kin, be commemorated.[39] Perhaps it vaulted Gorianin into the more prestigious *sinodik*. If so, I have been unable to locate it in Trinity's *sinodik* of 1575. For his significant gift, which he valued at 500 rubles to be paid to Trinity by his kin should they retain the village, Afanasii Karachev specified in detail the sort of commemoration he expected. He lived at least to 1546/47, when he wrote a testament confirming the grant to Trinity and its corresponding obligation to tonsure him, give him a monk's cell, and to pray for him. He apparently died soon after and, accordingly, Trinity inscribed Afanasii and his ancestors in its daily *sinodik*. His descendents also gave Trinity property. For that reason the Karachevs appeared in several entries in the *sinodik* of 1575.[40] Not only that; in return for Afanasii's donation, Trinity's sixteenth-century "Feast Book" (*kormovaia kniga*), a special *sinodik* recording benefactions made in exchange for commemorative feasts, recorded that it instituted a "minor feast" (*korm menshoi*) for the Karachevs.[41] I can identify many Karachev names in the *sinodik* with those in Trinity's charters, donation book, and feast book. The feast book and one Karachev entry in the *sinodik* mentioned a Semen, the name of Afanasii's grandfather recorded in a charter of the 1460s–80s;[42] the Aleksandr Semenovich, Afanasii's father, in the feast book also matches with a priest or presbyter (*ierei*) in another Karachev entry in the *sinodik*, and was recorded in charters of the 1470s–80s.[43] These were the "ancestors" for whom Afanasii requested commemorations. Afanasii cannot be identified with certainty with names in commemorative sources, but he was probably the monk named Akakii in one entry of the *sinodik* and Akadin in the feast book.[44] The *sinodik* also listed commemorations in the earliest Karachev entry for a Vasilii; it is probably the Vasilii identified as the monk Vas'ian in Trinity's donation book in relation to a grant made in 1551 and, alternatively, as Vasilii and as the monk Vas'ian in Karachev entries in the *sinodik*.[45] But in the three Karachev entries, and in many other instances, the *sinodik* had names that do not turn up in other sources. They included 11 in the earliest (unless its Oulita is the Iul'iana in the feast book), one in the second, and six in the third. These must have been children, spouses, or collateral relatives of Karachev donors of the 1540s and 1550s listed in the donation book, some of whom also cannot be identified in lists of those to be commemorated.

A statistical review confirms anecdotal evidence that Trinity instituted the same system of commemoration as that at the Iosifo-Volokolamsk Monastery, and at about the same time. Of 30 donations of 50 rubles or more made between 1499 and 1521, 18 were for exactly 50 rubles. In another instance a donor made three memorial donations in one year to go over 50 rubles, obtaining liturgical commemoration on the installment plan.[46] The database records many installment donors. To illustrate, one Ivan Kriachko Vorypanov from the Moscow land on 28 August 1550 paid Trinity 24 rubles and on 14 September of that year came up with another 26 to assure prayers for his wife Pelageia in the daily *sinodik*; Leontii Vladimirov syn Mansurov, also from Moscow, gave Trinity 30 rubles on 18 June 1554 and another 20 rubles on 24 March 1558 to commemorate his wife Nastas'ia.[47] The 50-ruble "admission fee" for the daily *sinodik* remained unchanged until the *oprichnina*. For example, in my database for the years 1547–64 (period 9), in addition to numerous 50-ruble donations accompanied by requests for prayers for specific persons, there were 89 donations of exactly 50 rules that undoubtedly were for commemorations even though the records do not contain such requests.

Gorianin Mordvinov's charter initiated a development that became commonplace. As Trinity and other houses bureaucratized the process of commemorating donors, in particular setting down specifically what a donor was expected to donate in return for a certain type of commemoration, donors began to write down more precisely and in more detail the nature and duration of the services they wished Trinity to perform. In the 83 years that followed, down to 1605, they did so in greater numbers than ever before.

* Appendix Table 1 indicates that, exclusive of immunities, in period 7 (August 1522–September 1533) Trinity received 139 donations, 27 more than in the preceding period. In period 8 (October 1533–46) it received 576 donations. In period 9 (1547–64) it received 796, and in period 10 (1565–18 March 1584, Ivan IVs death) it received 844! In period 11 (19 March 1584–13 April 1605, Godunov's death) it received 460 more donations. In all, from 1533 to 1605 Trinity received 2,676 donations. Muscovite Russia's sustained economic growth to midcentury in part explains the huge increase in the number of Trinity's benefactions. Political factors also came into play but are difficult to assess. During Ivan's minority, 1533–46, as boiar factions realigned, sought support, and struggled for preeminence, the state was unable or unwilling to restrain the alienation of private estates to monasteries. Compared to the previous period, land donations to Trinity more than doubled. Yet, in the succeeding period, 1547–64, in which an allegedly strong reform government restricted the acquisition of property by church institutions, donations of land more than doubled. Economic trends and political measures cannot by themselves explain this remarkable splurge. As I discuss below, donors from every class of free people used public benefactions to affirm their social identity as well as to satisfy traditional preoccupations about salvation.[48]

The same table indicates that, with the exception of period 10, donations of cash and moveable property, or combinations thereof, far outnumbered contributions in which land was the principal commodity. S. V. Nikolaeva's study of Trinity's donation books shows that between 1533 and 1560 of 1,170 donations, 867 were in cash. At their peak from 1538 to 1560, she calculated, Trinity collected between 900 and 2,963 rubles annually for a total of 34,345 rubles.[49] This reversed the pattern up to 1500, in which a land grant was the common form for benefactions. The reversal began in period 6, when the still-substantial number of donations involving land, 38, declined relatively to 33 percent of total donations. In period 7 grants of property fell to 24 percent of total donations and never went above that figure again. Even as donations of land more than doubled in period 8, their relative weight reached a low of 14 percent. And, although the number of donations involving land doubled again in period 9, that total was only 21 percent of total donations. More people were able to donate to Trinity, and to donate more. Russia's population increased, more lands went into agricultural production, and "national" income rose significantly, putting more cash into the hands of landowners. Land values also rose, making it advantageous for benefactors to hold onto their estates and instead give cash or moveable property. Trinity used its economic power to acquire lands by purchase, trade, and, occasionally, by judicial rulings. But in the boom years to 1564 the number of such acquisitions—18 parcels in period 7, of which 11 were purchases; 35 (15 purchases) in period 8; and 31 (22 purchases) in period 9—was not much different from the 26 they had picked up in period 6. In fact, the number of purchased properties is inflated in that some (many?) were donations concealed as sales to get around bans by Ivan IV and again by Fedor on giving hereditary domains to the church. For example, Trinity's copy of the purchase agreement shows that Ivan Shein-Kurbatov sold his village of Tentiukovo in Moscow District to Trinity for 50 rubles. The document said that his father Aleksandr had bequeathed the village to his mother Akulina, who then took the veil. At her death, Ivan stated, according to his father's testament, which Metropolitan Makarii affirmed with his signature and seal, the estate came to him and he turned it over to Trinity in 1562/63 for 50 rubles.[50] In all likelihood Aleksandr on his deathbed arranged with Trinity that it would obtain title to the estate, but that his wife would retain it to support herself until she died. Then her son and executor would hand it over. Its putative value, 50 rubles, was the exact sum needed to register her in Trinity's daily *sinodik* for perpetual commemoration, as Aleksandr no doubt intended. Trinity was not willing to invest its money in an expensive land market.

In the last two periods new political and economic factors came into play that changed both the number and nature of benefactions. Put simply, the Livonian War that began in 1558 and Ivan IV's *oprichnina* terror from 1565 into 1572 brought ruin and death to many landowners and caused Russia's economy to contract for years thereafter. The terror hit landowners hardest in certain areas, most notably striking princely elites of Vladimir, Starodub, and also Murom and Nizhnii Novgorod in the east, and in the northeast Tver' and Bezhetskii Verkh, through which Ivan's rapacious punitive expedition against Novgorod traveled in 1569–70.[51] As a result Trinity saw an increase in total donations in period 10 compared to the previous period only because donations of land increased by a ratio of 2.3 to 1. The murder or deportation of landlords and the ruin of their estates devastated land values and demoralized donor families. There were more dead whose souls had to be attended to, more survivors pressed to secure commemorations for the souls of the deceased and to make preparation in the event their lives were terminated. Only ruined estates emptied of peasant tillers remained as resources by which benefactions could secure commemorative prayers. Donations of cash and moveable property actually declined. At the same time Trinity used its cash reserves to advantage to acquire 78 properties in what had become an era of falling land values. It purchased 57 outright, many no doubt at fire-sale prices. Alternatively, it bargained with debt-ridden landowners to acquire their properties at advantageous prices. Thus, between 1573/74 and 1577/78, Aleksei Fedishchev-Zubatov, his brother Mikhail, and his mother Mavra, returning to Kostroma after the *oprichnina*, donated the sizeable villages of Zarech'e and Shipovo to Trinity. In return Trinity gave them 250 rubles to pay their debts, promised commemorative prayers for them and others of their family, and promised that Mavra's husband Kudash be buried at Trinity. Trinity also agreed that Aleksei might live on his estate until he died.[52]

Russia's economy, especially its agricultural sector, continued to contract during period 11 and the number and nature of donations reflected the diminished resources of benefactors.[53] As a proportion of total donations, land grants dropped off precipitously to 11 percent. This time it was not because of rising land values. Quite the contrary. Those who held workable farms held on to them in order to survive. Trinity's copybooks recorded numerous transactions from the 1570s down to 1605 that disguised commemorative gifts as sales, but on which "sellers" were allowed to remain until they died. This was a means to evade survival legislation by which the government in 1588–89 attempted to stop landowners from alienating taxable properties to the church, or at least to require monasteries like Trinity to farm such properties and pay taxes the state had levied. The majority of such charters provided the benefactor the security of living on his sale/grant without liability for taxes to the state so long as he or she lived, after which Trinity took control of the property. In a variant on this Trinity also began to give benefactors who made cash gifts the right to lifetime tenure (and income) from one of its estates.[54] Trinity also benefited. It acquired properties that were destitute of labor to work them; by leaving them for the subsistence of former owners, it avoided the obligation to invest scarce manpower and other resources to maintain them. Four records for period 11 record transfers of property, ostensibly for commemorations, in which the monastery in return gave the donors cash. Even the powerful played such games for a time: in 1585/86 the widow of Okol'nichii Mikhail Vasil'evich

Iakovlev (d. 1556), the nun Aksinia, gave Trinity a large village that included 19 hamlets in Bezhetskii Verkh. In return the monastery gave her 900 rubles to pay her deceased husband's debts; 700 went to his second cousin and brother of Ivan IV's first wife, Boiar Nikita Romanovich Iur'ev, and 200 back to the monastery.[55]

Most of Trinity's acquisitions for the period from 1522 on (see Appendix Table 2) were in the core area near the monastery (353), especially in the districts of Moscow (102), Pereiaslavl' (97), and Dmitrov (106). The pattern was identical to that in early stages of Trinity's growth. But Trinity also added significant properties around its more remote outposts. On the northern Volga, Trinity added 96. The increase was greatest in Kostroma (57). By 1605 Trinity owned more properties there than in the districts of Uglich, Rostov, and Iaroslavl' combined. In the western districts of Borovsk, Volok, Ruza, Zubtsov, and Vereia, it acquired 13 properties to add to the 6 it already had. To the south of Moscow, where before it had 6, Trinity added 29 parcels, mostly in Kolomna (18). The total was modest, but for the first time Trinity picked up land in Serpukhov, Obolensk, Tula, Novosil', and Kashira. Trinity also profited from Moscow's conquest of the Khanate of Kazan', acquiring 3 properties in Sviiazhsk and 13 in Kazan'.

Trinity's acquisitions immediately to the east of its core area, in the northern Trans-Volga and to the northwest, were particularly numerous, a trend brought on by the *oprichnina* and economic collapse. In the Trans-Volga, where previously it held 26 properties, 17 in Galich and 9 in Beloozero, in 1605 it owned 129. Trinity began moving into new areas after 1547 but acquired most of its properties there after 1564. By 1605 it held 6 in Vologda, 1 in Medyn', 3 in Tot'ma, 8 in Kholmogory, 1 in Sol'-Vychegovsk, and 60 in Varzuga. All but the latter were primarily commercial enterprises on the North Dvina route to the White Sea over which the *oprichnina* had been given administration. Varzuga was a remote area on the White Sea comprising much of the southern shore of the Kola Peninsula. Its inhabitants were free tax-payers who derived their income from salmon fishing. Each family owed shares, called *luks*, in fishing rights and plots of shoreline with hay fields. In 1568 an *oprichnina* detachment plundered Varzuga. Trinity's agents must not have been far behind. By the end of 1584 they acquired 52 *luks*, 40 by purchase. In period 11 they obtained eight more. In eastern districts, where many princely and boiar families initially stricken by the *oprichnina* had their roots, Trinity's acquisitions doubled in periods 10 and 11.[56] Of 88 acquisitions in period 10, 25 were in Vladimir and 13 in Starodub. Trinity also acquired 40 properties in Murom, a surprisingly high total given that it was neither an *oprichnina* district nor the home of many titled families or elite servicemen. No one, so far as I am aware, has examined the problem. Trinity's gains came between 1569 and 1580. So it is likely they were the result of the same forces that convulsed other areas. Finally, Trinity increased its holdings significantly in the northwest. Before 1522 Trinity had 37 properties, most of them in Bezhetskii Verkh. From 1522 on it acquired 214 more. Prior to the *oprichnina* Trinity obtained 8 properties in Novyi Torg, 7 in Kashin, 11 in Tver', its first properties in Staritsa (8), and an outpost in Novgorod. In the wake of the *oprichnina*, Trinity hit a bonanza; by 1584 it acquired 52 properties in Tver', 55 in Bezhetskii Verkh, seven in Novgorod and a factory in Pskov.

In each district Trinity acquired or established subsidiary monasteries and churches from which it ministered to the spiritual needs of its patrons as well to its economic empire. Near the great house it controlled four monasteries: Trinity acquired the Dormition Monastery on Voinovo Hill at the junction of the Kirzhach and Kliaz'ma rivers before 1425. It had its own abbot by the mid-fifteenth century, but Trinity administered it again in the sixteenth. Trinity administered the Monastery of the Annunciation in Kirzhach by 1430, the Monastery of the Dormition at Stromyn' on the Dubenka River by the 1440s, and the Trinity Monastery at Berezniki on the Voria River in the Moscow land from 1471. It also controlled two nearby houses that it converted into subsidiary convents; the Monastery of the Mother of God at Podsosenie in 1462–66 and the Monastery of the Intercession at Khot'kovo. By legend the latter had been the family monastery of Sergius's parents. Stefan was tonsured there and by 1506, it was thought to be where Sergius had buried his parents. It came under Trinity's administration as a convent in 1544.[57] In Priluki the Monastery of Christ's Nativity was headquarters for Trinity's affairs in Uglich and nearby districts as early as the 1420s. North of the Volga on the Sheksna River, Trinity at one time had two monasteries. That of St. Nicholas may have shut down by 1500 but the Monastery of St. George remained Trinity's base there. Trinity's base in Vladimir and Starodub was the St. George hermitage in Gorokhovets. In Bezhetskii Verkh by the 1440s Trinity administered churches dedicated to the Savior, St. Nicholas, and St. Il'ia in the town of Priseki near the Mologa River. In 1460, or shortly before that, Trinity built a subsidiary monastery dedicated to the Trinity and Sergius with a church of the Epiphany in the Moscow kremlin.[58] It became Trinity's spiritual outpost not only in the Moscow area, where it had other churches, but at the seat of Muscovite power. Finally, in 1554 a Trinity-Sergius Monastery, administered by the original Trinity-Sergius Monastery, was built in the Volga town of Sviiazhsk with a Church of St. Sergius, founded by Ivan IV as his jumping-off post to attack Kazan' in 1551. In addition, by 1605 Trinity had commercial properties in every major town from Kazan' in the east to Novgorod and Pskov in the west and from Kholmogory in the north to Kolomna in the south. It also had a large stake in salt works located in Sol'-Galich, Sol'-Pereiaslavl', Velikaia Sol', and in Nerekhta (Kostroma).[59]

When Boris Godunov died in1605 the Trinity-Sergius Monastery had accumulated a huge inventory of venerator-benefactors and property. In its numbers and geographical scope it dwarfed those of other prominent houses. We lack the data for comprehensive comparisons, but. S. B. Veselovskii showed that for 1551–90 Trinity acquired 392 properties, while 16 major houses, including Kirillov, Simonov, and Iosifo-Volokolamsk, together acquired 215. According to A. A. Zimin the Iosifo-Volokolamsk Monastery from its founding to 1597 acquired 244 properties in 11 lands. Most were in Volok or nearby. Published collections of its charters indicate that the Moscow Simonov Monastery, from its founding to 1605, acquired 76 properties in 19 lands. The Solovetskii Monastery, from its founding through 1571, acquired 158 properties; all but four were concentrated in the north. Published holdings for Kirillov end with 1505 and show 118 acquisitions, only 5 of which were outside of the Beloozero land (compared to Trinity's 309 in 21 lands by 1501).[60] Clearly, the Trinity-Sergius Monastery was the most revered house in Russia.

* From Ivan Svatko's donation in the early fifteenth century to those recorded in 1605, in addition to 1,698 requests for memorial prayers, the Trinity-Sergius Monastery received at least 124 requests for memorial feasts. The majority of these were in documents requesting memorial prayers but a few were not. We must assume that in many other instances where persons bestowed benefices on Trinity, they expected memorial prayers even if they did not specifically request them. Statistically, these requests represent the largest body of evidence we have of popular religiosity. From these and similar records from other monasteries, we may conclude that concerns about salvation, and a conviction that they could best be resolved at sites where saints were buried, were the most important elements in Russia's religious culture in the Middle Ages and at the dawn of the early modern era. Who were these people? What caused them to give so generously to Trinity? How did they understand what they were doing?

The first of these questions can be answered easily and unambiguously. Princes made almost 5.9 percent of the memorial donations. Elites (boiars and *okol'nichi*) made 13 percent, and state secretaries (*d'iaki*) another 6 percent. Landowners (*votchinniki*), great and small, were the largest category of donors, providing 47 percent of the memorial grants. Closely related to these families were military service people (*pomeshchiki*), who crop up as donors for the first time after 1533 and represent almost 2 percent of the donors. Their benefactions were mostly in cash in that their *pomestie* were held on conditional tenure. Many of the service people in my records were from families owing hereditary estates. It was not uncommon that family members donated property in their memory; a few *pomeshchiki* also held hereditary estates and made memorial donations. Townspeople made 3.73 percent of the donations. They appear in the records from 1501 on. Donations by clerics amounted to 9.5 percent overall. They were negligible until period 8 (1533–47), when there were 37 and period 9 (1547–64), when there were 54, comprising roughly 7 percent of the total in each. As Russia slid into crisis, clerical donations increased absolutely and as a percent of the total to 89 (10.5 percent) in period 10 (1565–84), and 93 (20 percent) in period 11 (1584–1605). The majority of these were from Trinity monks, many of whom had been landowner-benefactors who became monks to find spiritual and material sustenance within its walls. Memorial donations from peasants amount to just under 2 percent of the total; those from servants on boiar or monastic estates, 3.2 percent. They appear from period 7 (1522–33) on. Like those of clerics, their donations grew in number in periods 10 and 11. I cannot identify 7 percent of the donors by social class. But based on where they came from or held property, most evidently were landowners.[61]

To interpret these figures one needs realize that some persons and families made more than one memorial donation and that only those who possessed some sort of property could appear in Trinity's records. Yet I am convinced that the correspondence is not far off the mark when gauging the commitment of social groups to the culture of commemoration. The evidence shows that every social class, when it could, bought into the memorial culture at Trinity. Records for 1522–33, a "normal" period, indicate someone of unknown social origin, probably a small landowner in Tver', gave Trinity three horses, which he valued at just over 6 rubles, and one Isai Stroi Lachinov gave Trinity 13 rubles. At the other extreme, a will executed for Boiar Ivan Vasil'evich Pleshcheev, dated 8 March 1532, provided Trinity the villages of Dmitrievskoe and Timoshkino in Zvenigorod and their 29 hamlets. Yet each of these benefactors wanted the same thing. The anonymous donor said he gave Trinity the horses "for Iurii Malechkine" (*po Iur'e Malechkine*), probably a relative, and Lachinov made his donation "for my father the monk Gerasim" (*po ottse svoem inoke Gerasim*). Pleshcheev in his testament specified extravagant rituals of remembrance appropriate to his boiar rank. He gave Trinity one of the villages and its hamlets to Trinity "for Vasilii, for Ivan and for all their relatives" and the other "for Vasilii, for Anna, for Ivan and for all their relatives." The Ivan for whom he made these gifts was himself, while Anna and Vasilii were his father and mother. Trinity's donation book and feast book also record that Pleshcheev gave Trinity the village of Dmitrievskoe to underwrite an annual standard feast (*korm srednei*) at Trinity. The request specified the relatives to be commemorated: "Petr, Ivan, Mar'ia, Vasilii, Anna, Andrei. *Rod* Pleshcheev."[62] All three families appear in Trinity's daily *sinodik* because they made multiple donations. I can identify memorials to Gerasim Lachinov and the Pleshcheev family members mentioned in these charters, but not to Iurii Malechkin.[63] Whether rich or poor, the intent was the same.

Looking beyond the benefactors to examine whom they wished to commemorate when they gifted Trinity, one again is struck by the seamlessness of the memorial culture across the social hierarchy. I have chosen donations records for period 9 in the database for 1547–64 to illustrate this, because it had the largest number of memorial donations not influenced by the *oprichnina* and economic crisis. There were 796 donations, out of which 501 specified those to be commemorated). They recorded the relationship to the giver of those memorialized and whether the requests were for prayers or contained more elaborate—and expensive—requests for tonsure, burial, or feast. These records often set down who was to be memorialized, allowing us to compare whether the ruling elite—grand princes and tsars, appanage princes, boiars, state secretaries—requested different sorts of memorials or a different pattern of persons to be commemorated than did ordinary landowners, townsmen, clerics, service people or free peasants. There are problems with my classifications, differences in wealth and prestige of families of ordinary landowners being one. Nevertheless, the data confirm how little difference there was between whom the high and the mighty and the ordinary landowners memorialized and how they went about it. Elite donors requested 100 memorial prayers, ordinary donors 359, and the identity of 42 others who requested memorials is unknown. Elite donors requested prayers for themselves and their husbands or wives in 32 percent of the records; ordinary donors did so in 27 percent. Elite donors requested prayers for parents, grandparents, or ancestors in 16 percent of the records; ordinary donors did so in 30 percent. Records of donations for siblings were about the same (17 percent and 14 percent), as were those for children and grandchildren (9 percent and 10 percent) and for uncles, aunts, nephews, nieces, and cousins (6 percent and 4 percent). Finally, elite donors donated for persons of unknown kinship ties or none at all in 21 percent of the records; ordinary donors did so in only 14 percent.

The only significant differences in records of commemoration for elite and ordinary donors is in the memorializing of parents/ancestors and persons of unknown kinship. In the first instance I have no explanation, other than the statistical insignificance of the sample, because the rest of my evidence supports the contention that elites carefully defined their ancestry to maintain their social position. In the latter case records reveal that elite families felt obliged to memorialize members of other elite families. Often the memorials were for families related to them by marriage; for others I could find no evident relationship. Perhaps circumstances were such that the memorialized families lacked close relatives to do it for them. Then too, Tsar Ivan IV's custom of memorializing members of the service elite (10 of 32 such records) who died in battle or perished in his *oprichnina* terror inflated this category of memorialization for elites. My results and those presented by Daniel Kaiser contain the same categories of those memorialized.[64] This being the case, the degree of differentiation in percentages between categories of those memorialized in the studies are not so great that one cannot conclude that both ordinary donors and elites felt obliged to memorialize their kin; further, in carrying out such obligations, they exhibited patterns of memorialization so similar as to rule out the likelihood that social distinctions defined different levels of religious belief within the culture of commemoration.

It works out the same when we look at how they went about it. In this case, however, statistical comparisons are less instructive than the texts of commemoration charters. The reason is that burial or tonsure during the prime of life at Trinity were not options for members of the Muscovite royal line and voluntary tonsure was rare for boiars. What we have left are feasts, and elites asked for feasts in 12 percent of memorial requests, ordinary donors in 3.3 percent of theirs. The difference says more about wealth than about mentalities. But looking at the content of memorial requests, we find numerous records in which ordinary donors made commemoration requests or requests for feasts that were as detailed and elaborate as those of any boiar. In 1549 Marfa, the wife of Prince Petr Zasekin, gave 50 rubles to Trinity, instructing its officers, "and for this enter into the *sinodik* 29 names of our ancestors." In 1555/56 a Grigorii Spiridonov syn Arbuzov gave Trinity a village in Vladimir and asked that it commemorate "my ancestor the monk Dmitrii, Efrosin'ia, Spiridon, the nun Marem'iana, Ilarion, Leontii, Ignatii, Evdokhim, Irina, Fedor, Grigorii, Ul'iana, Oksen'ia."[65] Nor can I find any more elaborate request for commemoration than that which the wealthy but otherwise undistinguished Prince Semen Kiselev made in a will in 1547/48, and again in 1549/50 in a donation charter giving Trinity two villages—one hereditary, the other purchased—and 24 hamlets in Murom in 1549/50. According to these documents and Trinity's donation book, he requested commemorations for his grandparents Mikhail and the nun Marfa, for his parents Fedor and the nun Evdokiia, for himself and his wife the nun Agripena, his son Ivan, and for nuns (daughters?) Evfimiia and Nazariia. In the will Semen said that, as directed by his grandfather and father, he will give these properties to Trinity at the moment of his death, a stipulation repeated in the donation charter recorded in a Trinity copybook. When the time came, he continued, he asked that he be tonsured and provided a cell at Trinity and that, when he died, he be buried there. At that moment Trinity would assume responsibility for the requested commemorations, which were to take the form of "thrice annual standard feasts in memory of our parents, me and our entire line so long as the monastery exists." Its feast book records that Trinity arranged two major feasts and one standard feast each year for the Kiselevs, but only Semen, his father Fedor, and his grandmother "princess nun Marfa" are mentioned by name as objects of commemoration. I cannot decode satisfactorily the Kiselev entries in the daily *sinodik*, but the "monk Simeon," that is Semen, and the "nun Evdokhiia" seem certain; another is probably Eufimiia, and there is a monk Il'ia, who may have been Semen's son Ivan.[66]

But what of folk who did not have property or cash to secure a place in Trinity's *sinodiks*? The evidence is sparse, but it shows that they too participated in the same religious culture as their betters, and in much the same way. Documents of the second half of the fifteenth century and the first half of the sixteenth indicate that the great house and its outposts were scenes of regular public feasts, an important feature of which was the memorialization of ancestors. The earliest reference is in a charter from Grand Prince Vasilii II to Abbot Vassian Rylo of Trinity issued between 1455 and 1462:

> That anyone not a resident in your monastic village of Priseki in Bezhetskii Verkh or its hamlets, [including] my governor, agents, officers of the court, or servicemen, or any other of my people in Bezhetskii Verkh, is forbidden to come [to your properties] for beer without an invitation. And whoever should come uninvited to a feast [*pir;* elsewhere *bratchina* or fête], and initiate any kind of looting, I order that such loot be taken from him without trial or investigation.[67]

Ivan III issued charters in 1462–66 protecting Trinity's feasts in Radonezh, Pereiaslavl', Vladimir, and Suzdal'. Vasilii III, Ivan IV, and appanage princes Andrei Ivanovich and Vladimir Andreevich of Staritsa issued similar bans against uninvited guests at Trinity's feasts, extending them to its properties in Rostov, Staritsa, Vereia, Kostroma, Galich, and Iur'ev. Ivan IV also reaffirmed charters with these restrictions that his father and grandfather had issued.[68] They said who was not to attend feasts, but not who was invited or whether these gatherings included religious rites. The Russian word for fête, however, has a long history in which it signified a celebration connected to the cult of ancestors. The communal consumption of beer was a part of such celebrations and, traditionally, honored guests were invited. Religious institutions possessed the right to brew beer for religious and family holidays, as well as immunities on the profits they made from it. L. V. Cherepnin, commenting on these provisions in Trinity's charters, described them as village festivals, and in a sense they were. Yet in Christian times they were celebrated in the narthex and, occasionally, in the nave of a church.[69] In this context it is not unreasonable to infer that Trinity's more distinguished benefactors were the invited guests at such feasts and that they assembled in the refectory at Trinity or in the narthex of churches at its outposts to hear the reading of the *sinodik*, which was read during meals instead of in the liturgy. It is fair to assume that local peasants and townsmen also assembled to commemorate their ancestors by paying a nominal price for the beer that Trinity's brotherhood offered on such occasions. So said at least one late source, a directive issued in April or May 1590, by Archimandrite Kiprian, cellarer Evstafii Golovkin, treasurer Ignatii Lodygin, elder Vasunofii Iakimov, and Trinity's Council of Elders to several peasants by name, to Trinity's official in Kharitanovo, a village in Vladimir, "and to peasants of all [its] villages and hamlets." It said that "whatever peasant receives a special serving of beer, at celebrations of a birth or a commemoration of ancestors (*na rodinakh ili po roditelekh pominok*) for which our officer has received nothing, he shall for the fête (*s bratchiny*) be charged the sum of two *dengi*." The members of the church Council of One Hundred Chapters (*Stoglav*) of 1551 admitted the truth of Ivan IV's complaint that laity of all ranks constantly frequented feasts in Trinity's refectory, not to mention in cells of its monks, to commemorate their ancestors, often with excessive drinking.[70] Lay persons were active participants in the culture of commemoration.

* Making a commemorative donation, no matter its size, affirmed clan identities and gave the benefactor immortality. With a donation a beneficiary publicly bound Trinity's brotherhood to repeated commemoration and surviving family members and future generations to recall the memory of the deceased. Often overlooked is the fact that most charters, virtually all from the late fifteenth century on, mentioned the surname of the donor if he was

a male and, if not that, then the surname of the primary person to be prayed for. I shall say more about it in Chapter 6, but where females were donors, the documents identified them by the surname of their spouse, but often also that of their father. More importantly, Trinity's donation book recorded donations by surname. For example, the entry for the Pleshcheev clan, one of Trinity's earliest and most important patrons, mentions 21 different gifts and identifies 14 different donors to 1605. The collective identity that a surname provided established an individual's place in a social hierarchy. With repeated gifts members of a clan repeatedly and publicly reaffirmed who they were and where they stood among Trinity's community of venerators and in the world at large.[71] The donation of an inherited family property to Trinity rarely, if ever, was a private transaction between donor and monastery. Inheritance customs required that families give their consent to what, after all, was a claim of ownership that involved successive generations and, within each, lateral kinsmen. In the matter of Ivan Pleshcheev's testament (1532), for example, of three witnesses, two were kinsmen, Andrei Grigoriev syn Pleshcheev and Rychko Vorypaev syn Pleshcheev. Another example: in 1534/35 the Trinity monk Andreian, as a layman Andrei Ivanovich Golovkin, in his testament gave Trinity one-half of the hamlet of Iazvishch near Trinity's outpost in Bezhetskii Verkh. Two nephews, Ignatii and Iakov, sons of his oldest brother Semen, were his executors. For Andreian they made the donation to Trinity "to commemorate in the *sinodik* our uncle, the monk Andreian, and all his ancestors" (*po svoem diade vo inotsekh po Ondreiane i po vsem ego rodu . . . pozhalovati napisati diadiu nashego v senanik*). In addition to two priests who were Andreian's confessors, six Golovkins were listed in the testament as witnesses: his brothers Semen, Grigorii, and Gavriil; his nephews Iakov and Ignatii (Semen's sons); and Vasilii "Sviat" Danilovich, the great-grandson of Andreian's grandfather's brother.[72] That year Fedor and Stefan Golovkin, sons of Andreian's brother Boris, sold the other half of Iazvishch to Trinity for 25 rubles. The same six Golovkin family members who witnessed Andreian's testament witnessed this document. No record states how long Iazvishch had been in the family. We know, though, that about 1504 Ivan Osimovich, the father of Boris and Andreian, owned the entire settlement, because he divided it, giving his sons Andrei and Boris each a half. In this case Ivan's brother Matvei and his grandson Vasilii Timofeevich witnessed the charter.[73] Andreian and his nephews Fedor and Stefan must have held their halves of Iazvishch conditionally if, in order to give or sell their parts of the hamlet to Trinity, they had to have members of the family sign off on it. The Trinity Monastery, to gain "clear title" to the property, also had a stake in assuring that the family approved the donation and sale of Iazvishch.

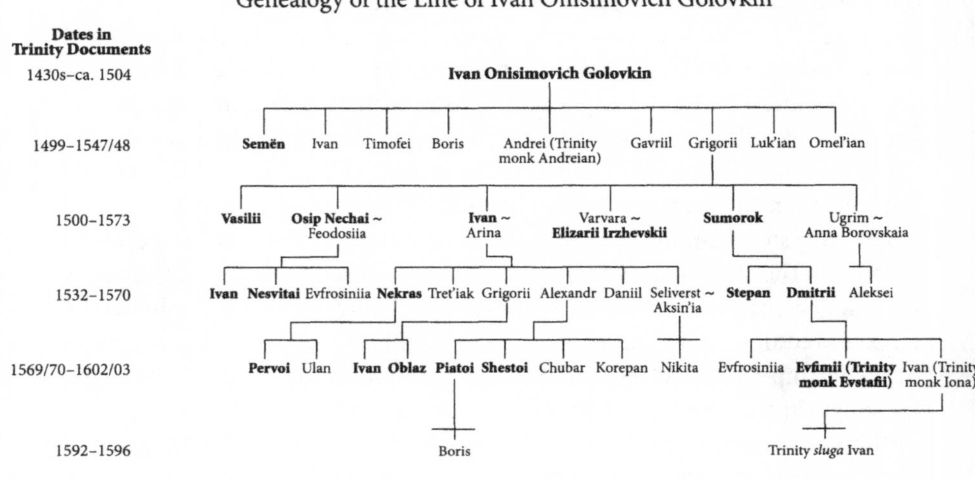

I know of no convention that required relatives with a specific kinship to the donor to witness the alienation of properties for commemorative purposes, certainly none so elaborate as those Stephen White worked out from documents regarding exchanges of property between families and religious institutions in western France of the twelfth and thirteenth centuries. Not infrequently no relative turns up in names of witnesses in Russian donation charters; but if not relatives, then, as in medieval France and Burgundy, close neighbors witnessed such transfers of property. So it was in Moscow's borderland of Bezhetskii Verkh in the fifteenth century when the Golovkin and Irzhevskii families witnessed their own and each other's donations and other transactions with Trinity's outpost.[74]

Andrei Golovkin's testament of 1534/35 specified that his memorial bequest of half of a village to Trinity was to be "without right of redemption" (*bez vykup*) by the Golovkin family. Andrei was by then the Trinity monk Andreian. By signing off on the testament, six Golovkin witnesses pledged that the family would not reassert its claim to the grant, thus giving Trinity security in its acquisition.[75] The term "redemption," appeared initially in testaments of the 1480s of appanage princes Andrei Vasil'evich of Vologda and Mikhail Andreevich of Vereia and Beloozero.[76] Each granted his relative Grand Prince Ivan III the right to redeem their bequests to Trinity. The absence of redemption clauses in fifteenth-century donation charters, excepting these, probably means that it was a nonissue; relatives of benefactors expected to shoulder obligations to respect such bequests and the obligations to pray for the souls of departed relatives. If this is so, then the appearance of a clause asserting the possibility of redemption in testaments of appanage princes, a component of a policy introduced by Ivan III designed to maintain his right to oversee property transfers of his junior relatives, marked a significant change. As land values rose, relatives of donor-landowners contemplated redeeming memorial grants to Trinity, and in more than a few cases did so.[77] Trinity's officers prepared for such eventualities by insisting that grants contain clauses disavowing encumbrances. At any rate, in 1506 Andrei, Ivan, and Il'ia Stogov gave Trinity a hereditary land and forest in Pereiaslavl' in return for prayers for their father Kuz'min and mother Nastas'ia. In doing so they donated "the land forever without redemption" (*vveki ta zemlia bez vykupa*) to Trinity. By the 1530s such clauses were commonplace. That is, unless a benefactor wrote into a charter the sort of proviso Gorianin Grigor'evich Mordvinov put in his memorial grant to Trinity of 1523/24 to the effect that a relative could reclaim the hamlet in question by paying Trinity 20 rubles.[78]

These formalities testify to the strength of the notion that a family had a claim to property donated for prayers, *unless* it repudiated it. And if a charter had such a clause, it in turn implied Trinity's commitment to pray forever for the souls of those whom benefactors specified. Benefactors were not slow to insist that such a clause be a component of commemorative grants. In a charter of 1529/30 giving Trinity a hamlet in Pereiaslavl' in return for prayers, Dmitrii Ivanovich Riabinin specified that the grant was unredeemable, and that Trinity's "abbot or brothers were not to sell, trade, or give away by redemption this hamlet, [but the] the monastery was to hold on to it" (*A toe derevni iguminu z bratami ni prodati ni promenit' ne v zakup ne dat', derzhati ee vo obiteli*).[79] A purchase charter dated 1547/48 by which Trinity sold the village of Podchertkovo in the Povel'skii district of Dmitrov to Fedor Ivanovich Sukin for 150 rubles contained another scenario illustrating the bonding nature of exchanges of property. Sukin was not an ordinary serviceman. In 1547 he was Ivan IV's treasurer and in 1563 he attained boiar rank. Nor was the property an ordinary holding. According to the purchase agreement, a Prince David Danilovich Khromyi-Iaroslavskii had donated it to Trinity. The "purchase" then was a contracted "lending out" of the property in return for a donation disguised as a purchase price. Sukin was to hold Podchertkovo until his death, at which time it was to be returned to the monastery.[80] The exchange of property was the glue that obligated the living to inaugurate prayers for the dead and the monastery to commemorate them in perpetuity, ensuring that the social identity of the clan was continually and publicly reconfirmed.

The exchange of land to make a contract between benefactor and Trinity took other forms. Sometimes a sale of family property to Trinity obligated the monastery to enter into complicated land settlements in order to obviate protests from an aggrieved family member. This was the case in two charters of 1529/30 involving the Shubin family, who were landowners in the Verkhdubin district of Pereiaslavl'.[81] According to the first, cellarer Vassian Korovin purchased for Trinity the hamlet of Maloe Sementsovo from Iurii Fedodrovich Shubin for 20 rubles. Four people witnessed the act, including a Petr Shemiakin syn Shubin, and Trinity elder Simon Grigorev syn Shubin. Following it in Trinity's earliest copybook was an exchange agreement by which Petr Shemiakin syn Shubin turned over the village of Bol'shoe Sementsovo to Trinity's treasurer in return for Maloe Sementsovo and the sum of 21 rubles. It explained that Petr's brother, meaning his cousin Iurii, had sold Maloe Sementsovo to Trinity. At the outset the agreement said the trade was made with treasurer Simon, meaning his kinsman Simon Grigorevich Shubin; elsewhere it said the treasurer was Serapion Kurtsev. The confusion is understandable because sometime before August 1533 Simon replaced Serapion when the latter became cellarer. The business makes sense if one believes that Simon managed these transactions to make equitable arrangements among kin so that they would agree to give the hamlet to Trinity. Petr's promise in the second charter that he would not alienate the family property of Maloe Sementsovo by sale, mortgage, or as a memorial grant suggests that this was so. Iurii's signature as witness to the exchange agreement indicates that he found the deal to be satisfactory.

* Once committed, property rights took on a social dimension that bound a clan to Trinity for generations. The relationship between Trinity and the Zabolotskii family, an offshoot of the Vsevolozh clan that produced several boiars, provides various examples. In his testament of 1547/48 the childless Timofei Vasil'ev syn Brazhnik-Zabolotskii requested tonsure as the monk Tikhon and memorial prayers. In return he gave Trinity the village of Golovkovo and the hamlet Krugloe in Dmitrov. A year later Trinity gave the properties to Bogdan Vasil'ev Zabolotskii, probably Timofei's brother, in exchange for one-half of the hamlet Mart'ianova and 50 rubles. At some point a Zabolotskii again used Krugloe and Golovkovo as a memorial donation because in the 1590s they were again registered to Trinity.[82] In another instance in 1562/63 the childless Danill Semenovich Ugrimov-Zabolotskii made a will giving the Trinity-Sergius Monastery the village of Novoe in

Pereiaslavl' in return for memorial prayers. Daniil, however, qualified the grant, saying that his nephews Vasilii and Fedor Ivanovichi Ugrimovy might redeem it for 111 rubles. The same year, lacking the necessary amount, Vasilii and Fedor pledged to Trinity their village of Shilkovo in Kolomna as security in return for Novoe and promised they would in no way encumber or alienate it. There is no record that Vasilii and Fedor ever obtained the cash to redeem Novoe. But somehow Trinity allowed the village to be used by Matrena, on the instructions of her husband Grigorii Ivanovich Drobnin Zabolotskii, as a donation for commemorative prayers for herself, her husband, and their children. As a result of the gift Matrena also was able to take vows and live out her life at one of Trinity's subsidiary convents. Vasilii Ugrimov was a witness to this.[83] In an analogous case a charter of 1555/56 indicates that the executors of the estate in Rostov of one Zakhar Panfilov at his request gave Trinity the village of Ponikarovo to commemorate him and his ancestors. It noted that earlier Trinity had sold the village to Zakhar. What is likely, but unstated, was that the sale was for lifetime tenure and the price, in effect, Zakhar's memorial gift to Trinity. We know too that Trinity initially came by Ponikarovo as a memorial grant in January 1529 from state secretary Danilo Kiprianov syn Mamyrev, a person quite unrelated to the Panfilovs.[84]

The importance of regular commemorations/affirmations cannot be overstated. If Trinity improperly alienated a donation, it might expect a storm of protest from an aggrieved beneficiary or his or her descendents. We know of just such a protest from a directive (*ukaznaia gramota*) of 7 May 1549 that was sent in Ivan IV's name to Trinity. It said that a very angry nun Aleksandra, formerly Agrafenia, the wife of Vasilii Ivanovich Volynskii, complained to him that Trinity had improperly given in redemption to Prince Konstantin Ivanovich Kurliatev for 200 rubles the village of Ostaf'evskoe in Kolomna. Agrafenia said she had stipulated in a donation charter of 1541, in which she gave Ostaf'evskoe to Trinity, that only a "near relative" might redeem her grant made for prayers for herself, her husband, and his and her parents, and for their respective ancestors, and that Kurliatev did not fall into that category. Ivan agreed and ordered Trinity to take back Ostaf'evskoe and refund Kurliatev his 200 rubles.[85] My examination of the relationship of those commemorated to their commemorators for 1547–64, and of kin who witnessed donation acts, demonstrates that donors drew clan boundaries and established clan identities on a "spine" of father-to-son relationships and usually involved close kin. The schemes were tightly cognatic. The witnesses were male and involved lateral kin with an interest in the contract, such as brothers, uncles, cousins, and nephews. The data show that donors memorialized both sets of their grandparents; they memorialized children of both sexes; and they often commemorated lateral kin such as brothers (less often sisters), uncles (occasionally aunts), cousins (usually male), and nephews and nieces. Rarely were witnesses affines or did memorials include affines. When they appeared, as I discuss in Chapter 6, they usually concerned a memorial involving a dowry property.[86]

When they could afford it, benefactors underwrote annual commemoration feasts for deceased family members. Their physical presence at Trinity reaffirmed in public ceremonies the social identity defined in a less grandiose manner by the ubiquity of surnames in Trinity's donation book and the lists of benefactors and those commemorated in donation charters. My database contains records of 124 or 125 feasts. Abbot Nikon inaugurated such public displays of generosity: the first three or four date from his tenure; six others occurred under his immediate successors. Moscow's grand princes, princes of Radonezh, or their boiars requested or were honored by the first seven feasts.[87] In all, Moscow's rulers, appanage princes, boiars, and state secretaries requested 67, or 54 percent of all feasts. When they could afford it, landowners of lesser service ranks arranged feasts too, leaving little doubt that donors of all ranks considered such occasions an important way to reaffirm kinship identities in a religious rite. As Emile Durkheim suggested, the participant in such periodic rites sought a "moral remaking" that endowed him or her with the strength to face the travails of profane society.[88]

References to ceremonies accompanying commemorative donations in the Latin West allow us to view them as customary occasions on which families displayed their identities. In Muscovite Russia rituals to seal a memorial donation, involving Trinity's officers, either at the great house or one of its subsidiary centers, and donor families, were also routine occasions. So much so that, excepting those of Moscow's rulers, no one thought them important enough to describe. But surely, what remained of the Morozov boiar clan must have been in attendance at the feast recorded in Trinity's feast book of 1674. It involved an office for the dead (*panikha*) and a mass (*obednia*) for 23 members of the venerable Morozov boiar family, and was paid for with two villages, 1,500 rubles, and a bejeweled icon cover. There is no other source for it, but it must have taken place when Mariia, the daughter of Iakov Morozov and wife of Molchan Aksent'ev, the final name in the list of those commemorated, made a memorial donation to Trinity in 1579/80.[89] Even ordinary folk reveled in commemorative fêtes that were part of the annual cycle at Trinity and its outposts, and there is evidence that other houses sponsored such events for persons of every social status. To sum up, it is likely that donations were the occasion of private rites involving a benefactor's family and Trinity's officers as well as public fêtes at which families were present as invited guests to commemorate their ancestors and parade their social status. Finally, those who could pay underwrote special feasts. They took place annually, even three times each year, and were public rites of varying complexity. These ceremonies did much to cement family ties and strengthen the social structure.[90]

Donation records indicate clans made repeated donations. It meant that their members participated in repeated ceremonies to secure the salvation of their ancestors and to reaffirm clan identities. Landowners, great and small, and religious communities like Trinity enjoyed an intimate relationship that succeeding generations reaffirmed with new donations. The frequency with which Pleshcheevs or Golovkins gifted Trinity shows how longstanding these relationships could be. Stephen White's observation that, "among lords and knights various forms of generosity were considered obligatory and were not merely performed out of habit," that giving to a holy site meant "obeying a divine command," held true of landowners who were Trinity's patrons throughout the sixteenth century. Clans were "moral persons" in exchanging property for commemorations and for arranging commemorative feasts.[91] From the Pereiaslavl' land alone different generations of the Skripitsyn clan between 1525/26 and 1600/1 made eight donations, members of the Kurtsev clan of state secretaries between 1534 and the end of the century made (or had made by others in their memory) 15, and the Butenevs between 1524/25 and 1573 made 11.[92] Year after year families proceeded to and from Trinity or to churches in its outposts for commemorative feasts. Given their ubiquity by the middle of the sixteenth century, Trinity began to regulate which families were entitled to them by specifying what size a land grant had to be in order to provide for minor, standard, or major feasts. Still, the frequency with which such rites occurred only increased. Coupled with the donations that fueled them, clans engaged generation after generation in formulaic responses of collective memory.[93]

As death approached and the preoccupations with securing one's salvation intensified, the importance of earthly identities receded. But of Moscow's grand princes (and well-to-do patrons of Catholic houses in the Middle Ages), the majority of whom were tonsured on their deathbed,[94] few of those who requested commemorative prayers and feasts at Trinity with bequests sought to end their days as monks there.

Although the sources are late, it is likely that Prince Semen Vladimirovich and his brother Andrei Vladimirovich of Radonezh requested tonsure at Trinity shortly before death in the plague year 1425. Three benefactors, Mikhail (Misail) Pleshcheev, Petr Morozov, and Vasilii (Vassian) Uvarov, became Trinity monks in the fifteenth century, but only the first and the last evidently did so in preparation for death.[95] The earliest record of a deathbed tonsure in Trinity's donation book is that of Boiar-Prince Dmitrii Pronskii on 18 January 1517; the first request for tonsure in a donation charter was made by Boiar Semen Ivanovich Vorontsov (the monk Serapion) in 1521 or 1522.[96] My records show two requests for period 7, nine for period 8, and 18 for period 9. In other words, there was a gradual increase in the number of benefactors who viewed tonsure, with its rejection of one's earthly identity and responsibilities, as an effective means to attain salvation. In period 9 the requests came from across the spectrum of Moscow's elite: one appanage prince, one boiar, two state secretaries, nine *votchinniki*, one cleric, two townspersons, one servant, and one person of unknown status. The price, if one can call it that, usually was the same as that for entry into the daily *sinodik*, 50 rubles. Thus, one Fedor Nefedev, the monk Feofilak, on 25 December 1548 gave Trinity 50 rubles to be tonsured "and for a cell 10 rubles."[97]

In periods 10 and 11 the number of donors seeking tonsure skyrocketed to 58 and 63, respectively. It is difficult not to conclude that *oprichniki* whips and plundering and the ensuing economic misery had much to do with this outburst of religious zeal. In period 10 the number of hereditary landowners who sought tonsure was 48; in period 11 only 8. But 19 seekers of tonsure were identified as peasants and 25 as servitors of landowners or the monastery. Not surprisingly, the "price" for tonsure dropped to 10 rubles, or less. In period 11, 17 donors also sought for themselves or their kin entry into service at the monastery. Obviously the category of servitor encompassed many ruined landlords. Orthodox Church law forbade the ownership of slaves by clerics or clerical institutions. The ubiquity of the "servant" (*sluga*, pl. *slugy*) in church records, particularly during hard times, can only mean that the church (and Trinity) took on dependents. Juridically the servant was not a slave. In one sense he was an employee, even one with considerable managerial authority. Servants could and often did obtain tonsure and burial at Trinity; and some had the cash to be its benefactors. Yet to some degree, perhaps to varying degrees, they were dependents.[98] It is unclear how the brotherhood determined who might be tonsured and who would enter its walls as a servant. There is no discernable pattern in the size of donations or, aside from high service ranks, in the social status of the donor that determined whether a petitioner became a monk or a servitor. Nor are the brotherhood's motives clear in deciding who gained tonsure and who did not. Was it that the brotherhood wished to limit its numbers, or was it unable physically to house a greater volume of aspiring monks? Or did it wish to use family members of impoverished benefactors in administrative or menial tasks? Trinity also accepted donation charters from its patrons, similar to those of Prince Semen Kiselev in 1549/50, Ivan Shein Kurbatov in 1562/63, or Aleksei Fedishchev-Zubatov in the 1570s (*see* above) that allowed the donor or a relative to retain and live on a property until death, at which time it passed to the monastery. The arrangement was a form of welfare for the well-to-do, assuring a donor a measure of security when he or she fell on hard times or was in his or her last years. In this it resembled *precaria* agreements providing a donor "lifetime" rent of a property common between houses and patrons in the medieval West.[99]

The simple prayer, "And when I die, say a prayer for my soul," with which Ivan Svatko had bequeathed Trinity three properties, had taken on a variety of functions, involving the monastery with a multitude of clans. But the concerns about salvation that caused Ivan to settle with Trinity at the outset of the fifteenth century were the same as those that that motivated patrons at the outset of the seventeenth to compose their complicated charters.

Chapter Five

Trinity's Monks

In 1572/73 Timofei Ivanovich Chashnikov, a landowner in Tver', prepared a charter giving the Trinity-Sergius Monastery the hamlet of Riabinino in exchange "for eternal peace"; that is, to assure him memorial prayers. To this he added, "And tonsure and succor me, Timofei, at the Lifegiving Trinity."[1] The desire to free himself from the desperate economic conditions in Tver' that followed from the ravages of Ivan IV's *oprichnina* army in 1570 probably leavened Timofei's pious request to be tonsured. Still, he followed a familiar path by taking tonsure as a monk while in his prime. At Trinity the tradition began with St. Sergius and his brother Stefan.

According to Epifanii the Wise, when Sergius became a monk in the mid-1340s around him "there gathered a few monks, but no more than twelve."[2] The next precise statement of the size of Trinity's brotherhood appeared in 1595, when the elder Varsunofii Iakimov dictated a testament in which he granted a ruble to each of Trinity's monks and meticulously recorded that the grant totaled 220.[3] Epifanii's 12 cast his hero in the image of his Savior; Varsunofii's 220 expressed a dying monk's affection for his brothers as he dispersed his estate. Only in 1641, at the behest of a commission established by Tsar Mikhail Fedorovich to survey the male population and resources of the Russian state, did the Trinity-Sergius Monastery prepare an inventory (*opis'*) of its property and brotherhood. S. V. Nikolaeva's analysis of the inventory sets the number of monks at Trinity in 1641 at 243 or 244, in addition to a large staff of servants, not to mention monks and nuns who lived in other houses under Trinity's jurisdiction or in its urban yards (*dvory*), salt works, and rural outposts scattered across Russia.[4] For the 255 years between Sergius's founding of Trinity and Varsunofii's testament four accounts by foreigners offered estimations of the size of Trinity's brotherhood. Based on conversations with Muscovite envoys in 1525, Johann Fabri in Tubingen said Trinity had 300 monks. Rafaello Barberini, visiting Russia in 1565, said it had up to 250. The Danish diplomat Jakob Ulfeldt, who stopped at Trinity in 1578, said it housed 300 monks. Antonio Possevino, who was in Russia in the 1580s, gave varying estimates of 200 and 350.[5] Fabri's figure, based on hearsay, and Ulfeldt's seem inflated; but Barberini and Possevino, in at least in one of his statements, provided totals that can be taken seriously and confirmed, if only approximately, in another way. Assuming that from four to six monks lived in a cell (a estimate perhaps derived from having lived in a Soviet student dormitory), Nikolaeva concluded that the number of monks said to be at Trinity in 1641 is in line with information in the inventory about the number of dormitory buildings, their size, and the number of cells in each. If we take these relationships and relate them to the amount of dormitory space that existed at Trinity a century earlier according to A. V. Gorskii's description of the monastery, then Pierre Gonneau's opinion that about 150 monks lived at Trinity in the 1530s seems reasonable.[6] Gorskii also showed that Trinity during the good times between then and the beginning of the *oprichnina* in 1565 built more living space, apparently enough to house the 220 monks who lived there in 1595.

From records of its property transactions, donation book, burial records, and *sinodik* I have compiled a reliable database listing Trinity's monks by name, office, and background from Sergius's time to 1605.[7] Along with narrative sources, they shed considerable light on the composition of the brotherhood and on governance at Trinity. It goes without saying that each genre of sources has its own problems of interpretation. Hagiographic sources provide names of Sergius's disciples but lack reliable chronological information. Documentary sources contain dates or can be dated from information in their texts, but provide little context about the people mentioned in them. For example, monks may have lived at Trinity long before or after the date of acts in which their names appeared. This is particularly true of Trinity's officers. Also, it would be misleading to count as resident monks all the benefactors requesting tonsure, because many (most?) did so shortly before death. The burial list, published in 1880, was said to derive from lists dating back to late in the seventeenth century.[8] Generically, the *sinodik* of 1575, with interpolations and continuations down to the 1680s, was a list of surnames. However, one often finds family names, titles, and occupations or other characteristics of those commemorated in the interstices. Moreover, a segment of the *sinodik* had at its core an older *sinodik* of Trinity's brothers. In the margin of its first folio page was the date 1495; but dates regularly appear in the margins and information in the interstices only from 1523 into the 1590s.[9] This section of the *sinodik* is a fruitful source for identifying Trinity monks, particularly those invisible in documentary sources: laborers and artisans. But it is a treacherous source in estimating the size of Trinity's brotherhood at any particular time.

I divide the database into 11 "generations." The first generation comprised monks who were with Sergius before his death in 1392. It probably is a complete roster. The second consists of monks living at Trinity under Abbot Nikon when Sergius's cult was established. Nikon died in 1428. I divide succeeding generations arbitrarily into chronological segments: the third includes monks who were at Trinity primarily from the 1430s to the early 1450s. It was a time of transition and division among the brothers that in some ways mirrored the struggles between contending parties in the Muscovite dynastic civil war. The next two generations lived at Trinity from the mid-1450s to 1475 and from 1476 to 1495, periods in which the state implemented policies to restrict the acquisition of property and immunities by monasteries. During that time the composition of the brotherhood itself began to change so that in the sixth generation (1496–1515) Trinity emerged as a rich community dominated by monks from families of landowner patrons. Generations seven (1516–33), eight (1534–53), and nine (1554–70) were at Trinity during Russia's economic boom years, during which the house became rich. Economic collapse shaped the fate of generations ten (1571–90) and eleven (1591–1605). Boris Godunov's coercive policies to halt the transfer of land and people to monasteries had a significant impact on generation eleven, even more on its leadership. Of course, monastic careers of individual monks rarely fit neatly into generational categories. Nevertheless, placing them in time frames that encompass the greater part of their tenure at Trinity provides a sample of the composition of its brotherhood at any one time.

My count, drawn from sources other than Trinity's *sinodik*, contains an inherent bias. From the second generation on it understates the number of monks living at Trinity, and over time, must fall short of reality in increasing amounts. The reason is that the database is weighted heavily with names of monks who appeared in documentary sources; that is, of administrators. Burial and donation records somewhat redress the balance by providing names of ordinary monks. Nevertheless, the database undercounts the common monks who performed liturgical duties or were cooks, artisans, and common laborers.[10] The undercount also exaggerates the percentage within the brotherhood of Trinity's officers and elders, virtually all of whose names appear in documentary sources, not to mention the percentage of the brotherhood that were from landowning families of Trinity's benefactors. To provide a "truer" profile of Trinity's brotherhood and its social origin, I provide a larger count by supplementing these names with those of monks recorded in the section of the *sinodik* based on the "brothers'" *sinodik* that have in the interstices above them identifiable family names or references to their place of origin, nickname, or trade. My reasoning is that persons so described were Trinity monks known to those who entered their names in the commemoration book. These entries begin only with generation six and peter out in generations ten and eleven, during which entries must be winnowed from a larger number of entries, most of which were not Trinity monks. In my narrative I provide the resulting "expanded" count in parentheses following the more reliable but biased smaller total.

On this basis I have 561–569 (1,269–1,284) monks who were at Trinity between the 1340s and 1605. In Sergius's time there were 21–24; during Nikon's abbacy 32. Regarding Sergius's cohort, Epifanii's life does not say whether the Mitrofan who tonsured Sergius remained as abbot or, as was likely, returned as abbot to the Khot'kov Monastery; secondly, the account of a disciple named Grigorii, who founded the Golutvin Monastery near Kolomna, may have been appended in later editions. I have names of 40 monks in the third generation, 39 or 40 in the fourth, 36 (38) in the fifth, and 50 (147) in the sixth. To the extent that these totals reflect the contours of the monastery's population, one must conclude that the state's policies of restricting donations of land to monasteries hindered Trinity's recruitment of monks down to the late 1490s. The seventh, eighth, and ninth generations were significantly larger, the totals being 80 (229), 86–89 (216–219), and 73 (321–329). The database contains the names of 72–75 (108–112) monks for generation ten and 82–84 (110–115) for generation eleven. Variables in the totals are the result of several factors: names appearing twice but at wide intervals in the database, the inability to connect surnames to family names, and, in names drawn form the *sinodik* alone, the problem of deciding whether monks said to have come from other houses actually lived at Trinity or had simply asked to be commemorated there. If the enhanced totals for generations seven, eight, and nine are indicative of Trinity's growing prosperity, a theme I discuss below, those for the last two generations in part were filled out by impoverished petitioners of all classes, who sought security by tonsure at Trinity. Some brought with them what remained of their fortunes. The large number of monks listed for generation eleven in the "basic" database reflects evidence in Trinity's donation book that monks began making memorial gifts of cash and personal belongings.[11]

S. V. Nikolaeva's discussion of the geographical and social composition of the brotherhood, based on the inventory of 1641, can help us to interpret data for earlier periods.[12] Among the monks listed in the inventory, she counted 74 with surnames, 97 with nicknames or surnames with geographical references, and 59 with nicknames indicating their office or occupational skill. Supplementing each category with other names from Trinity's donation book and in documentary sources, she drew a profile of the geographical origin of Trinity's monks. The largest cohort was from the vicinity of the monastery and the Moscow land. Others came from virtually everywhere Trinity owned property or was influential, "from Kiev in the south to Kargopol' in the north; from Novgorod in the west to Kazan' in the east."[13] From the large number of monks who were described by occupational skill (baker, farmer, icon painter) Nikolaeva concluded that up to 50 percent of the brothers were recruited from peasants of monastic villages or from its urban properties. Another 10 percent, she concluded, were of clerical origin, most from priestly families on its properties. Finally, a "significant number," which I interpret as about 35 percent, were by origin from the class of small and medium landowners or clerical officials that gave Trinity its properties and furnished most of its officers. Nikolaeva found no more than five monks in the inventory, and not many more in other documents, whose families were ranking members of Moscow's ruling elite.

The same methodology provides useful, albeit less definitive, generalizations about the social profile of Trinity's brotherhood, but a much less satisfactory profile of the geographical incidence of Trinity's recruitment generation by generation. In generation one Sergius and his brother Stefan and Stefan's son Ivan, tonsured as Fedor at Trinity, may be counted as coming from Moscow. Three more, living in Rostov, Dubno (in the southern reaches of the principality of Tver'), and Smolensk, got wind of Sergius's reputation for piety and joined him. Others must have been with Sergius for a time but were not so steadfast that Epifanii mentioned them in his life. Sergius, Stefan, and Fedor came from a landowning family. Five of Sergius's disciples were already monks or clerics whose search for Sergius's guidance was the culmination of a spiritual path already undertaken, perhaps in the same manner that Sergius had begun his. Mitrofan, the abbot of a nearby house, ruled Trinity until Sergius accepted that responsibility in 1353; sources also mention Simeon *Ekklisiarkh* (the administrator of a church or monastery), a hermit named Elisei, the deacon Onisim from Rostov, and a Simon who had been the archimandrite of a house in Smolensk. Vasilii *Sukhoi* apparently had been a townsman in Dubno.[14]

For monks of succeeding generations the sources provide few geographic nicknames. However, the surnames of some of the monks indicate they had been landowners, many of whom had owned properties in the vicinity of Trinity, in Pereiaslavl', or in the Moscow land. In the second generation four were "locals": one from Pereiaslavl', three from Moscow, and another from

Iur'ev. The monk Gerontii Likhorev came from Kostroma, where Trinity acquired villages between 1425 and 1432. Gerontii was an early disciple of Abbot Nikon. He came from a landowning family and was the first Trinity monk with the title of *posel'skii* or bailiff, but he did not hold that title in Kostroma.[15] Another monk was from Galich, which, along with Radonezh, was the patrimony of Trinity's patron Prince Iurii Dmitrievich and the site of the first of Trinity's remote holdings, properties that included lucrative salt works. Overall, 5 of the 32 monks categorized in generation two were from landowner families, 2 had been clerics, and 2 had been clerical administrators (*d'iaks*). The monk Efrem, in the secular world Ermolai Vaskin, was the progenitor of the Ermolin family of Moscow merchants. Another Moscow merchant, Ivan Surma, also became a monk. In the 1420s Nikon tonsured as the monk Gennadii a third Muscovite, the boiar Grigorii Ivanovich Buturlin.[16]

The third generation suffered through the Muscovite dynastic struggle between the late 1420s and the early 1450s, as a result of which Grand Prince Vasilii II of Moscow obtained jurisdiction over the monastery from the junior branch of the dynasty that had ruled Radonezh. I have identified 40 monks of this generation, suggesting that Trinity grew in numbers as well as in wealth, as each claimant to the throne sought favor there with land and privileges. Most of the monks were from neighboring districts: four from Radonezh, four from Pereiaslavl', three from Moscow, and one each from Dmitriev and Zvenigorod. The others were from outlying districts: four from Galich, one each from Suzdal' and Kostroma, and another from Beloozero, he being Martinian from the Ferapontov Monastery, whom Vasilii made Trinity's abbot in order to purge Trinity of monks who had supported Dmitrii Shemiaka. In this period the number of monks from the landowning elite rose significantly: Varsunofii (Vasilii Borisovich Kopnin) was a boiar of Radonezh princes, eight were from landowner and three from elite Moscow merchant families (one Surmin and two Ermolins). Martinian was a cleric, but his life, written a century after his death, said he was of peasant stock. In northern Russia peasants were freemen and often persons of means.[17]

Although it had become a famous shrine, the Trinity-Sergius Monastery occupied only a modest land area and had an unassuming physical presence. Nikon was said to have expanded the monastery with various constructions before his death in 1428, but aside from building the masonry Church of the Holy Trinity, what he did is unknown. Two years later a fire destroyed three structures at Trinity, including its refectory. These wooden buildings were replaced by other wooden buildings.[18] Before 1450 the monks probably erected a wooden church next to the Church of the Holy Trinity to house

Nikon's bones. The administrative system at Trinity was simplicity itself. In accord with Orthodox tradition, Sergius selected Nikon from among his brethren to be abbot, and Nikon's successors probably followed the same practice. In that its acts customarily stated that grants of property went to Trinity's abbot and brethren, it is fair to assume that that communality circumscribed the choice and the authority of the abbot except in matters where canon or custom assured him power over the lives of his brethren.[19] The elevation of an abbot at Trinity presumably had to have had the approval of the metropolitan and the temporal ruler of Radonezh, although there is no evidence about either. Sergius appointed the monk Il'ia (d. 1384) as his cellarer, an office that by midcentury was responsible for the house's business and judicial affairs. Nikon appointed as cellarer one Savva Arbuzov Chernikov as early as 1410. He held that office until Nikon's death, then became abbot (1428–32), no doubt on Nikon's initiative. Savva probably selected Zinovii (1432–45) as abbot in the same manner. In the dynastic civil war rivals for the title of grand prince found it hazardous to respect Trinity's autonomy. Zinovii's successor, Abbot Gennadii Samatov (1445–46), appointed when Vasilii II held the throne, and Dosifei Zvenigorodskii (1446–47), who replaced Gennadii when Dmitrii Shemiaka ousted Vasilii from power, enjoyed short tenures. Of course, after defeating Shemiaka, Grand Prince Vasilii II installed the northerner Martinian of Ferapontov (1547–55) as Trinity's abbot. Never again would Trinity's brotherhood have free rein to choose its abbot.

Nikon's successors as abbot probably also appointed their cellarers. An Afanasii served under Savva, and an Il'ia and an Ignatii served under Zinovii. Nikon's disciple Avraamii, the former Radonezh landowner Aleksei Voronin, was cellarer from 1445 to 1447. The monk Illarion served Martinian in that office and in the database for the first time some monks were known as elders (*startsy*). The title connoted respect due a senior monk. In a growing brotherhood a tonsuree might be under a double vow of obedience, one to the abbot, another to a charismatic elder-mentor. The title did not as yet pertain to membership in an elite governing body.[20] To 1447 Trinity evidently did not have a treasurer and the records mention only two bailiffs other than Gerontii Likhorev. One Aron served as such in Radonezh in the 1440s and a Neron was bailiff in Dmitrov from about 1450. Monks Aleksandr Rusin and Vassian appear as *zakazshchiki*, fiscal officers with judicial power over Trinity's people or property. Several monks were called or acted as scribes.[21] Nothing suggests other than that monks aspired to live in the image of angels as portrayed in Kievan and Byzantine monastic tradition. The ceremony of tonsure entailed, as Ludwig Steindorff has described it, a "social death" that resembled a wake. There survives no better description of it than Epifanii's account of Sergius's tonsure.[22] With tonsure the aspirant renounced participation in the property relations, politics, and family affairs of the secular world; the fledgling monk became an orphan (*sirota*) beholden to his abbot and, ultimately, to God. This had a physical component. For the pioneers it meant a life as a small collective of solitaries; for those who followed it meant a life of poverty, obedience, and sexual abstinence according to a simple regimen in a communal social order behind monastic walls.

In the third generation for the first time there was a noticeable increase in the relative number of Trinity's monks who were from the landholding elite. The change reflected Trinity's success in accumulating properties, whether in the form of commemoration grants or by purchase. The Voronin family from Pereiaslavl' mentioned in the previous chapter was only the first of landowner families that, in addition to grants, gave Trinity a son. He was Aleksei Bobosha, the monk Avraamii and one of Trinity's earliest cellarers. The only monk from a Moscow boiar family was Gennadii Buturlin. The Ermolins and Surmins, elite Moscow merchant families, sent two generations of monks to Trinity. Finally, the text of a miracle that Kloss dated to the years 1447–48 suggests that a larger component of monks from wealthy families in the third generation began to shake the egalitarian order that Sergius had established. Some time after his tonsure, it related, Dionisii Ermolin weakened in his vows; he left his cell improperly, broke the vow of silence, and criticized the rule Sergius had instituted, particularly its strictures against accepting alms or feasts provided by magnates and other laymen. By this account Martinian's attempt to reconcile Dionisii with Trinity's rule succeeded only when the monk underwent a miraculous transformation while at prayer before Sergius's tomb.[23]

* The three generations of monks who lived at Trinity between the mid-1450s and 1515 saw the monastery transformed. By 1515, the monastery had become sumptuous in appearance and ceremonial; its brotherhood manifested hierarchical social divisions not unlike those outside its walls and developed institutions of governance that reflected these changes.

One can define quantitatively the emergence of an elite cohort of monks from landowning families during these generations. In the fourth generation three of Trinity's monks were from Moscow boiar families, two Pleshcheevs (Mikhail Borisovich/Misail and Ivan Mikhailovich/Iona) and a Morozov (Petr Ignat'evich). A fourth, Semen/Sergii Andreevich Shumorovskii, was a descendent of Iaroslavl' princes. One monk was from Moscow's administrative elite (*d'iachestvo*); 10 others were from untitled landowning families. The fifth generation of Trinity's monks included two descendents of Muscovite boiar families, including another Pleshcheev (Veniamin), and two from families of the administrative elite: Isaia/Ivan Kurtsev and Feognost'/Fedor Kasha Dubenskii. Six were from hereditary landowning families. In the sixth there were three or four boiars or princes, including Ivan Iur'evich Patrikeev, whom Ivan III forcibly tonsured, possibly one *d'iak*, and 17–19 (17–21 adding names only in the *sinodik*) monks from landowning families. A cohort of monks from aristocratic background had emerged in a brotherhood, the size of which had grown little until sometime in the sixth generation. Trinity was not yet a large house.[24] Trinity's *sinodik* mentions at least 11 artisans who apparently were monks from the 1480s to 1515. Among them were a coppersmith, a carpenter, two sleigh makers, two turners, two cobblers, a fabricator of pectoral crosses of wood or bone, and a maker of ladles *(kovshechnik)*. It is the only source to mention artisan monks even though Trinity had become a center for the production of icons, manuscripts, and religious articles.[25] Remembering that these generations lived at a time when Ivan III and, initially, Vasilii III constrained immunities for monastic houses and placed obstacles in the way of their acquisition of property, Trinity's means to recruit and house more brothers probably was limited.

Most of those whose origins we can identify came from familiar recruiting grounds near the monastery: Moscow provided five in the fourth generation, four in the fifth and, after having swallowed up Radonezh, five (nine if we count those listed only in the *sinodik*) in the sixth. The totals for Pereiaslavl' were one, two, and four (or five), respectively, in the fourth, fifth, and sixth generations. Two monks in the fourth generation and six (or seven) in the sixth were from Dmitrov and four monks were from Galich and Uglich, where Trinity was well established. Eight to ten, however, came from areas where Sergius's cult had taken root more recently: one each from Murom and Iaroslavl' in the fourth; one each from Kostroma and Novgorod in the fifth; and in the sixth generation one each from Suzdal', Vladimir, and Bezhetskii Verkh, and perhaps one each from Kostroma and Tver'. About 80 percent of monks whose origins are known came from areas close by Trinity.

The differentiation in social background of Trinity's monks manifested itself in the way they lived, in how Trinity was ruled, and in how Trinity's properties were managed. For one thing the growing presence of monks who came from well-born or wealthy families and the growing communal wealth of the monastery undermined the rule Trinity's founder had established. No one event triggered the transformation but it is generally held that Vassian Rylo (1455–66) was the last abbot to maintain a strict communal rule. That it was no longer so was apparent when his successor Spiridon received a letter dated 21 May 1472 in which Metropolitan Filipp asked the brotherhood to forgive the transgression, whatever it was, of the Trinity elder Pamba.[26] Filipp added that, "regarding the possessions or horses taken from him, you my sons should respect my wishes [and] give back to him all that is his." To put it in context, Filipp admitted that the monastery "invited persons [into the brotherhood] according to their property" (*priglashati vsia po imeni*), according to Holy Scripture. Based on the context of the letter, it is likely that Pamba left Trinity as a result of some transgression. Although unsaid, Filipp wrote as if Pamba had enjoyed the use of his possessions (and income from estates?), something ostensibly prohibited by Trinity's cenobitic rule, and that by right he could take them with him when he left. Pamba probably came from a rich and well-connected family, one that could appeal his fate to the Muscovite court and cause the metropolitan "by the will of my son Grand Prince Ivan Vasil'evich" to request that Spiridon forgive the errant elder and return his property. It would seem that monks from wealthy families had become exempt from the "social death" that marked the transition of layman to monk. Pierre Gonneau argued persuasively that Pamba's claim to property he had given Trinity followed logically from a practice by which a benefactor-monk retained possession of his property until death, allowing his house periodic incomes from it, but full ownership only after his death. This compromise with the cenobite principal, he noted, had precedence and is attested in a contemporary deposition by monks and abbot of Trinity's subsidiary house, the Trinity Monastery in Berezniki (south of Radonezh), made before a judicial officer (*tiun*) of the metropolitan.[27] At the subsidiary, as at the great house, such arrangements created tension, the sources of which were not only in who controlled a monastery's resources, but in the relative social standing of monks within the brotherhood.

Although the number of monks remained relatively stable, by 1515 they lived in an expanded physical environment that exhibited unmistakable signs of opulence in its buildings and their decoration, attributes that impressed fifteenth-century pilgrims.[28] V. D. Ermolin, of the merchant family that provided Trinity with three monks, built a large masonry refectory to replace the wooden one opposite the Trinity church. He finished it in 1469 and it stood until the mid-eighteenth century, when it was taken down to make room for the bell tower that stands there today. The refectory had two stories, the first a dining hall, the second a great hall where the monks could host feasts for the grand prince and important personages. The seventeenth-century visitor Paul of Aleppo, who visited Trinity before the refectory was demolished, wrote that these spaces were built around a single large load-bearing column at their center. Paul marveled that, "there is nothing like this monastery not only in the Muscovite country, but in all the world." The Italian builders Marco Ruffo and Pietro Antonio Solari probably took the refectory as their model in building the great hall of the Palace of Facets in the Moscow kremlin two decades later. Subsequently builders built a one-columned hall for the refectory of the Solovetskii Monastery. There is iconographic evidence that Ermolin also built a masonry kitchen adjacent to the refectory and that a bell tower, possibly partly of stone or brick, was built at the center of the monastery (Frontispiece, nos. 3–4).[29] In 1486 Pskov masters, who later built the Church of the Dormition in the Moscow kremlin, constructed Trinity's second masonry church, a brick structure on the site of the original wooden Church of the Holy Trinity. Like Pskov churches, it had a single barrel-shaped tower that served as a belfry and was capped by a cupola. Known now as the Church of the Procession of the Holy Spirit, it was initially consecrated as the Church of the Holy Trinity.[30] Monastic cells, scattered about the central premises and along the walls, were of wood well into the sixteenth century.

Trinity also became a repository of decorated textiles, icons, crosses, manuscripts, and other religious articles. Most of the items in its inventory were the result of gifts. Among them was the ideologically "loaded" icon cloth that Grand Princess Sophia donated to herald Sergius's intercessory powers on behalf of her son Vasilii's birthright as grand prince. In the 1490s either the famous painter Dionisii or one of his apprentices executed a large icon of Sergius for the "local" row of the Church of the Trinity. Surrounding its portrait of Sergius were scenes from his life, including that of the apparition to him of the Mother of God.[31] From the 1450s Trinity's monks produced a variety of such items.[32] Among them were the chancel crosses of walnut, the first in the 1450s, the second late in the century, on which, among scenes from the New Testament, was one depicting the apparition to Sergius of the Mother of God, executed by the monk Amvrosii.[33] These works exhibited a new iconography and were attributes of an elaborate system of religious rituals at Trinity, not the least of which were feasts and prayer rituals for commemorating the dead.

The names recorded for each generation include virtually a complete roster of Trinity's governing and administrative elite. Between the mid-1450s and 1515, 38 percent of this elite were from landowning families, some of them of great wealth or prominence. Of 12 cellarers in generations four through six at least three—Veniamin Pleshcheev (1483/84–88), Varlaam Barakov (1490–91), and Vassian Kovezin (1495–1507)—and possibly two more—Login (1456–62) and Makarii Lipiatin (1454 or 1455)—came from families of landowner-patrons.[34] Beginning at midcentury Trinity's documents mention a treasurer (*kaznachei*), the first being Sergii, formerly Prince Semen Shumorovskii. For reasons implicit in the title, it became the third most important office after the abbot and the cellarer. After Sergii five monks held that rank to 1515; four of these were at other times cellarers; two became abbots. Makarii Lipiatin, who very likely was from a landowning family, held all three offices between 1454 and 1488; Pamba Moshnin, from a Dmitrov landowning family, was abbot in 1506, treasurer in 1506–7, and abbot again from 1508–15. In addition the database mentions a large roster of elders: 19 in the fourth generation, 21 in the fifth, and 13 in the sixth.

Most of the monastery's high officers were elders before assuming office; a few were elders after they retired. In this period the title of elder, in addition to its other connotations, came to designate members of a ruling body, one in which monks from elite families, whose loyalty to the house had become the bedrock of Trinity's existence, had a disproportionate presence. A reference to such a body refers to it acting with Abbot Martinian (1547–55) to receive a donation. Its provenance is suspect, but a charter issued between 1456 and 1462 clearly shows that by then elders were members of an administrative council acting with the abbot in economic matters. The charter recorded an exchange of land in Radonezh between Abbot Vassian Rylo for Trinity and Grand Prince Vasilii II, and concluded with the statement that it was executed in the presence of Vasilii's boiars and "the elders of Trinity—Cellarer Login, Pamba, Makarii Shchuka and Vissarion."[35] By 1500 many charters testify to the existence of a council of elders. One, for example, recorded an exchange of land carried out "with the blessing of our lord [and] father, the abbot of the Trinity-Sergiev Monastery Serapion (1496/97–1506) and cellarer Vas'ian [Kovezin] and the *entire holy council* [italics mine]." Other charters registered a list of elders who signed off on agreements.[36] At least 20 elders, or 38 percent of Trinity's leadership cadre, were from landowning families, although only Veniamin Pleshcheev was from a boiar family. Most, if not all, were Trinity's patrons. This being the case, it is unlikely that the abbot could arbitrarily define its membership. Henceforth, Trinity's cellarers and treasurers came from the council. In other words, it is likely that no abbot might act in economic affairs without its consent. For this reason it was an institution adept in fending off external intervention in Trinity's affairs. There is no way of telling how many elders were members of the council at one time. Throughout the sixteenth century the number of council elders (*sobornye startsy*) mentioned in Trinity's documents varied. The most, 18, were parties to an extraordinary decree of 1584 in which the council defined the authority of Trinity's superior. Iosif Volotskii's rule for his monastery set the number as ten; the council of the Solovetskii Monastery had 12 to 14 members.[37]

By 1515 Trinity's officers managed a bureaucracy-in-the-making.[38] The abbot's immediate subordinate was the cellarer. He was Trinity's business manager and, during interregnums, the acting abbot. The treasurer, next in the hierarchy, managed Trinity's funds and archives, and looked after the well-being of its monks. The lower administrative hierarchy of bailiffs and fiscal officers grew significantly during generations four through six. Laymen and monks filled these offices. In generation five there were at least six clerical bailiffs, one of whom, Feognost' Kasha Dubenskii, also was one of three fiscal officers. He held the latter position in Moscow. Before becoming a monk he had been the *d'iak* Fedor, serving Dmitrii Shemiaka, Vasilii II, and Ivan III from the 1440s to 1476. In the sixth I can identify six monk-bailiffs and a monk-fiscal officer. One of the former, Andronik Belin, held the title of "head [*bol'shoi*] bailiff," testifying to the layering that occurred in Trinity's bureaucratic ranks.[39]

Ten abbots presided over Trinity in generations four through six. But by 1447, when Vasilii II named Martinian as abbot-designate, the brotherhood obviously no longer had a free hand in the matter. Vasilii and his successors exercised oversight on Trinity's choices and occasionally imposed outsiders. When an abbot failed to choose his successor or the ruler's will was not unbending, the brotherhood made the choice by consensus, although by 1500 senior monks—the elders—acted for the brotherhood. There developed a tension as Moscow's princes, Trinity's abbots, or council of elders sought to determine major decisions and appointments and to exercise disciplinary power. The rivalry rarely became public, but when it did, it was over the grand prince's attempts to name and guide abbots.

At least four abbots, Vassian Rylo (1455–66), Spiridon (1467–74), Avraamii (1474–78), and Paisii (1478–82) were tonsured elsewhere and the first two were well regarded in Moscow before their appointment. Vassian, a disciple of St. Pafnutii of Borovsk and esteemed by Metropolitan Iona, was abbot before Ivan III came to power. He was a strong executive and subsequently became archbishop of Rostov and influential at the Muscovite court.[40] Paisii's appointment is a case apart. Like Martinian, he was from a northern house located on an island in Kubenskoe Lake near the Kirillo-Belozerskii Monastery. He mentored Nil Sorskii (ca. 1433–1508), the famed founder of a northern hermitage and proponent of a simple life, pious scholarship, and hesychast prayer, in the ways of an austere monastic existence. Ivan III, fresh from his conquest of Novgorod and the confiscation of its church lands, and concerned that monasteries in the core of his realm had become too wealthy and independent, asked Paisii to succeed the ailing Metropolitan Gerontii. Paisii said he would rather be abbot of Trinity "to restore the monks to God's path of prayer, fasting and chastity." Ivan concurred. Trinity's brotherhood, led by well-born elders, appreciated the significance of Paisii's appointment. To explain his departure from Trinity late in 1481, Paisii told Ivan that instead of accepting the monastic ideal he sought to establish, "[Trinity's brothers], not wanting to obey him, there being boiars and princes tonsured there, wanted to kill him, so that he abandoned his abbacy."[41]

Four of the five abbots who succeeded Paisii came from Moscow, but three originally were Trinity monks, suggesting that their selections were compromises between the court and Trinity's brotherhood. Simon Chizh, who presided from 1490 to 1495, was tonsured at Trinity in the 1480s, after which Ivan's councilor Ivan Patrikeev made use of his skills as a writer in Moscow. Simon was a talented executive and no one's subordinate. He also was a strong abbot and popular at Trinity. Writing to his successor Serapion, Simon appears as an upholder of monkish decorum who admonished Trinity's brothers for fornication, deplored strife among them, and exhorted them to seek unity and "spiritual love."[42] In 1495, after some hesitation, Ivan made him metropolitan. Indicative of the new order at Trinity was the grand procession Simon made to Moscow to be installed as metropolitan on 8 September 1495. Abbot Simon arrived in Moscow, like the magnate he was, accompanied by cellarer Vassian Kovezin, elders Savva, Veniamin Pleshcheev, Filipp Iznosok, and Feognost' Dubenskii, and Trinity's boiars and minor servitors. On 18 December 1498 his successor Serapion (1495–1505), his cellarer Vassian Kovezin, and elders Veniamin Pleshcheev, Savva, and Elisei lead an equally impressive procession to Moscow for the coronation of Ivan III's grandson Dmitrii.[43] Serapion was a Muscovite and former abbot of the Dormition-Stronym Monastery that Sergius had founded. As Trinity's abbot, Serapion could hardly have endeared himself to the grand prince when he succored Ivan Iur'evich Patrikeev after Ivan III dismissed and forcibly tonsured him in January 1499.[44] Three texts, two polemical and one hagiographical, written decades after the event, made Simon and Serapion leaders in defending monastic properties from confiscation by Ivan III and a church council convened in 1503. The Other Sermon (*slovo inoe*) and the life of Serapion portrayed him as the hero at the council of 1503 in opposing Ivan. The Other Sermon said Serapion protested when Ivan's judges decided for tax-paying peasants in a dispute with Trinity over property in the district of Ilemna in Vereia, fined the monastery, and had its monk Konon whipped. It also said that in late 1503 Ivan sought to inventory Trinity's charters and, when Serapion objected, ordered Trinity's officers to court. The third source, known as the Council's Response (*sobornyi otvet*), said Metropolitan Simon led the church in 1503 in opposition to Ivan.[45]

The first of seven abbots when Vasilii III was grand prince was Pamba Moshnin. His tenure marked the ascendancy of well-born brothers at Trinity. At least three generations of Moshnins had connections to Trinity before, during, or after Pamba's tenure.[46] They appeared in 1478 as witnesses to charters in Trinity's copybooks in Radonezh, Pereiaslavl', and Dmitrov, where they were small landowners. An Esip Moshnin was Trinity's bailiff in Maloiaroslavets in 1496–98; a Fedor Ivanovich Moshnin was witness to a donation to Trinity in Bezhetskii Verkh, then the monastery's bailiff in Nakhabino in the Moscow land between 1508 and 1518/19; Serko Vasil'evich Moshnin, a son of an early witness in Trinity's acts, was a monastic official in Novyi Torg and witness to Trinity's acts in Dmitrov and Moscow, and his brother Iusup sold his estate in Dmitrov to Trinity (1509–23/24). Brothers Ivan and Fedor, sons of early witness Grigor Moshnin, appeared as witnesses in Trinity's charter between 1518/19 and 1526/27. Serko's son Iakov sold an estate in Radonezh to Trinity in 1543; a Nikita Moshnin was a Trinity servant in 1532; a Savva Moshnin was a Trinity elder in 1548; and an Ivan Moshnin was a monk and head undercellarer (*bol'shoi podkelarnik*) there in 1571. Pamba Moshnin was abbot for one year in 1506, served as treasurer in 1506–7, and was abbot again from 1508 to 1515. He first appeared in charters as the lay bailiff Pavel (or Palka) Moshnin, who supervised Trinity's affairs between 1497 and 1500 in Priseki, Trinity's outpost in Bezhetskii Verkh.[47] Pamba's elevation as abbot was something of a precedent in that at least 6 of 13 successors down to 1554 were Trinity monks and at least 3 were from families that had been Trinity's patrons. His successor Iakov (1515–20) was a disciple of former abbot Serapion (whom Vasilii III allowed to retire to Trinity in 1511, having convened a synod to remove him as archbishop of Novgorod for refusing to relinquish spiritual jurisdiction over Iosif Volotskii's monastery). Porfirii (1521–24) came from a hermitage near Beloozero. Gonneau thought Vasilii appointed him to assert control over Trinity. Perhaps, but Vasilii subsequently acquiesced in the election as abbot of Trinity monks Arsenii Sakharusov (1525–27) and Ioasaf Skripitsyn (1529–39). Ioasaf, like Pamba, was from a local landowning family with a record of generosity to Trinity.[48]

Trinity's brotherhood grew in numbers to 80 (229) monks in the seventh generation (1516–33), 86–94 (210–219) in the eighth (1534–53), and 69 (321–329) in the ninth (1554–70). Trinity's physical space, measured by the stone walls built to encircle it from the 1540s, the construction of more wooden dormitories, a stone palace for the cellarer that included a stone hospital and the rapid rebuilding of Trinity after the fire of 1564, were commensurate.[49] These and the change in composition and structure of Trinity's brotherhood in the sixteenth century reflected its emergence as a spiritual and economic mega-institution.

We have a good sample—32–38 (80–94, including names in the *sinodik*) in the seventh generation, 50-63 (69–75) in the eighth, and 40-43 (134–160) in the ninth—from which to make judgments about the geographical origin of Trinity monks. In the seventh generation 21–26 (69–83) monks were from Moscow, Radonezh, Pereiaslavl', and Dmitrov; in the eighth 31–41 (41–57); and in the ninth 27–29 (95–108). Four of Trinity's abbots/archimandrites, 6 of its cellarers, 8 of its treasurers, and 21 elders were from this core area. In other words, most of Trinity's officers were local people. We have considerably more names of monks, 43–48 (50–55), from outlying areas than previously. Based on totals of firmly identifiable monks, they constituted 22–30 percent of the brotherhood and came from more areas than ever before, the largest total, 10 (19–21) from Bezhetskii Verkh. There were also monks from Rostov, Kostroma, Uglich, Suzdal', Iaroslavl', Beloozero, Tver', Kashin, Pskov, Sol'-Vychegodsk (from the Stroganov merchant family), Riazan', Obolenskoe, Vladimir, and Volok. If we add names from the *sinodik*, Trinity had monks from Galich, Kolomna, Viatka, Sviiazhsk, Tarusa, and Nizhnii Novgorod; also three monks said to be Greek and two from Mt. Athos and one from Mt. Sinai. Trinity had become an international community. But monks from peripheral parts of Russia furnished a smaller and declining proportion of Trinity's officers. There were from one to three elders in the seventh generation, six in the eighth, and four in the ninth; one became cellarer in the seventh generation, one in the eighth, and none at all in the ninth. In each generation there was a single treasurer from outlying areas. The preponderance of Trinity's officers who came from the core area around the monastery is even more striking in that Aleksei Pil'emov, from a landowning family in Rostov with a longstanding relationship with Trinity, between 1515/16 and 1520 being in succession an elder, treasurer, and cellarer, accounted for the one confirmed elder and both officers from peripheral areas in the seventh generation.[50]

I can draw a rough social profile of Trinity's brotherhood and an accurate social profile of its administrative elite during these generations. The data are unambiguous. At least 34 (39–47) monks in generation seven, 42.5–46 percent (17–21.5 percent), were from families of hereditary landowners or of the Muscovite service elite. In generation eight 55–59 (62–73), 58.5–70 percent (28–35 percent), were from these categories. In the ninth 34–38 (66–83), 49–55 percent (20–26 percent) were from this elite. Overall 42–48.5 percent (19–27 percent) of monks in the database for these generations were from landowner-service elite families. This represents an increase over the

36–38 percent (19.5–23 percent) of Trinity's monks of similar origin in generations four through six, the 24 percent in the transitional generation three, and the 14 percent in Trinity's first two generations of monks. The proportion of monks from elite families who were Trinity's officers (elders, treasurers, cellarers) between 1515 and 1570 was even greater.[51] In the seventh generation from 13–16, 59–73 percent of Trinity's 22 elders, were from families of the landowning-service elite; in the eighth 16 of 23 officers, 71 percent; and in generation nine 12 of 17 office holders, or 71 percent, were from elite families. Overall, for those three generations monks of the landowning-service elite comprised 66–68 percent of Trinity's officers, a significant increase over the 38 percent of Trinity's officers from elite families in generations four through six, the 23 percent for generation three, and the 20 percent for the two earliest generations. It is not overstating it to say that the Trinity-Sergius Monastery had become a haven for the well-to-do, and that they were even more dominant in its leadership than its rank and file. Correlating these statistics with previous observations about the geographical origin of Trinity's monks and leadership it is clear that Trinity became the domain of an elite that increasingly was Moscow-centered.

In generation seven only two or three monks came from princely families and families that produced boiar, or *okol'nichii* servicemen, one more if we count offspring of distinguished or wealthy families not then enjoying high service rank. There were five of such monks in the eighth generation and six or seven in the ninth generation. Pafnutii Pisemskii was an elder in the 1530s, Vassian Korovin was an elder between 1528 and 1546/47, Iona Pisemskii was elder then treasurer between 1542 and 1552/53, Iona Zabolotskii was an elder (1547/48–48/49) and Serapion Vorontsov and Iona (Prince Ivan Andreevich) Bulgakov were elders at Trinity in 1566–67.[52] The totals are small and their modest growth hardly reflected a growing influence at Trinity of the Muscovite state—some were there after being disgraced at court—or as the result of a new fashion of elite retirement, perhaps induced by the *oprichnina*. Yet Trinity was never without "friends" in Moscow. In addition to its court and church within the kremlin, Trinity maintained influential familial connections there. The most important of these were Trinity monks of the Kurtsev family, the genealogy and relationship to Trinity of which Stepan Veselovskii has delineated. Afanasiii Funik Kurtsev was an important state secretary in the 1530s and 1540s, and a patron of Trinity. His second of five sons, Nikita, was also a state secretary, then keeper of the seal (*pechatnik*) from the 1540s to his fall from power in 1570 in the *oprichnina* purge that brought down the tsar's cousin Prince Vladimir Andreevich Staritskii. He made several memorial donations to Trinity and was clerk and witness in charters involving Trinity, one being a purchase agreement by which Trinity obtained a village in Pereiaslavl' from Boiar Ivan Semenovich Vorontsov, and sold Trinity large villages in the Moscow and Vladimir lands shortly before Ivan IV executed him. Afanasii's third son, Konstantin, gave Trinity three memorial donations between 1543 and 1551 and, after serving as state secretary, became the monk Kornilii at Trinity and died there in 1561. Afanasii's fifth son, Daniil, became the Trinity monk Dorofei. Dorofei from 1558 was part of Trinity's governing elite, first as an elder, then treasurer in 1559/60 and cellarer from 1562/63 to 1566/67. Ivan had him killed along with his brother in 1570. There are other Kurtsevs in Trinity's records, whose ancestry cannot be established. Iov Kurtsev was monk from 1515/16, then elder, treasurer, and finally cellarer in 1523/24–28. He was among the monks who participated in the baptism of Ivan IV in 1530 at Trinity, and he died in 1539. Ivan Kushnik Petrovich Kurtsev was an important state secretary for over 30 years, from the late 1530s, and a generous benefactor of the Trinity Monastery. Before his death in 1571/72 he was tonsured there as the monk Iov. His brother took his vows at Trinity as Serapion and had a distinguished career as elder, treasurer (1530–32), cellarer (1533–39), abbot (1549–51), and later as archbishop of Novgorod and Pskov. The Trinity monk Ignatii Kurchev, who denounced former abbot Artemii as a heretic at the council of 1553, was probably a Kurtsev.[53]

Monks from landowning families, mentioned in Trinity's records of the last third of the fifteenth century, became ubiquitous in the sixteenth. Charters and Trinity's donation book record that in 1534/35 Ignatii and Iakov Semenovichi Golovkin executed the testament of their uncle, the Trinity monk Andreian, giving Trinity his half of Iazvishch village in Bezhetskii Verkh to commemorate his soul and those of his ancestors.[54] It was commonplace for monks at great houses to have personal property and money at their disposal that could be more than petty cash. Trinity's monks were no exception. Iov Kurtsev in 1538 on his death bed gave Trinity 50 rubles and a pall displaying Sergius's image. In 1540 the Trinity elder Ilinarkh Durov gave Trinity 45 rubles. In 1566 Elder Evstafii (Golovkin) executed the testament of Trinity's cellarer Dorofei Kurtsev, distributing his property, and Ilinarkh purchased for the Trinity-Sergius Monastery two villages in Bezhetskii Verkh to provide a commemorative feast for Dorofei, Iov Kurtsev, and other Kurtsev kin.[55] Subsequently, Evstafii made substantial memorial grants to Trinity. Five monks, priests, or deacons at Trinity of generation seven, 15 of generation eight, and 9 of generation nine made donations. Most of them were at the 50-ruble level. An elder Serapion from the Storozhevskii Monastery in generation nine made a donation of 50 rubles and another

100 so that he might have a "peaceful cell" (*keleinogo pokoia*) at Trinity.[56] Cellarer Andreian Angelov in the 1550s or 1560s gave Trinity a variety of manuscripts, one of them, dating from the end of the fifteenth century, a book of works attributed to John of Damascus.[57]

The gentrification of Trinity and the enjoyment of private wealth by its monks went hand in hand with the hardening of its institutional arrangements. Trinity's council of elders, now dominated by monks of the landowner-service elite, was party to decisions that shaped the monastery's existence. By the 1540s it was commonplace that the names of elders, the treasurer, and the cellarer who were council members appeared with that of the abbot in documents. Thus, not only Abbot Iona [Shchelepin] but Cellarer Panteleiman; Treasurer Merkurii; Butler (*chashnik*) Trifon; and Elders Simon Shubin; Gavrilo Bashmakov, Iona Zabolotskii, Arefa Koriakin, Varlaam Kashin, Dorofei Sechenoi, and Marko Shchelepin were parties to the agreement about the exchange of properties in Dmitrov with one Bogdan Vasil'evich Zabolotskii.[58] Frequently charters listed only two or three elders in addition to Trinity's abbot and officers, leading one to wonder whether Trinity's council of elders varied in size or whether it was customary that only those of its members concerned with the transaction signed off on it.[59] Or both. Often charters simply mentioned Trinity's officers, followed by a reference to the accord of its council of elders. Or, as a document dated 31 October 1555 had it, "The directive [*prigovor*] of the Council of the Trinity-Sergius monastery, Abbot Ioasaf, with Cellarer Andreian [Angelov] and with the council of elders, . . . orders" its officials not to allow sorcerers, minstrels, female fortune-tellers, thieves, or troublemakers on its properties around Priseki in Bezhetskii Verkh.[60] Documents recording participants in Trinity's administration indicate that abbots chose cellarers and treasurers solely from the ranks of council elders. Iov Kurtsev's career path from monk to elder, treasurer, and cellarer between 1515/16 and 1539, or Vassian Korovin's between 1528 and 1546/47 from monk to elder and in 1529/30 to cellarer, were typical.[61]

The butler (*chashnik*) was a new post in Trinity's hierarchy of administrative offices. Iona Shchelepin first held the title before becoming cellarer in 1538. Trifon was the second. The butler controlled Trinity's wine cellar, itself a sign of affluence. Another officer, the steward (*kliuchnik*) who controlled access to the monastery's food stores, is attested beginning in 1531 in the person of Mitka Kostkin. About this time the office of librarian came into being. The first monk to hold this post was a Kipriian who died in 1540.[62] The council of elders itself took on a hierarchical structure. By 1553 one of its members, Trifon, very possibly the monk who was Trinity's butler in

1547/48 and a member of the Karpov family of *okol'nichii* at the Muscovite court, held the title of Head Elder (*bol'shoi starets*).[63]

During these three generations Trinity had 20 abbots, until January 1561 when Ivan IV "with the advice of Metropolitan Makarii" raised Abbot Eleuferii to the rank of archimandrite in rank "highest of all archimandrites in the Russian state."[64] Nine or ten abbots or archimandrites had been monks at Trinity; only four can be identified as outsiders: Porfirii I (1521–24), Artemii (1551), and Ilarion (1554–55) were from northern houses and hermitages. Porfirii I and Ilarion were from Beloozero, and Artemii came from Pskov by way of a northern hermitage. Abbot Nikandr (1543–45) was from Iaroslavl' but had been tonsured at Trinity.[65] Ivan IV, we know, imposed Artemii on Trinity against the will of its elders, and within three months Trinity's elders drove him out. It is difficult to believe that any of Trinity's abbots/archimandrites wielded significant power over the brotherhood or could rule without the support of the council of elders, if only because, with but one exception, their terms of office were short. Abbot Ioasaf Skripitsyn, the exception, was a descendent of a landowning family in the Verkhduben district of Pereiaslavl' close by Trinity that had longstanding ties to the monastery; he rose through the ranks to become abbot for almost 11 years (1529–39), then metropolitan for 3. Abbots Iona Shchelepin (1547–49) and Serapion Kurtsev (1549–51) had similar career paths: they were from families of landowner-benefactors and had previously occupied the post of cellarer. Serapion's kinsman Iov was Ivan IV's godfather. The Shchelepins were small landowners in Dmitrov and patrons of Trinity; a Shchelepin, Andreian, had been a Trinity monk in 1470.[66]

In contrast to the short tenures of Trinity's abbots, the council of elders possessed continuity as an institution and a membership that had longevity as wielders of power: to name a few, Iov Kurtsev's tenure at Trinity is attested from 1515/16 to 1539, mostly as an elder or officer; Elder Iona Beleutov was at Trinity from 1517 to 1545; Elder Sil'vestr Upolovnikov was a Trinity monk from no later than 1525/26 to 1544/45, and Gavrilo Bashmakov from 1531 to 1555. Vassian Korovin was an elder or officer from 1528 to 1546/47, Arefa Tormosov from 1538/9 to 1567, and Dorofei Sechenoi from 1548/49 to 1572.

Monks of these generations, led by elders and officers from well-to-do families who themselves possessed or managed private fortunes, with the patronage of the court, transformed the internal life of the Trinity-Sergius Monastery, making it into a ceremonial center of the Muscovite elite. Feast days of the liturgical calendar were important events, particularly those of 5 July, celebrating the opening of St. Sergius's relics, and 25 September, the date of Sergius's death. Moscow's grand princes or tsars and their spouses made pilgrimages to Trinity to pray for an heir, for baptisms, or for commemoration of kin, and to give thanks for Sergius's intercessions on their behalf. They came with an entourage of courtiers by a route from Moscow served by way stations. Arriving, they passed through the great gate dedicated in 1512 by Vasilii III, atop which was a church dedicated to Sergius adjoined by a chapel to Vasilii's patron Saint Basil of Parius. They worshipped at Sergius's tomb in the Church of the Holy Trinity, and did homage to St. Nikon in the church, perhaps now of stone, that abutted the Trinity church. Often they stayed for a week or more, living in the ruler's residence at Trinity. Built in the sixteenth century on the north side of the square that was Trinity's center, it was a large wooden structure, containing the ruler's "cell" and quarters for his entourage. Thus, on 21 June 1547, "on Thursday of the fourth week of Peter's fast, the tsar and grand prince of all Russia Ivan Vasil'evich with much zeal and great faith went on foot to the life-giving Trinity-Sergius monastery with his tsaritsa and grand prince Anastasiia and his brother prince Iur'ii Vasil'evich to pray. At the [church] of the life-giving Trinity [he] attended the vespers and matins, the prayers of thanksgiving and the divine liturgy, and generously bestowed alms upon the abbot and brothers and feasted them, and returned to Moscow on Thursday, the 28th day of that same month."[67] In 1559, with funds from the Muscovite court, construction began on the largest ceremonial site of all, the Basilica of the Dormition of the Mother of God situated in the central square of the monastery. Trinity's "stable" of scribes, icon painters, and artisans skilled in the plastic arts grew accordingly[68] These grand events involved the entire monastic community.

Year in and year out magnates and their kin also visited Trinity for commemorative prayers and feasts. Since the monastery's founding its monks annually added commemorative feasts to its calendar. There were 41 or 42 by the end of 1547. On these occasions the kin of those memorialized, most of them rich, descended on Trinity to feast with its monks. The presence of so many laity and their behavior, as noted, caused Ivan IV disquiet, although he was the richest and most frequent of visitors. One of his first questions to the Stoglav council concerned frequent comings and goings of laity to great houses where superiors allowed benefactors free rein to move about and where monks entertained relatives, even women and children, in their cells, and desecrated their calling by immoderate drinking. Ivan blamed it on the culture of commemoration, or at least the propensity of magnates to become monks and to hold their family celebrations in the great houses. The council singled out the Trinity-Sergius Monastery, where "guests ceaselessly day and night" disregarded the monastic rule of the sanctity of the monk's cell.[69] Writing to Abbot Kozma of the Kirillov-Belozerskii Monastery in June 1571 to protest its tonsure of the disgraced fugitive Boiar Ivan Vasil'evich "Bol'shoi" Sheremetev, Ivan warned of the corrosive behavior caused by the presence of monks from great families. Ivan denigrated Sheremetev and other boiar-monks Varlaam (Vasilii Sobakin) and Ioasaf (Ivan Khabarov) as Judases who undermined the monastic rule that St. Kirill had established. Sheremetev, Ivan wrote, established his own rule and housed ten slaves in his establishment; he dined in his cell from his own pantry and ate better than did distinguished monks in the refectory. What else could one expect from a son of a demon (*ego besom zvali*), referring to his former serviceman Vasilii Andreevich Sheremetev, who in 1537/38 had been tonsured as Vassian at the Trinity-Sergius Monastery. At Trinity, Ivan said, the cellarer (1516–17, 1521–23) Nifont, who had formerly been a slave, "ate from the same plate" as (Boiar D. F.?) Bel'skii and Varlaam Lopotukhin, a monk of unknown origin, and sang in the choir alongside another Varlaam, a member of the Obolenskii boiar clan. When Vasilii/Vassian Sheremetev "arrived at the Sergiev monastery," Ivan fulminated, "he fell in with the Kurtsevs, and [Abbot] Ioasaf, who became metropolitan, and with the Korovins, causing quarrels to break out among them," with deplorable results. Ivan recalled seeing his *dvoretskii* Ivan Kubenskii stay on after a feast to eat and drink with Elder Simon Shubin and others when most had retired to their cells. "At Trinity," Ivan concluded, "piety withered and the monastery became impoverished."[70]

Well, not exactly. By 1564 there were 25 more commemoration feasts on Trinity's calendar. It meant that at least 66 days each year the monastery welcomed laity for memorial prayers. It wasn't unusual that elders who were their kin received the families that underwrote feasts. Varsunofii Zamytskii, for example, was a Trinity monk (later elder and treasurer) when in 1559/60 Princess Elena, the daughter of Ivan Andreevich Zamytskii and wife of Boiar Dmitrii Ivanovich Nemoi Telepnev Obolenskii, with the assent of Elena's brother Dmitrii, gave Trinity the village of Iarinskoe and its parish church and many hamlets. According to the charter, it had been given to Elena by her father, presumably as a dowry. The agreement specified she be allowed to live on the estate until her death, at which time she was to be buried at Trinity and an annual feast established in memory of her father and mother, her brother Iakov, and herself.[71] It is hardly possible that a humble monk could avoid the daily rounds of ceremonies that involved the brotherhood with the outside world.

By comparison, the brotherhood of the Iosifo-Volokolamskii Monastery was somewhat smaller in size than Trinity's. A. A. Zimin wrote that its brotherhood was dominated by monks who were from families of local landowner-patrons and, less so, of the service elite. Tom Dykstra's study provided a more precise profile of its brotherhood and leadership cohort: from its origin in 1479 to 1607, he estimated, monks from landowner and "noble" families numbered no more than 21 percent of the brotherhood and about 36 percent of its officers and elders.[72] The estimates are lower than mine for Trinity, but not so much to suggest that its *byt*, or way of life, and governance was much different. I cannot find comparable data about the Kirillo-Belozerskii Monastery, but a recent study of the Solovetskii Monastery indicates that 74 percent of its monks whose origin is known were from families of free peasants or urbanites in villages and towns of northern Russia.[73] Its social profile and ethos were considerably different than Trinity's.

* *Oprichnina* terror struck several important members of Trinity's brotherhood. On 13 November 1569 *oprichniki* arrested Trinity archimandrite Pamba, removed him to Novgorod, and imprisoned him in the Khutynskii Monastery.[74] A year later Ivan IV had the aforementioned elder Dorofei put to death. These acts were byproducts of Ivan's suspicions of others, rather than attacks on the monastery. Pamba's incarceration was part of a campaign to intimidate Kirill, Pamba's patron and predecessor as archimandrite, whom Ivan IV had chosen to replace the martyred Filipp Kolychev as metropolitan in 1568. Dorofei's death followed the execution of his brother the state secretary Nikita Afanas'evich Funikov Kurtsev.

The *oprichnina*, worsening economic circumstances, and Boris Godunov's unceasing efforts to stop the transfer of hereditary estates to Trinity and other monasteries decisively transformed patterns of recruitment of the last two generations of Trinity's brotherhood. I have identified 74–76 (110–112) monks who belonged to generation ten (1571–90), and 92 (117) in generation eleven (1591–1605). No doubt Trinity's brotherhood continued to grow into the mid-1590s; but the increasing number of ordinary monks recorded as benefactors in Trinity's donation book and listed in its burial records is the main reason for the increase in the names of monks for these generations known from sources other than the *sinodik*. The actual size of the brotherhood in 1595, found in Elder Varsunofii Iakimov's testament, was 220: 29–32 (54–64) monks were from nearby districts of Moscow, 13 or 14 (33–41) from Radonezh, 10–12 (13–15) from Pereiaslavl', 4 (6) from Dmitrov, and 2 from Iur'ev. For the first time Trinity recruited about as many monks from more remote districts, 29–31 (41–44). Some were from places where Trinity long had a presence: Bezhetskii Verkh, 8 (9); Novyi Torg, (perhaps 1); Galich, 3; Rostov, 1; Uglich, (1); Kostroma, 3 (6); and Suzdal', perhaps 1. Others were, to the west, from Novgorod, 3; Pskov, (3); Tver', 3; and Volok, 1. To the north, recruits came from Iaroslavl', 1 (2); Sol'-Vychegodsk, (1, another Stroganov); and Kholmogory, (1); to the south from Kashira, 1; Murom, 2 (3). Riazan' furnished possibly 1 recruit and Nizhnii Novgorod, 2. The trend indicated an extension of Trinity's prestige, one that certainly owed something to *oprichnina* campaigns, particularly in Volok, Tver', Bezhetskii Verkh, Novgorod, and Pskov, and in the north. These figures also reveal the decline in the number of well-born persons taking vows in central areas. This in turn may be explained by decrees against the alienation of properties to monasteries dating from Ivan IV's last years, and by Boris Godunov's policies.

The decline in the number and percentage of monks from landowner or service elite families in the final generation is striking. I count 39–44 (40–45) monks of the service, landowning elite, or from 51 –59 percent (36–41 percent) of the brotherhood, in the tenth generation. But in the eleventh only 24–25 (25–28) of 92 (117) monks, or no more than 27 percent (21%) were from elite families. Part of the explanation for this decline is that the database is richer in records of ordinary monks for this generation. The declining recruitment in central areas of well-born monks was another factor. One might see this as a lingering effect of *oprichnina* terror, but I think it had more to do with the economic conditions that followed. This line of reasoning with regard to both the social status and geographical origin of Trinity's brotherhood corresponds with data on requests for tonsure. Between 1584 and 1605, of 83 requests for tonsure, 5 came from townspeople, 4 from holders of conditional land grants by the state (*pomestie*), 19 from peasants, and 25 from servants of Trinity, other monasteries, or elite servicemen. The "price" for tonsure declined beginning in 1593/94. There was one substantial donation of cash and goods amounting to 208 rubles from a person described as a Trinity servant named Ivan Timonov in return for tonsure and memorial prayers. Two other initiates, townsmen in Sol'-Galich, came up with the traditional 50 rubles in property and five more donated 20–40 rubles each for tonsure—and often also for memorial prayers. One was in the form of 800 thin-cut boards.[75] Trinity tonsured the majority of the remaining initiates, 75 in all, and most of them servants or peasants on its lands, for 5–15 rubles.[76]

Given the number of persons of limited means who sought sustenance, spiritual or otherwise, within its walls, Trinity began to distinguish between applicants who paid between 5 and 10 rubles, accepting 19 donors, some as monks but others as servants at the great house or in its hospital. In Trinity's administration servants performed managerial as well as menial tasks. A notable name in this list of donors was that of Elder Iona Golovkin, who in 1596 gave Trinity ten rubles so that his son Ivan would be entered on the rolls as a servant.[77] It was a practice Trinity inaugurated in period 7 (1522–33) and continued on a modest basis until it peaked in period 11 (1584–1605) when Trinity tonsured 25 servants as monks and 17 others as servants. In the famine years, 1601/2–3/4, it enrolled 33 applicants as monks or servants. By social origin the recruits had been not only peasants and servants, but clerics and monks. Most of them had resided on its estates. For example, Trinity tonsured a deacon named Ivan from its village of Klement'evo for a donation of 10 rubles; state peasants Ermola Pakhomov from Pereiaslavl' for 15 rubles and a gelding assessed at 1 ruble; and Andrei Ivanov, said to be from Teshilovskie *volosti*, for 10 rubles and a skewbald horse.[78] Such recruitment was a form of welfare for those dwelling on Trinity's properties, most of whom had lived in areas close by and no longer were able to make a living. It had a democratizing effect on the brotherhood, if one can call it that; in other cases, such as that of the Golovkins, it was a means to assist members of once-wealthy families that benefited and served Trinity.[79] I have not been able to tease from the data criteria or a pattern in the levels of these modest payments that might explain to whom Trinity extended a welcoming hand and whom it left to his own fate.

If the nature of the brotherhood changed, the composition of its governing elite, and pattern of governance and ceremonial, did not. In generation ten there were many more elders or officers (other than archimandrite), 35 to 38. Of these 24–26, 63–74 percent, were from families of the landowning/service elite. But in generation eleven I have records for only 11 or 12 elders, not counting 11 from the earlier generation who lived on into this period. Six of the holdovers came from landowning-benefactor families; only two or three of the new elders or officers can be so identified. The reason for the precipitous decline in the number of elders and what it meant for Trinity's governance may be found in the documentary evidence. In 1584 the council of elders gave institutional form to its hegemony over matters regarding Trinity's properties and other matters in a "decree [*prigovor*] of the holy council of elders of the Trinity-Sergius Monastery regarding the preservation by new archimandrites of the monastic rule [*ustava zhitiia*] of previous abbots."[80] No earlier rule survives. But, coming as it did two months after Ivan IV's death, the beginning of Boris Godunov's administration for Tsar Fedor and Fedor's appointment of Mitrofan as Trinity's archimandrite (1584–88), and knowing Boris's determination to terminate the passing of private lands to monasteries, Trinity's elders obviously thought it expedient to put in written form what had been custom. Or, as they said in the declaration, "According to the rules [*ulozhen'iu*] of Trinity's elders and the entire holy council, how [previously] abbots conducted themselves [*kak igumenov zhiti*] at the Trinity-Sergius Monastery, and [how] now the archimandrite [should] conduct himself accordingly and according to the holy venerable fathers." The provisions defined the prayers and feasts the archimandrite should offer and for whom, his portion of fees for tonsure and burial, and incomes from which he was excluded. It affirmed his power to maintain a moral order for members of Trinity's brotherhood, one that included sobriety, the privacy of the monk's cell, and communal meals. But "in affairs of the monastery [the archimandrite] is not in anyway to interfere and, against those who transgress or complain, the archimandrite is to act [literally, to stand] with the cellarer, the treasurer and the elders of the council and nobody else"; further, "the archimandrite is to give approval without complaint wherever the cellarer and elders send an official on any monastic business whatsoever or on assignment"; "Nor is he to oppose the cellarer, treasurer and elders of the council regarding any monastic business." In other words, archimandrites were not to interfere with how the council of elders conducted Trinity's business.

Cellarer Evstafii (Golovkin), Treasurer-Elder Zakkhei (Surovtsev), Elder Varsunofii Iakimov, Elder Makarii Pisemskii, Elder Levkei Kondrat'ev, Elder Varlaam Nepeitsyn, Elder Tikhon Chashnikov, Elder Evfimii Meshcherskii, Elder Varlaam Meshcherskii, Elder Iona Surovtsev, Elder Ignatei Lodygin, Elder Gurii Aigustov, Elder Savatii Levon'tev, Elder Pafnutii Markov, Elder Feodosii Torgovanov, Elder Feodorit Matiunin, Elder Kirilo Lykov, and Elder Ferapont Zykov executed the decree (*u prigovoru sideli*). Rarely were all members of the council mentioned by name in Trinity's charters; never had there been as many as 18. Most, if not all, of the signers were longtime monks at Trinity and came from families that were its benefactors. Evstafii Golovkin, from a clan in Bezhetskii Verkh with ties to Trinity dating from before 1500, was cellarer for most of the period between 1569/70 and 1593, and was a Trinity monk until his death in 1602; Varsunofii Iakimov, a Trinity monk from 1570 to 1601, came from a benefactor family in Galich and held the title of "senior elder"; Makarii Pisemskii, as a laymen Mikhail, was from a family of landowners in Kostroma who gave Trinity numerous benefactions and several monks. He lived at Trinity from 1553 to 1587 and was its treasurer in 1572–73. Lev'kei Kondrat'ev was at Trinity from at least 1584 to 1592/93; he was from a family of servitors of the metropolitan of Rostov and one of his kin was a benefactor. Tikhon Chashnikov was the Tver' landowner mentioned at the outset of this chapter who in 1572/73 donated a village in order to be tonsured. Evfimii Meshcherskii had been a Trinity monk since 1571, and Varlaam since 1575/76. They were members of a family of princely benefactors in Iaroslavl'. Ignatii Lodygin and Gurii Aigustov, the former a Trinity monk and its treasurer 1587/88–92, the latter a monk from 1581 to 1597, were from families of landowner-benefactors, Ignatii's in Moscow, Gurii's in Pereiaslavl'. Pafnutii Markov's family owned land in Iaroslavl'. When he made a donation to Trinity in 1580 he was already an elder. Elder Kirill Lykov, a monk and benefactor in 1576, was probably from a family of landowners in Murom. Treasurer (1578–87) Zakkhei Surovtsev and several of his relatives were benefactors but I cannot identify their social or geographical origin. His brother Iona was at Trinity from 1584 to 1592. The Nepeitsyns were minor servitors in Novyi Torg. Only the reference to Elder Varlaam connects them to Trinity. I have no information about Ferapont Zykov, unless he was related to the townswoman Feodosiia Zykova from Balakhna, who twice donated to Trinity in 1538–39. I have no information regarding elders Savatii Leont'ev, Feodosii Torgovanov, and Fedorit Matiunin.[81]

In 1590 Trinity's elders still controlled the monastery's affairs. In an exchange of lands with one Andrei Petrovich Kleshnin in Tver' in 1586/87, five officers "and the entire council of elders with [Trinity's] monks" (*i vse startsy sobornye z* brat'eiu), in addition to Archimandrite Mitrofan, acted for Trinity. The officers were Cellarer Evstafii Golovkin, Treasurer Zakkhei Surovtsev, Elder Vasunofii Iakimov, and Elder Levkei Kondrat'ev, who had signed the decree of 1584, and Butler-Elder Feofilakt Ovsiannikov, who was from a landowner-benefactor family.[82] Subsequently Boris decisively restructured Trinity's elite. In a charter of 1594 by which a Tver' landowner gave Trinity an estate, Archimandrite Kirill II Zavidov, "Senior Elder" Vasunofii Iakimov, Cellarer-elder Isidor, Treasurer-elders Il'ia and Venedikt, and "the members of the Council of Elders" (*da pri startsakh pri sobornikh*) Akakii, Serapion Markov, Gurii Aigustov, and Zakkhei Kutuzov acted for Trinity. Varsunofii, Serapion, and Gurii were holdovers. Of the others, Zakkhei, whose family owned land in Volok and elsewhere, and probably Venedikt—who was immediately replaced by Il'ia, had been Trinity monks. After 1594 Serapion was no longer mentioned in Trinity's charters and Gurii was last mentioned in 1599. Varsunofii died in 1601 and Evstafii was no longer in office, although he lived on at Trinity. A testament of 21 February 1599 giving Trinity a property in Galich mentions elders Dement'ian "Vershin," Parmon Kniazhnin, and Nifont Snoksarov (or Sinaksarov) as witnesses. Nothing is known of Dement'ian and Parmon. A document of 1604/5 mentions four elders. One, Iona Skobel'tsyn, was from a Moscow clan of landowners with ties to Trinity; another, Gelasii Simonov, may have been from a Suzdal' landowning family.[83]

In addition to reducing Trinity's council by attrition, Boris arranged for the appointment of outsiders Kirill II Zavidov, Il'ia, and Isidor as Trinity's officers. Il'ia and Isidor arrived in 1594 from the Solovetskii Monastery at Tsar Fedor's order, meaning at Godunov's behest, and immediately became Trinity's cellarer and treasurer. Kirill, previously the archimandrite of the Anton'ev Monastery in Novgorod (where Ivan IV had exiled Trinity's Archimandrite Pamba in 1570), became Trinity's archimandrite in 1594 and retained the office until Godunov died in 1605. Il'ia remained treasurer until 1601, after which there was an interregnum until Godunov's death. Isidor's tenure as cellarer lasted only into 1595. There is no record of who, if anyone, was cellarer between 1595 and 1598. An Akakii Groznyi, origin unknown, was cellarer between 1598 and 1601. The next cellarer took office in 1605. Elder Nifont Snoksarev, mentioned in the charter of 1604/5, like Kirill, came to Trinity from the Anton'ev Monastery.[84] Godunov had reduced Trinity's governing elite to a shrunken core dominated by "outsiders" and limited in its ability to evade Godunov's restriction on donations of land. After that in Tver', mentioned above, Trinity received only 18 donations of land anywhere to 1605, a miniscule amount compared to in previous periods. It made a grim contrast to Boris Godunov's record of large memorial donations and the huge bell and extravagant cover for the Rublev's Trinity icon he brought to Trinity in the great pilgrimage of 1600 in gratitude for Trinity's support of his elevation to the throne.

* In 1596/97 Timofei Ivanovich Chashnikov, with whose request for tonsure I began this chapter, having been the Trinity monk Tikhon for 24 years and an elder since 1584, as death approached, had monastic servant Grisha Vasil'ev write down his last will and testament. In addition to the grant of Riabinino by which he had entered Trinity's brotherhood in 1572, Tikhon gave Trinity 40 rubles, some pieces of damask, a shoulder cape of velvet, and gold worth 13 rubles. Knowing that he no longer had kin to provide him with memorial prayers, Tikhon donated an altyn to each nun in Trinity's three subsidiary convents for memorial prayers and gave Trinity 25 rubles for five feasts by which his brothers might remember him. Moreover, Tikhon asked that Trinity's venerable elder Varsunofii Iakimov and its priest Seliverst, who had heard his confession, perform these rites. Tikhon further asked that modest sums be distributed among houses in Tver' to obtain memorial prayers for the souls of his ancestors, his brother, and himself, and that his estate give Trinity three more rubles to bury him.[85]

Tikhon's testament alluded to institutions and liturgical practices that were at the core of the monastery's operations. Tikhon's passing of the village of Riabinino to Trinity in the will, a grant promised long before in return for tonsure, restated what had become a common practice. As early as period

2 my records contain a request for tonsure that accompanied a donation. Thenceforth such requests cropped up sporadically. But only in period 8, in which I found nine requests, did their number increase significantly. Donation in order to become a monk had become custom and the practice grew rapidly. In period 9 requests for tonsure accompanied 18 donations; in period 10 there were 58; in period 11, 82! Rather than an increase in piety, it signaled that destitute landowners and peasants on Trinity's lands sought the security that being a monk at Trinity might afford them. Moreover, Trinity made it affordable for them to join its brotherhood.

An initiate promised property in return for tonsure but continued to enjoy its income while a monk. Only on his death did Trinity take possession of the grant and its income. It and probably other incomes assured Tikhon considerable personal wealth, evident in the substantial monies, gold, and clothing he willed Trinity for memorial prayers and feasts. In this he was not alone. Trinity's donation book for 23 June 1592 recorded two grants from Senior Elder Varsunofii Iakimov, the first of 200 rubles, 40 sable pelts, and various velvet and silk fabrics donated to secure memorial feasts for Tserevna Feodosiia, the daughter of Fedor Ivanovich, whom he had baptized, and for her mother Irina. The second consisted of the village of Medvedkovo and its 20 hamlets that he had purchased for 400 rubles from Boiar Grigorii Andreevich Bulgaka, and a bell weighing over three tons worth 520 rubles. In return he requested that on his death the monastery commemorate him annually with a major feast. Remember too that Varsunofii's testament provided 220 rubles to commemorate each of Trinity's brothers, and 92 rubles, one for each of his sisters in Trinity's subsidiary nunneries. On 9 October 1601, probably on his deathbed, Varsunofii left the house the huge sum of 800 rubles and a lavish inventory of goblets, bowls, cups, and clothing.[86]

Their contemporary, Cellarer Evstafii Golovkin, had an equal, if not greater, fortune. Born Evfimii Dmitrievich Golovkin, he was of the sixth generation of a clan of landowners with relations to Trinity's outpost in Bezheskii Verkh. Evfimii took his vows at Trinity in the 1560s; except for a few months in 1581–82, he was its cellarer from 1571 to 1593. According to the testament of his predecessor Dorofei Kurtsev, whom Ivan IV did away with in 1570, Evstafii purchased two villages in Bezhetskii Verkh for Trinity so that Dorofei, the monk Iov Kurtsev, and two kin Antipa and Anna be commemorated with a minor feast.[87] Sometime after 1571/72 Evstafii and Varsunofii gave Trinity the village of Oliavidovo in Dmitrov, which they purchased for 700 rubles from Vasilii Fedorovich Vorontsov in 1571/72 so that their brothers would memorialize them with a feast.[88] In 1586 Evstafii financed feasts for his kin and ancestors—"the monk Gurii, the monk Makarii, the monk Vassian, Iosif, the monk Feognei, the nun Evfrosiniia, the monk Evstafii, Anna, Ivan Kondratii, Evodkhiia, Kseniia, the infant Vassa, Aleksandr, the monk Andreian, the monk Iosif, the monk Rodion and the monk Dorofei Sechenii"—with the village of Krutets, the settlement Abalumtsovo, and land on the Kliaz'ma River in Vladimir. In 1592 he gave Trinity 200 rubles to inscribe him in the "old feast book"; and during the 1590s Evstafii painted and decorated the magnificent large icon of Sergius with scenes of his life to stand beside the saint's tomb in the Church of the Holy Trinity (fig. 12). On his deathbed in 1602 Evstafii gave Trinity two more grants: a sum of 259 rubles and four silver cups gilded with gold, and another 800 rubles so that he be inscribed in Trinity's permanent *sinodik*. In all he managed a personal fortune sufficient to give Trinity 1,500 rubles in donations, a huge sum in those days.[89] He also orchestrated his clan's relationship to Trinity. On his watch Okseniia, the widow of Evstafii's uncle Silvestr ("Selianin") Ivanovich, with her son gave Trinity a village in Bezhetskii Verkh, his brother Ivan made Trinity a gift of fishing rights and villages in Moscow and Dmitrov districts, and his sister Evrosiniia was a nun at an affiliated convent.[90] Lest one conclude that only a few elite monks owned property or had incomes, Trinity recorded donations from 16 monks between 1592 and 1605 that amounted to 50 rubles or more. Of these in 1594 the elder Serapion gave Trinity 205 rubles and a gelding; and an elder Iosif, previously Trinity's servant Ivan, gave Trinity 160 rubles. Elder Agafonik Ovsiannikov gave Trinity 250 rubles and a hamlet in four different donations between 1589 and 1600, and Elder Tikhon Kosarev gave Trinity one-forth of a salt works and a salt mine in Balakhna, in Nizhnii Novgorod, for memorials or for other reasons.[91] At least another 34 Trinity monks, priests, and deacons made donations of between 5 and 44 rubles in addition to horses or textiles in that same period.[92]

That a substantial part of Trinity's brotherhood could display such wealth, even in times of want, confirms Ivan IV's harangue of the 1570s about the lavish lifestyle of well-born monks at Russian houses. While the presence of laity at Trinity also was a familiar sight, it should be emphasized they came to Sergius's gravesite for holy purposes: to revere Sergius, especially on his feast days, to which on 14 August 1585 Tsar Fedor Ivanovich added a third, according to a document entitled "combined rule of the Trinity-Sergius and Kirillov Monasteries." The occasion was Fedor's presentation to Trinity of a new casket for its revered founder.[93] Tikhon Chashnikov, already an elder, was witness to the event. And day in and day out laity arrived to memorialize and feast their ancestors. Tikhon may not have had kin to participate in the feast he underwrote for himself. But Varsunofii Iakimov, Evstafii

Golovkin, and other monks were there to greet their kin and join them in commemorations. And when tsars arrived to worship Sergius or feast their kin, the entire brotherhood participated. No doubt some monks drank too much, or partied with relatives in their cells as Ivan had complained at the Stoglav 34 years previously. But we must remember that these were liturgical celebrations that often required prayer through the night and other strenuous devotions. In Tikhon's time they formed a vital part of the daily liturgical cycle for Trinity's brotherhood.

In noting that a monastic servant wrote Tikhon's testament, the document alluded, albeit indirectly, to the existence of the large numbers of scribes, artisans, and workers, both lay and clerical, who administered and maintained Trinity's properties and commercial ventures. From its abbot down to its local agents, the literate monks and lay clerks who wrote the documents, and to the many more who were artisans and laborers, Trinity's brotherhood was large enough and possessed the skills to make Trinity a resilient economic institution in the difficult times around 1600. Judicial charters indicate that Trinity never lacked personnel to contest, often with success, attempts to curtail its property rights and narrow its privileges. It also had agents to offset the decline in gifts of property by an aggressive policy of purchases of land and fishing rights, such as the eight parcels and fishing rights in Varzuga, three in Nizhnii Novgorod, two in Galich, and one each in Tver', Kholmogory, and Moscow that it obtained during period 11 (19 March 1584–13 April 1605). Until late in the sixteenth century the social profile of Trinity's monks and lay personnel was not significantly different than in the fifteenth century. Townsmen and peasants may not have been a significant part of the first generations of Trinity's brotherhood and only a relatively small, if growing, element in succeeding ones. But after 1500 Trinity's economy and liturgical duties became more complex. Both phenomena required a correspondingly more complex division of labor among its membership. It implied a rapid growth in the number of brothers of humble origin, one present although inadequately represented in my database. However, Trinity's leadership remained in the hands of elders who came from families of landowner-benefactors. Boris Godunov's measures to alter Trinity's governance died with him. Tikhon referred to nunneries that were subsidiaries of Trinity. That was but one of the gendered attributes characterizing Sergius's cult and Trinity's existence that I shall examine in the following chapter. Finally, Tikhon asked to be buried at Trinity. It was a logical request of one who found in Sergius an intercessor, and it will be the subject of my final chapter.

Chapter Six

Trinity's Female Venerators

In 1570/71 Boiarina Matrena Zabolotskaia dictated to her scribe a testament that began, "I Matrena, the wife of Grigor Ivanovich Zabolotskii, during my lifetime by the will and testament of my husband . . . give the village of Novoe to the House of the Life-giving Trinity."[1] The village was a substantial property in Pereiaslavl'. It included 12 hamlets, 6 settlements, and 2 uninhabited properties. On it stood a church dedicated to St. Nicholas. In the same testament, employing identical phrasing but surviving separately from the other document, Matrena bequeathed to Trinity a large hereditary estate in the Novosil' land, one that the tsar had given her husband in exchange for a hereditary estate in Dmitrov. The testament, recorded in both documents, requested that she, her husband, their children, and "all our ancestors" (*po nashikh po vsekh roditelekh*)—that is, Grigor's *and* Matrena's—be commemorated at Trinity. In addition she asked that "she be tonsured as a nun, and that Archimandrite Pamba and brothers . . . grant that wish to me [and] order the tonsure [to take place] at the convent of the [Dormition] of the Most Pure [Mother of God] 'Under the pine'" (*Pod sosnnoiu*); that is, in the village of Podsosenie.[2] Matrena's testament contains central (but not all of the) elements that defined the relationship of well-born women to the Trinity-Sergius Monastery. The property in each instance was that of her husband and she disposed of it according to his wishes. The grants were for commemorative prayers. Also, that Matrena commemorated her ancestors as well as Grigor's was not at all unusual. Trinity's charters attest to a tradition in which women commemorated their ancestors as well as their husbands'. Nor is there reason to believe that Matrena did not act on her own volition when she asked to be tonsured at one of Trinity's subsidiary convents. How the cult of St. Sergius and the monastery that maintained it gave meaning to the lives of women—and how women found ways to act in the public sphere by embracing the cult—is the subject of this chapter.

* Familial relations in medieval and early-modern Russia were patriarchal. That said, it is well known that women exercised considerable power, even in public affairs, but only in spheres defined by custom. The conventional wisdom is that over time, the rise in property values and the development of more sophisticated legal systems eroded women's independence.[3] It would be folly to look for a single cause for this. As in medieval and early-modern western Europe, patriarchy initially revealed itself in sources that document the settling of elites on agricultural estates in an era of rising land values and the growth of a money economy. Historians of the family in western Europe generally hold that the superimposition of patrilineal customs on older forms of spousal condominium in inheritance and control of property was a means to concentrate and preserve the unity of landed and commercial wealth.[4] This also held true in Muscovite Rus' in the economic expansion and money economy that appeared around 1500. Excepting the custom of transmitting property by partible inheritance, patrilineal customs and the modes of controlling property would be familiar to students of comparable trends in the West. Still, women wielded considerable control of property and my evidence offers little indication that it eroded over time.

Worshiping a saint was one of few ways in which women might assert themselves as individuals. This held true both in practical matters and in creative endeavors. As Peter Brown has observed, in worshiping saints "the compartments segregating sexes in public broke down"; in a society ordered by bonds of kinship, as Brown, citing St. Ambrose, so aptly noted, "saints were the only in-laws [women] were free to choose."[5] Even if Brown's emendation on St. Ambrose exaggerated, it remains that women became visible in ways that were unlikely, even unthinkable, in any other context. This was no more so than in the giving of commemorative benefices to enhance the political and social prestige of their line or that of their spouses.[6] Examining evidence of female devotion to Sergius we can discern the degree to which and under what circumstances women exercised control over property—be it dowry, family, or purchased. Worshipping Sergius's relics also exposed to public scrutiny women's concerns and obligations within kinship traditions in a manner not otherwise evident. We see this when we ask what special motives women had in making memorial donations. Whom did women memorialize? How did benefactors, male and female, memorialize women? And how might we understand requests by women for tonsure at one of Trinity's subsidiary convents? Women also found ways to become patrons of Sergius's cult; in fact, Moscow's royal women developed a special fertility cult around Sergius's intercessory powers to protect Moscow's dynasty.

* Women initiated 605 of 4,217 charters. Of the 3,135 acts that were donations, women initiated 537, or 17 percent. In each of ten time periods (except the statistically insignificant period 1) women initiated from 11 percent of donation charters (the lowest percentage being in period 11) to a high of 38 percent (period 3). Variances are random; they exceed or fall below the average in an equal number of periods and show no discernible trend over time. In 92 cases women acted jointly with spouses, sons, or other male relatives in issuing donation charters; but in 442, or more than 82 percent of charters initiated by women, women acted alone. Again there is no significant variation over time. However, the language of many charters, including Matrena's testament, shows that, when women initiated them, they frequently were widows acting "on the order" (*po prikazu*) of spouses who had departed before them. In 1570/71 Aksiniia Rogacheva with her son Vasilii gave Trinity the village of Kozlishchevo in Kostroma "according to the order" of her husband Tarasii so that she might be tonsured.[7] In many other charters by which women disposed of property, spousal orders were unstated, but assumed. The fate of Skovorodenskoe village in Medyn', which, together with immunities on it, Grand Prince Vasilii III gave one Dmitrii Ivanovich Miroslavov in 1515, illustrates this very well. The charter gave Dmitrii the right to dispose of the property as he saw fit and Vasilii reaffirmed the validity of the charter in 1532 after Dmitrii's death, saying that his wife Mariia Miroslavova might live on the property until her death. Mariia gave Trinity 50 rubles in 1531 for prayers for her late husband. And on her deathbed in 1535, her children no doubt having predeceased her, she gave Skovorodenskoe to Trinity, specifying that its brothers pray for her soul and bury her at Trinity.[8] In 1570/71, a widow Ekaterina and her son gave Trinity an estate in Iaroslavl' that her late husband Vasilii Arkhintorich had acquired so that he might be memorialized; in another, Anna, the widow of Andrei Voronov, in 1571/72 gave Trinity an estate of her late husband's in Kostroma. Anna might live there until, nearing death, Trinity tonsured her and, after her death, buried her.[9] Conventions and legal traditions, which changed little over time, dictated the parameters within which women initiated charters.

Yet within such parameters many women managed property, promoted their clan, or expressed themselves in a special religiosity. For example, there exist numerous charters similar to that by which the widow Feodora in 1432, acting alone, gave Trinity a large estate in Bezhetskii Verkh that must have belonged to her late husband "for [prayers] for my husband Aleksandr [Desiatinnich] and for my son Volodia." About then a woman from a family of humble origin but obvious means granted Trinity a quarter of a salt works at Sol'-Galich with the admonition that, "my husband Vasilii Mikhailovich [and] I, the nun Anna and my son Boris be written into the *sinodik*."[10] The statistical prominence of women donors of what were almost certainly properties of their spouses in the 1450s bears witness to the plight of widows, the only survivors in their families in a time of plague. It may well be that their husbands, before succumbing, had no time to draft a will directing surviving spouses regarding the disposal of their estates. Or, perhaps, they did so orally and, in an age in which charters were short and laconic, widows simply had set down how their late spouses' property was to be distributed without noting, as Matrena did, that it was according to the order of the deceased. Their prominent contemporary, the nun Mariia, widow of Prince Semen of Borovsk, however, stated that she acted on her mother's order (*po prikazu materi)*—in fact, that of her mother-in-law, the nun Evpraksiia, formerly Princess Elena, the daughter of Grand Prince Algirdas of Lithuania and wife of Prince Vladimir Andreevich of Serpukhov—in giving Trinity a village in Dmitrov "for [prayers for] the soul of my [Mariia's] husband's brother Prince Andrei Volodimerovich." Her brothers Semen and Andrei having predeceased her in 1426, Mariia acted as executor for her mother-in-law's estate, probably in 1454, or long after Evpraksiia's death in 1438.[11] Women in every period acted as Maria did but, as my database indicates, only in 27 instances did charters explicitly recognize their office. I know only one charter, a testament written in the 1430s or 1440s, in which a woman, "the elder Tamara" *(Tamavra staritsa)*, might have been a witness.[12]

Women, like men, made gifts primarily to endow memorials, but elite women were involved in 69 land transactions with Trinity that were not memorial donations. Of these 43 occurred before 1500 and Sofiia Vitovtovna (the mother of Grand Prince Vasilii II of Moscow) and Vasilii's wife Mariia issued 19 of them, 17 being immunity charters.[13] Because Sofiia and Mariia were otherwise patrons of Trinity, one may conclude that these were a form of donation. Mariia, whose father had been Trinity's lord until his appanage was liquidated, also signed four sets of instructions to local officials affirming Trinity's ownership or tax liabilities on specified properties that resembled acts coming from the grand princely chancellery. Mariia signed one even after she had taken religious vows. After her father's death she obviously exercised authority over his patrimonies. In an era when the distinction between personal and public property hardly existed, women like Sofiia and Mariia wielded considerable political power.[14] From the 1470s on, as Ivan III consolidated Moscow's authority over the appanages of his relatives, there were to be no more such charters.

Women, however, continued to be agents in a variety of private-property transactions. Between 1427/28 and 1432 widow Matrena Gnezdnikova and her son Ivan sold Trinity what must have been the family estate for 12 rubles and a cow; and in 1454 Mariia, widow of Boiar Vasilii Kopnin, sold Trinity an unoccupied plot near the monastery. That she did so might be explained by the fact that their children had predeceased her. Mariia's name appears again on a survey done in the 1480s or 1490s demarcating the boundaries of a property she had earlier donated to Trinity.[15] The name of Anna Skripitsyna is on two surveys, dated 1525/26. They set forth borders between her estate, estates of other owners in the Pereiaslavl' land, and the villages of Dulepovo and Rostokovo, which she had given Trinity. Two other Skripitsyns, Il'ia "Buchug" Aleksandrovich, the son of Anna's late husband's brother, and Ivan Fillipovich, whose relationship to Anna I cannot fix, witnessed the acts.[16] My database contains 21 more sales, exchanges, or surveys of property, mortgages, and contracts of indenture (*kabala*) to which women were parties between 1533 and 1605. In 1566/67 one Anna Shubina, her two brothers, and a Trinity servant named Stepan, son of Iurii, mortgaged her estate in Tver' with Treasurer Varsunofii Iakimov for 50 rubles. On 31 October 1586, Agaf'ia, identified as the daughter of Vasilii Suzdal'tsev and wife of Dmitrii Shemiakin, with her son Mikula sold Trinity two *luks* or shares in a communal salmon-fishing enterprise, along with hay fields in Varzuga, for four rubles.[17]

* The Trinity-Sergius Monastery was a major beneficiary of donation bequests of dowry property by women. Dowries were payments by a bride's family to a groom when they were married. In Muscovite Rus', as in western Europe, the payment constituted the bride's share of her family's estate. Trinity's records demonstrate that women exercised considerable control over dowries.[18] A prime example is in a series of charters involving several of Moscow's important families. It begins with a dowry agreement concluded in 1513/14 between Aksiniia, the widow of Fedor Pleshcheev, and the husband of her daughter Anastasiia, Prince Ivan Vasil'evich Kurlia Obolenskii. The Pleshcheevs and Obolenskiis were venerable clans. The agreement contains a meticulous inventory of contents: moveable property, including valuables such as an icon of the Mother of God with a jeweled silver cover and a variety of clothing; a list of slaves (*liudi*) who came with Anastasiia; and half of Bogoroditskoe village with its hamlets, and half of the settlement Koriakovskoe and its Dormition church in Pereiaslavl'. In the agreement Aksiniia agreed to pay debts her husband had incurred on these properties so that they came to the couple free and clear.[19] On 22 December

1515, Anastasiia purchased the other half of these villages in a complicated transaction. Evidently they had been part of the dowry of Anastasiia's sister Irina when she married Prince Petr Khovanskii. But, unlike the halves that had fallen to Anastasiia, they came encumbered with half of her late father's debt. In addition to sister Irina and brother-in-law Petr, Anastasiia had to pay off her father's executor, Prince Ivan Strigin Obolenskii, a relative who was also his creditor. The price was 200 rubles and a fur coat; 100 went to Strigin Obolenskii to satisfy her father's debt, while the remainder and the coat constituted the Khovanskii dowry. Anastasiia also pledged that neither she nor her children would sell, exchange, or otherwise alienate the property without her sister's and brother-in-law's consent.[20]

Next in the chain of documents is an affidavit of 1516/17. In it Prince Khovanskii acknowledged that he sold the two half-villages on behalf of his wife Irina to her sister Anastasiia. Irina's consent must have been necessary for the deal because Khovanskii said he was unable to complete the sale at the time agreed upon because she was ill.[21] According to an agreement of 1541/42 over boundaries, we know Anastasiia again divided the villages. Half went with her daughter as a dowry when she married Ivan Sobakin; the other half fulfilled the same function when her other daughter married Dmitrii Buturlin.[22] In 1570/71 Buturlin's sons Roman and Leontii gave their portion to Trinity, requesting tonsure and that the monastery "write them and their father Dmitrii in the [daily] *sinodik* and in the permanent *sinodik*."[23] At his death Sobakin's portion went to his widow. For some reason it then passed to the state, which in 1576 granted it in service tenure to another. In 1595 Tsar Fedor traded it to Trinity for another village.[24]

It is striking that as long as there were female descendants in the line stemming from Aksiniia, the dowry property remained intact. Anastasiia's "purchase" was a means of managing a common inheritance in the female line so as to underwrite the honor of her unmarried daughters. In this it resembles the donation of the village of Asanovo in Pereiaslavl' in 1528/29 Anna Skripitsyna made to Trinity to memorialize her daughter, Anastasiia, the wife of Aleksandr Mikhailovich Briukhov. Anna described the property as "my portion of the estate of my father" (*ee vyt' otsa ee otchiny*); a land survey executed by Anna and the Trinity Monastery in 1525/26 described it as "Anna's village Asanovo."[25] In 1536/37 Anna gave Trinity another gift of land in Pereiaslavl'. It was a hamlet titled variously as Elik or Elika Sovshina. Anna said it was her dowry property and that she made the gift for prayers "for my husband Foma Aleksandrov syn Skripitsyn Baluev." Her brother-in-law (*ziat'*) Vasilii Aleksandrovich Miakishev wrote the charter for her.[26] The nun Evdoksiia, widow of Fedor Strigin Obolenskii (the son of the above-mentioned Ivan), drew up a complex testament on 1 August 1513 by which she gave dowry properties to Trinity, to the Simonov Monastery, and to her cousin. Her village of Makha and its hamlets in Vladimir, she directed, were to go to the Trinity-Sergius Monastery during her lifetime. But should Grand Prince Vasilii III of Moscow seize this property, she requested that he pay 200 rubles to Trinity and 100 to her executors. From it they were to pay her debts and to distribute what was left to various monasteries so that they would memorialize her. She also directed her executors to donate a sum to Trinity so that it would memorialize her late husband and specified that Trinity elders Rodion Kostrov and Varsunofii Gomziakov were to recite the memorial prayers. Lastly, she told her executors to arrange that she be buried at Trinity.[27]

Women, especially widows, could manage and distribute dowry property virtually as they saw fit, although if they had living children it was more complicated. Thus, in a charter executed in 1532/33 Arina, the wife of Mikhail Neledinskii, with her children, three sons of Mikhail and another said to be the son of Andrei Plishin, whom Arina must have married on Mikhail's death and who then himself died, sold Trinity her dowry settlement of Staroe in Bezhetskii Verkh for 25 rubles. As in most dowries, it identified Arina's father, Iurii Pykhichev, who was its source. Lacking daughters to pass it to, Arina and her sons were free to take the money. Tretiak Neledinskii, Mikhail's brother and his two sons, witnessed the purchase and, in a rare example of female literacy, Arina signed off for her son Andrei, who was either too young to know how to write or simply illiterate.[28]

Throughout the sixteenth century and into the seventeenth Trinity received at least 11 other dowry properties. Although the charters recording them had common elements, each told a different story. In her testament of 1551 Princess Mariia, with her late husband Ivan Borisovich Gorbatyi's blessing, bequeathed Trinity the estate of Lumkhnoe in Iur'ev for memorial prayers for herself. The estate was large, consisting of a village with four churches and hamlets with three churches, and several other parcels. The testament said Ivan had purchased it with the 400 rubles Mariia's father Prince Petr Riapolovskii had given her as a dowry. Mariia added that, at her husband's order, she had already given Trinity 11 rubles to provide memorial prayers for his and her souls and for the souls of her spouse's father, mother, and brother.[29] In 1554/55 Avdotiia, the widow of Grigorii Tolbuzin, gave Trinity a dowry property in Ruza. She specified that she be allowed to live on it until death, at which time it was to pass to the monastery for memorial prayers. A dowry could serve multiple purposes, as seen in a testament of 1558/59 written by estate owner Vasilii Ivanovich Durov. Vasilii relinquished to his wife Evfimiia a dowry described as one-third of the village of Serino in Dmitrov, and her clothing and jewelry. Evfimiia, he said, might sell the goods for 50 rubles, but the third of a village at some point was to go to Nikifor, the eldest of their three sons, at which time she could live with the son of her choice and the others were to support her with annual payments of milled grain (100 *cheti vsiakago khleba*); if she chose to live alone, each was to give her 200 *cheti* of grain, 100 stacks of hay and firewood, and whatever else she required. Eventually Evfimiia was to be tonsured at a convent of her choice. They were to purchase a cell for her and continue to support her in the manner defined in the testament. A year later in another testament Princess Elena, the daughter of Ivan Zamytskii and wife of Dmitrii Telepnev Obolenskii, gave Trinity the dowry village of Iarinskoe in Dmitrov, which her father had given her. It was for memorial prayers and a feast for her father, mother, and brothers.[30] In 1569/70 Mariia Slizneva, already the nun Marem'iana, gave Trinity a village allotted her by her father for memorial prayers; and Irina, the widow of landowner Grigorii Elizar'ev and daughter of Iartsev Narmatskii, promised Trinity at her death her dowry consisting of hamlets in Pereiaslavl' and Radonezh. In return Trinity was to enter her and her son Boris in its *sinodik*.[31] Then there is a charter of 15 February 1582 by which free peasant Tretiak, son of Ivan, gave Trinity one *luk* of fishing rights and a hay field in Varzuga. In return he received 1.51 rubles. The charter says the property was a dowry of his wife Fekla, the daughter of Vasilii Suzdal'tsev. Although no memorial request accompanied the donation, it his likely that Fekla had passed away, that Tretiak acted for her, and that a memorial was intended.[32]

Other dowry transactions were more complex affairs in which the ability of women to control or manipulate the disposal of dowry property could be extraordinary. In 1574/75 Bogdan Volynskii and his wife Anna gave Trinity the village of Ekimatovo and several hamlets in Kolomna. The charter called it a dowry and implied that it came to her from her father Pavel Basin by describing it as an "old ancestral estate." While Anna lived the property was to be hers and Trinity was to tonsure her at its convent at Podsosenie and offer prayers for her health. When she died, the property was to go to Trinity, her remains were to be interred there, and its monks were to enter her into the "eternal" *sinodik*. In her study of women's property rights Ann Kleimola observed that the family of Anna's first husband Nikifor Durov long had owned Ekimatovo. Not only that; in 1571/72 Anna, "at my husband's order," already had given it to Trinity for memorial prayers for their souls and those of their daughter and ancestors, and to pay for Anna's burial. In 1574/75 Anna, having transformed a hereditary estate that came to her first husband into a dowry property belonging to her and her second husband, gave it to Trinity again.[33] No less complex was the donation in 1580/81 by Feodosiia, the daughter of Ermolai Khomutov and wife of Nikita Lebedev, of the hamlet of Brevnovo in Pereiaslavl'. It was called a dowry property, belonging to her alone, and said neither her brothers Ivan and Pospel nor her nephews had claims on it. The brothers signed off as witnesses. The act also said that Ermolai had obtained Brevnovo from a neighbor Fedor Kozlov, although how he did so it did not say.[34] An exchange of dowry properties that I cannot explain was one in which an Ivan Nazarevich Khlopov in 1577/78 gave Trinity the dowry estate in Tver' of the daughter of Fedor Kindyrev, perhaps Ivan's late wife, in exchange for another dowry property in Kolomna that Trinity had obtained from the wife of Iakov Godunov, Vasil'eva Naumovna.[35]

Finally, in 1590 Dariia, the wife of Petr Fedorovich Basmanov, descendent of a disgraced line of the Pleshcheev clan, executed a testament notable for its extravagant statement of faith in Sergius's power to save souls. It was notable too in the manner that Dariia disposed of her dowry while her husband was still alive. The dowry was an estate in Galich she had obtained from her mother Domna, the wife of Ivan Samsonovich Turenin, who was a member of the Obolenskii clan. Dariia gave it to Trinity and requested prayers for her soul and that of her mother, her ancestors, and possibly—the text is ambiguous—for her husband. She specified that her husband was to live on there until he died. At her death her estate was also to give Trinity 100 rubles and her personal belongings so that it perform three hymns (*stikhira*) at her burial, which we know from Trinity's donation book occurred at the monastery in proximity to her intercessor in 1602/3. Further, Dariia allocated 50 rubles for five memorial feasts and promised each of Trinity's brothers one grivna, a tenth of a ruble, in coin. Petr evidently was her executor; Trinity's donation book records that he gave her personal possessions to the monastery in 1602/3. They consisted of a piece of white damask; a cape (*oplech'e*) decorated with gold and silver thread sewn on red satin background; a cherry-colored lace head scarf (*kruzhevo*); some cherry-colored cotton fabric for lining or trim; several items of woman's summer clothing, one of gold fabric with a red background, another of red satin decorated with a pattern of circles; pieces of velvet (*voshvi*) decorated with gold and silver thread; and pieces of "German" brocade fabric. They were valued at 65 rubles and were to underwrite her burial.[36]

Trinity recorded other donations of estates for commemorations by women that may have been dowry properties but don't say so. A nun Evfrosiniia, for instance, once the wife of a Dmitrii Aleksandrovich Moklokov, in 1575/76 gave Trinity a village in Bezhetskii Verkh that had belonged to her father, Petr Pikhichev, for memorial prayers for herself and her kin (*roditelekh*). In the charter Evfrosiniia excluded her children, cousins, or living kin from claims to the proffered estate. Insofar as I can tell, none of the witnesses were related to her family or that of her husband.[37] Trinity's donation book also recorded the monastery's manipulation of dowry property that, on its face, cannot be reconciled with other sources. An entry said nun Evfrosiniia Ovinova gave cellarer Evstafii Golovkin the means to purchase the villages of Gorodishche and Naumovo in Moscow from Afanasii and Semen Fedorovich Nagoi so that Trinity would pray and hold a feast to commemorate her. Evfrosiniia made the donation between 1571, when Evstafii become cellarer, and 1574/75, the date on which this and many other donations of cash and personal property were recorded. The Nagois were uncles of Ivan IV's last wife-to-be, Mariia Nagaia. However, a donation act of 1576 said Semen Nagoi gave the villages and three mills to Trinity to assure the commemoration of his wife Mariia. The act explained that the villages had been Mariia's dowry from her father Andakan Tushin when she married Semen.[38] I can find no relationship between Evfrosiniia Ovinova and the Nagois that might explain her intervention. The donation charter, however, does say that in return for Mariia's dowry property, Semen Nagoi received 50 rubles from Trinity. Possibly, the "donation" was in fact a sale, a ruse to evade government restrictions on donations of land to the church. Evfrosiniia's gift of cash then would be the real donation, one that cellarer Evstafii used to pay Semen Nagoi. When women could choose, as was the case for dowry estates, they too opted to make donations that would provide commemorations. In this the Trinity-Sergius Monastery benefited immensely.

* Trinity's donation book also shows that women did not lack for means to underwrite commemorations.[39] Elite women like Dariia Basmanova utilized personal effects and created embroideries to demonstrate their devotion. The pious Mariia Miroslavova, mentioned above in another context, gave Trinity 200 rubles, stacks of rye and oats, and personal possessions, including a panagia of gold and silver, an icon "Vision of the Mother of God" edged in sliver, three rings, two necklaces, some "Lithuanian" pearls, and a variety of silver buttons, spoons, goblets, cups, and bowls, on her death bed in 1535. In 1541 Elena, her husband Boiar Ivan Andreevich Cheliadin having predeceased her, gave Trinity a silver goblet and a black ambler horse for prayers for her son Ivan. Only slightly more humble was Princess Mariia Bel'skaia's donation in 1602/3 of ten rubles, a piece of velvet cloth worth eight rubles, a damask fabric worth seven rubles, and a tablecloth.[40]

Embroideries, which were female crafts, figure prominently in Trinity's donation book.[41] One of the earliest was a purificator (*sudar'*), a cloth used at communion to wipe the chalice, that Evdokiia, wife of the Moscow treasurer and boiar Dmitrii Vladimirovich Khovrin, gave Trinity about 1495. Its primary image was that of the Lamb of God.[42] Another was an icon cloth containing images of several Iaroslavl' princes. An inscription describes the donor as a Princess Mariia Danilovna Aleksandrova, who cannot otherwise be identified, and her daughter. They gave it to Trinity in 1501.[43] In 1514 an ancestor by marriage of the aforementioned Evfrosiniia, Anastasiia Ovinova, the widow of former pro-Moscow Novgorod boiar Ivan Zakhar'inich, gave Trinity an icon cloth depicting the Lord's entombment, and two shrouds with crucifixion scenes. After Ivan's death Anastasiia settled in Moscow and in 1517, probably as death neared, also gave Trinity valuable personal possessions including a necklace and a gem-studded bracelet.[44] In 1524 a Matrena gave Trinity a shroud depicting Sergius's vision of the Mother of God, and the cross of Golgotha, on which was inscribed that she was the wife of a Fedor Vasil'evich Veprev.[45] Another affluent benefactor, Evdokiia, the wife of a Dmitrii Vladimirov, in 1530 gave Trinity two purificators done on silk, a munificent shroud mounted on a double layer of taffeta with an image of St. Sergius sewn in gold and silver thread, and a crown containing 3 rubies and 20 pearls. Two hundred and four pearls surrounded the crown; the border was hemmed in gold. Her husband was the Dmitrii for whom his brother Ivan on 3 June 1530 gave Trinity 20 rubles for memorial prayers.[46] Subsequently, owing to the *oprichnina* and a contracting economy, donations of embroideries fell off. As land prices declined, rich women, like rich men, donated estates. Only royal women or women in appanage lines could maintain embroidery workshops.

Among women whose devotion to the Trinity-Sergius Monastery we have measured in donations of property, Anna Skripitsyna and Princess Evfrosiniia Staritskaia were exceptional. I have already described Anna Skripitsyna as a manager of dowry property and executor of property surveys. She was the widow of a prominent Pereiaslavl' landowner and patron of Trinity, and very likely the mother of its abbot, and future metropolitan, Ioasaf Skripitsyn. In 1510/11 Anna and her son Andrei, a minor, purchased Dulepovo Village from the widow of her husband's brother and her children for 13 rubles. In turn she gave Dulepovo to Trinity in 1525/26 to secure her eternal remembrance. Should her relatives wish to redeem the property, she wrote, they must pay Trinity 25 rubles.[47] In 1525/26 Anna gave Trinity a second estate, one purchased by her late husband Foma, so that he, their parents, and son Andrei would be memorialized. And, as mentioned, in

1528/29 Anna gave Trinity her dowry village of Asanovo in Pereiaslavl' to memorialize her daughter, Anastasiia.[48] In 1533 she gave Trinity a stack of rye; in 1536 she provided the brothers with more rye; in 1540 she sent them still more; and in 1536/37 a dowry property to memorialize her husband.[49]

Princess Evfrosiniia Staritskaia's gifts to Trinity were of a wholly different dimension. Evfrosiniia was a Khovanskii princess and the wife of Ivan IV's uncle, Prince Andrei Ivanovich of Staritsa. In 1537 the regency, presided over by Ivan's mother during his minority, did away with Andrei and his claim to the throne, and imprisoned Evfrosiniia and her son Vladimir for almost four years. After her release Evfrosiniia and Vladimir lived in the kremlin near Trinity's compound under supervision and Evfrosiniia began to craft her donations to various holy places with a single-minded goal, to preserve the memory of her line and that of her husband.[50] In all she made three cash grants of 50 rubles to Trinity to assure that her kin be commemorated in the great daily *sinodik*: the first, undated, provided prayers for her late husband. She gave the second on 1 May 1547 to assure her own commemoration. Trinity received the third on 17 May 1555 for prayers for her mother, the nun Evfimiia. Trinity's donation book records that Evfrosiniia sent other, more lavish, gifts. On 1 June 1553 she, with her son Vladimir, gave Trinity 300 rubles, probably to underwrite services for Passion Week, and a silk shroud (*pokrov*) embroidered with a cross made of precious stones on an underlay of green taffeta. Trinity's inventory of 1574/75 of gifts other than land and cash recorded another crimson damask (*bagrova*) shroud embroidered with gold and silver thread. In 1558/59 she and her son donated 600 rubles for a new sarcophagus for Sergius's coffin and a gold ring set with a blue sapphire. In return the brotherhood was to undertake annual minor feasts, presumably to commemorate their line.[51]

Ivan IV's final move against the Staritskii clan began with the tonsure of Evfrosiniia in 1563 as the nun Evdokeia. He confined her in the Goritsy Resurrection Convent, a house she had founded in 1544 near the Kirillov Monastery. It concluded in 1569 with the death of her son Vladimir, poisoned while under guard en route to the headquarters of the *oprichnina* at Aleksandrovskaia Sloboda; he then had Andrei's wife and children and Evfrosiniia murdered. If Trinity's feast book is correct, Evfrosiniia anticipated the extermination of her line. For 5 August 1568 it records the endowment of a major feast to commemorate her husband Andrei on the date of his birth and an ordinary (*serednei*) feast for 3 December, said to be the date of his death. Those commemorated were Vladimir Andreevich, the "princess nun Evdokiia" (Evfrosniia), two princesses Evdokeia who had been Vladimir's wives, and a Princess Mariia and a Prince Vasilii, Vladimir's children.[52] Although the entry did not say who paid for the feasts and how much, with her son imprisoned, who else but Evfrosiniia could have been the benefactor? Evfrosiniia's workshop also produced shrouds depicting the apparition of the Mother of God to Sergius and Nikon, the first of which she sent to Trinity shortly before her death; the latter was for Trinity to fulfill Ivan IV's commission, probably in the same spirit that he memorialized other victims of his terror.[53]

The most remarkable of Evfrosiniia's gifts, however, was the large (174 x 276 cm) shroud executed in her workshop and sent to the Trinity-Sergius Monastery in 1561 with the title "The Entombment of the Blessed Jesus Christ" (fig. 9). It was one of four such shrouds her workshop produced during the 1560s depicting the entombment. No two of them alike. The other three she bestowed on the cathedral church of the Dormition in the Moscow kremlin, the Iosifo-Volokolamsk Monastery, and the Kirillov Monastery. The inscription sewn along the four borders of the Trinity shroud associated the fate of her husband's line to the central image of the entombment, leaving little to the imagination. In part it reads, "By the order of the pious Prince Vladimir Andreevich, the grandson of Great Prince Ivan Vasil'evich [III] and great grandson of Grand Prince Vasilii Vasil'evich [II] and his pious mother the Princess Evfrosniia [the wife] of Prince Andrei Ivanovich, [the shroud] is given in honor of and in homage to all Orthodox Christians and in memory of the last of the line for the eternal commemoration of their souls." Interspersed in the inscription are images appropriate to the line's dignity and ancestry: along the top of the embroidery the image of Rublev's Old Testament Trinity is flanked by images of the archangels. They have their parallel on the bottom border with an image of "The Sign" (*Znamenie*) with Madonna and Child flanked by Old Testament kings Solomon and David. The image of John Chrysostum, the name-saint of Ivan III, is on the left border and on the right is the image of Vasilii II's patron saint, Basil the Great. The embroidery, of exceptional quality, has an iconography drawn from the version of the entombment according to John 19:25–27, 38–41. Opposite the Mother of God, who cradles the head of the prostrate Jesus laid out on the tomb, and Mary, the wife of Clopas, bowed in reverence and partially covering her grief-stricken face with her hands, three males bow in reverence: the apostle John; Joseph of Arimathaea, who requested Jesus's body from Pilate for burial; and Nicodemus, who had brought a mixture of myrrh and aloes to anoint the corpse. Behind the two women, in a radiant blue cloak, stands a distraught Mary Magdalene (fig. 9a). It is tempting to speculate that Evfrosiniia saw herself in this figure, lamenting the fate of her husband and his illustrious line and, prophetically, that which soon befell her son. Evfrosiniia's generosity was an outpouring of a lifelong reservoir of grief and, at the same time, an affirmation of her family's distinction. This extraordinary woman used conventional forms of women's work and devotion to create the definitive iconography of the entombment in Russia. To this day historians—and filmmaker Sergei Eisenstein—cannot avoid reconstructing Evfrosniiia's image, usually as a "dangerous female" as Ann Kleimola put it, in bringing this period to life.[54]

Evfrosiniia's granddaughter Mariia followed her example. Ivan married Mariia into the Danish royal family to secure an alliance in the Livonian War. When her husband died and she returned in 1586, he had her tonsured as the nun Marfa at Trinity's subsidiary convent at Podsosenie in 1586. Trinity's donation book calls her Queen Marfa. In 1589 Queen Marfa gave Trinity 20 rubles for prayers for her grandmother Evfrosiniia. In 1597/98 Marfa gave Trinity chasubles, a cross, a bejeweled star, and a priest's stole (*patrakhil'*); in 1599 she gave Trinity a cup (*kubets*) of gold and silver and a wine bowl (*bratina*).[55]

* Sophia Palaeloga, Grand Prince Ivan III's second wife and descendant of Byzantine emperors, at a crucial moment in the dynastic crisis of 1499, presented Trinity with the icon cloth (fig. 7) I mentioned in Chapter 3. Into it Sophia's seamstresses sewed a complex ideological statement that drew together the biological welfare of Moscow's ruling family and Sergius's reputation as a miracle worker. The layout of the icon cloth resembled a biographical icon (*ikona s zhitiem*) in which a central figure is surrounded with small panels depicting scenes from his or her life. In Sophia's embroidery the cross, symbolizing Christ's promise of salvation, dominated the central panel. In the middle at the top appears the Old Testament Trinity of Rublev. This and the size of the cloth suggest that it was intended for that icon. To its left are images of the Mother of God and John Chrysostum; to the right are images of John the Baptist and the apostle Timothy. In parallel positions in the bottom row, the icon cloth contains at its center a panel depicting the apparition to Sergius of the Mother of God. To its left a panel contains images of the Moscow metropolitan-saints Petr and Aleksei; on the right the archangel Gabriel and Basil of Parius. Isolde Thyrêt has explicated that symmetry of these images. In the panels to the left of the central panels the Mother of God and the metropolitans assume traditional intercessory poses for the ruling house; John Chrysostum, Ivan III's name-saint, symbolized the grand prince's hope for a "true" heir. To the right on the top John the Baptist is the harbinger of good tidings and Timothy is the saint on whose day Ivan III was born, 18 January. On the right at the bottom are Gabriel, the herald

of the Miraculous Conception and Vasilii's name-day saint. Panels on the sides depict feasts of the calendar relevant to Sophia's ideological scheme: to the left the Annunciation and the Ascension, a promise and the result; to the right, the Father and Son (*Otechestvo)* and The Descent of the Holy Spirit to the Apostles. The former was a neat parallel to Ivan and Vasilii; the latter, in which a king stands before an altar holding a cloth on which were 12 wheels representing the peoples to whom the apostles preached, could be taken to symbolize the descent of divine grace on Moscow. A donation inscription along the bottom reads, "In 1499 this altar cloth was created under the pious Grand Prince Ivan Vasil'evich of all Rus' and under his son the Grand Prince Vasilii Ivanovich and in the reign of Metropolitan Simon by the will and at the inspiration of the Tsarevna of Tsargrad the Grand Princess of Moscow Sophia, [who] presented this icon cloth as a prayer to the life-giving Trinity and to the miracle worker Sergius."[56]

The icon cloth was visible to all who entered the Church of the Holy Trinity. It told visitors that through Sergius's intercession God provided Sophia with a son whom God ordained to rule Russia; also that the ruling dynasty recognized Sergius as intercessor for the continuation and well-being of the dynasty as well as for the Russian land. Finally, Thyrêt argued, Sophia's creation gave a gender-specific nuance to Sergius's cult, that of intercessor for her fertility.[57]

In the sixteenth century that is how Muscovites understood the image. In 1525 Vasilii's barren wife Solomoniia sent an icon cloth to Trinity depicting Sergius praying to the Mother of God. On it she had inscribed an appeal that the Lord grant her "the fruit of the womb." As in Sophia's icon cloth, smaller images of Solomoniia's and Vasilii III's name-saints surround the central image; and in the corners are biblical images of miraculous conception or miraculous birth.[58] Solomoniia remained barren and Vasilii divorced her, but the conviction that Sergius's intercessory power could assure the fertility of royal women retained its potency. Vasilii's second wife, Elena Glinskaia, according to a mid-seventeenth-century source, made a pilgrimage to Trinity and donated a pall (*pokrov*). Her visit was followed by the birth of Ivan the Terrible.[59] The narrative compresses events; Ivan was born five years after the divorce, remarriage, and otherwise undocumented pilgrimage, but a tradition linking them had come into being. The near-contemporary *Letopisets nachala tsarstva* said that in September 1547, eight months after marrying Ivan and showing no sign that she was pregnant, Tsaritsa Anastasiia made a pilgrimage with her husband to Trinity. Still without child in September 1548, she again made her way there to pray for an heir, this time on foot. The desperate Anastasiia solicited the intercession of Nikita of

6. Icon cloth (*pelena*), "The Apparition of the Mother of God to Sergius." ca. 1480s. 51 x 49 cm. Workshop of Grand Prince and Princess of Moscow. Museum of the Moscow Kremlin, no. 12663. N. A. Maiasova, *Drevnerusskoe shit'e* (Moscow, 1871), fig. 15.

7. Icon cloth (*pelena*), "Feasts and Saints." 1499. 103 x 122 cm. Gift of Grand Princess Sophia Palaeologa. Sergiev Posad Museum-Reserve, no. 413. N. A. Maiasova, *Drevnerusskoe shit'e* (Moscow, 1871), fig. 29.

8. Diptych (*ikona-skladen'*), "Old Testament Trinity" and "The Apparition of the Mother of God to Sergius." 1540. Wood. 7 x 5 x 1.8 cm. Gift of Vasilii (monk Vassian) Karacharov. Sergiev Posad Museum-Reserve, no. 90. T. V. Nikolaeva, *Sobranie drevnerusskogo iskusstva v Zagorskom Muzee* (Leningrad, 1968), 106.

9. Shroud (*plashchanitsa*), "The Entombment." 1561. 174 x 276 cm. Gift of Princess Evfrosiniia Staritskaia. Sergiev Posad Museum-Reserve, no. 408. T. V. Nikolaeva, *Sobranie drevnerusskogo iskusstva v Zagorskom muzee* (Leningrad, 1968), 145.

9a. Shroud, "The Entombment." 1561. Detail, "The Lamentation." Sergiev Posad Museum-Reserve, no. 408. T. V. Nikolaeva, *Sobranie drevnerusskogo iskusstva v Zagorskom muzee* (Leningrad, 1968), 145.

10. Basilica of the Dormition of the Mother of God, 1559–85. Trinity-Sergius Monastery. Photograph by William Brumfield.

11. The Trinity-Sergius Monastery. Contemporary view. Photograph by William Brumfield.

12. Cellarer Evstafii Golovkin. Icon, "St. Sergius with Scenes from His Life." 1591. 65 x 52.5 cm. Sergiev Posad Museum-Reserve, no. 279. T. V. Nikolaeva, *Sobranie drevnerusskogo iskusstva v Zagorskom muzee* (Leningrad, 1968), 88.

Pereiaslavl' and other miracle workers, as well as of Sergius, before giving birth to male children.[60] In the 1560s those around Metropolitan Makarii who wrote the Book of Degrees "embroidered" Sophia's donation of 1499 with a story according to which she too had made a pilgrimage to Trinity to pray for Vasilii's birth. En route she had a vision in which Sergius thrust a male child on her, a child to which Sophia subsequently gave birth after her prayers to Sergius. To corroborate the story, the author said Vasilii III related the tale to Metropolitan Ioasaf who, of course, had been Trinity's abbot.[61] In 1585 Tsaritsa Irina, urged by husband Tsar Fedor, walked to Trinity to attend the translation of Sergei's relics to a new casket and to pray for a child. Queen Elizabeth's ambassador Giles Fletcher, who arrived in Moscow in 1588, noting that Sergius's reputed intercessory power had yet to make her pregnant, reported that 5–6,000 ladies-in-waiting and 4,000 soldiers attended Irina on her journey.[62] In 1588 and 1591 Trinity cellarer Evstafii Golovkin painted two icons on which he inscribed appeals that Sergius grant Irina and Fedor an heir.[63] Trinity's brotherhood made common cause with the Muscovite court in perpetuating the myth that reverence to Sergius was the way to royal motherhood.

* The record of women's devotion to Sergius's cult in donations raises questions as to whether there were gendered differences in those whom women and men memorialized. Males acting alone or with other males initiated 2,598 donations to Trinity, 83 percent of the total number of such acts; women were acting participants in 537 donations, or 17 percent of the total. Of these, women were sole agents in initiating 444, almost 83 percent of these. In the 93 others they acted jointly; in 30 instances with their spouses, in 41 with their sons, and in 22 with a variety of people, both male and female. Males and females made far fewer donations that contained statements regarding who was to be memorialized: 1,369 by men, 324 by women. Of these, the percentage in which women acted alone was roughly the same as that of the total number of acts in which women were agents.

Looking at donations in which benefactors specified who was to be memorialized, the most glaring gender difference is that males requested memorials for themselves in 31 percent of the acts they initiated, while females did so only in 21 percent of theirs; conversely females requested memorials for their spouses in 32 percent of their acts or for their spouse and themselves in 25 percent, while males memorialized their spouses alone in only 9 percent of their acts and they and their spouses in 4 percent. But did gendered preferences drive these choices? When women acted alone to obtain memorial prayers for their souls, they undoubtedly acted independently. To some degree women also acted independently to obtain memorials for their spouses and children. Thus, the poignant grief that drove widow Evdokiia Bulgakova-Shibaeva underlies the laconic entry in Trinity's donation book that records her gift of 100 rubles in 1573 for prayers commemorating her husband Frol, children Nikita and Elena, and eight unnamed infants who probably died at birth. Frol probably was one of the Bulgakov clan of Riazan' landholders whom, with their families, Ivan IV killed off in the mid-1560s.[64] But we know too that husbands frequently died before their spouses and, before doing so, directed them to obtain memorial prayers for their immediate family. It is likely also that the greater frequency with which women memorialized children—in 35 percent of their acts, while males memorialized children in only 9 percent of theirs—indicates a mixture of motives, ranging from maternal grief to spousal directives, that cannot be untangled. Mothers and fathers alike, however, memorialized sons almost three times as often as daughters. Here a gender preference seems obvious.

I can detect only two obvious shifts over time in male and female preferences for memorializing themselves, their spouses, or their children. Through period 5, ending in 1501, the number of charters in which men or women designated whom they wished memorialized is small; of those in which they memorialized themselves, or themselves and their spouses, the number is even smaller and without a discernable pattern. Thenceforth the number of memorial donations increased significantly each period until the final one, when overall donations were down. What is clear is that, beginning in the second quarter of the sixteenth century, men with increasing frequency memorialized their wives. The first to do so was Boiar Andrei Aleksandrovich Kvashnin, who on 7 June 1531 gave Trinity 50 rubles "in memory of my wife."[65] Was it the harbinger of an emerging respect for one's wife? Whatever, males memorialized their spouses more rarely than their spouses memorialized them, if only because women tended to outlive men. Another new phenomenon appeared in records for period 10 (1565–18 March 1584). On the face of it men memorialized themselves in 53 percent of their memorial charters and women did so in 69 percent of theirs. The difference may not be so great, however, when one realizes that in their charters women memorialized spouses as well as themselves 62 percent of the time. The *oprichnina* took a heavy toll on male landowners in this period; and women, more than at any other time, acted according to testaments left by departed spouses and generated a large proportion of memorials for both husband and wife. The steady—even precipitous—increase in requests by both sexes for memorial prayers for themselves illustrates a peculiar paradox:

as Muscovite Russia was evolving into a caste society, men and women of the landowning class exhibited a greater sense of individual identity.[66]

In a significant number of memorial requests men and women asked that Trinity's brotherhood pray for the souls of parents, grandparents and *roditeli*, a term that in most contexts referred to ancestors, but which could refer to only parents. They did so in virtually equal proportion, women doing so in almost 44 percent of their charters, males in just over 46 percent of theirs.[67] Without doubting the depth of the spiritual concerns motivating such requests, there is overwhelming evidence that benefactors memorialized their kin at Trinity as a means to establish their social identity and give public recognition to their lines. Gender was an important criterion in measuring the obligation to make such donations. Males requested prayers for their parents, grandparents, and ancestors in 45 percent of memorial donations; by contrast, they requested prayers for the line of their spouses in only .8 percent of such charters and for both their own and their spouse's line in .4 percent. Females similarly were committed to commemorating their parents, grandparents, and ancestors, doing so in 30 percent of their memorial donations. In 3 percent of memorial donations they requested prayers for their line and that of their spouses; and in 10 percent they requested prayers for their spouse's ancestors alone. That husbands who predeceased their spouses frequently instructed them in making memorial donations explains the larger percentage of female requests for prayers for their spouse's line. The entry in Trinity's donation book for 25 October 1549, however, recorded no such instruction when Princess Marfa, the wife of Petr Zasekin, gave Trinity 50 rubles so that its brothers would inscribe in its *sinodik* the names of 25 of their ancestors.[68] Her request was atypical only in its specificity.

That ancestral lines contained both males and females only adds to the complexity of any understanding of the influence of gender preferences in making memorial donations. Male benefactors, for example, requested prayers for their parents in 527 instances. In 255 of these they requested prayers for both parents. But of the remainder, requests for prayers for fathers (and in one instance for a stepfather), 199 to be exact, outnumbered the 73 for mothers by a ratio of well over two to one. Of 71 requests by women to memorialize their parents, 9 memorialized fathers only, 2 mothers only. Most memorialized both. But in 7 of the 21 memorial donations that women made to memorialize the parents of their spouses, they requested prayers for fathers; they did so only in two instances for mothers. Male and female benefactors unambiguously favored male parents with their memorials. Figures for grandparents are too small to allow an analysis of gender preferences. Those for ancestors generally did not differentiate by gender.

Men and women also requested memorial prayers for a variety of persons other than immediate family members or direct ancestors. In 68 records of memorial donations, women memorialized mainly an assortment of collateral relatives. In this statistical sample there is no clear evidence of gender preference: thus, for period 3 (1445–61) women made memorial donations for grandchildren, a daughter-in-law, a son-in-law, and a grandson; for period 9 (1547–64) they commemorated three grandchildren, three daughters-in-law, a niece, a son-in-law, and a monk. In a significant number of the 269 records in which men were benefactors, donations memorialized persons of the same social class who were not relatives. In period 8 (1533–47), for example, male estate holders memorialized 15 other landowners, state secretaries memorialized five others in the same office, and clerics memorialized seven clerics. In addition, men initiated seven memorials for uncles. In some of these men were executors of testaments of neighboring estate owners; in others they may have memorialized relatives by marriage. There also were approximately 14 memorials that Ivan IV made in period 10 (1564–18 March 1584) for men he had done away with during the *oprichnina*.

The data regarding the identities of those memorialized suggests that women, like men, contracted for memorial prayers for their souls, those of their ancestors, and those of their spouse with an acute awareness that memorials affirmed their social status. Witness the testament of 1 August 1513 of the nun Evdoksiia, the widow of Prince Fedor Strigin Obolenskii. Being childless, Evdoksiia had numerous dowry properties to distribute and Trinity was one of the monasteries she gifted in return for prayers "for the soul of my lord Prince Fedor Ivanovich, for my own soul and for all our ancestors." Evdoksiia's will ends with the statement that after her donations were made and her debts paid she held "her lord and husband's brother Prince Vasilii Ivanovich Obolenskii 'Shekhe' Strigin [the same Obolenskii mentioned above in another act as executor and creditor] and elders Rodion Kostrov and Varsonofii Gomzaikov of the Trinity Monastery" responsible for her memorial. On the back of the will, Prince Vasilii attested before Metropolitan Varlaam that he had distributed her estate in accord with her wishes. At her request, he continued, he gave Trinity 25 rubles for five feasts, a ruble for four offices for the dead (*panikhidy*), and .2 ruble for candles. Following his statement Trinity's treasurer noted that he had received the memorial donation. Evdoksiia's lavishness was in accord with the high status and the wealth of her husband's family and that of her father Ivan Kuritsyn. What was unusual was the meticulous care with which the dying Evdoksiia set down how her property was to be distributed, who was to be memorialized, and how her soul was to be set at peace—and who was to do it.[69] With much the same motivation men overwhelmingly memorialized only themselves and their kin. Women, much more frequently than men, memorialized children. But where distinctions were made, women memorialized boys more than girls. Similarly, men and women thought it more important to memorialize fathers than mothers. Finally, men frequently memorialized unrelated men of the same social class; women never memorialized women of the same class who were not family members. The statistical patterns I have described also suggest that both male and female donors conventionally memorialized lines descending to them through their mothers as well as through their fathers.

* It was not unusual that Evdoksiia Strigina Obolenskaia became a nun after her husband's death or that Ivan IV housed the widowed "Queen Marfa" at a convent. In 1558/59, for example, Vasilii Durov wrote a testament in which he gave his wife Evfimiia her dowry. It consisted of one-third of Serino Village near Dmitrov and "her choice of either clothes or 50 rubles," adding that if she didn't like the clothes, they should be sold. Further, Vasilii said that her share of the village should go to his son Nikifor and that Evfimiia could live with whatever son she wished, or alone, and that they would support her. And should she wish to be tonsured, they were to "purchase a cell for her in a house of her choice," and that the terms for her support should remain in place. Evfimiia must have chosen to live out her life at a convent that was subsidiary to the Trinity-Sergius Monastery, because by 1600 Serino belonged to Trinity.[70] In my database at least 71 female donors or women otherwise mentioned in donations were said to be nuns or candidates for tonsure. Such references occur in every period.

Convents were of two types: some were, like male houses, independent and subject to local bishops or lay patrons; others were subsidiaries of male monasteries. In the sixteenth century, convents comprised an estimated 14 percent of all monasteries. Other than that, and information about one or two wealthy convents, we know next to nothing about them, including those belonging to Trinity.[71] The testaments of senior elder Varsunofii Iakimov (10 April 1595) and of Trinity monk Tikhon Chasnikov (1596/97) reveal that Trinity had three subsidiary convents. Varsunofii said that at his death, in addition to money distributed from his estate to Trinity's monks, "a ruble each [was to go] to nuns at Khot'kovo, of whom there were 36, to nuns at Klement'evo of whom there were 34, . . . and also a ruble each to the 22 nuns at the [convent] of the most-pure Mother of God at Podsosenie." Tikhon asked that his estate grant .03 rubles to each nun at the same convents, whose numbers he put at 37, 33, and 27.[72] These were small convents.

No act survives recording how and when Trinity acquired the village of Bogorodtskoe "*Pod sosnoiu*," where a convent of the same name came into being. Several immunity charters, the earliest issued by Grand Prince Ivan III between 1462 and 1466, indicate that Trinity owned the property located in Radonezh on the Voria River seven kilometers to the southeast.[73] V. V. Zverinskii's list of Russian houses said it was a convent named the Dormition of the Mother of God and said Trinity took it over by 1561. It already was a subsidiary convent of the Trinity-Sergius Monastery in 1558/59, however. According to a charter of that date, Arina, the wife of Pavel Zvorykin and daughter of Andrei Polkov, together with her son, gave Trinity her share of a family estate in Vladimir for memorial prayers and so that she "might find peace at the [convent] of the [the Dormition] of the Mother of God at Podsosenie" (*pokoiti u Bogoroditsu pod Sosnoiu*).[74] Klement'evo Village, the site of a second subsidiary convent, was immediately south of the Trinity-Sergius Monastery. It was one of Trinity's oldest properties, having come to it in 1425 or 1426 from the estate of Prince Andrei of Radonezh. At that time a monastery was said to be there, but I know no act by which it became a Trinity subsidiary.[75] The Monastery of the Intercession at Khot'kovo near Radonezh was ancient. Epifanii wrote that Sergius's brother Stefan was tonsured there, probably in the 1330s. By 1506 it was thought to be where Varfolomei/Sergius had buried his parents, although Epifanii in describing their tonsure and burial did not name it as the site of either.[76] If Sergius's parents were tonsured there, it must have housed both sexes. Probably in 1454 Trinity elder Nifont Skobel'tsin donated a "waste," a plot of land that had ceased to be farmed, to the Monastery of the Intercession in Khot'kovo. The act, written by a cleric and witnessed by three Trinity monks, said Nifont contracted to be its priest. In 1472/73 the priest Andreian of the Monastery of the Intercession purchased a nearby waste, specifying at his death it go to Trinity. Neither act said unambiguously that the monastery in Khot'kovo had come under Trinity's administration. On 1 August 1544 Ivan IV issued a charter placing the monastery at Khot'kovo and its properties under Trinity's jurisdiction and specifying that it was to house only women.[77]

Women frequently entered convents as they approached death or at the death of their spouse. Trinity's records contain 27 such cases between 1392 and 1533; that is, either of donors or of those memorialized who were or became nuns. Most of them, it is clear, lived in houses unconnected to Trinity. Nor do I have evidence regarding who lived in the convents at Klement'evo or Khot'kovo then or later, or how these houses were organized and governed.

In Trinity's donation book the earliest request for tonsure at the Intercession Convent in Khot'kovo dates to 1621, when one Efim Skobeev gave Trinity five rubles so that it would take his daughter, the nun Taiseia. The few references to the Skobeevs in Moscow's service books indicate that they were provincial servicemen and officials. Trinity's donation book mentions several other requests like that of Efim's in the seventeenth century: in 1644 a serviceman at the Muscovite court, Vasilii Fedorovich Ianov, together with his wife and son, donated 1,000 rubles to construct a stone church of the Intercession "over the [graves of] the parents of the miracle worker Sergius." In the sixteenth century the church, a smaller winter church, and cells at the Intercession Convent were of wood. None of its few residents, so far as I know, came from a distinguished family.[78] I have no records, even for the seventeenth century, regarding nuns at the Klement'evo Convent or requests for tonsure there. The land cadastre of 1573/74 said it had a wooden church dedicated to the Dormition of the Mother of God with an auxiliary chapel and a wooden winter church dedicated to St. Nicholas, as well as a wooden bell tower and cells.[79] I do have evidence regarding nuns at the Dormition Convent in Podsosenie. It consists of nine donation grants like that which Arina Zvorykina made to Trinity in 1558/59 so that it would tonsure her there. The others date from 1567/68 to 1599/1600. Six other charters, beginning with a testament of 1558/59 by which Vasilii Durov disposed of dowry property in Dmitrov of his wife Evfimiia, indicated residence at one of Trinity's convents, although they did not give it a name. The Durov testament did specify that Evfimiia be buried at Trinity when she died and, as noted above, the village in question belonged to Trinity by 1592–94.[80] In another of the six, one Matvei D'iakov wrote Trinity's officers in 1599/1600 to confirm the contract between his father Stepan and the monastery by which it had received the village of Korobaeva, a hamlet and two wastes (probably in Moscow) in return for the tonsure of his mother and one of his sisters (and to arrange the marriage of a another). In Tsar Fedor's time the convent at Podsosenie consisted of the Church of the Dormition, a wooden Church of the Resurrection, cells, several tilled fields, hay fields, forests, and a water mill.[81]

The acts reveal a good deal about why Trinity established subsidiary convents and how it maintained them. For one, the women in Trinity's convents were well born. From 12 to 17 were from provincial landowning families in Pereiaslavl' (4), Dmitrov (4), Moscow (4), Kostroma (2), and Bezheskii Verkh, Vladimir, and Iaroslavl' (1 each), lands where Trinity had properties. Three came from boiar families and one, Queen Marfa, the daughter of Vladimir of Staritsa, was an appanage princess whom Ivan IV had ordered tonsured. Not only were they from the same class from which Trinity recruited many of its monks and most of its officers; they were from the same families. Thus, in 1567/68 Dmitrii Lodygin gave Trinity two hamlets in Moscow. In return he asked that he and his wife Matrena be tonsured at Trinity and his sons be taken in as servants and, if they so desired, tonsured there. Lodygins appear in Trinity documents starting in the late fifteenth century, and two of them—a Zhuk and a Denis Afanas'ev—were Trinity servants. Ignatii Lodygin was an elder and treasurer at Trinity between 1584 and 1592. Matrena was a descendent of a Muscovite *d'iak* of the early sixteenth century named Boldyr' Paiusov; the Lodygins were likely of the same bureaucratic milieu. I have no idea what caused the dramatic change in the fate of this family, but the date of the donation suggests it was related to the *oprichnina*.[82] Another example: in 1574/75 Mariia, the wife of Bogdan Semenovich Zamytskii, and her son Ivan gave Trinity an estate comprising a village with a Church of St. Nicholas, 8 hamlets, and 11 forested plots on the Nerl' River in Pereiaslavl'. "And when God [says] her time has come," she dictated to her scribe, Trinity's archimandrite "is to tonsure me at the Convent of the Mother of God at Podsosenie." Many Zamytskiis had been boiars and its members held high service ranks in the late sixteenth century. Zamytskii estate owners in Pereiaslavl' made commemorative grants to Trinity beginning in 1560/61 and especially in the *oprichnina* years. An Elisei Zamytskii became Trinity monk Elizarei and from 1570/71 to 1577/78 was a member of its council of elders and momentarily its cellarer.[83]

Then there is the woman with whose donation grant I began this chapter. After the death of her husband Grigorii Ivanovich Drovnin Zabolotskii, the widow Matrena wrote two donation charters in 1470/71 and one in 1471/72 granting Trinity significant properties in the districts of Pereiaslavl' and Novosil' in return for memorial prayers and feasts. In those of 1470/71 she said it was her wish to be tonsured at Trinity's Convent of the Mother of God at Podsosenie. She became the nun Marem'iana and abbess of the house. The Zabolotskii clan had provided the Muscovite court with boiars and high-ranking commanders and servitors from the late fifteenth century but saw their positions and hereditary properties in Pereiaslavl' liquidated by the *oprichnina*. Their patronage of Trinity had begun in 1512; an Iona Zabolotskii was a monk there in the late 1540s; an Alipii Terent'evich Zabolotskii was buried there as a monk in 1566.[84] Finally, in 1580/81 an Anna, the daughter of Mikhail Skripitsyn from Pereiaslavl', requested tonsure at Podsosenie and burial at the great house.[85] Nuns at Trinity's subsidiary convents, or at least that in Podsosenie, like monks at the great house, were from the same landowning families whose hereditary lands were close by Trinity or one of its outposts and who were Trinity's patrons.

Following Matrena's request for tonsure and to be a nun in the Novosil' act was the phrase, "and implement these [requests] to give support [*obrochnaia dat'*] as set forth in the charter."[86] I take this to mean that Matrena/Mirem'iana intended that her land grant support her during her time as a nun and go to Trinity only at her death (when it would provide a suitable commemoration and burial as provided in the document). The subsequent disposition of the property that Vasilii Durov gave Trinity in 1558/59 to finance his widow's tonsure supports my interpretation, and other documents are explicit about this. In 1569/70 Irina, the widow of Grigorii Elizar'ev and daughter of Iartsev Narmatskii, in promising her dowry of several hamlets in Radonezh and Pereiaslavl' to Trinity at her death, directed that until then Trinity was to "give her a cell" at its Convent of the Mother of God at Podsosenie.[87] The widow Anna Voronova gave Trinity "her husband's" village of Dmitreevo in Kostroma District. According to the terms of the grant, Anna could live there until near death, at which time Trinity was to tonsure her at Podsosenie. Monastic peasants were to till the estate and annually deliver to her 20 *chetverti* (a *chetvert'* as a dry measure = 210 liters) of rye and 40 *chetverti* of oats. As death neared, the monastery was to tonsure her. After she became a nun, "as set down in the books, it was to provide fully for her, just as [the monastery] supported the nun Akulina Chiubatova."[88] Land cadastres reveal that income from the mill at Podsosenie went to the maintenance of Queen Marfa and that the village housed 12 persons attached to her service. In 1598 Boris Godunov made a pilgrimage to the convent to give thanks after having recovered from illness.[89]

The 15 women described as nuns or requesting tonsure were not only widows; they were old. Or most of them were. One or two probably became nuns on their death bed. Knowing this, and that family incomes supported their tenure, one might describe the convent at Podsosenie, and probably the others, as the equivalent of a contemporary nursing home. But this was only part of the story: in 11 of the records, widows chose a nun's life independent of instructions from their late or dying spouses. As Matrena Zabolotskaia dictated to her scribe, "I wish to be tonsured a nun" (*I pokhochiu si postric' v chernitsy*).[90] In the time that was left to them these women chose to break with routines and duties of family life (although, like many of Trinity's monks, they probably enjoyed the frequent company of kin) in order to prepare for their salvation by a life of prayer at a site proximate to their intercessor. Their donations made it possible. This is a partial answer to the question I posed at the outset, paraphrasing Brown, about a woman's freedom to choose.

* In Trinity's charters women figure prominently as initiators of memorial grants of property to Trinity. In fact, they made about 17 percent of such grants, almost always acting within conventions outside their control, frequently as companions of their spouse, more often as widows. They did what they did because custom dictated that they act for themselves and minor children to provide suitable memorials for a dead spouse, or because they were the only member of their immediate family alive and able to meet its obligations. It is worth repeating that widows often said they made memorial donations at the express will of dying husbands; in early periods often they were executors or co-executors of their late husbands' testaments. In this Muscovite Russian women were not so different from the women described by Samuel Cohn in Tuscany and Umbria who were redactors of from 30 percent to 48 percent of surviving wills. By contrast to Italy and France, where the percentage of donations by women declined from the tenth through the twelfth century, but like trends in Germany, Russian women maintained the same right to dispose of property in the final periods of my study as in earlier ones.[91] In the matter of dowries, however, Anastasiia Obolenskaia's management of the dowry her mother arranged with her spouse, and the degree of control Anastasiia subsequently exercised over the property to preserve it in the female line across several generations, was unusual even in an all-European perspective. This and other evidence I have presented about donations of dowry property to Trinity, interpreted in the light of what we know about Muscovite dowries in general, leave little doubt that when women could choose, they acted tenaciously to retain for themselves the means to provide memorial prayers at Trinity or to ensure that their female descendents could do so.

Sergius's cult elicited from women an unusual range of personal expression. Anna Skripitsyna's frequent gifts, great and small and often without mention of a memorial, were simple expressions of devotion. From the numerous cases where widows made lavish gifts to Trinity, with or without memorial requests attached to them, we may infer too that, in addition to whatever spiritual value they might have sought, women were as determined as men to call attention to their social standing and that of their family. Few other sites could bring their acts such notoriety. Princess Evfrosiniia of Staritsa thought so and her generosity to Trinity, calibrated to exalt her family's station, was an ingredient in a complex campaign of giving to religious centers to ensure that it would not be forgotten. Women, operating within the same memorial culture as men, sent distinctly gendered commemorative requests with their donations at Sergius's tomb—requests that, among other things, demonstrated that honor descended through matrilineal as well as patrilineal lines. Finally, Tsaritsa Sophia's resort to embroidery (a woman's métier) and donation (an accepted woman's sphere of public action) for an impassioned political statement of her son's claim to the throne was an assertion of family place quite out of the ordinary. The bookmen who transformed Sophia's wiles into invented tradition had their own concerns. But they made it possible for royal women with analogous aspirations to emulate what they thought Sophia had done, thereby making the extraordinary ordinary.

Chapter Seven

INTERMENT AT TRINITY

In a donation charter of 1523/24, having requested prayers for his soul and those of his ancestors, and that he be tonsured, Gorianin Mordvinov, a landowner in Rostov, added, "And [when] God sends for [my] soul, for me Gorianin . . . , then bury me at the house of the Life-giving Trinity."[1] Gorianin was not the first person to be buried at Trinity; nor was he the first of its patrons to make such a request. Trinity's inventory, published in 1880, of those buried at Trinity, together with the location of their graves, contains names of many persons from whom we have no requests. By 2002 excavations revealed over 275 complete or fragmentary gravestones in the collection of the Sergiev Posad Museum-Reserve and more digging will undoubtedly uncover more. These finds confirm the burial sites of some of those in the inventory, but also contain names of the interred about whom the inventory is silent.[2] We probably will never have an inventory of Trinity's graves that is accurate and complete. One reason is that we cannot expect to recover anywhere near the sum of stones that were laid down or to decipher fully inscriptions on fragmentary finds. The markers were of soft limestone and highly perishable. Nor did it help that eighteenth-century builders used old gravestones as construction material.[3] Nevertheless, the body count in the inventory alone, amounting to 952 names, leads us to the realization that in 1880 at Trinity the dead outnumbered the living by a ratio of three or four to one! Even for the period from Trinity's foundation to the beginning of the *smuta* in 1605 the number of burials within Trinity's walls recorded in the inventory, in chronicles, or on gravestones, 339, was far greater than the 220 who then resided at Trinity.[4] By any standard we may conclude that in Muscovite society the cohabitation of the living and the dead at Trinity and other holy sites was accepted as normal.

* From late antiquity the conviction that burial in hallowed ground was beneficial for the salvation of one's soul became rooted in Christian tradition. This being so, it is not the least surprising that in the Middle Ages a monastery might become a favored burial site, particularly if it contained the relics of a saint. Saints, after all, "hovered near the ultimate source of all power."[5] Might not that same power be inherent in their relics? Relics made a house, observed Barbara Rosenwein writing about the monastery of Cluny in Burgundy, a sacred place that "could mediate between the natural and supernatural world." In western Christendom the dead had prominent places in and around churches and monasteries and elites marked such sites with gravestones and sarcophagi into the modern era. The same could be said about the Trinity Monastery that housed the relics of its founder, Sergius of Radonezh. The Orthodox Church in Rus' introduced norms for burial in and around urban churches and at proliferating monastic establishments in the fourteenth century.[6] We know too that requests for burial were an element of the new culture of memorializing the dead. "Gravemarkers (*doski*) became the pages of an immense stone *sinodik*," wrote archaeologist L. A. Beliaev.[7] As in the medieval West this culture, in which people sought burial within monastic walls, generated relations between monasteries and laity that were driven by complex motives on both sides.

Sergius's grave was the epicenter of Trinity's sacred space and provided the *raison d'être* for the others. He died in 1392, but after the Tatar destruction of Trinity in 1408, the location of his grave supposedly was lost; that is, until 1422, when Abbot Nikon miraculously discovered it. The timing could not have been better to attract the patronage for a new stone church of the Holy Trinity from Prince Iurii Dmitrievich of Zvenigorod and Galich, the younger brother and political rival of Grand Prince Vasilii I of Moscow, and one whom Sergius had baptized. He was present when Nikon translated Sergius's remains to the new church and established a feast honoring him as a miracle worker.[8] In 1426 plague took Trinity's lord and patron Prince Andrei Vladimirovich of Radonezh and also his brother Prince Semen of Borovsk. Although the earliest sources told different stories, it was probably Andrei whom Nikon buried in the southwest corner of the Trinity Church.[9] The brothers were sons of Vladimir Andreevich, the hero of the Kulikovo victory, and Vasilii's cousins once removed. In one stroke Nikon had obtained for his house the favor of the ruling family of Radonezh and distanced it from Iurii's patronage. On both counts it was an outcome that would win favor at the Muscovite court. When Nikon died in 1427, the monks built a wooden chapel adjacent to Trinity to house his remains. Then or soon thereafter they interred there 12 of Sergius's disciples and his first hagiographer

Epifanii the Wise. There is no record that these people requested burial at Trinity; rather we should interpret their interments as steps in the founding of Sergius's cult.[10] Nor, with one exception, is there evidence that the other 33 persons whom the inventory said were interred at Trinity before 1490 requested burial there.[11] Yet, because virtually all of them had been Trinity monks, it is likely that they expected it would happen. And knowing what the norm became by 1500, one might suppose that those in the inventory such as Cellarer Avraamii Voronin, whose family first donated land to Trinity in Nikon's time, made donations with the intent of being tonsured and buried there. This was also likely to have been the case for monks Grigorii Buturlin and Petr Ignat'evich Morozov, and Cellarer Veniamin Pleshcheev, members of prominent Muscovite families who had benefited Trinity as early as the 1440s.[12] Many places were available. So patrons probably did not think it necessary to make provision for burial in donation charters or testaments, at least until late in the century.

By then members of elite families in Muscovite society sought burial at Trinity and said so. The compilation of 1518 says that, having been tonsured as the monk Varsunofii on 5 June 1490, two days before his death, the prominent state secretary Vasilii Mamyrev was laid to rest at Trinity. Other evidence comes from gravestones. The earliest is dated 1480. It marked the resting place of Vasilii Beda, who was a favored state secretary of Grand Prince Vasilii II. Another gravestone commemorated Iurii Romanov syn Alekseev, a landowner and son of an important Muscovite *d'iak*, who was buried at Trinity in 1493/94. Trinity's donation book recorded Iurii's grants in Rostov and Borovsk and, according to T. V. Nikolaeva, Trinity's *sinodik* noted his right to a feast and burial. A third gravestone marked the grave of Trinity monk and former Archbishop of Novgorod Sergii. It is dated 1495.[13] Five other stones dating from the early sixteenth century marked graves of members of Moscow boiar families or, in one case, of a member of a prominent princely family from Suzdal', Prince Semen Borisovich. Between 1508 and 1511 Semen gave his estate of Okaemovo to Trinity for prayers for his soul and those of his wife and ancestors. By the time he wrote this he had been tonsured there as the monk Sergius. Of the boiars, a stone dated 1517 marked the grave of Prince Dmitrii Pronskii, who had requested tonsure at Trinity. Another, dated 1519, commemorated Ivan Ivanovich Kholmskii. And a fragmentary stone has a partial inscription saying that Princess Anna Vorotinskaia, the wife of Ivan Ivanovich Vorotynskii—whose stone of 1535 is adjacent to it—commemorated their dead child. It is undated, but is similar to a nearby gravestone of 1508. A fourth, dated 1512, marked the grave of Semen Ivanovich Ugrimov Zabolotskii. Five other gravestones of the late fifteenth or early sixteenth century lack legible inscriptions.[14] Nun Evdoksiia, the widow of the late Boiar Prince Fedor Ivanovich "Sheka" Strigin Obolenskii, concluded her elaborate testament of 1 August 1513 with the request that, "when God calls for my soul . . . , my executors shall petition that my bones be carried to the monastery of the Life-giving Trinity." This was the earliest charter containing a request for burial.[15] By 1500, if not before, laity began to think it important to seek burial at Trinity; not only that, but to have their name inscribed on a burial stone.

I know of 27 requests for burial between 1522 and 1565. Their incidence became more frequent over time, but nothing like that which characterized the period from 1565 to the death of Tsar Ivan IV in 1584, when requests for burial at Trinity skyrocketed to 70, a total that can be supplemented with names on gravestones of six persons not in the inventory. A determination by estate owners to specify exactly what a donation grant was to give them accounts in part for the increase in burial requests. Yet it could hardly have been a coincidence that 1565 marked the beginning of the *oprichnina* terror that brought a deluge of land acquisitions to Trinity—and a corresponding escalation in requests for burial there. Burial requests had the same geographical incidence as land acquisitions. For example, of 119 acquisitions that followed in the wake of the devastating campaign of Ivan's *oprichniki* in 1569 through Tver', Kashin, Staritsa, and Bezhetskii Verkh to Novgorod, 15 were memorial grants that included requests for burial. In reading the documents, it takes little imagination to appreciate the violence that overtook these families and the poignant fate of those who survived. Thus in a testament of 1573/74 one Nastasiia gave Trinity one-half of the village of Mikhailovskoe in Staritsa together with its Church of the Annunciation and four hamlets. In return she asked that memorial prayers be said and an annual feast be held at the monastery for her late husband and his ancestors. Nastasiia was the widow of Stepan Ivanovich Zhitov. Her testament was so much a memorial for her husband's line that Stepan may have dictated its contents before he died during the *oprichnina* army's march through Staritsa. Although the other half of Mikhailovskoe had belonged to their son Luk, Nastasiia wrote that it was to pass to his wife Mariia, allowing us to suppose that Luk and other children had perished with him, and that the task of memorializing the family fell to Stepan's widow. The testament specified that she be allowed to live on in her half of Mikhailovskoe and, when death neared, Trinity was to bury her at the monastery. Another memorial grant of 1594 indicates that by then she had taken the veil as the nun Pelageia at Trinity's Podsosenie Convent.[16] Her request to be buried at Trinity was truly a request to be buried by the only family she had left, her brothers and sisters of Trinity's community. From the death of Ivan IV to the death of Boris Godunov in 1605, there were 34 more requests for burial at Trinity and four gravestones marking additional interments.

To sum up, requests for burial to 1605 appeared in 141 charters. As the burial inventory and gravestones reveal, there were more requests that went unrecorded in charters or in the monastery's donation book or, if they were recorded, have dates that cannot be reconciled. It is also apparent that charters containing burial requests made up a small part, 4 percent, of the 3,135 donations in my database. In this Trinity's experience differed little from what Barbara Rosenwein found at the Cluny Monastery, where in the almost 3,000 donation charters recorded between 909 and 1049, only in the final half century did requests for burial reach 17 percent of the total.[17] What we can say is that the practice of requesting burial at Trinity in a donation charter began shortly before 1500, quickly became well established, and appeared with increasing frequency to 1605. Even if the number of requests under-represents the sum of those who sought and received burial at Trinity, one must conclude that only a small number of those who were Trinity's patrons thought it important or possible to seek burial there.

* Most of the people who requested burial at Trinity were not so alone in the world as Nastasiia/Pelageia when they contemplated the hour of their death. Most did so while residing in the bosom of their family. Some made their decision while actively involved in public life and conscious of their standing in society. If we put aside the special conditions of the *oprichnina* years, we must look to the memorial culture that had grown up among landowners and monasteries to understand why requests for burial appeared in the sixteenth century, who made such requests, and what they expected from them. During the sixteenth century, we know from the increasing specificity of donation acts that benefactors developed a more complex sense of familial or, even, individual identity. The gravestone, dated 1573, of the monk Ioasaf [Iakov] Vasil'evich Volynskii was the first to contain an inscription saying that the burial was at a reserved plot (*zaniatom meste*); sometime later in the century his kinsman Fedor Andreevich Volynskii was buried nearby and his stone bears the same notation. The practice of reserving a plot began at least by the middle of the sixteenth century. The burial inventory records the presence, side by side, of graves of family members who died at different times. This could only have happened if early on someone, wishing to maintain a visual reminder of clan solidarity while yet alive, reserved a plot or row for future graves of family members.[18] The first surviving document in which a living person reserved plots for him- or herself and family within

the walls of the Trinity-Sergius Monastery is the testament signed by Boiar Fedor Ivanovich Khvorostinin in 1602/3.[19] Requests for family plots were part of a culture that provided for regular commemoration of the departed. Within this culture, burial, like memorial prayers or tonsure, came at a price. It could range from 2 rubles to 500 rubles, but 50 rubles was common. At a monastery the brotherhood and their benefactors created a self-affirming community linked by spiritual, cultural, and economic bonds.[20]

Those at the top of the social order frequently made arrangements for memorial prayers at more than one monastery. But they could be tonsured or buried only at a single house. I already have demonstrated that landowners in Muscovite Rus' often took their vows when anticipating death while but a few well-born men and women did so while in their prime, and that those that did often were involved in familial concerns pertaining to the distribution of properties to ensure that living family members and ancestors were properly memorialized. Well-born men and women who took vows when in their prime also were active when it came to burying them. There is no better example of this than Trinity's cellarer Evstafii Golovkin. Soon after the completion of the Basilica of the Dormition at Trinity in 1585, Evstafii planned his family's interment, and his own. In 1586 he made a donation to memorialize his sister and, according to the inventory, that same year she was buried at Trinity within the new church on its southwest wall. At that time Evstafii, following a tradition that had taken shape in the sixteenth century and that he had fostered, reserved a site in front of and to the west of the main entrance to the basilica, where brother Ivan Golovkin, Akseniia Golovkina (the wife of his uncle), and he were to be buried. There they could count Trinity's community of liturgical specialists who were his surrogate family to pray for their souls until the Day of Judgment. A gravestone there, dated 1586, marks the resting place of Akseniia. More recently, stones marking the graves of Evstafii and his brother Ivan Golovkin have been found adjacent to it. Trinity's inventory records Ivan's burial but does not give it a date. Although his final gift to Trinity was in 1579/80, Ivan's burial—or reburial—on that site could only have taken place after 1585. When Evstafii died in 1602, Trinity's brothers interred him beside his brother and Oksiniia as had been planned 17 years earlier.[21]

It is worth repeating that death rituals in the Middle Ages were "not so much a question of dealing with a corpse as of reaffirming the secular and spiritual order by means of a corpse."[22] Funerals were occasions that reminded society of the rank and lineage of the deceased and strengthened family solidarity. Excepting that of Sergius, we have no description of a burial service at Trinity. But, arguably, choosing where one's line was buried was more important than the rite itself in securing these ends. Monastic ground was hallowed. There, memorial prayers had a greater resonance because the erstwhile beneficiary lay near his or her hoped-for intercessor. There, a family assembled for feasts honoring its ancestors; and it was there that the family returned to bury succeeding members of its line. Names of estate owners who lived near Trinity or one of its outposts and who were its patrons, and provided a high proportion of its brothers, fill the burial inventory; for example, 3 Butenevs, 4 Aigustovs, and 4 Kurtsevs from Pereiaslavl', 13 Durovs from Dmitrov; also 3 Pisemskiis, 3 Golovkins, and 5 Tatevs from not-so-nearby Kostroma, Bezhetskii Verkh, and Starodub.[23] The more powerful the reputation of the miracle worker, the more prestigious the site.[24] It is safe to say that, because of Sergius's reputation, the Trinity-Sergius Monastery was the most prestigious place for aristocrats to bury their dead. A. A. Zimin's monograph on the Muscovite elite lists 137 families in which one or more members obtained boiar rank to 1605; Trinity's inventory indicates that 43 buried one or more of its members there.[25]

One might also assume that great families would expect the monastery to recognize their status by providing burial sites for their members as close as possible to that of Sergius. As Peter Brown observed, the cult of saints localized the holy as a place where those who sought a saint's intercessory powers could find the "joy of proximity." He called it a "therapy of distance" that made it possible for the corpse laid to rest near the tomb of a saint to rise again at the resurrection.[26] Status was important at Trinity, as it was at other houses or in the secular world. But when it came to burial sites, the reality was more complicated. It does not surprise us that, at least for over a century, the remains of Prince Andrei Vladimirovich rested in the Trinity Church, the holiest site in the monastery. The inventory insists that his brother Semen was there too. It also said that in the sixteenth century Trinity put to rest four members of the Gorbatyi princely line—Boris, his son Aleksandr, Aleksandr's wife Anastasiia, and their son Petr—in the same location. How does one account for this? One ingredient certainly was the clan's meteoric rise in status at the Muscovite court. Boris was a boiar by 1513, the first of his line to hold that rank. He remained a boiar until 1534/35. Boris died about 1538 and by 1544 his son Aleksandr was a boiar. Aleksandr brought the family to the pinnacle of success at court by a series of advantageous marriages: he married the daughter of Treasurer Peter Ivanovich Golovin of the Khovrin boiar clan and arranged the marriage of their oldest daughter to Nikita Romanovich Iur'ev, the brother of Tsar Ivan's wife Anastasiia. The clan's downfall was abrupt, Aleksandr and son Petr being among the first victims of Ivan's *oprichnina* in 1565.[27] The other factor that assured the Gorbatyi clan a place of honor at Trinity was its intimate and longstanding involvement in Sergius's cult. Before death Boris took the habit at Trinity as the monk Bogolep. On 31 March 1539, soon after Boris's death, Aleksandr gave Trinity his estate of Mikhailovskoe and its four hamlets in Rostov to memorialize his father, his mother, himself, and their ancestors. A church dedicated to Sergius stood on the estate, indicating that for some time previously he had been the object of Gorbatyi reverence. In 1546 Aleksandr gave Trinity another 50 rubles, and after his death his wife took the habit, probably at a house affiliated with Trinity, as the nun Nataliia before being buried alongside her husband and son in 1573.[28]

Three other boiar lines had graves in the Trinity Church: two Vorotinskii graves are there, but from the 1550s, excepting one other burial elsewhere at Trinity, the clan buried its dead at the Kirillov Monastery. Ivan IV's uncle Prince Mikhail L'vovich Glinskii, Mikhail's wife, two sons (one of whom was tonsured at Trinity before dying), and one of their wives also rested there. Then there was Ivan Iur'evich Patrikeev, his grandson Prince Mikhail Ivanovich Bulgakov-Golitsa (d. 1558), founder of the Golitsyn clan, and Boiar Prince Ivan Iur'evich Golitsyn (d. 1603). Grand Prince Ivan III, having deprived Ivan Patrikeev of his influence at court, forcibly tonsured him at Trinity as the monk Ioasaf in 1499, and there he died. Between 1552 and 1560 Mikhail too was a Trinity monk. Like the Gorbatyi clan, these families maintained a serious, although not an exclusive, commitment to Trinity's religious life in order to be buried next to Sergius. By the time Ivan Glinskii took the habit there in 1602 the line had given Trinity two considerable properties, a lavish inventory of clothes, jewels, and personal property, and the prodigious sum of 1,995 rubles.[29] Four prominent churchmen also rested in the sacred confines of the Trinity Church: Archbishop Ioasaf of Vologda (d. 1571); his predecessor Aleksei (d. 1565), who had been abbot of Kirillov and then a monk at Trinity; Kipriian Balakhonets (d. 1594), an archimandrite of Trinity; and the Trinity elder Varsunofii Iakimov (d. 1601). The graves of Metropolitan (1461–64) Feodosii (d. 1575), who lived the last 10 years of his life at Trinity; Serapion (d. 1516), a former abbot and archbishop of Novgorod; and former abbot and metropolitan Ioasaf Skripitsyn were in what the inventory described as Sergii's cell adjacent to the Trinity church. Now Ioasaf Skripitsyn rests in the Chapel of St. Nikon, as, probably, do the others. Finally, the name of Archbishop Sergii of Novgorod and the burial date, 10 April 1495, is on a gravestone located to the east of the central apse of the Trinity Church. Sergiii was tonsured at Trinity. Grand Prince Ivan III had designated Sergii archpriest of the Dormition Cathedral in the Moscow kremlin and in 1483, after his conquest of Novgorod, its archbishop. Unpopular there, Ivan III having deposed its last locally chosen archbishop and seized his treasury, Sergii returned to Moscow in 1484 and lived out his life at Trinity.[30]

The inventory grouped the names of others interred within the monastery according to the location of their graves and, in general, by the priority of the locations from highest to lowest. Obviously, Trinity's administrators created guidelines by which to allocate burial sites. They may have been imprecise, but they were far from arbitrary. People were buried at sites with people more or less like them in social rank and in their record of generosity or service to Trinity. It made for an order of precedence in which the most distinguished groups rested closer to Sergius and those less so in less exalted places, one more example of the Muscovite custom of creating hierarchy based upon service.

The Nikon chapel was the second most prestigious site. It contained the graves of Sergius's disciples, of members of several boiar lines—the Saltykovs, two Basmanovs, Iurii Dmitrievich Shein—and of the monk Ioasaf of the Volynskii family of landowners, who was not of boiar rank. These lines benefited Trinity, some over an extended period: from 1529 to 1600 the Saltykovs made 13 gifts to Trinity amounting to 619 rubles and several donations of personal property; the Basmanovs between 1544 and 1603/4 gave Trinity 470 rubles in cash or goods; over a period from 1506/7 to 1558 the Shein clan gave Trinity two villages in Beloozero, 149 rubles, and personal items of unspecified value; six Volynskii patrons between 1541 and 1586 gave Trinity a village in Kolomna and 520 rubles.[31]

The next most proximate burial site, unknown to the compilers of the inventory, extended from the Chapel of St. Nikon to the entrance of the metropolitan's residence (*mitropolich'i pokoi*), where investigators found 30 gravestones, 16 of which have legible inscriptions. The earliest, dated 1480, was the resting place of State Secretary Vasilii Beda; the latest was dated 1604. The site was primarily the chosen resting place of prominent boiar clans: the Pleshcheevs (eight stones), the Vorontsovs (two stones), and the Zabolotskiis (two stones). Each was bound to the Trinity-Sergius Monastery by patronage and longstanding personal ties.[32]

Four stones were for Fedor Grigor'evich Ochin Pleshcheev (1560), his wife Anna (second half of 16th century), and their sons Iurii (1550) and Ivan (1560). Two others have the names of wives Anna (1603) and Ul'iana (1565) of Fedor's nephews Nikita and Zakharii Ivanovichi. Andrei and Nikifor, the monk Nikandr (1594), Ivanovichi Okhotin Pleshcheev rest there too. Andrei certainly and Nikifor probably were nephews of Fedor Grigor'evich. At least three Pleshcheevs were Trinity monks in the fifteenth century, and one, Veniamin, its cellarer. From 1508 until 1603 Pleshcheevs gave Trinity 30 donations, including gifts of 50 rubles in 1557 by Fedor Pleshcheev, and 50 rubles in 1565 in memory of Ul'iana by a kinsman of her husband, Boiar Aleksandr Danilovich Basmanov. In 1587/88 Andrei Ivanovich gave Trinity a village in Bezhetskii Verkh in memory of his wife, Mariia. It may well be that her name is on one of the gravestones with illegible inscriptions. Altogether the Pleshcheev clan gave Trinity two villages in Zvenigorod, villages in Bezhetskii Verkh and Vladimir, seven donations of personal property, 220 gold coins (*zolotye*), and 1,799.61 rubles. Stones for the Zabolotskiis, rich landowners in Pereiaslavl' of the highest service ranks at the Muscovite court, were also in this area. The two identifiable gravestones were for Semen Ivanovich Ugrimov Zabolotskii (1512) and the nun Aleksandra (1563), formerly Akulina, the wife of Semen Konstantinovich. Three other Zabolotskiis were Trinity monks, an Iona from the 1540s to the 1560s, another Iona who was buried there at an unknown site in 1597, and an Alipii Terent'evich who died about 1566. Between 1512, when a gift of 90 rubles was recorded to commemorate a Gleb Zabolotskii, and 1571/72 the clan gave Trinity two villages in Pereiaslavl', two in Dmitrov, and one in Novosil', two gifts of personal property, and 380 rubles. Of this amount, on her deathbed Akulina Zabolotskaia gave Trinity 30 rubles. In 1565 this was supplemented by a gift in her memory of 20 rubles by her nephew Danilo Vladimirovich Zabolotskii. In 1570 Zakharii Semenovich Zabolotskii gave Trinity another 15 rubles "in memory the elder Aleksandra."[33] Two Vorontsovs were buried here—the stones contain names of serviceman and estate owner in Pereiaslavl' Ivan Dmitrievich (1572) and of Ul'iana (1553), the wife of Boiar Ivan Mikhailovich.

Three other Vorontsovs, according to Trinity's inventory, were buried in an only slightly less prestigious site between the churches of the Holy Trinity and the Procession of the Holy Spirit (completed in 1476) between 1568 and 1578. From 1522 to 1586 Vorontsovs gave Trinity 13 extensive properties in Dmitrov, Kashin, Tver', Moscow, Bezhetskii Verkh, and Borovsk, three gifts of personal property, 969.38 rubles, and 50 Hungarian gold pieces. One gift alone in Trinity's donation book in memory of Ivan Dmitrievich by his cousin ("brother" in the donation book) Vasilii Fedorovich Vorontsov in 1571/72 included villages in Tver', Kashin, Bezhetskii Verkh, Borovsk, and Moscow![34] At this site too were 25 graves of persons whose families were hardly less distinguished at court. Among them were seven members of the Rostovskii clan, four Khvorostinins, and four Buturlins, families that boasted one or more persons of boiar rank and had been important *oprichniki*. All benefited Trinity beyond the norm. Grigorii Buturlin, whom Abbot

Nikon tonsured as the monk Gennadii, between 1428 and 1432 gave Trinity a village in Uglich. Buturlins between 1550/51 and 1570/71 gave Trinity two other properties and a memorial gift of 50 rubles. Members of various branches of the Rostovskii clan gave Trinity 37 donations between 1523 and 1602/3. They included a yard in Moscow, a village worth 150 rubles in Dmitrov, a trove of personal property, and cash totaling 1,286 rubles. The Khvorostinin clan was a benefactor of Trinity from 1517 to 1604/5. It gave Trinity 750 rubles and three gifts of personal items. That few individuals from these clans—only Grigorii/Gennadii Buturlin and Semen/Serapion Vorontsov—became Trinity monks probably accounts for the burial of such prominent persons in less distinguished ground than the equally distinguished clans resting near the Nikon chapel. The site also contained five graves of Tatevs. Like the Rostovskiis and Khvorostinins, the Tatevs were a princely line related to the Riapolovskiis. Several became commanders (*voevody*) but no Tatev held more than minor ranks. The Tatevs gave Trinity only 200 rubles in the sixteenth century; their great generosity to Trinity in the first half of the seventeenth probably accounts for their being buried alongside the other families.[35]

The Church of the Procession of the Holy Spirit was next in precedence as a burial site. Maxim the Greek was buried within and by 1605 around it there were 26 graves of members of noble families. Most were prominent in patronage and in taking vows at Trinity. From clans that had placed individuals in the highest service ranks were Ivan Andreevich Bulgakov, who was tonsured in 1505; Prince Andrei Riapolovskii (d. 1570); Marfa (d. 1568), the wife of Prince Ivan Dmitrievich Bel'skii and daughter of Vasilii Vasilevich Shuiskii; Prince Iurii Ivanovich Kashin Obolenskii (d. 1564); and the nun Marfa (d. ca. 1570), previously Mariia, the wife of Ivan Vasilevich Kashin Obolenskii. Between 1549 and 1591 Trinity's donation book recorded eight Bulgakov donations consisting of 300 rubles in cash, personal property, and an estate in Borovsk valued at 502 rubles. Members of the Riapolovskii clan gave Trinity 166.66 rubles, some personal property, and a large dowry estate in Iur'ev between 1534 and 1556. From the Bel'skii clan Trinity received seven donations from 1534 to 1602/3 that came to 509 rubles, personal property valued at 15 rubles, and one and one-half villages with 13 hamlets in Tver'. The large Obolenskii clan outdid them all: from 1513 to 1605 various members made 59 donations amounting to 1,996.25 rubles, 12 gifts of personal items, a village in Vladimir, two villages in Obolensk (one controlling 52 hamlets), and two villages and three hamlets in Pereiaslavl'.[36] Among those from less exalted service ranks were a Grigorii Khitrii (d. 1580), the Trinity monk Serapion Solovtsov (d. 1555), and four members of the

Pisemskii clan. The Pisemskiis, rich Kostroma landowners, some of whom had important service ranks, were intimately tied to Trinity. Between 1546 and 1600/1 Pisemskii benefactors gave ten donations to Trinity: three villages and numerous hamlets, two caches of personal property, and cash totaling 160 rubles. An Iona Pisemskii was a Trinity monk in the 1540s, a Pafnutii Pisemskii in the 1550s, and four other Pisemskiis known to be buried at Trinity had been monks there. One, Makarii, was Trinity's treasurer in the 1570s. Grigorii Khitrii was from a family of minor servicemen in Viaz'ma. There is no record that he or a relative was tonsured at Trinity, but between 1547 and 1581 Khitriis gave Trinity eight donations totaling 322 rubles. Trinity monk Serapion, formerly Semen Solovtsov, evidently was from a family of minor service men in Pskov and Novgorod, and then Rostov. But between 1536 and 1555 members of the clan made ten gifts to Trinity of 449.94 rubles and opulent personal items.[37]

The next sites mentioned in the inventory were areas next to the present Church of St. Mikhei, the Refectory Church of St. Sergius, and between the latter and the main gate. These sites were further removed from Sergius's remains. For the period up to and including 1605 there were 23 graves in the first of these, 35 at the second, and ten at the third, as well as undated graves of an undetermined number of peasants from Trinity's estates. In these sites one finds the names of local landowning families such as the Aigustovs (three), the Kurtsevs (four), the Stogovs (three), the Butenevs (three) from Pereiaslavl', the Zlobin-Osor'ins (four), the Zacheslomskiis (two) from Dmitrov, and the Durovs (14!) from Kolomna. The Kurtsevs were famous, some as powerful officials at the Muscovite court, others as officers of the Trinity-Sergius Monastery. The earliest Kurtsev grave was Iov's (d. 1539). He had been Trinity's cellarer from 1524 to 1528 and participated in Ivan IV's baptism. Next was that of State Secretary Konstantin Afanas'evich Kurtsev, who died as the Trinity monk Kornilii in 1562. Daniil Kurtsev, the Trinity monk Dorofei and its treasurer and cellarer whom Ivan IV executed, was buried at Trinity in 1570. Finally, State Secretary Ivan Kushnik Kurtsev, who entered Trinity as the monk Iov by 1570, died and was buried there, probably in 1572. The Aigustovs were the most giving, providing Trinity with two monks, Gurii (1580–82/83) and the Elder Feognost' (1573/74–79/80), and 627 rubles. Relatively few members of the other families, however, became monks at Trinity, and their gifts, although often frequent, were modest compared to those buried at sites closer to Sergius. The Butenevs, for example, gave Trinity 288 rubles and some personal property in 12 gifts between 1524/25 and 1570. There was a Durov monk and at least one Zlobin-Osor'in monk at Trinity, but none from the other families.[38]

The inventory's concluding section contained 62 names of those thought to have been buried at Trinity up to 1605 but whose gravesites were unknown. Most were monks, some (e.g., Grigorii Buturlin) said to be disciples of St. Nikon who were buried in the fifteenth century; others, like abbot Pamba Moshin (1506, 1508–15), Treasurer Varsunofii Zamytskii (d. 1572), Andreian Angelov, Arefa Tormosov, and Simon Shubin, had been Trinity's officers in the sixteenth. One also finds names of members of elite clans who had requested tonsure at Trinity or one of its convents, such as Sheremetev, Bel'skii, Zasekin, Zabolotskii, Romandonovskii, and Obolenskii (including the nun Evdoksiia). Here the inventory noted that Trinity had buried more patrons who are not on the list because there is no record of their burial.[39]

Immediately preceding the list of those whose resting place was unknown were names of another group that by composition and burial site was exceptional. The site was the Basilica of the Dormition. It was special because the basilica, when completed in 1585, became the monastery's liturgical center. The inventory and gravestones thus far uncovered mark 33 graves dating from before 1605 in the church or in front of it. The heterogeneous origin of those buried there is also exceptional.[40] As I mentioned earlier, Trinity's cellarer Evstafii Golovkin buried Evfrosiniia Golovkina along its southwest wall and arranged his burial in 1602 in a family plot he had selected as the basilica was being completed. It was a conspicuous site near its main entrance where he had buried his brother and the wife of his uncle. Evfrosiniia's grave within the basilica was an anomaly in that other sites there were filled during the Time of Troubles and after by Tsar Vasilii Shuiskii and the Romanovs with "exiles" from the kremlin's imperial necropolis in the Church of Michael the Archangel. Shuiskii, in September 1606, reburied the Godunovs—Tsar Boris (d. 13 April 1605 as the monk Bogolep), his wife Mariia (a Skuratov), and his son Fedor—in the west entryway (*papert'*) to the basilica. At the same time he arranged that Fedor's sister Kseniia as the nun Ol'ga take up residence at Trinity's Podsosenie convent and at her death in 1622, she was laid to rest with the others. In 1613 Trinity buried Queen Marfa Staritskaia who, like Kseniia, had been living at Trinity's convent at Podsosenie, in the basilica. She rested alongside her daughter Evdokiia, who had at age 10 died in 1589. She may have been the only member of an outcast line interred there before 1605.[41]

Outside the basilica with the Golovkins were the remains of members of landowning families, some of them prominent, others not. They had in common a generosity to Trinity and most of them had taken tonsure there or at one of its convents, or counted members of their family who had done so. The inventory said Elizar, Vasilii, Nosnik, and Mikhail, the children of

Aleksandr Novosil'tsev, and Boris Domashnovich Novosiltsev in 1576 gave Trinity the estate in Tver' they had inherited from their grandmother, so that they could be buried at the Trinity-Sergius Monastery. Trinity's donation book confirms the grant but not the details. In 1529 a member of the clan gave Trinity 50 rubles.[42] Nearby rested two women of the Pushkin clan, Anisiia Ivanovna (d. 1595) and Mariia (d. 1605), the wife of Gavriil Grigor'evich. I cannot link their burial to a specific grant, but the donation book recorded six Pushkin grants made between 1547 and 1594/95; the penultimate in 1579/80 was an uncultivated parcel in Pereiaslavl', and the last was the small sum of ten rubles for the nun Anna Pushkina by the nun Pelageia/Nastasiia Zhitova, who very likely had occupied a cell in the same convent at Podsosenie. Pelageia, who had provided for her burial at Trinity in 1573/74, was buried nearby in 1601.[43] The monk Iosif (Ivan Andreevich Aminev, d. 1603) and the monk Iov (Ivan Fedorovich Mansur Opochinin, d. 1605) occupied plots in the same row of graves. They probably were deathbed tonsures. The donation book recorded five Aminev grants for commemorations between 1557/58 and 1574/75 to Trinity, three being large properties in Kostroma and another in Dmitrov. The Opochinins made five grants between 1576 and 1605/6 to Trinity. That of 100 rubles, which Ekaterina Opochinina made to Trinity in 1604/5, was to secure Iov's commemoration and burial.[44]

Of nine gravestones uncovered southwest of the Dormition Cathedral adjacent to the Chapel over the Well, a late seventeenth-century structure, five can be identified. The most notable were for graves of three Volynskiis, one of whom the inventory said had been interred at the Nikon chapel. Two had been Trinity monks. The stone of an "Abbess" Zabolotskaia, dated 1601, marked the grave of Matrena/Marem'iana, who in the 1570s had requested burial and also tonsure at Trinity's Podsosenie convent. Other stones marked the resting places of the monk Varlaam Putiatin (1570) and of the monk and deacon Mikhail "Kolomiatin" (from Kolomna, 1533). The dates suggest they might have been initially interred elsewhere, then reburied at this site when the Dormition Cathedral was completed. According to the inventory, three rows of unnamed servants, who had resided in a special servant's quarter outside the walls, were buried southwest of the Dormition Church. These ranks surely included many of those who gave Trinity modest sums in order to enter its service in the two decades ending in 1605.[45]

* So, yes, Trinity's assignment of burial sites took into consideration the distinction of families that sought places there. We may also conclude that individuals made their commitment to Trinity with an eye toward having

their line celebrated publicly at as important a site as possible. But, as in the dispensation of rank at the Muscovite court, in these transactions there existed a tension between secular realities of a family's social distinction and power, and others that one would term spiritual. They were defined in a variety of ways: by a record of longstanding generosity, by a tradition of taking the habit at Trinity, or by service to that house. It was in all of these traits that devotees of St. Sergius established the closest pattern of intimacy with the miracle worker and the house that held his relics.

CONCLUSION

"Here [at the Trinity-Sergius monastery] beats the pulse of Russian history . . . , here Russia reifies itself in its entirety."[1]
—Father Pavel Florenskii

Father Florenskii wrote this paean, equating Sergius's Trinity Monastery with what it meant to be Russian, in 1919. It came at a time when it seemed that the Bolsheviks were about to eradicate the monastery in order to give new meaning to being Russian. If this is a fair assessment, then it is not unfair to assert that the Bolsheviks accorded the Trinity-Sergius Monastery the same transcendental significance as did the visionary father.

In 1605 the Trinity-Sergius Monastery, second only to the Muscovite state, was the richest and the most respected institution in the land. By 1613 its heroic resistance to foreign invasion and its leadership in Russia's liberation during the Time of Troubles achieved for Trinity a popular adulation that was unequaled. Armies of the Polish crown and the second pretender besieged Trinity for 15 months, from 23 September 1608 to 1 December 1610. In 1618 to early 1619 in his cellarer's office at Trinity, Avraamii Palitsyn finished the earliest version of his description of the siege and its aftermath. The testimony of many eye-witnesses gave his tale a sense of its writer having been there (which Avraamii hadn't); it also gave authenticity to instances in which he claimed that SS. Sergius and, secondarily, Nikon alerted the defenders to attacks, encouraged them with prophesies of their rescue, and interceded to secure the retreat of besieging Polish forces. Avraamii wrote as if Sergius were instrumental in the re-creation of the Russian tsardom and the Trinity Monastery crucial to a definition of Russianness. He called his native land *Rosi(i)a* seven times, referred to its components as the lands and states of the r*osiiskoe derzhavy* twice, and said he lived in the *rosiiskikh stranakh*.[2]

In 1611 and 1612 Trinity's Archimandrite Dionisii and Avraamii signed appeals to areas and towns of Russia not under foreign control, to unite to drive the Poles from Moscow and reconstitute Russia's shattered political order. Avraamii ended his tale with stories of how Sergius brought bread to starving Moscow and prophesied to Archbishop Arsenii, a Greek hierarch, then in besieged Moscow, that a relieving army would storm the *Kitai gorod* and rid Moscow of its Polish occupiers. The army of liberation that Trinity had helped to summon billeted at the monastery en route to liberate Moscow. The New Chronicle, a court history crafted in the patriarchal chancellery by 1630 for the new Romanov dynasty, said that Dionisii and the brothers met this host with icons of the Trinity and of Sergius and Nikon, and blessed it with a cross and holy water. Thereupon, tbe New Chronicle reported, Sergius "turned fear into bravery," after which the army marched on Moscow and liberated it.[3]

Few families of Moscow's governing elite were prominent in the liberation army. Rather, one finds names of provincials like the merchant Kuz'ma Minin and Prince Dmitrii Pozharskii, of servicemen, townsmen, Cossacks, and peasants. Subsequently, as Avraamii intended, the Russian people accepted the saga of the Trinity-Sergius Monastery as the expression of its own aspirations. Adoration for Sergius and Trinity was greater than ever and the Romanov dynasty adopted their prestige to underwrite its own. As I write these words, I can see a print made at Trinity on 14 September 1859 that hangs above my desk. It depicts three mounted monks, Mikhei, Varfolomei, and Naum, riding out of Trinity unscathed through the Polish lines to Moscow for help. The text explains that Sergius arranged their safe passage and the success of their mission.[4] The image was printed many times over, one of many testimonies to the continuity of Trinity's centrality to how Russians envisioned their collective identity.

Since then Russia's rulers, and clerical and secular thinkers, in advancing policies for modernization, repeatedly altered their attitudes toward traditional religion. These turns inevitably affected Sergius's cult and Trinity's status. For most of the seventeenth century Trinity's wealth increased and its prestige remained undiminished. Census books (*perepisnye knigi*) of 1646 reveal that there were 16,811 peasant households on Trinity's properties, twice the number living on lands of other great landowners, the ruling dynasty, and the patriarchate. The Trinity-Sergius Monastery also witnessed an unparalleled record of construction: a hospital and church of SS. Zosima and Savvatii (1635–38), a huge and sumptuous refectory with its Church of St. Sergius (1686–92), the gate church of St. John the Baptist, and a residence (*chertog*) for the tsar (1692–99). The walls and towers that distinguish the monastery today also went up in the seventeenth century.[5] Trinity's sacristy (*riznitsa*) was a treasure house, and its library, according to the monastic inventory of 1641, bulged with manuscript books.[6] From an extended residence in Russia in the 1630s and 1640s in missions for the Duke of Holstein,

Adam Olearius knew of the monastery's wealth and reputation as a center of Russian resistance to the Poles. He also knew of Sergius's reputation as a miracle worker in defense of Russia, although his reckoning of when Sergius lived was off by two centuries. Archdeacon Paul of Aleppo, who visited Russia in 1655 in the delegation of the patriarch of Antioch, was astonished by Trinity's wealth and splendor. He said Moscow's rulers habitually lavished gifts on it and that in its splendor it had no equal in Muscovy or in the whole world.[7] The dynasty viewed Sergius as patron and protector and the monastery as its sanctuary. It was to Trinity that the imperial children Sofiia, Ivan, and Petr (the future Petr I the Great) fled from Khovanskii's *strel'tsy* revolt in 1682; in August 1689, Petr again found sanctuary there from Sofiia and her *strel'tsy* allies, after which he returned on 16 November 1691 to pray and to donate 1,000 rubles for a bell. At that time, probably for Petr, bookmen at Trinity made a copy of the late sixteenth-century illuminated life of Sergius.[8]

The Petrine state's attack on religious institutions and "prejudices" put an end to official support for Sergius's cult for 100 years.[9] Petr I assumed financial control over monastic properties and put monks on fixed incomes in 1701; in 1721 he placed Trinity and other houses that were allowed to survive under his Holy Synod; and by the Spiritual Regulation of 1722 he asserted the state's right to regulate tonsure in order to reduce the number of monks. The Petrine state also discouraged its armies from displaying religious symbols on campaign. Peter even "borrowed" 400,000 rubles from Trinity to pay for the construction of St. Petersburg. Empress Anna Ivanovna (1730–40) tightened the screws by prohibiting monasteries from acquiring new lands or recruiting monks (unless they were widowed priests or retired soldiers). Trinity remained wealthy—in 1742 housed a seminary and in 1744 became a *lavra*, the highest class for a monastery in the Orthodox world. This world crashed with Catherine the Great's decree in 1764 secularizing monastic estates (albeit with some compensation in monies and state serfs). Trinity lost its economic empire and brotherhood was limited to 100 monks. Peter's cultural revolution also meant that fewer of Russia's elite privileged monasteries in their family rites. Trinity's inventory of graves recorded 48 burials in the eighteenth century, a sharp decline from totals of the seventeenth century. Only 28 of the graves contained bodies of lay persons.[10]

Yet Sergius's cult remained alive in elite and popular consciousness. In the Great Northern War (1700–21) Petr I's commanders carried with them the triptych icon painted by Evstafii Golovkin (1588), the central and largest image of which was that of the appearance of the Mother of God to Sergius.[11] The illuminated life of Sergius, copied in the early 1590s, found its way into Petr's library in St. Petersburg. Also, state and church cooperated in building, reconstructing, or refurbishing structures at Trinity between 1740 and 1770. The imperial family itself provided funds to construct a great bell tower. Other new edifices were a church dedicated to St. Mikhei (1734), the disciple with whom Sergius shared the vision of the Mother of God; a church to house the Smolensk icon of the Mother of God (1746–48); and a new metropolitan's residence (*mitropolich'i pokoi*, 1778).[12]

The nineteenth century witnessed a resurgence of religiosity among all classes and the government eased restrictions against monastic landowning. Trinity benefited enormously. In 1814 the Moscow Theological Academy made its home there, donations poured in, and the brotherhood grew in size. Its inventory of graves recorded that Trinity buried 239 Russians between 1800 and 1880, the year the inventory was published. Historians, utilizing the historical texts of the sixteenth century, wrote Sergius into popular narratives as having inspired the monastic expansion that spread Orthodoxy across Russia and interceded to free Russia from the Mongols, assure victory over the Khanate of Kazan', and protect Russia from all its enemies.[13] These printed works reached thousands of readers. In 1839 Nicholas I laid the cornerstone for the Church of Christ the Savior on the Moscow River as a memorial to those who had fallen in the "Great Fatherland War" to liberate Russia from Napoleon. Completed in 1880 and consecrated in the presence of Tsar Alexander III in 1883, it was the largest church in Russia, and a visual complement to the nearby kremlin. Its north façade contained the building's most famous sculptures: one in high relief depicted Sergius blessing Dmitrii Donskoi in 1380 before his campaign against the Mongols and giving him warrior monks Peresvet and Osliabia to fight with him. Another depicted Archimandrite (by then Saint) Dionisii at Trinity blessing Minin and Pozharskii before they set off to liberate Moscow from the Poles in 1612. Artist V. P. Vereshchagin did a painting in the church that paired Sergius blessing Dmitrii with the prophet Samuel anointing King David. The public made the church a place of pilgrimage.[14] During the nineteenth century commanders repaired to Trinity for blessings before their campaigns and Trinity produced icons and other religious objects that troops carried into battle. Golovkin's triptych icon accompanied Russian armies in 1812 against Napoleon, in the Crimean War (1853–56), in the Russo-Turkish War (1877–78), in the Russo-Japanese War (1904–05), and in 1914, when Russia entered World War I. Mass printings of *Troitskie listi* (Trinity leaflets) with stories of the saint found an avid readership with an increasingly literate public. Between the 1860s and the 1890s the number of pilgrims passing through the new railroad station in Sergiev Posad grew from a quarter million to over half a million.[15]

These developments culminated in the celebration of the 500th anniversary of St. Sergius's death in September 1892. Well described by Scott Kenworthy, popular excitement transformed the brotherhood's plan for a local celebration into a national holiday. An estimated 100,000 pilgrims made part of or the entire journey from Moscow to the Trinity-Sergius *lavra*. At the Moscow Theological Academy on 26 September 1892, the day after Sergius's feast day, historian Vasilii Kliuchevskii made a memorable speech in which he asked his audience to share in his image of an imaginary chronicler, "an eternal and immortal observer [who] could tell how for five hundred years people worshiped at the grave of the Venerable Sergius, [and] what thoughts and feelings they carried with them when they returned to all corners of the Russian land."[16] Like Pavel Florenskii, Kliuchevskii was steeped in a nineteenth-century tradition that privileged Orthodoxy in defining Russian national identity. His survey of Russian history was notable for its focus on the people rather than the state and was very popular; in perhaps its most famous chapter Kliuchevskii portrayed Sergius as catalyst for monastic expansion that brought Orthodoxy and Russianness to pagan peoples of northern Rus'. Russians glorified Sergius's heritage in 1892 for a variety of reasons: to assert Moscow's primacy over St. Petersburg as Russia's "true" capital, to express a resurgent nationalism independent of state and synod, and to use Sergius's popularity as a foil to secular critics of Orthodoxy. For most publicists it was a celebration of the unity of Orthodoxy and Russianness. In the lead-up to the celebration the Moscow Gazette called Sergius the "creator of the Russian land," to whom Russians turned in time of peril. But Kenworthy is probably correct in concluding that most pilgrims came to Trinity seeking the "miracle-worker who could provide spiritual and physical healing and consolation in their life's troubles."[17] More resplendent than ever, the monastery housed 252 monks and 150 novices; it managed a home for the poor, a complex of orphanages, a hospital, and a hostel for monks; it controlled two subsidiary houses and four hermitages, and had offices in St. Petersburg and Moscow.[18]

The Bolshevik victory in 1917 brought a wave of attacks against church persons and property, followed by official measures nationalizing church property and forbidding public religious instruction and observance. But the Soviet government realized that Trinity required special handling. As a result the Commissariat of Education established a Commission for the Preservation of Art Objects and Antiquities of the monastery. Its members were believing intellectuals, one of whom was the expert on icons and manuscripts Iurii Olsuf'ev; Florenskii was another. At the height of the civil war in 1919, however, Bolsheviks everywhere attacked cults of saints. Rumors that the local soviet intended to open Sergius's coffin to "prove" that he was but a man precipitated popular protests in Sergiev Posad. Nevertheless, in April ex-priest and militant atheist M. B. Galkin and a team from the "Liquidation Section" of the Commissariat of Justice in Moscow came and did just that. On 3 November at three in the morning, by order of the Soviet government, Red Army units surrounded the monastery, expelled all but four of its monks and its archimandrite, and closed the monastery to prevent pilgrimages. Three times in November, mobilized by rumors that the Bolsheviks intended to remove Sergius's remains to a museum in Moscow, angry citizens gathered around the town hall. Iurii Olsuf'ev, with the consent of Patriarch Tikhon, removed Sergei's skull from the coffin to preserve it. He replaced it with that of a Prince Trubetskoi. Which prince specifically, we do not know; four Trubetskoi princes, including Dmitrii (d. 1625), one of the commanders of the liberation army in 1612, were buried during the seventeenth century in the Trinity Church. In April 1920 the government decreed the liquidation of the brotherhood and the closing of Trinity's churches. Once the Easter holidays were over, it quietly implemented the decree. At the height of the purges in 1937, police arrested for counter-revolutionary agitation and executed 10 former Trinity monks and Archimandrite Kronid, who had continued to live nearby. Florenskii and Olsuf'ev died in the purges in 1937 and 1938. The monastery became a museum. The transition contained several ironies: one was that Sergius's relics remained at Trinity until the German advance on Moscow caused them to be evacuated for safekeeping in 1940.[19] The other was that the Zagorsk (now Sergiev Posad) Museum-Reserve, to which authorities entrusted the monastery, became a zealous preserver of its treasures. On the other hand, on 5 December 1933 Stalin dynamited the Church of Christ the Savior, with its famous reliefs, to make room for a gigantic palace of Soviets that was never built.

During World War II Stalin decided that the Orthodox Church should be restored, ostensibly as an independent entity. He may have done so to court popular support; but he chose the People's Commissariat of Internal Affairs (NKVD) to bring it about, indicating that, properly controlled, the church was to be an institution to legitimatize the regime at home and abroad.[20] Concomitant to this, he ordered that the Trinity-Sergius Monastery be reconstituted. It reopened on 8 October (25 September according to the ecclesiastical calendar) 1945, Sergius's feast day; by 1946 it again functioned as a monastery. Sergius's skull, hidden for 26 years, was restored to its body. In 1948 the government reestablished the Moscow Theological Academy and Seminary at the monastery and authorized it to train priests. I first visited Trinity in November 1963. I was unaware of it, but my visit coincided with the fiercest period of Nikita Khrushchev's anti-religious campaign, one element of a quixotic effort to thrust the Soviet Union into communism. At Trinity a red banner, fluttering across the main avenue within the monastery, read "Forward to the Victory of Communism." A stream of pilgrims moved under the banner and into the Church of the Holy Trinity; others were already sprawled on the floor within the church. They were Russia's proverbial simple folk, dressed in worn clothes of grey, brown, and black. They looked exhausted. But they sang out their prayers as they moved one after the other to kiss Sergius's casket under the supervision of a representative of Soviet power dressed in the clinical white of a medical orderly. After each kiss, he swabbed the casket with disinfectant as if to break the communication that had been established. In 1991, in the final months of the existence of the Soviet Union, its ideologues—seeking again to buttress Soviet power by appropriating Russia's religious heritage—issued a series of five postage stamps entitled "History of Russian Culture." The third of the series reproduced the earliest image of St. Sergius on the embroidery of the 1420s below a picture of his monastery; the fourth reproduced Rublev's icon of the Trinity, the monastery's signifier.

Since Communism's fall Trinity has been regilded (fig. 11), its continual services are well attended, and its seminary overflows with aspirants for the priesthood. Russians celebrated the 600th anniversary of Sergius's death with new printings of his life, and with reprinted and original scholarly and popular articles and picture books about him.[21] Hoping that it might appropriate some of the saint's charisma, Boris El'tsin's fledgling democratic government of a truncated Russia joined the patriarchate on 8 October 1992 (congruent with 25 September in the ecclesiastical calendar) in a formal reception in the Great Kremlin Place to celebrate the 600th anniversary of Sergius's death. The correspondent for the newspaper *Krasnaia Zvezda*, Aleksandr Bondarenko, in describing the occasion, gave words to the sponsors' hopes, writing that "throughout the country exhibitions, readings, and many other events are taking place dedicated to the memory of this man with whose name is connected the very idea of the independence of the Russian state, its unity, its integrity and its power." [22] This was followed by a two-day popular festival of music, sponsored by State and Church, in the Kremlin Palace of Congresses in Moscow on 10 and 11 October. Its promoters named the festival "The Awakening" (*Probuzhdenie*), and it included a number of prominent rock bands. [23] In 1990 the church received permission to build a new Church of Christ the Savior in Moscow on the site of the old one. Construction, financed in part by public contributions, especially from Russia's newly rich, and the support of President Boris El'tsin and Moscow

Mayor Iurii Luzhkov, began in 1994. It was completed in 2000. In style and decorations that celebrated Sergius as Russia's protector, it was a replica of the original, except that the external reliefs were in bronze.[24]

* If what I have set forth in preceding chapters is at all creditable, by 1605 Sergius's cult had entered into scenarios of Russian historical consciousness and was an object of veneration up and down the social order. His monastery had become what historian Pierre Nora has called a "memory site"; that is, a place that gave meaning to countless families and the manner in which they constructed social identities in rites of commemoration, tonsure, and burial.[25] Finally, the Trinity-Sergius Monastery was an economic engine, second only to the state, that drove the formation of a national economy and integrated generations in the use of a common Russian language.

First, the centrality of Sergius, his cult, and the Trinity-Sergius Monastery within Russian culture: when Sergius died in 1392, Trinity's brotherhood; its lord Vladimir Andreevich and his family; Metropolitan Kipriian and members of the clergy; the sons of Dmitrii Donskoi, Vasilii and Iurii; and their courts revered Sergius for his piety and moral vision. Sergius also was the most famous of the God- seekers who extended a semi-cenobitic form of monasticism into rural areas of northern Rus'. About 1412 Epifanii wrote in his encomium that Sergius was revered "in this country"—meaning Trinity's immediate environs—but also "in other towns and in distant countries and among pagans, even from sea to sea, not only in Constantinople but in Jerusalem." Sergius, he wrote, "lived among mortals as an angel, perceived as a bright star in the Russian land."[26]

By 1422 Abbot Nikon and monks who had known Sergius viewed his deeds and qualities as extraordinary, so much so that they found explanations for them in the idiom of miracles. Nikon discovered Sergius's relics, for which the brotherhood built a new Trinity church of stone and inaugurated a feast on 5 July at which, Pakhomii the Serb wrote, their patron Prince Iurii Dmitrievich of Zvenigorod was present. For this generation, Sergius's sanctity was that expressed in the face of the ascetic hermit with cavernous cheeks and sunken eyes on the pall (fig. 4) crafted, probably, at Prince Iurii's behest to cover his casket. Thanks to Sergius's intercessory power, Nikon rejoiced, the Trinity Monastery enjoyed the protection of the Mother of God. There was something of "invented tradition" in Nikon's management of these events: they, after all, inaugurated a memorial culture for which the monastery solicited grants of land and the first burials near Sergius's tomb. Eric Hobsbawm defined "invented tradition" as a means to solidify conservative norms of social relations in a changing industrial world. Nikon's vision, in fashioning Sergius's cult and using it to introduce a culture of commemoration, was well within Orthodox tradition and all the more potent in that it had roots in East Slavic ancestor worship. In the 1420s only those who worshipped at Trinity thought Sergius a saint. As yet their number did not include the grand prince of Moscow.[27]

In Orthodox Russia as in the Catholic West, beginning with Christ's death and resurrection, "the [dead's] fate in the afterlife was the hub around which the theology of the Church revolved and evolved."[28] In fifteenth-century Rus' it took form in a new culture of commemoration. The presence of Sergius's bones and the claims for their sanctity made the Trinity Monastery a place where a supplicant in search of salvation for oneself or one's kin might find a mediator who could connect him or her to the supernatural world. Nikon created the formulae by which supplicants forged a connection to the saint through the exchange of gifts for prayers; his successors built on this foundation. Appendix Table 1 shows how quickly the culture of commemoration grew around Sergius's tomb. By the 1450s the pattern of patronage for prayers attracted provincial landowners like Boiar Vasilii Borisovich Kopnin; or the Kuchetskii and Voronin families, who lived in Radonezh; or the Redrikovs in Pereiaslavl'. By then contending branches of the Muscovite ruling family and their boiars were exchanging gifts for prayers at Trinity.[29] Appendix Table 2 records the spread of Trinity's holdings, and the cult's expansion: from its center in Radonezh and nearby parts of Moscow, Pereiaslavl' and Dmitrov, it found benefactors to the north in Uglich and Galich; in Vladimir, Starodub and Suzdal' to the east; and to the northwest in Bezhetskii Verkh and Novyi Torg. Pakhomii's Third Edition of Sergius's life described a miracle that occurred to a visiting archimandrite from Novgorod named Ignatii, and miracles added to it in 1448–49 said pilgrims "from various towns and lands, not just from [those in] in Moscow but from neighboring [ones], that is, from Lithuania, Riazan' and Tver'" journeyed to the Trinity Monastery for the feast of Pentecost and throughout the year to venerate Sergius.[30] Trinity was attracting more pilgrims and gifts from more people from a wider area than any other cult center in Russia. And while elites sought commemorative prayers at more than one holy site, more of them went (and more often) to Trinity than anywhere else.

By the 1450s no churchmen questioned the proposition that Sergius inspired the many monastic foundings in northern Rus'. The cult explained why Metropolitan Aleksei had asked his help in establishing the Monastery of Our Savior (Andronikov) near Moscow (1366) and why princes looked to Sergius to found monasteries in Serpukhov (1374), at Stronym (1378/79), and the Golutvin Monastery in Kolomna (1385). In addition Sergius established s house at Kirzhach (1377) in Pereiaslavl'. By Sergius's death or soon after the faithful had come to believe that numerous other houses owed their foundation to him: the Simonovskii Monastery near Moscow by his nephew Fedor (1379), the house his disciple Dmitrii founded at Priluki near Vologda (1389), Kirill's house near Beloozero, the monasteries of St. Nicholas in Dmitrov (1361), and the Storozhevskii near Zvenigorod with Sergius's disciple Savva as its abbot (1398–99). There were others in the Rostov and the Nizhnii Novgorod principalities.

In 1447 or 1448 the Russian Orthodox Church recognized Sergius an "all-Russian" saint.[31] In his model of the emergence of a Russian ethos, G. M. Prokhorov in 1992 argued that Sergius's cult coalesced at a key moment in which the triumph of faith, with its aspiration to eternity, emancipated society from a stagnant past and set it on a dynamic path. Prokhorov's formulation is metaphysical in the extreme; but in Sergius's cult, which was at the core of this phenomenon, it found human expression.[32] At midcentury Pakhomii's editions of Sergius's life contributed to fresh currents of optimism that followed the splintering of Mongol power by explaining with the logic of miracle the emergence of Muscovite power; namely, Sergius's intercession that assured Dmitrii Donskoi's victory over the Mongols in 1380. Sergius's cult permeated Muscovite self-consciousness when the compiler of the first all-Russian codex around midcentury assimilated Pakhomii's invention into his narrative. Sergius's cult became a lively component of popular religiosity that explained Moscow's emergence as the hub of the Russian state. It was a robust consciousness at the center, weaker and more differentiated at the periphery.

Appendix Table 2 shows that in the latter half of the fifteenth and the sixteenth century, Sergius's cult spread inexorably with the expansion of the Muscovite state. From 1445 to 1501 Trinity acquired 81 properties in lands proximate to the monastery, this despite Grand Prince Ivan III's policies to restrict the transfer of land to religious corporations. Between 1501 and 1605 Trinity acquired 381 more properties in the central lands of the Muscovite state. Along the northern Volga it added 49 parcels between 1445 and 1501, and 107 more to 1605. To the northwest Trinity gained 19 properties between 1445 and 1501, including 2 in Tver', and by 1605 it added 228 more: 101 in Bezhetskii Verkh, where the cult had taken root early on, 110 in Tver' and its appanages of Staritsa and Kashin, and 11 in Novgorod and Pskov. North of the Volga to the White Sea Trinity acquired 10 properties from 1445 to 1501 and thereafter 106: 25 in Galich and 18 on the Sukhona-Northern Dvina from Vologda, through Tot'ma and Sol'-Vychegovsk to Kholmogory. Trinity also established its presence in Medyn' and in Varzuga, but its acquisitions were more by purchase than by cult-driven donations. Eastward Trinity's reach extended out of Vladimir-Suzdal'-Starodub to Murom (3) by 1501, and from 1501 to 1605 it added 132 properties: 47 in Murom, 25 in Nizhnii Novgorod. Further east on the Volga River Trinity secured 16 parcels in and around Sviiazhsk and Kazan'. Measured in the same terms, Sergius's cult resonated more faintly in the west: from 1445 to 1501 it acquired three properties in Vereia and Borovsk. From 1501 to 1605 it added 16 in these lands and in Volok, Zubstov, and Ruza. Trinity's aura extended south of the Oka River with 5 donations of property in Maloiaroslavets from 1445 to 1501, and 30 more after that to 1605 in Serpukhov, Kashira, Kolomna, Obolensk, Novosil', and Tula. By my calculation (see Appendix Table 1, excluding immunity charters) donors gave Trinity 251 gifts of all kinds from 1501 to 1533; 1,372 from 1533 to 1564; and 842 from 1565 to 1584. From 1584 to 1605 it received 460 despite a chaotic economy and government restrictions against property donations. S. V. Nikolaeva's tally of donations, with a different periodization, is comparable.[33] My data for the period 1584–1605 records 387 gifts of cash and goods from people in the core area (133 being Trinity monks or dependents); from Vladimir-Suzdal'-Starodub (13), Murom (3), Sviazhsk (1), Riazan' (8), Nizhnii Novgorod (4) and Siberia (2) in the east; from Tver'-Staritsa-Kashin (11), Bezhetskii Verkh (10), and Novyi Torg (3) in the northwest; from Vorotynsk, Rzhev, Volok, and Mozhaisk (1 each) in the west; and from Galich (1), Iaroslavl' (6), Vladimir (5), and Kostroma (4) in the north. The number, amounts, and geographic incidence of gifts to Trinity can be described as national. In these categories no other cult center comes close.

The Trinity-Sergius Monastery was a cult center of national proportions in three other respects. First, its brotherhood, like Trinity's benefactors, hailed from every part of Russia. Second, sixteenth-century hagiographers, writing about semi-legendary hermits of an earlier age who founded monasteries in the far north—Avraamii at Chukhomsk, Sil'vestr and Pavel on the Obnora River, and Sergii on the Nurma River—thought it natural (necessary?) to claim Sergius as their mentor.[34] In the 1440s Pakhomii initiated a variant on the theme of Sergius as progenitor of the expansion of Christianity in his Third and Fourth Editions of Sergius's life. Pakhomii said that St. Stefan of Perm (d. 1396), who brought Christianity and an alphabet to the Zyrians, a Finnic people of the far north, "had love for our blessed father Sergius." While traveling between Perm' and Moscow, he wrote, Stefan paused near Sergius's monastery and hailed him. Sergius alone, of all his brothers eating in the refectory, heard Stefan's salute and uttered a prayer of blessing to Stefan, then explained to them the reason for his outburst. The episode became part of the lore of Russian history in the sixteenth century. Both the Prologue Edition and the many copies of the Extended Edition of Sergius's life repeated Pakhomii's account; it entered the Sofiia Second Chronicle under 1395/96 in an entry recording Stefan's death and was retold in the illuminated life of Sergius produced at Trinity in the 1590s.[35] Third, by 1600 churches or chapels dedicated to Saint Sergius existed throughout Russia; in Bezhetskii Verkh (several), on the Northern Dvina, and in Kazan', Moscow, Novgorod, Dmitrov, Rostov, Sevezh (south of Pskov), Staritsa, Starodub, and Sviiazhsk.[36]

Finally, my database and narrative sources indicate veneration for Sergius up and down the social order. Of Trinity's benefactors who can be identified, provincial landowners or servicemen holding a *pomestie* (who may also have been landowners or donated cash) dominated, comprising over 53 percent of the total. Moscow's ruling family, and *udel* princes made six percent of all donations to Trinity. Tsars Ivan IV, his son Fedor, and Boris Godunov were exceedingly generous. By my calculation Ivan IV assuaged his guilt at Trinity to the tune of at least 26,011 rubles; 18 properties; and 20 items such as icons, icon covers, embroideries, church vestments, and liturgical plate.[37] Benefactors in high service ranks, boiars, and *okolnichii*, made 14 percent of all donations. Some gave generously and often. Comparing Trinity's burial record with Zimin's list of the Muscovite service elite, almost a third of the families that sent members to the Boiar Duma chose to bury one or more of their dead at Trinity. In my database *d'iaki* were six percent, clerics ten percent, townspeople four percent, and peasants two percent of Trinity's benefactors. Remembering that these totals reflect the only the small minority of persons in these categories rich enough to make gifts in return for commemorations, and that Trinity held regular feasts attended by common folk at the great house and on its other properties, these figures show only the tip of a huge iceberg of ordinary people who venerated Sergius. By any measure, in what mattered most to a believer—that is, in prayers and acts to secure salvation—people of every social class and throughout Muscovite Russia turned to Sergius to be their intercessor. Sigismund Herberstein, imperial envoy to Moscow in 1517 and 1526, wrote, "The chief monastery in Muscovy was that of the Holy Trinity. . . . St. Sergius who is buried there, it is said, performed many miracles, causing huge numbers of tribes and peoples to throng [to the monastery] to venerate him. The ruler himself often is there and ordinary people gather there annually on appointed days to partake of the monastery's bountiful feasts."[38] The Papal envoy Antonio Possevino, who got only as far as Staritsa in 1581 to meet Tsar Ivan IV and stayed no more than four weeks, had heard of a miracle worker "the monk

Sergius, who had died 190 years earlier and was buried at the Trinity Monastery located 60 Italian miles from their capital." The monastery, he reported, "was the premier [house] in Muscovy."[39]

As a result Trinity's sacristy (*riznitsa*) overflowed with icons, relics, crosses, textiles, and liturgical books from devotees from all over Russia.[40] Pierre Gonneau's catalog of images of Sergius in icons, frescoes, or textiles comes to 98 items up to 1605. Of these, 38 were prepared at or around Trinity, 34 in Moscow, another five in Rostov, Iaroslavl', Kostroma, or Suzdal', 11 in the monasteries at Beloozero or elsewhere in the north, and 10 from the Novgorod region. The list is hardly exhaustive; researchers continue to find images of Sergius at Trinity and elsewhere.[41] Most images of Sergius, unlike that on the pall of the 1420s, displayed the face of a St. Sergius, uniformly rendered and recognizable to venerators throughout Russia who had never seen him. Venerators rejoiced in tracing his life and miracles in services on feast days and on icons, such as that Dionisii's disciples drew at the end of the fifteenth century for the iconostasis of the Church of the Holy Trinity, in which scenes of the saint's life rimmed the borders. Evstafii Golovkin painted another in 1591. In the interim someone in Dmitrov painted a third such icon (now in Rublev Museum in Moscow). One of Trinity's monks also prepared a richly illuminated life of Sergius by 1592 that is housed in its sacristy. It and the hagiographical icons were more than windows to the divine; they were lessons in life (such as the image in which Dmitrii Donskoi sought and received Sergius's blessing before defeating the Mongols in 1380), meant to be "read" and meditated on. Images of the apparition of the Mother of God to Sergius were ubiquitous at Trinity and throughout the realm.[42]

Is it possible that by 1605 citizens without a modern consciousness or language of national identity thought themselves a people or members of a Russian empire? I think one can answer in the affirmative if one accepts, like K. Anthony Appiah writing about African folktales, that, "traditional stories, widely shared, enmesh people in a single society by transmitting shared pictures of how the world is or ought to be."[43] By the mid-sixteenth century Moscow's ideologues and diplomats customarily described their state as the Russian tsardom. And its bookmen regularly invoked a pantheon of national saints as its intercessors: they mentioned Varlaam Khutynskii of Novgorod—particularly if the fate of that city was at stake—or Kirill Belozerskii, but invariably they invoked and gave precedence to the names of Sergius and metropolitans Petr and Aleksei, who were (with Kirill) the first Muscovites to be recognized by the church as saints.[44] More specifically, they created stories in which Sergius and Sergius alone prophesied or miraculously assured the Russian tsardom victories over Lithuanian enemies, such as that at Sevezh, or over the Tatars. In such tales the conquest of the Kazan' khanate in 1552 validated the hegemony of the Russian state and its ruler over neighboring rivals (and former oppressors); it also legitimized the notion that Orthodox Russia was God's instrument in the world. Sergius's intercession to bring Dmitrii Donskoi victory at Kulikovo in 1380 was deeply ingrained in Muscovite thinking by the sixteenth century and inspired stories of Sergius's intercession to bring victory over Kazan'. One version, admittedly of uncertain date, of the "History of Kazan'" explicitly drew the parallel.[45] No wonder that ordinary Russians might assume that Sergius's cult and his Trinity Monastery would be instrumental in their salvation during the Time of Troubles.

* Sergius's cult forged physical as well as cultural bonds among his devotees. Orthodox believers in Russia were complicit in constructing it and transforming Sergius's cult in ways that provided them a collective identity. Lay involvement with Trinity "did not begin and end with a gift," to quote Barbara Rosenwein's observation regarding Cluny's involvement in the wider world; it was a glue that strengthened clan solidarity, united donors with witnesses, and linked clans from disparate areas and rival political factions in common bonds of liturgical celebration.[46] Worshipers of every social class assembled at Trinity on feast days. Clans assembled at Trinity to bury and commemorate their dead. Trinity recruited monks and nuns for its subsidiary houses, monastic servants, and tenants from benefactor families, creating for them a common identity as brothers and sisters. Trinity as hub of a large artificial group of devotees was a significant element in the emergence of Russian society.

We are familiar with how clans arranged marriages to cement and prolong kinship alliances to their mutual advantage, and about the long-term effect of such unions in creating a complex social fabric and political order.[47] Similarly, Trinity cemented bonds among local families and made them part of a larger world centered on the monastery. There is no better example than that of the Skripitsyn clan and its neighbors in the Verkhduben district of Pereiaslavl'. A Foma Skripitsyn appeared in Trinity's earliest copybook as witness to a purchase about 1470. Foma, elsewhere called Tarbei Skripitsyn syn Baluev or Foma Aleksandrovich Skripitsyn Baluev, in 1491/92 purchased the hamlet Oziminskaia from Filipp Bursev syn Skripitsyn and his sons Ivan and Vasilii. In 1510/11, apparently after Foma/Tarbei's death, his widow Anna arranged with her mother-in-law Tatiana, Aleksandr's wife, and Foma's brothers Il'ia Buchug and Semen Shiba, the division of Skripitsyn properties. Then Anna and her son Andrei donated land to Trinity and were parties to surveys, purchases, and exchanges involving Trinity, Tat'iana, and Foma's brother Il'ia Buchug down to 1525/26.[48] Filipp Burtsev was the scion of another Skripitsyn line, his father Burets being one of six sons of an Ivan Skripitsyn.[49] One can trace the Baluev and Ivan Skripitsyn lines into the mid-sixteenth century, and Skripitsyns crop up in Trinity's records to 1600/1.[50] Anna was the first Skripitsyn to give Trinity a memorial grant in 1525/26 and, as I noted in Chapter 6 she repeatedly bestowed gifts on Trinity. Between her first grant and Bova Skripitsyn's in 1599/1600, Trinity's donation book lists eight gifts of land, cash, or goods worth 50 rubles or more.[51] Between 1432 and 1445, before they were benefactors and involved in Trinity's land transactions, a Veniamin Skripitsyn was a Trinity monk. Ioasaf Skripitsyn was Trinity's abbot from 1529 to 1539, when numerous donations flowed in from Anna and other Skripitsyns. He was metropolitan of Russia, 1539–42. In 1542 he retired to Trinity and was buried there in 1555. In 1580 Mikhail Andreevich "Menshikov" Skripitsyn on his death bed gave Trinity a village in return for tonsure. Within a year his daughter Anna gave Trinity a grant so that she could become a nun at its Convent of the Mother of God at Podsosenie and, when she died, be buried at the main house.[52] The Skripitsyns repeatedly proclaimed their clan solidarity in memorial bequests, in witnessing one another's contracts with Trinity, and in blending their identity with that of Trinity's brotherhood.

Other clans of the Verkhduben district—the Upolovnikovs, Redrikovs, Butenevs, Miakishevs, Briukhovs, and Riabinins, along with the Skripitsyns—figured in these acts and in exchanges, sales, surveys, and divisions of property with one another and with Trinity, and served as witnesses to one other's deals.[53] Being neighbors and intermarrying contributed to their closeness. Anna Skripitsyna referred to Vasilii Aleksandrovich Miakishev as her brother-in-law in one document and to Aleksandr Briukhov as the husband of her late daughter Anastasiia in another; Solomonida, the daughter of Ivan Riabinin, was the wife of Il'ia Buchug Aleksandrovich Skripitsyn Baluev. Trinity involved them in a web of land deals and insisted they witness one another's acts. In doing so it created obligations among them and to Trinity that lasted for generations. Thus, in 1530/31 Ivan Riabinin's daughter Solomonida, according to the will of her husband Il'ia Buchug Aleksandrovich Skripitsyn Baluev, gave Trinity half of her meadow of Il'inskoe. She and her children retained the other half on the condition that they make mortgage payments to Trinity. Three Upolovnikovs, a Redrikov, and a Riabinin witnessed the transaction, and a Dmitriii Ivanov syn Riabinin wrote it.[54] Some of these families died out or lost their hereditary lands and become servicemen elsewhere. But there were still Skripitsyns and Miakishevs in the Pereiaslavl' land cadastres of 1592–94.[55] By then the Trinity-Sergius Monastery transformed them into a community of venerators.[56] In 1530/31 a Mitia Riabinin wrote a charter by which Vasilii Semenov syn Redrikov gave Trinity a hamlet in return for prayers for his health and, when he died, for his soul and for tonsure there. The gift bound Trinity to his family for another generation in that only his sons might redeem the hamlet by paying Trinity 13 rubles.[57] Vasilii's tonsure was not at all unusual. Asaf and Sil'vestr Upolovnikov, Bogdan/Varfolomei Miakishev, and two Butenevs, Fedor/Feognost' and Stepan/Sergii, became monks—the first two, like Vasilii Redrikov, well before their hour of death.[58] Two Skripitsyns other than Ioasaf, three Butenevs, and many Redrikovs (all but one having died after 1605) were in Trinity's burial records.[59]

The Golovkin clan's involvement with Trinity can be traced through six or seven generations; it typified the manner in which Trinity brought together families of benefactors in distant areas, and turned them to the monastery and the wider society in the making. I have traced the interaction between the Golovkins and the Irezhskiis from early in the fifteenth century, when they were landowners in Bezhetskii Verkh when it was a borderland between Novgorod and the grand principality of Vladimir. Another clan, the Michurins, beginning in 1503/4 became involved in transactions with the Irezhskiis and the Golovkins, and with Trinity.[60] The Irezhskii clan no longer appeared in Trinity's records after the 1520s; the Michurins and the Golovkins remained interlocked in dealings with Trinity throughout the sixteenth century. Like Golovkins, Michurins became monks at Trinity: an Elder Paisii Alekseev syn Michurin gave the estate of Guznishchevo in Bezhetskii Verkh to his monastery in 1562/63 in return for memorial prayers for himself and his ancestors. Of 13 witnesses, four were Michurins and four were Golovkins. In 1569/70 when Boris Piatoi syn Golovkin gave Trinity an estate in return for enrollment as its servant and then tonsure, a Kostantin Semen syn Michurin was a witness. By 1577 Paisii was Trinity's treasurer; from the 1570s into the 1590s a Varlaam Michurin was a Trinity elder. Through 1605 the Michurins gave Trinity eight more gifts.[61]

One can trace similar relationships between Trinity and clans of state secretaries—the Kurtsevs, Klobukovs, and Toporkovs, who owned estates in Moscow, Pereiaslavl' and elsewhere; the Aigustov and Sharapov clans in Pereiaslavl'; the Lodygin and Skobel'tsin clans in Moscow (including Radonezh); the Rugotin, Zamytskii, Bobrov, Bashenin, Skobeev, Shchel-epin, Durov, Tat'ianin, and Moshnin clans in Dmitrov; the Pisemskii and Likhorev clans in Kostroma; the Pil'emov clan in Rostov; and the Kindyerev clan in Tver'. Excluding possibly the Durovs, Skobeevs, and Tat'ianins, they each provided Trinity with at least one monk. During and after the *oprichnina*, Trinity was a self-interested welfare agency on a national scale for landowner-benefactors and their families threatened with the loss of their estates or their ruination: it gobbled up their lands as donations, but returned them to their benefactors (with monastic immunities) to live out their lives. Often these deals were disguised as purchases to get around the state's ban on alienating taxable properties. The practical effect was that Trinity provided its destitute patrons with land to till and with cash payments. It tonsured members of impoverished families; others—very likely the propertyless—it enrolled as servants. Other great houses did the same, but only Trinity was capable of transforming provincial-based identities into national ones on a grand scale. In times of political and social chaos it was an institution providing social cohesion.[62]

Few clans that made up the Muscovite ruling elite were as devoted to the Trinity-Sergius Monastery as the Zabolotskiis, although the Pleshcheevs and Obolenskiis were not far behind. There was a Zabolotskii boiar about 1460; subsequently Zabolotskiis continued to hold high service ranks. Between the first in 1512 and the last in 1571/72 Zabolotskiis made 18 gifts to Trinity; at least three became monks and another was in its service. Four Zabolotskiis were buried there.[63] The loyalties of most boiar clans, however, were more complicated than those of the Zabolotskiis or of provincial landowning families. They made memorial donations to more than one religious institution, and few members of elite clans became monks except on their deathbed. Nevertheless, most elite clans sought prayers at Trinity. A significant number made Trinity their primary beneficiary and scheduled commemorative feasts there. Many buried their dead there. These were long-term commitments, played out over many generations. The custom could only contribute to a collective consciousness among the ruling elite that they belonged to a common social organism. One can appreciate how this worked by juxtaposing donation records at Trinity for lines that descended from Andrei Ivanovich Kobyla, one of the first Muscovite boiars (1340s). His son Fedor Koshka commissioned the magnificent *Apraksos* that his son Fedor Goltiai gave to Trinity probably in 1422. Fedor Goltiai's widow Mariia and their son Andrei gave Trinity Fedor's estate. Mariia was a Vel'iaminov, yet another clan of Moscow boiars with a history of memorial gifts to Trinity (not to mention fraternal bonds to Sergius's family). Andrei's widow bequeathed the Goltiai estate of Tarbeevo to Trinity.[64] The Bezzubtsov and Sheremetev lines that descended from Fedor Goltiai's brother Alekesandr Bezzubets were also Trinity's benefactors. Five Sheremetevs were buried at Trinity.[65] The Zakharin line, including Iur'evs and the Iakovlevs, gave a dozen donations to Trinity, but there is no record they became monks or were buried there.[66]

Of all elite clans, Moscow's, then Russia's, ruling house to 1598 established the most vital and long lasting bond with Trinity. During the Muscovite civil war (1425–53) contending branches of the Danilovichi vied in their patronage to secure Trinity's support. Subsequently, Moscow's grand princes and tsars baptized most of their children at Trinity, made it the primary destination for pilgrimages, lavished more wealth on it than on any other house, and made Sergius the primary intercessor for the clan's well-being. Beginning with Sophia Palaeologa, grand princesses and tsarinas made Sergius's grave the site of a fertility cult. Adjunct branches of the clan, whom Vasilii III, Ivan IV, Fedor, and Boris Godunov considered rivals—witness Princess Evfrosiniia Staritskaia—were equally devoted to Sergius's cult and monastery. Neither Trinity nor any other house rivaled the state—in its opportunities for reward, in its service muster (*razriad*) based on the award of temporary tenure land grants, and in its coercive power—as an agent transforming provincial-based social loyalties into national ones. But can anyone doubt that Trinity was second to the state in this respect?

* Engendered by Sergius's cult and fertilized by gifts of properties and immunities, the Trinity-Sergius Monastery built an enormous economic empire. In the statistical appendices to her two books, M. S. Cherkasova provides us with as detailed a description of Trinity's properties as we are likely to get. At the end of the sixteenth century Trinity owned 310 villages and parts of 21 others in 40 districts of Russia, from Novgorod in the west to Kazan' in the east and from Beloozero in the north to Obolensk, Vereia, and Novosil' in the south. These villages had 1,609 outlying hamlets and 15 *pogosti* (churches and surrounding buildings in Novgorod and the north), 72 new settlements (*pochinki*), and 1,401 parcels of uncultivated land. Of the villages 88 were small, having 10 or fewer households; 165 villages had between 11 and 79 households; 56 had 80 or more households. Anomalies in her tables make it difficult to assess the vitality of Trinity's holdings: some villages were without households, yet had cultivated fields of varying size and output; also, entries lump together the households of several, probably adjoining, villages, making it impossible to ascertain the average number of households per village. In the 1590s Trinity controlled from 8.2 percent of cultivated land in Moscow to 21.6 percent in Pereiaslavl' and 29.1 percent in Iur'ev. To the east it held 11.9 percent and 29.3 percent of cultivated land in Vladimir and Suzdal', respectively, and 9.4 percent in Kazan'. E. I. Kolycheva's breakdown of the same data is not comparable with Cherkasova's, but yields

similar results. Cherkasova concluded that Trinity owned 12.1 percent of all the cultivated land in Russia; only the state owned more.[67]

We have no way to estimate the annual income of Trinity's holdings, as A. G. Man'kov did for other big monasteries, or to assess its importance to the growth of a national economy. This is because in 1746 fire destroyed Trinity's *krepostnoi* archive in which its treasurers kept running accounts of expenses and incomes.[68] We know Russia's economy, having experienced significant growth well into the sixteenth century, was in a free fall from the 1570s on. And we may be certain that Trinity's income fell well short of its potential in 1605. Stepan Veselovskii's description of the hard times experienced by the county (*volost'*) of Ilemna in Vereia needs no embellishment. Trinity long had owned the entire county, having received it from Ivan III in 1467. It was highly lucrative: in 1544 Trinity's official administered the county from Troitskoe, one of its two villages. It consisted of Trinity's compound, two yards attached to its Church of the Mother of God, and 18 peasant households; 3 dwellings for Trinity officials. 36 peasant households were in the neighboring village of Egor'evskoe. Together, the villages controlled over 39 hamlets with 430 households. Each year they produced surplus grain that was shipped by water routes to Moscow and the monastery. According to the inventory of 1592–94, hard times reduced the households in Troitskoe to 13 and in Egor'evskoe to 25, and the number of their hamlets to 20, with 249 households. Ilemna still had significant lands in cultivation, enough to be a profitable grain exporter, if on a reduced scale. In central Russia, where the crisis was more severe, even Trinity, with its means and tax immunities, could not retain or recruit enough peasant households to cultivate its lands. To keep land under cultivation, the monastery instituted welfare measures that allowed former owners of donated property to remain on the land and to farm it.[69] On any balance sheet, it is only fair to point out that the diminution in Trinity's income was offset by its ability, despite the state's countervailing efforts, to use the misfortunes of others to increase its holdings. It is also difficult to evaluate the impact of government inventories of Trinity properties and immunities, and its edicts of 1551, 1580, and 1584, on Trinity's acquisition of tax-paying estates and its tax liabilities. Veselovskii thought 1584 a watershed after which the number of Trinity's acquisitions declined precipitously. Yet he recognized that Russia's tsars often exempted Trinity's acquisitions from these measures and continued to issue immunity charters for new acquisitions, especially for Trinity's network of urban yards.[70]

Trinity controlled 17 subsidiary monasteries and yards in important towns, including Novgorod, Kholmogory, Kazan', and Sviiazhsk, or their suburbs (*slobodki*) in the sixteenth century. These and its large rural holdings, such as those in Ilemna and Shukobalovo, were trade centers that enjoyed charters allowing them to ship goods to the monastery duty-free. Trinity's salt-boiling enterprises in Sol'-Pereiaslavl', Sol'-Galich, Sol'-Nerekhta, and Sol'-Velikaia in Kostroma, and Balakhna in the Nizhnii Novgorod land, dominated salt production in central Russia and could ship salt to the monastery and elsewhere duty-free. But Trinity never had a monopoly and had to pay a tax on salt it sold. The tsar's charters of 1553 and 1575, discussed below, giving Trinity a monopoly to brand and collect branding fees on Nogai horses in Kazan' and Sviiazhsk, reveal that the monastery had a similar privilege in Moscow. Trinity was also an important producer and trader of honey and wax and its outposts had fishing rights on the Kliaz'ma, Moscow, Velia, Dubna, and Sheksna rivers, and on the upper Volga. In hard times Trinity increased its urban holdings and they showed continued economic vitality. For example, an inventory of 1588 shows that Medna, a commercial village in Novyi Torg on the route to Novgorod that paid *obrok* to Trinity, contained the monastery's yard, 4 church courts, 10 cells for the poor (*kellii nishchikh*), 23 households of farming peasants and 76 households of non-agricultural peasants. This was not one of Trinity's major centers. Yet its residents included eight bakers, seven of whom were purveyors of a special bread (*kalachniki*); a brewer; two butchers; a producer of malts; two salt traders; five tailors; two fisherman; four shoemakers; a rug maker; a maker of bast shoes; a tanner of lambskins; seven carpenters; two blacksmiths; a saddler; a maker of lathing; a herdsman; three Cossacks; and one clown.[71]

In 1547/48 Ivan IV freed Trinity outposts at Ust'-Kur'ia and Gorki in the Dvina land from the jurisdiction of his courts and accorded them the right to mount annual trade expeditions duty-free from the monastery through Vologda on the Sukhona and the Northern Dvina rivers to the White Sea and back. These expeditions sold bread, honey, and hops in the north and purchased fish, salt, and other goods there.[72] In 1554 the state increased by half the quantity of goods it might move south to 400 sleighs of salt and 50 sleighs of fish. The exemption from duties applied to goods used at the monastery and to surplus salt it might sell once a year in Moscow. While the economy of the central part of the state became crisis-ridden, the economy in the north remained dynamic. Trinity used its resources to expand operations there dramatically, and the state, perhaps to better feed hungry central Russia, was willing to assist it. Ivan IV issued a directive on 6 April 1580 that forbade tax collectors on the Dvina, in Vologda, Ustiug, and Tot'ma, from levying duties of Trinity's merchandise, the limits of which were to be 360,000 pounds (10,000 *poods*) of salt and 100 sleighs of fish. In 1581/82 he issued a charter doubling the number of expeditions Trinity might send on the Dvina with immunities. Tsar Fedor ratified the agreement in 1586 and increased four times the number of expeditions Trinity could send through Vologda. And no limit was set on the amount of fish and salt Trinity might sell in Moscow. To fuel this trade Trinity enjoyed fishing rights for its compound in Kholmogory on the Northern Dvina and in 1580/81 obtained the first of many rights to fish for salmon in Varzuga.[73] The value of these fishing rights appreciated significantly, encouraging Trinity aggressively to buy up more properties.

Ivan IV gave Trinity the land to establish a monastery in Sviiazhsk on the Volga west of Kazan' on 17 March 1554, and with it land, forests, and fishing rights; in Kazan' Trinity obtained many residences in return for memorial prayers or by purchase in 1553–54 from servicemen who had been given these properties by the state for their participation in the conquest. On 1 February 1553 Ivan gave Trinity land in Kazan' for a compound and a church.[74] From these outposts Trinity built a commercial empire on the central and lower Volga and to the east. Money flowed in, and in large amounts. The Nogai Horde, nomads of the steppe to the east of the lower Volga, sold up to 20,000 horses annually in Kazan' destined for the Russian market. In February 1553 the tsar gave Trinity a monopoly to brand and collect a branding fee on Nogai horses of .04 rubles (and .03 more for the imperial treasury) per horse. In 1575 the tsar reaffirmed and expanded Trinity's privileges to include Russian as well as Nogai horses branded in Sviiazhsk as well as Kazan'.[75] Ivan IV on 8 July 1578 ratified an earlier charter that shows just how important Trinity's base in Kazan' was for trade on the Vol'ga. The monastery could send two ships annually via Nizhnii Novgorod, Cheboksary, Sviiazhsk, and Kazan' to Astrakhan to pick up salt and fish and return duty-free. The charter set no limit on the cargo, but it was to be for consumption at the monastery. A charter of 11 November 1585 imposed limits on the quantity of goods Trinity might haul, but they seem generous to the extreme: no more than 720,000 pounds (20,000 *pood*) of salt on one vessel and 10,000 sturgeon on the other. It also mentioned a fishing camp below Kazan' on the Volga, where fishermen hauled in duty-free 2,000 fish annually for Trinity's consumption. Later charters, drawn up in different terms, reaffirmed these quantities and provided further concessions.[76] These charters mentioned only goods that Trinity shipped duty-free. One wonders what Trinity's consumption requirements were, or whether a portion of the catch found its way to the market.

Although we cannot estimate the brotherhood's contribution to the creation of a national economy, the size of its land fund, the vitality of its commercial enterprises, and the fact that they could be found in every part of Russia leave no doubt that it was very important. The state was the only institution to surpass Trinity in the volume and geographical scope of its economic activity.

* The majority of sources used in this study are private charters—donation, purchase, and exchange agreements, and testaments that defined the relationship between thousands of persons, most of them lay men or women, and the Trinity-Sergius Monastery. It is to those private charters that I return to argue the monastery's energizing power in the creation of "Russianness." Put simply, by insisting that property transactions be documented, Trinity compelled those with whom it did business to learn how to read and to write in Russian. Memory was impermanent; it depended on the presence of partners and witnesses to an agreement. But a written act (even a forgery) was definitive, impersonal, capable of being organized, and portable over space and time. Creating a legal record of its acquisitions and the terms by which they were acquired empowered Trinity in its relations with benefactors, their relatives and descendants, and with other parties, including the state. Contracting parties learned they had best master rudimentary skills of reading and writing if they were to be partners with Trinity in the exchange of property and intangible goods.[77] And so they did.

Appendix Table 3 shows that increasing numbers of those who entered into transactions with Trinity learned to read and write in a simple administrative language. Its simplicity was in its limited, repetitive vocabulary and formulaic syntax. In period 1, of 27 charters, only one was written by a benefactor. It was a donation of several meadows in Dmitrov between 1398 and 1421 by one Dmitrii Ivanovich, described in Trinity's oldest donation book. It consisted of one sentence, named two witnesses, and concluded: "And Dmitrii himself wrote the charter."[78] Benefactors signed two others and 13 affixed their seals or made their mark. None of the 106 witnesses to these charters were apparently literate, although eight affixed seals or marks. In the next six periods, to 1533, the number of charters increased significantly and the percentage of donors or their relatives who wrote their charters rose from 9 percent to 31 percent. The number of initiators of charters who signed, in addition to those who wrote theirs, rose even more, to 54 percent. For some reason the number of benefactors who wrote their own charters declined after 1533. But this did not indicate a decline in secular literacy. In periods 8, 9, 10, and 11, in which there were significantly more charters, 73 percent, 85 percent, 80 percent, and 84 percent of them signed.

Increases in the number of witnesses who signed charters betoken the same growth in practical mastery of the printed word. Throughout the fifteenth century and down to 1533 the number of signers rose from none at all in period 1 to 38 percent in period 7 (1522–33). In the four subsequent periods (1533–1605), with a much larger body of documents, the number of witnesses who signed their names was 55 percent, 71 percent, 71 percent, and 79 percent. The totals attest to the same level of literacy indicated by the number if initiators who signed charters. One may have reservations about the level of their comprehension and ability to express themselves. So too, the percentage of signing witnesses undoubtedly was greater than the percentage of literate laymen. One often encounters the same witnesses on different acts. No doubt those arranging transactions rounded up literate neighbors or relatives as witnesses. But if the "rounding up of the usual witnesses" inferred illiteracy, it also valued literacy of others within the same social milieu.

This worked in several ways. A Fedor Il'in syn Zheltukhin wrote a survey of the boundary between his property and Trinity's in Moscow in 1528. Elder Sil'vestr Upolovnikov acted for Trinity, and Fedor's uncle Aleksei Grigor'ev *syn* Zheltukhin, Aleksei's sons Semen Bol'shoi and Semen Menshoi, Fedor Aleksandr *syn* Rugotin, and some state peasants were witnesses. All but the peasants signed. In the Golovkin clan's many dealings with Trinity, literacy was handed down from father to son in certain lines, such as that of Ivan Onisimovich Golovkin (see p. 130) but not in others. The literate wrote and witnessed acts for their illiterate uncles and brothers. Ivan Onisimovich wrote or signed five documents between the 1430s and 1504. Only the literacy of Semen, the eldest of his nine sons, can be verified, even though another became a Trinity monk. Ivan's seventh son, Grigorii, witnessed eight acts and was a party to another between 1500 and 1547/48, but signed none of them. Yet all but the youngest of Grigorii's five sons, Osip Nechai, Vasilii, Ivan, Sumorok, and Ugrim, could read and write, and his daughter Varvara married a neighbor, Eliazar Irzhevskii, who was literate. Vasilii witnessed with his signature ten acts, one for his brother, three for three different uncles, two for an uncle once removed, one for his brother-in-law Eliazar, and two for neighbors; he also wrote a donation charter and witnessed one of Varvara's. In the fourth generation Osip Nechai's two sons, Ivan and Nesvitai, could write; Vasilii evidently had no sons; Ivan's two sons Aleksandr and Daniil left no trace of literacy, nor did Ugrim's son Aleksei. But Sumorok's sons Stepan and Dmitrii were literate. I can trace into the sixth generation only the two sons and the daughter of Dmitrii Sumorokovich. Evfimii in 1560 was tonsured as the Trinity monk and cellarer Evstafii, and was highly literate. Of Ivan I know nothing, although he probably was the Trinity monk Iona Golovkin mentioned in 1596. Evfrosiniia became a nun and Evstafii buried her at Trinity.[79]

Looking at my largest sample, that for period 10 (1565–18 March 1584), initiators wrote 41 of 446 charters (9.2%) and 360 signed them. Appendix Table 3 shows that there existed almost from the beginning a class of professional scribes and that in period 10 lay clerks (*d'iaki*), by then a well-established class of literate citizens, wrote 94. Moreover, most of the 251 unidentifiable writers of charters must have been laymen. Finally, in period 10, 1,126 (71%) witnesses signed the charters. In my data for Trinity's transactions in Varzuga a smaller, but significant, number of free peasants was literate. In the early 1580s they were party to 62 charters. Forty-seven of them were sales agreements, ten were donation charters, and five were contracts of debt slavery. Nine parties to these agreements—one being a cleric, the others laymen—signed them. Four peasants and one cleric wrote charters, but most were written by clerks, the most active being a Nikita Mironov syn, the *d'iachek* of the Church of St. Nicholas. Of 124 lay witnesses, 16 signed their names. Evidence of female literacy in Trinity's documents is all but nonexistent. All the more remarkable then was the elaborate testament, discussed in an earlier chapter, that Dariia, the daughter of Ivan Samsonovich and Domna Ivanovna Turenin and wife of Petr Fedorovich Basmanov, "in her own hand" (*svoeiu rukoiu*) wrote in 1590 making her husband executor for her dowry. Dariia's family was a branch of the Pleshcheev clan and her husband the descendent of a boiar during the *oprichnina*.[80] One can only wonder whether among elite women she was exceptional, and whether women of less distinguished origin were literate at all.

The formulaic nature of charters, especially of the simple, earlier ones, suggests that at first writing had a totemic relationship to oral culture that relied on memory, that it was symbol rather than a new mode of communication. That a significant number of initiators of charters and their witnesses signed with marks or seals supports this line of argument. But not always. At the conclusion of his testament giving Trinity property between 1417 and 1427, Vasilii Iakovlia Pliasets Voronin, a Pereiaslavl' landowner, noted, "and I wrote the charter myself, and sealed this charter with a cross."[81] As more people wrote charters, and more initiators and witnesses signed them, the use of seals and marks to record one's assent to a charter and its veracity dropped away. Also, charters became longer and more complex. Those who wrote them had developed a practical literacy; that is, of one capable of reading and writing in transacting business.[82] In western Europe practical literacy usually indicated a facility in the use of a vernacular language rather than of Latin. There was no parallel in Russian Orthodoxy, although some linguists have argued for a similar diglossia between the practical Russian of the clerks and the Church Slavonic literacy of clerics. This contrast is hardly apt for Muscovite Russia; sophisticated theological texts were rare; most religious literature consisted of popular texts, such as chronicles and lives of saints. Their language was in various gradations between the extremes, with most comprehensible (in various gradations?) to one literate in business Russian. However one may define it, the written documentation of land transactions became well established in the sixteenth century, and a large part of the landowning population could use it.

Our evidence for practical literacy had parallels in the Byzantine Empire and in Western Europe. Robert Browning has concluded that in good times and bad there was a wider spread of functional literacy in the Byzantine Empire than has been supposed. In France, beginning in the eleventh century, lay aristocrats turned to the use of the written word in situations requiring "authority and commitment," in the words of Brigitte Bedos-Rezak. She had in mind situations of a legal and bureaucratic character such as I describe above. The use of writing accelerated from the end of the twelfth century. M. T. Clanchy traces this phenomenon in England. Between the mid-eleventh and the late fourteenth century the number of written parchments increased many times over and their use expanded throughout the social order and territorially. By the late fourteenth and the fifteenth century literacy had become indispensable in order to function in a complex economy or in politics. The volume and variety of written materials surviving in the West are greater than those extant in Russia, but the pattern is the same.[83]

The Muscovite state's introduction of judicial codes of 1497 and 1550, its establishment of local government institutions in the 1550s, and the development of service registers and surveys of lands supporting service greatly encouraged the development of a literate culture in Russia. A state office known as the *Razriadnyi prikaz* came into being to keep up the registers. It became the largest government bureaucratic organ, and for servicemen the most important. To present claims for land allotments, rank, and appointment, servicemen had to be able to read registry documents, prepare genealogical books describing the service ranks and appointments of their relatives and descendents, and petition the state to assert their claims or seek redress. Those of high rank also had to read and to write to perform their duties. The result was an explosion of literacy of landowners great and small, the rapid expansion of a class of clerks, and a situation in which facility with the written word became a factor promoting social differentiation.[84] These were elements apparent in the evidence for literacy in Trinity's records that began over a century earlier. Both cases, however, contain synchronous evidence for the rapid development of literacy in the sixteenth century.

The Golovkin clan provides a "micro model" of the consequences of the growth of literacy.[85] The clan began as provincials from Bezhetskii Verkh, and none of its members appeared in service registers before 1605, although later Golovkins held distinguished service ranks. The first Golovkin to sign his name was Ivan Osimovich. He wrote and signed documents between the 1440s and the end of the century, but there is no evidence that his four cousins were literate. I can identify 22 members of the third generation in Trinity's documents from 1470 and 1548; only two signed their names, and one had another sign for him. Of 31 male Golovkins in the fourth generation in documents dating from 1499 to 1565/66, 13 of them, or 42 percent, signed their names. Of the 23 males in the fifth generation, 10 were literate and only 1 was clearly illiterate. There were 14 male Golovkins in the sixth generation; 6, almost half, signed their names. The survey reveals a growth of literacy within the Golovkin clan in the sixteenth century; yet by 1600 probably no more than half of them could read or write. But, of course, Trinity monk Evstafii in the sixth generation not only could read and write, but elevated his level of literacy into a higher sphere. As cellarer Evstafii lived in a world of written complicated commercial and real-estate transactions his literacy transcended the merely functional, judging by the fact that he added more property to Trinity's holdings than any cellarer before or after, and to his death in 1602 actively supervised his family's fortunes. Sources reveal him as a spiritual advisor to Ivan IV and a painter of complex icons, skills that required literacy in the world of religious texts—what Malcolm Parkes has called that of a cultivated reader, a literacy of "recreation," if not quite that of a man of letters.[86]

Trinity's numerous and bulky copybooks and the state's archive of charters are evidence that the monastery made a culture of reading and writing indispensable to landowners in fulfilling their social function and made it possible for individuals such as Evstafii Golovkin to enter a higher sphere of literacy. Writing standardizes languages and this correlates with the development of complex societies in which ruling elites and value systems took form in many places and in different ages.[87] Trinity's generation of practical literacy pioneered and continued to contribute to a process of social formation and self-definition of a society that was on the cusp of calling itself Russian.

* The debate in our time as to the debt modern nationalism owes, consciously or otherwise, to the detritus of cultural tradition, social-economic and political formations, the evolution of written language, and geographical

and demographic imperatives put in focus my argument for the importance of Sergius's cult and the Trinity-Sergius Monastery in the formation of Russia and a Russian national identity. Simon Franklin and Emma Widdis introduced their book about national identity in Russian culture with the observation that identity is not a thing; rather it depends on how one perceives oneself "as an individual, in relation to a group or groups, and by contrast with other individuals and groups." Benedict Anderson said much the same thing in describing national identity as an "imagined community." Anthony D. Smith and John Armstrong have taken exception to Ernest Gellner's instrumentalist explanation of the origin of modern notions of national identity; to wit, that nations are "not there to be awakened." Rather, they insisted, ideologues appropriate ethnic trappings to create national belief systems to legitimize modern states. The critique Smith and Armstrong undertook follows from the belief that notions of national identity are compelling only if they take familiar forms rooted in tradition that distinguish a people from "the Other," in political structures (real or imagined), a sense of religious uniqueness, economic institutions, bonds of kinship, and common modes of expression and ritual.[88] All these features, from which later generations constructed and reconstructed their identity as Russians, were present around 1600; and Sergius's cult and his Trinity Monastery were integral parts of all of them.

APPENDIX

TABLES 1–3

TABLE 1—Donations to the Trinity-Sergius Monastery by Type, 1392–1605

Period	1. Landed Property	2. Immunity Charters	3. Money a. ≥50 rubles	3. Money b. >49 rubles	4. Moveable Property	5. Type Unknown	COMBINATIONS OF 1, 3, 4	1 & 3a	1 & 3b	3a & 4	3b & 4	1 & 4	Total
1392–1422	14	5	0	0	5	0	0	0	0	0	0	0	24
1423–1445	61	35	0	0	2	0	0	1	0	0	0	2	101
1446–1461	44	40	0	0	2	0	0	0	0	0	0	1	87
1462–1478	37	58	0	0	1	0	0	0	0	0	0	0	96
1478–1501	23	35	3	0	11	0	0	0	1	0	0	0	73
1501–1522	37	31	27	22	15	0	0	1	0	4	6	0	143
1522–1533	31	18	34	41	25	0	0	1	2	2	3	0	157
1533–1546	82	54	162	192	118	0	0	0	1	7	14	0	630
1547–1564	168	39	357[a]	194[a]	64	1	0	4	1	4	1	1	835
1565–1584	386	42	290[b]	91[b]	42	1	2	7	5	5	11	2	886
1584–1605	51	15	132	171	68	0	0	4	0	17	17	0	475
Total	**934**	**372**	**1005[c]**	**711[c]**	**353**	**2**	**2**	**18**	**10**	**39**	**52**	**6**	**3507**

[a]= +one of unknown amount[b]= +2 of unknown amount[c]= +3 of unknown amount

TABLE 2—Acquisitions of Property by the Trinity-Sergius Monastery (Donations, Purchase, Exchange, or Judicial act) According to Location, 1392–1605

LOCATION	PERIOD											SUBTOTAL
	1	2	3	4	5	6	7	8	9	10	11	
	1392–1422	1423–45	1445–61	1462–78	1478–1501	1501–22	1522–33	1533–47	1547–64	1565–84	1584–1605	
Center	**16**	**55**	**36**	**29**	**16**	**28**	**27**	**51**	**94**	**143**	**38**	**533**
Moscow	1	13	9	8	6	11	2	19	30	37	14	150
Radonezh	2	6	5	3	0	1	2	5	5	7	2	38
Pereiaslavl'	10	27	12	11	3	6	16	13	22	35	11	166
Dmitrov	3	9	10	5	4	9	4	13	30	55	4	146
Iur'ev	0	0	0	2	3	1	2	0	4	9	4	25
Zvenigorod/ Klin	0	0	0	0	0	0	1	1	3	0	3	8
North Volga	**8**	**19**	**15**	**7**	**27**	**11**	**8**	**20**	**27**	**36**	**5**	**183**
Rostov	0	1	1	0	2	2	7	9	5	1	1	29
Uglich	8	11	6	5	3	4	0	2	2	4	0	45
Kostroma	0	6	8	2	22	4	1	7	16	29	4	99
Iaroslavl'	0	1	0	0	0	1	0	2	4	2	0	10
Northwest	**0**	**4**	**7**	**9**	**3**	**14**	**16**	**27**	**26**	**127**	**18**	**251**
Bezhetskii Verkh	0	3	5	8	1	10	9	10	14	55	3	118
Novyi Torg	0	1	1	1	1	1	0	3	0	2	0	10
Staritsa	0	0	0	0	0	0	2	6	1	6	1	16
Kashin	0	0	0	0	0	3	3	4	7	4	0	21
Tver'	0	0	1	0	1	0	2	4	3	52	12	75
Novgorod	0	0	0	0	0	0	0	0	1	7	2	10
Pskov	0	0	0	0	0	0	0	0	0	1	0	1
Trans-Volga	**1**	**12**	**1**	**4**	**5**	**3**	**0**	**3**	**12**	**67**	**21**	**129**
Beloozero	0	1	1	3	3	1	0	0	1	0	0	10
Galich	1	11	0	1	2	2	0	2	2	8	11	40
Vologda	0	0	0	0	0	0	0	0	4	1	1	6
Tot'ma	0	0	0	0	0	0	0	0	0	3	0	3
Kholmogory	0	0	0	0	0	0	0	0	5	2	1	8
Varzuga	0	0	0	0	0	0	0	0	0	52	8	60
Medyn'/Sol'-Vychegovsk	0	0	0	0	0	0	0	1	0	1	0	2

TABLE 2 *(Continued)*—Acquisitions of Property by the Trinity-Sergius Monastery (Donations, Purchase, Exchange, or Judicial act) According to Location, 1392–1605

LOCATION	PERIOD											
	1	2	3	4	5	6	7	8	9	10	11	SUBTOTAL
	1392–1422	1423–45	1445–61	1462–78	1478–1501	1501–22	1522–33	1533–47	1547–64	1565–84	1584–1605	
East	**0**	**9**	**11**	**4**	**2**	**5**	**1**	**7**	**16**	**88**	**15**	**158**
Vladimir	0	4	3	1	0	3	0	1	4	25	3	44
Suzdal'	0	3	6	0	0	1	1	0	1	0	1	13
Starodub	0	2	1	3	0	0	0	1	6	13	0	26
Murom	0	0	1	0	2	1	0	0	3	40	3	50
Nizhnii Novgorod	0	0	0	0	0	0	0	5	2	10	8	25
East Volga	**0**	**0**	**0**	**0**	**0**	**0**	**0**	**0**	**12**	**3**	**1**	**16**
Sviiazhsk	0	0	0	0	0	0	0	0	1	1	1	3
Kazan'	0	0	0	0	0	0	0	0	11	2	0	13
West	**0**	**0**	**0**	**2**	**1**	**3**	**0**	**3**	**4**	**4**	**2**	**19**
Borovsk	0	0	0	0	1	1	0	2	0	3	0	7
Ruza	0	0	0	0	0	1	0	0	3	1	1	6
Zubtsov	0	0	0	0	0	0	0	0	0	0	1	1
Vereia	0	0	0	2	0	0	0	1	1	0	0	4
Volok	0	0	0	0	0	1	0	0	0	0	0	1
South	**0**	**0**	**1**	**0**	**4**	**1**	**0**	**3**	**11**	**13**	**2**	**35**
Serpukhov	0	0	0	0	0	0	0	0	0	3	0	3
Kashira	0	0	0	0	0	0	0	0	1	0	0	1
Kolomna	0	0	0	0	0	1	0	3	6	7	2	19
Obolensk	0	0	0	0	0	0	0	0	3	2	0	5
Maloiaroslavets	0	0	1	0	4	0	0	0	0	0	0	5
Novosil	0	0	0	0	0	0	0	0	0	1	0	1
Tula	0	0	0	0	0	0	0	0	1	0	0	1
Unknown	**0**	**0**	**1**	**0**	**0**	**0**	**1**	**1**	**2**	**0**	**0**	**5**
TOTAL	25	99	72	55	58	65	53	115	204	481	102	1324

TABLE 3—The Evidence for Secular Literacy in Private Charters of the Trinity-Sergius Monastery, 1392–1605

	# of charters	*Giver*	*Cleric*	*Clerk*	*Other*	*# of givers signing (% of charters)*	*seal*	*Acts with witnesses*	*# of witnesses*	*# of witnesses signing*	*Signers as % of witnesses*	*# of witness' seals*
1392–1422	27	1 (4%)	8 (30%)	4 (15%)	5 (19%)	2 (7%)	13	23	106	0	—	8
1423–1445	91	8 (9%)	22 (24%)	10 (11%)	34 (37%)	3 (3%)	33	81	323	2	(.6%)	5
1446–1461	74	9[a] (12%)	14 (19%)	12 (16%)	26 (35%)	2 (3%)	17	61	232	5[b]	(2%)	4
1462–1478	69	5 (7%)	3 (4%)	19 (28%)	28 (41%)	5 (7%)	23	58	287	8	(3%)	5
1478–1501	77	13 (17%)	4 (5%)	6 (8%)	43 (56%)	14 (18%)	19	73	314	30	(10%)	2
1501–1522	144	32[c] (22%)	8 (6%)	24 (17%)	68 (47%)	47 (33%)	23	135	668	249	(37%)	1
1522– 1533	114	35[d] (31%)	0 (0%)	17 (15%)	56 (49%)	61 (54%)	3	113	613	233	(38%)	1
1533–1547	162	32[e] (20%)	2 (1%)	15 (9%)	101 (63%)	118 (73%)	6	153	691	382	(55%)	2
1547–1564	230	28[f] (13%)	7 (3%)	25 (11%)	161 (70%)	148[g] (85%)	6	225	937	666	(71%)	3
1565– 1584	447	41[h] (10%)	6 (2%)	94 (24%)	251 (64%)	360[i] (80%)	2	432	1590	1126	(71%)	0
1584– 1605	74	4[j] (5%)	0 (0%)	19 (26%)	47 (64%)	62[k] (84%)	0	69	245	193	(79%)	0.
Total	**1510**	**206**	**74**	**246**	**819**	**824 (55%)**	**145**	**1429**	**6006**	**2894**	**(48%)**	**31**

a= includes 1 cleric / b= includes 1 grand prince's ***d'iak***, Met. Feodosii / c= includes 2 by kin / d= includes 4 by kin / e= includes 10 by kin / f= includes 6 by kin / g= includes 4 by priest for giver / h= includes 1 by son-in-law, 2 by kin / i= includes 87 clerics, 3 executors, 19 kin for giver / j= includes 1 by kin / k= includes 3 Trinity monks, ll kin, 9 clerics for giver

Notes

ABBREVIATIONS USED

AAE	Akty, sobrannye v bibliotekakh i arkhivakh Rossiiskoi imperii arkheograficheskoiu ekspeditsieu Imp. Akademii nauk.
AE	Arkheograficheskii ezhegodnik.
AFZiKh	Akty feodal'nogo zemlevladeniia i khoziaistva XIV–XVI vekov.
AGR	*Akty, otnosiashchiesia do grazhdanskoi raspravy drevnei Rossii,* comp. A. Fedotov-Chekhovskii.
AI	Akty istoricheskie, sobrannye i izdannye Arkheograficheskoiu kommissieiu.
AN	Akademiia nauk.
ARG	Akty russkogo gosudarstva, 1505–1526 gg.
ASEI	Akty sotsial'no-ekonomicheskoi istorii severo-vostochnoi Rusi, kontsa XIV–nachala XVI v.
AZKh	L. A. Kirichenko, *Akty zemlevladeniia i khoziaistva Troitse-Sergieva monastyria, 1584–1641.*
BAN	Biblioteka Akademii nauk.
ChOIDR	Chteniia v imperatorskom Obshchestva istorii i drevnostei rossiiskikh pri Moskovskom universitete.
DDG	ANSSSR, In-t ist. *Dukhovnye i dogovornye gramoty velikikh i udel'nykh kniazei XIV–XVI vv.*
DRI. Sergii	Drevnerusskoe iskusstvo. Sergii Radonezhskii i khudozhestvennaia kul'tura Moskvy XIV–XV vv.
FOG	Forschungen zur osteuropäischen Geschichte.
GKE	Gramoty "Kollegii ekonomii."
IT	Kloss, B. M., *Izbrannie trudy.*
IZ	Istoricheskie zapiski.
JGO	Jahrbücher für Geschichte Osteuropas.
"KhP"	"Khronologicheskoi perechen' immunitetnykh gramot XVI veka."
Legenden	*Die Legenden des Heiligen Sergij von Radonež, Nachdruck der Ausgabe von Tichonravov,* ed. Ludolf Müller.

LZAK	*Letopis' zaniatii Arkheograficheskoi kommissii.*
OU	*Opisanie aktov sobraniia grafa A. S. Uvarova. Akty istoricheskie opisannye I. M. Kataevym i A. K. Kudanovym.*
PAA	*Perechen' aktov Arkhiva Troitse-Sergieva monastyria, 1505–1537*, ed. S. M. Kashtanov.
"Perechen'"	"Perechen' immunitetnykh gramot 1584–1610."
PK	*Pistsovye knigi Moskovskogo gosudarstva*, ed. N. K. Kalachev.
PLDR	*Pamiatniki literatury Drevnei Rusi, XIV–seredina XV veka*, ed. L. A. Dmitriev, D. S. Likhachev.
PRP. RK	*Pamiatniki russkoi pis'mennosti XV–XVI vv. Riazanskii krai.*
PSRL	Polnoe sobranie russkikh letopisei.
RGADA	Rossiiskii gosudarstvennyi arkhiv drevnikh aktov.
RIB	*Russkaia istoricheskaia biblioteka.*
RORGB	Rukopisnyi otdel Rossiiskoi gosudarstvennoi biblioteki.
SA	Sovetskaia arkheologiia.
SbGKE	Sbornik gramot Kollegii ekonomiki.
SbL	*Sbornik aktov sobrannykh N. P. Likhachevom.*
SbM	*Sbornik Mukhanova.*
Slovar'	*Slovar' knizhnikov i knizhnosti Drevnei Rusi*, ed. D. S. Likhachev.
SobB	*Sobranie istoriko-iuridicheskikh aktov I. D. Beliaeva*, comp. D. Lebedev.
Soobshcheniia	*Soobshcheniia Sergievo-Posadskogo* (formerly *Zagorskogo gosudarstvennogo istoriko-khudozhestvennogo) muzeia-zapovednika* (alternately, *Sergievo-posadskii muzei zapovednik. Soobshcheniia*).
SP	Spisok pogrebennykh v Troitse-Sergievoi Lavre ot osnovaniia onoi do 1880 goda.
TK/DT	Tysiachnaia kniga 1550 g. i Dvorovaia tetrád' 50-kh godov XVI v.
TL	Troitskaia letopis': Rekonstruksiia teksta.
TODRL	Trudy Otdela drevnerusskoi literatury.
T-SL	*Troitse-Sergieva lavra v istorii, kul'ture i dukhovnoi zhizni Rossii.* 4 vols. to date.
VK	*Vkladnaia kniga Troitse-Sergieva Monastyria.* ed. E. N. Klitina.

VMCh	Velikiia minei chetii, sobrannyia Mitropolitom Makariem.
ZOR	Zapiski Otdela rukopisei. Rossiiskoi gosudarstvennoi biblioteki (formerly Gosudarstvennaia biblioteka im. Lenina).

INTRODUCTION

1. V. O. Kliuchevskii, *Drevnerusskie zhitiia sviatykh kak istoricheskii istochnik* (Moscow, 1871; repr. The Hague, 1968, and Moscow, 1988), 88–138; E. Golubinskii, *Prepodobnyi Sergii Radonezhskii i sozdannaia im Troitskaia Lavra* (Moscow, 1892).

2. I. I. Bureichenko, "K voprosu o date osnovaniia Troitse-Sergieva Monastyria," *Soobshcheniia*, vyp. 2 (1958): 3–22; idem, "K istorii osnovaniia Troitse-Sergieva Monastyria," *Soobshcheniia*, vyp. 3 (1960): 5–40; V. A. Kuchkin, "Sergii Radonezhskii," *Voprosy istorii* (1992), no. 10: 75–92; Pierre Gonneau, *La Maison de la Sainte Trinité: Une Grand-monastére Russe du Moyen-âge Tardif (1345–1533)* (Paris, 1993), 111–38; B. M. Kloss, *IT,* 2 vols. (Moscow, 1998–2001), 1: 22–60, esp. 54–56; K. A. Aver'ianov, *Sergii Radonezhskii, lichnost' i epokha* (Moscow, 2006), 406–7, said Sergius was born in 1322. N. S. Borisov, *Russkaia tserkov v politicheskoi bor'be XIV–XV vekov* (Moscow, 1986), 87–91; idem, *Sergii Radonezhskii* (Moscow, 2001), 68–104, said 1314. Borisov dated Trinity's founding to 1337, Kuchkin to 1342, Aver'ianov to 1344–45, Gonneau and Bureichenko to 1345. Gonneau thought Sergius became a monk in 1339, Borisov 1341, Kuchkin and Kloss 1342, Aver'ianov 1344, Bureichenko 1345–46. Most agreed that he became abbot in 1353, Aver'ianov said 1354.

3. G. M. Prokhorov, *Povest' o Mitiae: Rus' i Vizantiia v epokhu Kulikovskoi bitvy* (Moscow, 1978); Kuchkin, "Sergii," 83–89; Aver'ianov, *Sergii*, 239–95; Jean Meyendorff, *Byzantium and the Rise of Russia: A Study of Byzantino-Russian Relations in the Fourteenth Century* (Cambridge, Eng., 1981), 200–41; Borisov, *Russkaia tserkov'*, 100–30.

4. B. M. Kloss, "Zhitiia Sergiia i Nikona Radonezhskikh v russkoi pis'mennosti XV–XVII vv.," in *Metodicheskie rekomendatsii po opisaniiu slaviano-russkikh rukopisnykh knig*, vyp. 3 (Moscow, 1990): 271–96; *IT* 1: 155–223; V. M. Kirillin, "Epifanii Premudryi kak agiograf prepodobnogo Sergiia Radonezhskogo: problema avtorstva," *Germenuvtika drevnerusskoi literatury* 7, pt. 2 (1994): 264–75. The incomplete Epifanii text, *IT* 1: 285–341; repeated in the Extended Edition through the chapter "About the Shabbiness of Sergei's Clothes and about a Certain Peasant," *PLDR* (Moscow, 1980), 256–358. Cf. Aver'ianov, *Sergii*, 3–8.

5. *IT* 1: 160–212; cf. A. G. Bobrov, G. M. Prokhorov, S. A. Semiachko, "Imitatsiia nauki: o knigi V. M. Klossa 'Izbrannye trudy,' v. 1: 'Zhitie Sergiia Radonezhskogo. Rukopisnaia traditsiia, zhizn' i chudesa, teksty,'" *TODRL* 53 (2003): 418–45; V. A. Kuchkin's intemperate but often acute critique on this (and most of Kloss's work), "Antiklossitsizm," *Drevniaia Rus'. Voprosy medievistiki* (pts. 1–3, 2002, nos. 2–4; pts. 4–7, 2003, nos. 1–4).

6. Ludolf Müller, introduction, v–liii, and appendix, 90–91, to *Legenden*, the reprinting of N. S. Tikhonravov's collection of many editions of Sergius's life (1892), set forth the schemes by which scholars have ordered these works; V. Iablonskii, *Pakhomii*

Serb i ego agiograficheskie pisaniia. Biograficheskii i bibliograficheski-literaturnyi ocherk (St. Petersburg, 1908); V. P. Zubov, "Epifanii Premudryi i Pakhomii Serb," *TODRL* 9 (1953): 145–58; Gonneau, *La Maison*, following Ortrud Appel, *Die Vita des hl. Sergij von Radonež. Untersuchungen zur Textgeschichte* (Munich, 1972).

7. M. D. Priselkov, *Istoriia russkogo letopisaniia*. Repr. of Leningrad ed., 1940 (The Hague, 1966), 128–64; Ia. S. Lur'e, *Obshcherusskie letopisi XIV–XV vv.* (Leningrad, 1976), 17–121; *IT* 1: 96–130, 241–67; A. S. Bobrov, "Letopisnyi svod Mitropolita Fotiia (Problema rekonstruktsii teksta," *TODRL* 52 (2001): 98–137.

8. Kuchkin, "Sergii;" idem, "Dmitrii Donskoi i Sergii Radonezhskii v kanun kulikovskoi bytvy," in *Tserkov', obshchestvo i gosudarstvo v feodal'noi Rossii*, ed. A. I. Klibanov (Moscow, 1990), 103–26; idem, "Russkie istoriki o Sergii Radonezhskom," *Otechestvo: Kraevedcheskii al'manakh* 3 (1992): 5–28; idem, "Nachalo moskovskoi Simonova monastyria," in *Kul'tura srednevekovoi Moskvy XIV–XVII vv.*, ed. L. A. Beliaev (Moscow, 1995), 113–22; idem, "Sergii Radonezhskii i bor'ba za mitropolich'iu kafedru vseia Rusi v 70–80e gody XIV v.," in *Kul'tura Slavian i Rus'*, ed. Iu. S. Kukushkin (Moscow, 1998), 353–60; *IT* 1: 22–60; David B. Miller, "The Cult of Saint Sergius of Radonezh and Its Politcal Uses," *Slavic Review* 52 (1993): 680–99; Borisov, *Sergei*; Aver'ianov, *Sergii*.

9. Edward Shils, *Center and Periphery: Essays in Macrosociology* (Chicago, 1975), 38.

10. Emile Durkheim, *The Elementary Forms of Religious Life* (London, 1915), 243–44.

11. Aviad Kleinberg, *Prophets in Their Own Country: Living Saints and the Making of Sainthood in the Later Middle Ages* (Chicago, 1991), 1–21ff.

12. Evfimii: I. U. Budovnits, *Monastyri na Rusi i bor'ba s nimi krest'ian v XIV–XVI vv.* (Moscow, 1966), 156–58. Cenobite rules: *PSRL* (2d ed., 4 vols. to date, St. Petersburg-Petrograd-Leningrad, 1908–) 15 pt. 1: 105–6, 121, 123, 129; L. A. Beliaev, *Drevnie monastyri Moskvy po dannym arkheologii* (Moscow, 1994), 153–54. Cf. Golubinskii, *Prepodobnyi Sergii*, 25–26, 35–36, 46–48, 54–57, giving Sergius maximum credit for monastic foundings, and the more cautious Kuchkin, "Sergii," 88–89; Borisov, *Sergii*, esp. 120–28.

13. Clifford Geertz, "Centers, Kings, and Charisma: Reflections on the Symbolics of Power," in *Culture and Its Creators: Essays in Honor of Edward Shils*, ed. Joseph Ben-David and Terry Nichols Clark (Chicago, 1977), 150–71; repr. in *Rights of Power: Symbolism, Ritual and Politics Since the Middle Ages*, ed. Sean Wilentz (Philadelphia, 1985), 13–38, esp. 13–14.

14. S. A. Shumakov, *Obzor "Gramot kolegii ekonomii,"* 6 vols. (Moscow, 1899–1917); idem, *Tverskie akty*, 2 vols. (1996–97), 1: *Akty 1506–1647*; idem, *Uglichskie akty 1400–1749 gg.* (Moscow, 1899); idem, *Sotnitsy, gramoty i zapisi*, 4 vols. (Moscow, 1902–1911); also Nataliia D. Shakhovskaia's unsatisfactory survey of Trinity's properties, *V monastyrskoi votchine XIV–XVII vv. (Sv. Sergii i ego khoziaistvo)* (Moscow, 1916).

15. *SbGKE*. 2 vols. (Peterburg, Leningrad, 1922, 1929).

16. *ASEI*, 3 vols., v. 1 ed. S. B. Veselovskii, vols. 2–3 ed. I. A. Golubtsov (Moscow, 1952–54).

17. *AFZiKh*, 3 vols., ed. L. V. Cherepnin (Moscow, 1951–1961).

18. *PAA* (Moscow, 2007); *ARG*, ed. S. B. Veselovskii (Moscow, 1975); S. M. Kashtanov, *Aktovaia arkheografiia* (Moscow, 1998), 234–35.

19. "KhP," pts. 1–2, ed. S. M. Kashtanov, *AE za 1957 god* (1958), 302–76 and *AE za 1960 god* (1962), 129–200; pt. 3, ed. Kashtanov, V. D. Nazarov and V. N. Floria, *AE za 1966 god* (1968), 197–253. "Perechen," 2 pts., ed. D. A. Tebekin, *AE za 1978 god* (1979), 191–235 and *AE za 1979 god* (1980), 210–55; *AZKh* (Moscow, 2006).

20. Gonneau, *La Maison*, has a different periodization to 1533.

21. Barbara H. Rosenwein, *To Be the Neighbor of Saint Peter: The Social Meaning of Cluny's Property, 909–1049* (Ithaca, NY, 1989); Megan McLoughlin, *Consorting with Saints: Prayer for the Dead in Early Medieval France* (Ithaca, NY, 1994); also Ludwig Steindorff on the memorial culture of the Iosifo-Volokolamsk monastery, *Memoria in Alt-russland. Untersuchungen zu den Formen christliches Totensorge* (Stuttgart, 1994).

22. Durkheim, *Elementary Forms*, 38.

23. Ludwig Steindorff, "Einstellungen zum Monchtum im Spiegel altrussischen Quellen," *Archiv für Kulturgeschichte* 75 (1993): 65–90.

24. Peter Brown, *The Cult of the Saints: Its Rise and Function in Latin Christianity* (Chicago, 1981), 44; David B. Miller, "Motives for Donations to the Trinity-Sergius Monastery, 1392–1605: Gender Matters," *Essays in Medieval Studies* 14 (1998): 91–106.

25. Philippe Ariès, *The Hour of Our Death*, transl. Helen Weaver (New York, 1981); idem, *Western Attitudes Toward Death: From the Middle Ages to the Present*, transl. Patricia M. Ranum (Baltimore, 1974); R. C. Finucan, "Sacred Corpse, Profane Carrion: Social Ideals and Death Rituals in the Later Middle Ages," in *Mirrors of Mortality: Studies in the Social History of Death*, ed. Joachim Whaley (New York, 1981), 40–60.

26. Pierre Nora, "Between Memory and History: Les lieux de Memoire," *Representations* 26 (1989): 7–25; David I. Kertzer, *Ritual, Politics, and Power* (New Haven, 1988), 9–12.

1—THE HISTORICAL SERGIUS

1. *IT* 1: 286; *PLDR*, 256. Sergius died 25 September 6900, *TL*, 440–41; *IT* 1: 22–23; B. M. Kloss, 'K izucheniiu traditsii knigopisaniia v Troitse-Sergievom monastyre," *Istoriia i paleografiia* (1993), 23–26.

2. Janet Martin, *Medieval Russia, 980–1584* (Cambridge, Eng., 1995), 145ff.; V. V. Kargalov, *Vneshnepoliticheskie factory razvitiia feodal'noi Rusi: Feodal'naia Rus' i kochevniki* (Moscow, 1967), 133ff.; Cherepnin, *Obrazovanie*, 551–663, 715–34; David B. Miller, "Monumental Building as an Indicator of Economic Trends in Northern Rus' in the Late Kievan and Mongol Periods, 1138–1462," *American Historical Review* 94 (1989): 368–72; V. A. Kuchkin, "Goroda severo-vostochnoi Rusi v XIII–XV vekakh (chislo i politiiko-geograficheskoe razmeshchenie)," *Istoriia SSSR* (1990), no. 6: 72–85; B. A. Rybakov, *Remeslo drevnei Rusi* (Moscow, 1948), 593ff.; John T. Alexander, *Bubonic Plague in Early Modern Russia* (Baltimore, 1980), 11–16; *TL*, 418–28, 431–31.

3. Kloss, "K izucheniiu traditsii," 11; Kuchkin, "Sergii Radonezhskii," 75–76; Aver'ianov, *Sergii*, 25–32, based largely on Epifanii's word that Sergius died at age 70.

Borisov, *Sergii*, 13–14, 280–82, following Pakhomii's report that Sergius lived 78 years, said he was born in 1314, gave earlier dates for most events known only from the life.

4. Kuchkin, "Sergii Radonezhskii," 75–76; Miller, "Monumental Building," 368–73; *TL*, 327–28, 338–39, 345–46, 347–48, 352, 353, 355, 356–57, recorded 10 Mongol expeditions in northeastern Rus', 1262–1322.

5. *PSRL* 18: 89, and 4, pt. 1: 256–58; J. L. I. Fennell, *The Emergence of Moscow, 1304–1359* (Berkeley, 1968), 91–92; V. A. Kuchkin, *Formirovanie gosudarstvennoi territorii severo-vostochnoi Rusi v X–XIV vv.* (Moscow, 1984), 264–66.

6. *IT* 1: 303–4; *PLDR*, 288–90.

7. *PSRL* 1 (2d ed.): 531 (Mariia's marriage to Konstantin); *TL*, 358–59 (Fedorchuk's invasion), 361 (famine), 364–65 (Kalita's death, Semen's installation as grand prince). Cf. Borisov, *Sergii*, 18–33; *IT* 1: 27–28; Kuchkin, "Sergii Radonezhskii," 76; idem, "Antiklossitsizm," pt. 1, 122; idem, "Zemel'nye priobreteniia moskovskikh kniazei v Rostovskom kniazhestve v XIV v.," in *Vostochnaia Evropa v drevnosti i srednevekov'e*, ed. L. V. Cherepnin (Moscow, 1978), 185–92; Bureichenko, "K istorii," 13–17; Gonneau, *La Maison*, 111–13; K. A. Aver'ianov, "O stepeni dostovernosti 'Zhitiia Sergiia Radonezhskogo'," *Germenevtika drevnerusskoi literatury* 12 (2005): 835–48; idem, *Sergii*, 39–48.

8. *IT* 1: 30, 32, 304; *PLDR*, 290; *DDG* (Moscow-Leningrad, 1950), 7–8 (no. 1); Aver'ianov, "O stepeni," 838–41; idem, *Sergii*, 34–52; L. A. Beliaev, "Sobor Bogoiavlenskogo Monastyria za Torgom i Troitskii sobor Troitse-Sergievoi Lavry (Istoriko-khudozhestvennye paralleli)," in *DRI. Sergii* (Moscow, 1998), 402; S. B. Veselovskii, *Issledovaniia po istorii klassa sluzhilykh zemlevladel'tsev* (Moscow, 1969), 211–12.

9. Borisov, *Sergii*, 28–33, drew the same conclusion, but his Sergii was a lad of 14.

10. Priselkov's intro. to *TL*, 16–33; idem, *Istoriia*, 113–40; Lur'e, *Obshcherusskie letopisi*, 36–49; idem, *Dve istorii Rusi XV veka* (St. Petersburg, 1994), 57–63; Kloss, "Zhitiia," 291–92; idem, "Determining the Authorship of the Trinity Chronicle," in *Medieval Russian Culture* 2, ed. Michael S. Flier and Daniel Rowland (Berkeley, 1994), 57–72; *IT* 1: 100–7, 241–55. I argue in the next chapter that news of Sergius's purported diplomacy in Nizhnii Novgorod for Dmitrii under 1363 in the compilation of 1448, *PSRL* 39: 113–14, reflected the cult rather than reality.

11. L. L. Murav'eva, "O nachale letopisaniia v Troitse-Sergievom monastyre," in *Kul'tura srednevekovoi Moskvy, XIV–XVII vv.*, ed. L. A. Beliaev (Moscow, 1995), 4–22.

12. *TL*, 396–97; T. Vesuolkina, "Vysotsky Monastery in Serpukhov founded by St. Afanasy," *The Journal of the Moscow Patriarchate* (1992), no. 4: 34–35.

13. *IT* 1: 290–92; *PLDR*, 264–68; Aver'ianov, *Sergii*, 29–32; Kuchkin, "Sergii Radonezhskii," 75; idem, "Antiklossitsizm," pt. 1: 120–22; Borisov, *Sergii*, 13–14.

14. *IT* 1: 297–301; *PLDR*, 278–84.

15. *IT* 1: 28–29, 305–6; *PLDR*, 290–92.

16. *IT* 1: 29–30, 306–7; *PLDR*, 292–94, 302; cf. Kuchkin, "Antiklossitsizm," pt. 2: 121.

17. *IT* 1: 30–32, 278; *PLDR*, 294–302; *Legenden* 1: 15; Kuchkin, "Sergii Radonezhskii," 77–78; Pakhomii's Third Ed. of the life, 1448–49, and an insertion in

ms. of Epifanii's life said Sergius was 23; *IT* 1: 310, 384. Cf. Aver'ianov. who, having dated Sergius's move to Radonezh to 1341, said 1345, "O stepeni," 850, and *Sergii*, 52–76, as did Bureichenko, "K voprosu," 6–7, and Gonneau, *La Maison*, 13–15. Borisov, *Sergii*, 37–43, dated it 1337.

18. *IT* 1: 32; Kloss, "K izucheniiu," 11; G. P. Fedotov, *The Russian Religious Mind*, vol. 2: *The Middle Ages: The Thirteenth to the Fifteenth Centuries*, ed. Jean Meyendorff (Cambridge, Mass., 1966), 204–7. Texts: *IT* 1: 313–18; *PLDR*, 606–16.

19. *IT* 1: 32, 311–12, 318–22; *PLDR*, 302–4, 318–22; Borisov, *Sergii*, 58–63, said Sergius from about 1344 was Trinity's "de facto" abbot.

20. Bureichenko, "K istorii," 17–26; Budovnits, *Monastyri*, 82–84, 87; the Zubachev estate: *ASEI* 1: 29, 34–35, 591–92 (nos. 6, 16–17).

21. *IT* 1: 318, 322; *PLDR*, 316, 322.

22. *IT* 1: 32–33, 322–26; *PLDR*, 322–28.

23. Aleksei's trips: *PSRL* 15, pt. 1: 62–65. Aver'ianov, *Sergii*, 87–92; Borisov, *Sergii*, 68–69; Bureichenko, "K voprosu," 10–11; Golubinskii, *Prepodobnyi Sergii*, 15; Gonneau, *La Maison*, 116–17; *IT* 1: 33. Kuchkin, "Sergii Radonezhskii," 78, dated it to the fall of 1353.

24. *IT* 1: 330–32; *PLDR*, 338–42.

25. *IT* 1: 328; *PLDR*, 334; *PSRL* 15, pt. 1: 65, 68, 73; Kuchkin, "Sergii Radonezhskii," 78–79; cf. Aver'ianov, *Sergii*, 92–95.

26. *IT* 1: 329–30; *PLDR*, 336, 338.

27. *TL*, 392; Kuchkin, "Sergii Radonezhskii," 79; Aver'ianov, *Sergii*, 104–5, dated it to the earlier famine of 1364; *TL*, 379–80.

28. *IT* 1: 34–35, 332–41; *PLDR*, 340–58; *TL*, 396–97; Kloss, "Determining," 63–64; Kuchkin, "Sergii Radonezhskii," 79–80.

29. Kuchkin, "Sergii Radonezhskii," 91, no. 28; idem, "Sergii Radonezhskii i bor'ba," 353–54, 356. Kipriian's entreaties to them: "Thus, was there nobody left in Moscow concerned about the soul of the Grand Prince and his inheritance?" and "If you are concerned with the soul of the Grand Prince and all his inheritance, why did you remain silent?", *RIB* 6 (2d ed.), app., no. 20, col. 175; Prokhorov's version, *Povest'*, app., 196, omitted quotation two; English transl., Meyendorff, *Byzantium*, app., 293–94.

30. About Kipriian: Dmitri Obolensky, "A Philorhomaios anthröpos: Metropolitan Cyprian of Kiev and All Russia," *Dumbarton Oaks Papers* 32 (1979): 79–98.

31. *TL*, 397–98, put the assembly in the fall prior to the baptism, but did not mention Aleksei's or Kipriian's presence as did *PSRL* 15, pt. 1: 105, which placed the assembly in the spring. Fedor as confessor: *PSRL* 15, pt. 1: 141–42; Kuchkin, "Nachalo," 113–22. Mikhail as confessor: Prokhorov, *Povest'*, app. 3, 219.

32. *IT* 1: 308–9, 329–32; *PLDR*, 296–98. Cf. Aver'ianov, *Sergii*, 95–101; Kuchkin, "Sergii Radonezhskii, 77–78; Nancy Kollmann, *Kinship*, 128–30; Beliaev, "Sobor," 400–9.

33. *DDG*, 14 (no. 3).

34. *PLDR*, 334–36.

35. *PSRL* XV, pt. 1: 65; *TL*, 375. Borisov, *Sergii*, 114–16, following from his early dating of Sergius's birth, dated Stefan's return as 1447–48 (and termed his relationship to Moscow's ruler and Sergius amicable). Aver'ianov, *Sergii*, 96–101, accepted the date in the chronicle but, elsewhere, 137–38, 207, argued that the chronology from 1327 in the chronicle was inexact. Cf. Fennell's dating to 1353–54, *The Emergence of Moscow*, 292–93 and Kuchkin, "Sergii Radonezhskii," 78–79. On court politics: Hartmut Rüss, "Der Kampf um das Moskauer Tysjackij-Amt im 14. Jahrhunderts," *JGO* 22 (1974): 481–93; Nancy Shields Kollmann, "The Boyar Clan and Court Politics: The Founding of the Muscovite Political System," *Cahiers du monde russe et soviétique* 23 (1982): 12–17.

36. Kloss's scheme for Pakhomii's editions, *IT* 1: 160–89. Texts described the event identically; *IT* 1: 362–63; *Legenden*, 1: 47–51; *PLDR*, 370–74.

37. Pakhomii's First Edition: *IT* 1: 364–65, and *Legenden*, 1: 46–47; Extended Ed., *PLDR*, 368–70. Pakhomii's Second Ed., *Legenden*, 1: 118, altered only the rhetoric.

38. *IT* 1: 364–65; *Legenden*, 1: 47–51; *PLDR*, 370–74, are identical.

39. *Legenden*, 1: 52–54, 124–27; *PLDR*, 382–84; Kuchkin, "Sergii Radonezhskii," 83; idem, "Nachalo," 113–22; Ivina, *Krupnaia votchina*, 30–38.

40. Golubinskii, *Prepodobnyi Sergii*, 20–25; Meyendorff, *Byzantium*, 132–36; Bureichenko, "K istorii," 26–33; Borisov, *Sergii*, 91–100, 114–19; also Gonneau, *La Maison*, 117–21. The date 1355 is impossible; by then Callistos (1354–1363) had replaced Philotheos as patriarch.

41. The cross/reliquary: Vorontsova, *Prepodobnyi Sergii*, cat., no. 3, illustrations nos. 1–2; the martyrdom: *PSRL* 7: 214. O. A. Belobrova, "Posol'stvo Konstaninopol'skogo Patriarkha Filofeiiu k Sergiiu Radonezhskomu," *Soobshcheniia* 2 (1958): 112–18; T. V. Nikolaeva, *Proizvedeniia russkogo prikhladnogo iskusstva*, 32–33 (no. 2); Meyendorff, *Byzantium*, 134–35, no. 62, thought the cross fabricated in Rus'.

42. *RIB* 6, no. 21: 187–90; Aver'ianov, *Sergii*, 208–9.

43. Kuchkin, "Sergii Radonezhskii," 80–82; Meyendorff, *Byzantium*, 132–38, 204–5; Prokhorov, *Povest'*, 8–49.

44. *IT* 1: 38–41.

45. *TL*, 379; Kloss, *IT* 1: 43, for the first reference to Gerasim as archimandrite of the Chudovskii monastery in a manuscript of Pakhomii's first edition of Sergius's life, dated 1365.

46. Kuchkin, "Sergii Radonezhskii," 82, citing V. V. Zverinskii, *Materialy dlia istoriko-topograficheskogo izsledovaniia o pravoslavnykh monastyriakh v Rossiiskoi imperii*, 3 vols. (St. Petersburg, 1890–97), 2: 202; *IT* 1: 82.

47. Meyendorff, *Byzantium*, 148–205; V. A. Kuchkin, "Sergii Radonezhskii i filofeevskii krest," in *DRL. Sergii*, 16–22, esp. 19–20.

48. *PSRL* 15, pt. 1: 105, 116; *RIB* 6, app., no. 33: 202, 204. Aver'ianov, *Sergii*, 205–11; Kuchkin, "Sergii Radonezhskii," 81–82; poke holes in Prokhorov's dating Kipriian's visit to March, 1376, *Povest'*, 57–58.

49. Miller, "Monumental Building," 367–74; Carsten Goehrke, *Die Wüstungen in der Moskauer Rus': Studien zur Siedlungs-, Bevölkerungs- und Sozialgeschichte*

(Wiesbaden, 1968); Langer, "Plague," 351–68; A. L. Shapiro, *Problemy sotsial'no-ekonomicheskoi istorii Rusi XIV–XVI vv.* (Leningrad, 1977).

50. Meyendorff, *Byzantium*, 122–24; Kloss, "K izucheniiu biografii," 11–14; *IT* 1: 46–53, esp. 46, on Aleksei's initiative in introducing it; cf. Kuchkin, "Antiklossitsizm," pt. 3, 112–13.

51. V. O. Kliuchevskii, "Kurs russkoi istorii," in *Sochineniia*, 8 vols. (Moscow, 1956–59), 2: 244–75, the classic account of the spread of rural monasteries. Borisov, *Russkaia tserkov'*, 87–94; idem, *Sergii*. 96–104, argued that Sergius's zeal for cenobite reform was self-generated.

52. *PSRL* 15, pt. 1: 129; Beliaev, *Drevnie monastyri*, 152–57.

53. *IT* 1: 38–42, 56, 366–67, 370–71; *PLDR*, 376–80: Aver'ianov, *Sergii*, 157–78. Cf. Kuchkin, "Iz literaturnogo," 242–56; idem, "Antiklossitsizm," pt. 3, 100–7.

54. *IT* 1: 38–46; Golubinskii, *Prepodobnyi Sergii*, 35–36, 53–63; Budovnits, *Monastyri*, 77–111; Gonneau, *La Maison*, 122–27.

55. *PLDR*, 372–74; G. P. Chiniakova, "Zhitie Prepodobnogo Romana, igumena Blagoveshchenskogo Kirzhachskogo monastyria, uchenika Prepodobnogo Sergiia," *Makarievskie chteniia* 5 (1998): 226–27.

56. *IT* 1: 46; Kuchkin, "Nachalo," 113–22; Ivina, *Krupnaia*, 35–39.

57. *IT* 1: 59, 411–12; *PLDR*, 388–90; Kloss, "K izucheniiu biografii," 14; Kuchkin, "Sergii Radonezhskii," 88–89.

58. Kuchkin, "Sergii Radonezhskii," 88–89; *IT* 1: 59–60; Golubinskii, *Prepodobnyi Sergii*, 56; Aver'ianov, *Sergii*, 152–55.

59. *TL*, 418; *PSRL* 15, pt. 1: 137–38.

60. Kuchkin, "Sergii Radonezhskii," 86–87; idem, "Dmitrii Donskoi," 121; *IT* 1: 58–59; Kloss, "K izucheniiu biografii," 14; Borisov, *Sergii*, 126–27, 176–77, 182–87; Golubinskii, *Prepodobnyi Sergii*, 46–48. S. Z. Chernov, "Uspenskii Dubenskii Shavykin Monastyr' v svete arkheologicheskikh dannykh," in *Kul'tura srednevekovoi Moskvy*, ed. Beliaev, 125–55, showed only that a second Dubenka monastery might have existed.

61. *IT* 1: 60–61; *Zhitie Savvy*, 26–29; Aver'ianov, *Sergii*, 395–400, agreed on this.

62. *IT* 1: 61; Budovnits, *Monastyri*, 153–55; Zverinskii, *Materialy*, 1: 217–19.

63. *IT* 1: 61–62; Kliuchevskii, *Drevnerusskie zhitiia*, 122–23.

64. *TL*, 404–7.

65. Meyendorff, *Byzantium*, 173–241.

66. Ibid., 183; *PSRL* 15, pt. 1: 94–95, 105–6.

67. *RIB* 6, app., no. 30: 167–72; Prokhorov, *Povest'*, 25–32; Kuchkin, "Sergiii Radonezhskii i bor'ba," 354–56; Meyendorff, *Byzantium*, 200–3.

68. *RIB* 6, app., no 30: 173–74; Eng. transl., Meyendorff, *Byzantium*, 304; cf. Kuchkin, "Sergii Radonezhskii i bor'ba," 353–57; Borisov, "Moskovskie," 40–42.

69. Prokhorov, *Povest'*, 4–79, 219; *TL*, 407–8.

70. *IT* 1: 368–69, 406–7; *Legenden* 1: 132–35; *PLDR*, 392.

71. Prokhorov, *Povest'*, 219; Aver'ianov argued that Aleksei and Philotheos anticipated the former's death and nominated Sergius in 1374 to ensure the continuity of a united see and an anti-Mongol orientation, *Sergii*, 221–34, 247–55. He had no

evidence for this, only an unrealistically elevated sense of Sergius's importance.

72. Prokhorov, *Povest'*, 195; Meyendorff, *Byzantium*, 292.

73. *PSRL* 15, pt. 1: 116; Kuchkin, "Sergii Radonezhskii i bor'ba," 356–57.

74. Prokhorov, *Povest'*, 195–201, esp. 196, 201; Meyendorff, *Byzantium*, 293–99.

75. Prokhorov, *Povest'*, 59–60, 202; *IT* 1: 369; cf. Kuchkin, "Sergii Radonezhskii i bor'ba, 358, with B. V. Krichevskii, *Russkie mitropolity (Tserkov' i vlast' XIV veka)* (St. Petersburg, 1996), 169–85.

76. *PLDR*, 394–96; Borisov, *Russkaia tserkov*, 111–13; idem, *Sergii*, 172–76; *IT* 1: 35–36, 372–73; Aver'ianov, *Sergii*, 366–68.

77. Prokhorov, *Povest'*, 66–82, 221–22; *PSRL* 15, pt. 1: 126–27.

78. *RIB* 6, app., no. 33: 205–16; partial Eng. transl., Meyendorff, *Byzantium*, 307–8; Kuchkin, "Sergii Radonezhskii i bor'ba," 357; Obolensky, "O Philorhomaios," 89

79. Prokhorov, *Povest'*, 222–23; *PSRL* 15, pt. 1: 128–31; *RIB* 6, app., no. 33: 206–16. Cf. Prokhorov, *Povest'*, 74–101; Meyendorff, *Byzantium*, 214–21.

80. Cf. Prokhorov, *Povest'*, 101–24; Kuchkin, "Sergii Radonezhskii i bor'ba," 359–59; idem, "Sergii Radonezhskii," 87–89, with Aver'ianov, *Sergii*, 295–303, relying on the sixteenth-century Nikon chronicle, *PSRL* 11: 49, dating Kipriian's return in 1380 *before* Kulikovo, to claim that Sergius reconciled Kipriian (and himself) with Dmitrii.

81. *PSRL* 15, pt. 1: 141–42, 143, 148.

82. Ibid., 144, 147; *TL*, 423–25; *PSRL* 6: 122.

83. *PSRL* 15, pt. 1: 142; *TL*, 421.

84. *PSRL* 15, pt. 1: 150.

85. Ibid., 151; *TL*, 429; *DDG*, no. 10: 29–30 (the pact of 1381 or 1382); A. E. Presniakov, *Obrazovanie velikorusskogo gosudarstva* (Petrograd, 1918), 326–29: Golubinskii, *Prepodobnyi Sergii*, 46.

86. *PSRL* 15, pt. 1: 156; *TL*, 434.

87. *PSRL* 15, pt. 1: 155, 157; *TL* 433, 435; *DDG*, nos. 7, 11, 13, 23–24, 30–33, 37–39; Presniakov, *Obrazovanie*, 171–82; V. A. Kuchkin, "Spodvizhnik Dmitriia Donskogo," *VI* (1979), no. 8: 114–15; A. L. Khoroshkevich, "K vzaimootnosheniiam kniazei moskovskogo doma vo vtoroi polovine XIV–nachale XV veka," 6 (1980), no. 6: 170–71.

88. *TL*, 435–36; *PSRL* 15, pt. 1: 152–53, 157–59; Meyendorff, *Byzantium*, 239–41, 244–52.

89. Life of Nikon Radonezhskii in Pachomij Logofet, *Werke in Auswahl. Slavische Propyläen* 1, ed. Dmitrij Tschiżewskij (Munich, 1963): lxix-lxxiv; *Zhitie Savvy*, ed Timoshina, 28.

90. *PSRL* 15, pt. 1: 163–64; *TL*, 440–41.

91. *IT* 1: 246–47.

92. *IT* 1: 66–68, and Arsenii, "O votchinykh vladenii," 141–75, regarding Dmitrii Donskoi's spurious grant of immunities for Trinity's properties, *ASEI* 1: 25–26 (no. 1). Cf Bureichenko, "Monastyrskoe zemlevladenie;" Budovnits, *Monastyri*, 105–11; Kuchkin, "Antiklossitsizm," pt. 5, 127–30, with Aver'ianov, *Sergii*. 376–95, arguing

the existence of the charter, if not with the immunities later attributed to it; also that villages historians considered a gift in 1426 from Prince Andrei Vladimirovich were hereditary holdings of Sergius's family, and that Semen Fedorovich Morozov gave "to elder Sergius and abbot Nikon" one half of a salt works in Sol'-Galich in 1392 [*ASEI* 1: 27 (no. 3)]. The reference to Sergius must be rhetorical. This Morozov was killed in 1433; he may not even have been born in 1392.

2—SERGIUS THE SAINT

1. Pakhomii's life of Nikon (1440s) said Nikon refused to become abbot for six years until Trinity's brotherhood urged him to do so; only Savva's biography (sixteenth century) says he held office in that interval. Pachomij, *Werke*, lxxii–lxxiii; Zhitie Savvy, ed. Timoshina, 28. I cite the extended edition of Nikon's life (sixteenth century); the original is unpublished; *IT* 1: 235–40. Kuchkin, "Antiklossitsizm," pt. 5: 131–32, without proof, said Savva's tenure is a myth. Cf. *IT* 1: 286, on Epifanii's recollection of when he started collecting material about Sergius.

2. *PSRL* 15, pt. 1: 179–85; Epifanii's letter to Archimandrite Kirill of the Spaso-Afanas'ev Monastery in Tver', *PLDR*, 446; life of Nikon in Pachomij, *Werke*, lxxiv–lxxv; Kloss, "K izucheniiu," 17; Gorskii, *Opisanie* 1: 73.

3. Kleinberg, *Prophets*, 5–21ff.; L. M. Vorontsova, "K voprosu o skladyvanii pochitanii prepodobnogo Sergiia Radonezhskogo v XV v.," in Sergievo-posadskii muzei-zapovednik, *Trudy po istorii Troitse-Sergievoi Lavry* 7 (Moscow, 1998), 11–14

4. Cf. *IT* 1: 92–97, Kloss, "Zametki," 4–5, with Kuchkin, "Antiklossitsizm," pt. 6: 112–14.

5. *IT* 1: 271–83, esp. 279 (text), 17, 100, 145–54 (commentary); *PSRL* 25: 240; E. M. Vereshchagin, "K istolokovaniiu imeni Epifanii Premudrogo (v sviazi istokami stilia 'pleteniia sloves')," *Izvestiia RAN, Seriia literatury i iazyka* 52, no. 2 (1993): 65–76; Kuchkin, "O vremeni," 407–15; idem, Antiklossitsizm," pt. 6: 15–17, said Epifanii wrote the encomium in 1422 to commemorate the translation of Sergius's relics to the new stone church, citing Epifanii's reference to viewing Sergius's relics, his statement in the life that nothing previously was written about him, and Byzantine sources dating Anna's trip in 1414; Bobrov, Prokhorov and Semiachko, "Imitasiia nauki," 418–45, concurred. Cf. A. S. Sedel'nikov, "Iz oblasti literaturnogo obshchenia v nachale XV veka (Kirill Tverskoi i Epifanii 'Moskovskoi')," *Izvestiia Otdeleniia russkogo iazyka i slovestnosti* 31 (1926): 159–76; Kliuchevskii, *Drevnerusskie zhitiia*, 62–63, on the authenticity of the reference to Epifanii's trip.

6. Cf. *TL*, 440–41; encomium, *IT* 1: 271–74; Kloss, "Determining the Authorship," 66–67.

7. *IT* 1: 279.

8. *IT* 1: 274.

9. S. Elesevich, "'Sluzhba prepodobnomu Sergiiu' sviashchenno-inoka Pakhomiia Serba i ei predshestvuiushchie gimnograficheskie formy," in *T-SL* 3: 121–32.

10. Pachomij, *Werke*, lxxv–lxxvi; *IT* 1: 86–88, 98–99; V. N. Lazarev, *Andrei Rublev i ego shkola* (Moscow, 1966), 33–34; G. V. Popov, "Dve drevneishie ikony 'Vetkhozavetnoi Troitsy' iz Troitse-Sergieva lavry (vopros proiskhozhdeniia i datirovki," in *Troitse-Sergieva lavra v istorii, kul'tury i dukhovnoi zhizni Rossii. Tezisy dokladov* (Sergiev Posad, 1998), 56–57; idem, "Daniil i Andrei Rublev v Troitse-sergievom monastyre," in *T-SL* 3: 220–21; E. Ia Ostashenko, *Andrei Rublev: paleologicheskie traditsii v moskovskoi zhivopisi kontsa XIV–pervoi treti XV veka* (Moscow, 2005, 131–39. N. A. Maiasova, "O datirovke drevnei kopii 'Troitsy' Andreia Rubleva iz ikonostasa Troitskogo sobora," *Soobshcheniia* 3 (1960): 170–74, argued that another Old Testament Trinity icon, "The Hospitality of Abraham" (*gostopriimstvo Avraamiia*), graced the wooden church; cf. E. K. Guseva, "Ob ikone Troitsy iz Dukhovskogo khrama (v sobranii Sergiev-Posadskogo muzeia)," in *T-SL* 1: 223–25; idem, "Nekotorye voprosy izucheniia 'Troitsy' Andreia Rubleva," in *Troitse-Sergieva lavra v istorii, kul'ture i dukhovnoi zhizni Rossii. Tezisy dokladov* (Sergiev Posad, 2000), 63–66; cf. the icons, Baldin and Manushina, *Troitse-Sergieva Lavra*, figs. 203–4; V. D. Kuzmina, "Drevnerusskie pis'mennye istochniki ob Andree Rubleve," in *Andrei Rublev i ego epokha. Sb. statei*, ed. M. V. Alpatov (Moscow, 1971), 111–12.

11. David B. Miller, "Counting Monks: Towards an Estimation of the Size and Composition of the Monastic Community of the Trinity-Sergius Monastery in the First One Hundred Sixty Years of Its Existence," *FOG* 58 (2001): 175–84.

12. Lazarev's exegesis of the icon: *Andrei Rublev*, 35–42; Adela Spindler Roatcap, "The Iconography of Saint Sergius of Radonezh," PhD diss., Stanford Univ. (Stanford, Cal., 1974), 27–34, quote, 32; O. S. Popova, "Russkie ikony epokhi Sv. Sergiia Radonezhskogo i ego uchenikov. Pravoslavnaia dukhovnost' XIV v. i ee russkii variant," in *DRI. Sergii* (St. Petersburg, 1998), 27–38; E. S. Smirnova, *Moscow Icons 14th-17th Centuries*, transl. Arthur Sklarovsky-Raffé, (Leningrad, 1989), 25.

13. Iurii's presence in 1422 attested in what Kloss, *IT* 1: 60–61, 168–69, 418–19, called Pakhomii's Third Ed. of ca. 1442; V. V. Kavel'makher, "Zametki o proiskhozhdenii 'Zvenigorodskogo china,'" in *DRI. Sergii*, 202–6; N. N. Voronin, *Zodchestvo severo-vostochoi Rusi*, 2 vols. (Moscow, 1960–62), 2: 290–306; Petr's patronage: *ASEI* 1: 33, 47 (nos. 13, 40); that Savva was an intermediary between Iurii and Nikon, Gonneau, *La Maison*, 158–59; idem, "Functions," 302–5; Paul Bushkovitch, "The Limits of Hesychasim: Some Notes on Monastic Spiritualism in Russia, 1300–1500," *FOG* 38 (1986): 97–98, 101, n. 9.

14. *IT* 1: 286, 96–99, 155–59; Kliuchevskii, *Drevnerusskie zhitiia*, 67–68.

15. *IT* 1: 287; *PLDR*, 258–60.

16. *IT* 1: 290–97; *PLDR*, 264–78; Fedotov, *Russian Religious Mind* 2: 200–1.

17. Book learning: *IT* 1: 298–301; *PLDR*, 280–84. Asceticism and trials: *IT* 1: 310- 18, 332–41; *PLDR*, 302–16, 340–50. Epithets: *IT* 1: 309, 289; *PLDR*, 300, 262.

18. *IT* 1: 160–69; Kloss, "Zhitiia Sergiia i Nikona," 276–80, 289–90; Aver'ianov, *Sergii*, 8–14.

19. *IT* 1: 343–48; *Legenden* 1: 12, and 2: 10, and *VMCh* for 25–30 September (St. Petersburg, 1883), col. 1413, mentioned the move without reference to Moscow's initiative.

20. *IT* 1: miracles, 354–56, 360–62, 369–74; quote, 374.

21. *IT* 1: 165–67; *Legenden* 1: 70–144, esp. 143–44.

22. *IT* 1: 377-439, esp. 418–19 (translation), 419–20 (Nikon's death, references to the Mother of God), 421–39 (new miracles).

23. Pachomij, *Werke*, lxxiv–lxxvii; B. M. Kloss, "Zametki po istorii Troitse-Sergievoi Lavry XV–XVII vv.," *Trudy po istorii Troitse-Sergievoi Lavry* 2 (1998): 5–6, said Nikon died in 1428; cf. Pierre Gonneau, "Fonctions de l'iconographie dans la diffusion du culte des saints moines Russes (XIVe-XVIe S.)," in *Fonctions sociales et politques de culte des saints dans les sociétés de rite grec et latin au Moyen Âge et à l'époque moderne*, Marek Derwich and Michel Dmitriev, eds. (Wroclaw, 1999), 158, 236 (1427).

24. Baldin and Manushina, *Troitse-Sergieva Lavra*, 263–71, figs. 20, 203–4, 208; G. I. Vzdornov, *Troitsa Andreia Rubleva. Antologiia*, 2d ed. (Moscow, 1989), 5–10; Guseva, "Nekotorie voprosy," 63–65; idem, "Tsarskie vrata kruga Andreiia Rubleva," in *DRI. Sergii*, 295–311; cf. V. I. Antonova, "O pervonachal'nam meste 'Troitsy' Andreia Rubleva," *Gosudarstvennaia Tret'iakovskaia Galereia: Materialy i issledovaniia* 1 (1956): 21–43; *IT* 1: 86–88, saying Rublev's icon was not initially in the iconostasis.

25. T. V. Nikolaeva, *Drevnerusskaia zhivopis' Zagorskgo muzeia* (Moscow, 1977), 62, 65 (nos. 64, 69); G. V. Popov, "Daniil i Andrei," esp. 217–27; Ostashenko, *Andrei Rublev*, 279–350; S. S. Churakov, "Otrazhenie rublevskogo plana rospisi v stenopisi XVII v. Troitskogo sobora Troitse-Sergievoi lavry," in *Andrei Rublev. Sb. Statei*, ed. Alpatov, 194–212; Gonneau, *La Maison*, 302–5.

26. T. V. Nikolaeva, *Sobranie drevnerusskogo iskusstva v Zagorskom muzee* (Leningrad, 1968), 110–12, nos. 53, 54; Baldin and Manushina, *Troitse-Sergieva Lavra*, 346, fig. 275, the "idealized" Sergius (Pakhomiian?) on a pall, ca. 1450, p. 347, fig. 257; T. V. Nikolaeva, *Drevnerusskaia zhivopis'*, 62, 65 (nos. 64, 69); N. A. Maiasova, "Khudozhestvennye shit'e," in *Troitse-Sergieva Lavra*. ed. Voronin and V. V. Kostochkin, 118–19 (nos. 133–35); idem, *Drevnerusskoe shit'e* (Moscow, 1971), 11–12; idem,"Obraz prepodobnogo Sergiia Radonezhskogo v drevnerusskom shit'e (K voprosu ob ikonografii)," in *DRI. Sergii*, 42–43; V. V. Nartsissov, "Problemy ikonografii Prepodobnogo Sergiia Radonezhskogo," DRI. Sergii, 54.

27. *IT* 1: 354–58 (Pakhomii); *PLDR*, 358–66 (Epifanii). The second episode in the Extended Ed. is like Pakhomii's, but shorter; the third episode in the Extended Ed. was rhetorically richer, but changed or added nothing to Pakhomii's versions.

28. *IT* 1: 360–61, 393 (Pakhomii's First, Third Eds.); *Legenden* 1: 111–13 (Pakhomii's Second).

29. *IT* 1: 361–62, 405–6; *Legenden* 1: 113–15.

30. *IT* 1: 371–73, 408–9; *Legenden* 1: 138–41.

31. *IT* 1: 373–74, 409–10; *Legenden* 1: 141–42.

32. Jostein Børtnes, *Visions of Glory. Studies in Early Russian Hagiography* (Oslo, 1988), 182–84; cf. "light" imagery: Pachomij, *Werke*, in lives of Kirill Belozerskii, xv [*vidit svet velii siaiushch* (apparition to him of the Mother of God)]; of Nikon, lxxiv (*i iavishas emu presvetli svetilnitsi velitsyi erarsi Petr i Aleksei s nimizhe i blazhennyi Sergie*); in *Zhitie sviatogo Stefana, episkopa Permskago napisannoe Epifaniem Premudrym*,

repr. and intro. Dmitrij Čiževskij from ed. V. G. Druzhinin, St. Petersburg, 1897 ('S-Gravenhage, 1959). Light imagery in earlier hagiography; eg., the patericon of the Kievan Caves Monastery, *The Paterik of the Kievan Caves Monastery*, transl. Muriel Heppell (Cambridge, Mass., 1989), 14, 48–49, does not compare to Pakhomii's artful employment of it to highlight Sergius's miracles.

33. Kloss, "K izucheniiu biografii," 14; Aver'ianov, *Sergii*, 366–68; *SP* (Moscow, 1880), 11, 31; *TL*, 421, 429, 432.

34. T. V. Nikolaeva, *Sobranie*, 26–27, no. 2.

35. E. K. Guseva, "Osobennosti slozheniia ikonografii 'Sergieva videniia' ('Iavleniia Bogomateri prepodobnomu Sergiiu," *Iskusstvo srednevekovoi Rusi. Materialy i issledovaniia* 12 (1999): 136; David B. Miller, "The Origin of Special Veneration of the Mother of God at the Trinity-Sergius Monastery: The Iconographical Evidence," *Russian History* 28 (2001): 303–14.

36. 1442: *PSRL* 23: 150, and Pierre Gonneau "The Trinity-Sergius Brotherhood in State and Society," in *Moskovskaia Rus (1389-1584): Kul'tura i istoricheskoie samosoznanie*, eds. A. M. Kleimola and Gail. D. Lenhoff (Moscow, 1997), 129. 1446: *PSRL* 18: 198; 26: 201–2.

37. T. V. Nikolaeva, *Proizvedeniia melkoi plastiki XII–XVII vekov v sobranii Zagorskogo muzeia. Katalog* (Zagorsk, 1960), 59–63, 313 (no. 155b), 324 (no. 157/10); Miller, "The Origin," 306–7.

38. Archimandrite Matvei, "Liturgicheskie traditsii Troitse-Sergievoi Lavry," *Bogoslovskie trudy* 29 (1989): 197–98; Gorskii, *Opisanie*, 1: 73–4.

39. See chapter 5, on Trinity's monks.

40. *ASEI* 1: 40–1 (no. 29); *DDG*, 50 (no. 17).

41. *ASEI* 1: 27 (no. 3); *IT* 1: 66–68.

42. Properties: *VK*, 29; *IT* 1: 68; Cherkasova, *Zemlevladenie*, 65–66. Tonsure and burials: *PSRL* 26: 184; *PSRL* 28: 97, 263; *SP*, 3; Kloss, "O sud'be zakhoroneniia Kniazia Andreia Radonezhskogo," in *T-SL* 1:24–28; cf. Gonneau, "The Trinity Sergius Brotherhood," 126–27; idem, "Les relations entre le temporel et le spirituel dans la Russie muscovite: Pistes de recherche," Revue des Études Slaves 70 (1998): 492–93.

43. *ASEI* 1: 27–48, 50, 53–58, 63–65, 70–71, 96–97, 94, 100, 114–15, 117–18 (nos. 4–8, 10–16, 18–19, 20–28, 30, 32–33, 36–39, 40–42, 45, 51, 53–54, 56, 58–61, 70–73, 83, 85, 119, 122–24, 129 154, 160); Semenchenko, "O khronologii aktov severo-vostochnoi Rusi XV v.," 105, 107–9; idem, "O khronologii Troitskikh aktov kontsa XIV–pervoi polovine XV v.," 62; V. I. Koretskii, "Pravaia gramota ot 30 noiabria 1618 g. Troitse-Sergievu monastyriu (Iz istorii monastyrskogo zemlevladeniia XIV–XVI vv.," *ZOR* 21 (1959): 173–84; Gonneau, *La Maison*, 236–40.

44. *IT* 1: 35–36, n. 27; L. I. Lifshits, "Ikonografiia Iavleniia Bogomateri prepodobnomu Sergiiu Radonezhskomu i motify teofanii v iskusstve kontsa XIV–XV vv.," in *DRI. Sergii*, 79–82, quote n. 23, 93; ROBIL, F. 304.1, <www.stsl.ru/manuscripts/index.php>, no. 746, f. 336v (quote), ff. 361v–63 (the miracle); Arsenii, "Opisanie slavianskikh rukopisei biblioteki Sviato-Troitskoi Sergievoi lavry," *ChOIDR* (1879), pt. 3, 141 (no. 746); *Afonskii Paterik: ili, zhizneopisanii sviatykh na sviatoi Afonskoi gorie*

prosiiavshikh, 2 pts. in one vol., repr. of 7th ed. of 1897 (Moscow, 1994), pt. 2: 26–28.

45. E. S. Ovchinnikova, "Novyi pamiatnik stankovoi zhivopisi XV veka kruga Rubleva," in *Drevne-russkoe iskusstvo XV–nachala XVI vekov*, ed. V. N. Lazarev (Moscow, 1963), 94–117, illustrations, 95, 98.

46. E. S. Smirnova, "Bogomater' s Mladentsem na prestole, s arkhangelom i prepodobnym Sergiem Radonezhskim—ikona pervoi treti XV v. Istoki i smysl ikonografii," in *Russkoe podvizhnichestvo*, ed. T. V. Kniazhevskaia (Moscow, 1996), 124–35. 47. Richard D. Bosley, "The Changing Profile of the Liturgical Calendar in Muscovy's Formative Years," in *Moskovskaia Rus'*, ed. Kleimola, Lenhoff, 33.

48. *IT* 1: 414–15.

49. *IT* 1: 423–25.

50. *IT* 1: 427–29. A. A. Gorskii, *Moskva i Orda* (Moscow, 2000), 142–44; Jaroslaw Pelenski, *Russia and Kazan: Conquest and Imperial Ideology (1438–1560s)* (The Hague, 1974), 24, 179–80.

51. IT 1: 413–14, 421–23, 425–27, 429–33.

52. *PDPI*, 394–96; *IT* 1: 160–223, described 203 versions of Sergius's life with the episode.

53. *ASEI* 1: 256–57 (no. 350).

54. Maiasova, "Obraz," 48–50; David B. Miller, "Rublev's Old Testament Trinity and the Appearance of the Mother of God to Saint Sergius: Dual Iconographic Signifiers of the Trinity-Sergius Monastery in the First Centuries of Its Existence," *Symposiom* 7–12 (2002–2007): 47–65.

55. Cf. Charles J. Halperin, "The Russian Land and the Russian Tsar: The Emergence of Muscovite Ideology, 1380–1408," *FOG* 23 (1976): 7–103; *Kulikovskaia bitva: Sbornik statei*, ed. L. G. Beskrovnyi (Moscow, 1980); *Skazaniia i povesti o Kulikovskoi bitve*, ed. L. A. Dmitriev, O. P. Likhacheva (Leningrad, 1982); *Kulikovskaia bitva v istorii kul'ture nashei rodiny*, ed. B. A. Rybakov (Moscow, 1983); *Zhizn' i zhitie Sergiia Radonezhskogo*, ed. V. V. Kolesova (Moscow, 1991); *Sergii Radonezhskii*, ed. V. A. Desiatnikov (Moscow, 1991); Kuchkin, "Dmitrii Donskoi."

56. Cf. the attention in the USSR on the 600th anniversary of the Kulikovo battle described by Yitzhak M. Brudny, *Reinventing Russia: Russian Nationalism and the Soviet State, 1953–1991* (Cambridge, Mass., 1998), 181–91.

57. *PSRL* 4, pt. 1: 311–25; repr. from Karamzin ms., *PLDR*, 112–30; Lur'e, *Obshcherusskie letopisi*, 67–121; idem, *Dve istorii*, 15–16; M. A. Salmina, "'Letopisnaia povest' o Kulikovskoi bitve i 'Zadonshchina', in "*Slovo o polku Igoreve*" *i pamiatniki Kulikovskogo tsykla*, ed. D. S. Likhachev, L. A. Dmitriev (Moscow-Leningrad, 1966), 370–72; M. A. Shibaev, "Redaktorskie priemy sostavitelia Sofiiskoi I letopisi," in *Opyty po istoichnikovedeniiu. Drevniaia russkaia knizhnost': redactor i tekst* (St. Petersburg, 2000), 376–93, esp. 381–82.

58. *IT* 1: 369–70.

59. *Legenden* 1: 136–38.

60. *IT* 1: 403–5.

61. *PDPL*, 118; *PSRL* 39: 120.

62. Kuchkin, "Dmitrii Donskoi," 115–16; *IT* 1: 110, 116–17; Bobrov, Prokhorov and Semiachko, "Imitatsii nauki," 418–19.

63. Salmina, "Letopisnaia povest'," 344–84, esp. 355–64, 370–72; idem, "Eshche raz o datirovke 'Letopisnoi povesti' o Kulikovskoi bitve," *TODRL* 32 (1977): 1–39, esp. 1–5; and her reconsiderations cited by Charles Halperin, "Text and Textology: Salmina's Date of the Chronicle Tales about Dmitrii Donskoi," *Slavonic and East European Review* 79 (2001): 248–63; David B. Miller, "Prepodobnyi Sergii Radonezhskii, zastupnik Russkoi zemli," *Makarievskie chteniia* 4, pt. 2 (1996): 16–22; cf. Borisov, *Sergii*, 172–82, arguing the historicity of Sergius's vision of the Mother of God and intercession for Dmitrii.

64. *PLDR*, 112–14.

65. Cf. *PLDR*, 386 (Epifanii) and 146 (The Tale): *Poidi, gospodine, na poganye polovtsi, prizivaia boga, i gospod' bog budet ti pomoshchnik i zastupnik*; M. A. Salmina, "K voprosu o datirovke 'Skazaniia o Mamaevom poboishche'," *TODRL* 29 (1974): 98–124, esp. 102–8; Kuchkin, "Dmitrii Donskoi," 109–14; Ia. S. Lur'e, *Rossiia drevniaia i Rossiia novaia* (St. Petersburg, 1997), 147–48; B. M. Kloss, "Ob avtore i vremeni sozdaniia 'Skazaniia o mamaevom poboishche," in *In Memorium. Sbornik pamiati Ia. S. Lur'e*, comps. N. M. Botvinnik, E. I Vaneev (St. Petersburg, 1997), 253–62. Cf. Aver'ianov, *Sergii*, 303–39, arguing the primacy of the Tale for Sergius's intervention.

66. Cf. *IT* 1: 404 (Pakhomii), and *PLDR*, 388.

67. *TL*, 419–20.

68. re. Leontii/Savva: *TL*, 418; *IT* 1: 58–59, 405; *PLDR*, 388; Gonneau, *La Maison*, 136–39; Aver'ianov, *Sergii*, 395–400.

69. A. A. Gorskii, *Moskva i Orda*, 93–152; Lur'e, *Dve istorii*, 86–93; Miller, "Monumental Building," 367–90.

70. Max Weber, *Essays in Sociology*, transl., ed. H. H. Gerth and C. Wright Mills (New York, 1946), 245–52, esp. 245.

71. Garry Wills, *What Jesus Meant* (New York, 2006), xxvi–xxvii; Eric Hobsbawm, "Introduction: Inventing Traditions," in *The Invention of Tradition*, ed. Eric Hobsbawm and T. Ranger (Cambridge, Eng., 1983), 1.

72. *IT* 1: 432–39; cf. version, unknown to Kloss, in sixteenth-century miscellany (Hilandar ms. 485), Predrag Matejic, "Rediscovered Texts from the Life of St. Sergius of Radonezh. Understanding Russia and Russian Orthodoxy in the 16th century," in *The Trinity-Sergius Lavra in Russian History and Culture*, ed. Vladimir Tsurikov (Jordanville, NY, 2005), 251–98.

73. Simeon's tale in two eds.: V. Malinin, *Starets Eleasarova monastyria Filofei i ego poslaniia* (Kiev, 1901), app., 89–11; John Fennell, *A History of the Church in Russia to 1448* (London, 1995), 170–83.

74. Ia. S. Lur'e, "Kak ustanovilas' avtokefaliia russkoi tserkvi v XV v., *Vospomogatel'nye istoricheskie distsipliny* 23 (1991): 181–98.

75. *PSRL* 15, pt. 1: 177, 186.

76. *ASEI* 1: 41–43, 47–48 (nos. 30–31, 34–35, 41–42).

77. Marriage: *PSRL* 25: 250; Kloss *IT* 1: 70–71; *ASEI* 1: 65–66 (no. 74), 70–71,

84, 88 (nos. 84, 104, 109); also Gonneau, *La Maison*, 161–62.

78. *PSRL* 25: 250; *PSRL* 26: 189.

79. *PSRL* 25: 251; *PSRL* 26: 190; *DDG*, 82–83 (no. 32).

80. *IT* 1: 71; Gonneau, *La Maison*, 161, 163–64; Gorskii, *Opisanie* 1: 66–71; *ASEI*, 1: 101–3 (nos. 132–33), 107 (no. 139); *PSRL* 12: 40.

81. *ASEI* 1: 120–22 (nos. 164–65); Kashtanov, *Ocherki*, 348–51 (no. 6).

82. *PSRL* 6: 170; *PSRL* 23: 151; *DDG*, 107–17 (no. 38); *IT* 1: 71.

83. Durkheim, *Elementary Forms*, 362; Miller, "The Cult," 687–88; Gonneau, *La Maison*, 162–65.

84. *IT* 1: 71.

85. *PSRL* 26: 196–200; Cherepnin, *Obrazovanie*, 768–71, 787–808.

86. *PSRL* 26: 200; Miller, "The Cult," 689.

87. *PSRL* 23: 152; Pakhomii's miracles of 1448–49 in *IT* 1: 442–48, also 68, 70; Cherepnin, *Obrazovanie*, 791, 793.

88. *PSRL* 23: 152; *PSRL* 20: 259; Gonneau, *La Maison*, 165–66; Miller, "The Cult," 689–90.

89. *PSRL* 6: 172–74, *PSRL* 18: 196–98; *PSRL* 26: 200–2; re. Dosifei: *ASEI* 1: 129–30 (no. 179); *IT* 1: 71; Gonneau, *La Maison*, 166; idem, "The Trinity-Sergius Brotherhood," 131.

90. *PSRL* 23: 153. Robert Romanchuk, *Byzantine Hermeneutics and Pedagogy in the Russian North: Monks and Masters at the Kirillo-Belozerskii Monastery, 1397*–1501 (Toronto, 2007), 172–74, said Simon came from Trinity.

91. *PSRL* 26: 207; *PSRL* 27: 114.

92. Gorskii, *Opisanie* 1: 69–72; E. E. Shevchenko, "Prepodobnye Ferapont i Martinian Belozerskie," in *Prepodobnye Kirill, Ferapont, i Martinian Belozerskie*, 2d ed., ed. G. M. Prokhorov (St. Petersburg, 1994), 190–95; Miller, "The Cult," 690–91.

93. *IT* 1: 442–47.

94. *AI* 1 (St. Petersburg, 1841): 75–83 (no. 40); *DDG*, 150–55 (no. 51).

95. Iona, initially Shemiaka's nominee as metropolitan, came over to the winning side. *PSRL* 8: 120–22; Gustave Alef, "Muscovy and the Council of Florence," *Slavic Review* 20 (1961): 397–401; Lur'e, "Kak ustanovilas'," 181–98.

96. Meeting: *PSRL* 23: 154; betrothal and marriage: *PSRL* 26: 205, 212.

97. *PSRL* 25: 272; *PSRL* 26: 212; *PSRL* 6: 179; Gonneau, *La Maison*, 169.

98. *ASEI* 1: 143, 158 (nos. 200, 222); Gonneau, *La Maison*, table 9, no. 73, and table 28.

99. Chalice: T. V. Nikolaeva, *Proizvedeniia melkoi plastiki*, 54–55 (no. 34); Gorskii, *Opisanie* 1: 44. Properties: *DDG*, 178 (no. 57); *ASEI* 1: 171–72 (no. 244). Semenchenko, "O khronologii nekotorykh gramot," 54–55, dating Martinian's departure and Vassian's (who as bishop of Rostov in 1480 famously urged Grand Prince Ivan III to resist the Mongols on the Ugra river) appointment. Previously historians dated the change in abbots to 1455.

100. Vasilii II: *ASEI* 1: 134–44, 150–51, 154–58, 160–61, 170–73 (nos. 189, 191–92, 195, 197, 199–200, 202, 215, 219, 221, 225–26, 243–45); *AAE* 1 (1836): 32–33, 38–39

(nos. 43, 52); Gonneau, *La Maison*, table 9, nos. 70, 72–75, and table 28; Kashtanov, *Ocherki*, 363–65 (nos. 11–12). Sofiia Vitovtovna: *ASEI* 1: 152–54, 166–69 (nos. 217–18, 237, 239). Mariia Iaroslavna: *ASEI* 1: 174–78 (nos. 246–48); *AAE* 1: 39–40 (no. 53).

101. *PSRL* 23: 156; *PSRL* 25: 277.

102. *DDG*, 155 (no. 51); cf. *AI* 1: 86–87 (no. 43).

3—SERGIUS, A RUSSIAN ICON

1. *PSRL* 28: 337.

2. *Legenden* 2: 3–60, Fourth Ed.; *Legenden* 2: 61–100, Fifth Ed.; *VMCh*, 25 vols. (St. Petersburg, 1868–1917), 3 (25–30 Sept.), cols. 1408–63; Kloss, "Zhitiia Sergiia," 280–86; *IT* 1: 170–212.

3. *Legenden* 2: 50, 81 (Iurii), 37–39, 70–73 (Kulikovo). Pakhomii's Fifth Ed., crafted before Grand Prince Vasilii II's death in 1462, repeated, with some emendations, the miracle recorded in the Third Ed. "About the warrior saved from the pagans," with its double-edged denouement affirming Sergius's solicitude for Moscow but warning that it depended on its patronage of Trinity, *Legenden* 2: 92–95.

4. *PLDR*, 386–88; *IT* 1: 213–23, esp. 217; Morozov, *Litsevoi svod*, 172–75, 177, 179, 181; O. A. Belobrova, "O litsevom spiske Zhitiia Sergiia Radonezhskogo v biblioteke Petra I," *T-SL* 3: 176–78; Kleinberg, *Prophets*, 153.

5. *IT* 1: 423–25 (Borozdin), 448–49 (pilgrims).

6. Grant: RORGB, F. 303, no. 519, f. 5; Gonneau, *La Maison*, 184–85, table 3, no. 166. Immunities: *ASEI* 1: 209–11, 214 (nos. 294–98, 303); *AAE* 1: 56–58 (nos. 78–79).

7. *ASEI* 1: 1: 155–56 (no. 220); *PSRL* 16: 199; E. A. Ozerskaia, "Obraz grada bozh'ego v stenakh zhitiia Sergiia Radonezhskogo iz Sergievskoi tserkvi novgorodskogo detintsa," *DRI. Sergii*, 95–97.

8. *Prepodobnye Kirill, Ferapont i Martinian Belozerskie*, 2d ed., ed. G. M. Prokhorov (St. Petersburg, 1994), 9, 17–18, 66; Gonneau, *La Maison*, 122–23; Kliuchevskii, *Drevnerusskie zhitiia*, 103–5.

9. Gonneau, "Fonctions," 289, 291–92, 305–7, 309–10, 315–16 (table).

10. Golubinskii, *Prepodobnyi Sergii*, 56–57; *IT* 1: 61; Kliuchevskii, *Drevnerusskie zhitiia*, 169–72, 186–87, 211, 229–30.

11. Iu. A. Degtev, *Riazan' pravoslavnaia* (Riazan', 1993), 41–42, 53–55.

12. Patrick Geary. *Phantoms of Remembrance: Memory and Oblivion at the End of the First Millennium* (Princeton, NJ, 1994), 6.

13. By 1462 Tver' and Novgorod called the Moscow ruler "elder brother"; *PSRL* 18: 212; *PSRL* 23: 155; *PSRL* 26: 217; *ASEI* 1: 189–91 (nos. 260–2). Cf. Gonneau, *La Maison*, 171–73; idem, "The Trinity-Sergius Brotherhood," 131, with Cherkasova, *Zemlevladenie*, 90, n. 160; *Poslaniia Iosifa Volotskogo*, ed. A. A. Zimin and Ia. S. Lur'e (Moscow-Leningrad, 1959), 201–2, 209.

14. *RIB* 6: 643, 658–59, 664–64 (nos. 86, 88); Gonneau, "The Trinity-Sergius Brotherhood," 141–42.

15. *PSRL* 4, pt. 1: 292; *PSRL* 5: 230; *PSRL* 39: 113–14.

16. *PSRL* 15, pt. 1: 74–75; *TL*, 379. Cf. Kuchkin "Dmitrii Donskoi," 119–21, with Gonneau, *La Maison*, 129–31; *IT* 1: 34, 43, 365; Aver'ianov, *Sergii*, 115–55 (positing two missions to Nizhnii Novgorod, one in 1363 and Sergius's in 1365).

17. *PSRL* 25: 183; *PSRL* 8: 13; *PSRL* 11: 5.

18. *PSRL* 25: 202–3.

19. *PLDR*, 144–48, 172, 174, 182, 184; Kloss, "Ob avtore," 253–62; David M. Goldfrank, ed. and transl., *The Monastic Rule of Josef Volotsky* (Kalamazoo, Mich., 1983), 196, on the *khlebets*.

20. Kuchkin, "Dmitrii Donskoi," 104–7; *PSRL* 15, pt. 1: 140; *TL*, 448.

21. L. A. Dmitriev, "Obzor redaktstii Skazaniia o Mamaevom poboishche" and "Opisanie rukopisnykh spiskov Skazaniia o Mamaevom poboishche," in *Povesti o Kulikovskoi Bitve*, ed. M. N. Tikhomirov (Moscow, 1959), 449–509; Salmina, "K voprosu," 102–8; *PSRL* 11: 46–49; Kloss, "Ob avtore," 254–62.

22. *PSRL* 25: 310–11; also Gonneau, "Fonctions," 305–6.

23. *PSRL* 26: 266–73, esp. 273.

24. Maiasova, *Drevnerusskoe shit'e*, 15 (no. 15); idem, "Obraz," 48; Guseva, "Osobennosti," 122–23.

25. Gonneau, *La Maison*, 276–85, 388–94, 423–29, 433–37, tables 11–16; S. M. Kashtanov, *Sotsial'no-politicheskaia istoriia Rossii kontsa XV-pervoi poloviny XVI veka* (Moscow, 1967), 12–20, 70–78, 170–86, 218–38; Alekseev, *Agrarnaia i sotsial'naia istoriia*, 68–96; Cherkasova, *Zemlevladenie*, 90–104.

26. Gonneau, *La Maison*, 309–11, table 17, graph below table 18.

27. *ASEI* 1: 241–42 (no. 333); cf. 77–79, 123 (nos. 94–97, 168); Semenchenko, "O khronologii Troitskikh aktov," 104.

28. *ASEI* 1: 318–20 (no. 430), 188–89 (no. 259); Gonneau, *La Maison*, 311–37, table 25.

29. *ASEI* 1: 399–401, 413–20, 464–90, 551–54 (nos. 523, 537–40, 583–94, 639–40); cf. 149 (no. 213).

30. Kashtanov, *Ocherki*, 377–83 (nos. 19–22), confirming, defining existing immunities. Ibid., 375–77, 391–93 (nos. 18, 29); *ASEI* 1: 292–93, 305–6, 324–25 (nos. 400, 416, 433) granting new, limited immunities; cf. objections of Mark D. Zlotnik, "Immunity Charters and the Centralization of the Muscovite State. PhD diss., Univ. of Chicago (Chicago, 1976), 22–23, to Kashtanov's emphasis on primacy of politics in defining immunity policy.

31. *PSRL* 28: 156; Gonneau, *La Maison*, 422.

32. *ASEI* 1: 299–300 (no. 409); *PSRL* 8: 177; Gonneau, *La Maison*, 186–87.

33. *PSRL* 23: 179 and *PSRL* 25: 275 (Dmitrii), 323 (Vasilii), 333 (Ivan *vnuk*); *PSRL* 6: 223 (Iurii).

34. Documents: *Poslanie Iosifa*, 322–26 (*Sobornyi otvet*), 366–69 (*Pis'mo o neliubkakh*); N. A. Kazakova, *Vassian Patrikeev i ego sochineniia* (Moscow, Leningrad, 1960), 275–281 (*Prenie s Iosifom Volotskim*), esp. 279; K. I. Nevostruev, ed., "Zhitie prepodobnogo Iosifa Volokolamskogo," *Chteniia Obshchestva liubtelei drevnei pis'mennosti* 2 (1865): 112–20; Iu. K. Begunov, "'Slovo inoe'—novonaidennoe proizvedenie russkoi

publitsistki XVI v. o bor'be Ivan III s zemlevladeniem tserkvi," *TODRL* 20 (1964): 351–64; G. N. Moiseeva, "Zhitie arkhiepiskopa novgorodskogo Serapiona," *TODRL* 21 (1965): 147–65. Cf. Ia. S. Lur'e, *Ideologicheskaia bor'ba v russkoi publitsistike kontsa XV–nachala XVI veka* (Moscow-Leningrad, 1960), 407–17; R. G. Skrynnikov, "Ecclesiastical Thought in Russia and the Church Councils of 1503 and 1504," *Oxford Slavonic Papers* 25 (1992): 43–54; N. V. Sinitsyna, "Tipy monastyrei i russkii asketicheskii ideal (XV–XVI vv.)," in *Monashestvo i monastyri v Rossii X–XX veka*, ed. Sinitsyna (Moscow, 2002), 137–42, A. I. Alekseev, *Pod znakom kontsa vremeni: Ocherki russkoi religioznosti kontsa XIV–Nachala XVI vv.* (St. Petersburg, 2002); 245–301; idem, "Kogda nachalas' polemika 'Iosiflian' i 'nestiazhatelei'?" in *Nil Sorskii v kul'ture i knizhnosti Drevnei Rusi*, ed. Alekseev (St. Petersburg, 2008), 29–40; with A. I. Pliguzov, *Polemika v russkoi tserkvi pervoi treti xvi stoletiia* (Moscow, 2002), 330–86; Donald Ostrowski, "500 let spustia: Tserkovyi sobor 1503 g.", *Palaeoslavica* 11 (2003): 214–39.

35. *PSRL* 28: 337.

36. In 1502 Grand Princess Sophia Palaeologa and her boiar allies demanded that Ivan III name her son Vasilii as his successor. Faced with the prospect of civil war, Ivan gave in. John V. A. Fine Jr., "The Muscovite Dynastic Crisis of 1497–1502," *Canadian Slavonic Papers* 8 (1966): 198–215; Nancy Shields Kollmann, "Consensus Politics: The Dynastic Crisis of the 1490s Reconsidered," *Russian Review* 45 (1986): 235–67; idem *Kinship*, 135–42.

37. Maiasova, *Khudozhestvennoe shit'e*, 21–22 (no. 29); Baldin and Manushina, *Troitse-Sergieva Lavra*, 347, 357–59 (figs. 285–87); T. V. Nikolaeva, *Proizvedeniia prikhladnogo iskusstva*, 65–66; Isolde Thyrêt, "'Blessed is the Tsarisa's Womb': The Myth of Miraculous Birth and Royal Motherhood in Muscovite Russia," *Russian Review* 53 (1994): 481–86.

38. *PSRL* 28: 337. Vasilii's handlers may also have arranged the appointment of Mitrofan, whom Kloss believed had been tonsured at Trinity, "Ob avtore," 253–62, as archimandrite of the Andronikov monastery and Ivan III's confessor.

39. Kertzer, *Ritual*, 9–10 (first quote); Geertz, "Centers," in Rites, ed. Wilentz, 13–14; cf. Durkheim, *Elementary Forms*, 431–36.

40. Miller, "The Cult," 696–97.

41. *VK*, 26, 45; cf. Veselovskii, *Issledovaniia po istorii klassa sluzhilykh*, 452–53; Nikolaeva, *Proizvedeniia prikladnogo iskusstva*, 76, 147 (no. 70).

42. Kashtanov, *Sotsial'no-politicheskaia istoriia*, 239–74; idem, "The Centralized State and Feudal Immunities in Russia," in *Major Problems in Early Modern Russian History*, ed. Nancy Shields Kollmann (London, 1992), 118–20; Gonneau, *La Maison*, 211–24; Zlotnik, "Immunity Charters," tables A. 1–20.

43. Gorskii, *Opisanie*, 2: 177; Miller, "The Cult," 697; *IT* 1: 135–36.

44. 1518: *PSRL* 6: 261; 1524: Gorskii, *Opisanie*, 1: 75–79; 1530: *PSRL* 6: 265; *PSRL* 13, pt. 1: 48; 1532: *PSRL* 8: 276, *PSRL* 13, pt. 1: 56; 1531–32: *PSRL* 6: 261, 266, *PSRL* 8: 280, 285, *PSRL* 13, pt. 1: 66; 1533: *PSRL* 6: 271–72, 274–76, *PSRL* 29: 9–10.

45. *PSRL* 39: 149–58 (other saints, 153–54: Metropolitans Petr, Aleksei; Leontii of Rostov, Kirill, Nikita of Pereiaslavl, and Varlaam Khutynskii of Novgorod); Lur'e,

Dve istorii, 123–67; Gail D. Lenhoff, Janet Martin, "Marfa Boretskaia, *Posadnitsa* of Novgorod: A Reconsideration of Her Legend and Her Life," *Slavic Review* 59 (2000): 343–68.

46. *PSRL* 6: 150–51; *PSRL* 20, pt. 1: 242–44; *Legenden* 2: 92–95; *IT* 1: 258, 427–29.

47. *PSRL* 6: 261; *PSRL* 28: 354–55.

48. In addition, it repeated entries from earlier chronicles mentioning prayers at Sergius's tomb, along with prayers to other saints, for aid against Novogord, and Vasilii's trip in 1518 to Trinity before confronting the Poles: *PSRL* 11: 127–47, esp. 144–45; *PSRL* 12: 171; *PSRL* 13, pt. 1: 29; *IT* 1: 258; B. M. Kloss, *Nikonovskii svod i russkie letopisi XVI–XVII vekov* (Moscow, 1980), 19–189.

49. RORGB, F. 303, no. 518 (copybook of 1534). Charters reaffirmed: *ASEI*, 1, nos. 307, 309–10, 316, 318–19, 346, 349, 351–54, 356, 358, 388, 403, 412, 414, 417, 455, 462, 491–95 497–98, 516, 519, 530–31, 534, 561, 567–68, 573, 621, 637, 653; *ARG*, nos. 15, 19, 23, 29, 32–34, 83–84, 86, 89, 99, 107, 118–19, 133, 135–37, 146–47, 175, 185, 193, 205–6, 211, 220, 280; "KhP" 1, nos. 4, 42, 46, 51–52, 67, 99, 111, 134, 153, 157, 163–64, 207, 228, 246, 282–83, 288; Kashtanov, "Kopiinye knigi," 3–14. Cf. Veselovskii, "Monastyrskoe zemlevladenie," 95–97, still the best analysis of state land policies; Kashtanov, *Sotsial'no-politicheskaia istoriia*, 275–326, Cherkasova, *Zemlevladenie*, 118–29; Zlotnik, "Immunity Charters," 88–103.

50. *SbGKE*, 2 vols. (Petrograd, Leningrad, 1922–29), 2: 827–30 (no. 118a); *SobB*, comp. D. Lebedev, (Moscow, 1881), 21 (no. 86); "KhP" 1: 374 (no. 578).

51. Kashtanov, *Sotsial'no-politicheskaia istoriia*, 327–74; idem, "The Centralized State," 121–24; Zimin, *Reformy*, 348–54, 375–94; E. I. Kolychevka, *Agrarnyi stroi Rossii XVI veka* (Moscow, 1987), 121–25.

52. Reaffirmed (*=curtailed privileges): *ASEI* 1, nos. 92 [of 1432–45 with false signature, S. M. Kashtanov, "Monastyrskie dokumenty o politicheskoi bor'be serediny XVI v.," *AE za 1973 god.* (1974), 33–34], 246–47, 304, 318–19, 346, 354, 356, 403, 412, 414, 417, 455, 462, 491–92, 497–98, 518–19, 530, 561, 568, 631; *ARG*, nos. 19, 23*, 32–33, 84, 89*, 99, 107, 133*, 136–37, 147, 175, 185, 193, 205–6, 211, 220*, 280; "KhP," pt. 1, nos. 42*, 46, 52, 67, 99*, 111, 134, 153, 157, 164, 207*, 246*, 283, 288*, 318*, 319, 322–23, 326–28, 330–33*, 339*, 343, 359, 362, 368, 383–84*, 452, 456*–57*, 474, 491, 494, 510*, 518, 524*, 538*, 549, 555*, 564–65*, 571*; pt. 2, nos. 610*, 624–25*, 631*; pt. 3, no. I–280.

53. Kashtanov, *Ocherki*, 166–217; idem, "Obshchie zhalovannye gramoty Troitse-Sergievu monastyriu 1550, 1577 i 1578 gg.," *ZOR* 28 (1966): 104–41; 1550 charter: "KhP" 2: 134–35 (no. 625), *SobB*, 23 (no. 97); 1571 charter: P. A. Sadikov, "Iz istorii Oprichniny XVI v.," *Istoricheskii arkhiv* 3 (1940): 257–58 (no. 52). 1577 charter: "KhP" pt. 2: 185 (no. 1024). 1578 charter: *SbGKE* 1: 865–68 (no. 220a); "KhP" pt. 2: 187 (no. 1039).

54. Act of 1554: Dvina: *SbGKE* 1: 557–63 (no. 137a); "KhP" 2: 141–42 (no. 688); Kazan': RORGB, F. 303, no. 526: 20–20v; "KhP" 2: 140 (no. 676); S. M. Kashtanov, "Deiatelnost' pravoslavnykh monastyrei v Srednem Povolzh'e v epokhu Ivana Groznogo (1551–1556 gg.)," *FOG* 63 (2004): 293–309.

55. Ivan's government orchestrated the Stoglav; but Ivan's pique resonated in the text of what probably was a prepared speech and in his interjections; E. B. Emchenko, *Stoglav, Issledovanie i tekst* (Moscow, 2000), 256–59, 328–35, 342–43 (quote), 408–9 (restricting acquisitions of urban settlements), 413–16 (prohibiting purchases of secular holdings without government permission).

56. *PSRL* 29: 62 (Serapion's appt., itself temporary; in 1552 he was replased by Pimen, tonsured at a trans-Volgan hermitage); Zimin, *Reformy*, 389; Kashtanov, "Monastyrskie dokumenty," 29–42; Cherkasova, *Zemlevladenie*, 130.

57. *AAE* 1: 167 (no. 190); Gorskii, *Opisanie* 2: 177–79; Baldin and Manushina, *Troitse-Sergieva lavra*, 30110–11, 114–16; recently V. V. Kavel'makher, "Nikonovskaia tserkov' Troitse-Sergieva monastyria: Avtor i data postroiki," in *Kul'tura srednevekovoi Moskvy. XVII vek*, ed. L. A. Beliaev (Moscow, 1999), 40–95, esp. 40, 78, concluded that the architecture of the church of St. Nikon is better dated to 1623 and that the chronicle entry was a fabrication.

58. *PSRL* 6: 304; *PSRL* 13, pt. 1: 120, 130, 231; *PSRL* 29: 27, 30, 33–35, 37–38, 41, 43–47, 49–51, 56, 111–12, 206, 210–11, 231, 247, 249–50, 274, 280, 290, 297, 323, 334–35, 337, 341, 346–48, 350, 352, 354; Gorskii, *Opisanie*, 1: 8; Nancy Shields. Kollmann, "Pilgrimage, Procession and Symbolic Space in Sixteenth-Century Russian Politics," in *Medieval Russian Culture* 2: 163–81; Miller, "The Cult," 698; *IT* 1:72–3. Cf. Florenskii, "Troitse-Sergieva Lavra," 21–23, regarding Trinity Day.

59. *PSRL* 29: 47.

60. *PSRL* 29: 210–11; *PSRL* 13, pt. 1: 239.

61. *PSRL* 29: 56, 111–12; *PSRL* 6: 314; *VK*, 27; T. V. Nikolaeva, "Oklad s ikony 'Troitsa' pis'ma Andreia Rubleva," *Soobshcheniia* 2 (1958): 31–38; *IT* 1: 73–85; Baldin and Manushina, *Troitse-Sergieva lavra*, 466–69 (figs. 409–16), 478; A. N. Nasonov, "Novye istochniki po istorii Kazanskogo 'vziatiia,'" *AE za 1960 god.* (1962), 10.

62. Kloss, "Ikony Ivan Groznogo i ego sem'i v Troitse-Sergievom monastyre," in *T-SL* 3: 290–301; M. Spirina, "Ikona 'Bogomater' Odigitriia (Smolenskaia)' XVI v. iz sobraniia Sergievo-Posadskogo muzeia-zapovednika," *Soobshcheniia* (2000), 221–42.

63. *PSRL* 13, pt. 1: 273; *PSRL* 29: 249–50; Gorskii, *Opisanie* 2: 178; Golubinskii, *Prepodobnyi Sergii* (1909), 205; Baldin and Manushina, *Troitse-Sergieva lavra*, 116, 121.

64. Visits: *PSRL* 13, pt. 2: 320; *PSRL* 29: 280–81. Anastasiia's death, *PSRL* 13, pt. 2: 328. Cf. Gorskii, *Opisanie* 1: 89; Golubinskii, *Prepodobnyi Sergii* (1909), 182–83, 205; Baldin and Manushina, *Troitse-Sergieva lavra*, 121.

65. Gorskii, *Opisanie* 1: 176–83, esp. 180; *PSRL* 29: 290.

66. *PSRL* 13, pt. 2: 386–87; *RIB* 3 (St. Petersburg, 1880): 233.

67. *VK*, 26–29, 50, 58, 75, 82–83, 99, 102, 121, 144; "KhP" pt. 1: 352, 356, 362, 364, 366, 368, 372–74 (nos. 384, 386, 474, 491, 510, 524, 564–65, 573, 578), pt. 2: 133, 135, 140, 157, 160, 182 (no. 610, 631, 673, 816, 840, 1000); Shumakov, *Obzor* 4: 463 (no. 281); *SbGKE* 2: 827–30 (no. 118a); *SobB*, 32 (no. 157); ROGPB, F. 303, no. 519, ff. 62v–63v, and no. 530, ff. 1250v–51.

68. Kazan: RORGB, F. 303, no. 519, ff. 99v–101v, 105–8v; "KhP" 2: 181–82 (nos. 998, 1000–1); Astrakhan': RORGB, F. 303, no. 519, ff. 127–31; "KhP" 2: 188 (no. 1045).

Varzuga: "KhP" 2: 193 (no. 1087); Kolycheva, *Agrarnyi stroi*, 125–42.

69. Copybook no. 519: RORGB, F. 303; Kashtanov, "Kopiinye knigi," 32–41; Veselovskii, "Monastyrskoe zemlevladenie," 95–116; Cherkasova, *Zemlevladenie*, 146–61; Kolycheva, *Agrarnyi stroi*, 142–60.

70. Calculations of A. I. Alekseev, "K izucheniiu vkladnykh knig Kirillo-belozerskogo monastyria," in *Sikh zhe pamiat' prebyvaet vo veki (memorial'nyi aspect v kul'ture russkogo pravoslavia)*, ed. A. I. Alekseev (St. Petersburg, 1997), 77; Ludwig Steindorff, "Mehr als seine Frage der Ehre. Zum Stifterverhalten Zar Ivans des Schrechlichen," *JGO* 51 (2003): 343–66.

71. Julian Pitt-Rivers, "Postscript: The Place of Grace in Anthropology" in *Honor and Grace in Anthropology*, ed. J. G. Peristiany and Pitt-Rivers (New York, 1992), 217–225 (quote 222); Marcel Mauss, *The Gift: Forms and Functions for Exchange in Archaic Societies*, transl. Ian Cunnison (New York, 1967); Nancy Shields Kollmann, *By Honor Bound. State and Society in Early Modern Russia* (Ithaca, NY, 1999).

72. Ivan's character: *Russian History, Ivan the Terrible: A Quarcentenary Celebration of His Death* 14 (1987), esp. Richard Hellie, "What Happened? How Did He Get Away with It?: Ivan Groznyi's Paranoia and the Problem of Institutional Restraints," pp.199–24; Nancy Shields Kollmann, "The Grand Prince in Muscovite Politics: The Problem of Genre in Sources on Ivan's Minority," 293–313; also David B. Miller, "Creating Legitimacy: Ritual, Ideology, and Power in Sixteenth-Century Russia," *Russian History* 21 (1994): 289–315.

73. Texts: I. V. Dergacheva, *Stanovlenie povestvovatel'nykh nachal v drevne-russkoi kul'ture XV–XVII vv. (na materiale sinodika)* (Munich, 1990), 34–35; *VK*, 28–29; Veselovskii, *Issledovaniia po istorii Oprichniny* (Moscow, 1963), 337–40; Kloss, "Zametki," 9–10.

74. Kashtanov, "Kopiinye knigi," 41–44; Cherkasova, *Zemlevladenie*, 168–80; idem, *Krupnaia feodal'naia votchina*, 28–32, 54.

75. *PSRL* 29: 221–22.

76. *PSRL* 29: 218–19; Gorskii, *Opisanie* 1: 8; A. V. Gorskii and K. I. Novostruev, *Opisanie slavianskikh rukopisei moskovskoi sinodal'noi biblioteki*, 3 vols. (Moscow, 1855–1917, repr. in 4 vols., Wiesbaden, 1964), 2: 382 (no. 400).

77. T. V. Nikolaeva, *Drevnerusskaia zhivopis'*, 138.

78. Gorskii, *Opisanie* 1: 97; *Skazanie Avramiia Palitsyna*, ed. and commentary O. A. Derzhavina and E. V. Kolosova (Moscow-Leningrad, 1955), 102.

79. *VK*, 28; *AI* 1: 434–36 (no. 229); Gorskii, *Opisanie* 2: 63–64; Manushina, *Khudozhestvennoe shit'e*, 70–72 (nos. 15–16); N. A. Maiasova, "Khudozhestvennye shit'e," in *Troitse-Sergieva Lavra. Khudozhestvennye pamiatniki*, ed. Voronin and Kostochkin, 130–32 (nos. 158–60); Cherkasova, *Zemlevladenie*, 164.

80. *VK*, 29; Gorskii, *Opisanie* 2: 62–63; cf. Grigorii's gift, *VK*, 122; A. A. Zimin, *V kanun groznykh potriaseii: Predposylki pervoi krest'ianskoi voiny v Rossii* (Moscow, 1986), 17, 112ff.

81. Cherkasova, *Zemlevladenie*, 192, n. 125.

82. *PSRL* 34: 202; *PSRL* 14: 56, 62.

83. *VK*, 28–29, 99 (dating bell to 1602/3); Shumakov, *Obzor* 4, no. 509; T. V. Nikolaeva, "Oklad s ikony," 32–35; Maiasova, "O datirovke," 170–74. Ivan's cover probably was transferred to the other Old Testament Trinity icon in the iconostasis of the Trinity church.

84. William Parry, *A New and Large Discourse of the Travels of Sir Anthony Sherley by Sea and over Land to the Persian Empire* (London, 1601), 36–38; Russian transl.: "Proezd cherez rossiiu persidskogo posolstva v 1599–1600 godakh," *ChOIDR* (1899), bk. 4, pt. 3, 7–9.

85. Maiasova, "O datirovke," 172; S. V. Nikolaeva, "Vklady i vkladchiki v Troitse-Sergiev Monastyr' v XVI–XVII vekakh," *Tserkov' v istorii Rossii* 2 (1998): 94.

86. Continuations of the Nikon Chronicle, the illuminated codex: Kloss, *Nikonovskii svod*, 190–252; Morozov, *Litsevoi svod*, esp. 11–39. The Book of Degrees: David B. Miller, "The *VMCh* and the *Stepennaia Kniga* of Metropolitan Makarii and the Origins of Russian National Consciousness," *FOG* 26 (1979): 315–17; N. N. Pokrovskii and Gail D. Lenhoff, eds., *Stepennaia kniga tsarskogo rodosloviia po drevneishim spiskam: Teksty i kommentarii*, 3 vols. (Moscow, 2007–), 1: 89–114; A. V. Sirenov, *Stepennaia kniga: Istoriia teksta* (Moscow, 2007), esp. 5–51, 371–409. The History of Kazan' (*Kazanskaia istoriia*): Pelenskii, *Russia and Kazan*, esp. 104–5, n. 1, 124–35; Frank Kämpfer, "Die Erobergung von Kazan 1552 als Gegenstand der zeitgenöischen russischen Historiographie," *FOG* 14 (1969), 7–161; cf. T. F. Volkova, "Letopisets nachala tsarstva Tsaria Ivana Vasil'evicha" i Troitskoe sochinenie o vziatii Kazani kak istochniki teksta 'Kazanskoi istorii,'" in *Drevnerusskaia literatura. Istochnikovedenie. Sb. nauchnykh trudov*, ed. D. S. Likhachev (Leningrad, 1984), 172–87; S. I. Kokorina, "K voprosu o sostave i plane avtorskogo teksta 'Kazanskoi istorii,'" *TODRL* 12 (1956): 576–85; Edward L. Keenan Jr., "Coming to Grips with the Kazanskaya Istoriya: Some Observations on Old Answers and New Questions," *The Annals of the Ukrainian Academy of Arts and Sciences in the United States* 11, pts. 1–2 (1964–68): 143–83. Also David B. Miller, "Official History in the Reign of Ivan Groznyi and its Seventeenth Century Imitators," *Russian History* 14 (1987): 333–60.

87. *PSRL* 11: 67–68, 127–47, esp. 144–45; *PSRL* 21, pt. 2: 396–98, also 350, 357–58, 360–61, 363, 415; *IT* 1: 258–60; *IT* 1: 258–60; Kloss, "Zhitiia," 293–96; Kloss, *Nikonovskii svod*, 190–74; Miller "The *VMCh*", 347.

88. Cf. *PSRL* 21, pt. 2: 592–95 (quotes, 592–93), with *PSRL* 13, pt. 1: 27; *Ioasafovskaia letopis'*, ed. A. A. Zimin (Moscow, 1957), 171.

89. *PSRL* 21, pt. 2: 599–604; *PSRL* 13, pt. 1: 37–43, esp. 40 (on Varlaam as intercessor), cf. p.142, n. 45. Like most chronicles, it failed to mention that Moscow bought off the Tatar army with a ransom. A. A. Zimin, "K izucheniiu istochnikov Stepennoi knigi," *TODRL* 13 (1957): 225–30.

90. *PSRL* 29: 25; *PSRL* 21, pt. 2: 634; Miller, "Prepodobnyi Sergii," 23.

91. *PSRL* 21, pt. 2: 605–15; *PSRL* 13, pt. 1: 48–53, 75–77 (Shumilovskii ms.).

92. *PSRL* 6: 267–76; N. N. Rozov, "Pokhval'noe slovo velikomu kniaziu Vasiliiu III," *AE za 1964 god* (1965), 278–89.

93. *PSRL* 21, pt. 2: 607–8, 610–15; Ihor Ševčenko, "A Neglected Byzantine

Source of Muscovite Political Ideology," *Harvard Slavic Studies* 2 (1954): 161–63; idem, "Gleanings, pts. 1–2," *Palaeoslavica* 6 (1998): 294.

94. *PSRL* 6: 271–72.

95.*PSRL* 21, pt. 2: 612–14; *PSRL* 6: 273–74; Miller, "Creating Legitimacy," 295–97.

96. Cf. *PSRL* 29: 49–51 with *PSRL* 29: 148; *PSRL* 13, pt. 2: 450–51.

97. T. V. Nikolaeva, *Sobranie*, 200 (no. 106); Trinity's donation book, perhaps mistakenly, said one image was the Crucifixion, not the Trinity, *VK*, 81.

98. Nasonov, "Novye istochniki," 3–26, esp. 10–11, 18–19, 21–22. Another version said Andreian brought Ivan the image of Sergius's vision of the Mother of God and a gold reliquary cross; G. Z. Kuntsevich, "Dva rasskaza o pokhodakh Tsaria Ivana Vasil'evicha Groznogo na Kazan' v 1550 i 1552 godakh," *Pamiatniki drevnei pismennosti i iskusstva* 130 (St. Petersburg, 1898): app., 23–35, esp. 33; Arkhimandrit Makarii (Veretennikov), *Moskovskii Mitropolit Makarii i ego vremia* (Moscow, 1996), 175–85; *IT* 1: 137–38; Daniel Rowland, "The Memory of St. Sergius in Sixteenth Century Russia," in *The Trinity-Sergius Lavra in Russian History and Culture*, ed. Vladimir Tsurikov (Jordanville, NY, 2005), pp. 56–63, a sensitive portrayal of the use of Sergius's imagery in descriptions of the conquest.

99. Nasonov, "Novye istochniki," 9; *PSRL* 29: 61.

100. Nasonov, "Novye istochniki," 17–20; *PSRL* 29: 87–88, 93–94, 96–97, 100, 106, 110–12.

101. *PSRL* 13, pt. 1: 164, 194, 201, 204–5, 209, 216, 223, 231–32, and pt. 2: 497–98, 500, 505, 511, 517, 522–23; *PSRL* 6: 310–12; *PSRL* 29: 117; *PSRL* 21, pt. 2: 646, 651–52; Miller, "Prepodobnyi Sergii," 23.

102. *PSRL* 19: 62–63. 173. 432. 434. 439–40; Volkova, "Letopisets," 172–87.

103. *PSRL* 19: 137, 455–56; Kuntsevich, "Dva rasskaza," 32–33; Nasonov, "Novye istochniki," 18–19.

104. *PSRL* 19: 137–38, 473–74.

105. *PSRL* 19: 143; Pelenski, *Russia and Kazan*, 229.

106. *PSRL* 29: 221, 307, 314–15; *PSRL* 14: 11–12; Miller, "Prepodobnyi Sergii," 23.

4—TRINITY'S PATRONS

1. *ASEI* 1:32 (no. 12).

2. Before 1422: *ASEI* 1: 29, 30–33, 41–42, 117–18 (nos. 6, 7, 10–11, 14, 30, 160); *VK*, 161; Semenchenko, "O khronologii Troitskikh aktov," 103–4; Gorskii, *Opisanie*, 1: 39–41; T. V. Nikolaeva, *Proizvedeniia prikladnogo iskusstva*, 52 (no. 30). In 1422 or 1423–27: *ASEI* 1: 27, 37–39, 45–46, 593 (nos. 3, 21–22, 26, 36–38); *VK*, 145–46, 159; Gonneau, *La Maison*, table 2, no. 5; V. D. Nazarov, "Razyskaniia o drevneishikh gramotakh Troitse-Sergieva monastyria. II: Vklad Kniazia Fedora Andreevicha Starodubskogo," in *T-SL* 1: 30–41; Gorskii, *Opisanie* 1: 6; Maiasova, "Khudozhestvennye shit'e," 118–19 (no. 133), illus. opp. 28; T. V. Nikolaeva, *Prikladnoe iskusstvo moskovskoi Rusi* (Moscow, 1976), 160–65; *VK*, 149.

3. *ASEI* 1: 37, 39, 117 (nos. 21, 26, 160); L. I. Ivina, *Vnutrenee osvoenie zemel' Rossii v XVI v.* (Leningrad, 1985), 34–36.

4. Anastasiia's donation: *ASEI* 1: 200 (no. 279); Miller, "Donors," 461.

5. *ASEI* 1: 74–5 (no. 90); *VK*, 162–63; T. V. Nikolaeva, *Proizvedeniia prikladnogo iskusstva*, 32–34, 53, 85–86, 154–55 (nos. 2, 31, 84, 85).

6. Gorskii, *Opisanie* 2: 47, 50–54, 75; *ASEI* 1: 48, 58, 63–65, 69, 86–87, 115, 120, 129 (nos. 41, 61, 70–71, 81, 108, 155, 164, 178); *PSRL* 26: 184; Kloss, "O sud'be," 24–25; Cherkasova, *Zemlevladeniia*, 65–66, 68, 73, 75, 81, 83, 202.

7. Miller, "Donors," 467–68; Veselovskii, *Feodal'noe zemlevladenie*, 166–77; Bobosha: *ASEI* 1: 45–46 (nos. 36–38).

8. Langer, "Plague," 351–68; V. A. Kruglik, "Zemlevladenie Troitse-Sergieva monastyria v periode feodal'noi voiny (1425–1452 gg.)," in *Agrarnoi stroi v feodal'noi Rossii XV–nachalo XX v.* (Moscow, 1986), 4–25; Ivina, *Vnutrenee osvoenie*, 10–30.

9. Some church lands were taxable, albeit at lower levels than lands owned by the laity.

10. *ASEI* 1: 209–11 (nos. 295–98); Kashtanov, *Ocherki*, 381–83 (no. 22); "KhP" 3: 201–2 (no. I–28).

11. *VK*, 38–39, 40, 44; *Akty sluzhilykh zemlevladel'tsev XV–Nachala XVII veka*, 2 vols., ed., A. V. Antonov and R. V. Baranov (Moscow, 1997–98) 1: 130–33 (no. 158); *PSRL* 13, pt. 1: 14; *PSRL* 28: 343–44; T. V. Nikolaeva, *Proizvedeniia prikladnogo iskusstva*, 73–74 (no. 66).

12. Ludwig Steindorff, *Memoria;* idem, "Commemoration and Administrative Techniques in Muscovite Monasteries," *Russian History* 22 (1995): 433–54; idem, "Sravnenie istochnikov ob organizatsii pominaniia usopshikh v Iosifo-Volokolamskom i Troitse-Sergievom monastyriakh v XVI veke," *AE za 1996 god* (1998), 65–78; idem, "Princess Mariia Golenina: Perpetuating Identity through 'Care for the Deceased,'" in *Moskovskaia Rus'*, Kleimola and Lenhoff, eds., 557–77; A. Alekseev, *Pod znakom*, 131–80; idem, "O skladyvanii pominal'noi praktiki na Rusi" and "K izucheniiu vkladnykh knig Kirillo-Belozerskoiogo monastyria," and Steindorff, "Pominanie usopshikh kak obshchee nasledie zapadnogo srednevekoviia i Drevnei Rusi," in "Sikh zhe pamiat'"), ed. Belonenko, 5–10, 68–85, 40–46. Daniel H. Kaiser, "Death and Dying in Early Modern Russia," in *Major Problems*, ed. Kollmann, 217–57; Russell Martin, "Gifts for the Dead. Kinship and Commemoration in Muscovy," *Russian History* 26 (1999): 171–72.

13. Mauss, *The Gift*, 37–80; A. Ia. Gurevich, *Categories of Medieval Culture*, transl. G. L. Campbell (London, 1985), 221–26.

14. I. Ia. Froianov, *Kievskaia Rus': Ocherki sotsial'no-politicheskoi istorii* (Leningrad, 1980), 74–76, 139–46.

15. Julian Pitt-Rivers, "Postscript," 217–31, quoting, 222, from Louis Ott, *Précis de theologie dogmatique*, transl. Marcel Grandclaudon (Moulhouse, 1955), 314, and Maria Pia di Bella, "Name, Blood and Miracles: The Claims to Renown in Medieval Sicily," 157–58, in *Honor and Grace in Anthropology*, ed. J. G. Peristiany and Pitt-Rivers (Cambridge, Eng., 1992); McLauglin, *Consorting*, 138–41.

16. Bruce Gordon and Peter Marshall note that in pre-Reformation Catholicism commemoration practices amounted to "a cult of the living in service to the dead,"

The Place of the Dead: Death and Remembrance in Late Medieval and Early Modern Europe, ed. Bruce Gordon and Peter Marshall (Cambridge, Eng., 2000), 3; Stephen D. White, *Custom, Kinship and Gifts to Saints: The "Laudatio Parentum" in Western France, 1050–1150* (Chapel Hill, NC, 1988), 40–85.

17. *ASEI* 1: 27–28 (no. 4); Nazarov, "Razyskaniia," 30–41. Cf. McLaughlin, *Consorting*, 2–9; Otto G. Oexle, "Die Gegenwart der Toten," in *Death in the Middle Ages*, ed. H. Braet and W. Verbeke (Louvain, 1983), 19–77.

18. Hartmut Rüss, *Herren und Diener. Die soziale und politische Mentalität des russischen Adels, 9.-17. Jahrhundert* (Cologne, 1994), 202–9; Brown, *The Cult*, 18–20.

19. Thomas Head, *Hagiography and the Cult of Saints: The Diocese of Orléans, 800–1200* (Cambridge, Eng., 1990), 17; Brown, *The Cult*, 1; Rosenwein, *Neighbor*, 35–43, 144–50; Sharon Farmer, *Communities of Saint Martin: Legend and Ritual in Medieval Tours* (Ithaca, NY, 1991), 1–2.

20. *ASEI* 1: 200 (no. 279); cf. Rosenwein, *Neighbor*, 109; Kaiser, "Death and Dying," 245.

21. Steindorff, *Memoriia*, 119–54. Byzantium: Michael Angold, *Church and Society in Byzantium under the Comneni, 1081–1261* (Cambridge, Eng., 1995), 265–382, 442–57; John R. Thomas, *Private Religious Foundations in the Byzantine Empire*, Dumbarton Oaks Studies, 24 (Washington, D. C., 1987), 171–74, 214–53; Rosemary Morris, *Monks and Laymen in Byzantium, 843–1118* (New York, 1995), 90–142, 166–99. Pre-Mongol Rus': Golubinskii, *Istoriia russkoi tserkvy*, 2 vols. (Moscow, 1900–11), 1, pt. 2: 655–703; Vladimir Vodoff, *Naissance de la Chrétienté russe, la conversion du prince Vladimir de Kiev (988) et ses conséquences (XIe-XIIIe siècles)* (Paris, 1988), 155–85.

22. Clive Burgess, "'Longing to Be Prayed for': Death and Commemoration in an English Parish in the Later Middle Ages," in *The Place of the Dead*, ed. Gordon and Marshall, 44–48; Geary, *Phantoms*, 18–22; Eamon Duffy, *The Stripping of the Altars. Traditional Religion in England, c. 1400–c. 1580* (New Haven, 1992), 220; Peter Marshall, *Beliefs and the Dead in Reformation England* (Oxford, Eng., 2002), 6.

23. I. I. Sreznevskii, *Materialy dlia slovaria drevnerusskogo iazyka*, 3 vols. (St. Petersburg, 1893–1903), 3: 465; Kaiser, "Death and Dying, 235–41; Steindorff, *Memoria*, 103–18; Sazonov, "K probleme vospriiatiia smerti v srednevekovoi Rusi," in *Russkaia istoriia: Problemy mentaliteta*, ed. V. A. Barchenkova (Moscow, 1994), 49; John Meyendorff, *Byzantine Theology* (New York, 1974), 220–22; Angold, *Church and Society*, 442–46.

24. S. V. Sazonov, "'Molitva mertvykh za zhivikh' v russkom letopisanii XII–XV v.," in *Rossiia v X–XVIII vv. Problemy istorii i istochnikovedeniia* (Moscow, 1995), 508–17; *PSRL* 2 (2d. ed.): cols. 911–25, esp. 921–24; Alekseev, *Pod znakom*, 131–46; idem, "O skladyvanii," 5–7; M. S. Cherkasova, "Pozemel'nye akty kak istochnik dlia izucheniia religioznogo soznaniia srednevekovoi Rusi," *Drevniaia Rus'. Voprosi medieavistiki* (2000), no. 2: 35–47.

25. Sixteenth-century Rus' experienced 14 years of famine, five incidences of Plague and typhus, and the burden of frequent wars: Kaiser, "Death and Dying, 219–20.

26. Brown, *The Cult*, 30.

27. Duffy, *Stripping*, 303.

28. Rus': Sazonov, "K probleme," 47–9; idem, "Molitva," 514–15; Miller, "Donors," 464–65. West: Rosenwein, *Neighbor*, esp. 35–48; Constance Bouchard, *Sword, Miter, and Cloister: Nobility and the Church in Burgundy, 980–1198* (Ithaca, NY, 1987), 125–89; Farmer, *Communities*, 67–75; McLaughlin, *Consorting*, 69–79, 125–32, 165–77.

29. A. Alekseev, *Pod znakom*, 142–51; Kazakova, *Vassian*, 342–57; A. A. Zimin, "O politicheskoi doktrine Iosifa Volotskogo," *TODRL*, 9 (1953): 168–69.

30. RORGB, F. 304/III, no. 25; partial transcription by Iu. A. Olsuf'ev, RORGB, F. 173/II, no. 226; described by S. V. Konev, "Sinodikologiia, pt. 1: Klassifikatsiia istochnikov," *Istoricheskaia genealogiia* 3 (1993): 10–15; N. V. Ponyrko, "Sinodiki," in *Slovar' knizhnikov i khizhnosti*, ed. D. S. Likhachev 2, pt. 2 (St. Petersburg, 1988): 339–44; S. V. Nikolaeva, "Tri sinodika Troitse-Sergieva monastyria XVI–XVII vv." in *Tserkov' v istorii Rossii* 3 (Moscow, 1999): 69–98; Steindorff, "Commemoration," 433–34; Dergacheva, "Stanovlenie," 34–35.

31. Konev, "Sinodikologiia," pt. 1: 10–12.

32. *ASEI* 1: 39 (no. 26).

33. *ASEI* 1: 39, 114, 97 (nos. 26, 154, 124). *Roditeli* in commemorations often extended beyond father and mother to include distant kin: Sreznevskii, *Materialy* 3:131; Kaiser, "Death," 245.

34. *ASEI* 1: 131 (no. 182).

35. *ARG*, 223 (no. 221).

36. *ARG*, 235 (no. 232).

37. *Obikhod* in Golubinskii, *Istoriia* 2, pt. 2, 577–82; *Poslaniia Iosifa Volotskogo*, ed. Zimin and Lur'e, 179–83; Steindorff, *Memoria*, 163–83; idem, "Princess Mariia Golenina," 557–75; idem, "Commemoration," 434–35; cf. McLaughlin, *Consorting with Saints*, 90–101; Arnold Angenendt, "Theologie und Liturgie der mittelalterlichen Toten-Memoria," in *Memoria. Der geschichtliche Zeugniswert des liturgischen Gedenkens im Mittelalter*, ed. K Schmid and J. Wollasch (Munich, 1984), 79–199.

38. Cherkasova, *Zemlevladeniia*, 55; Konev, "Sinodikologiia," pt. 1: 14; Alekseev, "O skladyvanii," 7; S. V. Nikolaeva, "Vklady," 88.

39. *VK*, 88, 155; *ARG*, 261–62 (no. 256).

40. Acts: *ARG*, 235–36 (no. 232); RORGB, F. 303, no. 532, ff. 374v–75v; Donation book: *VK*, 81; *Sinodik*: RORGB, F. 304/III, no. 25, ff. 144, 204v, 208v.

41. Gorskii, *Opisanie* 2: 52.

42. Gorskii, *Opisanie* 2: 52; RORGB, F. 304/III, no. 25, f. 208v; *ASEI* 1: 284–285 (n. 392).

43. Gorskii, *Opisanie* 2: 52; RORGB, F. 304/III, no. 25, f. 144; *ASEI* 1: 296, 363–64, 427–28 (nos. 404, 481, 549).

44. Gorskii, *Opisanie* 2: 52; RORGB, F. 304/III, no. 25, f. 208v.

45. RORGB, F. 304/III, no. 25, ff. 144, 204v, *VK*, 81.

46. *VK*, 38–39, 41, 44–49, 51, 160, 195.

47. *VK*, 70, 85. Nastas'ia Mansurova in the daily *sinodik*: RORGB, F. 304/III, no. 25, f. 210v, and possibly ff. 88v 147, 195, 211. I cannot locate Pelagaia. Installment donations: *VK*, 69 (Aigustov), 77 (Romandonovskii), 79 (Butenev), 83 (Durov), 100 (Pozharskii), 104 (Kosmynin and Adashev), 106 (Pushkin), 107 (Epokhov), 108 (Bulgakov), 120 (Tormosov), 127 (Zubov).

48. A. L. Shapiro *et al.*, *Agrarnaia istoriia Severo-Zapada Rossii XVI veka*, 2 vols. (Leningrad, 1974–78), esp. 1: 293–99; Cherkasova, *Zemlevladenie*, 118–61, on economic trends noted here and below. Politics: Zimin, *Reformy*, 222ff; Kollmann, *Kinship*, 161–80.

49. S. V. Nikolaeva, "Vklady," 83–84, 86–91.

50. RORGB, F. 303, no. 520, ff. 125v–27v.

51. Veselovskii, "Monastyrskoe zemlevladenie," 95–116; R. G. Skrynnikov, *Tragediia Novgoroda* (Moscow, 1994), es81–83.

52. *VK*, 120; RORGB, F. 303, no. 557, ff. 62–63v and 541, f. 255 (inc.); Shumakov, *Obzor* 4: 60–61 (no. 79), 63 (no. 92); Veselovskii, "Monastyrskoe zemlevladenie," 105–6.

53. Only towns on the Volga and to the east seem to have prospered; cf. references, n. 49.

54. RORGB, F. 303, no. 522, ff. 130v–32 (V. I. Zhikharev, 1573/74); Shumakov, *Obzor* 1: 28 (no. 2) (E. V. Voekov, 1578); Shumakov, *Tverskie akty* 1: 160–61 (no. 72) (K. Kherov, 1598/999); temporary land grant for cash in 1583/4 to Fedor Shestunov: RORGB, F. 303, no. 532 Dmitrov, ff. 590–90v; L. A. Kirichenko, *Aktovye material Troitse-Sergieva monastyria 1584–1641 gg. kak istochnik po istorii zemlevladeniia i khoziaistva* (Moscow, 2006), 72, 91–92; Cherkasova, *Zemlevladenie*, 171–72.

55. Aksinia: RORGB, F. 303, no. 524, ff. 187v–90; Shumakov, *Obzor* 1: 18 (no. 79); Kollmann, *Kinship*, 101. Matvei Zheltukhin (1586/87): RORGB, F. 303, no. 530, ff. 597v–98; Shumakov, *Obzor* 4: 285 (no. 899), *VK*, 240. Vasilii Panov 1589/90: RORGB, F. 303, no. 530, ff. 86v–87; Kiselevskie townsmen (1592): RORGB, F. 303, no. 532, ff. 1017v–18; Shumakov, *Obzor* 4: 65 (n. 102); *VK*, 231.Cf. Cherkasova, *Zemlevladeniia*, 165, 181.

56. Janet Martin, "Economic Development in the Varzuga Fishing Volost' During the Reign of Ivan IV," *Russian History* 14 (1987): 315–32; A. I. Kopanev, "Nezemledel'cheskaia volost' v XVI–XVII vv., " in *Krest'iansvto i klassovaia bor'ba v feodal'noi Rosii*, ed. N. E. Nosov (Leningrad, 1967), 176–94; R. G. Skrynnikov, *Nachalo Oprichniny* (Leningrad, 1966), 271–306; Veselovskii, "Monastyrskoe zemlevladenie," 97–100.

57. *ASEI* 1: 47–49, 53, 67–69, 101–3, 114, 164, 293–94, 300, 305–6, 532–33 (nos. 41–43, 50, 77, 80, 132–33, 153, 232, 401, 410, 416, 621); *ASEI* 3: 447 (nos. 463–64); *ARG*, 24–25 (no. 15), 303; "KhP," pt. 1: 362 (no. 474); Shumakov, *Obzor* 4: 277, 284 (nos. 878, 897); Kashtanov, "Obshchie zhalovannye gramoty," 141; Gonneau, *La Maison*, 174, 194, 234–35, 251–52, 264; Cherkasova, *Zemlevladenie*, 101–3, 184, 192, 253; *IT* 1: 28–9; idem, *Krupnaia feodal'naia votchina*, 303–4 (table 3), 346 (map); L. M. Spirina, *Pokrovskii Monastyr' v Khot'kove* (Sergiev Posad, 1996), 7–8; Chernov,

"Sel'skie monastyri," 117–19, 121–22; Zverinskii, *Materialy*, 3: 198–99 (no. 2182).

58. *PSRL* 23: 156; Zverinskii, *Materialy*, 3: 29 (no. 1436).

59. *AI* 1: 434–36 (no. 229); *ASEI* 1: 67, 77, 82, 224, 241, 244 (nos. 76, 94, 102, 313, 333, 337); ARG, 186–90 (no. 190); "KhP," pt. 3: 140 (no. 673); Zverinskii, *Materialy* 3: 191 (no. 2148); Cherkasova, *Zemlevladenie*, 120–22; idem, "Aktovye istochniki o gorodskikh vladeniiakh Troitse-Sergieva monastyria v XV–XVII vekakh," in *Ekonomika, upravlenie, demografiia gorodov evropeiskoi Rossii XV–XVIII vekov* (Tver', 1999), 109–14; idem, *Krupnaia feodal'naia votchina*, 304 (table 3); Gonneau, *La Maison*, 377–79, table 28.

60. S. B. Veselovskii, "Monastyrskoe zemlevladenie v Moskovskoi Rusi vo vtoroi polovine XVI v." *IZ* (1941), 101; A. A. Zimin, *Krupnaia feodal'naia votchina i sotsial'no-politicheskaia bor'ba v rossii (konets XV–XVI v.)* (Moscow, 1977), 170–188; Simonov: *ASEI* 2, *AFZiKh* 4, comp. L I. Ivina (Leningrad, 1983); L. I. Ivina, *Krupnaia votchina severo-vostochnoi Rusi kontsa XIV–pervoi poloviny XVI v.* (Leningrad, 1979), 177–99; Solovki: *Akty Solovetskogo monastyria 1479–1571gg.*, comp. I. Z Liberzon (Leningrad, 1988); Kirillov: *ASEI* 3: 15–299.

61. S. V. Nikolaeva confirmed these trends, "Vklady," 92–95. Zimin, *Krupnaia feodal'naia votchina*, 105–53, concluded that, as at Trinity, local *votchinniki* were the Iosifo-Volokolamsk monastery's chief benefactors and that initially its prince and, later, the Muscovite ruler and his elite were generous contributors. My estimate from the property records cited in n. 60 is that princes and boiar elites contributed 12% of Simonov's properties, 11% of Kirillov's (through 1505), and 2% of acquisitions at the Solovetskii Monastery (1472–1571). At Solovki free peasants constituted most of its benefactors; elsewhere local *votchinniki* outnumbered other categories of donors.

62. *VK*, 67, 41; RORGB, F. 303, no. 518, ff. 271–71v; Gorskii, *Opisanie* 2: 52; Cherkasova, *Zemlevladenie*, 107.

63. RORGB, F. 304/III, ff. 87v (Pleshcheevs), 185 (Gerasim Lachimov).

64. Kaiser, "Death," 243–44; Ludwig Steindorff, "Mehr als seine Frage," 342–66.

65. *VK*, 87, 157–58.

66. *VK*, 52; *SbL* 1: 18–21; RORGB, F. 303, no. 522, ff. 41–45; Gorskii, *Opisanie* 2: 55; RORGB, F. 173 (Olsuf'ev), f. 88, and RORGB, F. 304/III, no. 25, f. 75; *TK/DT*, ed. Zimin, 157.

67. *ASEI* 1: 192 (no. 264).

68. *ASEI* 1: 220–21, 223–25, 231–32, 237, 260–62, 264–65, 304, 348–50, 390–91, 410–11, 445–47 (nos. 309, 312, 315, 322, 327, 354, 356, 361, 414, 462–63, 516, 534, 567–68); Kashtanov, *Ocherki*, 404–6 (n. 37); *ARG*, 31–32, 38–39, 40, 49–50, 251–52 (nos. 23, 32, 34, 43, 249); *AAE* 1: 206–7 (no. 217).

69. S. Solov'ev, "Bratchiny," *Russkaia Beseda* (1856), no. 4: 108; Gonneau, *La Maison*, 90–91, 431–32; Cherepnin, *Obrazovanie*, 308–11; A. L. Khoroshkevich, ""Nezvanyi gost' na prazdnikakh srednevekovoi Rusi," in *Feodalism v rossii: Sb. statei vospominanii posv. Pamiati Akad. L. V. Cherepnina*, ed. V. L. Ianin (Moscow, 1987), 184–92.

70. *AAE* 1: 420–21 (no. 348); Emchenko, *Stoglav*, 342–43; Paul Bushkovitch, *Religion and Society in Russia: The Sixteenth and Seventeenth Centuries* (New York,

1992), 35–36.

71. *VK*, 41–42; Rosenwein, *Neighbor*, 199–200; Bouchard, *Sword*, 29; Shields Kollmann, *By Honor Bound*, 62.

72. Pleshcheev will: RORGB, F. 303, no. 518, ff. 271–72v. Golovkin will: RORGB, F. 303, no. 524, ff. 161–63; RGADA, F. 281 (GKE), Bezhetsk, no. 74/1178; Shumakov, *Obzor* 1: 5 (no. 18); *VK*, 131. Andreian's commemoration: RORGB, F. 304/III, no. 25, f. 94; cf. Ludwig Steindorff. "Kto blizhnie moi? Individ i kul'tura pominoveniia v Rossii rannego novogo vremeni," in *Chelovek i ego blizkie na zapade i vostoke Evropy*, ed. Iurii Bessmertnyi and Otto Gerhard Oexle (Moscow, 2000), 208–239.

73. Sale: RORGB, F. 303, no. 524, ff. 163–65; RGADA, F. 281 (GKE), Bezhetsk, no. 73/1177; Shumakov, *Obzor* 1: 39 (no. 8). Division: *ASEI* 1: 581 (no. 657); Veselovskii, *Feodal'noe zemlevladenie* 1: 169–77.

74. *ASEI* 1: 63, 119–20, 187–88, 202, 327–28, 330, 335–36, 357–58, 536–37, 561–63, 581 (nos. 69, 163, 258–58a, 281, 438, 440, 443, 447, 472, 626, 644–45, 657); *ARG*, 8, 52, 113, 178–79, 239 (nos. 1, 47, 110, 180, 237); Miller, "Donors," 467–68; White, *Custom*, 86–107; Rosenwein, *Neighbor*, 56–75; Steindorff, "Genealogy," 284–302.

75. Shumakov, *Obzor* 1: 5 (no. 18); RORGB, F. 303, no. 524, ff. 161–63.

76. *DDG*, 276–77, 304 (nos. 74, 80); Cherkasova, *Zemlevladenie*, 115.

77. Cherkasova, *Zemlevladenie*, table 4, 227–28.

78. *ARG*, 22–23, 223 (nos. 12, 221).

79. Shumakov, *Obzor* 4: 268 (no. 854); RORGB, F. 303, no. 523, ff. 190–91v.

80. RORGB, F. 303, no. 521, ff. 146–48; Shumakov, *Obzor* 3: 9 (no. 34); *Razriadnaia kniga 1475–1598 gg.*, ed. V. I. Buganov (Moscow, 1966), 10ff., 223.

81. ROGPB, F. 303, no. 518, ff. 489–89v, 490–90v.

82. RORGB, F. 303, no. 521, ff. 60–61, 144–46; Shumakov *Obzor* 3: 9–10 (no. 35), 62 (no. 206); *VK*, 42–43; *PK*, pt. 1: 782–83; Veselovskii, *Issledovaniia po istorii klassa sluzhilykh*, 351; Iu. G. Alekseev, *Agrarnaia i sotsial'naia istoriia severo-vostochnoi Rusi XV–XVI vv.: Pereiaslavskii uezd* (Moscow-Leningrad, 1966), 137–38; cf. Rosenwein, 78–122.

83. Shumakov, *Obzor* 4: 274 (no. 870), 277 (no. 878), 402–3 (no. 1117); RORGB, F. 303, no. 521, ff. 186v–88v, and no. 523, ff. 111–113v; *VK*, 43; Veselovskii, *Issledovaniia po istorii klassa sluzhilykh*, 357–58.

84. Panfilov: RORGB, F. 303, no. 520, ff. 241v–43; *VK*, 103. Mamyrev: RORGB, F. 303, no. 518, ff. 437v–38; Veselovskii, *D'iaki*, 316; Cherkasova, *Zemlevladenie*, 108–9.

85. Agrafenia's grant, 2 January 1541: ROGPB, F. 303, no. 521, ff. 168v–69v; *ARG*, 327; Ivan's directive and examples of Trinity's improper alienation of donations: S. N. Kisterev, "Delo Agrafeny Volynskoi i 'Otvet' Mitropolita Makariia Ivanu IV," *AE za 1998 god* (1999), 71–74.

86. Cf. White, *Custom*, 86–105.

87. Gorskii, *Opisanie* 2: 47 (Pr. Andrei of Radonezh, c. 1425), 50 (Zubachevs, ca. 1400–10?; Grand Pr. Vasilii II, 1432; Radonezh boiar Vasill Kopnin, ca. 1428–32; Vasilii Kuchetskii, 1444–47; Andrei Sharapov, 1432–45), 52 (Moscow boiar Ivan

Kriukov Fominskii, 1427/28; Moscow boiar Ivan Buturlin, 1444), 53 (Grand Pr. Vasilii I, bef. 1425), 53–54 (Pr. Dmitrii Krasnyi, 1440).

88. Durkheim, *Elementary Forms*, 420–32, esp. 427; Steindorff, "Kloster," 349–53.

89. L. A. Kirichenko and S. V. Nikolaeva, *Kormovaia kniga Troitse-Sergieva monastyria 1674 g. Issledovanie i publikatsiia* (Moscow, 2008), pp.192–93, 319–20, 370. The recorded donation was the sum total of Morozov gifts beginning with Ivan Grigor'evich Morozov's first gift of 15 May 1522. Cf. *VK*, 54; RORGB, F. 303, no. 522, ff.4v–6. Kollman, *Kinship*, 219.

90. Kaiser, "Death," 241–44; David G. Mandelbaum, "Social Uses of Funeral Rites," *The Meaning of Death*, ed. Herman Feifel (New York, 1959), 189–98; cf. Ludwig Steindorff, "Kto blizhnie moi?," 216–18; T. I. Shablova, "Praktika pominoveniia v Kirillo-belozerskom monastyre v vtoroi polovine XVI–pervoi polovine XVII vekov," in "*Sikh zhe pamiat*"', ed. Belonenko, 46–67; White, *Custom*, 161–76.

91. White, Custom, 75 (first two quotes); Mauss, *The Gift*, 3 (third quote).

92. VK, 66 (Anna Skripitsyna, wife of Foma Tarbeev), 90–91 (Skripitsyns), 68 (Kurtsevs), 79 (Butenevs).

93. Cherkasova, *Zemlevladenie*, 55.

94. Michael Cherniavsky, *Tsar and People: Studies in Russian Myths* (2d ed., New York, 1969), 34ff. Tonsured: Daniil, Ivan I, perhaps Semen, Ivan II, Vasilii III, Ivan IV, Fedor I, Boris Godunov. No record of tonsure: Dmitrii Donskoi (but eulogized as living a monk's existence), Vasilii I, Vasilii II and Ivan III; cf. McLaughlin, *Consorting with Saints*, 165–77.

95. Gorskii, *Opisanie* 2: 47, 50–51; *ASEI* 1: 169–70, 270, 337–38 (nos. 241, 370, 450), 609; Cherkasova, *Zemlevladeniia*, 65–66; Veselovskii, *Issledovaniia po istorii klassa sluzhilykh*, 202, 253–54.

96. *VK*, 45; RORGB, F. 303, no. 525, ff. 33v–36; Kollmann, *Kinship*, 238.

97. *VK*, 233.

98. Richard Hellie, *Slavery in Russia, 1450–1725* (Chicago, 1982J), 474–75; Tom Dykstra, *Russian Monastic Culture: "Josephism" and the Iosifo-Volokolamsk Monastery, 1479–1607* (Munich, 2006), 104–6.

99. Bouchard, *Sword*, 93–95.

5—TRINITY'S MONKS

1. Shumakov, *Tverskie akty* 1: 91–92 (no. 35).

2. *PLDR*, 320.

3. Arsenii, "Letopis,"' 92–93.

4. S. V. Nikolaeva, "Sostav monasheskoi bratii Troitse-Sergieva monastyria v XVII v. (Po Opisi 1641 g. i Opisi 1701 g.)," *Trudy po istorii Troitse-Sergievoi Lavry* 7 (1998): 34–55, esp. 44.

5. Nikolaeva, "Sostav," 35, citing J. Fabri, "Donesenie d. Ioanna Fabri ego vysochestvu Ferdinandu," *Otechestvennye zapiski* 25 (1826): 285–327, and 27 (1826):

46–67; Raffaello Barberini, *Relazione di Moscovia scritta di Rafelleo Barberini (1565)* (Palermo, 1966), 61; Jacob Ul'fel'dt, *Puteshestvie v Rosiiu* (Moscow, 2002), 191, 250, 314; A. Possevino, *Istoricheskie sochineniia o Rossii XVI v.* (Moscow, 1983), 32, 212.

6. Nikolaeva, "Sostav," 43–45; Gonneau, *La Maison*, 360; Gorskii, *Opisanie* 1: 6–8. From illuminations in T. Sidorova, "Realisticheskie cherty v arkhitekturnyh izobrazheniiakh drevne-russkikh miniatiur," *Arkhitekturnoe nasledstvo* 10 (1958): 76–78; Goldfrank, ed. and transl., *The Monastic Rule*, 36, wrote that a cell held two monks. Distortions in perspective and scale in the illuminations are too great to make a judgment.

7. A preliminary survey, Miller, "Counting Monks," 175–84; also Arsenii, "Letopis'"; Gonneau, *La Maison*; V. G. Briusova, "Spiski igumenov Troitse-Sergieva monastyria pervoi poloviny XVI v.," *AE za 1969 god* (1971): 292–95; Veselovskii, *Issledovaniia po istorii klassa sluzhilykh*; Cherkasova, *Zemlevladenie*; L. A. Kiripchenko, "Aktovyi material Troitse-Sergieva monastyria kontsa-XVI–serediny XVII v. kak istochnik sostava monastyrskoi administratsii," *Soobshcheniia* (2000): 38–65.

8. *SP* (Moscow, 1880).

9. RORGB, F. 304/III, no. 25. ff. 72–81 (sinodik of Trinity's brothers); S. V. Nikolaeva, "Pominanie inokov Troitse-Sergieva monastyria v Sinodike 1375 g.: k voprosu o bratskom sinodike," *Soobshcheniia* (Moscow, 2006), 29–48; idem, "Sinodik Troitse-Sergieva monastyria 1575 g.: k voprosu o strukture i istochnikakh," in *T-SL* 4: 130–37.

10. Cf. Gonneau, *La Maison*, 355–59.

11. *VK*, 191–92, 194–98.

12. Nikolaeva, "Sostav," 38–45.

13. Ibid., 41.14. *PLDR*, 300–4, 320, 334; *PSRL* 11: 132, 135, 137, 141.

15. *ASEI* 1: 39, 71 (nos. 26, 85); Semenchenko, "O khronologii aktov kontsa XIV–pervoi poloviny XV v.," 107; Cherkasova, *Zemlevladenie*, 84, 211 (no. 77).

16. *Legenden*, pt. 2: 158–59, *IT* 1: 442, 444 (the merchants); *ASEI* 1: 59 (no. 63), Cherkasova, *Zemlevladenie*, 84 (Buturlin).

17. Shevchenko, "Ferapont i Martinian," 191–92; *Slovar'* 2: pt. 2: 104.

18. *IT* 1: 70.

19. Cf. Gonneau, *La Maison*, 341–61; idem, "Les trublions au monastère (*bezčinniki monastyrskie*): Indiscipline et partage du pouvoir à la Trinité-Serge au XVe siècle," *Revue des études slaves* 63 (1991): 195–206.

20. The meaning of *starets* depended upon the source. In Trinity's donation book the terms *starets* and *monk* might be interchangeable; in narrative sources *starets* usually denoted an unusually holy or senior monk; in documentary sources *starets* came to mean membership in a governing body of senior monks. Cf. Dykstra, *Monastic Culture*, 90–96; Robert Romanchuk, on elders as mentors at the Kirillov monastery, *Byzantine hermeneutics*, 170–72.

21. *ASEI* 1: 39, 43, 50, 54, 57–61, 65–66, 71–73, 84, 89, 93–97, 109, 111–13, 123, 126, 130, 133, 138, 143 (nos. 26, 32, 45, 53, 59, 61, 63–64, 66, 72, 75, 85, 87, 89, 103, 111, 116, 119–23, 143–44, 147, 149–51, 168, 173, 180, 187, 193, 201).

22. Steindorff, "Einstellungen", 66–89; *PLDR*, 300.

23. *Legenden*, pt. 2: 158–65; *IT* 1: 442–47.

24. My database undercounts the number of landowners because many monks named in Trinity's documents cannot be identified. And, to repeat, the number of monks recorded in generations four and five represents an undercount in that written sources other than the *sinodik* rarely mentioned monks who served outside the administrative sphere; E. I. Kolycheva, "Pravoslavnye monastyri vtoroi poloviny XV–XVI veka," in *Monashestvo i monastyri v Rossii XI–XX veka*, ed. N. V. Sinitsyna (Moscow, 2002), 89–95, has no estimates for the fifteenth century.

25. T. V. Nikolaeva, *Prikladnoe iskusstvo*, 24–47; RORGB, F. 304/III, no. 25, ff. 72–74v.

26. *RIB* 6 (2d ed.): 733–36 (no. 104).

27. Gonneau, "Les trublions," 202–3.

28. Baldin and Manushina, *Troitse-Sergieva Lavra*, 38, 40, 92, 99–103 (fig. 86), 238 (fig. 195).

29. Paul of Aleppo, *Puteshestvie antiokhiiskogo Patriarkha Makariia v Rossii v polovine XVII veke*, transl. G. Murkos (Moscow, 1898; repr. and condensed, Moscow, 2005), 430–31; N. N. Voronin, "Litsevoe zhitie Sergiia kak istochnik dlia otsenki stroitelnoi deiatel'nosti Ermolinykh," *TODRL* 14 (1958): 573–75; cf. V. N. Lazarev about Italian influence on the hall of the Palace of Facets, *Vizantiiskoe i drevnerusskoe iskusstvo: Stat'i i materialy* (Moscow, 1978), 286, 289; V. V. Skopin, *Solovki: Istoriia, arkhitektura, priroda* (Moscow, 1994), 98–103.

30. *PSRL* 24: 195; Trofimov, *Pamiatniki*, 59–62.

31. T. V. Nikolaeva, *Sobranie*, 74–75 (no. 34); I discuss Sophia's icon cloth in Chapter 6.

32. Baldin and Manusheva, *Troitse-Sergieva lavra*, 243–48, 252–92 (icons, esp. figs. 223–24), 340–51, 357 (textiles, esp. fig. 285), 409–32 (plastic arts, esp. figs. 357–65), 433–70 (metallic objects).

33. Miller, "The Origin"; T. V. Nikolaeva, *Proizvedeniia melkoi plastiki*, 59–65, 313–14, 318–20, 324 (nos. 155, 157/10).

34. Gonneau, *La Maison*, table 25; *ASEI* 1: 387 (no. 510) Veniamin Pleshcheev; 428 (no. 550) Varlaam Barakov; 458 (no. 580) ff., Vassian Kovezin; 184 (no. 255) Makarii (Lipiatin?); 188 (no. 259) ff., Login.

35. *ASEI* 1: 149 (no. 212), 198 (no. 277); Gonneau, "Les troublions," 204.

36. *ASEI* 1: 498 (no. 601, 1495–1506); cf. Shumilov, *Obzor* 3: 62; RORGB, F. 303, no. 521, ff. 144–46 (1548/49).

37. Kiripchenko, "Aktovyi," 51.

38. To 1533: Gonneau, *La Maison*, 341–61; for later years Kiripchenko, "Aktovyi material," 38–65; S. B. Veselovskii, "Krepostnoi arkhiv Troitse-Sergievoi lavry," in idem, *Trudy po istochnikovedeniiu i istorii Rossii perioda feodalizma* (Moscow, 1978), 150–55.

39. *ASEI* 1: 563–64, 579–81 (nos. 646, 655–56); *ARG*, 81–84 (no. 77).

40. Gorskii, *Opisanie* 1: 77–80; Gonneau, *La Maison*, 344–46, table 25.

41. *PSRL* 6: 236; *PSRL* 28: 152; Gonneau, *La Maison*, 188–91; G. M. Prokhorov, "Paisii Iaroslavov" in *Slovar'* 1, pt. 2: 156–60; E. V. Romanenko, "Istoricheskie realii zhitii Nila Sorskogo," and David Goldfrank, "Etapy i itogi poluvekovoi istorii issledovanii o Nile Sorskom i perevodov ego sochinenii," in *Nil Sorskii*, ed. A. Alekseev, 22–24, 9–19.

42. Gonneau, *La Maison*, 199–201; Kloss, "Ob atributsii nekotorykh poslanii iz formuliarnika mitropolita Simona," *Tserkov' v istorii Rossii* 1 (1997): 30–55; *IT* 1: 133–36.

43. *PSRL* 23: 195; *PSRL* 22, pt. 1: 513; Gonneau, *La Maison*, 200, 202.

44. *PSRL* 28: 331; Gonneau, *La Maison*, 202–6; Cherkasova, *Zemlevladenie*, 99–100.

45. *Poslaniia Iosifa*, 291, 322–26 (*sobornyi otvet*); Begunov, "'Slovo inoe,'" 351–64; Moiseeva, "Zhitie Serapiona," 147–65.

46. Moshnins: *ARG*, nos. 27, 52, 167, 172, 201, 255, 281, 285, 307; *VK*, 15, 37, 173, 196, 239; Gonneau, *La Maison*, 344–45.

47. Pavel/Palka/Pamba Moshnin, *ASEI* 1: 525, 536–37 (nos. 613, 626–27), and perhaps 198 (no. 277); *ARG*, 22–23, 33, 51–54f. (nos. 12–13, 25, 46–50f.), 307. The Pamba of Metropolitan Filipp's letter of 1472 to Trinity abbot Spiridon, *RIB*, 6: (2d ed.): 733–36 (no. 104), was a different person.

48. Skripitsyns: *VK*, 37, 45, 66, 90–91, 173; *ASEI* 1: nos. 577, 582; *ARG*, nos. 9, 67, 72, 168, 226 (?), 238, 259–61, 302.

49. Gorskii *Opisanie*, 2: 177–79.

50. *ASEI* 1: 332–33, 336 (nos. 445, 448); *ARG*, 125, 147–48, 150–52, 162, 166–70, 173–74, 179–83, 212–13, 226 (nos. 126, 152–53, 157–58, 167, 172, 174, 178, 181, 183–84, 210, 226).

51. These calculations include only elders appearing in Trinity's administrative documents.

52. RORGB, F. 303, no. 518, ff. 34–35, 538–38v, 489–89v; no. 521, ff. 144–46, no. 530, ff. 1436–36v; RGADA, F. 281, Bezhetskii Verkh, no. 1245; *SP*, 71–72 (no. 784); *VK*, 191, 197; Cherkasova, Zemlevladenie, 131, 143; Kollmann, *Kinship*, 238–39, 240–41.

53. *ARG*, 125, 212, 219, 227–28, 262, 265–66, 280, 289, 292–99 (nos. 126, 210, 217, 225–26, 256, 260, 262, 278, 290, 293–99, 301); RORGB, F. 303, no. 518, ff. 30v–31, 490–90v; no. 519, ff. 119–22, 162v64v; no. 520: 299–301v; Shumakov, *Obzor* 4: 56; *PSRL* 6: 265; *SP*, 35 (no. 361); Veselovskii, *D'iaki*, 280–82; Veselovskii, *Issledovaniia po istorii Oprichniny*, 404–5; Arsenii, "Letopis,'" 92; RORGB, F. 303, no. 525, ff. 74v–75v; V. B. Kobrin, "Iz istorii zemel'noi politiki v gody oprichniny," *Istoricheskii arkhiv* (1958), no. 3: 1158–60; *SP*, 35 (nos. 362–65); Hugh Graham, ed. and transl., "'The Brutal Rule of Vasil'evich Tyrant of Muscovy' (Albert Schlichting on Ivan Groznyi)," *Canadian-American Slavic Studies* 9 (1975): 262; Skrynnikov, *Tragediia Novgoroda*, 110, 112–13; idem, *Oprichnyi terror*, 59, n. 3; Kashtanov, "Monastyrskie dokumenty," 36–39; *AAE* 1: 252 (no. 238).

54. RORGB, F. 303, no. 524, ff. 161–63; Shumakov, *Obzor* 1: 5 (no. 18); RGADA, F. 281, Bezhetskii Verkh, no. 74/1178.

55. *VK*, 68, 83; Gorskii, *Opisanie* 2: 62. Cf. books donated to Iosifo-Volokolamsk Monastery by its brothers: R. P. Dmitieva, T. V. Dianova, L. M. Kostiokhina, *Knizhnye tsentry Drevnei Rusi: Iosifo-Volokolamskii monastyr'* kak tsentr knizhnosti (Leningrad, 1991), 24–116.

56. *VK*, 183, 191, 195–96.

57. Arkhimandrit Makarii (Veretennikov), "Kelar' Troitse-Sergievoi obiteli starets Andreian Angelov, *Al'fa i omega* (1995), no. 2, 125.

58. RORGB, F. 303, no. 521, ff. 144–46; Shumakov, *Obzor* 3: 62.

59. Shumakov, *Uglichskie akty*, 103 (no. 56, 1540/41); RGADA, F. 281, Bezhetskii Verkh, no. 115/1219 (1547/48).

60. *SbL* 1: 9 (no. 2); *AAE* 1: 267 (no. 244).

61. Regarding Kurtsev and Korovin: 187–88 and nn. 52, 53; RORGB, F. 303, no. 523, ff. 164–66v; Shumakov, *Obzor* 4: 336.

62. Iona and Trifon: RORGB, F. 303, no. 520, ff. 135–37, no. 521, ff. 144–46; Mitka: Shumakov, *Obzor* 1: 65 (no. 3); RGADA, F. 281, Bezhetskii Verkh, no. 62/1166; Arsenii, "Letopis"," 121.

63. *VK*, 81; Kollmann, *Kinship*, 208–9.

64. *PSRL* 29: 290.

65. Arkhimandrit Makarii (Veretennikov), "Svidetel'stva istochnikov o rostovskom arkhiepiskope Nikandre (1549–1566), *Tserkov' v istorii Rossii* 2 (1998): 66–67.

66. Gorskii, *Opisanie*, 1: 84–88. Skripitsyns: Iu. Alekseev, *Agrarnaia*, 52, 130, 132, 135–36, 155–57, 166, 195, 202, 208–9. Shelepins: Veselovskii, *Issledovaniia po istorii Oprichniny* (Moscow, 1963), 473.

67. *PSRL* 29: 155.

68. Baldin and Manusheva, *Troitse-Sergieva lavra*, 115–30, 248–49.

69. Emchenko, *Stoglav*, 256, 258–59 (questions 8, 15, 17), 339–43 (chapter 52), esp. 342.

70. *AI* 1: 379–80, 382, 385 (no. 204); Skrynnikov, *Oprichnyi terror*, 137–38. Monk, 1528–1546/47, elder and cellarer, 1529/30–31,Vassian Korovin was from a Moscow landowning family.

71. Shumakov, *Obzor* 2: 12 (no. 47); RORGB, F. 303, no. 521, ff. 72–74v; Cherkasova, *Zemlevladenie*, 143. The agreement said her children might redeem the village for 300 rubles, yet maintain her commemoration, which they did.

72. A. A. Zimin, *Krupnaia feodal'naia votchina*, 105–65, esp. 112–18, 154; Dykstra, *Russian Monastic Culture*, esp. 121–35.

73. Jennifer B. Spock, "The Solovki Monastery, 1450–1645" (PhD diss., Yale Univ., 1999), 183–85.

74. *Novgorodskiia letopisi*, ed. A. F. Bychkov (St. Petersburg, 1879), 100.

75. *VK*, 192, 224, 236, 240–41, 263.

76. *VK*, 57, 192, 197–98, 216, 224, 233, 236, 240–41, 256, 259, 261–64.

77. Probably Iona before tonsure was Ivan Dmitrievich, donor to Trinity of Moscow and Dmitriev hamlets, and fishing rights on the Staritsa River (1579/80); *VK*, 132; RORGB, F. 303, no. 520, ff. 199–200v.

78. *VK*, 57, 69, 192, 198, 233, 240–41, 256, 259, 261–64, esp. 216, 236; cf. Veselovskii, "Krepostnoi arkhiv," 152–53.

79. Also Trinity Elder Nifont Snokarev, of a landowing family. In 1595/96 he came from the Anton'ev monastery in Novgorod (*VK*, 197, Shumakov, *Obzor* 4: 74–75; *Slovar'* 2, pt. 2: 141); the servant Merkurii Aigustov (1599/1600), from the same family as the elder Gurii (*VK*, 240); Fedor Ovsianikov, accepted into service in 1593/94, five years after Trinity Elder Anofrii Ovsianikov gave his house, property, and money for a family feast (*VK*, 197, 240; Gorskii, *Opisanie* 2: 63).

80. *Akty otnosiashchiesia do iuridicheskogo byta drevnei Rossii,* 3 vols., ed. Nikolai Kalachev (St. Petersburg, 1857–1884) 3: 25–28 (no. 274); David B. Miller, "How the Trinity-Sergius Monastery Got Governance, Got Godunov's Wrath and Got New Life," *Russian History* 33 (2006): 447–53; Kiripchenko, "Aktovyi material," 59–60; idem, *Aktovyi material,* 144–48.

81. Golovkin: *VK*, 132; David B. Miller, "Troitse-Sergieva lavra kak ob'ediniaiushchii tsentr Russkoi zemli," in *T-SL* 1:7–23; T. V. Nikolaeva, "Troitskii zhivopisets XVI veka Evstafii Golovkin," in *Kul'tura drevnei Rusi,* ed. A. L. Mongait (Moscow, 1966), 177–93; Kiripchenko, "Aktovyi," 52–53. Iakimov: Arsenii, "Letopis,'" 33–34, *VK*, 186; Shumakov, *Obzor* 4: 285; *Tverskie akty* 1: 111–13 (no. 52); Kiripchenko, "Aktovyi," 53–54. Zakkhei and Iona Surovtsev: *VK*, 186; Arsenii, "Letopis,'" 35. Makarii Pisemskii: Arsenii, "Letopis,'" 34; *VK*, 92; RORGB, F. 303, no. 520, 129v–32, 223v–24v; Kondrat'ev: *TK/DT*, ed. Zimin, 240–41; *VK*, 130. Varlaam Nepeitsyn: *TK/DT*, ed. Zimin, 199; Veselovskii, *Issledovaniia po istorii Oprichniny*, 122. Chashnikov: cf. n. 1. Meshcherskiis: *VK*, 196; Veselovskii, *Issledovaniia po istorii Oprichniny,* 127. Lodygin: *VK*, 130; Arsenii, "Letopis,'" 35; *TK/DT*, ed. Zimin, 139. Aigustov: *VK*, 609; *SP*, 33 (no. 328); Alekseev, *Agrarnaia istoriia*, 134–7ff. Zykov: *VK*, 228.

82. Shumakov, *Tverskie akty* 1: 168–70 (no. 75); cf. n. 72. Ovsiannikovs: RORGB, F. 303, no. 532 Dmitrov, ff. 591–91v; Cherkasova, *Zemlevladenie*, 204; Gorskii, *Opisanie* 2: 63; *VK*, 199.

83. Charters: Shumakov, *Obzor* 4: 74–75 (no. 147); RORGB, F. 303, no. 530 Vladimir, ff. 874–75. Nifont: cf. chapter 5, n. 79; Skobeltsyn(s): *VK*, 104, 186; Gelasii: perhaps *TK/DT*, ed. Zimin, 242.

84. Shumakov, *Tverskie akty* 1: 111–13 (no. 52); RGADA, F. 281 Tver', no. 64/12557; also Gorskii, *Opisanie* 1: 91 (Kirill); Arsenii, "Letopis,'" 23, 35 (Il'ia, Venedikt, Isidor); *VK*, 197, and RORGB, F. 532 Sol'-Galich, ff. 1011v–12 (Venedikt, Serapion and Gurii). RORGB, F. 303, no. 541, ff. 286–87; RORGB, F. 303, no. 532 Dmitrov, ff. 591–91v, and Galich, ff. 1018–18v (Zakhei and Akakii). n. 82 (Nifont).

85. Shumakov, *Tverskie akty* 1: 133–36 (no. 65).

86. *VK*, 186; Gorskii, *Opisanie* 2: 56–57, 63–64; Arsenii, "Letopis," 92–93; Cherkasova, *Zemlevladenie*, 143.

87. *VK*, 68.

88. This was a donation disguised as a purchase to get around the state's ban on donations of land. The property also served a double purpose: it secured Vasiliii a memorial for himself and his kin; it also provided the capital for the elders to secure

their own feast. Sadikov, "Iz istorii," 250–52 (no. 55); *VK*, 132; Gorskii, *Opisanie* 2: 61–62; Cherkasova, *Zemlevladeniia*, 148–49.

89. *VK*, 132; T. V. Nikolaeva, "Troitskii zhivopisets," 177–83.

90. *VK*, 132; less likely, the epithet "sister" referred to Evfrosiniia's having taken vows; if so, she probably was the Evfrosiniia Iakovlevna, Evstafii's aunt mentioned in RGADA, F. 281, Bezhetskii Verkh 151/1255. Cf. Miller "Troitse-Sergieva lavra," 7–23; Samuel K. Cohn Jr., "The Place of the Dead in Flanders and Tuscany: Towards a Comparative History of the Black Death," in *The Place of the Dead*, ed. Gordon and Marshall, 27–43, about family management east and west.

91. *VK*, 186, 97–8; Gorskii, *Opisanie* 2: 63.

92. *VK*, 130, 173, 192, 197–8, 216.

93. Gorskii and Nevostruev, *Opisanie* 1: 382 (no. 400).

6—TRINITY'S FEMALE VENERATORS

1. Shumakov, *Obzor* 4: 277 (no. 878); RORGB, F. 303, no. 523, f. 691.

2. Sadikov, "Iz istorii Oprichniny," 252–53 (no. 48).

3. Isolde Thyrêt, *Between God and Tsar: Religious Symbolism and the Royal Women of Muscovite Russia* (DeKalb, Ill., 2001), 17 for the paradigm. Also Ann Kleimola, "'In accordance with the canons of the Holy Apostles': Muscovite Dowries and Women's Property Rights," *Russian Review* 51 (1992): 204–29; N. L. Pushkareva and Eve Levin, "Zhenshchina v srednevekovom Novgorode XI–XV vv.," *Vestnik Moskovskogo universiteta,* Ser. 8: *Istoriia* 3 (1983): 78–89; Sandra Levy, "Women and the Control of Property in Sixteenth-Century Moscow," *Russian History* 10 (1983): 201–12; Carsten Goehrke, "Die Witwe in alten Russland," *FOG* 38 (1986): 64–96.

4. David Herlihy, *Women, Family and Society in Medieval Europe* (Providence, 1995), 44–55, 135–53; Diane Owen Hughes, "From Brideprice to Dowry in Mediterranean Europe," in *The Marriage Bargain: Women and Dowries in European History*, ed. Marian A. Kaplan (New York, 1985), 13–58; Anthony Molho, *Marriage Alliance in Late Medieval Florence* (Cambridge, Mass., 1994); Jack Goody, *The Development of the Family and Marriage in Europe* (New York, 1983), esp. 66–67, 118–22, 240–61; Samuel K. Cohn Jr., *The Cult of Remembrance and the Black Death: Six Renaissance Cities in Central Italy* (Baltimore, 1992), 11–28, 162–201.

5. Brown, *The Cult*, 44.

6. Cohn, *Cult of Remembrance*, 195–201, saw much the same pattern in fourteenth-century Tuscan and Umbrian towns; June Hall McCash, "The Cultural Patronage of Medieval Women: An Overview," in *The Cultural Patronage of Medieval Women*, ed. McCash (Athens, Ga., 1996), 16–19; J. S. W. Helt, "Women, Memory and Will-Making in Elizabethan England," in *The Place of the Dead,*" ed. Gorden and Marshall (2000), 188–205.

7. Shumakov, *Obzor* 4: 59 (no. 73); *VK*, 156.

8. *ARG*, 120 (no. 119), 315; *SbL* 1: 10–12 (no. 3); *VK*, 64; T. V. Nikolaeva, *Proizvedeniia prikladnogo iskusstva*, 60 (no. 42).

9. RORGB, F. 303, no. 520, ff. 302–4; Shumakov, *Obzor* 4: 60 (no. 78); McCash, "Cultural Patronage," 9–13.

10. Anna: *ASEI* 1: 59–60 (no. 64). Fedora: *ASEI* 1: 110–11 (no. 146); Semenchenko, "O khronologii Troitskikh aktov kontsa XIV–pervoi poloviny XV veka," 106.

11. *ASEI*, 1: 164 (no. 231), 612; Semenchenko, "O khronologii Troitskikh aktov vtoroi poloviny XV veka," 46.

12. *ASEI* 1: 114 (no. 153), pointed out to me by Elena Pavlova.

13. *ASEI* 1: 100–2 (nos. 131–33), 152–54 (nos. 217–18), 158 (no. 222), 166–69 (nos. 237, 239), 174–78 (nos. 246–48), 237 (no. 327), 249–50 (no. 341), 255–56 (no. 349), 269–70 (no. 369), 288–92 (nos. 397, 399); Kashtanov, *Ocherki*, 365 (no. 13); T. V. Nikolaeva, *Proizvedeniia prikladnogo iskusstva*, 54–55 (no. 34).

14. Isolde Thyrêt, "The Cultural Politics of the Grand Princesses of Moscow and the Emergence of the Muscovite Dynasty," *Russian History* 33 (2006): 339–52.

15. *ASEI* 1: 94–95 (no. 119), 133–34 (no. 267), 344–45 (no. 457); *ASEI* 3: 449 (no. 467); Veselovskii, *Feodal'noe zemlevladenie*, 149, n. 3.

16. *ARG*, 265–67 (nos. 260, 262).

17. Shumakov, *Tverskie akty*, 153–54 (no. 68); *SbGKE* 1: 297 (no. 307); also 6 in Varzuga, 1582–83; RORGB, F. 303, no. 519: 194–94v, 199–99v, 213v–15; *SbGKE* 1: 257–58 (no. 269); 4 in Pereiaslavl': 1540/41, 1543/44, 1560/61, 1592/93 Shumakov, *Obzor* 4: 333–35, 432, 338 (nos. 981–82, 1210, 988); 2 in Iur'ev, 1560s *Akty sluzhilykh zemlevladel'tsev XV–nachala XVII veka*, 2 vols. ed. A. V. Antonov, K. V. Baranov (Moscow, 1997–98) 2: 253–54 (no. 284); 2 in Moscow: 1563–64; RORGB, F. 303, no. 520, ff. 137–39v; no. 530, f. 47v; 1 each in Staritsa (1542/43), Galich (1555), Bezhetskii Verkh (1592/3), and Tver' (1576/7): ROGPB, F. 303 no. 532, ff. 563–63v, Shumakov, *Obzor* 4: 132–33 (no. 362), 88 (no. 190) and 1: 34, 44 (nos. 1–2); Shumakov, *Tverskie akty*, 154–55 (no. 69).

18. Kleimola, "In accordance," 205.

19. *ARG*, 113–14 (no. 111); Kollmann, *Kinship*, 222–14, 227–28.

20. *ARG*, 122–23 (no. 123); Kleimola, "In accordance," 207–9.

21. *ARG*, 137–38 (no. 141).

22. Shumakov, *Obzor* 4: 316 (no. 950); RORGB, F. 303, no. 530 Pereiaslavl', ff. 604v–6v.

23. Shumakov, *Obzor* 4: 276–77 (no. 877); RORGB, F. 303, no. 523, ff. 111–13v.

24. RORGB, F. 303, no. 530 Pereiaslavl', ff. 610–11.

25. Shumakov, Obzor 4: 268 (no. 853); RORGB, F. 303, no. 518, ff. 480–80v; *ARG*, 266–67 (no. 262).

26. RORGB, F. 303, nos. 523, ff. 192–92v, and 530, f. 1437v.

27. *ARG*, 109–12 (no. 108); Kleimola, "In accordance," 212–13.

28. RORGB, F. 303, no. 518, ff. 34–35; Shumakov, *Obzor* 1: 39 (no. 7); cf. *ARG*, 55–56 (no. 53), in which a father created a dowry for his daughter; dowries naming fathers of female actors: *ARG*, 107 (no. 105); for 1553: RORGB, F. 303, no. 524, ff. 43v–45v; Shumakov, *Obzor* 1: 7 (no. 26).

29. *SbL*, 21–24 (no. VII).

30. Avdotiia: RORGB, F. 303, no. 521, ff. 238v–40; Evfimiia: Shumakov, *Obzor* 3: 34–35 (no. 124), RORGB, F. 303, no. 532, ff. 481–83v; Elena: RORGB, F. 303, no. 521, ff. 72–74v, Shumakov, *Obzor* 2: 12 (no. 47), Cherkasova, *Zemlevladenie*, 143.

31. Slizneva: RORGB, F. 303, no. 521, ff. 75–77v; Irina: Shumakov, *Obzor* 4: 276 (no. 875); RORGB, F. 303, no. 520, ff. 68–69v, and no. 521, 30v–31; *VK*, 138; Iu. Alekseev, *Agrarnaia i sotsial'naia istoriia*, 195.

32. RORGB, F. 303, no. 519, 189v–90v.

33. Cf. *PRP. RK*, ed. E. I. Kotkova (Moscow, 1978), 51 (no. 39); RORGB, F. 303, no. 530 Kolomna, ff. 413v–14v, with *PRP. RK*, 47 (no. 36); RORGB, F. 303, no. 521, ff. 166–67; Kleimola, "In accordance," 213; *ARG*, 315.

34. Shumakov, *Obzor* 4: 284 (no. 896); RORGB, F. 303, no. 530 Pereiaslavl', ff. 599–600.

35. Shumakov, *Tverskie akty* 1: 167–68 (no. 74); RORGB, F. 303, no. 532, ff. 301v–2.

36. RORGB, F. 303 Sol'-Galich, no. 532, ff. 1038–40v; *VK*, 99; V. P. Kobrin, *Materialy genealogii kniazhesko-boiarskoi aristokratii XV–XVI vv.* (Moscow, 1995), 118, 131.

37. RORGB, F. 303, no. 524, ff. 126–28v.

38. *VK*, 44, 70; RORGB, F. 303, no. 520, f. 48v; Veselovskii, *Feodal'noe zemlevladenie*, 1: 201.

39. In 1550 five women donated 15 to 50 rubles for memorials; *VK*, 56, 79, 81, 108, 112.

40. *VK*, 64, 90; Kollmann, *Kinship*, 164, 203; a rich donation, 1551, of nun Kilikeia, widow of Prince Ivan Ushatyi, *VK*, 98; Zimin, *Formirovanie*, 89, 96–97; a crucifix icon with a bone and silver cover and three other covers from the widow of Boiar Fedor Ivanovich Khvorostinin, ca. 1570, *VK*, 46.

41. *VK*, 68, 76, 117–18, 223.

42. T. V. Nikolaeva, *Proiskhozhdeniia prikladnogo iskusstva*, 63–64, 137 (no. 48).

43. Maiasova, *Khudozhestvennoe shit'e*, 113.

44. *VK*, 44; T. V. Nikolaeva. *Proizvedeniia prikladnogo iskusstva*, 61, 72–73, 142 (nos. 43, 65); Maiasova, "*Khudozhestvannoe shit'e*," 123–24.

45. *VK*, 148–49; T. V. Nikolaeva, *Proizvedeniia prikladnogo* iskusstva, nos. 73–74; Maiasova, "*Khudozhestvennoe shit'e*," 124–25; The donation book's entry said Fedor was a boiar; in fact only a distant ancestor had held that rank, Veselovskii, *Issledovaniia po istorii klassa sluzhilykh*, 365, 367, 369.

46. *VK*, 63.

47. *ARG*, 77 (no. 72), 264–65 (no. 259). Anna and Ioasaf had identical family names, and Anna was an unusually devoted patron and a chronological "fit" to be his mother. Also, Trinity abbots often were from families of landowner/ patrons and the Skripitsyns were certainly that; *VK*, 66. 90–91, *ASEI* 1, nos. 216, 380, 565, 577, 582; *ARG*, nos. 9, 67, 72, 75, 114, 128, 168, 232, 238, 260–62, 269, 284, 302.

48. *ARG*, 266 (no. 261); Shumakov, Obzor 4: 268 (n. 853); RORGB, F. 303, no. 518, ff. 480–80v; *VK*, 45. The Anna, Andrei, and Anastasiia in numerous Skripitsyn entries in Trinity's *sinodik* also appeared in Trinity's documents, and the Filipp in the

sinodik possibly was Foma's name as a monk; RORGB, F. 304/III, no. 25, f. 66.

49. *VK*, 66; RORGB, F. 303, nos. 523, ff. 192–92v, and 530, f. 1437v.

50. Kollmann, *Kinship*, 158, on the travails of the Staritskiis; Ann Kleimola, "Women's Cultural Patronage in Early Modern Rus': Was Muscovy Europe?," in *Mesto Rossii v Evrope (Materialy mezhdunarodnoi konferentsii)*: Knigi po rusistike 5 (Budapest, 1999): 103–7.

51. *VK*, 28; Gorskii, *Opisanie* 2: 58; possible *sinodik* entries for Andrei Ivanovich and Vladimir Andreevich, RORGB, F. 304/III, no. 25, f.11. I cannot locate those for Evfrosiniia/Evdokiia or other clan members.

52. Gorskii, *Opisanie* 2: 55; Skrynnikov, *Oprichnyi terror*, 272; Graham, "The Brutal Rule," 263, n. 174.

53. *VK*, 28; Maiasova, "Khudozhestvennoe shit'e," nos. 143, 155; Maiasova, "Masterskaia, 41–64; Kleimola, "Women's Cultural Patronage," 104–7; Baldin and Manushina, *Troitse-Sergieva Lavra*, 356, 382 (illus. 308).

54. Maiasova, *Drevnerussoe shit'e*, 28 (no. 44); Maiasova, "Khudozhestvennoe shit'e," 127–28; These three women were in the entombment shroud prepared for the Kirillo-Belozerskii monastery, Maiasova, "Drevnerusskoe litsevoe shit'e iz sobraniia Kirillo-Belozerskogo Monasteria," in *Drevnerusskoe iskusstvo: Khudozhestvennye pamiatniki russkogo Severa*, ed. G V. Popov (Moscow, 1989), 214; Kleimola, "Women's Cultural Patronage," 104.

55. *VK*, 30, 212; Zimin, *V kanun*, 140.

56. Maiasova, *Drevenrusskoe shit'e*, 21–22 (no. 29); Baldin and Manushina, *Troitse-Sergieva lavra*, 347, 357–59 (nos. 285–87); Thyrêt, "'Blessed,' 481–86; Thyrêt, *Between God and Tsar*, 22–25; cf. Western parallels: Madeline H. Caviness, "Anchoress, Abbess, and Queen: Donors and Patrons or Intercessors and Matrons," 124–43, and Miriam Shadis, "Piety, Politics, and Power: The Patronage of Leonor of England and Her Daughter Berenguela of León and Blanche of Castile," 202–17, in *The Cultural Patronage*, ed. McCash.

57. N. A. Khlebnikova, "Maloizvestnye proizvedeniia masterskoi Sof'ii Paleolog," in *Pamiatniki kul'tury. Novye otkrytiia. Ezhegodnik 1976 g.* (Moscow, 1977), 196; Thyrêt, "'Blessed,'" 488–89. Sophia gave Trinity two cerements, The Crucifixion and The Lamb of God, and a liturgical cuff (*poruch*) with an image of The Annunciation flanked by Saints Florus and Laurus; Baldin and Manushina, *Troitse-Sergieva lavra*, 347, 360–62 (nos. 288–90). She very likely also donated an icon of the Mother of God with a cover of Byzantine origin that hung near Sergius's tomb; Guseva "Ob ikona," 267–77.

58. T. V. Nikolaeva, *Sobranie*, 138–39 (no. 68); Thyrêt, "Blessed," 486–87.

59. *PSRL* 34: 194; *VK*, 26; Maiasova, "Khudozhestvennoe shit'e," 125–26; Thyrêt, *Between God and Tsar*, 28–30.

60. *PSRL* 29: 56; Thyrêt, "Blessed," 489–92.

61. *PSRL* 21, pt. 2: 554; *PSRL* 12: 190–91; Miller, "Motives," 96; Thyrêt, "Blessed," 488–89.

62. *PSRL* 29: 218–19; Lloyd E. Berry and Robert O. Crummey, eds., *Rude & Barbarous Kingdom: Russia in the Accounts of Sixteenth-Century English Voyagers* (Madison, 1968), 217–18.

63. T. V. Nikolaeva, *Drevnerusskaia zhivopis'*, 137–39; Thyrêt, "Blessed," 494.

64. *VK*, 108; Veselovskii, *Issledovaniia po istorii Oprichniny*, 207–8.

65. *VK*, 64; cf. *VK*, 42 (Rychko Pleshcheev), 45 (Petr Pronskii), 49 (Mikhail Glinskii), 51 (Ivan Mezetskii), 55 (Aleksandr and Nikita Rostovskii), 58 (Petr Strigin and Nikita Obolenskii), 68 (Fedor Chelishchev and Nikita Kurtsev), 95 (Fedor and Grigorii Kurakin), 101 (D'iak Posnik Gubin), 106 Iakov Poroshin, 107 (Nekliud Erokhov).

66. Richard Hellie, "The Great Paradox of the Seventeenth Century. The Stratification of Muscovite Society and the Individualization of the High Culture, Especially Literature," in *O Rus! Studia litteraria slavica in honorem Hugh McLean*, ed. Simon Karlinsky *et al.* (Oakland, Calif., 1995), 116–28.

67. Women did so in 142 of 324 memorial requests, males in 648 of 1369.

68. *VK*, 87. The Zasekins were Iaroslavl' Princes, Veselovskii, *Issledovaniia po istorii Oprichniny*, 385–86. I cannot locate a Zasekin entry in the *sinodik*.

69. *ARG*, 109–12 (no. 108); Kollmann, *Kinship*, 222–23; Veselovskii, *D'iaki*, 278–80.

70. Shumakov, *Obzor* 3: 34–35 (no. 124); Cherkasova, *Zemlevladenie*, 259.

71. Emchenko, "Zhenskie monastyri v Rossii," in *Monashestvo i monastyri v Rossii XI–XX veka: Istoricheskii ocherki*, ed. N. V. Sinitsyna (Moscow, 2002), 245–58.

72. Arsenii, "Letopis"," 92–93; Shumakov, *Tverskie akty* 1: 134 (no. 65).

73. *ASEI* 1: 220 (no. 309), 261 (no. 355, 1467–74), 373–74 (no. 494, 7 July 1481). Arsenii, "Selo Podsosen'e," *Moskovskie eparkhial'nye vedomosti* 34 (1878): 300–5, and Gonneau, *La Maison*, 253, 483 (n. 556), confuse this Bogoroditskaia with a waste of that name in Pereiaslavl' that an Ivan Afanas'ev gave Trinity in 1433, *ASEI* 1: 69 (no. 80).

74. Zverinskii, *Materialy* 3: 198–99 (no. 2182); RORGB, F. 303, no. 522: 155–56, *VK*, 80.

75. *VK*, 29; Arsenii, "O votchinykh," 144–45; Arsenii, "Selo Klement'evo," *CHOiDR* (1887), bk. 2, 1–61; Cherkasova, *Zemlevladeniia*, 65–66; *ASEI* 1: 220–21 (no. 309); cf. Aver'ianov, *Sergii*, 276–95.

76. Zverinskii, *Materialy* 3: 399; *ARG*, 24–25 (no. 15), 303; *PLDR*, 294.

77. *ASEI* 1: 164 (no. 232), 300 (no. 410); "KhP" 2: 362 (no. 474); Chernov, "Sel'skie monastyri," 22–25; Spirina, *Pokrovskii monastyr'*, 7–8.

78. *VK*, 128 (Skobeev), 72–73 (Ianovs), 82, 141, 213; Veselovskii, *D'iaki*, 478; *Razriadnaia kniga*, ed. Buganov, 524; *PK*, 2 vols., ed. N. V. Kalachev (St. Petersburg, 1872–1877), 1: 79, 239; Spirina, *Pokrovskii monastyr'*, 8–10.

79. *PK*, ed. Kalachev, 1: 82.

80. See earlier this chapter.

81. RORGB, F. 303, no. 530, f. 1456; *PK*, ed. Kalachev, 1: 81, 286.

82. RORGB, F. 303, no. 520, ff. 75v–78; *ARG*, 159, 320 (no. 165); Veselovskii, *D'iaki*, 403; Ignatii: RORGB, F. 303, no. 532 Sol'-Galich, ff. 1017v–18; *Akty, otn. do iuridicheskogto byta*, ed. Kalachev, 3: 28; Arsenii, "Letopis"," 35.

83. Shumakov, *Obzor* 4: 280–81 (no. 887); RORGB, F. 303, no. 323, ff.

78–81; *RK*, ed. Buganov, esp. 112; Zimin, *Formirovanie*, 164, 167; Iu. G. Alekseev, *Agrarnaia i sotsial'naia istoriia*, 59, 147–48, 190–92.

84. Shumakov, *Obzor* 4: 277–78 (nos. 878, 881); Sadikov, "Iz istorii," 252–53 (no. 48); RORGB, F. 303, no. 523, ff. 69–71v; RORGB, F. 303, no. 530, item 175, ff. 733v–34; *VK*, 42–43; Cherkasova, *Zemlevladeniia*, 148; V. I. Vishnevskii, "Srednevekovye belokamennye nadgrobiia nekropolia Troitse-Sergieva monastyria (nakhodki 1998–1999 gg.)" *Soobshcheniia*, (2000): 24–25, 27; Veselovskii, *Issledovaniia po istorii klassa sluzhilykh*, 357–58; Zabolotskii monks: RORGB, F. 303, no. 524, ff. 135–36v; no. 521, ff. 144–46; *SP*, 71–72 (no. 784).

85. Shumakov, *Obzor* 4: 284 (no. 897); RORGB, F. 303, no. 530, Pereiaslavl', ff. 557v–58.

86. Sadikov, "Iz istorii," 252.

87. Shumakov, *Obzor* 4: 276 (no. 875); RORGB, F. 303, no. 520, ff. 68–69v; *VK*, 138; Iu. G. Alekseev, *Agrarnaia i sotsial'naia istoriia*, 195.

88. Shumakov, *Obzor* 4: 60 (no. 78).

89. *PK*, ed. Kalachev 1: 81, 286; Cherkasova, *Zemlevladenie*, pp.192, 253.

90. Shumakov, *Obzor* 4: 277 (no. 878).

91. Cohn, *Cult of Remembrance*, 197–8; David Herlihy, "Land, Family and Women in Continental Europe, 701–1200," in *Women in Medieval Society*, ed. Susan Mosher Stuart (Philadelphia, 1976), 13–45.

7—INTERMENT AT TRINITY

1. *ARG*, 223 (no. 221).

2. *SP*; "Spisok nadgrobii Troitskago-Sergieva monastyria, sostavlennyi v XVII veke," *ChOIDR* (1846), bk. 2, pt. 1, 33–50, and *ChOIDR* (1879), bk. 2, 79–107; T. V. Nikolaeva, "Novye nakhodki na territorii Zagorskgo muzeia," *SA* (1957), no. 1, 251–55; idem, "O nekotorykh nadgrobniakh XV–XVII vv. Zagorskogo muzeia-zapovednika," *SA* (1958), no. 3, 170–79; idem, "Nadgrobie novgorodskogo arkhiepiskopa Sergiia," *SA* (1965), no. 3, 266–69; idem, "Nadgrobnye plinty pod zapadnym pritvorom Troitskogo sobora," *Soobshcheniia* 2 (1958): 92–106; idem, "K izucheniiu nekropolia Troitse-Sergievoi lavry," *Soobshcheniia* 3 (1960): 181–90; idem, "Novye nadpisi na kamennykh plitakh XV–XVII vv. iz Troitse-Sergievoi lavry," *Numizmatika i epigrafika* 6 (1966): 207–55; V. B. Girshberg, "Nadpis' 1501 g. na Troitse-Sergievoi lavry," *SA* (1959), no. 3, 227–29; V. I. Vishnevskii, "Novye nakhodki srednevekovykh nadgrobii nekropolia Troitse-Sergieva monastyria," *Trudy po istorii Troitse-Sergievoi Lavry* 7 (1998): 72–87; idem, "Srednevekovye," 17–37; idem, "O nekotorykh osobennostiakh srednevekovykh nadgrobii Troitse-Sergieva monastyria (po materialam arkheologicheskikh issledovanii 2001 g.)," in *T-SL* 3: 97–110; idem, "Srednevekovye nadpisi-graffiti na nadgrobiiakh iz Troitse-Sergieva Monastyria," in *Troitse-Sergieva lavra v istorii, kul'ture i dukhovnoi zhiznii Rossii IV Mezhdunarodnaia konferentsiia. Tezisy dokladov*, ed. G. S. Isaakov (Sergiev Posad, 2004), 14–15.

3. L. A. Beliaev, *Russkoe srednevekovoe nadgrobie* (Moscow, 1996), 17–19.

4. Testament of Varsonofii Zamytskii, 10 April 1595, in Arsenii, *Letopis' namestnikov*, 33–34.

5. R. C. Finucan, "Sacred Corpse, Profane Carrion: Social Ideals and Death Rituals in the Later Middle Ages," in Joachim Whaley, ed., *Mirrors of Mortality: Studies in the Social History of Death* (New York, 1981), 40–60, esp. 52; Cf. Philippe Ariès, *The Hour of Our Death*, transl. Helen Weaver (New York, 1981), 29–92; idem, *Western Attitudes Toward Death: From the Middle Ages to the Present*, transl. Patricia Ranum (Baltimore, 1974), 14–22; McLaughlin, *Consorting with Saints*, 44–54; Oexle, "Die Gegenwart," 46–48.

6. Rosenwein, *Neighbor*, 5; A. E. Musin, "Pogrebal'nyi obriad drevnei Rusi kak arkheologicheskaia i liturgicheskaia problema, in "Sikh zhe pamiat,"" ed. Belonenko, 28–34; Ariès, *The Hour*, 32–33; Brown, *The Cult*; Geary, *Living with the Dead*; Marshall, *Beliefs*, 7, 22–24; Miller, "Pogrebeniia riadom s Sergiem: pogrebal'nye obychai v Troitse-Sergievom monastyre, 1392–1605 gg.," in *T-SL* 2: 74–89.

7. Beliaev, *Nadgrobie*, 264; Kaiser, "Death and Dying," 233–35; idem, "Marking a Life: The History and Meaning of Muscovite Gravestones," paper read at meeting of the Amer. Assoc. for the Advancement of Slavic Studies, St. Louis, Mo., 19 November 1999.

8. Pakhomii's Third Ed. of Sergius's life, *IT* 1: 418–19; above, chapter 2.

9. The compilation of 1477, *PSRL* 26: 184, recorded both deaths and said Semen, tonsured as the monk Sava, was buried at Trinity. The Moscow compilation of 1477, *PSRL* 25: 247 recorded only Andrei's death and said he was tonsured as Sava (which is unlikely) and buried at Trinity. Subsequent Moscow chronicles repeated this entry. Trinity's later burial record, *SP*, 1, said both were buried there although in the sixteenth century their remains were moved to the Archangel Cathedral in the Moscow kremlin, the dynasty's burial church; Kloss, "O sud'be," 24–5. It is possible that both Andrei and Semen were initially interred at Trinity.

10. Iliia, Simon of Smolensk, Simeon "Ekklisiarkh", Makarii, Iakov, Naum, Ioanikii, Mikhei, Isaakii Molchal'nik, Vasilii, Onisim, Varfolomei, Elisei; *SP*, 11–12.

11. Akakii, Antonii, Sava Arbuzov-Cherikov, Grigorii Buturlin, Varlaam, Avraamii Voronin, Gerontii, Prince Ivan Iur'evich Patrikeev (listed as a Golitsyn), Grigorii, Feogost' Dubenskii, Zinovii, Zosima, Ignatii, Filipp Iznosok, Ilarion, Irinarkh, Iosif, Simeon Kushelev, Martirii, two Matveis, Mina, Mikhail (Bishop of Smolensk), Petr Morozov, Pakhomii the Serb, Pimen, Veniamin Pleshcheev, Prokhor, Sergius (Archbishop of Novgorod), Simon, Vassian Uvarov, Feognost', and (Metropolitan) Feodosii Byval'tsev; also *PSRL* 25: 231 (Mikhail); *PSRL* 24: 330, the burial in 1483 of Trinity monk Sergius, a 34th person unless it is the Sergius of Novgorod who died in 1485.

12. Voronins: *ASEI* 1: 45–46, 50, 54–55 (nos. 36–38, 45, 53); Semenchenko, "O khronologii aktov kontsa XIV," 104; Veselovskii, *Feodal'noe zemlevladenie* 1:166–68; Gonneau, *La Maison*, 237–8. Buturlin: *ASEI* 1: 59 (no. 63); *VK*, 113; Zimin, *Formirovanie*, 170; Cherkasova, *Zemlevladenie*, 84. Pleshcheev: *ASEI* 1: 131, 299, 377–78 (nos. 181, 212, 499). Morozov: *ASEI* 1: 169–70, 252–4 (nos. 241, 346–7); Cherkasova, *Zemlevladeniia*, 94.

13. Vishnevskii, "O nekotorykh," 100–1; *PSRL* 28: 320; T. V. Nikolaeva, "O

nekotorykh," 171–2; *VK*, 146; *SP*, 64; *T. V. Nikolaeva*, "Nadgrobie," 210–11.

14. *ARG*, 51–52 (no. 46); *VK*, 28; Cherkasova, *Zemlevladenie*, 109; T. V. Nikolaeva, "Novye nadpisi," 212, 218, 220, 251; Vishnevskii, "O nekotorykh," 98, 105; Vishnevskii, "Srednevekovye," pp.18, 30–31; Zimin, *Formirovanie*, 108, 112–13, 114, 116–17, 130, 132–34, 227–28; Kollmann, *Kinship*, 209, 229, 240–41.

15. *ARG*, 110 (no. 108); *VK*, 57; above, chapter 6.

16. *VK*, 152–53; ROPGB, F. 303, no. 532, Staritsa ff. 365–6v, 368–69; Cherkasova, *Zemlevladenie*, 151; Veselovskii, *Issledovaniia po istorii Oprichniny*, 166.

17. Rosenwein, *Neighbor*, 16, 41–42.

18. Vishnevskii, "Srednevekovye," 18–19, 26–27, 29–30; cf. idem, "Novye nakhodki," 76–77; *SP*, 50 (Golovkins), 35 (Butenevs), 27 (Buturlins), 31 (Vorontsovs), 35–36 (Durovs), 35 (Kurtsevs), 18 (Pisemskiis).

19. Vishnevskii, "Srednevekovye, 26–27; idem, "O nekotorykh," 107–8; RORGB, F. 303, no. 541, f. 394.

20. V. A. Tkachenko, "Vkladnye knigi 1638/1639 i 1672/1673 gg. kak istochniki po istoriii nekropolia Troitse-Sergievoi lavry," *T-SL* 3: 152–65, esp. 156. For interments in the west: Rosenwein, *Neighbor*, 38–43, 48; McLaughlin, *Consorting*, 68–79, 125–77; Peter-Johannes Schuler, "Das Anniversar. Zu Mentalität und Familienbewusstsein im Spätmittelalter," in *Die Familie als sozialer und historischer Verband. Untersuchungen zum Spätmittelalter und zur frühen Neuzeit*, ed. Schuler (Sigmaringen, 1987), 67–117. In Russia: Steindorff, *Memoria*; idem, "Princess Mariia Golenina;" idem, "Sravnenie," 65–78; Miller, "Donors;" Sazonov, "K probleme," 47–52; S. V. Nikolaeva, "Tri sinodika," 69–98.

21. Vishnevskii, "Novye nakhkodki," 76–77; *SP*, 50, 53. V. A. Tkachenko showed me Evstafii's gravestone and its original site.

22. Finucan, "Sacred Corpse," 41 (quote, 44–45); Daniel Kaiser, "Social Cohesion and Death Rituals in Early Modern Russia," paper read at meeting of Amer. Historical Assoc., Chicago, 28 December 1984.

23. Bushkovitch, *Religion and Society*, 36–37; cf. *SP*, 18, 29–30, 33, 35, 53, with *VK*, 68 (Kurtsevs), 83 (Durovs); Miller, "Troitse-Servieva Lavra" (Golovkins); Cherkasova, *Zemlevladenie*, 131, 153 (Pisemskiis); Iu. G. Alekseev, *Agrarnaia i sotial'naia istoriia*, 79f. (Butenevs), 137f. (Kurtsevs); *TK/DT*, ed. Zimin, 58, 63 (Tatev).

24. Finucan, "Sacred Corpse," 44–45; Ariès, *Hour*, 40–42, 62–71.

25. Cf. *SP*, index, 85–97, with A. A. Zimin, "Sostav boiarskoi dumy v XV–XVI vekakh," *AE za 1957 god* (Moscow, 1958), 83–87.

26. Brown, *The Cult*, 87–88ff; McLauglin, *Consorting with Saints*, 44–54, 184–94, 212–34; Cohn, "Place of the Dead," 27; Steindorff, "Sravnenie istochnikov," esp. 69–74; Kaiser, "Death and Dying," 233–35.

27. *SP*, 1; Veselovskii, *Issledovaniia po istorii Oprichniny*, 146–47, 374–75; Zimin, "Sostav," 52, 54, 58; Kollmann, *Kinship*, 208.

28. *VK*, 102; RORGB, F. 303, no. 520, ff. 238–39; Ivan IV, having executed Aleksandr, donated 200 rubles to Trinity to commemorate him. The donation book said that Ivan IV earlier made commemorative donations for Ivan Gorbatyi, his wife Mariia, and their parents, and that in 1574 the elder-nun Varsunof'iia, the wife of

Vasilii Gorbatyi, commemorated the elder-nun Aleksandra.

29. *SP*, 2–5; Vishnevksii, "Srednevekovye nadpisi," 14; *VK*, 48, 50–51, 135, 160; Kollmann, *Kinship*, 79, 207, 225–26. The Vorotynskiis were infant Praskoviia (buried in 1522), Ivan Mikhailovich (d. 21 July 1535), Fedora, the wife of his grandson (buried 20 April 1586).

30. *SP*, 8–10; T. V. Nikolaeva, "Nadgrobie Sergiia," 266–69. The treasury was returned to Novgorod when Makarii became its archbishop in 1524, *PSRL* 8: 203 and 4: 286.

31. *SP*, 11–14; *VK*, 60–61, 88, 97, 99; Kollmann, *Kinship*, 221; Veselovskii, *Issledovaniia po istorii Oprichniny*, 428; Vishnevskii, "Srednevekovye, 17–20, finding Ioasaf's gravestone elsewhere, speculated that Ioasaf's remains were moved after 1880, when the list appeared. But the stone says that it is at a "reserved site." This, and the presence nearby of another Volynskii grave, suggests the list erred.

32. Vyshnevskii, "O nekotorykh," 97–110.

33. *VK*, 41–44; Kobrin, *Materialy*, 150, 154–55; Kollmann, *Kinship*, 227–28, 240–41.

34. *SP*, 30–31; *VK*, 52–53; Kollmann, *Kinship*, 66, 238–39.

35. The inventory listed the site of Gennadii Buturlin's grave as unknown. *SP*, 26–31, 69; *VK*, 46–47, 52–53, 56–57, 77–78, 113; *ASEI* 1: 59 (no. 63); Nancy Kollmann, *Kinship*, 203 (Buturlins), 231–32 (Rostovskiis); Veselovskii, *Ocherki po istorii Oprichniny*, 208–9 (Buturlins), 209–10 (Vorontsovs), 235–36 (Khvorostinins), 435–36 (Rostovskiis); *TK/DT*, 58, 63, and Razriadnaia *kniga*, ed. Buganov, 123f. (Tatevs). Ivan Bakhteiarov Rostovskii (1587) and a Tatev (1586) were tonsured on their deathbed.

36. *SP*, 14–23; *VK*, 108 (Bulgakov), 90 (Bel'skii), 57–59, 101–2 (Obolenskii), 74; *SbL*, 21–24 (Riapolovskii); Kollmann, *Kinship*, 204–5, 209, 222–26, 230.

37. *SP*, 14–22; "Spisok nadbrobii," pt. 2, 96; *VK*, 92, 75, 105–8; P. A. Sadikov, *Ocherki po istorii Oprichniny* (Moscow-Leningrad, 1950), 139 (Pisemskii); *TK/DT*, 78, 190 (Khitrii), 85, 142 (Solovtsov).

38. *SP*, 31–37; *VK*, 57, 69, 79, 83, 95, 107; Iu. G. Alekseev, *Agrarnaia i sotial'naia istoriia*, 129–30, 136, 160.

39. *SP*, 68–82, also said Petr Morozov, Veniamin Pleshcheev, Avraamii Voronin, and Pakhomii the Serb were interred at unknown sites.

40. *SP*, 38, 46–54; Vishenskii, "Srednevekovye belokamennye nadgrobiia," 17–37.

41. *Rude and Barbarous Kingdom*, ed. Berry and Crummey, 315–17; Zimin, *V kanun*, 140; *SP*, 47–48; The Staritskiis and Godunovs, of course, had been among Trinity's most generous patrons.

42. Of those in the inventory, it mentioned Vasilii and an Elizarei, said to be his brother, and that the grant was to commemorate themselves and their parents; *SP*, 52; *VK*, 61.

43. *SP*, 53; *VK*, 106.

44. *SP*, 54; *VK*, 128, 148.

45. *SP*, 54; *VK*, 239–41; Vishnevskii, "Srednevekovye," 18–31, 33.

CONCLUSION

1. Florenskii, "Troitse-Sergieva Lavra," 4.

2. *Skazanie Avraamiia*, 139–40, 142–43, 147–48, 170–71, 197–98 (Siege); 101, 105, 116, 128, 194, 212, 230 (appellations for Russia); Kloss, "Zametki," 6–9; *IT* 1.

3. *PSRL* 14: 95, 123–24 (quote); *Skazanie Avraamiia*, 213–15 (rallying resistance), 215–17 (the liberation army), 225–30 (freeing Moscow), 139; Miller, "Prepodobnyi Sergii," 23; idem, "Official History," 333–60; S. F. Platonov, *Drevnerusskie skazaniii i povesti o smutnom vremeni XVII kak istoricheskii istochnik* (St. Petersburg, 1888).

4. *Osada Troitskoi Lavry v 1608 godu*, print (Sergieva Troitskaia Lavra, 14 September 1859).

5. Baldin and Manushina, *Troitse-Sergieva lavra*, 132–242.

6. Over 8,000 manuscript books; G. Luchinskii, "Troitse-Sergieva Lavra" in *ZOR* 22 (1960): 74–194; Arsenii, "Opisanie slavianskikh rukopisei biblioteki Sviato-Troitskoi Sergievoi lavry," *ChOIDR* (1878), bk. 2, 1-xix, 352, bk. 4, 1–24, (1879), bk. 2, 1–267; T. A. Popesku, "Opisi Troitse-Sergieva monastyria kak istochnik po istorii monastyrskoi biblioteki," in *T-SL* 1: 156–67; T. V. Ukhova and S. A. Klepikov, "Katalog miniatiur, ornamenta i graviur sobranii Troitsi-Sergievoi lavry i Moskovskoi dukhovnoi akademii, *ZOR* 22 (1960): 74–194.; cf. A. G. Luchinskii, "Troitse-Sergieva Lavra" in *Entsiklopedicheskii slovar*", 82 vols., ed. F. A. Brokhaus and I. A. Efron' (St. Petersburg, 1890–1904), 33: 872–73.

7. *The Travels of Olearius in 17th-Century Russia*, transl. Samuel H. Baron (Stanford, Calif., 1967), 259–60; Paul of Aleppo, *Puteshestvie*, 431.

8. Its illuminations remain incomplete, *VK*, 275; O. A. Belobrova, "O litsevom spiski Zhitiia Sergiia Radonezhskogo v biblioteke Petra I," in *T-SL* 3: 175–203.

9. Scott Kenworthy, "The Revival of Monasticism in Modern Russia: The Trinity-Sergius Lavra," PhD diss., Brandeis University (Waltham, Mass., 2001), 48–55; A. S. Lavrov, *Koldovstvo i religiia.v Rossii, 1700–1740 gg.* (Moscow, 2000), 39–60, 267–340.

10. *SP*, 85–97.

11. G. P. Cherkashina, "Ikony Troitse-Sergieva monastyria—svideteli i uchastniki voennykh sobytii XVIII–nachala XX v.," in *Troitse-Sergieva Lavra v istorii, kul'tury i dukhovnoi zhizni Rossi*, ed. T. N. Manushina (Sergiev Posad 2002), 464–65, 474n.11; Baldin and Manushina, *Troitse-Sergieva Lavra*, 320, illus. 244–48.

12. Belobrova, "O litsevom spiske," 198–99; Kenworthy, "Revival," 48–55; Baldin and Manushina, *Troitse-Sergieva lavra*, 215–34.

13. Robert F. Byrnes, "Kliuchevskii on the Multi-National Russian State"; Seymour Becker, "Contributions to a Nationalist Ideology: Histories of Russia in the First Half of the Nineteenth Century"; Carl Reddel, "S. M. Solov'ev and Multi-National History"; and Edward Thaden, "V. N. Tatishchev, German Historians, and the St. Petersburg Academy of Sciences," *Russian History* 13 (1986): 313–98.

14. Konstantin Akinsha, Gregory Kozlov with Sylvia Hochfield, *The Holy Place. Architecture, Ideology, and History in Russia* (New Haven, 2007), esp. 62–63; E. T. Kirichenko, *Khram Khrista Spasitelia v Moskve* (Moscow, 1992), esp. 76, picture 82–83, 107.

15. Scott M. Kenworthy, "Memory Eternal: The Five-hundred Year Commemoration of St. Sergius of Radonezh, 25 September 1892," in *The Trinity-Sergius Lavra in Russian History and Culture*, ed. Vladimir Tsurikov (Jordanville, NY, 2005), 27.

16. V. O. Kliuchevskii, "Znachenie Preopodobnogo Sergiia dlia russkogo naroda i gosudarstva," *Bogoslovskii vestnik* (1892), no. 11, 1; 24–55: Kenworthy, "Memory," 24–55.

17. Kenworthy, "Memory," quotes, 32, 55.

18. *SP*, 85–97; Kenworthy, "Revival," 15–23, 56–93; Cherkashina, "Ikony," 462–76.

19. M. A. Gaganova, "Sud'ba moshchei prepodobnogo Sergiiia (sobytiia 1919–1921 gg.)," in *T-SL* 3: 84–94; Igumen Andronik (Trubachev), "Sud'ba glavy Prepodobnogo Sergiia," *Zhurnal Moskovskoi Patriarkhii* (2001), no. 4: 1–16; Kenworthy, "Revival," 391–403, 417; burial record, *SP*, 7–8.

20. Tatiana A. Chumachenko, *Church and State in Soviet Russia: Russian Orthodoxy from World War II to the Khrushchev Years*, transl. Edward E. Roslof (Armonk, NY, 2002), 15–86.

21. Arkhimandrit Makarii (Veretennikov), "Pervyi namestnik vozrozhdennoi Lavry," in *T-SL* 2: 185–92; *Zhizn' i zhitiia*, ed. Kolesov, and *Sergii*, ed. Desiatnikov, appeared in 1991; "Pamiati Sergiia Radonezhskogo (assessments of Sergius by Kuchkin, I. I. Kostomarov, A. I. Ilovaiskii and Kliuchevskii) in *Otechestvo: Kraevecheskii al'manakh* 3 (1992): 5–28; a collection of gravures for popular consumption: S. Kharlamov, *Prepodobnyi Sergii Radonezhskii* (Moscow, 1992); the stamps; Simon Franklin, "Russia in Time," in Franklin and Emma Widdis, eds., *National Identity in Russian Culture* (Cambridge, Eng., 2004), 20–24.

22. Aleksandr Bondarenko, "Podvizhnik zemli russkoi," *Krasnaia Zvezda* (KZV, no. 229, 8 October 1992), Eastview Information Services.

23. Program cover, *Music Festival 'Probuzhdenie', Dedicated to the 600th Anniversary of the Venerable Sergius, Abbot of Radonezh and Miracleworker of All Rus'*, (Moscow, Kremlin Palace of Congresses, 10–11 October 1992), and explanation, both courtesy of Marianna Tax Choldin.

24. Akinsha, Kozlov and Hochfield, *The Holy Place*, 154–61.

25. Pierre Nora, "Between Memory and History: les Lieux de Memoire." *Representations* 26 (1989): 7–35.

26. *IT* 1: 273–74.

27. *IT* 1: 68–70; Maiasova, *Drevnerusskoe shit'e*, 11–12, fig. 7; Maiasova, "Khudozhestvennoe shit'e," 118–19, figs. 133–35; Vorontsova, "K voprosu," 11–19, esp. 16; Mariia G. Gal'chenko, "Troitse-sergievskie rukopisei kontsa XIV–pervoi poloviny XV v. i problema vtorogo iuzhnoslavianskogo vliianiia," pt. 1: "Konets XIV–pervaia chetvert' XV vv.," *Palaeoslavica* 8 (2000): 18–21; Matvei, "Liturgicheskie traditsii," 197–98.

28. Marshall, *Beliefs*, 6.

29. See above, chapter 2; cf. Kloss, *IT* 1: 66–72; Miller, "Donors," 455–74.

30. *IT* 1: 169, 422; *Legenden*, 2: 107.

31. Gonneau, *La Maison*, 166–70; Evgenii Golubinskii, *Istoriia kanonizatsii sviatykh v russkoi tserkvi* (Farnborough, Eng., 1969; repr. of Moscow, 1903 ed.), 72.

32. G. M. Prokhorov, "Vnutrenniaia dinamika drevnerusskoi kul'tury ili Nadsoznanie Drevnei Rusi," in *La cultura spirituale russa*, ed. Luigi Magarotto and Daniela Rizzi (Trento, 1992), 218–26.

33. 172 gifts, 1500–1532; 1,170 gifts, 1533–1560; 788 gifts, 1561–1584; 621 gifts, 1585–1612; S. V. Nikolaeva, "Vklady," 82–95.

34. Golubinskii, *Prepodobnyi Sergii*, 56–57; Kloss, *IT* 1: 56, 63.

35. *IT* 1: 202, 214, 258 (commentary), 398–99 (text); *PLDR*, 374–76; *PSRL* 6: 129.

36. *VK*, 63, 87, 102, 114, 154, 229; RORGB, F. 303, no. 522, ff. 138–40, 151–53v; Ozerskaia, "Obraz," 95; *PSRL* 29: 25, 52, 61, 132, 152, 192, 205.

37. Cf. Steindorff, "Mehr al seine Frage der Ehre," 342–63, that Ivan IV was no less generous to the Iosifo-Volokolamsk and Kirillov monasteries in commemorating *oprichnina* victims.

38. Sigismund Herberstein, *Zapiski o Moskovii*, transl. A. I. Maleina and A. V. Nazarenko (Moscow, 1988), 106.

39. Possevino, *Sochineniia*,, 9–10, 32.

40. L. M. Vorontsova, "Riznitsa Troitse-Sergieva monastyria. K voprosu o sostave i istorii formirovaniia," in *T-SL* 3: 228–39.

41. Gonneau, "Fonctions," 283–307.

42. T. V. Nikolaeva, *Sobranie* 88–89 (no. 42); L. M. Evseeva, "K voprosu o datirovke ikony 'Sergii Radonezhskii s 18 kleimami zhitiia' iz nadvratnoi tserkvi Troitse-Sergieva monastyria," I. A. Shalina, "Ikona-Moshchevik 'Prepodobnyi Sergii Radonezhskii s zhitiem' nachala XVI v. iz sobraniia V. A. Bondarenko," and I. L. Buseva-Davydova, "Novootkrytye ikony s izobrazheniem Prepodobnogo Sergiia Radonezhskogo iz chastnykh sobranii," in *T-SL* 4: 31, 32–34, 37–40; Vorontsova *et al.*, *Prepodobnyi Sergii*. Miller, "The Origin," 304–14; Rowland, "Memory," 56–69; Robert Bird, at the Norman Ingham workshop, Univ. of Chicago, 21 April 2006, inspired my reading of narrative images.

43. K. Anthony Appiah, review of *Nelson Mandela's Favorite African Folktales*, ed. Nelson Mandela, in *The New York Review of Books* (18 December 2003): 46.

44. Cf. *PSRL* 29: 25 (Sebezh miracle), 307–8, 314 (the term "Russian tsardom" and the invocation of saintly intercessors).

45. *PSRL* 19: 138 (Chap. 68, Solovetskii ms.); Pelenski, *Russia and Kazan*, 22; John Armstrong, *Nations Before Nationalism* (Chapel Hill, NC, 1982), 131–67, about the nexus of religion and national identity.

46. Rosenwein, *Neighbor*, 4, 48.

47. Valerie A. Kivelson, "The Effects of Partible Inheritance: Gentry Families and the State in Muscovy," *Russian Review* 53 (1994): 206; Janet Martin, "Mobility, Forced Resettlement and Regional Identity in Muscovy," in *Moskovskaia Rus'*, Kleimola and Lenhoff, eds. 431–49.

48. *ASEI* 1: 277, 444, 456, 460 (nos. 380, 565, 577, 582); *ARG*, 73–74, 77, 79

162–63, 264–67 (nos. 67, 72, 75, 168, 259–62); Iu. G. Alekseev, *Agrarnaia*, 130, 156–57.

49. *ASEI* 1: 444, 456, 460 (nos. 567, 577, 582); *ARG*, 17–18, 236, 240, 265–67, 272, 285 (nos. 9, 232, 238, 260–62, 269, 284); Shumakov, *Obzor* 4: 279 (no. 883), 284 (no. 897), 319 (954); Iu. G. Alekseev, *Agrarnaia*, 155, 195.

50. Trinity's purchase, 1540/1, of village from Solomonida, wife of Il'ia Buchug Skripitsyn and their sons Matvei and Fedor Buchugin (four Skripitsyn witnesses), Shumakov, *Obzor* 4: 333 (no. 981); Anna Mikhailovna Skripitsyna's grant (1580/1), Shumakov, *Obzor* 4: 284 (no. 827); jeweled ornament from Bova Skripitsyn in 1600/1, *VK*, 91.

51. *VK*, 37, 66, 90–91 (Skripitsyns, Tarbeevs).

52. *ASEI* 1: 84 (no. 103); Shumakov, *Obzor* 4: 283–4 (nos. 896–97).

53. Acts, conclusion, nn. 47–49; *ASEI* 1: 456 (no. 577), one Skripitsyn, two Redrikov witnesses; *ARG*, 240 (no. 238), Butenev purchase, two Skripitsyn and four Upolovnikov witnesses, written by an Upolovnikov, 243 (no. 244), Butenev exchange with four Upolovnikovs, eight Butenev witnesses, 245–8 (no. 245), Butenev-Upolovnikov exchange, three Upolovnikov and seven Butenev witnesses; 291 (no. 292), Riabinin-two Upolovnikov exchange; five Upolovnikov and one Miakishev witnesses, Shumakov, *Obzor* 4: 333 (no. 981), Trinity purchase from Solomonida arranged by monk Seliverst Upolovnikov, four Skripitsyn witnesses.

54. RORGB, F. 303, no. 518, ff. 483–83v, and F. 303, no. 523, ff. 192–92v; *VK*, 45; Shumakov, *Obzor* 4: 268–69 (nos. 853, 856).

55. *PK*, ed. Kalachev, 1: 20, 188, 821, 823–24, 840, 916, and 2: 193, 644, 646, 648–50.

56. Donations: *VK*, 45 (Briukhovs); 79 (Butenevs), 85–86 (Redrikovs), 120 (Miakishevs), 143 (Riabinins); Iu. G. Alekseev, *Agrarnaia*, 52, 136, 156–57, 203–5.

57. Shumakov, *Obzor* 4: 268–69 (no. 855).

58. RORGB, F. 303, no. 518, ff. 490–90v, 492–93v; Shumakov, *Obzor* 4: 268–69 (no. 855); *VK*, 79.

59. *SP*, 9, 20–21, 35, 54.

60. Miller, "Donors," 467–68. Michurins: *ASEI* 1: 561–63 (nos. 644–45); *ARG*, 178–79 (no. 180), 242 (no. 241).

61. Shumakov, *Obzor* 1: 4–5 (no. 2), 7–8 (no. 30), 10–11 (no. 44), 13 (no. 56; RGADA, F. 281 (GKE), Bezhetskii Verkh, nos. 177/1281, and 223/1329; *VK*, 126–27; *PK*, ed. Kalachev 2: 18.

62. See chapters 4, 5; Veselovskii, "Monastyrskoe zemlevladenie," 99–104; Cluny's analogous experience, Rosenwein, *Neighbor*, 47–48.

63. Kollmann, *Kinship*, 240–41; *VK*, 42–43; *SP*, 71–72; Vishnevskii, "O nekotorykh," 98, 105.

64. Kollmann, *Kinship*, esp. 35, 101 (fig. 7: Koshkin Clan), 211–16; the *Apraksos* in VK, p.149 under *Rod Goltievykh*, T. V. Nikolaeva, *Prikladnoe iskusstvo*, 160–65; *VK*, 82 (Vel'iaminovs) 149, 163; *ASEI* 1: 56 (no. 56), 128–29 (no. 177).

65. *VK*, 66–67, 78; *SP*, 73–74.

66. *VK*, 98–99, 101, 118.

67. Cherkasova, *Zemlevladenie*, table 10, 248–81; idem, "Akty," 71–72; idem, *Krupnaia feodal'naia votchina*, esp. table 6, 307; Kolycheva, *Agrarnyi stroi*, 195–200.

68. A. G. Man'kov, *Tseny i ikh dvizhenie v russkom gosudarstve XVI veka* (Moscow-Leningrad, 1951); Veselovskii, "Krepostnoi arkhiv," 152–53.

69. Veselovskii, *Selo*, 72–102, esp. 81–84, and "Monastyrskoe zemlevladenie," 95–116; Cherkasova, *Zemlevladenie*, 281; Kolycheva, *Agrarnyi stroi*, 195–200; Zimin, *Reformy*, 117–66, regarding earlier growth.

70. Cherkasova, "Akty," 172; Veselovskii, "Monastyrskoe zemlevladenie," 114–16; Kashtanov, "Obshchie zhalovannye gramoty," 96–137.

71. Cherkasova, *Krupnaia feodal'naia votchina*, table 3, 303–4; idem, "Aktovye," 109–14; Gonneau, *La Maison*," 418–54; Kirichenko, *Aktovyi material*, 108–10; Kashtanov, "Zemel'no-immunitetnaia politika russkogo pravitel'stva v Kazanskom krae v 50-kh godakh XVI v.," *Uchenye zapiski Kazanskogo pedagoicheskogo institute (Iz istorii Tatarii)* 80 (1970): 165–66; *AAE* 1: 239 (no. 235); *AI* 1: 360 (no. 194); "KhP," pt. 2, 140 (nos. 676–77).

72. *SbGKE* 1: 587–63 (no. 137a); L. A. Kirichenko, "Torgovye ekspeditsii Troitse-Sergieva monastyria po aktovomu materialu kontsa XVI–nachala XVII v.," in *T-SL* 3: 52–55; Veselovskii, *Selo*, 93–94.

73. *SbGKE* 1: 222–23 (no. 228), 244–46 (no. 254), 246–47 (no. 255), 454–55 (no. 141); Kirichenko, *Aktovyi material*, 113-14; Martin, "Economic Development," esp. 327–29; N. E. Nosov, *Stanovlenie soslovno-predstaveitel'nye uchrezhdenii v Rossii* (Leningrad, 1969), 240–366.

74. *PSRL* 29: 61; "KhP," 2: 140 (nos. 673 675); Cherkasova, *Zemlevladenie*, 132–34; RORGB, F. 303, nos. 526, ff. 40–48v, and 530, ff. 1401v–42v; Kashtanov, "Zemel'no-immunitetnaia politika," 164–203, regarding Trinity's economic privileges on the central Volga; Kirichenko, *Aktovyi material*, 125–26.

75. "KhP," 2: 140 (nos. 676–77); RORGB, F. 303, no. 526, ff. 20–20v.; *AAE* 1: 239 (no. 235); *AI* 1: 360 (no. 194); B.-A. B. Kochekaev, *Nogaisko-russkie otnosheniia v XV–XVIII vv.* (Alma-Ata, 1988), 83; I. P. Ermolaev, *Kazanskii krai vo vtoroi polovine XVI–XVII vv. (Khronologicheskii perechen' dokumentov)* (Kazan', 1980), 23 (no. 112).

76. RORGB, F. 303, no. 519, ff. 127–131, 271–73v; *AAE* 1: 405–7 (no. 336), 411–12 (no. 339); Tebekin, "Perechen'," 2: 217–18 (no. 178); Ermolaev, *Kazanskii krai*, 25–26, 34, 49–50 (nos. 126, 135, 192–93, 296); Kirichenko, "Torgovye ekspeditsii," 55–56; Ann Kleimola, "Good Breeding, Muscovite Style: 'Horse Culture' in Early Modern Rus'," *FOG* 50 (1995): 202–16.

77. Ruth H. Finnegan, *Literacy and Orality: Studies in the Technology of Communication* (Oxford, 1988), 10–12, 45–85, 110–23; M. T. Clanchy, *From Memory to Written Record, England 1066–1307* (2d ed., Oxford, 1993), esp. 328; by Trinity's scribes, A. A. Zimin, "Aktovye poddelki Troitse-Sergieva monastyria 80-kh godakh XVI v.," in *Voprosy sootsial'no-ekonomicheskoi istorii i istochnikovedeniia period feodalizma v Rossii*, ed. N. V. Ustiugov (Moscow, 1961), 247–52; Kashtanov, "Kopiinye knigi," 3–47; Kashtanov, "Ocherki," 266–68; Koretskii, "Pravaia gramota," 173–219.

78. *ASEI* 1: 33 (no. 14).

79. The survey: ROGPB, F. 303, no. 518, ff. 536v–38. Golovkins: Miller, "Troitse-Sergieva lavra," 7–23. Charters: *ASEI* 3: 450 (no. 468); *ARG*, 140 (no. 144), 153 (no. 159), 156–7 (no. 162), 178–79 (no. 180), 239 (no. 237), 242 (no. 241), *GKE*, F. 281,

Bezhetskii Verkh, 55/1159, 65/1169, 108/1212, 113/1217, 135/1239, 146/1250, 161/1265, 177/1281; RORGB, F. 303, no. 524, ff. 195v–96v.

80. RORGB, F. 303, no. 532 Sol'-Galich, ff. 1038–40v; *VK*, 99; Kobrin, "Materialy," 118.

81. *ASEI* 1: 46 (no. 38); Matthew Innes, "Memory, Orality and Literacy in Early Medieval Society," *Past and Present* 158 (Feb., 1998): 3–10; cf. Clanchy, *Memory* (2d ed.), 308–17; Brigitte Bedos-Rezak, "Medieval Identity: A Sign and a Concept," *American Historical Review* 105 (2000): 1490–31 (seals as symbols of identity in medieval French charters).

82. Malcolm B. Parkes, "The Literacy of the Laity," in *Literature and Western Civilization: The Medieval World*, ed. D. Daiches and M. Thorlby (New York, 1973), 555–63; Franz H. Baüml, "Varieties and Consequences of Medieval Literacy and Illiteracy," *Speculum* 55 (1980): 237–42.

83. Robert Browning, "Literacy in the Byzantine World," *Byzantine and Modern Greek Studies* 4 (1978): 39–54; Bedos-Rezak, "Medieval Identity," 1490 (quote), 1505–1511; Baüml, "Literacy," 243–49; Clancy, *Memory*, 2ff.; Parkes, "Literacy," 555–70.

84. Marshall Poe, "Elite Service Registry in Moscovy, 1500–1700," *Russian History* 21 (1994): 251–88.

85. Miller, "Troitse-Sergeieva lavra," 7–20.

86. Parkes, "Literacy," 555–57.

87. Brian Stock, *The Implications of Literacy: Written Language and Models of Interpretation in the Eleventh and Twelfth Centuries* (Princeton, New Jersey, 1983), 19–30; Innes, "Memory," 9; Finnegan, "Literacy," 139–45.

88. Simon Franklin and Widdis, eds., *National Identity*, xii; Benedict R. Anderson, *Imagined Communities: Reflections on the Origin and Spread of Nationalism* (rev. ed., London, 1991), 6–36; Armstrong, *Nations*; Anthony D. Smith, *The Ethnic Origins of Nations* (Oxford, 1986); also Dimitri Obolensky, "Nationalism in Eastern Europe in the Middle Ages," in Obolensky, *The Byzantine Inheritance in Eastern Europe* (London, 1982), 1–16.

Bibliography

Manuscripts

Rossiiskii gosudarstvennyi arkhiv drevnikh aktov. Fund 281 (*Gramoty "Kollegii ekonomii"*).

Rukopisnyi otdel Rossiiskoi gosudarstvennoi biblioteki. Fund 173, no. 226 (*Sinodik Troitse-Sergievoi Lavry 1575 goda*, incomplete), with index of names and notations. Comp. Iu. A. Olsuf'ev, 11 February 1923.

Rukopisnyi otdel Rossiiskoi gosudarstvennoi biblioteki. Fund 303, nos. 518–20, 522–23, 530, 532, 536 (*Akty Troitse-Sergievoi lavry*).

Rukopisnyi otdel Rossiiskoi gosudarstvennoi biblioteki. Fund 304.I, no. 746 <www.stsl.ru/manuscripts/index.php>.

Rukopisnyi otdel Rossiiskoi gosudarstvennoi biblioteki. Fund 304.III, no. 25 (*Sinodik* of 1575).

Printed Primary and Secondary Sources

Afonskii Paterik: ili zhizneopisanii sviatykh na sviatoi Afonskii gorie prosiiavskikh. 2 pts. in one vol. Repr of 7th ed. of 1897. Moscow, 1994.

Akinsha, Konstantin, and David Kozlov, with Sylvia Hochfield. *The Holy Place. Architecture, Ideology, and History in Russia*. New Haven, 2007.

Akty feodal'nogo zemlevladeniia i khoziaistva XIV–XVI vekov. Vols. 1–3, ed. L. V. Cherepnin. Moscow, 1951–61. Vol. 4, comp. L. I. Ivina. Leningrad, 1983.

Akty istoricheskie, sobrannye i izdannye Arkheograficheskoiu kommissieiu. 6 vols. St. Petersburg, 1841–42.

Akty, otnosiashchiesia do iuridicheskogo byta drevnei Rossii. 3 vols. Ed. Nikolai Kalachov. St. Petersburg, 1857–1884.

Akty russkogo gosudarstva, 1505–1526 gg. Ed. S. B. Veselovskii. Moscow, 1975.

Akty sluzhilykh zemlevladel'tsev XV–nachala XVII veka. 2 vols. Ed. A. V. Antonov, K. V. Baranov. Moscow, 1997–98.

Akty, sobrannye v bibliotekakh i arkhivakh Rossiiskoi imperii Arkheograficheskoiu ekspeditsieiu Imp. Akademii nauk. 4 vols. St. Petersburg, 1836.

Akty Solovetskogo monastyria 1479–1571 gg. Comp. I. Z. Liberzon. Leningrad, 1988.

Akty sotsial'no-ekonomicheskoi istorii Severo-vostochnoi Rusi, kontsa XIV–nachala XVI v. 3 vols. Ed. S. B. Veselovskii and I. A. Golubtsov. Moscow, 1952–64.

Alef, Gustave. "Muscovy and the Council of Florence," *Slavic Review* 20 (1961): 389–401.

Alekseev, A. I. "K izucheniiu vkladnykh knig Kirillo-Belozerskogo monastyria," in *"Sikh zhe pamiat' prebyvaet vo veki": (Memorial'nyi aspekt v kul'ture russkogo pravoslaviia)*. Ed. V. S. Belonenko. St. Petersburg, 1997. 68–85.

———. "Kogda nachalas' polememika 'iosiflian' i 'nestiazhatelei'?" in *Nil Sorskii v kul'ture i knizhnosti Drevnei Rusi*. Ed. A. I. Alekseev. St. Petersburg, 2008. 29–40.

———. "O skladyvanii pominal'noi praktiki na Rusi," in *"Sikh zhe pamiat prebyvaet vo veki": Memorial'nyi aspekt v kul'ture russkogo pravoslaviia*. Ed. V. S. Belonenko. St. Petersburg, 1997. 5–10.

———. *Pod znakom kontsa vremen: Ocherki russkoi religioznosti kontsa XIV–nachala XVI vv.* St. Petersburg, 2002.

Alekseev, Iu. G. *Agrarnaia i sotsial'naia istoriia severo-vostochnoi Rusi XV–XVI vv: Pereiaslavskii uezd*. Moscow-Leningrad, 1966.

Alexander, John T. *Bubonic Plague in Early Modern Russia*. Baltimore, 1980.

Anderson, Benedict R. *Imagined Communities: Reflections on the Origin and Spread of Nationalism*, rev. ed. London, 1991.

Andronik (Trubachev), Igumen. "Sud'ba glavy Prepodobnogo Sergiia," *Zhurnal Moskovskoi Patriarkhii* no. 4 (2001): 1–16.

Angenendt, Arnold. "Theologie und Liturgie der mittelalterlichen Toten-Memoria," in *Memoria. Der geschichtliche Zeugniswert des liturgischen Gedenkens im Mittelalter*. Ed. K. Schmid and J. Wollasch. Munich, 1984. 79–199.

Angold, Michael. *Church and Society in Byzantium under the Comneni, 1081–1261*. Cambridge, Eng., 1995.

Antonova, V. I. "O pervonachal'nom meste 'Troitsy' Andreia Rubleva," *Gosudarstvennaia Tret'iakovskaia Galereia: Materialy i issledovaniia* 1 (1956): 21–43.

Appel, Ortrud. *Die Vita des hl. Sergij von Radonež. Untersuchungen zur Textgeschichte*. Munich, 1972.

Appiah, K. Anthony. "Review of *Nelson Mandela's Favorite African Folktales*, ed. Nelson Mandela," *The New York Review of Books*, 18 December 2003, 46–47.

Ariès, Philippe. *The Hour of Our Death*. Transl. Helen Weaver. New York, 1981.

———. *Western Attitudes Toward Death: From the Middle Ages to the Present*. Transl. Patricia M. Ranum. Baltimore, 1974.

Armstrong, John A. *Nations before Nationalism*. Chapel Hill, N.C., 1982.

Arsenii. "Letopis' namestnikov, kelarei, kaznacheev, riznichikh, ekonomov i bibliotekarei Sviato-Troitskoi Sergievoi Lavry," in *Letopis' zaniatii Arkheograficheskoi kommissii* 4, pt. 2 (1865–66): 62–130.

———. "O votchinykh vladeniiakh Troitskago monastyria pri zhizni ego osnovatelia prepodobnago Sergiia," *Letopis' zaniatii Arkheograficheskoi kommissii* 7 (1884): 139–75.

———. "Opisanie slavianskikh rukopisei biblioteki Sviato-Troitskoi Sergievoi lavry," *Chteniia v imperatorskom Obshchestve istorii i drevnostei rossiiskikh pri moskovskom universitete* no. 2 (1878): i–xix, 1–352; no. 4 (1878): 1–240; no. 2 (1879): 1–267.

———. "Selo Klement'evo," *Chteniia v imperatorskom Obshchestve istorii i drevnostei rossiiskikh pri moskovskom universitete* no. 2 (1887): 1–61.

———. "Selo Podsosen'e," *Moskovskie eparkhial'nye vedomosti* 34 (1878): 300–305.

Aver'ianov, K. A. "O stepeni dostovernosti 'Zhitiia Sergiia Radonezhskogo,'" *Germenevtika drevnerusskoi literatury* 12 (2005): 833–54.

———. *Sergii Radonezhskii, lichnost' i epokha*. Moscow, 2006.

Baldin, V. I., and T. N. Manushina, *Troitsa-Sergieva Lavra. Arkhitekturnyi ansambl' i khudozhestvennye kollektsii drevnerusskogo iskusstva XIV–XVII v.* Moscow, 1996.

Barberini, Raffaello. *Relazione di Moscovia scritta di Rafelleo Barberini (1565)*. Palermo, 1996.

Baüml, Franz H. "Varieties and Consequenses of Medieval Literacy and Illiteracy," *Speculum* 55 (1980): 237–65.

Becker, Seymour. "Contributions to a Nationalist Ideology: Histories of Russia in the First Half of the Nineteenth Century," *Russian History* 13 (1986): 331–53.

Bedos-Rezak, Brigitte, "Medieval Identity: A Sign and a Concept," *American Historical Review* 105 (2000): 1489–1533.

Begunov, Iu. K. "'Slovo inoe'—novonaidennoe proizvedenie russkoi publitsistiki XVI v. o bor'be Ivana III s zemlevladeniem tserkvi," *Trudy Otdela Drevnerusskoi Literatury* 20 (1964): 351–64.

Beliaev, L. A. *Drevnie monastyri Moskvy po dannym arkheologii*. Moscow, 1994.

———. *Russkoe srednevekovoe nadgrobie*. Moscow, 1996.

———. "Sobor Bogoiavlenskogo monastyria za Torgom i Troitskii sobor Troitse-Sergievoi lavry (Istoriko-khudozhestvennye paralleli)," in *Drevnerusskoe iskusstvo: Sergii Radonezhskii i khudozhestvennaia kul'tura Moskvy XIV–XV vv.* St. Petersburg, 1998. 400–409.

Belobrova, O. A. "O litsevom spiske Zhitiia Sergiia Radonezhskogo v biblioteke Petre I," in *Troitse-Sergieva lavra v istorii, kul'ture i dukhovnoi zhizni Rossii*, vol. 3 (2004). 176–203.

———. "Poslanie Epifaniia Kirillu Tverskomu," in *Sbornik proizvedenii literatury Drevnei Rusi*. Moscow, 1969. 398–403.

———. "Posol'stvo Konstantinopol'skogo Patriarkha Filofeiiu k Sergiiu Radonezhskomu," *Soobshcheniia Zakorskogo Gos. Istoriko-khudozhestvennogo muzeia-zapovednika* 2 (1958): 12–18.

Berry, Lloyd E., and Robert O. Crummey, eds. *Rude & Barbarous Kingdom: Russia in the Accounts of Sixteenth-Century English Voyagers*. Madison, Wis., 1968.

Bobrov, A. G. "Letopisnyi svod Mitropolita Fotiia (Problema rekonstruktsii teksta)," *Trudy Otdela drevnerusskoi literatury* 52 (2001): 98–137.

Bobrov, A. G., Prokhorov, G. M., and A. A. Semiachko. "Imitatsiia nauki: o knigi V. M. Klossa "Izbrannye trudy," t.1: "Zhitie Sergiia Radonezhskogo. Rukopisnaia traditsiia, zhizn' i chudesa, teksty," *Trudy Otdela drevnerusskoi literatury* 53 (2003): 418–45.

Bondarenko, Aleksandr. "Podvizhnik zemli russkoi," *Krasnaia zvezda*, no. 229 (8 October 1992). East View Information Services.

Borisov, N. S. "Moskovskie kniaz'ia i russkie mitropolity XIV veka," *Voprosii istorii* no. 8 (1986): 30–43.

———. *Russkaia tserkov' v politicheskoi bor'be XIV–XV vekov*. Moscow, 1986.

———. *Sergii Radonezhskii*. Moscow, 2001.

Børtnes, Jostein. *Visions of Glory. Studies in Early Russian Hagiography*. Oslo, 1988.

Bosley, Richard. "The Changing Profile of the Liturgical Calendar in Muscovy's Formative Years," in *Moskovskaia Rus' (1359–1584): kul'tura i istoricheskoe samosoznanie*. Ed. A. M. Kleimola, G. D. Lenhoff. Moscow, 1997. 26–38.

Bouchard, Constance. *Sword, Miter, and Cloister: Nobility and the Church in Burgandy, 980–1198*. Ithaca, NY, 1987.

Brown, Peter. *The Cult of the Saints: Its Rise and Function in Latin Christianity*. Chicago, 1981.

Browning, Robert. "Literacy in the Byzantine World," *Byzantine and Modern Greek Studies* 4 (1978): 39–54.

Briusova, V. G. "Spiski igumenov Troitse-Sergieva monastyria pervoi poloviny XVI v.," *Arkhiegraficheskii ezhegodnik za 1969 god* (1971): 292–95.

Brudny, Yitzhak M. *Reinventing Russia: Russian Nationalism and the Soviet State, 1953–1991*. Cambridge, Mass., 1998.

Budovnits, I. U. *Monastyri na Rusi i bor'ba s nimi krest'ian v XIV–XVI vv*. Moscow, 1966.

Bureichenko, I. I. "K istorii osnovaniia Troitse-Sergieva monastyria," *Soobshcheniia Zagorskogo gosudarstvennogo istoriko-khudozhestvennogo muzeia-zapovednika* 3 (1960): 5–40.

———. "K voprosu o date osnovaniia Troitse-Sergieva monastyria," *Soobshcheniia Zagorskogo gosudarstvennogo istoriko-khudozhestvennogo muzeia-zapovednika* 2 (1958): 3–12.

Burgess, Clive. "'Longing to be Prayed for': Death and Commemoration in an English Parish in the Later Middle Ages," in *The Place of the Dead: Death and Remembrance in Late Medieval and Early Modern Europe*. Ed. Bruce Gordon, Peter Marshall. Cambridge, Eng., 2000. 44–65.

Buseva-Davydova, I. L. "Novootkrytye ikony s izobrazheniem Prepodobnogo Sergiia Radonezhskogo iz chastnykh sobranii," in *Troitse-Sergieva lavra v istorii, kul'ture i dukhovnoi zhizni Rossii. IV mezhdunarodnaia konferentsiia, 29 sentiabria-1 oktiabria 2004 g. Tezisy dokladov*. Ed. G. S. Isaakov. Sergiev Posad, 2004. 37–40.

Bushkovitch, Paul. *Religion and Society in Russia: The Sixteenth and Seventeenth Centuries*. New York, 1992.

———. "The Limits of Hesychasm: Some Notes on Monastic Spirituality in Russia, 1300–1500," *Forschungen zur osteuropäischen Geschichte* 38 (1986): 97–109.

Byrnes, Robert F. "Kliuchevskii on the Multi-National Russian State," *Russian History* 13 (1986): 313–30.

Caviness, Madeline H. "Anchoress, Abbess, and Queen: Donors and Patrons or Intercessors and Matrons?" in *The Cultural Patronage of Medieval Women*. Ed. June Hall McCash. Athens, Ga., 1996. 104–54.

Cherepnin, L. V. *Obrazovanie russkogo tsentralizovannogo gosudarstva v XIV–XV vekakh*. Moscow, 1960.

———. *Russkie feodal'nye arkhivy XIV–XV vekov*. 2 vols. Moscow-Leningrad, 1948–51.

Cherkashina, G. P. "Ikony Troitse-Sergieva monastyria—svidteli i uchastniki voennykh sobytii XVIII–nachala XX v.," in *Troitse-Sergieva Lavra v istorii, kul'tury i dukhovnoi zhizni Rossi,* vol. 2 (2002). 462–76.

Cherkasova, M. S. "Aktovye istochniki o gorodskikh vladeniiakh Troitse-Sergieva monastyria v XV–XVII vekakh," in *Ekonomika, upravlenie, demografiia gorodov evropeiskoi Rossii XV–XVIII vekov.* Tver', 1999. 109–14.

———. "Akty Troitse-Sergieva monastyria XIV–XVI vv. kak istochnik po istorii ego zemlevladeniia," *Vestnik Moskovskogo gosudarstvennogo universiteta,* Ser. 8: *Istoriia* 4 (1981): 71–82.

———. "Formy raschislennoi sobstvennosti v votchine Troitse-Sergieva monastyria XV–XVI vv.," in *Feodalizm v Rossii.* Ed. V. I. Ianin. Moscow, 1987. 41–44.

———. *Krupnaia feodal'naia votchina v Rossii kontsa XVI–XVII vekov.* Moscow, 2004.

———. "Pozemel'nye akty kak istochnik dlia izucheniia religioznogo soznaniia srednevekovoi Rusi," *Drevniaia Rus'. Voprosi medievistiki,* no. 2 (8) (2002): 35–47.

———. "Rostovskie votchiny Troitse-Sergieva monastyria v nachale XVII vv.," in *Istoriia i kul'tura Rostovskoi zemli. 1993 god.* Rostov, 1994. 86–90.

———. "Zemlevladenie Troitse-Sergieva monastyria v iugo-podmoskov'e v XV–nach. XVII vv.," in *Monastyri v zhizni Rossii.* Comp. V. I. Osipov. Kaluga-Borovsk, 1997. 39–47.

———. *Zemlevladenie Troitse-Sergieva monastyria v XV–XVI vv.* Moscow, 1996.

Cherniavsky, Michael. "The Reception of the Council of Florence in Moscow," *Church History* 24 (1955): 347–59.

———. *Tsar and People: Studies in Russian Myths,* 2nd ed. New York, 1969.

Chernov, S. Z. "Rod Kutuzovykh i ego zemlevladenie na volokolamskom uezde v XV–XVI vv.," *Istoricheskaia genealogiia* 4 (1994): 49–59.

———. "Sel'skie monastyri XIV–XV vv. na severo-vostoke moskovskogo kniazhestva po arkheologicheskim dannym," *Rossiiskaia arkheologiia* 2 (1996): 111–30.

———. "Uspenskii Dubenskii Shavykin monastyr' v svete arkheologicheskikh dannykh," in *Kul'tura srednevekovoi Moskvy XIV–XVII vv.* Ed. L. A. Beliaev. Moscow, 1995. 123–55.

———. "Voskresenskaia zemlia Troitse-Sergieva monastyria: K integratsii metodiki arkheologii i spetsial'nykh istoricheskikh distsiplin," *Arkheograficheskii Ezhegodnik za 1981 god* (1982): 95–109.

———. "Votchina Voroninykh (po aktam Troitse-Sergieva monastyria)," *Vestnik Moskovskogo gosudarstvennogo universiteta,* Ser. 8: *Istoriia* no. 6 (1982): 84–95.

Chiniakova, G. P. "Zhitie Prepodobnogo Romana, igumena Blagoveshchenskogo Kirzhachskogo monastyria, uchenika Prepodobnogo Sergiia," *Makarievskie chteniia* 5 (1998): 222–35.

Chumachenko, Tatiana A. *Church and State in Soviet Russia: Russian Orthodoxy from World War II to the Khrushchev Years.* Transl. Edward E. Roslof. Armonk, NY, 2002.

Churakov, S. S. "Otrazhenie rublevskogo plana rospisi v stenopisi XVII v. Troitskogo sobora Troitse-Sergievoi lavry," in *Andrei Rublev i ego epokha. Sb. Statei.* Ed. M. V. Alpatov. Moscow, 1971. 194–212.

Clanchy, M. T. *From Memory to Written Record, England, 1066–1307*, 2nd ed. Oxford, 1993.

Cohn, Samuel K. Jr. *The Cult of Remembrance and the Black Death: Six Renaissance Cities in Central Italy*. Baltimore, 1992.

———. "The Place of the Dead in Flanders and Tuscany: Towards a Comparative History of the Black Death," in *The Place of the Dead: Death and Remembrance in Late Medieval and Early Modern Europe*. Ed. Bruce Gordon, Peter Marshall. New York, 2000. 17–43.

Degtev, Iu. A. *Riazan' pravoslavnaia*. Riazan', 1993.

Dergacheva, I. V. *Stanovlenie povestvovatel'nykh nachal v drevne-russkoi kul'ture XV–XVII vv. (na materiale sinodika)*. Munich, 1990.

Dmitriev, L. A. "Obzor redaktsii Skazaniia o Mamaevom poboishche," in *Povesti o Kulikovskoi Bitve*. Ed. M. N. Tikhomirov. Moscow, 1959. 449–80.

———. "Opisanie rukopisnykh spiskov Skazaniia o Mamaevom poboishche," in *Povesti o Kulikovskoi Bitve*. Ed. M. N. Tikhomirov. Moscow, 1959. 481–509.

Dmitrieva, R. P., T. V. Dianova, and L. M. Kostiukhina. *Knizhnye tsentry Drevnei Rusi: Iosifo-Volokolamskii monastyr' kak tsentr knizhnosti*. Leningrad, 1991.

Duffy, Eamon. *The Stripping of the Altars. Traditional Religion in England, c. 1400–c. 1580*. New Haven, 1992.

Dukhovnye i dogovornye gramoty velikikh i udel'nykh kniazei XIV–XVI vv. Ed. L. V. Cherepnin. Moscow-Leningrad, 1950.

Durkheim, Emile. *The Elementary Forms of Religious Life*. London, 1915.

Dykstra, Tom E. *Russian Monastic Culture: "Josephism" and the Iosifo-Volokolamsk Monastery, 1479–1607*. Munich, 2006.

Elesevich, S. "'Sluzhba prepodobnomu Sergiiu' sviashchenno-inoka Pakhomiia Serba i ei predshestvuiushchie gimnograficheskie formy," in *Troitse-Sergieva lavra v istorii, kul'ture i dukhovnoi zhiznii Rossi*, vol. 3 (2004). 121–32.

Emchenko, E. B. *Stoglav. Issledovanie i tekst*. Moscow, 2000.

———. "Zhenskie monastyri v Rossii," in *Monashestvo i monastyri v Rossii XI–XX veka: istoricheskie ocherki*. Ed. N. V. Sinitsina. Moscow, 2002. 245–84.

Ermolaev, I. P. *Kazanskii krai vo vtoroi polovine XVI–XVII vv. (Khronologicheskii perechen' dokumentov)*. Kazan', 1980.

Evseeva, A. M. "K voprosu o datirovke ikony 'Sergii Radonezhskii s 18 kleimami zhitiia' iz nadvratnoi tserkvi Troitse-Sergieva monastyria," in *Troitse-Sergieva lavra v istorii, kul'ture i dukhovnoi zhiznii Rossii*, vol. 4. Ed. G. S. Isaakov. Sergiev Posad, 2004. 31.

Farmer, Sharon. *Communities of Saint Martin: Legend and Ritual in Medieval Tours*. Ithaca, NY, 1991.

Fedotov, G. P. *The Russian Religious Mind. 2: The Middle Ages, the Thirteenth to the Fifteenth Centuries*. Ed. John Meyendorff. Cambridge, Mass., 1966.

Fedotov-Chekhovskii, A., comp. *Akty, otnosiashchiesia do grazhdanskoi raspravy drevnei Rossii*. 2 vols. Kiev, 1860.

Fennell, J. L. I. *The Emergence of Moscow, 1304–1359*. Berkeley, 1968.

Fine, John V. A., Jr. "The Muscovite Dynastic Crisis of 1497–1502," *Canadian Slavonic Papers*, 8 (1966): 198–215.

Finnegan, Ruth H. *Literacy and Orality: Studies in the Technology of Communication*. Oxford, Eng., 1988.

Finucan, R. C. "Sacred Corpse, Profane Carrion: Social Ideals and Death Rituals in the Later Middle Ages," in *Mirrors of Mortality: Studies in the Social History of Death*. Ed. Joachim Whaley. New York, 1981. 40–60.

Florenskii, Pavel. "Troitse-Sergieva Lavra i Rossiia," in *Komissiia po okhrane pamiatnikov iskusstva i stariny Troitse-Sergievoi Lavry*. Moscow, 1919. 3–29.

Franklin, Simon, and Emma Widdis, eds. *National Identity in Russian Culture*. Cambridge, Eng., 2004.

Froianov, I. Ia. *Kievskaia Rus': Ocherki sotsial'no-politicheskoi istorii*. Leningrad, 1980.

Gaganova, M. A. "Sud'ba moshchei prepodobnogo Sergiia (sobytiia 1919–1921 gg.)," in *Troitse-Sergiev Lavra v istorii, kul'ture i dukhovnoi zhizni Rossii*, vol. 3 (2002). 84–94.

Gal'chenko, Mariia G. "Troitse-Sergievskie rukopisi kontsa XIV–pervoi poloviny XV v. i problema vtorogo iuzhnoslavianskogo vliianiia," pt. 1: "Konets XIV–pervaia chetvert' XV vv.," *Palaeoslavica* 8 (2000): 18–96.

Geary, Patrick. *Living with the Dead in the Middle Ages*. Ithaca, NY, 1994.

———. *Phantoms of Remembrance: Memory and Oblivion at the End of the First Millennium*. Princeton, NJ, 1994.

Geertz, Clifford. "Centers, Kings, and Charisma: Reflections on the Symbolics of Power," in *Rites of Power: Symbolism, Ritual, and Politics since the Middle Ages*. Ed. Sean Wilentz. Philadelphia, 1985. 13–38.

Girshberg, V. B. "Nadpis' 1501 g. na Troitse-Sergievoi lavry," *Sovetskaia arkheologiia* no. 3 (1959): 227–29.

Goehrke, Carsten. "Die Witwe im alten Russland," *Forschungen zur osteuropäischen Geshichte* 38 (1986): 64–66.

———. *Die Wüstungen in der Moskauer Rus': Studien zur Siedlungs-, Bevölkerungs- und Sozialgeschichte*. Wiesbaden, 1968.

Goldfrank, David. "Etapy i itogi poluvekovoi istorii issledovanii o Nile Sorskom i perevodov ego sochinenii," in *Nil Sorskii v kul'ture i knizhnosti Drevnei Rusi*. Ed. A. I. Alekseev. St. Petersburg, 2008. 9–19.

———, ed. and transl. *The Monastic Rule of Josef Volotsky*. Kalamazoo, Mich., 1983.

Golubinskii, Evgenii. *Istoriia russkoi tserkvi*. 2 vols. Moscow, 1900–11.

———. *Prepodobnyi Sergii Radonezhskii i sozdannaia im Troitskaia Lavra*. Moscow, 1892.

Gonneau, Pierre. "Fonctions de l'iconographie dans la diffusion du culte des saints moines Russes (XIVe–XVIe S.)," in *Fonctions sociales et politiques du culte des saints dans les sociétés de rite grec et latin au Moyen Âge et à l'époque moderne*. Ed. Marek Derwich and Michel Dmitriev. Wroclaw, 1999. 283–325.

———. *La Maison de la Sainte Trinité: un grand-monastère Russe du moyen-âge tardif (1345–1533)*. Paris, 1993.

———. "Les relations entre le temporel et le spirituel dans la Russie muscovite. Pistes de recherche," *Revue des études slaves* 70 (1998): 485–95.

———. "Les trublions au monastère (bezčinniki monastyrskie): Indiscipline et partage du pouvoir à la Trinité-Saint Serge au XVe siècle," *Revue des études slaves* 63 (1991): 195–206.

———. "The Trinity Sergius Brotherhood in State and Society," in *Moskovskaia Rus' (1389–1584): Kul'tura i istoricheskoe samosoznanie*. Ed. A. M. Kleimola, G. D. Lenhoff. Moscow, 1997. 118–45.

Goody, Jack. *The Development of the Family and Marriage in Europe*. New York, 1983.

Gorskii, A. A. *Moskva i Orda*. Moscow, 2000.

Gorskii, A. D. "Dinamika bor'by krest'ian za zemliu v severo-vostochnoi Rusi XV–nachala XVI veka," *Istoriia SSSR* no. 3 (1972): 85–105.

Gorskii, A. V. *Istoricheskoe opisanie Sviato-Troitskiia Sergievy Lavry v 1841 g.* 2 vols. Moscow, 1890.

Gorskii, A. V., and K. I. Nevostruev. *Opisanie slavianskikh rukopisei Moskovskoi Sinodal'noi biblioteki*. 3 vols. Moscow, 1855–1917. repr. Wiesbaden, 1964.

Graham, Hugh, ed. and transl. "'The Brutal Rule of Ivan Vasil'evich Tyrant of Muscovy' (Albert Schlichting on Ivan Groznyi)," *Canadian-American Slavic Studies* 9 (1975): 204–72.

Gurevich, A. Ia. *Categories of Medieval Culture*. Transl. G. L. Campbell. London, 1985.

Guseva, E. K. "Nekotorye voprosy izucheniia 'Troitsy' Andreia Rubleva," in *Troitse-Sergieva Lavra v istorii, kul'ture i dukhovnoi zhizni Rossii. Tezisy dokladov*. Ed. K. V. Bobkov. Sergiev Posad, 2000. 63–66.

———. "Ob ikone Troitsy iz Dukhovskogo khrama (v sobranii Sergievo-Posadskogo muzeia)," in *Troitse-Sergiev Lavra v istorii, kul'ture i dukhovnoi zhizni Rossii*, vol. 1 (2000). 223–38.

———. "Osobennosti slozheniia ikonografii 'Sergieva videniia' ('Iavleniia Bogomateri prepodobnomu Sergiiu)," *Iskusstvo srednevekovoi Rusi. Materialy i issledovaniia* 12 (1999): 120–38.

———. "Tsarskie vrata kruga Andreiia Rubleva," in *Drevnerusskoe iskusstvo. Sergii Radonezhskii i khudozhestvennaia kul'tura Moskvy XIV–XV vv.* St. Petersburg, 1998. 295–311.

Halperin, Charles J. "Text and Textology: Salmina's Dating of the Chronicle Tales about Dmitrii Donskoi," *Slavonic and East European Review* 79 (2001): 248–63.

———. "The Russian Land and the Russian Tsar: The Emergence of Muscovite Ideology, 1350–1408," *Forschungen zur osteuropäischen Geschichte* 23 (1976): 7–103.

Head, Thomas. *Hagiography and the Cult of Saints: The Diocese of Orléans, 800–1200*. Cambridge, Eng., 1990.

Hellie, Richard. "The Great Paradox of the Seventeenth Century: The Stratification of Muscovite Society and the Individuation of High Culture, Especially Literature," in *O Rus! Studia litteraria slavica in honorem Hugh McLean*. Ed. Simon Karlinsky et al. Oakland, Calif., 1995. 116–28.

———. *Slavery in Russia, 1450–1725*. Chicago, 1982.

———. "What Happened? How Did He Get Away with It?: Ivan Groznyi's Paranoia and the Problem of Institutional Restraints," *Russian History* 14 (1987): 199–24.

Helt, J. S. W. "Women, Memory and Will-Making in Elizabethan England," in *The Place of the Dead: Death and Remembrance in Late Medieval and Early Modern Europe*. Ed. Bruce Gorden, Peter Marshall. Cambridge, Eng., 2000. 188–205.

Herberstein, Sigismund. *Zapiski o Moskovii*. Transl. A. I. Maleina, A. V. Nazarenko. Moscow, 1988.

Herlihy, David. "Land, Family and Women in Continental Europe, 701–1200," in *Women in Medieval Society*. Ed. Susan Mosher Stuard. Philadelphia, 1976. 13–45.

———. *Women, Family and Society in Medieval Europe*. Providence, 1995.

Hobsbawm, Eric. "Introduction: Inventing Traditions," in *The Invention of Tradition*. Ed. Eric Hobsbawm, T. Ranger. Cambridge, Eng., 1983. 1–14.

Hughes, Diane Owen. "From Brideprice to Dowry in Mediterranean Europe," in *The Marriage Bargain: Women and Dowries in European History*. Ed. Marian A. Kaplan. New York, 1985. 13–58.

Iablonskii, V. *Pakhomii Serb i ego agiograficheskie pisaniia. Biograficheskii i bibliograficheski-literaturnyi ocherk*. St. Petersburg, 1908.

Innes, Matthew. "Memory, Orality and Literacy in Early Medieval Society," *Past and Present* 158 (Feb. 1998): 3–36.

Ioasafovskaia letopis'. Ed. A. A. Zimin. Moscow, 1957.

Ivina, L. I. "Kopiinye knigi aktov Troitse-Sergieva monastyria XVII v.," *Zapiski Otdela rukopisei Gosudarstvennoi biblioteki im. V. I. Lenina* 24 (1961): 5–44.

———. *Krupnaia votchina servero-vostochnoi Rusi: kontsa XIV–pervoi poloviny XVI v*. Moscow, 1979.

———. "Troitskii sbornik materialov po istorii zemlevladeniia russkogo gosudarstva XVI–XVII vv.," *Zapiski Otdela rukopisei Gosudarstvennoi biblioteki im. V. I. Lenina* 27 (1965): 149–63.

———. *Vnutrennee osvoenie zemel' Rossii v XVI v*. Leningrad, 1985.

Kaiser, Daniel H. "Death and Dying in Early Modern Russia," in *Major Problems in Early Modern Russian History*. Ed. Nancy Shields Kollmann. New York, 1992. 217–57.

———. "Marking a Life: The History and Meaning of Muscovite Gravestones." Paper read 19 November 1999 at convention of the American Association for the Advancement of Slavic Studies, St. Louis, Mo.

———. "Social Cohesion and Death Rituals in Early Modern Russia." Paper read 28 December 1984 at meeting of the American Historical Association, Chicago.

Kämpfer, Frank. "Die Eroberung von Kazan 1552 als Gegenstand der zeitgenössischen russischen Historiographie," *Forschungen zur osteuropäischen Geschichte* 14 (1969): 7–161.

Kargalov, V. V. *Vneshne-politicheskie faktory razvitiia fedoal'noi Rusi: Feodal'naia Rus' i kochevniki*. Moscow, 1967.

Kashtanov, S. M. *Aktovaia arkheografiia*. Moscow, 1998.

———. "The Centralized State and Feudal Immunities in Russia," in *Major Problems in Early Modern Russian History*. Ed Nancy Shields Kollmann. New York, 1992. 109–28.

———. "Deiatel'nost' pravoslavnykh monastyrei v Srednem Povol'zhe v epokhu Ivana Groznogo (1551–1556 gg.)," *Forschungen zur osteuropäischen Geschichte* 63 (2004): 293–309.

———. *Iz istorii russkogo srednevekovogo istochnika. Akty X–XVI vv.* Moscow, 1996.

———. "K istorii feodal'nogo zemlevladeniia v sviiazhskom uezde v 70-kh godakh XVI v.," *Uchenye zapiski Kazanskogo gosudarstvennogo pedagogicheskogo instituta (Istoriografiia i istochnikovedenie: Voprosy metodologii issledovaniia)* 184 (1978): 134–42.

———. "Kopiinye knigi Troitse-Sergieva monastyria XVI veka," *Zapiski Otdela rukopisei Gosudarstvennoi biblioteki im. V. I. Lenina* 18 (1956): 3–47.

———. "Monastyrskie dokumenty o politicheskoi bor'be serediny XVI v.," *Arkheograficheskii ezhegodnik za 1973 g.*, 1974: 29–42.

———. "Obshchie zhalovannye gramoty Troitse-Sergievu monastyriu 1550, 1577, i 1578 gg.," *Zapiski Otdela rukopisei Gosudarstvennoi biblioteki im. Lenina* 28 (1966): 104–41.

———. *Ocherki russkoi diplomatiki*. Moscow, 1970.

———. "Po sledam Troitskikh kopiinykh knig XVI v.," *Zapiski Otdela rukopisei Gosudarstvennoi biblioteki im. V. I. Lenina* 38 (1977): 30–63; 40 (1979): 4–58; 42 (1981): 5–63; 43 (1982): 4–37.

———. *Russkaia diplomatika*. Moscow, 1988.

———. *Sotsial'no-politicheskaia istoriia Rossii kontsa XV–pervoi poloviny XVI veka*. Moscow, 1967.

———. "Vnutrennaia torgovlia i spros krupnykh zemlevladel'tsev na predmety potreblenii XIV–XV vv.," *Istoriia SSSR*, no. 1 (1977): 144–60.

———. "Vozniknovenie russkogo zemlevladeniia v Kazanskom krae (dokumenty)," *Uchenye zapiski Kazanskogo gosudarstvennogo pedagogicheskogo instituta (Iz istroii Tatarii)* 116 (1973): 3–35.

———. "Zemel'no-immunitetnaia politika russkogo pravitel'stva v Kazanskom krae v 50-kh godakh XVI v.," *Uchenye zapiski Kazanskogo gosudarstvennogo pedagogicheskogo instituta (Iz istorii Tatarii)* 80 (1970): 164–203.

Kavel'makher, V. V. "Nikonovskaia tserkov' Troitse-Sergieva monastyria: Avtor i data postroiki, in *Kul'tura srednevekovoi Moskvy XVII vek*. Ed. L. A. Beliaev. Moscow, 1999. 40–95.

———. "Zametki o proiskhozhdenii 'Zvenigorodskogo china,'" in *Drevnerusskoe iskusstvo. Sergii Radonezhskii i khudozhestvennaia kul'tura Moskvy XIV–XV vv.* St. Petersburg, 1998. 196–216.

Kazakova, N. A. *Vassian Patrikeev i ego sochineniia*. Moscow-Leningrad, 1960.

Keenan, Edward L. "Coming to Grips with the Kazanskaya Istoriya: Some Observations on Old Answers and New Questions," *The Annals of the Ukrainian Academy of Arts and Sciences in the United States* 11, pts. 1–2 (1964–68): 143–83.

Kenworthy, Scott M. "Memory Eternal: The Five-Hundred Year Commemoration of

St. Sergius of Radonezh," in *The Trinity-Sergius Lavra in Russian History and Culture*. Ed. Vladimir Tsurikov. Jordanville, NY, 2005. 24–55.

———. "The Revival of Monasticism in Modern Russia: The Trinity-Sergius Lavra." Ph.D. dissertation, Brandeis University. Waltham, Mass., 2001.

Kertzer, David I. *Ritual, Politics and Power*. New Haven, 1988.

Khlebnikova, N. A. "Maloizvestnye proizvedeniia masterskoi Sof'ii Paleologi," in *Pamiatniki kul'tury. Novye otkrytiia. Ezhegodnik 1976 g.* (1977): 196–203.

Khoroshkevich, A. L. "K vzaimootnosheniiam kniazei moskovskogo doma vo vtoroi polovine XIV–nachale XV veka," *Voprosy istorii* no. 6 (1980): 170–74.

———. "'Nezvanyi gost" na prazdnikakh srednevekovoi Rusi," in *Feodalizm v Rossii*. Ed. V. L. Ianin. Moscow, 1987. 184–92.

"Khronologicheskoi perechen' immunitetnykh gramot XVI veka," pt. 1, ed. S. M. Kashtanov, in *Arkheograficheskii ezhegodnik za 1957 g.*, 1958: 302–76; pt. 2, ed. S. M. Kashtanov, in *Arkheograficheskii ezhegodnik za 1960 g.*, 1962: 129–200; pt. 3, ed. S. M. Kashtanov, V. D. Nazarov and V. N. Floria, in *Arkheograficheskii ezhegodnik za 1968 g.*,1968: 197–253.

Kirichenko, E. I. *Khram Khrista Spasitelia v Moskve*. Moscow, 1992.

Kirichenko, L. A. *Aktovyi material Troitse-Sergieva monastyria 1584–1641 gg. kak istochnik po istorii zemlevladeniia i khoziaistva. Moscow, 2006.*

———. "Aktovyi material Troitse-Sergieva monastyria kontsa XVI–serediny XVII v. kak istochnik sostava monastyrskoi administratsii," *Soobshcheniia Sergievo-posadskogo muzeia-zapovednika* (2000): 38–65.

———. *Akty zemlevladeniia i khoziaistva Troitse-Sergieva monastyria, 1584–1641.* Moscow, 2006.

———. "Torgovye ekspeditsii Troitse-Sergieva monastyria po aktovomu materialu kontsa XVI–nachala XVII v.," in *Troitse-sergieva lavra v istorii, kul'ture i dukhovnoi zhizni Rossii*, vol. 3 (2004). 51–61.

Kirichenko, L. A., and S. V. Nikolaeva. *Kormovaia kniga Troitse-Sergieva monastyria 1674 g. Issledovanie i publikatsiia*. Moscow, 2008.

Kirillin', V. M. "Epifanii Premudryi kak agiograf prepodobnogo Sergiia Radonezhskogo. Problema avtorstva," in *Germenevtika drevnerusskoi literatrury* 7, pt. 2 (1994): 264–75.

Kisterev, S. N. "Delo Agrafeny Volynskoi i "Otvet" Mitropolita Makarii Ivanu IV," *Arkheograficheskii ezhegodnik za 1998 g.* (1999): 71–77.

Kivelson, Valerie A. "The Effects of Partible Inheritance: Gentry Families and the State in Muscovy," *Russian Review* 53 (1994): 197–212.

Kleimola, Ann. "'In Accordance with the Canons of the Holy Apostles': Muscovite Dowries and Women's Property Rights," *Russian Review* 51 (1992): 204–29.

———. "Good Breeding, Moscow Style: 'Horse Culture' in Early Modern Rus'," *Forschungen zur osteuropäischen Geschichte* 50 (1955): 199–233.

———. "Women's Cultural Patronage in Early Modern Rus': Was Muscovy Europe?," in *Mesto Rossii v Evrope (Materialy mezhdunarodnoi konferentsii)*: *Knigi po rusistike* 5. Budapest, 1999. 103–7.

Kleinberg, Aviad. *Prophets in Their Own Country: Living Saints and the Making of Sainthood in the Later Middle Ages*. Chicago, 1992.

Kliuchevskii, V. O. *Drevnerusskie zhitiia sviatykh kak istoricheskii istochnik*. Moscow, 1871; repr. The Hague, 1968, Moscow, 1988.

———. *Sochineniia*. 8 vols. Moscow, 1956–1959.

———. "Znachenie Prepodobnogo Sergiia dlia russkogo naroda i gosudarstva," *Bogoslovskii vestnik* no. 11 (1892): 1–15.

Kloss, B. M. "Determining the Authorship of the Trinity Chronicle," in *Medieval Russian Culture*, vol. 2. Ed. Michael S. Flier and Daniel Rowland. Berkeley, 1994. 57–72.

———. "Ikony Ivana Groznogo i ego sem'i v Troitse-Sergievom monastyre," in *Troitse-Sergieva Lavra v istorii, kul'ture i dukhovnoi zhizni Rossii*, vol. 3 (2004). 290–301.

———. *Izbrannye trudy*. 2 vols. Moscow, 1998–2001.

———. "K izucheniiu biografii prepodobnogo Sergiia Radonezhskogo," in *Drevnerusskoe iskusstvo: Sergii Radonezhskii i khudozhestvennaia kul'tura Moskvy XIV–XV vv.* St. Petersburg, 1998. 11–15.

———. "K izucheniiu traditsii knigopisaniia v Troitse-Sergievom monastyre," *Istoriia i paleografiia*, 1993: 23–26.

———. *Nikonovskii svod i russkie letopisi XVI–XVII vekov*. Moscow, 1980.

———. "Ob atributsii nekotorykh poslanii iz formuliarnika mitropolita Simona," *Tserkov' v istorii Rossii* 1 (1997): 30–55.

———. "Ob avtore i vremeni sozdaniia 'Skazaniia o mamaevom poboishche,'" in *In Memoriam. Sbornik pamiati Ia. S. Lur'e*. Ed. N. M. Botvinnik, I. I. Vaneev. St. Petersburg, 1997. 253–62.

———. "O sud'be zakhoroneniia Kniazia Andreia Radonezhskogo," in *Troitse-Sergieva Lavra v istorii, kul'tury i dukhovnoi zhizni Rossii*, vol. 1 (2000). 24–28.

———. "Zametki po istorii Troitse-Sergievoi Lavry XV–XVII vv.," Trudy *po istorii Troitse-Sergievoi Lavry* 7 (1998): 4–11.

———. "Zhitiia Sergiia i Nikona Radonezhskikh v russkoi pis'mennosti," in AN SSSR, In-t. slavianovedeniia i balkanistiki. *Metodicheskie rekomendatsii po opisaniiu slaviano-russkikh rukopisnykh knig*. Moscow, 1990. 271–96.

Kobrin, V. B. "Iz istorii zemel'noi politiki v gody oprichniny," *Istoricheskii arkhiv* no. 3 (1958): 152–60.

———. *Materialy genealogii kniazhesko-boiarskoi aristokratii XV–XVI vv.* Moscow, 1995.

———. *Vlast' i sobstvennost' v srednevekovoi Rossii*. Moscow, 1985.

Kochekaev, B.-A. B. *Nogaisko-Russkie otnosheniia v XV–XVIII vv.* Alma-Ata, 1988.

Kokorina, S. I. "K voprosu o sostave i plane avtorskogo teksta 'Kazanskoi istorii,'" *Trudy Otdela drevnerusskoi literatury* 12 (1956): 576–85.

Kollmann, Nancy Shields. *By Honor Bound. State and Society in Early Modern Russia*. Ithaca, NY, 1999.

———. "Consensus Politics: The Dynastic Crisis of the 1490s Reconsidered," *Russian Review* 45 (1986): 235–67.

———. *Kinship and Politics: The Making of the Muscovite Political System, 1345–1547*. Stanford, 1987.

———. "Pilgrimage, Procession and Symbolic Space in Sixteenth-Century Russian Politics," in *Medieval Russian Culture*, vol. 2. Ed. Michael S. Flier and Daniel Rowland. Berkeley, 1994. 163–81.

———. "The Boyar Clan and Court Politics: The Founding of the Muscovite Political System," *Cahiers du monde russe et soviétique* 23 (1982): 5–31.

———. "The Grand Prince in Muscovite Politics: The Problem of Genre in Sources on Ivan's Minority," *Russian History* 14 (1987): 293–313.

Kolycheva, E. I. *Agrarnyi stroi Rossii XVI veka*. Moscow, 1987.

———. "Pravoslavnye monastyri vtoroi poloviny XV–XVI veka," in *Monashestvo i monastyri v Rossii, XI–XX veka*. Ed. N. V. Sinitsyna. Moscow, 2002. 81–115.

Konev, S. V. "Sinodikologiia, pt. 1: Klassifikatsiia istochnikov," *Istoricheskaia genealogiia* 1 (1993): 7–15.

Kopanev, A. I. *Istoriia zemlevladeniia Belozerskogo kraia XV–XVI vv.* Moscow-Leningrad, 1951.

———. "K voprosu o strukture zemlevladeniia na Dvine v XV–XVI vv.," in *Voprosy agrarnoi istorii. Materialy nauchnoi konferentsii po istorii sel'skogo khoziaistva i krest'ianstva evropeiskogo severa SSSR*. Vologda, 1968. 442–62.

———. "Nezemel'cheskaia volost' v XVI–XVII vv.," in *Krest'ianstvo i klassovaia bor'ba v feodal'noi Rossii*. Ed. N. E. Nosov. Leningrad, 1967. 176–94.

Koretskii, V. I. "Pravaia gramota ot 30 noiabria 1618 g. Troitse-Sergievu monastyriu (Iz istorii monastyrskogo zemlevladeniia XIV–XVI vv.)," *Zapiski Otdela rukopisei Gosudarstvennoi biblioteki im. V. I. Lenina* 21 (1959): 173–219.

Krichevskii, B. V. *Russkie mitropolity (tserkov' i vlast' XIV veka)*. St. Petersburg, 1996.

Kruglik, G. M. "Zemlevladenie Troitse-Sergieva monastyria v period feodal'noi voiny (1425–1453 gg.)," in *Agrarnyi stroi v feodal'noi Rossii XV–nachalo XX vv.* Moscow, 1986. 4–25.

Kuchkin, V. A. "Antiklossitsizm," *Drevniaia Rus'. Voprosy mediavistiki*, pt. 1, no. 1 (2002): 113–23; pt. 2, no. 3 (2002): 121–29; pt. 3, no. 4 (2002): 98–113; pt. 4, no. 1 (2003): 112–18; pt. 5, no. 2 (2003): 127–33; pt. 6, no. 3 (2003): 112–30; pt. 7, no. 4 (2003): 100–22.

———. "Dmitrii Donskoi i Sergii Radonezhskii v kanun Kulikovskoi bitvy," in *Tserkov', obshchestvo i gosudarstvo v feodal'noi Rossii*. Ed. A. I. Klibanov. Moscow, 1990. 103–25.

———. *Formirovanie gosudarstvennoi territorii severo-vostochnoi Rusi v X–XIV vv.* Moscow, 1984.

———. "Goroda severo-vostochnoi Rusi v XIII–XV vekakh (Chislo i politiko-geograficheskoe razmeshchenie," *Istoriia SSSR* no. 6 (1990): 72–85.

———. "Nachalo moskovskogo Simonova monastyria," in *Kul'tura srednevekovoi Moskvy XIV–XVII vv.* Ed. L. A. Beliaev. Moscow, 1995. 113–22.

———. "O vremeni napisaniia Slovo pokhval'nogo Sergiiu Radonezhskomu Epifaniia Premudrogo" in *Ot Drevnei Rusi k Rossii novogo vremeni*. Ed. A V. Iurasov. Moscow, 2003. 407–19.

———. "Russkie istoriki o Sergii Radonezhskom," *Otechestvo: Kraevedcheskii al'manakh*, 3 (1992): 5–28.

———. "Sergii Radonezhskii," *Voprosy istorii* no. 10 (1992): 75–92.

———. "Sergii Radonezhskii i bor'ba za mitropolich'iu kafedru vseia Rusi v 70–80e gody XIV v." in *Kul'tura slavian i Rus'*. Ed. Iu. S. Kukushkin. Moscow, 1998. 353–60.

———. "Sergii Radonezhskii i 'Filofeevskii krest'" in *Drevnerusskoe iskusstvo: Sergii Radonezhskii i khudozhestvennaia kul'tura Moskvy XIV-XV vv.* St. Petersburg, 1998. 16–20.

———. "Spodvizhnik Dmitriia donskogo," *Voprosy istorii* no. 8 (1979): 104–16.

———. "Zemel'nye priobreteniia moskovskikh kniazei v Rostovskom kniazhestve v XIV v.," in *Vostochnaia Evropa v drevnosti i srednevekov'e*. Ed. L. V. Cherepnin. Moscow, 1978. 185–92.

Kulikovskaia bitva. Sbornik statei. Ed. L. G. Beskrovnyi. Moscow, 1980.

Kulikovskaia bitva v istorii i kul'ture nashei rodine. Ed. B. A. Rybakov. Moscow, 1983.

Kuntsevich, G. Z. "Dva rasskaza o pokhodakh Tsaria Ivana Vasil'evicha Groznogo na Kazan' v 1550 i 1552 godakh," *Pamiatniki drevnei pis'mennosti i iskusstva* 130. St. Petersburg, 1898. Appendix, 23–35.

Kuzmina, V. D. "Drevnerusskie pis'mennye istochniki o Andree Rubleve," in *Andrei Rublev i ego epokha. Sb. statei*. Ed. M. V. Alpatov. Moscow, 1971. 103–24.

Langer, Lawrence N. "Plague and the Russian Countryside: Monastic Estates in the Late Fourteenth and Fifteenth Centuries," *Canadian-American Slavic Studies* 10 (1976): 351–68.

Lavrov, A. S. *Koldovstvo i religiia v Rossii, 1700–1740 gg.* Moscow, 2000.

Lazarev, V. N. *Andrei Rublev i ego shkola*. Moscow, 1966.

———. *Vizantiiskoe i drevnerusskoe iskusstvo: Stat'i i materialy.* Moscow, 1978.

Lenhoff, Gail D., and Janet Martin. "Marfa Boretskaia, *Posadnitsa* of Novgorod: A Reconsideration of Her Legend and Her Life," *Slavic Review* 59 (2000): 343–68.

Levy, Sandra. "Women and the Control of Property in Sixteenth-Century Moscow," *Russsian History* 10 (1983): 201–12.

Lifshits, L. I. "Ikonografiia Iavleniia Bogomateri prepodobnomu Sergiiu Radonezhskomu i motify teofanii v iskusstve kontsa XIV–nachala XV v.," in *Drevnerusskoe iskusstvo. Sergii Radonezhskii i khudozhestvennaia kul'tura Moskvy XIV–XV vv.* St. Petersburg, 1998. 79–94.

Likhachev, D. S., and Ia. S. Lur'e. *Poslaniia Ivana Groznogo*. Moscow, 1951.

Luchinskii, G. "Troitse-Sergieva Lavra" in *Entsiklopedicheskii slovar,*" 82 vols. Ed. F. A. Brokhaus and I. A. Efron'. St. Petersburg, 1890–1904. 33: 872–73.

Lur'e, Ia. S. *Dve istorii Rusi XV veka*. St. Petersburg, 1994.

———. *Ideologicheskaia bor'ba v russkoi publitsistike kontsa XV–nachala XVI veka.* Moscow-Leningrad, 1960.

———. "Kak ustanovilas' avtokefaliia russkoi tserkvi v XV v., *Vospomogatel'nye istoricheskie distsipliny* 23 (1991): 181–98.

———. *Obshcherusskie letopisi XIV–XV vv.* Leningrad, 1976.

Maiasova, N. A. *Drevnerusskoe shit'e.* Moscow, 1971.

———. "Drevnerusskoe litsevoe shit'e iz sobraniia Kirillo-Belozerskogo monastyria," in *Drevne-russkoe iskusstvo: Khudozhestvennye pamiatniki russkogo severa.* Ed. G. V. Popov. Moscow, 1989. 203–33.

———. "Khudozhestvennoe shit'e," in *Troitse-Sergieva Lavra. Khudozhestvennye pamiatniki.* Ed. N. N. Voronin, V. V. Kostochkin. Moscow, 1968. 112–39.

———. "Masterskaia khudozhestvennogo shit'ia kniazei Staritskikh," *Soobshcheniia Zagorskogo gosudarstvennogo istoriko-khudozhestvennogo muzeia-zapovednika* 3 (1960): 41–64.

———. "O datirovke drevnei kopii 'Troitsy' Andreia rubleva iz ikonostasa Troitskogo sobora," *Soobshcheniia Zagorskogo gosudarstvennogo istoriko-khudozhestvennogo muzeia-zapovednika* 3 (1960): 170–74.

———. "Obraz prepodobnogo Sergiia Radonezhskogo v drevnerusskom shit'e (K voprosu ob ikonografii)," in *Drevnerusskoe iskusstvo. Sergii Radonezhskii i khudozhestvennaia kul'tura Moskvy XIV–XV vv.* St. Petersburg, 1998. 40–53.

Makarii (Veretennikov), Archimandrit. "Kelar' Troitse-Sergievoi obiteli starets Andrian Angelov, *Al'fa i omega* no. 2 (1995): 117–25.

———. *Moskovskii Mitropolit Makarii i ego vremia.* Moscow, 1996.

———. "Pervyi namestnik vozrozhdennoi Lavry," in *Troitse-Sergieva lavra v istorii, Kul'ture i dukhovnoi zhizni Rossii*, vol. 2 (2002). 185–192.

———. "Svidetel'stvo istochnikov o rostovskom arkhiepiskope Nikandre (1549–1566)," *Tserkov' v istorii Rossii* 2 (1998): 66–80.

Malinin, V. *Starets Eleazarova monastyria Filofei i ego poslaniia.* Kiev, 1901.

Mandelbaum, David G. "Social Uses of Funeral Rites," in *The Meaning of Death.* Ed. Herman Feifel. New York, 1959. 189–217.

Man'kov, A. B. *Tseny i ikh dvizhenie v russkom gosudarstve XVI veka.* Moscow-Leningrad, 1951.

Manushina, T. N. *Khudozhestvennoe shit'e drevnei Rusi v sobranii Zagorskogo muzeia. Katalog.* Moscow, 1983.

Marshall, Peter. *Beliefs and the dead in Reformation England.* Oxford, 2002.

Martin, Janet. "Economic Development in the Varzuga Fishing Volost' During the Reign of Ivan IV," *Russian History* 14 (1987): 315–32.

———. *Medieval Russia, 980–1584.* Cambridge, Eng., 1995.

———. "Mobility, Forced Resettlement and Regional Identity in Muscovy," in *Moskovskaia Rus' (1389–1584): Kul'tura i istoricheskoe samosoznanie.* Ed. A. M. Kleimola, G. D. Lenhoff. Moscow, 1997. 431–49.

Martin, Russell. "Gifts for the Dead: Death, Kinship and Commemoration in Muscovy," *Russian History* 26 (1999): 171–202.

Matejic, Predrag. "Rediscovered Texts from the *Life of St. Sergius of Radonezh.* Understanding Russia and Russian Orthodoxy in the 16th Century," in *The Trinity-Sergius Lavra in Russian History and Culture.* Ed. Vladimir Tsurikov. Jordanville, NY, 2005. 251–98.

Matvei, Arkhimandrit. "Liturgicheskie traditsii Troitse-Sergievoi Lavry, *Bogoslovskie trudy* 29 (1989): 194–200.

Mauss, Marcel. *The Gift: Forms and Functions for Exchange in Archaic Societies*. Transl. Ian Cunnison. New York, 1967.

McCash, June Hall. "The Cultural Patronage of Medieval Women: An Overview," in *The Cultural Patronage of Medieval Women*. Ed. June Hall McCash. Athens, Ga., 1996. 1–49.

McLaughlin, Megan. *Consorting with Saints: Prayer for the Dead in Early Medieval France*. Ithaca, NY, 1994.

Meyendorff, John. *Byzantine Theology*. New York, 1974.

———. *Byzantium and the Rise of Russia: A Study of Byzantino-Russian Relations in the Fourteenth Century*. Cambridge, Eng., 1981.

———. "O vizantiiskom isikhazme i ego rol' v kul'turnom i istoricheskom razvitii vostochoi Evropy v XIV veke," *Trudy Otdela drevnerusskoi literatury* 29 (1974): 291–305.

Miller, David B. "Counting Monks: Towards an Estimation of the Size and Composition of the Monastic Community of the Trinity-Sergius Monastery in the First One Hundred Sixty Years of its Existence," *Forschungen zur osteuropäischen Geschichte* 58 (2001): 175–84.

———. "Creating Legitimacy: Ritual, Ideology, and Power in Sixteenth-Century Russia," *Russian History* 21 (1994): 289–301.

———. "The Cult of Saint Sergius of Radonezh and Its Political Uses," *Slavic Review* 52 (1993): 680–99.

———. "Donors to the Trinity-Sergius Monastery as a Community of Venerators: Origins, 1360s–1462," in *Moskovskaia Rus' (1359–1584): kul'tura i istoricheskoe samosoznanie*. Ed. A. M. Kleimola, G. D. Lenhoff. Moscow, 1997. 540–74.

———. "How the Trinity-Sergius Monastery Got Governance, Got Godunov's Wrath and Got New Life," *Russian History* 33 (2006): 447–53.

———. "Monumental Building as an Indicator of Economic Trends in Northern Rus' in the Late Kievan and Mongol Periods, 1138–1462," *American Historical Review* 94 (1989): 360–90.

———. "Motives for Donations to the Trinity-Sergius Monastery, 1392–1605: Gender Matters," *Essays in Medieval Studies* 14 (1998): 91–106.

———. "Official History in the Reign of Ivan Groznyi and Its Seventeenth-Century Imitators," *Russian History* 14 (1987): 333–60.

———. "The Origin of Special Veneration of the Mother of God at the Trinity-Sergius Monastery: The Iconographical Evidence," *Russian History* 28 (2001): 303–14.

———. "Pogrebeniia riadom s Sergiem: pogrebal'nye obychai v Troitse-Sergievom monastyre, 1392–1605," in *Troitse-Sergieva Lavra v istorii, kul'ture i dukhovnoi zhizni Rossii*, vol. 2 (2002). 74–89.

———. "Prepodobnyi Sergii Radonezhskii, zastupnik Russkoi Zemli," *Makar'evskie chteniia* 4, pt. 2 (1996): 16–26.

———. "Rublev's Old Testament Trinity and the Appearance of the Mother of God to

Saint Sergius: Dual Iconographic Signifiers of the Trinity-Sergius Monastery in the First Centuries of Its Existence," *Symposiom* 7-12 (2002–2007): 47–65.

———. "Troitse-Sergieva lavra kak ob'ediniaiushchii tsentr Russkoi zemli," in *Troitse-Sergieva lavra v istorii, kul'ture i dukhovnoi zhizni Rossii*, vol. 1 (2000). 7–23.

———. "The *Velikie Minei Chetii* and the *Stepennaia kniga* of Metropolitan Makarii and the Origins of Russian National Consciousness," *Forschungen zur osteuropäischen Geschichte* 26 (1979): 263–382.

Moiseeva, G. N. "Zhitie novgorodskogo arkhiepiskopa Serapiona," *Trudy Otdela drevnerusskoi literatury* 26 (1965): 147–65.

Molho, Anthony. *Marriage Alliance in Late Medieval Florence*. Cambridge, Mass., 1994.

Morozov. V. V. *Litsevoi svod v kontekste otechestvennogo letopisaniia XVI veka*. Moscow, 2005.

———. "Miniatiury zhitiia Sergiia Radonezhskogo iz Litsevogo letopisnogo svoda XVI v.," *Materialy i soobshcheniia po fondam Otdela rukpisnoi i redkoi knigi Biblioteki AN SSSR 1985* (1987): 71–87.

Morris, Rosemary. *Monks and Laymen in Byzantium, 843–1118*. New York, 1995.

Müller, Ludolf, ed. "Introduction," in *Die Legenden des Heiligen Sergij von Radonež, Nachdruck der Ausgabe von Tichonravov. Slavische Propyläen*, no. 17. Munich, 1967. v–liii.

Murav'eva, L. L. "O nachale letopisaniia v Troitse-Sergievom monastyre," in *Kul'tura srednevekovoi Moskvy XIV–XVII vv.* Ed. L. A. Beliaev. Moscow, 1995. 4–22.

Musin, A. E. "Pogrebal'nyi obriad drevnei Rusi kak arkheologicheskaia i liturgicheskaia problema," in "*Sikh zhe pamiat prebyvaet vo veki": (Memorial'nyi aspekt v kul'ture russkogo pravoslaviia)*. Ed. V. S. Belonenko. St. Petersburg, 1997. 11–38.

Nasonov, A. N. "Novye istochniki po istorii Kazanskogo 'vziatiia'," *Arkheograficheskii ezhegodnik za 1960 god*, (1962): 3–26.

Nastol'naia kniga dlia sviashchenno-tserkovno-sluzhitelei, 2nd ed. Comp. S. V. Bulgakov. Khar'kov, 1900.

Nartsissov, V. V. "Problemy ikonografii Prepodobnogo Sergiia Radonezhskogo," in *Drevnerusskoe iskusstvo. Sergii Radonezhskii i khudozhestvennaia kul'tura Moskvy XIV–XV vv*. St. Petersburg, 1998. 54–62.

Nazarov, V. D. "Razyskaniia o drevneishikh gramotakh Troitse-Sergieva monastyria. II: Vklad Kniazia Fedora Andreevicha Starodubskogo," in *Troitse-Sergieva Lavra v istorii, kul'ture i dukhovnoi zhizni Rossii*, vol. 1 (2000). 29–58.

Nevostruev, K. I., ed. "Zhitie prepodobnogo Iosifa Volokolamskogo, sostavlennoe neizvestnym," *Chteniia Obshchestva liubitelei drevnei pis'mennosti* 2 (1865): 77–152.

Nikolaeva, S. V. "K voprosu o sostave bratii Troitse-Sergieva monastyria v XV–XVI vv.," *Sergievo-posadskogo muzeia-zapovednika. Soobshcheniia* (2000): 66–80.

———. "Pominanie inokov Troitse-Sergieva monastyria v Sinodike 1575 g.: k voprosu o bratskom sinodike," *Sergievo-Posadskii muzei-zapovednik. Soobshcheniia* (2006): 29–48.

———. "Sinodik Troitse-Sergieva monastyria 1575 g.: k voprosu o structure i istochnikakh," in *Troitse-Sergieva lavra v istorii, kul'ture i dukhovnoi zhizni Rossii*, vol. 4 (2007). 130–37.

———. "Sostav monasheskoi bratii Troitse-Sergieva Monastyria v XVII V. (Po Opisi 1641 g. i Opisi 1701 g.)," *Trudy po istorii Troitse-Sergievoi Lavry* 7 (1998): 34–55.

———. "Tri sinodika Troitse-Sergieva Monastyria XVI–XVII vv.," *Tserkov' v istorii Rossii* 3 (1999): 69–98.

———. "Vklady i vkladchiki v Troitse-Sergiev monastyr' v XVI–XVII vekakh," *Tserkov' v istorii Rossii* 2 (1998): 81–108.

Nikolaeva, T. V. *Drevnerusskaia zhivopis' zagorskogo muzeia*. Moscow, 1977.

———. "K izucheniiu nekropolia Troitse-Sergievoi lavry," *Soobshcheniia Zagorskogo gos. istoriko-khudozhestvennogo muzeia-zapovednika* 3 (1960): 181–90.

———. "Nadgrobie novgorodskogo arkhiepiskopa Sergiia," *Sovetskaia arkheologiia* no. 3 (1965): 266–69.

———. "Nadgrobnye plinty pod zapadnym pritvorom Troitskogo sobora," *Soobshcheniia Zagorskogo gos. istoriko-khudozhestvennogo muzeia-zapovednika* 2 (1958): 92–106.

———. "Novye nadpisi na kamennykh plitakh XV–XVII vv. iz Troitse-Sergievoi lavry," *Numizmatika i epigrafika* 6 (1966): 207–55.

———. "Novye nakhodki na territorii Zagorskgo muzeia," *Sovetskaia arkheologiia* no. 1 (1957): 251–256.

———. "O nekotorykh nadgrobniakh XV–XVII vv. Zagorskogo muzeia-zapovednika," *Sovetskaia arkheologiia* no. 3 (1958): 170–79.

———. "Oklad s ikony 'Troitsa' pis'ma Andreia Rubleva," *Soobshcheniia Zagorskogo gos. istoriko-khudozhestvennogo muzeia-zapovednika* 2 (1958): 32–34.

———. *Prikladnoe iskusstvo Moskovskoi Rusi*. Moscow, 1976.

———. *Proizvedeniia melkoi plastiki XII–XVII vekov v sobranii Zagorskogo muzeia. Katalog*. Moscow, 1960.

———. *Proizvedeniia russkogo prikladnogo iskusstva s nadpisiami XV–pervoi chetverti XVI v.* AN SSSR, In-t Arkheologii. *Svod arkheologicheskikh istochnikov*, E1–49. Moscow, 1971.

———. *Sobranie drevnerusskogo iskusstva v Zagorskom muzee*. Leningrad, 1968.

———. "Troitskii zhivopisets XVI veka Evstafii Golovkin" in *Kul'tura drevnei Rusi*. Ed. A. L. Mongait. Moscow, 1966. 177–93.

Nikol'skii, N. K. *Kirillo-Belozerskii monastyr' i ego ustroistvo do vtoroi chetverti XVII veka (1397–1625)*. 2 vols. St. Petersburg, 1897, 1910, 2006.

Nora, Pierre. "Between Memory and History: Les Lieux de Memoire," *Representations* 26 (1989): 7–25.

Novgorodskiia letopisi. Ed. A. F. Bychkov. St. Petersburg, 1879.

Obolensky, Dimitri. "Nationalism in Eastern Europe in the Middle Ages," in *The Byzantine Inheritance of Eastern Europe*. Ed. Dimitri Obolensky. London, 1982. 1–16.

———. "A Philorhomaios anthröpos: Metropolitan Cyprian of Kiev and All Russia,"

Dumbarton Oaks Papers 32 (1979): 79–98.

Oexle, Otto G. "Die Gegenwart der Toten," in *Death in the Middle Ages*. Ed. H. Braet, W. Verbeke. Louvain, 1983. 19–77.

Opisanie aktov sobraniia A. S. Uvarova. Akty istoricheskie, opisannye I. M. Kataevym i A. K. Kudanovym. Ed. M. V. Dovnar-Zapol'skii. Moscow, 1905.

Osada Troitskoi Lavry. Print. Sergieva-Troitskaia Lavra, 14 September 1859.

Ostashenko, E. Ia. *Andrei Rublev: palaologicheskie traditsii v moskovskoi zhivopisi kontsa XIV–pervoi treti XV veka*. Moscow, 2005.

Ostrowski, Donald. "500 let spustia: Tserkovnyi sobor 1503 g.," *Palaeoslavica* 11 (2003): 214–39.

Ott, Louis. *Prècis de theologie dogmatique*. Transl. Marcel Arandchaudon. Mulhouse, 1955.

Ovchinnikova, E. S. "Novyi pamiatnik stankovoi zhivopisi XV veka kruga Rubleva," in *Drevne-russkoe iskusstvo XV–nachala XVI vekov*. Ed. V. N. Lazarev. Moscow, 1963. 94–117.

Ozerskaia, E. A. "Obraz grada bozh'ego v stenakh zhitiia Sergiia Radonezhskogo iz Sergievskoi tserkvi novgorodskogo detintsa," in *Drevnerusskoe iskusstvo. Sergii Radonezhskii i khudozhestvennaia kul'tura Moskvy XIV–XV vv*. St. Petersburg, 1998. 95–107.

Pachomij Logofet. *Werke in Auswahl, Slavische Propyläen*, no. 1. Ed. Dmitrij Tschiževskij. Munich, 1963.

"Pamiati Sergiia Radonezhskogo," *Otechestvo. Kraevedcheskii al'manakh* 3 (1992): 5–28.

Pamiatniki literatury Drevnei Rusi, XIV–seredina XV veka. Ed. L. A. Dmitriev, D. S. Likhachev. Moscow, 1981.

Pamiatniki russkoi pis'mennosti XV–XVI vv. Riazanskii krai. Ed. S. I. Kotkova. Moscow, 1978.

Pamiatniki sotsial'no-ekonomicheskoi istorii moskovskogo gosudarstva XIV–XVII vv. Ed. S. B. Veselovskii, A. I. Iakovlev. Moscow, 1929.

Parkes, Malcolm. "The Literacy of the Laity," in *Literature and Western Civilization: The Medieval World*. Ed. D. Daiches, A. Thorlby. New York, 1973. 555–77.

Parry, William. *A New and Large Discourse of the Travels of Sir Anthony Sherley by Sea and over Land to the Persian Empire*. London, 1601.

———."Proezd cherez Rossiiu persidskogo posolstva v 1599–1600 godakh," *Chteniia v imperatorskom Obshchestve istorii i drevnostei rossiiskikh pri moskovskom universitete*, 1899, bk. 4, pt. 3: 3–9.

The Paterik of the Kievan Caves Monastery. Transl. Muriel Heppell. Cambridge, Mass., 1989.

Paul of Aleppo. *Puteshestvie antiokhiiskogo Patriarkha Makariia v Rossiiu v polovine XVII veka*. Transl. G. Murkos. Moscow, 1898; repr. Moscow, 2005.

Pelenski, Jaroslaw. *Russia and Kazan: Conquest and Imperial Ideology (1438–1560s)*. The Hague, 1974.

Perechen' aktov Arkhiva Troitse-Sergieva monastyria, 1505–1537. Ed. S. M. Kashtanov. Moscow, 2007.

"Perechen' immunitetnykh gramot 1584–1610 gg." Ed. D. A Tebekin. Pt. 1: *Arkheograficheskii ezhegodnik za 1978 g.* (1979): 191–235; Pt. 2: *Arkheograficheskii ezhegodnik za 1979 g.* (1981): 210–55.

Petukhov, E. V. *Ocherki iz literaturnoi istorii sinodiki*. St. Petersburg, 1895.

Pia di Bella, Maria. "Name, Blood and Miracles: The Claims to Renoun in Medieval Sicily," in *Honor and Grace in Anthropology*. Ed. J. G. Peristiany, Julian Pitt-Rivers. Cambridge, Eng., 1992. 151–65.

Pistsovyia knigi Moskovskogo gosudarstva. Ed. N. V. Kalachov. 2 vols. St. Petersburg, 1872–1877.

Pitt-Rivers, Julian. "Postscript: The Place of Grace in Anthropology," in *Honor and Grace in Anthropology*. Ed. J. G. Peristiany, Julian Pitt-Rivers. Cambridge, Eng., 1992. 217–25.

Platonov, S. F. *Drevnerusskie skazaniia i povesti o smutnom vremeni kak istoricheskii istochnik*. St. Petersburg, 1888.

Pliguzov, A. I. *Polemika v russkoi tserkvi pervoi treti XVI stoletiia*. Moscow, 2002.

Poe, Marshall. "The Elite Service Registry in Muscovy, 1500–1700," *Russian History* 21 (1994): 251–88.

Pokrovskii, N. N. *Aktovye istochniki po istorii chernososhnogo* zemlevladeniia *v Rossii XIV–nachala XVI v.* Novosibirsk, 1973.

Pokrovskii, N. N., and Gail D. Lenhoff, eds. *Stepennaia kniga tsarskogo rodosloviia po drevneishim spiskam: Teksty i kommentarii*. 3 vols. Moscow, 2007–.

Polnoe sobranie russkikh letopisei. 41 vols. to date. Moscow-St. Petersburg-Leningrad, 1846–, and 2nd ed. 4 vols. to date. St. Petersburg-Petrograd-Leningrad, 1908–.

Ponyrko, N. V. "Sinodiki," in *Slovar' knizhnikov i khizhnosti*, vol. 2, pt. 2. Ed. D. S. Likhachev. St. Petersburg, 1988. 339–44.

Popesku, T. A. "Opisi Troitse-Sergieva monastyria kak istochnik po istorii monastyrskoi biblioteki," in *Troitse-Sergieva lavra v istorii, kul'ture i dukhovnoi zhizni Rossii*, vol. 1 (2000). 156–67.

Popov, G. V. "Daniil i Andrei Rublev v Troitse-Sergievom monastyre," in *Troitse-Sergieva lavra v istorii, kul'ture i dukhovnoi zhizni Rossii*, vol. 3 (2004). 217–27.

———. "Dve drevneishie ikony 'Vetkhozavetnoi Troitsy' iz Troitse-Sergieva lavry (vopros proiskhozhdeniia i datirovki)," in *Troitse-Sergieva lavra v istorii, kul'tury i dukhovnoi zhizni Rossii. Tezisy dokladov*. Sergiev Posad, 1998. 56–57.

Popova, O. S. "Russkie ikony epokhi Sv. Sergiia Radonezhskogo i ego uchenikov. Pravoslavnaia dukhovnost' XIV v. i ee russkii variant," in *Drevnerusskoe iskusstvo. Sergii Radonezhskii i khudozhestvennaia kul'tura Moskvy XIV–XV vv.* St. Petersburg, 1998. 27–39.

Poslaniia Iosifa Volotskogo. Ed. A. A. Zimin, Ia. S. Lur'e. Moscow-Leningrad, 1959.

Possevino, A. *Istoricheskie sochineniia o Rossii XVI v.* Transl. L. N. Godovikovaia. Moscow, 1983.

Prepodobnye Kirill, Ferapont i Martinian Belozerskie, 2nd ed. Ed. G. M. Prokhorov. St. Petersburg, 1993.

Presniakov, A. E. *Obrazovanie velikorusskogo gosudarstva*. Petrograd, 1918.

Priselkov, M. D. *Istoriia russkogo letopisaniia*. Leningrad, 1940; repr. The Hague, 1966.
Program Cover, *Music Festival "Probuzhdenie," Dedicated to the 600th Anniversary of the Venerable Sergius, Abbot of Radonezh and Miracleworker of All Rus'*. Moscow, Kremlin Palace of Congresses, 10–11 October 1992. Electronic copy and explanation, Marianna Tax Choldin.
Prokhorov, G. M. "Keleinaia isichastkaia literatura v biblioteke Troitse-Sergievoi Lavry s XIV do XVII veki," *Trudy Otdela drevnerusskoi literatury* 28 (1974): 317–24.
———. *Povest' o Mitiae: Rus' i Vizantiia v epokhu Kulikovskoi bitvy*. Moscow, 1978.
———. "Vnutrenniaia dinamika drevne-russkoi kul'tury, ili nadsoznanie Drevnei Rusi," in *La cultura spirituale russa*. Ed Luigi Magarotto, Daniela Rizzi. Trento, 1992. 211–32.
Pushkareva, N. L., and Eve Levin. "Zhenshchina v srednevekovom Novgorode XI–XV vv.," *Vestnik Moskovskogo universiteta*. Ser. 8: *Istoriia* 3 (1983): 78–89
Razriadnaia kniga 1475–1598 gg. Ed. V. I. Buganov. Moscow, 1966.
Reddel, Carl. "S. M. Solov'ev and Multi-National History," *Russian History* 13 (1986): 355–66.
Roatcap, Adela Spindler. "The Iconography of Saint Sergius of Radonezh," Ph.D. dissertation, Stanford Univ. Stanford, 1974.
Romanchuk, Robert. *Byzantine Hermeneutics and Pedagogy in the Russian North: Monks and Masters at the Kirillo-Belozerskii Monastery, 1397–1501*. Toronto, 2007.
Romanenko, E. V. "Istoricheskie realii Zhitiia Nila Sorskogo," in *Nil Sorskii v kul'ture i knizhnosti Drevnei Rusi*. Ed. A. I. Alekseev. St. Petersburg, 2008. 20–28.
Rosenwein, Barbara H. *To Be the Neighbor of Saint Peter: The Social Meaning of Cluny's Property, 909–1049*. Ithaca, NY, 1989.
Rowland, Daniel. "The Memory of St. Sergius in the Sixteenth Century," in *The Trinity-Sergius Lavra in Russian History and Culture*. Jordanville, NY, 2005. 56–69.
Rozhkov, N. A. *Sel'skoe khoziaistvo Moskovskoi Rusi v XVI v*. Moscow, 1899.
Rozov, N. N. "Pokhval'noe slovo velikomu kniaziu Vasiliiu III," in *Arkheograficheskii ezhegodnik za 1964 g*. Moscow, 1965. 278–89.
Rüss, Hartmut. "Der Kampf um das Moskauer Tysjackij-Amt im 14. Jahrhundert," *Jahrbücher für Geschichte Osteuropas* 22 (1974): 481–93.
———. *Herren und Diener: Die soziale und politische Mentalität des russischen Adels, 9–17 Jahrhundert*. Cologne, 1994.
Russkaia istoricheskaia biblioteka. 39 vols. St. Petersburg, Petrograd, Leningrad, 1872–1927.
Rybakov, B. A. *Remeslo drevnei Rusi*. Moscow, 1948.
Sadikov, P. A. "Iz istorii oprichniny XVI v.," *Istoricheskii arkhiv* 3 (1940): 113–303.
———. *Ocherki po istorii Oprichniny*. Moscow-Leningrad, 1950.
Salmina, M. A. "Eshche raz o datirovke 'Letopisnoi povesti' o Kulikovskoi bitve," *Trudy Otdela drevnerusskoi literatury* 32 (1977): 1–39.
———. "K voprosu o datirovke 'Skazaniia o Mamaevom poboishche,'" *Trudy Otdela drevnerusskoi literatury* 29 (1974): 98–124.
———. "'Letopisnaia povest' o Kulikovskoi bitve i 'Zadonshchina,'" in *"Slovo o polku*

Igoreve" i pamiatniki Kulikovskogo tsykla. Ed. D. S. Likhachev, L. A. Dmitriev. Moscow-Leningrad, 1966. 344–84.

Sazonov, S. V. "K probleme vospriiatiia smerti v srednevekovoi Rusi," in *Russkaia istoriia: Problemy mentaliteta.* Ed. V. A. Barchenkova. Moscow, 1994. 47–52.

———. "'Molitva mertvykh za zhivikh' v russkom letopisanii XII–XV v.," in *Rossiia v X–XVIII vv. Problemy istorii i istochnikovedeniia.* Moscow, 1995. 508–17.

———. "O vidakh sinodika-pamiatnika," in *Istoriia i kul'tura Rostovskoi zemli.* Rostov, 1993. 110–12.

Sbornik aktov, sobrannykh N. P. Likhachevom. 2 pts. St. Petersburg, 1895.

Sbornik gramot Kollegii ekonomiki. 2 vols. Petrograd, Leningrad, 1922–29.

Sbornik Mukhanova, 2nd ed. St. Petersburg, 1866.

Schuler, Peter-Johannes. "Das Anniversar. Zu Mentalität und Familienbewusstsein im Spätmittelalter," in *Die Familie als sozialer und historischer Verband. Untersuchungen zum Spätmittelalter und zur frühen Neuzeit.* Ed. Peter-Johannes Schuler. Sigmaringen, 1987. 67–117.

Sedel'nikov, A. S. "Iz oblasti literaturnogo obshcheniia v nachale XV veka (Kirill Tverskoi i Epifanii Moskovskoi)," *Izvestiia Otdeleniia russkogo iazyka i slovestnosti* 31 (1926): 159–76.

Semenchenko, G. V. "O khronologii aktov severo-vostochnoi Rusi XIV–XV vv.," *Arkheograficheskii ezhegodnik za 1988 god* (1989): 31–40.

———. "O khronologii aktov severo-vostochnoi Rusi XV v.," *Arkheograficheskii ezhegodnik za 1989 god* (1990): 55–64.

———. "O khronologii nekotorykh gramot upominaiushchikh 'Velikgo Kniazia' Ivana III Vasil'evicha," *Arkheograficheskii ezhegodnik za 1983 god* (1985): 53–67.

———. "O khronologii Troitskikh aktov kontsa XIV–pervoi poloviny XV v.," *Arkheograficheskii ezhegodnik za 1984 god* (1986): 100–9.

———. "O khronologii Troitskikh aktov vtoroi polovine XV v.," *Arkheograficheskii ezhegodnik za 1987 god* (1988): 45–53.

Sergii Radonezhskii. Ed. V. A. Desiatnikov. Moscow, 1991.

Ševčenko, Ihor. "A Neglected Byzantine Source of Muscovite Political Ideology," *Harvard Slavic Studies* 2 (1954): 41–79.

———. "Gleanings, 1–2," *Palaeoslavica* 6 (1998): 291–97.

———. "Intellectual Repercussions of the Council of Florence," *Church History* 24 (1955): 291–323.

Shablova, T. I. "Praktika pominoveniia v Kirillo-belozerskom monastyre vo vtoroi polovine XVI–pervoi polovine XVII vekov," in *"Sikh zhe pamiat' prebyvaet vo veki": (Memorial'nyi aspect v kul'ture russkogo pravoslaviia).* Ed. V. S. Belonenko. St. Petersburg, 1997. 46–67.

Shadis, Miriam. "Piety, Politics and Power: The Patronage of Leonor of England and Her Daughter Berenguela of León and Blanche of Castile," in *The Cultural Patronage of Medieval Women.* Ed. June Hall McCash. Athens, Ga., 1996. 202–17.

Shakhovskaia, N. D. *V monastyrskoi votchine, XIV–XVII veka. Sv. Sergii i ego khoziaistvo.* Moscow, 1915.

Shalina, A. "Ikona-Moshevik 'Prepodobnyi Sergii Radonezhskii s zhitiem' nachala XVI v. iz sobraniia V. A. Bondarenko," in *Troitse-Sergieva Lavra v istorii, kul'ture i dukhovnoi zhizni Rossii. IV mezhdunarodnaia konferentsiia, 29 sentiabria-1 oktiabria 2004 g. Tezisy dokladov.* Ed. G. S. Isaakov. Sergiev Posad, 2004. 32–34.

Shapiro, A. L. *Problemy sotsial'no-ekonomicheskoi istorii Rusi XIV–XVI vv.* Leningrad, 1977.

Shevchenko, E. E. "Prepodobnye Ferapont i Martinian," in *Prepodobnye Kirill, Ferapont, i Martinian Belozerskie*, 2nd ed. Ed. G. M. Prokhorov. St. Petersburg, 1994. 189–95.

Shibaev, M. I. "Redaktorskie priemy sostavitelia Sofiiskoi I letopisi," in *Opyty po istochnikovedeniiu. Drevniaia russkaia knizhnost': redactor i tekst*. St. Petersburg, 2000. 368–94.

Shils, Edward A. *Center and Periphery: Essays in Macrosociology*. Chicago, 1975.

Shumakov, S. A. *Obzor Gramot "Kolegii ekonomii,"* 4 vols. Moscow, 1899–1917.

———. *Tverskie akty*, 2 vols. Moscow, 1896–1897.

———. *Uglichskie akty 1400–1749 gg.* Moscow, 1899.

Siderova, T. "Realisticheskie cherty v arkhitekturnykh izobrazheniakh drevnerusskikh miniatiur," *Arkhitekturnoe nasledstvo* 10 (1958): 73–100.

Sinitsyna, N. V. "Tipy monastyrei i russkii asketicheskii ideal (XV–XVI vv.)," in *Monashestvo i monastyri v Rossii XI–XX veka*. Ed. N. V. Sinitsyna. Moscow, 2002. 116–49.

Sirenov, Aleksei V. *Stepennaia kniga: Istoriia teksta*. Moscow, 2007.

Skazanie Avramiia Palitsyna. Ed. and commentary O. A. Derzhavina, E. V. Kolosova. Moscow-Leningrad, 1955.

Skazaniia i povesti o Kulikovskoi bitve. Ed. L. A. Dmitriev, O. P. Likhacheva. Leningrad, 1982.

Skopin, Vladimir. *Solovki: Istoriia, arkhitektura, priroda*. Moscow, 1994.

Skrynnikov, R. G. "Ecclesiastical Thought in Russia and the Church Councils of 1503 and 1504," *Oxford Slavonic Papers* 25 (1992): 34–60.

———. *Nachalo Oprichniny*. Leningrad, 1966.

———. *Oprichnyi terror*. Leningrad, 1969.

———. *Tragediia Novgoroda*. Moscow, 1994.

Slovar' knizhnikov i knizhnosti Drevnei Rusi. Ed. D. S. Likhachev. Vol. 2, pts. 1–2, and vol. 3, pt. 1. St. Petersburg, 1988–90.

Smirnova, E. S. "Bogomater' s Mladentsem na prestole, s arkhangelom i prepodobnym Sergiem Radonezhskim—ikona pervoi treti XV v. Istoki i smysl ikonografii," in *Russkoe podvizhnichestvo*. Ed. T. V. Kniazhevskaia. Moscow, 1996. 124–35.

———. *Moscow Icons 14th-17th Centuries*. Transl. Arthur Sklarovsky-Raffé. Leningrad, 1989.

Smith, Anthony D. *The Ethnic Origins of Nations*. Oxford, 1986.

Sobranie istoriko-iuridicheskikh aktov I. D. Beliaeva. Ed. D. Lebedev. Moscow, 1881.

Solov'ev, S. "Bratchiny," *Russkaia Beseda* no. 4 (1856): 108.

Spirina, L. M. "Ikona 'Bogomater Odigitriia (Smolenskaia)' XVI veka iz sobraniia

Sergievo-Posadskogo muzeia-zapovednika," *Soobshcheniia Sergievo-posadskogo muzeia-zapovednika* (2000): 221–42.

———. *Pokrovskii Monastyr' v Khot'kove.* Sergiev Posad, 1996.

"Spisok nadgrobii Troitskago Sergieva monastyria, sostavlennyi v polovine XVII veka," pt. 1, *Chteniia v imperatorskom Obshchestve istorii i drevnosteei pri moskovskom universitete* (1846) bk. 2: 33–50; and pt. 2, *Chteniia v imperatorskom Obshshestve istorii i drevnostei pri moskovskom universitete* (1879), bk. 2: 79–107.

Spisok pogrebennykh v Troitse-Sergievoi Lavre ot osnovaniia onoi do 1880 goda. Moscow, 1880.

Spock, Jennifer. "Community Building and Social Identity: Donations to the Solovki Monastery, 1460–1645," *Jahrbücher für Geschichte Osteuropas* 55 (2007): 534–65.

———. "The Solovki Monastery, 1450–1645. Ph.D. dissertation, Yale Univ., 1999.

Sreznevskii, I. I. *Materialy dlia slovaria drevnerusskogo iazyka,* 3 vols. St. Petersburg, 1893–1903.

Steindorff, Ludwig. "Commemoration and Administrative Techniques in Muscovite Monasteries," *Russian History* 22 (1995): 433–54.

———. "Einstellungen zum Mönchtum im Spiegel altrussischen Quellen," *Archiv für Kulturgeschichte* 75 (1993): 66–90.

———. "Klöster als zentren der Totensorge in Altrussland," *Forschungen zur osteuropäischen Geschichte* 50 (1995): 337–53.

———. "Kto blizhnie moi? Individ i kul'tura pominoveniia v Rossii rannego novogo vremeni," in *Chelovek i ego blizkie na zapade i vostoke Evropy.* Ed. Iurii Bessmertnyi and Otto Gerhard Oexle. Moscow, 2000. 231–58.

———. "Mehr als eine Frage der Ehre. Zum Stifterverhalten Zar Ivans des Schrechlichen," *Jahrbücher für Geschichte Osteuropas* 51 (2003): 342–66.

———. *Memoria in Altrussland: Untersuchungen zu den Formen christlicher Totensorge.* Stuttgart, 1994.

———. Pominanie usopshikh kak obshchee nasledie zapadnogo srednevekov'ia i Drevnei Rusi," in "Sikh zhe pamiat' prebyvaet vo veki": (memorial'nyi aspect v kul'ture russkogo pravoslaviia). Ed. V. S. Belonenko. St. Petersburg, 1997. 39–45.

———. "Princess Mariia Golenina: Perpetuating Identity through 'Care for the Deceased,'" in *Moskovskaia Rus' (1359–1584): Kul'tura i istoricheskoe samosoznanie.* Ed. A. M. Kleimola, G. D. Lenhoff. Moscow, 1997. 557–77.

———. "Sravnenie istochnikov ob organizatsii ponimaniia usopshikh v Iosif-Volokolamskom i Troitse-Sergievom monastyriakh v XVI veke," *Arkheograficheskii ezhegodnik za 1996 god* (1998): 65–78.

Stock, Brian. *The Implications of Literacy: Written Language and Models of Interpretation in the Eleventh and Twelfth Centuries.* Princeton, 1983.

Stroev, P. M. *Spiski ierarkhov i nastoiatelei monastyrei Rossisskoi tserkvi. St Petersburg,* 1877; repr. Köln, 1990.

Thaden, Edward. "V. N. Tatishchev, German Historians, and the St. Petersburg Academy of Sciences," *Russian History* 13 (1986): 367–98.

Thomas, John R. *Private Religious Foundations in the Byzantine Empire.* Dumbarton Oaks Studies, no. 24. Washington, D. C., 1987.

Thyrêt, Isolde. *Between God and Tsar: Religious Symbolism and the Royal Women of Muscovite Russia*. DeKalb, Ill., 2001.

———. "'Blessed is the Tsaritsa's Womb': The Myth of Miraculous Birth and Royal Motherhood in Muscovite Russia," *Russian Review* 53 (1994): 479–96.

———. "The Cultural Politics of the Grand Princesses of Moscow and the Emergence of the Muscovite Dynasty," *Russian History* 33 (2006): 339–52.

Tkachenko, V. A. "Vkladnye knigi 1638/1639 i 1672/1673 gg. kak istochniki po istorii nekropolia Troitse-Sergievoi lavry," in *Troitse-Sergieva lavra v istorii, kul'ture i dukhovnoi zhizi Rossii*, vol. 3 (2004). 152–65.

The Travels of Olearius in 17th-Century Russia, Transl. Samuel H. Baron. Stanford, 1967.

Trofimov, I. V. *Pamiatniki arkhitektury Troitse-Sergievoi Lavry. Issledovaniia i restavratsii*. Moscow, 1961.

Troitse-Sergieva Lavra. Khudozhestvennye pamiatniki. Ed. N. N. Voronin, V. V. Kostochkin. Moscow, 1968.

Troitse-Sergieva lavra v istorii, kul'ture i dukhovnoi zhizni Rossii. Materially II mezhdunarodnoi konferentsii. Ed. T. N. Manushina, S. V. Nikolaeva. Sergiev Posad, vol. 1, 2000; vol. 2, 2002; vol. 3, 2004; vol. 4, 2007.

Troitskaia letopis': Rekonstruktsiia teksta. Ed. M. D. Priselkov. Moscow-Leningrad, 1950.

Troitskii paterik. Sergiev Posad, 1896.

Tysiachnaia kniga 1550 g. i Dvorovaia tetrad' 50-kh godov XVI v. Ed. A. A. Zimin. Moscow-Leningrad, 1950.

Ukhova, T. V., and S. A. Klepikov. "Katalog miniatiur, ornamenta i graviur sobraniia Troitse-Sergievoi Lavry i Moskovskoi dukhovnoi akademii," *Zapiski Otdela rukopisei Gosudarstvennoi biblioteki im. V. I. Lenina* 22 (1960): 74–194.

Ul'fel'dt, Jacob. *Puteshestvie v Rossiiu*. Moscow, 2002.

Velikiia minei chetii sobranyia Vserossiiskim Mitrolpolitom Makariem. 25 vols. St. Petersburg, 1868–1917.

Veselovskii, S. B. *Feodal'noe zemlevladenie v severo-vostochnoi Rusi*. Moscow-Leningrad, 1947.

———. *D'iaki i pod'iachie XV–XVII vv*. Moscow, 1975.

———. *Issledovaniia po istorii klassa sluzhilykh zemlevladel'tsev*. Moscow, 1969.

———. *Issledovaniia po istorii Oprichniny*. Moscow, 1963.

———. "Krepostnoi arkhiv Troitse-Sergievoi lavry," in *Trudy po istochnikovedeniiu i istorii Rossii perioda feodalizma*. Ed. S. B. Veselovskii. Moscow, 1978. 150–55.

———. "Monastyrskoe zemlevladenie v moskovskoi Rusi v vtoroi polovine XVI v.," *Istoricheskie zapiski* 10 (1941): 95–116.

———. *Selo i derevnia v severo-vostochnoi Rusi XIV–XVI vv*. Moscow-Leningrad, 1936.

Vesyolkina, T. "Vysotsky Monastery in Serpukhov Founded by St. Afanasy," *Journal of the Moscow Patriarchate* no. 4 (1992): 34–36.

Vishnevskii, V. I. "Novye nakhodki srednevekovykh nadgrobii nekropolia Troitse-Sergieva monastyria," *Trudy po istorii Troitse-Sergievoi Lavry* 7 (1998): 72–87.

———. "O nekotorykh osobennostiakh srednevekovykh nadgrobii Troitse-Sergieva monastyria," in *Troitse-Sergieva lavra v istorii, kul'ture i dukhovnoi zhizni Rossii*, vol. 3 (2004). 97–110.

——. "Srednevekovye belokamennye nadgrobiia nekropolia Troitse-Sergieva monastyria (nakhodki 1998–1999 gg.)," *Soobshcheniia Sergievo-posadskogo muzeia-zapovednika* (2000): 17–39.

——. "Srednevekovye nadpisi-graffiti na nadgrobiiakh iz Troitse-Sergieva monastyria," *Troitse-Sergieva lavra v istorii, kul'ture i dukhovnoi zhiznii Rossii. IV Mezhdunarodnaia konferentsiia, Tezisy dokladov.* Ed. G. S Isaakov. Sergiev Posad, 2004. 14–15.

Vkladnaia kniga Troitse-Sergieva Monastyria. Ed. E. N. Klitina. Moscow, 1987.

Vodoff, Vladimir. "Les transports dans le vie economique des monastères de la russie du nord-est au XVe siècle," *Annales de Bretagne et des pays de l'Ouest (Anjou, Maine, Touraine)* 85, no. 2 (1978): 315–36.

——. *Naissance de la Chrétienté russe, la conversion du prince Vladimir de Kiev (988) et ses conséquences XIe-XIIIe siècles).* Paris, 1988.

Volkova, T. F. "'Letopisets nachala tsarstva Tsaria i Velikogo Kniazia Ivana Vasil'evicha' i Troitskoe sochinenie o vziatii Kazani kak istochnik teksta 'Kazanskoi istorii,'" in *Drevnerusskaia literatura. Istochnikovedenie. Sb. Nauchnykh trudov.* Ed. D. S. Likhachev. Leningrad, 1984. 172–87.

Voronin, N. N. "Litsevye zhitia Sergiia kak istochnik dlia otsenki stroitel'noi deiatel'nosti Ermolinykyh," *Trudy Otdela drevneirusskoi literatury* 14 (1958): 573–75.

——. *Zodchestvo severo-vostochoi Rusi.* 2 vols. Moscow, 1960–62.

Vorontsova, L. M. "K voprosu o skadyvanii pochitaniia prepodobnogo Sergiia Radonezhskogo v XV veka," *Trudy po istorii Troitse-Sergievoi Lavry* 7 (1998): 11–19.

—— et al. *Prepodobnyi Sergii Radonezhskii v proizvedeniiakh russkogo iskusstva XV–XIX vekov. Katalog.* Moscow, 1992.

——. "Riznitsa Troitse-Sergieva monastyria. K voprosu o sostave i istorii formirovaniia," in *Troitse-Sergieva Lavra v istorii, kul'ture i dukhovnoi zhizni Rossii*, vol. 3 (2004). 228–39.

Vzdornov, G. I. *Troitsa Andreia Rubleva: Antologiia*, 2nd ed. Moscow, 1989.

——. "Knigopisanie i khudozhestvennoe oformlenie rukopisei v moskovskikh monastyriakh do kontsa pervoi treti XV v.," *Trudy Otdela drevnerusskoi literatury* 22 (1966): 119–44.

Weber, Max. *Essays in Sociology.* Transl. and ed. H. H. Gerth and C. Wright Mills. New York, 1946.

Weinstein, Donald, and Rudolph M. Bell. *Saints and Society: The Two Worlds of Western Civilization, 1000–1700.* Chicago, 1982.

White, Stephen D. *Custom, Kinship and Gifts to Saints: The "Laudatio Parentum" in Western France, 1050–1150.* Chapel Hill, NC, 1988.

Wills, Garry. *What Jesus Meant.* New York, 2006.

Zhitie Savvy Storozhevskogo. Ed. L. A. Timoshina. Moscow, 1994.

Zhitie sviatogo Stefana, episkopa Permskago napisannoe Epifaniem Premudrym. "Introduction" by Dmitrij Čiževskij. Ed. V. G. Druzhinin. St. Petersburg, 1897; repr. 'S-Gravenhage, 1959.

Zhizn' i zhitiia Sergiia Radonezhskogo. Ed. V. V. Kolesov. Moscow, 1991.

Zimin, A. A. "Aktovye podelki Troitse-Sergieva monastyria 80-kh godakh XVI v." in *Voprosy sotsial'no-ekonomicheskoi istorii i istochnikovedeniia perioda feodalizma*. Ed. N. V. Ustiugov. Moscow, 1961. 247–52

———. *Formirovanie boiarskoi aristokratii v Rossii*. Moscow, 1988.

———. "K izucheniiu istochnikov Stepennoi knigi," *Trudy Otdela drevnerusskoi literatury* 13 (1957): 226–30. ———. *Krupnaia feodal'naia votchina i sotsial'no-politicheskaia bor'ba v Rossii (konets XV–XVI v.)*. Moscow, 1977.

———. "O politicheskom doktrine Iosifa Volotskogo," *Trudy Otdela drevnerusskoi literatury* 9 (1953): 159–77.

———. *Oprichnina Ivana Groznogo*. Moscow, 1964.

———. *Reformy Ivana Groznogo*. Moscow, 1960.

———. "Sostav boiarskoi dumy v XV–XVI vekakh," *Arkheograficheskii ezhegodnik za 1957 g.* (1958): 41–87.

———. *V kanun groznykh potriasenii; Predposylki pervoi krest'ianskoi voiny v Rossii*. Moscow, 1986.

Zlotnik, Marc D. "Immunity Charters and the Centralization of the Muscovite State." Ph.D. dissertation, Univ. of Chicago. Chicago, 1976.

Zubov, V. P. "Epifanii Premudry i Pakhomii Serb," *Trudy Otdela drevnerusskoi literatury* 9 (1953): 145–58.

Zverinskii, V. V. *Materialy dlia istoriko-topograficheskogo izsledovaniia o pravoslavnykh monastyriakh v Rossiiskoi imperii*. 3 vols. St. Petersburg, 1890–97.

Index

CPSIA information can be obtained
at www.ICGtesting.com
Printed in the USA
BVHW030255131221
623904BV00001B/39

9 780875 804323